LONG-RANGE FORECASTING
From Crystal Ball to Computer

LONG-RANGE FORECASTING
From Crystal Ball to Computer

J. SCOTT ARMSTRONG
Wharton School
University of Pennsylvania

Second Edition

A WILEY-INTERSCIENCE PUBLICATION

JOHN WILEY & SONS, New York ● Chichester ● Brisbane ● Toronto ● Singapore

This publication is designed to provide accurate and
authoritative information in regard to the subject
matter covered. It is sold with the understanding that
the publisher is not engaged in rendering legal, accounting,
or other professional service. If legal advice or other
expert assistance is required, the services of a competent
professional person should be sought. *From a Declaration
of Principles jointly adopted by a Committee of the
American Bar Association and a Committee of Publishers.*

Library of Congress Cataloging in Publication Data:

Armstrong, Jon Scott, 1937–
   Long-range forecasting.

   "A Wiley-Interscience publication."
   Includes indexes.
    1. Forecasting. 2. Business forecasting. I. Title.
H61.4.A76 1985   338.5′442   85-3292

ISBN 0-471-82360-0
ISBN 0-471-82260-4 (pbk.)

Printed in the United States of America

10 9 8 7 6 5 4 3 2 1

To
Murrl J. Anderson, my father-in-law,
who helped me to accept the future

PREFACE

Things are more like they are now than they ever were before.

Dwight David Eisenhower

Research on forecasting has been growing rapidly—more so than in most other areas of the social and management sciences. It seemed appropriate, then, to revise *Long-Range Forecasting*.

This second edition of *Long-Range Forecasting* improves upon the first edition in the following manner:

First, it indicates where *recent research* has made significant contributions, either supporting or refuting conclusions from the first edition. (This research is integrated into the text and described in the updated bibliography.)

Second, the updated bibliography compiles the most important research on forecasting since the first edition was published seven years ago. It includes over 350 books and papers. References to these works are easily found in the text as they are cross-referenced. The LAST NAMES OF THE AUTHORS have been capitalized to help the reader find the latest research.

Third, the *graphics* have been improved. Shaded areas set off descriptions of empirical research. Exhibits have been redrawn for better readability.

Fourth, while corrections had been made in each of the seven printings of the first edition, this edition makes extensive *revisions*. To
ensure that my summaries of the research were accurate, I tried to
contact all of the authors cited in *LRF* for old as well as new citations.
Most authors were cooperative, so almost all interpretations of studies
in *LRF* have met with the approval of their original authors. This
effort not only led to corrections, but also informed me about the most
recent work by these authors. Extensive revisions were also made to
the People and Subject Indexes.

Fifth, additions were made. These include a more thorough discussion on the relationship between planning and forecasting, a synthesis
of surprising findings on the use of scenarios, a quantitative review of
all empirical studies examining sophisticated approaches to extrapolation, some benchmarks for assessing forecast accuracy, new results
on the use of role playing to predict the outcome of conflicts, suggestions
on how to present the forecast in an effective manner, and guidelines
for auditing the forecasting process in an organization.

Philadelphia, Pennsylvania   J. SCOTT ARMSTRONG
April 1985

ACKNOWLEDGMENTS

Thanks to all those who helped with this second edition. Useful suggestions were provided on various chapters by Dennis A. Ahlburg, Colin Camerer, Jay Christensen-Szalanski, Gregory W. Fischer, Baruch Fischhoff, David Kasiarz, Hans Levenbach, Essam Mahmoud, Ruth Pagell, Asani Sarkar, Kranti Toraskar, Dick Torburg, by the students in my classes at the Wharton School, IMEDE, the University of Hawaii, and by many others. Particularly helpful was Everette Gardner, Jr. who made many excellent suggestions for the chapter on extrapolation methods. I owe a great debt to libraries; these include the University of Pennsylvania, Drexel University, IMEDE, and especially the University of Rochester. Stephen Kippur at John Wiley encouraged me to do this revision. Regina Loro typed most of the changes and managed to eliminate some of my new errors in the process. Martha Lightwood greatly expanded, reorganized, and clarified the subject index. Malcolm Davidson reviewed the page proofs and prevented many errors. I have gained much from my association with my colleagues at the International Institute of Forecasters, Robert Fildes, Bob Carbone, and Spyros Makridakis. Finally, my wife, Kay, provided advice, emotional support, and, during times of crisis on the revision, helped with the details. Also helping during these crises were my sister, Bonnie, and my daughters, Kathy and Jennifer. (Why did the crises arise? Could it have been poor forecasting?)

J.S.A.

PREFACE TO FIRST EDITION

For one who has no objective, nothing is relevant.

Confucius

This is a book about forecasting methods. The emphasis is on methods for long-range forecasting. The methods are applicable to all areas of the social, behavioral, and management sciences.

Much is known about forecasting methods, but little is used. Why? Because what is known in one field is unknown in another. Because what is known frequently contradicts our common sense. Because what is known challenges our beliefs and our behavior.

Long-Range Forecasting is a book for "doers," the people who have done or who are doing forecasting. These doers may be in business, in government, in academia, or in consulting. Doers may also be students working on forecasting projects in courses such as finance, marketing, economics, or sociology, or in those increasingly popular courses dealing with the future.

Some of the doers have little expertise, and some have much. If you have a lot of expertise, you will find many things to disagree with in this book. That is how it should be; if there is nothing in a book that challenges your beliefs, then there is no opportunity to learn. Of course, you will also find things to make you feel good about your current beliefs, but you will not learn much from these things. The way to learn is to find ideas that you disagree with—and then to suspend judgment and experiment with these ideas.

Long-Range Forecasting is a guide to forecasting methods. Although it is designed to be read, it can also be used as a reference book. The book:

1. Tells how to structure a forecasting problem so that alternative forecasting methods can be developed and evaluated effectively.
2. Discusses how to implement new forecasting methods.
3. Explains how to get forecasts accepted.
4. Describes a variety of forecasting methods, discusses their strengths and weaknesses, explains how to use them effectively, and tells where to find out more about the technical details. In keeping with my aim not to duplicate material already published, I have omitted technical details that are easily available from other sources. In effect, this book is more of a blueprint than a tool kit.
5. Helps you to select the most appropriate methods for a given forecasting problem.
6. Tells how to evaluate forecasting models. This is useful in selecting the most appropriate method for a particular problem, in trying to improve a given model, or in evaluating models developed by others.
7. Suggests what research on forecasting methods will have the greatest, and the least, payoff.
8. Summarizes and synthesizes research from a variety of areas. My review of this literature covered about 1300 books and articles primarily from the social and behavioral areas: economics, sociology, psychology, marketing, production, finance, demography, transportation, international business, politics, education, and social psychology. Occasional references are also made to work in medicine, meteorology, agriculture, and technology.

In addition, I think you will find the book enjoyable to read. The first draft was very technical and obscure. By this fifth and final draft, I was able to express my ideas in a form that is easier to understand and more precise. Most readers prefer this—and so do I. To my surprise, I found that many of the fancy ways of saying things were not necessary. Occasionally I had said something in a complex way because I did not know what I was talking about.

This book is readable. I checked it with the Flesch readability index (Flesch, 1956) and obtained a rating of 66 or "standard." This is about the same as the readability of a newspaper such as the *Wall Street Journal*. Similar results were obtained with the Gunning Fog Index (Gunning, 1959); this yielded a score of 13, which corresponds roughly to the educational level in school needed to comprehend the writing. In short, the book is much more readable than other scientific works. (Science is not big words, despite what some people think.)

One of my original objectives was to write the world's first obscene technical book. It did not turn out obscene, but I think it is fun to read. Research tells us that humor does not add to or detract from learning (Markiewicz, 1974); so why not have a bit of fun?

I am optimistic about the current state of knowledge about forecasting. After you read this book, I think you will agree that it would be difficult to find a situation where forecasting could not be improved with existing methods.

Philadelphia, Pennsylvania J. SCOTT ARMSTRONG
November 1977

ACKNOWLEDGMENTS FOR FIRST EDITION

Seventeen years: that's how long I spent on the preparation and writing of this book. The work was done as a staff analyst in industry, as an educator, and as a consultant in business and government. My experience included forecasting projects in many areas: photographic film processing, camera sales, steel production, production costs for a photographic manufacturer, political candidates and issues, construction contracts, finished goods inventory for duplicating machine parts, automobile sales, the selection of supermarkets by families, passenger travel by air, a proposed system for urban transportation, gasoline sales at various sites, steel drums, breakfast cereals, electrical components for military aircraft, job success for production workers, profits for automobile dealerships, choice of a brand of toothpaste, forest products, nonresponse bias in mail surveys, effects of educational experiments, lodging industry sales, and the health of "very important people" around the world.

In the course of these efforts, I received much help. The help came from business firms, especially

Eastman Kodak, Xerox, and Polaroid. It came from philanthropic institutions, especially the Ford Foundation, which supported this work when I was at M.I.T.; the National Science Foundation, which provided support for a summer so that I could conduct a literature search on forecasting methods in the social sciences; and the U.S. Government Work Study Program, which allowed me to hire some good people, especially Bill Tamulonis, Steve Lanset, and John O'Gorman.

Certain consulting contracts provided me with problems and with time to work on forecasting methods; these were with the Management Science Center at the University of Pennsylvania, the University City Science Center (Philadelphia), the C.I.A., and the U.S. Department of Transportation.

Various educational institutions also helped. M.I.T. provided me with money, help, and freedom. The Stockholm School of Economics provided time and a beautiful environment. The University of Pennsylvania provided an opportunity to experiment with *Long-Range Forecasting* as a text over a 7-year period, as well as a sabbatical in 1977 so that I could complete the book.

Libraries played a big part in my work. Most of the work was done at the University of Pennsylvania library. It is a bureaucratic nightmare and requires far too much time to find anything; despite this, it has some very helpful people who rise above the situation. The University of Rochester library, where I spent many vacations, is wonderful; it has a large and well-organized collection. The Stockholm School of Economics was outstanding in its ability to track down articles and to save time for me. Help was also received from the libraries at M.I.T., Drexel University, Carnegie-Mellon University, and the University of Hawaii.

The computer centers at M.I.T. and at the University of Pennsylvania were helpful for many of the analyses that are summarized in this book.

My most valuable help came from individuals, especially from two individuals. Don Peters, Corporate Director of Information Systems at EG&G in Boston, spent much time in discussions with me and worked on two early drafts of *Long-Range Forecasting (LRF)*. Don was good at telling me what I was really trying to say—and when I was going beyond the data.* Carl Harrington, a marketing manager from General Foods, played a big part in making improvements in the final version. He did some of the analyses and greatly improved the writing.

---

*A special thanks to Don because he convinced me that footnotes are not needed if you work hard enough on your writing. Footnotes interfere with communication.

Fritz Dressler from the University City Science Center, Rusty Scheewe of the University of New Hampshire, Tom Tessier of Arthur Andersen, and Mike Grohman of IBM each commented on two versions of *LRF*.

Comments on versions of *LRF* were provided by Ralph Day from Campbell Soup; Al Davis from the U.S. Air Force; Rolf Ruhfus from McKinsey Consulting (Germany); Frank Husic from Donaldson, Lufkin, and Jenrette; John Ferguson, Doug Crocker, and Bill Mountain from Eastman Kodak; Robert Fildes from Manchester University in England; George Wehrlin from Loeb, Rhoades; Ed Lusk from the Wharton School; Jan-Erik Modig from the Stockholm School of Economics; Lester Sartorius from the University of Texas; Jim Utterback from M.I.T. and Harvard; Andrew Sage from the University of Virginia; and Justis Muller from the University of Hawaii.

Some people were especially helpful in providing advice and support in early stages of this book. These were John Little and Paul MacAvoy from M.I.T., Ezra Krendel from Wharton, and David Pyle from the University of California at Berkeley.

Many people commented on specific chapters. Paul Kleindorfer, Tom Robertson, Alan Shapiro, Jerry Wind, Paul Green, Ron Frank, Len Lodish, Hank Brown, David Hildebrand, Dick Clelland, Morris Hamburg, Jean Crockett, Randy Batsell, Neil Beckwith, Howard Kunreuther, Andy Van de Ven, and Lawrence Klein, all from Wharton, were helpful. So were Paul Slovic and Robyn Dawes from Decision Research; Jim Castellan from Scott Paper; Frank Wolek from the U.S. Department of Commerce; Rich Bartlett from Bell Labs; Dick Cryer from Scholastic, Inc.; Mel Hirst from the University of Warwick (England); Joel Huber from Purdue; Gerry Barrett from the University of Akron; Carter Franklin from the University of Houston; Johan Arndt from the Norwegian School of Economics; Jeff Miller from Harvard; Franz Ettlin from the Stockholm School of Economics; Bob Brienholt from the Center for Professional Studies (Philadelphia); Stelios Kourakis, industrialist from Athens, Greece; and Gordon Welty from the Brookings Institution.

Thanks are due also to the many people who answered my letters for information, to Larry Robbins, who worked to improve my writing style, and to students at Wharton who provided comments, especially Kevin O'Keefe and Chuck Neul.

Typing on the first drafts of *LRF* was supervised by Anna-May Busch; this was truly fine service. The final draft was done by two of the best typists I know—Gwen Shannon and Aileen Cummings. The copy editor, Ruth Flohn, was outstanding; she found thousands of ways to improve the writing in *LRF*.

I am grateful to Ron Brennan of Wiley-Interscience for having faith and for allowing me to apply my strange style to this book.

My wife, Kay, provided comments on the book and helped me to live through the tough times that arise when one spends so many years writing a book.

Many others also helped. In all, well over 100 people provided criticisms and suggestions. The book owes a great deal to these people. Without their help the book would have been finished 5 years ago—but it wouldn't have been very good.

I learned (I think it was in 1958) that not everything written in books is true. This was a big discovery for me. This book is no exception. I have tried hard, and so did the people mentioned here. Still, the book contains mistakes. I will feel bad when they are found—but not as bad as I would have felt had I not warned you. I could have spend another 10 years on the book, but as my friend John Cronin told me, "If God had waited until he got everything right, we wouldn't be here."

J.S.A.

INSTRUCTIONS TO THE READER

1. Although much time and effort went into putting the pages in the order you find them, readers who have not had much experience with forecasting problems may want to read Part III, "Evaluation," before reading Part II, "Forecasting Methods."

2. The book can be used as a reference book (preferably after you have read it). A detailed table of contents is provided at the start of each chapter to help you. Also, annotated references, a list of exhibits, a glossary and indexes for people and subjects are included.

3. The book summarizes the existing empirical evidence. Descriptions of these studies are enclosed within the shaded boxes. You may skip the shaded material and still retain the train of thought. It is most important to read the shaded material when you disagree with the conclusions. (The conclusions will be stated before the shaded text).

4. Many of the technical details are easily found in previously published papers. If a source was difficult to obtain, I did discuss the details.

5. Good stopping places are at the ends of chapters except for Chapters 6 and 8, where intermissions are provided.

6. A glossary is provided because terminology varies among fields. The glossary also defines the symbols and abbreviations used in the book. (These terms are presented in boldface with a superscript "G" when they first appear in the text.)

7. The best way to learn from the book is to be considering a forecasting problem while you are reading the book.

8. Sometimes my humor is built around tongue-in-cheek comments where I overstate my case. This should cause no problem because the evidence behind the statement is presented in the book and you can reach your own conclusion. In fact, this humor has an advantage; it informs you of my opinions and biases. I have avoided the use of irony, so the meaning is never the opposite of that which is stated (except as noted in the book).

9. Tell all your friends about the good book you are reading.

CONTENTS

PART IV   COMPARING METHODS

PART V   COMMENCEMENT

EXHIBITS

This list will help you to use *LRF* as a reference book. It will be of most value to you after you have read the book. The exhibits include all cartoons, figures, photographs, and major tables.

LONG-RANGE FORECASTING
From Crystal Ball to Computer

Part I

GETTING STARTED

An overview of the book and a discussion of key concepts are provided in Part I. It includes four chapters. Chapter 1 defines the scope of the book and provides a brief overview. The systems approach is described in Chapter 2, along with a discussion of how it may be applied to forecasting problems. Chapter 3 discusses the most important aspects of forecasting—how to get people to adopt new methods and how to gain acceptance of forecasts. Finally, some general research strategies for model building and evaluation are discussed in Chapter 4.

Part I is more general than the rest of the book. Although the ideas in it may seem simple, to use them requires ingenuity. Part I is also less empirical than the rest of the book. I was inspired in this by Tukey (1962), who wrote, "Far better an approximate answer to the right question, which is often vague, than an exact answer to the wrong question, which can always be made precise."

It is hoped that the right questions have been addressed in Part I. Certainly the answers are approximate.

One

INTRODUCTION

Contents

If a man gives no thought about what is distant, he will find sorrow near at hand.

                                                                    Confucius

I could begin by telling you that times are becoming more turbulent and, as a result, our forecasts are becoming poorer. Hence, we need to put more emphasis on forecasting. *But that would be wrong.* From the evidence that I have been able to find (e.g., DAUB and PETERSON [1981]*), times have not become more turbulent and our forecasts have not become less accurate. So here is the new beginning: Think about the wonderful advances in management and social sciences. . . . How long did that take you? James LEE spent much time thinking about this issue in his book, *The Gold and the Garbage in Management Theories and Prescriptions*. He reached some dismal conclusions: Most of the important techniques have been known for many decades or even centuries, while many of the recent "advances" have proven to be of little value.

However, the situation in forecasting is different. Almost all significant research in the field has been done since 1960, and the results of this research have been remarkable. That is what this book is about. We can now make better forecasts and we also know more about how to convince people to act on these forecasts.

Chapter 1 is short. It relates forecasting to planning and decision making, and it also outlines what the rest of the book is about.

THE SCOPE OF THIS BOOK

To study long-range forecasting, we need to know where we are starting from and to be able to forecast for the short and intermediate terms. I could have called the book *Measurement and Forecasting Up to and Including Long-Range Forecasting,* but that is not a catchy title, to say the least. In any event, the book considers forecasting methods in general, but it has a bias toward long-range forecasting because research in this area has been especially useful.

Long-Range Forecasting (LRF) describes methods that can be used

---

*The references in capitals are in the UPDATED BIBLIOGRAPHY. The lower case references are from the original edition and they are located in the References. (The year of publication is indicated in the parentheses).

to forecast anything in the social, behavioral, or management sciences. Although the language differs greatly among fields, the techniques are similar. Forecasting sales of photographic goods draws upon many of the same techniques as forecasting the health of certain Very Important People around the world or forecasting gasoline sales at various sites.

How long is long range? That depends upon the situation; for example, a time period that is short range for the lumber industry is long range for the personal computer industry. I have struggled with various definitions—for example, "long range" is the length of time required for all parts of the system to react to given stimuli (in economics, this would be stated as the length of time it takes for supply to adjust to changes in demand); it is anything over 2 years in the future; it is the length of time over which large changes in the environment may be expected to occur. The last one is my favorite and I will use the terms "large changes in the environment" and "long range" interchangeably.

The definition of long range is not as clear as I would like it to be. You probably have your own idea of what long range means, but if you don't, the Wizard of Id certainly does, as shown in Exhibit 1-1.

The terms forecasting and prediction are used interchangeably in this book. Some writers make a big fuss over the differences between these terms. Neither Webster nor I see a difference that makes much difference. "Forecasting" seems to have a narrower meaning, connoting a statement about a future event, whereas "prediction" can refer to any unknown situation, past or future. But this is not an important point.

Exhibit 1-1   THE MEANING OF LONG-RANGE FORECASTING

THE WIZARD OF ID   by Brant parker and Johnny hart

Source.   "The Wizard Of Id," by permission of Johnny Hart and Field Enterprises, Inc.

Forecasting vs. Planning

Forecasting is often confused with planning. When the leader of an organization says that he would like a forecast, he often means that he wants a plan. He wants to make something happen, and he uses this plan to provide a target for people in his organization. This book is about forecasting, not planning.

Although *LRF* is not about planning, it is useful to consider how forecasting relates to planning. Forecasting is concerned with determining what the future *will* look like, rather than what it *should* look like. The latter is the job of planning. The forecast is an input to the planning model. A forecasting model can be used in an attempt to find out what the world will look like if you leave it alone ... or if you make different assumptions about the future ... or if you make changes.

The key steps in the planning process, illustrated in Exhibit 1-2, are to gain commitment to the process, to specify objectives, to generate strategies, to evaluate strategies, and to monitor results.

The argument is sometimes raised that planning is of prime importance while forecasting is of minor importance. As long as a reasonable forecast can be made, the argument goes, there is little gain from improved accuracy. The major benefits come from the development of a better and a more consistent plan and from a comparison of alternative plans under a given set of assumptions about the future. In my opinion, this argument has little merit. Even if forecasting were less important than planning, it would not follow that forecasting is unimportant in an absolute sense. It may be worthwhile to spend money on both planning and forecasting.

Don't get me wrong. I am also an advocate of formal planning. So, apparently, are many others, as this has been a rapidly growing activity in organizations. Also, I have reviewed the empirical evidence

---

Exhibit 1-2   STEPS IN THE PLANNING PROCESS

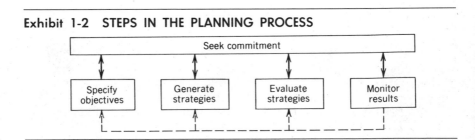

and have concluded that firms using explicit approaches to long-range planning do better than those that do not (ARMSTRONG [1982c], SHRADER, TAYLOR, and DALTON [1984].) Firms also do better after they start using explicit approaches to long-range planning than before using them. So planning is useful as well as popular.

The interest in long-range planning and its apparent success should lead to an increased interest in long-range forecasting. This appears to be the case. For example, there has been a marked increase in the number of firms that claim to engage in long-range forecasting. Jantsch (1967, p. 27) refers to a survey by the McGraw-Hill Economics Department that estimated that in 1947 approximately 20% of all firms attempted forecasts over time spans of 3 years or longer while about 90% did so in 1966. This growth led to the formation of the International Institute of Forecasters in 1982.

Forecasting and Decision Making

A forecast is often required whenever a decision is made. This is especially true for decisions that have long term consequences. Organizations must make decisions involving the location of facilities, the hiring of key personnel, the types of products to provide, contracts with suppliers and unions, and financing. Individuals must make decisions involving expenditures for college, the choice of a career, health treatments, marriage, running for public office, buying a house, writing a book on long-range forecasting, and so on. Because such decisions must be made, it is desirable to forecast their consequences.

Exhibit 1-3 summarizes the various types of forecasts needed within the firm. For example, General Motors would need forecasts of the environment (e.g., GNP and tariffs), the industry (total auto sales), their own actions (possible marketing strategies and likelihood of successful implementation), competitors' actions (reactions to GM strategies), market share (relative prices of competitors' products), sales (calculated from preceding forecasts), costs, and results (e.g., profits, recalls, law suits, customer satisfaction, and employee layoffs). A more complete discussion of this framework is provided in ARMSTRONG [1983a].

Of course, it is often possible to avoid forecasting. ACKOFF [1983, p. 6] points out that if we can control the future, we do not need to forecast (just as we do not need to forecast the weather inside our houses). To the extent that we can respond rapidly, we need no forecasts (as in driving an automobile). FILDES [1982] discusses other ways to

Exhibit 1-3   NEED FOR FORECASTS IN A FIRM

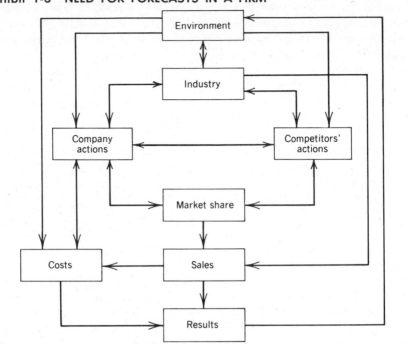

avoid forecasts, such as buying insurance, diversifying one's strategy, and hedging one's bets. Contingency planning, illustrated by Wee Pals in Exhibit 1-4, provides still another way.

THE APPROACH USED IN *LRF*

I draw upon my experience in this book. Although experience is a great motivator of learning, it is an inefficient way to learn, and I, like others, tend to see what I want to see. So when I draw *only* upon my experience in *LRF,* I will let you know. In this manner you will at least be aware of my biases.

Much of what is reported in this book goes beyond my experience to report on research. I have done some of the research, but most of it has been done by others. This research is examined, summarized, and occasionally reanalyzed in an attempt to draw conclusions about forecasting methods. For some critical areas, I hired research assistants to code independently the empirical studies to determine how the con-

Exhibit 1-4 CONTINGENCY PLANNING AS A SUBSTITUTE FOR FORECASTING

Source. "Wee Pals" comic strip, by permission of Morrie Turner. © 1970, The Register and Tribune Syndicate.

clusions related to certain hypotheses. I also asked the original authors whether my interpretation was correct. In addition, I received critiques from about 100 people who read early drafts of *LRF*, from 40 reviews of the first edition, and from many who reviewed the second edition.

The most useful type of research for *LRF* was that which used **multiple hypotheses**[G] and empirical research. For example, studies that compared the effectiveness of two or more forecasting methods in an actual forecasting situation were of immense value. These studies and others are described in the annotated references at the end of *LRF* and in the UPDATED BIBLIOGRAPHY.

AN OVERVIEW OF THE BOOK

This book is divided into five parts—"Getting Started," "Forecasting Methods," "Evaluation," "Comparing Methods," and "Commencement." The relationships among these sections are illustrated in Exhibit 1-5. Note that Parts II and III may be read in either order.

Part I, "GETTING STARTED," presents a short introduction to the book, a description of how to implement different methods of long-range forecasting, and a discussion of the systems approach and its relevance to long-range forecasting. Some general research strategies are then described.

[G] Boldface type with the superscript G is used in *LRF* to indicate some of the terms defined in the glossary. It is used only when it is felt that different readers may have different definitions and then only for the *first appearance of the term* in *LRF*.

Part II, "FORECASTING METHODS," examines methods one might use in long-range forecasting. Consideration is given to the most effective way to use judgmental, extrapolation, econometric, and segmentation methods, as well as combinations of these methods. The use of combined forecasts is also examined.

Part III, "EVALUATION," discusses how to evaluate forecasting models and processes. This includes how to analyze inputs to a model, as well as how to analyze the outputs from it. The section on evaluating outputs may be used to select the best method for a given problem. It also describes how to conduct an audit on the forecasting process used by an organization.

Part IV, "COMPARING METHODS," examines the relative advantages of each of the forecasting methods. I have presented evidence to identify the methods that are best in each situation. A guide is constructed to help you to select the methods most appropriate for your problem.

Part V, "COMMENCEMENT," discusses which forecasting methods will prove to be more popular and more useful in the future. It also suggests areas where further research on forecasting methods will be most valuable—and what research areas will have the smallest payoffs.

SUMMARY

There were few surprises in Chapter 1. The primary objective was to tell you what the book will cover. It covers forecasting methods . . .

Exhibit 1-5   PLAN FOR THIS BOOK

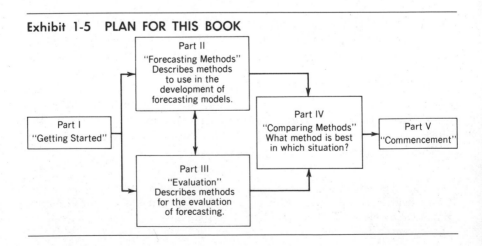

and evaluation . . . from short- to long-range, with the emphasis on the latter . . . in the social, behavioral, and management areas. It does not cover planning or decision making, although it is closely related to both.

The approach used in this book is primarily to test hypotheses by examining all relevant empirical evidence. This evidence is fully disclosed.

An overview of the book appears in Exhibit 1-5.

Two

THE SYSTEMS
APPROACH

Contents

Having lost sight of our objective, we redoubled our efforts.

Old Adage

This chapter presents a simple idea. I call it the systems approach. The systems approach is described here because it is important for the development, evaluation, and implementation of forecasting methods. It will also help you understand how I reach some of the more unorthodox conclusions found in this book.

Although operational steps will be described and examples presented, you will not learn how to use the systems approach by reading this chapter. However, people have *used* this description and have learned to make it work—and that's what the "other good advice" at the end of the chapter is about.

DESCRIPTION OF THE SYSTEMS APPROACH

The systems approach uses two basic ideas. First, one should examine objectives before considering ways of solving a problem; and, second, one should begin by describing the system in general terms before proceeding to the specific. These ideas are illustrated in Exhibit 2-1. The arrows indicate time priorities, and the boxes indicate the separate steps of the approach. Thus the first step is the identification of the objectives of the system, and the last step is the development of an operational program.

A separate time period should be allocated to each step in the systems approach. This is important because most of us feel more comfortable when working on the operational program. Time spent on the

Exhibit 2-1   THE SYSTEMS APPROACH

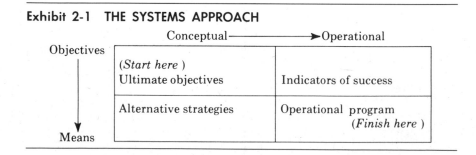

Objectives	Conceptual ————————→ Operational	
	(*Start here*) Ultimate objectives	Indicators of success
Means	Alternative strategies	Operational program (*Finish here*)

other stages often appears to be wasted; it creates tension, especially for experts. However, dramatic gains are often made by working on the three other stages, and that is where creative people spend more time. Therefore it is generally wise to allocate a significant portion of time to each of the four stages. Each step should be done independently of the one following. Most importantly, the identification of objectives should proceed without consideration being given to the steps that follow. Each step should be carried out in an explicit manner with a written summary.

Identifying Objectives

"Cheshire-Puss," she [Alice] began, "Would you tell me, please, which way I ought to go from here?"

"That depends a good deal on where you want to get to," said the Cat.

Lewis Carroll

One interesting thing about this section is that it is written not for us, but for other people. We all have a good ability to recognize the objectives of a system. I must confess, however, that I, like those others, often ignore the advice in this section, sometimes to my lasting regret.

The first step in the systems approach is to identify the ultimate objectives of the system. This analysis should start at the highest conceptual level. Common sense, certainly; but those *other people* don't follow it. Therefore we pay experts like Ted Levitt to spend their lives telling other people about this idea. Incidently, Ted Levitt wrote what is probably the most famous article in the field of marketing. This article stresses the importance of beginning with ultimate objectives rather than with operational goals. (Actually, I think he stole the idea from the Bible or from Shakespeare . . . or was it Adam Smith?) In any event, you can read his article (Levitt, 1960), or you can read a book about the article (Levitt, 1962). His advice is sound, simple, and generally ignored by other people.

No consideration should be given to alternative strategies during the initial phase. Set up a separate time period for this analysis. Write a separate report on objectives. Review the objectives to ensure that they do not imply strategies. This advice is also simple. Why is it often ignored? Perhaps because we are taught to accept tradition. Tradition tells us how, not why.

An example from marketing may help to illustrate the analysis of objectives. One of my projects involved making forecasts for the cereal market. It was possible to recast this problem in more general terms by looking at needs such as nourishment. Man's need for nourishment has been studied extensively, and it changes slowly; however, his preference for different types of foods, such as cereals, changes rapidly. Ccreals are a means to an end; substitutes for cereals include eggs, instant breakfasts, pills, or fasting. In our problem, it helped first to go back to consider the ultimate needs served by the product.

One technique for identifying objectives is the stakeholder analysis. The first step in a stakeholder analysis is to identify all the groups (or individuals) who may possibly be affected by a change in the system. **Brainstorming**[G] can help in compiling a list of these groups. Another approach is to publicize the fact that changes are being considered in the organization and see who responds. Still another alternative is to consult experts.

When the list of interest groups has been identified, the objectives of each group should be listed. This may also be done by brainstorming. Even better, one can survey people from each group in order to determine their objectives.

Although *LRF* relates to means (forecasting methods) rather than to objectives (decision making), this book places much emphasis on objective-setting. One small example: I make a distinction between "forecasting models" and "measurement models." The objectives of this book relate to forecasting models. Measurement models are only a means to the development of forecasting models.

The preceding paragraph is probably not much clearer than a passage from *Alice in Wonderland*. We call forecasting models "forecasting models" because that is what they are. Most people who discuss forecasting models *don't* call them forecasting models. They find other names such as regression, computer, judgmental, or econometric models. In short, they name the model not for its objective but for its method. The fact that the model is named on the basis of means rather than ends tends to divert the researcher's attention from what he is trying to do, to how he does it—an unfortunate, but certainly not uncommon, consequence.

My associate, Fritz Dressler, has generalized about the researcher's devotion to method rather than objectives and has developed the *rainmaker theories*. Here are some examples:

Rainmaker Theory Number One. "The rainmaker gets so involved with the dance that he sometimes forgets that he has to make rain."

Rainmaker Theory Number Two. "Yes, I know it didn't rain—but didn't you like the dance?" In other words, the successful rainmaker is the one who can convince his client that he really didn't want rain—he wanted to watch the dance.

Rainmaker Theory Number Three. "Who cares why it rains?" The science of rainmaking evolves into the science of rainmaking dances.

Here is a rain dance example. Once upon a time, I was on an admissions committee for a graduate business school. The committee used a weighting scheme to predict which students would successfully complete the graduate program. Someone (probably I) suggested that we take a broader view of our objectives. For example, what should people be like after they finish the program? In what ways do we or can we help people? What benefits do they receive? The proposal was roundly shouted down. We spent about an hour discussing whether we could devote 15 minutes to assessing objectives—then voted not to spend the 15 minutes. The consensus was: "I've been in discussions like this before and nothing fruitful ever comes of them." The chairman summed up things this way: "First we'll figure out how to admit students. If we have any time, we'll come back and examine why we're admitting them." And he was serious! This is only one of many similar experiences I have encountered in both business and academic life. For further reading, try Vonnegut's *Player Piano,* Kafka's *Amerika,* or Heller's *Catch-22.* For further evidence, look at your own organization; note that you generally have no problems if you fail to reach the ultimate goal of the organization. But what happens if you fail to use the prescribed method?

The identification of objectives is probably the most important step in the systems approach. This is especially true because it is the most widely ignored step. Further consideration will be given to this idea in Chapter 3.

Indicators of Success

Before charging off after the objectives, you should decide what point you are trying to reach, and how you would know if you ever got there. In other words, it is important to establish explicit indicators of success.

The list of objectives from the preceding section serves as the starting point in the development of indicators of success. In this step, procedures are developed to measure how changes in the system will affect each of the objectives. This phase is difficult and requires a lot of psychic energy.

It is desirable to find measures that can be quantified and, better still, measures that can be *accurately* quantified. In the example that described procedures for admission to graduate school, the success of students was quantified by grades in courses. However, faculty grades of students lack **reliability.**[G] Different raters usually provide widely different grades for the same piece of work if the ratings are done independently.

The measures should relate to the objectives of the forecasting exercise. This is a question of **validity.**[G] Do the indicators measure what they are intended to? As to the prediction of student success, grades by teachers have been shown to lack validity. A brief summary of the evidence on this issue is provided by ARMSTRONG [1980c]. (What *do* grades by faculty measure, you ask? Probably obedience, ability to follow directions, flattery, and cheating. Oh, where have you gone, Joe DiMaggio? Is it true you're Mr. Coffee now?)

Alternative Strategies

It is important to prepare more than one strategy for meeting the objectives. Sometimes it helps to obtain suggestions from different people, especially from those with different types of expertise. This process can be improved further by using brainstorming.

Ideally, the various strategies should differ substantially. Unfortunately, we are usually trained in narrow specialties and consequently become experts in only a small number of strategies. One of the objectives of *LRF* is to help you go beyond your current area of expertise.

Developing Programs

At this stage, a preliminary screening can be conducted to reduce the alternative strategies to a manageable number. This can be done by rating the alternative strategies against one another, using the indicators of success as the criteria. You could set minimum acceptable targets for each indicator and then see which strategies can exceed each of these minimums. (This approach is known as **satisficing.**[G]) Another approach is to compare programs using a subjective unit weighting scale of better (+ 1), even (0), or worse (− 1), and summing the total.

The more promising strategies can then be translated into an operational program. **Scenarios**[G] may be useful at this point to help ensure that each aspect of the program has been adequately covered. Scenarios are stories describing the environment, how a strategy can be implemented, and what results are likely.

Further screening may then follow, using the same procedures as above. Satisficing can be applied with new minimum levels, and the unit weighting scheme can also be used. At this point, however, choices among different strategies become more difficult to make. One solution is to try to translate each indicator into a common unit of measure, such as dollars. This requires weighting the various objectives of stakeholders to provide what is essentially a cost-benefit analysis. (Encel, Marstrand, and Page, 1975, provide a lengthy discussion of cost-benefit analysis.)

An alternative solution is to carry along more than one strategy, perhaps on an experimental basis. Alternative strategies can also serve as contingency plans. If the preferred strategy does not perform as hoped, or if conditions change, the contingency plan can be used.

Comparisons among alternative programs can also be aided by presenting the scenarios to the stakeholders for their reactions. This topic is discussed further in Chapter 3.

Ideally, this step would complete the systems analysis. In practice, however, it is frequently necessary to return to earlier steps once this point is reached. In other words, the systems approach is used in an iterative manner.

VIOLATING THE SYSTEMS APPROACH

What happens when the systems approach is violated in forecasting? That's simple: you are more likely to get poor forecasts, and there is a greater probability that someone will criticize your work in a book on forecasting methods.

Hacke (1967) demonstrated what can happen when the systems approach is ignored. He provided a nine-year forecast of transistor production. Although the forecast was published in 1967, it had actually been based on data through 1957 and the forecast was made for 1966.

The forecast was made by extrapolating historical data on transistors. Forecasters using the systems approach would find this odd because consumers have no basic need for transistors. They have need for things like visual and audio entertainment, and thus for TVs and radios, but not for transistors. Transistors represent only a means to an end. Furthermore, substitutes for transistors, such as vacuum tubes, existed.

The growth rate of transistors was about 230% per year. As a result, the direct extrapolation forecasted a sizable production for 1966. After playing with different extrapolation techniques, Hacke predicted (i.e., with 95% confidence limits) that the U.S. production rate in 1966 would be between 6 billion and 690 billion units. Now wouldn't you say that this is a rather large confidence interval?

Contrast the direct model in Hacke's example with one that initially forecasts at a slightly higher conceptual level by considering the market for transistors *and* its close substitute, vacuum tubes. Certainly this model is closer to representing the visual and audio entertainment market. An analysis of the data for this market, using the 1941–1957 period, indicated that the growth rate was 11% per year. On the basis of this growth rate, a market forecast could be prepared.

This forecast for transistors can be made by forecasting the transistor market share and multiplying it by the market forecast. The market share was only 6% in 1957, but it had been growing rapidly. On the assumption that growth would continue, the market share could be between 6% and 100% in 1966. Let's choose the midpoint, 53%, as the 1966 forecast. Using this simple model, transistor production would grow from 30 million units in 1957 to 700 million units in 1966. This forecast is substantially less than the minimum forecast of 6 billion units based on the direct extrapolation.

The actual production of transistors in 1966 was about 850 million units. The industry grew at about the same rate, and the market share for transistors increased from about 6% to about 60%. This actual value was 14% of Hacke's minimum prediction and less than 1% of the most likely prediction.

The prediction from the simple model that was formulated in more general terms proved to be much more accurate. Furthermore, given the market forecast, the assumption of growth, and the limits on market share, it would have been impossible to miss the prediction as badly as did the direct extrapolation in the illustration by Hacke.

OTHER GOOD ADVICE

I have never been able to teach anyone how to use the systems approach. A few people have learned how to use it; sometimes they said I helped. But the biggest problem is simply a matter of trying.

Everyone likes to read about general laws in a book like this. So I will tell you about a law that has inspired me to get over my natural tendency to say "no." It's the well-known Gerstenfeld's *law of trying*. It was discovered one night by my friend, Art Gerstenfeld, upon returning home from work. Gerstenfeld's son met him at the door, and the following exchange took place between the two:

"Daddy, fix my bike for me."

"I don't know anything about bikes."

"Daddy, please fix my bike."

"I don't know how to fix your bike!"

"Daddy, *please* fix my bike!"

"I don't know *how* to fix your bike!"

PAUSE

"But, Daddy, you can try, can't you?"

ANOTHER PAUSE

"Yes, I suppose that I can try."

Exhibit 2-2   THE DISCOVERY OF GERSTENFELD'S LAW OF TRYING

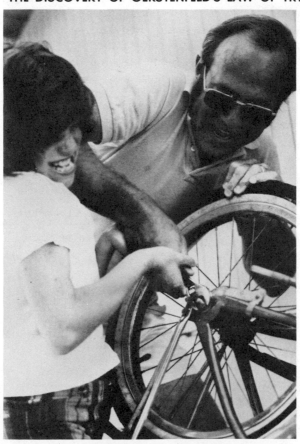

"And you know," said my friend Gerstenfeld later, "I did fix that bike." Exhibit 2-2 reenacts the discovery of Gerstenfeld's law of trying (by the real Gerstenfeld and his son).

SUMMARY

In this chapter the systems approach was proposed as a way to structure forecasting problems. This calls for an evaluation of objectives before means, and for a consideration of the general before the specific. It is carried out in four steps as shown in Exhibit 2-3. This exhibit also contains a checklist of procedures that might be used in each step. In addition, four general procedures carry across all four steps:

1. Write it! (An average person with time, a pencil, paper, and a systematic approach will beat a smart person who "thinks on his feet.")
2. Plan separate time periods for each step.
3. Omit reference to steps that come later.
4. Remember that objectives come first and the program comes last.

Finally, the issue is not whether we understand this approach (most of us do), but whether we use it (most of us don't). Gerstenfeld's law of trying was suggested to inspire use of the systems approach.

Exhibit 2-3 CHECKLIST FOR THE SYSTEMS APPROACH

Steps	Checklist of Procedures	Done?
Identify objectives	Start at highest conceptual level	____
	Use stakeholder analysis	____
Develop indicators of success	Build in reliability	____
	Build in validity	____
Generate alternative strategies	Use experts from different areas	____
	Use brainstorming	____
Develop and select programs	Write scenarios	____
	Satisfice or use unit weights	____

Three

IMPLEMENTATION

Contents

If you're not part of the solution, you're part of the problem.

Source Unknown

A youth group at a church was asked to participate in a study (Batson, 1975). As part of this study, they were asked to indicate how strongly they believed Jesus Christ to be God. They were then told that some documents had recently been discovered by archeologists. The documents were said to be correspondence that took place among the apostles after Christ died. The basic theme was similar to a Watergate cover-up: now that Christ has died, people will realize that he is not God; what can we do to fool them? The apostles concluded that people want to believe Christ is God, so the deception could be carried on.

The members of the church youth group were told that *The New York Times,* under pressure from the World Council of Churches, was withholding the story. Their reactions were being studied to see what would happen should *The New York Times* release the story. After learning about the documents, the youth group members completed a second questionnaire that asked how strongly they now believed that Christ was God.

What happened? In general, this disconfirming evidence led the believers to *increase* their belief that Christ was God. Furthermore, the increase was greatest for members who had initially felt most strongly that Christ was God. Finally, the increase was strongest for the people who believed that the information was authentic!

Readers who are familiar with **cognitive dissonance**[G] studies may not find these results surprising. There have been other studies with similar findings. People who believe in the rational man may, however, be surprised.

Even a person who is familiar with cognitive dissonance studies will find that the above results are depressing. In every organization that I have worked for, the official approach to change is based on the assumption that man is rational. "If you present evidence that the new way is better than the old, then people will accept the new way." This works for unimportant changes, but not for changes that are important to people. So we cling to the model of rational man and go around saying things like "People are resistant to change." Dramatic examples of such resistance are provided in MOSTELLER and TUKEY [1977] and ROGERS [1983]. For example, in 1601, lemons were found to be an effective way to prevent scurvy, but it was 264 years before this finding was adopted by the British Merchant Marine.

Fortunately, there has been much research on how to implement change. The research is not new; it has been going on for half a century. It is extensive and offers clear guidelines on how to implement change. A summary of the research is included in this chapter.

Unfortunately, the answer does not lie in the presentation of empirical evidence. People's attitudes toward change are analogous to the attitudes of the youth group members that Christ is God. Thrusting disconfirming evidence upon them will only strengthen their present beliefs.

If you already know how to implement change, you have just finished this chapter. If, on the other hand, you are interested in improving your techniques you may be able to make this chapter work for you.

Although you can branch around this chapter without losing the train of thought, you should recognize one thing: surveys of problems in the use of forecasting methods (e.g., Wheelwright and Clarke, 1976) indicate that implementation problems are probably the most important reasons for failure. The surveys are right.

If you want to branch around this section, go to Chapter 4, p. 51.

Chapter 3 presents a framework for implementing changes in forecasting methods. The framework builds upon the discussion of the systems approach in the preceding chapter. Consideration is also given to the way people use forecasts.

A FRAMEWORK FOR IMPLEMENTATION

Let's start with a problem—the COMPU-HEART Case. A description is presented here. As you read it, write out the strategy that you would use to solve it. As motivation, I can tell you that this problem has been used often as a role-playing case. Although people are sometimes given a few days to think about the case, it is a rare individual who produces a strategy that is successful in the role play.

The COMPU-HEART Case

To provide space for its outpatient facilities, Rosemont Hospital had examined its inpatient program. When considering the whole system, they concluded that there were clear-cut benefits for reducing the space allotted to patients with heart problems. In fact, they were excited about a program called COMPU-HEART, that provided home treatment for heart patients. This could be done by paramedics who visit the patient, perform some simple tests, and ask questions of the patient. The paramedics then call a time-sharing computer system that suggests what steps should be taken (e.g., "do nothing," "send patient to hospital," "contact personal physician," "eliminate drug X" . . .). This program was developed by modeling the decisions used by a committee composed of 10 of the best heart specialists in the world. The computer is already used by Rosemont for other purposes, so the startup costs would not be large.

An experimental study run at a hospital in Los Angeles found that use of COMPU-HEART resulted in:

1. Fewer fatalities,
2. Faster recovery rate for patients,
3. More satisfaction among patients, and
4. *Much* lower costs.

However, you realize that when previous suggestions of a similar nature had been made, the doctors were skeptical. So, even though the doctors are currently overworked and this proposal would save time for them, you expect them to resist this change. The doctors prefer to have the patients in the hospital where they can see them and talk with them. They do not trust paramedics or computers to handle the situation.

You have scheduled a meeting with the doctors' decision-making committee. You would like to convince them to accept the COMPU-HEART program.

STOP!! Write out your strategy before proceeding.

That's the problem—and we'll solve it before the chapter ends. (Fortunately, I have heard Chekhov's advice to writers. As I remember, he said, "If you describe a house, and within that house you describe the living room, and within the living room you describe the fireplace, and then you go into detail about the gun that hangs over the fireplace, be sure the gun fires before the story ends!")

The framework for implementing changes in forecasting methods (actually, you can use it for implementing any type of change) is illustrated in Exhibit 3-1. This framework draws heavily upon the systems approach. The four rectangles follow the four-step procedure of the systems approach, but the approach is translated into one that is useful for implementation. The rules for application also follow those for the systems approach:

1. Write your analysis!
2. Use separate time periods for each step.
3. Omit references to steps that come later.
4. Objectives come first and programs come last.

In practice, some iteration is generally necessary. The two way arrows in Exhibit 3-1 indicate where iteration is needed most often. Note that the research, for example, the development of new forecasting methods, does not start until after commitment has been reached. This

Exhibit 3-1   FRAMEWORK FOR IMPLEMENTING NEW METHODS

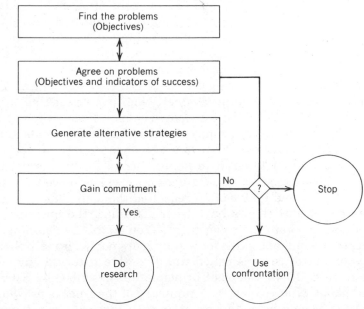

procedure will cause a bit of stress in the organization because managers will be reluctant to commit themselves before they have "all the facts."

The following discussion is organized according to the steps in the four rectangles in Exhibit 3-1. Consideration is also given to the choices involved when one fails to reach commitment.

FINDING PROBLEMS

This section examines the procedure for finding problems. First, consider what not to do. Do not think about solutions at this point. Be problem-minded rather than solution-minded. This is easier said than done; what is needed are some positive steps.

The first step in finding the problem is to meet with the client and listen to her viewpoint. Unfortunately, the identity of the client is not always obvious. Let me tell you about one of my failures. My colleagues and I were asked by a large food processor to evaluate some forecasting models and to recommend improvements. The man who requested the study said that he would make the decision. He was backed up by a sign in his office saying "The Buck Stops Here." After we were well into the analysis, we learned that a decision had already been made in this case, and it had been made by someone other than our buck-stopper. (How did the story end? Our analysis conflicted with the decision. We were given the option of changing our conclusion to keep the dollars rolling in to us. Instead, we presented our analysis as we saw it, . . . becoming poorer but happier in the process.)

One technique for identifying the client is the stakeholder analysis. As described in the preceding chapter, this involves listing all the groups that will be affected by a proposed change. For new forecasting methods, the affected groups will typically include users and producers such as those listed in Exhibit 3-2. It is a good idea to start off assuming that all groups are interested in being clients. In my work, I have occasionally ignored some of these groups because I assumed they would have no interest, and I have often regretted the omissions.

After the various clients have been identified, the question then arises of how to obtain their viewpoints. You do this by listening. But listening is difficult, and skills for listening are not intuitively obvious. One helpful set of rules is called **nondirective interviewing**[G]. According to LEE [1980], the basic principle was described by King Issi of Egypt about 4700 years ago. A summary of the rules is provided in Exhibit 3-3. People have told me that with these rules, a **learning partner**[G] and a tape recorder, they have been able to master nondi-

---

**Exhibit 3-2   A CHECKLIST OF STAKEHOLDERS
IN FORECASTING PROBLEMS**

Users

 Accounting
 Finance
 Management
 Marketing
 Personnel
 Production
 Research and development

Producers

 Analysts with competing proposals
 Computer and software groups
 Developers of the current method
 Groups responsible for new methods
 Preparers of the forecasts
 Suppliers of data

---

rective interviewing in about one day. If you do not want to do that, you can hire an expert in nondirective interviewing (available at your local marketing research firm). It is much more practical to learn how to use nondirective interviewing yourself. There are two key ideas behind the rules for nondirective interviewing. First, your role is to listen, and second, you should not evaluate what is said. More is said about each of the rules in the following paragraphs.

Describe the purpose of the meeting.   There's nothing devious here. You tell the clients why you are meeting with them. You are there primarily to listen during this meeting. You want to find out how they

---

Exhibit 3-3   RULES FOR NONDIRECTIVE INTERVIEWING

Do	Don't
Describe purpose of meeting	Evaluate
Check your understanding	Interrupt
Follow up on areas of interest	Introduce your ideas
Take notes	Worry about pauses

view the problem (e.g., "Because you are a user of this forest products forecast, I'm interested in finding out what problems you see with it").

Problems can also be viewed as the difference between where one is now and where one would like to be. Thus you can ask the client to describe her objectives and where she feels she is now. The problems are later inferred by the analyst from the equation: *problems = objectives − current situation.*

People often have difficulty in discussing objectives. Try to probe at this point by asking *why,* or by asking what measures would define an ideal state for them. Your aim is to develop some indicators of success from this interview.

The discussion of the current situation for forecasting problems involves such things as the methods presently used, the current level of accuracy, the cost, and the purposes for which the forecasts are now being used. A good analysis at this stage will help you to avoid reinventing the current solutions.

Don't evaluate.   The analyst should not evaluate what is said. You should avoid positive as well as negative evaluation.

Don't interrupt.   Your job is to listen. It helps when the clients talk, so don't stop them.

Don't introduce your ideas.   Thinking about your own ideas will make it harder for you to listen. Talking about your own ideas will make it difficult for the client to speak.

Don't worry about pauses.   There seems to be a Parkinson's law of conversations: words expand to fill the time allowed. Silence embarasses people. The problem is especially severe with only two people in a meeting; one talks and one listens with the result that neither one has much time to think. In any event, with some practice, you will find that pauses do not bother you. In fact, they often occur when the client is thinking or when she is mulling over the possibility of telling you something important. You will be able to tell whether she is thinking or whether it is time for you to talk.

Check your understanding.   As the interview proceeds, summarize what you have heard to see whether you have understood correctly. This does two things: it helps you to listen and it lets the speaker know that you are interested in what she says.

Follow up on areas of interest. If the client mentions an area that is of particular interest and you would like to know more, ask! For example, "You say that you've been having trouble understanding the assumptions behind the forecasts. Could you say more about that?" This also does two things: it helps you to listen, and it lets the speaker know that you are interested in what she says.

Take notes. Again, this does two things: it helps you remember important points, and it lets the speaker know that you are interested in what she says.

Thank the respondent. She is helping you.

Be sure to allow ample time for the interview. I generally prefer to allocate 2 hours; 1½ hours is sometimes adequate; 1 hour is often too short. Nobody said finding problems was cheap.

AGREEING ON PROBLEMS

Consider the following problem (adapted from Maier and Solem, 1952). "A man bought a horse for $60 and sold it for $70. Then he bought it back again for $80 and sold it for $90. How much money did he make in the horse business?" (STOP! Record your answer here _____ unless your library "cautions the careless reader against the marking of books.")

Now consider another problem. "A man bought a horse for $60 and sold it for $70. Then he bought a *pig* for $80 and sold it for $90. How much money did he make in the animal business?" Record your answer here _____ .

For a number of people, the two answers above will be different. In fact, Maier and Solem found that fewer than half the people who were asked the horse question got the right answer (see Appendix F for the answer). I have used the animal question and found that almost everyone gets the correct answer.

Here we have a simple problem in arithmetic. Yet the way the problem is stated affects the answer. The statement of the problem would be expected to be even more important in complex situations.

Problem statements can mislead us in many ways. The problem can be intentionally disguised to make the client look good (I learned this as an industrial engineer); the problem statement may be constrained because it has to be acceptable to the organization; or the problem may carry emotional overtones. Probably the most serious difficulty is that the statement of the problem often implies a solution.

A useful technique for avoiding difficulties in the statement of the problem is to state it in different ways. This can be done by obtaining viewpoints of the problem from different people. It can be done by having a brainstorming session on "stating the problem."

These statements of the problem should be reported to the clients. This allows them to see the problem as viewed by different people. At this point, you can also present your own views on the problem. The clients should then reach a consensus on the problems to be examined. One approach to reaching a **consensus**^{G} is provided in the glossary. You may have your own style for running meetings in order to gain a consensus. (My own style follows Maier, (1963), a highly pragmatic and useful book.) Whatever your style, avoid voting and, instead, work toward a consensus.

A good job of identifying the problems will reduce the likelihood of **Type III errors**^{G}. (Type III errors are good solutions to the wrong problems.)

PROPOSING ALTERNATIVE SOLUTIONS

The clients will generally be interested in making proposals about possible solutions. You can get them to generate ideas here by using brainstorming. The brainstorming sessions will not only help to discover ideas but will also allow the clients to keep control of the change process. This is an important part of what Kurt Lewin referred to as the unfreezing phase in his unfreezing, change, and refreezing model. Evidence on the importance of unfreezing is provided in GINZBERG [1979] and ZAND and SORENSEN [1975].

For the part of the problem relating to specific forecasting methods, the clients will probably rely on you as the analyst. You can use the methodology tree (Exhibit 5-2, page 77) as a checklist. Specific techniques are described in Chapters 6 through 10.

GAINING COMMITMENT

Commitment is aided by use of the problem identification stages. If the client defines the problem and suggests possible methods, she will be more interested in the solution. Returning to the "COMPU-HEART Case", the assumptions the role players make about how the problem was defined are important. When a person proposes a new technique, he may refer to "our previous meeting, where you stated that we should look into ways of solving our problem of the shortage of space."

The likelihood of gaining the client's commitment to solutions can be increased by use of the three guidelines outlined in Exhibit 3-4. Some participants in the COMPU-HEART Case were given 10-minutes of instruction in these rules; these participants were generally successful in gaining management's agreement to run an experiment. Additional support is found in the results of tests reported in ARMSTRONG [1982a]. This strategy also worked in the study from which the problem was drawn (Marrow and French, 1945). Management did try an experiment, and it led to change.

**Exhibit 3-4   GUIDELINES FOR GAINING COMMITMENT
             TO SOLUTIONS**

---

1. Don't sell the change; sell an experiment
2. Stakeholders should participate in the experiment:
    (a) Setting criteria
    (b) Describing constraints
3. Provide feedback to stakeholders

The guidelines for commitment are based on a simple philosophy: people who are affected by a change should have control over the change process whenever feasible (and it is usually feasible). The control should be real, not merely an illusion of control. (It is seldom that clients can be tricked in this respect, and then only once.) Techniques for implementing these guidelines are described in the following section. For want of a better name, I refer to this as the Delta Technique.

Experimentation

The resistance to *experimentation* is lower than the resistance to change. Most people like to view themselves as being open to new ideas.

The experiment should allow for a comparison between the proposed methods and the method that is currently being used; this will give the various stakeholders a chance to examine the new method in a factual way. The experiment should also be small scale in order to reduce risk for the stakeholders. They can experience the new method without having to make a substantial investment.

In addition to giving clients control over the change, the experiment may lead to revisions that improve the proposed method. These revisions can be made before everyone gets committed to doing things in a particular way. Also, what if the proposal doesn't work the way everyone expected that it would? The experiment allows the proposal to be dropped in a graceful and face-saving way, and it saves the organization from making an ineffective change.

The term "experiment" is used in a general sense here. We need an answer to this question: "What information do you need to convince *you* that the current methods should be replaced by the proposed methods?" In most circumstances, this question would imply the need for an experiment. Sometimes, however, it may call for an analysis of historical data, a summary of evidence from analogous situations, results from laboratory experiments, or a trial run.

Participation

The role of the analyst (the one proposing a new forecasting method) is that of a **helper**[G] to the clients. The experiment should be under the control of the clients. More specifically, it should be under the control of the stakeholders who feel that they have an interest and a legitimate right to participate in running the experiment. Many people will not want to participate, but a few will.

The obvious way to find out who is interested is to review the proposal with the various stakeholders. Sometimes, however, this is not wise. You may not have time or money for such a review; you may wish to avoid early commitment or a quick dismissal of a proposal; groups may not know how they would react, or they may be unwilling to disclose their true feelings; or competitive secrets may be involved. **Role playing**[G] offers an alternative technique for situations where one or more of the above problems exist. The proposed method can be presented to subjects, who are asked to play the role of selected stakeholders and to act as they would act in the given situation. This procedure will help to identify areas of resistance which, in turn, may lead to modifications in the proposed method, in the experiment, or in the approach used with various stakeholders. Role playing identifies areas for participation and helps one to understand the viewpoints of other stakeholders. It does not, however, substitute for participation.

The critical area for participation lies in setting criteria for the experiment. A prior commitment should be made by the clients as to what constitutes success and what constitutes failure for a proposed method. This prior commitment should be worked out in detail so that agreement exists on what decisions will be made, given various outcomes from the experiment. For example, it might be specified that a new forecasting method will be adopted if it leads to a statistically significant reduction in error, if this reduction in error is at least 10%, and if the cost does not exceed that of the current method.

It may be difficult for the clients to propose criteria because they do not fully understand their own criteria. One solution to this problem is to present hypothetical outcomes to the experiment. The clients may then be asked what decision they would make, given each outcome.

The clients should also describe any constraints on the experiment. There may be certain beliefs that the clients are unwilling to change, no matter what the outcome (as in the Jesus Christ study). It is a good idea to get a list of these before starting the experiment.

The clients may also have suggestions on how the experiment should be run. A serious attempt should be made to incorporate all suggestions.

Much of the earlier advice in this chapter was based on folklore and on personal experience. The evidence on participation, however, is well documented. Most of this research was done on changes in work procedures for blue-collar workers; occasionally it involved managerial people [Carter (1971) and WEDLEY and FERRIE [1978] present some examples.] The conclusion is fairly clear cut: most people want to participate in changes that affect them (see Blumberg, 1968). Some of the early studies are described here:

Lewin (1947) compared lecture vs. group decision in trying to introduce change in the use of various foods by housewives. Group decision was superior. Similar results were obtained by Levine and Butler (1952) with factory workers, and by Bennett (1955) with college students.

Coch and French (1948) varied the amount of participation among groups of factory workers when a change in work procedure was to be made. When no participation was allowed, group productivity initially dropped to about 70% of its previous rate. Much hostility was also encountered; for example, grievances increased and employee turnover rose. When total participation was allowed, there was a small drop in productivity, but it rapidly recovered and exceeded the previous rate. There were no signs of hostility.

French, Kay, and Meyer (1966) found that participation in goal setting by a subordinate manager increased the likelihood that the subordinate would achieve these goals. Improvements were found only when specific goals were established with time deadlines and when the criteria had been agreed upon. The change was also more successful if the subordinate did not feel threatened. Similar results were obtained by Bass and Leavitt (1963) in a laboratory study.

Lawler and Hackman (1969) found that part-time building cleaners were willing to adopt a new incentive pay plan when they participated in the design of the plan. Resistance occurred during the first two meetings, but after that the change went smoothly. Productivity in this experimental group was higher than that in another group where an identical pay plan was imposed by management. A follow-up of this study is reported in Scheflen, Lawler, and Hackman (1971).

More recent evidence is provided by LONNSTEDT [1975], ZAND and SORENSEN [1975], BASS [1977], ROSENBERG and RO-SENSTEIN [1980], and ARMSTRONG [1982a].

Participation is often resisted initially; thus at first it looks like a failure. This initial resistance may occur because the people involved have not previously participated in this type of decision and they have some initial doubts as to whether the persons proposing participation can be trusted.

Feedback

Successful managers need to learn about the success or failure of their actions. Therefore it is important that they be kept informed of the progress of the experiment. Do not let anyone be "surprised;" prepare an explicit project plan that includes regularly scheduled reports.

Feedback helps the managers maintain control over the experiment. In other words, the feedback reinforces the principle of participation. If the managers really are in control of the project step by step, they will remain committed to the original guidelines of the experiment. Wouldn't it seem strange for them to agree step by step, and then fail to act according to the plan?

Feedback should be provided frequently because early results may be dramatic enough to allow for a quicker decision or for necessary changes to be made in the experimental design.

Finally, feedback to all parties who are affected helps to reduce the unfounded fears that people may falsely associate with the change (assuming that there are no grounds for fears). Although the provision of feedback can be time-consuming and costly, it is an important step in the introduction of important changes.

"Knowledge of results" has been found to lead to better performance in laboratory experiments and in experiments done with factory workers. The following study is also relevant:

Mann (1957) examined the introduction of an attitude survey for employees in six accounting departments of a company. Much feedback from the survey was provided to those involved in four of the departments. The resulting changes in these departments proved to be favorable in comparison to those in the other two departments, where the feedback was more limited.

Additional studies on the value of feedback are provided in Harris and Chaney (1969), McFall (1970), and BECKER [1978].

WHEN COMMITMENT FAILS

The discussion so far has assumed that the clients are interested in change. Of course, sometimes they are not willing to consider changes, and as a result commitment is not reached. There are three basic options at this point: (1) to terminate the project, (2) to try to redefine the problem, or (3) to use confrontation.

The strategy of termination when commitment fails has its disadvantages: for consultants it means no further income and for the client it means no improvements. On the other hand, there are advantages: the consultant avoids frustration and a sense of failure and the client saves time and money. In my opinion, termination, though often desirable, is used too rarely. Many consultants and staff members are willing to plunge ahead without commitment, armed with vague statements by the clients such as "We certainly are interested in obtaining more information on this problem," or "We are entirely willing to change if that is what the study suggests." Such remarks are the kiss of death for projects involving important changes.

Often a failure to reach commitment occurs because the clients feel threatened. This is easy to understand; they selected the current methods because they felt that they were the best ones for the circumstances. The proposal of a new method could be interpreted as, "You dummies! You are using X, while the best method is Y." Such a reaction is likely to occur if clients do not feel that they are fully in control of the change process. Because the conflict usually is focused on methods, it may be helpful at this point to redefine the problem and to start over. In other words, rather than argue about methods, discuss problems.

If commitment cannot be reached even after an attempt to redefine the problem, and if the problem is too important to terminate, then it may be fruitful to create a confrontation. Some of the most beneficial changes in this world have been achieved through confrontation. It is a last-ditch effort, and it is frequently successful. It is also hard on the change agent (for examples, see Nader, Petkas, and Blackwell, 1972). Usually you get the chance to make only one big change in an organization, so choose wisely.

Because *LRF* is a friendly book, I will not discuss strategies for confrontation. Furthermore, use of the procedures in this chapter generally eliminates any need for confrontation. If you decide on such a route, however, consult Saul Alinsky's work. His strategy is simple and effective. One of the reasons it worked was that the target groups were unaware of Alinsky's strategy. For a description of this strategy, see Bailey (1974) and Alinsky (1971).

GAINING ACCEPTANCE OF THE FORECAST

In 1872, there was a German invasion of Britain. The British armies and fleet, it will be remembered, were at that time scattered across the world—putting down mutiny in India, protecting Canada from the United States, and guarding Ireland against Emperor Napoleon III. As a result, the home defenses were minimal on that morning in March when the German boats set out across the North Sea. What Royal Navy was left in British waters soon succumbed to the German mines and torpedoes—weapons that had been developed in secrecy. British land forces suffered not only from lack of numbers, but also from inadequate training and discipline, combined with an outdated philosophy of warfare. The great stand at the Battle of Dorking failed: the Germans conquered the British.

This story is completely false. It was written by G. T. Chesney, a historian of the future and was published in *Blackwood's Magazine* in 1871. At that time, it was a plausible forecast. The publication of "The Battle of Dorking" created a political sensation. Prime Minister Gladstone attacked both the plausibility of the forecast and the wisdom of publishing such an alarmist view. A wide-ranging debate followed, and some changes took place as a result. (The story has been passed along by Encel, Marstrand, and Page, 1975, pp. 63–64.)

The earlier discussion in this chapter concerned the introduction of new methods into an organization, however, the Battle of Dorking raises a new issue. How does one persuade people to use the forecasts? Three issues are described here: (1) prior commitment, (2) scenarios, and (3) presentation strategies.

Prior Commitment

Prior commitment should be used to gain acceptance of forecasts. This advice is simple. The clients are asked (1) what forecasts they expect? and (2) what decisions will be made given various possible forecasts? If the decisions do not vary when the forecasts vary, then there is no need to spend the money on forecasting.

Formal questionnaires can be administered to the clients, asking them to record their forecasts and confidence intervals. Also, the questionnaire could sketch out possible forecasts and ask the clients what decisions they would make. As an alternative to questionnaires, the process might be conducted in structured meetings.

Prior commitment to the forecasting process is also important. If the stakeholders feel that the process is rational and fair, then they are more likely to accept the forecasts.

Forecasts are most likely to be useful when they are surprising. Yet without prior commitment, the forecast is unlikely to be regarded as different or surprising, as shown in the "hindsight studies" (Fischhoff, 1975; Fischhoff and Beyth, 1975; SLOVIC and FISCHHOFF, [1979]; ARKES, [1981]). People rationalize that the forecast provides nothing new and so no action is needed. The rationalization may be that they knew-it-all-along [WOOD, 1978] or it may be that they do not believe the forecast.

Scenarios

Forecasts with unpleasant consequences often create problems. Rather than changing the plans, attempts are often made to change the forecasts (as was done by Gladstone in the Battle of Dorking). It is like changing the reading on your thermometer in an attempt to improve the weather. Unfortunately, this type of irrational behavior occurs often. Examples include the U.S. government's failure to use forecasts that indicated bombing North Vietnam would be ineffective; the Boeing Aerospace Company's refusal to accept forecasts that the U.S. public would tire of the space program; and the Ford Motor Company's ignoring unfavorable forecasts of the economy at the time it introduced the Edsel.

Unpleasant forecasts are ignored even though they have potential usefulness. For example, BAKER [1979] found that valid hurricane warnings are frequently ignored. GRIFFITH and WELLMAN [1979] found that hospitals purchased forecasts and then ignored those with pessimistic outcomes.

The scenario technique is useful in helping people to confront unpleasant forecasts. A scenario is a story about the future. It can integrate a number of different forecasts about a situation and present them in an interesting and comprehensible manner. The Battle of Dorking is an example of a scenario.

The scenario-writing process described here calls for an initial suspension of evaluation so that the group members may discuss the unthinkable. It requires a well-defined structure, acceptance by the group, and a group leader. Scenarios may be used not only to examine what will happen, but also to consider what might be done by the organization. The idea may be expressed this way (adapted from George Bernard Shaw):

Some see the world as it is and ask, "Why?"
Some see the world as it could be and ask, "Why not?"

My structure for scenario writing is presented in Exhibit 3-5. This was used extensively by one organization, and it led to worthwhile changes.

The basic building blocks for the scenario process are presented above the dashed line in Exhibit 3-5. Examples are presented below the dashed line. The example was expanded for the least favorable environmental forecast, but a similar process could be used for the most likely environment and for the most favorable environment.

Exhibit 3-5 BUILDING BLOCKS FOR SCENARIO WRITING

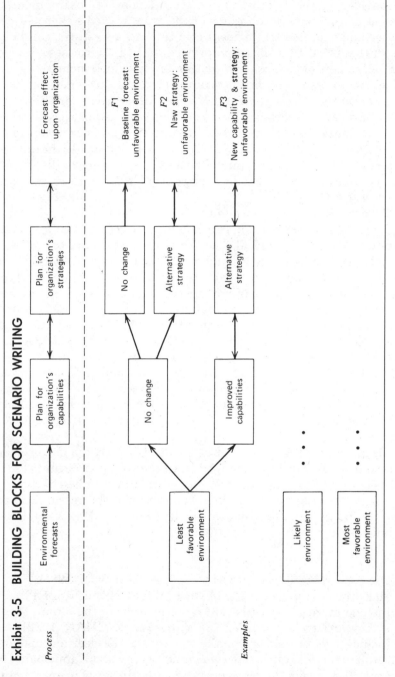

Process

Environmental forecasts → Plan for organization's capabilities → Plan for organization's strategies ↔ Forecast effect upon organization

Examples

Least favorable environment → No change → No change ↔ F1 Baseline forecast: unfavorable environment

Least favorable environment → No change → Alternative strategy ↔ F2 New strategy: unfavorable environment

Least favorable environment → Improved capabilities → Alternative strategy ↔ F3 New capability & strategy: unfavorable environment

Likely environment

Most favorable environment

Considering the forecast of the least favorable environment, the analyst can prepare descriptions of the organization's expected capabilities and expected strategies. From this, a forecast, $F1$, can be prepared; this is called a "baseline projection" or a "surprise-free projection." Members of the scenario-writing group, which include the major stakeholders, can then brainstorm alternative strategies under the assumption that the organization's capabilities are fixed. They should be encouraged to freewheel and to develop wild and provocative ideas. These changes are then translated by the analyst or by a forecasting model into a revised forecast ($F2$). The scenario group also brainstorms to consider what changes might be made in the capabilities of the organization. The result can be used to develop new strategies, leading to forecast $F3$.

The arrows running from right to left in Exhibit 3-5 suggest another approach: the scenario group can imagine a forecast (e.g., $F3$) that its members consider to be ideal. They then work backward to brainstorm changes in strategies that could yield such a forecast, and then to brainstorm the changes in capabilities that would be required to carry out these strategies. This use of the scenario process helps the group to forget about constraints in creating the type of future it wants.

The scenario process should help the members to use information that is contrary to their current views of the world. This procedure gives them control over the change process and allows them to discuss the unthinkable in a context that is socially approved by the group.

The difference between the scenario process suggested here and that used in the Battle of Dorking is that the latter stressed confrontation. In my opinion, the participative approach is more effective and less expensive.

The original edition of LRF stated that little research had been done on scenarios. Things have changed since then. Some relevant research has been done, and the scenario has been shown to be effective as a technique for gaining acceptance. For example, the research implies that the impact of the scenario can be heightened by the following techniques:

1. Use *concrete examples* [READ, 1983; ANDERSON, 1983b]
2. Make the description *vivid* [HAMILL, WILSON and NISBETT, 1980]
3. Include events that will seem *representative* of the situation, even if they are irrelevant [TVERSKY and KAHNEMAN, 1982]
4. Include events that will make it easy for the decision makers to recall *available supporting evidence* (Tversky and Kahneman, 1973)
5. *Link the events by showing causality* in a plausible manner

[KAHNEMAN and TVERSKY, 1979; TVERSKY and KAHNE-
MAN, 1983]
6. Include *commensurate measures* across alternative scenarios, even
   if these measures are irrelevant [SLOVIC and McPHILLAMY, 1974]
7. Ask the decision makers to *project themselves* into the situation
   [ANDERSON, 1983a]
8. Ask the decision makers to *predict how they would act* in the scenarios [SHERMAN, 1980]

These techniques can make a scenario more plausible, increasing its
chances of being taken seriously and perhaps leading the organization
to develop contingency plans.

Note the dangers of the scenario, however. Scenarios could seriously
distort judgmental forecasts [GREGORY, CIALDINI, and CARPEN-
TER, 1982]. Furthermore, the experiment by ANDERSON [1983b] suggests that the scenario will unduly increase perceived probabilities
even in cases where the forecaster is provided with information that
the situation is unlikely. It would be easy to "lie with scenarios"—
easier, perhaps, than lying with statistics:

GREGORY, CIALDINI, and CARPENTER [1982] conducted four
experiments on scenarios. In this context, scenarios meant short
stories, written by the experimenters, where the subjects were
asked to imagine that the events were actually happening to
them. It was hypothesized that subsequent predictions of the likelihood of the event will be increased because knowledge of the
event is more easily *available*. Here is a brief overview of the
results of the four experiments where the scenario groups imagined the event happening to them, but the control groups did not:

Experiments	Subjects	Predicted Likelihood	
		Control %	Scenario %
1. "How likely is it that you might someday be arrested for armed robbery regardless of whether you are innocent or guilty?"	48 college psychology students	9	18

| | | Predicted Likelihood | |
| | | Control | Scenario |
Experiments	Subjects	%	%
2. "What is the perceived probability that you will win a vacation trip?"	100 high school psychology students	23	38
3. "How likely is it that you might be arrested for shoplifting or petty theft?"	39 college psychology students	2	16
4. Percentage of subjects who actually subscribed to cable TV within six weeks	79 residents of two middle class neighborhoods	20	47

Alternative explanations were examined in the four studies, but the "availability" hypothesis held up well. In my opinion, however, experiment four expands the notion of availability to include saliency. This was the only experiment in which the information was the same for both experimental and control groups (thus it was equally available). The experimental group, however, imagined themselves to be experiencing the benefits of cable TV. This increased saliency had a substantial effect. The practical implications are important. By putting information in the form of a plausible story, you can increase a person's perceived probability that the event will occur. The likelihood can be increased even more if the person will imagine that the event is actually happening. The latter implication is relevant not only for planning but for practical marketing problems, as shown by the cable TV study. In that study, the subscription rates were about double those that had been experienced in the area by the cable TV company.

In ANDERSON [1983b], subjects were presented with evidence that a fire fighter trainee's preference for risk is predictive of his subsequent success. Half were told high risk taking leads to success and the other half were told it leads to failure. This "evidence" was presented in two ways, either as two concrete examples, or as abstract statistical data on 20 trainees. The subjects were then told that the evidence was bogus and were asked what they thought to be the true relationship. Interestingly, the bogus information had a strong effect both when asked immediately and when asked a week later. If told that risk aids success, then told to ignore the statement, the subject continued to believe it, and vice versa. The concrete examples (sample of 2 cases) showed a much stronger impact than the statistical data (sample of 20 cases), and this effect was just as strong one week later. The study has implications for the presentation of forecasts. Concrete examples have a stronger impact than do statistical data, apparently because it is easier for readers to construct causal explanations to support the prediction. Perhaps J. B. Watson knew this in the early 1900s. He built his fame as a psychologist with a study on conditioning that used one subject, a baby known as Little Albert. Watson's fame continued to grow over the years despite evidence that there was no Little Albert study [SAMELSON, 1980]. An interesting extention of Anderson's study would be to see if the effect holds if the subjects were told in advance (as we do in scenarios) that the predictions are hypothetical.

Presenting the Forecast

"The forecast should be presented clearly": ( ) TRUE ( ) FALSE

If you have an important forecast and want to implement change, the answer is "true." But if your concern is to gain respect as a successful forecaster, the answer is "false." Or, so it seems if one can generalize from the Dr. Fox studies.

Dr. Fox was an actor who looked distinguished and sounded authoritative. Armed with a fictitious but impressive resume, he lectured on a subject about which he knew nothing. The lecture, "Mathematical Game Theory as Applied to Physician Education," was delivered on three occasions to a total of 55 psychologists, educators, psychiatrists, social workers, and administrators. The talk lasted an hour and was followed by 30 minutes of questions and answers. It consisted entirely of double talk, meaningless words, false logic, contradictory statements, irrelevant humor, and meaningless references to unrelated topics. According to a questionnaire administered at the end of the session, the audience found the lecture to be clear and stimulating. They had a high regard for Dr. Fox. None of the subjects realized that the lecture was pure nonsense [NAFTULIN, et al. 1973]. In a follow-up study, I found that researchers who write in a style that is difficult to understand are more highly regarded [ARMSTRONG, 1980a].

The Dr. Fox studies yield practical advice to those concerned about personal advancement. I call it bafflegab:

- "If you have nothing to say, make sure you do not say it clearly."
- "If your forecast is unpleasant, make sure no one understands it."

For further advice, see Exhibit 3-6.

Exhibit 3-6   ON PRESENTING BAD NEWS

Source. "THE WIZARD OF ID," by permission of Parker and Hart, and Field Enterprises, Inc.

This advice runs counter to doing an effective job, so I urge you not to use bafflegab. However, recognize that others may use it.

Forecasts should be presented in a clear fashion. The purpose of statistics is to simplify and to aid in understanding—not to create false confidence. Clients often have difficulty in using even the simplest statistical concepts [ROSENBLATT, 1968].

Here are some guidelines for the presentation of forecasts:

1. Eliminate unnecessary information
2. Round numbers to two significant digits
3. Organize numbers in a meaningful way [WAGENAAR and VIS-SER, 1979]
4. Present current status first [WAGENAAR and VISSER, 1979]
5. Present estimates of uncertainty with the forecasts

Remember that less is more [WAGENAAR and VISSER, 1979].

For additional ideas on presentation see ASCHER and OVERHOLT [1983] and EHRENBERG [1981].

The above rules are not overly expensive. Clarity comes from organization and simplicity. You do not need to mount an elaborate production with expensive visual aids and professional delivery. Consider the weather forecaster, one of America's highest paid professions. Is it all for entertainment? And what about computer graphics?

Do these wonderful TV shows with maps and TV stars do better at communicating the forecast than is done on radio? No, according to WAGENAAR, SCHREUDER, and VAN DER HEIJDEN [1985]. Low recall of the forecasts occurred (typically about 25% of the message) for TV as well as for radio. This was true even for highly motivated subjects. Part of the problem seemed due to the large amount of irrelevant information. Reductions in the length of the forecast led to a higher percentage of items recalled (the number of items recalled stayed about the same). Written summary statements helped, as did animated pictograms that emphasized key elements of the forecast.

Computer graphics are becoming increasingly popular. I was quite pleased by this and expected that it would lead to substantially better communication and, consequently, to better forecasting and decision making. Thus, I was surprised when I read the research in this area. A comprehensive review of the evidence is provided by DeSANCTIS [1984]. Graphics do not seem to be more effective than tables. There seems to be no question that graphics are more attractive, but features that make a graph visually attractive, such as color, design, complexity, and realism may detract from comprehension. (In addition to DeSANCTIS, see DICKSON, et al. [1977] and LAWRENCE et al. [1985].)

Exhibit 3-7   IMPLEMENTATION PROCESS

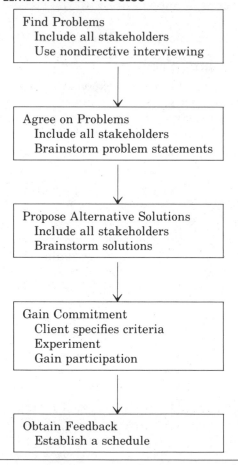

Find Problems
     Include all stakeholders
     Use nondirective interviewing

Agree on Problems
     Include all stakeholders
     Brainstorm problem statements

Propose Alternative Solutions
     Include all stakeholders
     Brainstorm solutions

Gain Commitment
     Client specifies criteria
     Experiment
     Gain participation

Obtain Feedback
     Establish a schedule

SUMMARY

Implementation is the Achilles' heel of forecasting. Attempts to impose forecasting methods or forecasts upon other people in an organization can be expected to fail, unless the changes are unimportant and the forecasts provide only confirming evidence. To judge by the Jesus Christ study, such attempts are likely to increase people's confidence in their current beliefs rather than to result in change.

An explicit process for the implementation of new methods was presented. It parallels the steps in the systems approach, but is adapted to gain the participation of the stakeholders in the organization. The steps, are summarized in Exhibit 3-7.

A prior commitment to accept the forecasts should be obtained from the stakeholders. This includes a commitment to the forecasting process (is it reasonable?), to the confidence intervals (what forecasts would be surprising?) and to decision making (if the forecast were X, what decision would you make?).

Scenarios were proposed to gain acceptance of forecasts with unfavorable outcomes. Recent research on this topic provided a set of specific rules for heightening the impact of a scenario.

Finally, it was suggested that the forecast be clear and simple. Specific suggestions were made for implementing this useful, often ignored, and potentially dangerous piece of advice.

Four

RESEARCH
STRATEGIES

Contents

"No data yet," he answered. "It is a capital mistake to theorize before you have all of the evidence. It biases the judgment."

– Sherlock Holmes
A Study in Scarlet (1886)
Arthur Conan Doyle

Sherlock Holmes was wrong. He should have listened to JEVONS [1877]. Research over the past century has supported Jevons. This research has much to say about when to theorize. The first part of the chapter discusses the use of theory in forecasting.

Another strategy discussed here is breaking down a problem to solve it by its parts. You will get some ideas about how, why, and when to decompose.

Finally, the strategy of **eclectic research**^{G} will be described. What is it and when should it be used?

Each of these three strategies is used at various places in this book. They are all relevant for developing and evaluating forecasting models.

USING THEORY

Actually, Sherlock Holmes was not completely wrong. The development of a theory does bias the judgment (Chapman and Chapman, 1969; Wason, 1960, 1968a,b; Pruitt, 1961; Rosenthal and Rosnow, 1969; Geller and Pitz, 1968), but biases can be reduced by specifying alternative theories. (I'll have more to say about this in Chapter 17.) But, my dear fellow Sherlock, what data are to be collected? How do I purge my mind of that half-baked theory I have? How do I incorporate my ideas into the picture after I have the data? (Sherlock obviously had no idea what he was getting into when he made that remark.)

There are few cases in the social sciences where we have "no data yet." Researchers have experience, they have done experiments, they have read the literature, and they feel that this background is relevant to the new situations they encounter. Most people feel that this information should be used in some way. The question is how to use these subjective data most effectively. Should subjective information be used before analyzing the problem or after? This question has been debated in many fields. Currently, for example, the conclusion in psychology is to use the theory before the data. In economics there is a bit of hypocrisy, students are taught to use theory first, but practicing economists insist on using it afterward.

Here is what has happened in economics. Theoretical econometricians have advocated a prior use of theory. In fact, often they never get around to using any data at all. Those working on practical economic problems initially had little faith in prior theory; they used the exploratory approach. Such an approach was used in the 1930s and 1940s. For example, Burns and Mitchell (1946) conducted a famous study that was almost devoid of prior theory. Koopmans (1947) criticized this work—rightly so, I believe. The Rayco Case indicates the low regard that some analysts held for the use of prior theory:

> In the case of the Rayco Seat Cover Company (Hummel, 1961), 300 variables were selected to "explain" variations in automobile seat cover sales per square mile. Simple plots of each variable against the sales measures for 150 sales offices eliminated 226 variables that appeared to be unrelated to sales. A **stepwise regression**[G] then reduced the remaining 74 variables down to the best 37. This model was shown to produce an excellent fit to the data, but there was no evaluation of its usefulness in a predictive situation.

What happens when researchers fail to use their information before examining the data? They show great creativity afterward in using their subjective information. Economists use a fancy name for this, **a posteriori analysis**[G], but that does not help much. See Lucy; she is in Exhibit 4-1. Then see Tom Swift . . . and Solow:

Exhibit 4-1 *A POSTERIORI* ANALYSIS: LUCY'S VIEWPOINT

PEANUTS ® By Schulz

Source. Copyright 1956, United Feature Syndicate, Inc.

In this adventure of Tom Swift (see Armstrong, 1970b), we find Tom explaining differences in sales of caribou chips among 31 countries. An excellent explanation of the data was obtained by using a stepwise regression and selecting 8 predictors from a possible set of 30. The adjusted R^{2G} was 85%, . . . which is interesting because the data were all drawn from a table of random numbers. The data produced a theory, but it was useless.

Solow (1957) analyzed data from 1909 to 1949. These data fell along a straight line with the exception of those for the years 1943–1949. The 1943–1949 data were parallel to the other data but shifted above them. Solow devoted about one-half page to a hypothesis about this "structural shift." He even drew upon other literature to support his hypothesis (he did, however, regard the hypothesis with a healthy amount of suspicion). A reply to Solow's paper by Hogan (1958) indicated that, rather than a "structural shift," the results were due to mistakes in arithmetic.

These studies show what can go wrong. What about studies that contrast theory and no theory? I examined this issue:

In Armstrong (1968a, pp. 160–165), two models were developed to forecast camera sales per capita in each of 11 countries. Each of these models was developed using data from 19 other countries. The exploratory model used little prior theory. Stepwise regressions were run, drawing from a set of 15 variables, and the model with the highest $\overline{R}^2$ was selected as the forecasting model. A theory-based model was also developed by selecting seven variables, by putting a *priori* constraints on the signs, and by incorporating prior estimates of magnitudes. Although the exploratory model provided the best fit to the 19-country analysis data ($\overline{R}^2$ of 99.8% vs. 99.6%), its performance in forecasting for the 11-country validation sample was inferior; the mean absolute percentage error ($\overline{\textbf{MAPE}}^G$) was 52% vs. 31% for the theory-based model. The average percentage error ($\textbf{APE}^G$) of the theory-based model was also lower, −5% vs. 38%.

The evidence cited was drawn from economics and closely related fields. What about other areas? Sociologists and psychologists have also examined this issue.

I was impressed by the theoretical arguments of Francis (1957), a sociologist. He concluded that the theory should precede the data. It was difficult, however, to find empirical studies on this issue. Reiss (1951) provided indirect evidence. His evidence is consistent with the hypothesis that one should use prior theory:

Reiss (1951) studied whether juvenile delinquents would commit crimes again after they were released. Although a larger number of variables improved the fit of a model to the analysis sample, the predictive power dropped for the validation sample when the number of predictors was increased above four. Presumably, one could improve accuracy by using prior theory to reduce the number of predictor variables.

Three studies were found in psychology. These studies provide indirect evidence that is consistent with the greater value of *a priori* analysis relative to *a posteriori* analysis. In these studies, the judges used their implicit subjective theories after they analyzed the data. The result was a loss of predictive power:

Kelly and Fiske (1950) used objective tests to predict the success of students in a training program in clinical psychology. When the test data were examined by analysts who had interviewed the candidates, the resulting predictions were inferior to those provided by tests alone.

Harris (1963) examined the effects of using subjective methods, after using objective methods, in predicting football scores. The judges, who were sportswriters and football coaches, could not improve upon the forecasts made by an objective extrapolation known as the Litkenhous formula. The judges toned down the objective forecasts, and the forecasts from the "formula followed by subjective analysis" were less accurate than the "formula only" forecasts.

MILSTEIN [1980, 1981] found personal interviews to be worthless for predicting which applicants would be successful at the Yale School of Medicine.

Einhorn (1972b) discussed the dangers of proceeding without a theory and illustrated these hazards by reviewing the literature and by using simulations based upon random data. Stone and Brosseau illustrated these dangers without even trying to do so:

Stone and Brosseau (1973), in a study of student success in a medical training program, used 115 variables in a stepwise regression to explain differences among 19 subjects. This exploratory model was then used to predict success for 18 new subjects, and an R^2 of 76% was obtained. For this they won the "Tom Swift Award for Data Abuse" (Armstrong, 1975a); if one assumed that the data were random, the expected R^2 would have been higher than 76%. (For the 1978 Award, see BUHMEYER and JOHNSON [1978])

This evidence, although uniformly favoring the *a priori* over the *a posteriori* analysis, is limited. One study examined the question directly; one study found that *a priori* analysis made things better; and four studies found that *a posteriori* analysis made things worse. Practicing econometricians will continue to be skeptical. I think that they are wrong, and I'll tell you why . . . but I won't tell you until Chapter 8 (on econometric methods).

The researcher can use theory in many ways to develop a forecasting model. Many resources and sources of information exist that can be used in this *a priori* analysis. The details will be presented in Part II of *LRF*. Three of the important resources, however, are illustrated in Exhibit 4-2; they are (1) paper, (2) pencils, and (3) books. Another tool is time.

It would be nice to provide additional studies on the value of *a priori* analysis, but I have been unable to find any. Perhaps they do not exist; more likely, I have been looking in the wrong places.

Does this evidence mean that researchers should not use subjective inputs after analyzing the data? I think that it does. However, another good rule is never to say "always" or "never." Always remember the story about the young economist who analyzed U.S. economic

Exhibit 4-2   A PRIORI ANALYSIS: AUTHOR'S VIEWPOINT

Photograph by Kay Armstrong.

data from 1930 to 1978. He found some dramatic deviations of the data from the model during the years 1940–1945. On reading the literature, he discovered that World War II occurred during this period.* In such a case, it is reasonable to revise the model.

Don't laugh. The WW II example is not so strange as it may sound. Evans (1974, p. 174) cited the thesis written by a Ph.D. candidate at the University of Pennsylvania. The model failed to show any economic downturn during the Great Depression.

DECOMPOSITION

The spirit of decision analysis is to divide and conquer: Decompose a complex problem into simpler problems, get one's thinking straight in these simpler problems, paste these analyses together with logical glue. . . .

Raiffa (1968, p. 271)

*This example and the Lucy cartoon (Exhibit 4-1) were passed on to me by Franklin Fisher at M.I.T.

Raiffa tells us to use **decomposition**^G for decision analysis. This section of Chapter 4 suggests that decomposition is also applicable in forecasting problems. It is useful in structuring forecasting models, obtaining forecasts, assessing uncertainty, and evaluating forecasting models.

Decomposition has a number of advantages. It allows the forecaster to use information in a more efficient manner. It helps to spread the risk; errors in one part of the problem may be offset by errors in another part. It allows the researchers to split the problem among different members of a research team. It makes it possible for expert advice to be obtained on each part. Finally, it permits the use of different methods on different parts of the problem.

The advantages of decomposition are impressive but probably a bit vague. When I was lecturing to a group of students about the benefits of decomposition, someone asked me, "How do you know?" After thinking about this, I concluded that I knew because other people had told me. I was once an industrial engineer and, as such, made much use of the strategy of decomposition. But I was surprised that I could not find empirical support for my belief. As a result, we conducted our own study. It supported two hypotheses:

1. Decomposition will improve judgmental predictions
2. Decomposition is of greatest value when uncertainty is high

Armstrong, Denniston, and Gordon (1975) randomly split 151 subjects into two groups. One group received some questions directly; the other group received a decomposed version. The groups were asked to make predictions for five problems ranging from areas where uncertainty was low to others where it was high. These questions were asked (paraphrased here):

1. How many families were there in the United States in 1970?
2. How many high school dropouts were there in 1969?
3. How many packs of Polaroid color film were used in the United States in 1970?
4. How many pounds of tobacco were produced in the United States in 1969?
5. In 1972, a Philadelphia radio station asked high school students to submit postcards with the message "Carefree Sugarless Gum." There was no limit to the number of cards per

student. The school that submitted the most postcards would have a free rock concert by the Grass Roots band. The contest was heavily promoted. How many cards were submitted?

The decomposed versions contained a series of questions on parts of the problem. These were used by the researchers to compute the overall prediction. For example, the Polaroid questions were:

1. How many people were living in the United States in 1970?
2. What was the average size of a family?
3. What percentage of families owned cameras?
4. Of those families owning cameras, what percentage owned Polaroid cameras?
5. What was the average number of packs of film used per Polaroid camera owner?
6. What percentage of Polaroid film sales were color film?

The decomposed version yielded more accurate forecasts for all questions, and the improvements were much greater for the questions where uncertainty was high, especially for the chewing gum contest. (The answers to the questions on the preceding page can be found in Appendix F.)

ASCHENBRENNER and KASUBEK [1978] provided additional support for decomposition. However, more research is needed. For example, omissions of key elements seem to be difficult to detect [FISCHHOFF, SLOVIC, and LICHTENSTEIN, 1978]. Also causal reasoning would seem helpful in decomposition, yet in BURNS and PEARL [1981] it did not lead to improved accuracy.

A most useful forecasting application has been to consider separately the current status and the change. This split is illustrated in Exhibit 4-3.

Forecasting errors are often caused by failure to know the starting point, that is, the current status. Morgenstern (1963) provided evidence on the difficulties that economists have in measuring current status. Thompson (1961) cited this as a major problem in weather forecasting. PALMORE [1979] showed its importance in predicting health changes for elder citizens. Hedlund et al. (1973) provided evidence about the analogous problem of the base rate in trying to predict which mental patients are dangerous.

Exhibit 4-3   FORECASTING BY PARTS: CURRENT STATUS AND CHANGE

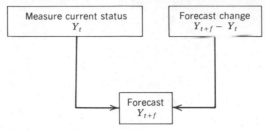

Some specific examples are cited to show how serious the problems can be in measuring current status:

A problem with the estimation of the base rate was found in Bakwin's (1945) study of tonsillectomies. A sample of 1000 eleven-year-old children was examined by a group of physicians, and 61% were selected to have their tonsils removed. The remaining 39% were then examined by another group of physicians, and 45% were selected for tonsillectomies. The remaining children were examined by still another group of doctors, and 46% were selected. Notice that the base rate depended on the physicians, not on the children in the sample. (Incidentally, in case you don't already know this, children should rarely have their tonsils removed. The operation is dangerous, and it often does nothing worthwhile for the child.)

Bell (1962, pp. 152–153) discussed problems in measuring the current crime rate in New York City. The "crime rate" increased drastically when all complaints were phoned into a central switchboard. Before this time, the calls had gone to local precincts, and not all calls had been recorded there. This caused the crime rate to appear lower, which, in turn, made the police chiefs happy.

The U.S. Bureau of the Census (1967) found that the number of dilapidated housing units in 1960 was probably closer to 3.4 million than to the 1.9 million previously reported. This led the

Bureau to change its original conclusion that 1950 to 1960 was a period of progress in housing developments.

Cole (1969) estimated that about 40% of the errors in 1-year forecasts of the GNP are due to errors in measuring the current GNP.

Breaking the problem down into current status and change can alert the researcher to serious difficulties in the measurement of current status. This aspect of the problem is often overlooked.

Different methods might be used for estimating current status than for predicting change. For example, judgment might be used to assess the current status of a person's health, and segmentation methods to forecast the change in this person's health over the next 20 years. Another example, judgment methods might be used to assess current sales of breakfast cereals and extrapolation methods to forecast change.

Other types of decomposition have also been employed with apparent success in forecasting problems. For example, WARSHAW [1980] obtained improved predictions of actual purchase behavior for branded products by asking detailed questions about the purchase situation:

In WARSHAW [1980], sixty housewives were asked about their intentions to purchase various brands of soft drinks over a five-day period. Global intentions were asked: "What is the probability that you will purchase brand X between now and next Monday morning?" Also, a decomposed version was asked of the same subjects with questions about location and about the purchase of multiple brands. The decomposed version (which Warshaw refers to as a "derived intention") was significantly more accurate in predicting actual purchase behavior.

Of particular importance is the breakdown between industry sales and market share. Many organizations follow this practice. (Such a breakdown proved useful in the reanalysis of Hacke's transistor forecast from *LRF* p. 20.) For economic problems, this breakdown can be used in conjunction with the breakdown between current status and change, yielding four separate parts of the forecasting problem.

ECLECTIC RESEARCH

It was six men of Indostan
     To learning much inclined,
Who went to see the Elephant
     (Though all of them were blind),
That each by observation
     Might satisfy his mind.

The First approached the Elephant
     And, happening to fall
Against his broad and sturdy side,
     At once began to bawl:
"God bless me, but the Elephant
     Is very like a wall!"

The Second, feeling the tusk,
     Cried, "Ho! what have we here
So very round and smooth and sharp?
     To me 'tis very clear
This wonder of an Elephant
     Is very like a spear!"

The Third approached the animal
     And, happening to take
The squirming trunk within his hands,
     Thus boldly up he spake:
"I see," quoth he, "the Elephant
     Is very like a snake!"

The fourth reached out an eager hand,
     And felt about the knee:
"What most the wondrous beast is like
     Is very plain," quoth he;
" 'Tis clear enough the Elephant
     Is very like a tree!"

The Fifth, who chanced to touch the ear,
     Said, "E'en the blindest man
Can tell what this resembles most;
     Deny the fact who can:
This marvel of an Elephant
     Is very like a fan!"

The Sixth no sooner had begun
     About the beast to grope
Than, seizing on the swinging tail
     That fell within his scope,
"I see," quoth he, "the Elephant
     Is very like a rope!"

And so these men of Indostan
    Disputed loud and long,
Each in his own opinion
    Exceeding stiff and strong.
Though each was partly in the right,
    They all were in the wrong!

"The Parable of the Blind Men and the Elephant"
John Godfrey Saxe

Each blind man of Indostan used only one approach. In contrast, eclectic research requires the researcher to utilize a set of very different methods in solving a problem. In other words, the research budget should be split so that a variety of approaches can be used. This is the strategy used by my boyhood friend, Perry Mason (you know, the lawyer).

Eclectic research can be applied in a variety of ways in forecasting. It can be used to measure variables in a forecasting model . . . or relationships in a forecasting model . . . or it can be used to assess the validity of a relationship . . . or the uncertainty involved with a forecast. An illustration of how eclectic research might be used to measure a relationship is provided in Exhibit 4-4.

Using a combination of all five approaches rather than a single approach increases the likelihood of obtaining a valid estimate of the relationship shown in Exhibit 4-4. For a given research budget, it may be better to use a number of different approaches, even though crudely done, than a single approach, done well. This is especially true in situations where measurement is difficult.

An analogy may help to clarify this argument. Assume that a hunter is about to shoot at a bird. Unfortunately for him, he cannot see his target directly. However, he does have some idea as to the general location of the target because he saw the bird go into the bush, he can hear the bird, and he can see some branches moving. Since it is getting late, he decides at this time to try to shoot the bird. The question he now faces is whether to use his rifle or his shotgun.

If he uses the rifle, he is likely to miss the target altogether, and the bird will fly away. If he does hit the bird, it is likely that the shot will kill the bird. If he uses the shotgun, he is more likely to hit the bird with some of the buckshot. In this case, he has a higher likelihood of hitting the bird, although the shot may not kill it. By wounding the bird, however, he will get further information as to its location and can then move in for the kill.

**Exhibit 4-4   ECLECTIC RESEARCH FOR MEASURING RELATIONSHIPS:
AN EXAMPLE**

The Relationship   Measurement Approaches

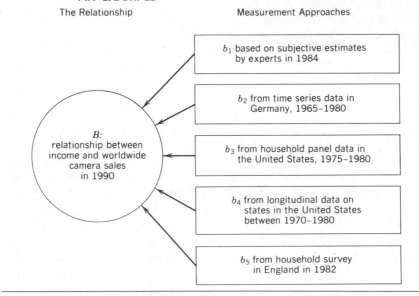

b_1 based on subjective estimates by experts in 1984

b_2 from time series data in Germany, 1965–1980

B: relationship between income and worldwide camera sales in 1990

b_3 from household panel data in the United States, 1975–1980

b_4 from longitudinal data on states in the United States between 1970–1980

b_5 from household survey in England in 1982

The rifle is analogous to **intensive research**^{G}. When aimed in exactly the right direction, it does the job and does it well. If not aimed correctly, however, it does little good. The shotgun, analogous to eclectic research, is likely to do some good if aimed in the *general* direction of the target. It may down the bird or, at least, maim the bird and allow for a second shot.

Importance of Eclectic Research

Social scientists often refer to the physical sciences for their research methods. However, two major differences affect the transfer of methods from the physical to the social sciences. First, it is generally more difficult to develop the desired controls when running experiments in the social sciences. And, second, there is more uncertainty about measurement in the social sciences. Of course, it is all a matter of degree.

Sometimes the differences are illusory. People often reject experimental findings in the social sciences because the results challenge their current beliefs. On the other hand, we do not often get upset about an experimental finding on the strength of materials because a belief in this area is not an important part of our attitudes. However, an expert in the strength of materials may get upset and react emotionally. (I'll show you an example soon of how physical scientists can do this.) Furthermore, the presumed accuracy of the physical sciences is often an illusion. Why, we did not even know where the sun was until 1961! (Maybe we still don't).

> Macdonald (1972) examined studies by W. J. Youden on the distance from the earth to the sun. Of 15 observations published from 1895 to 1961, each worker's estimated value was outside the certainty limits set by his immediate predecessor.

Macdonald (1972) also had a recommendation for the physical sciences—eclectic research! He suggested that the quantity in question should be measured with a different technique, one that operates on a different principle. This contrasts with the earlier position of Bridgman (1927), a well-known physical scientist who said, "If we have more than one set of operations, we have more than one concept, and strictly there should be a separate name to correspond to each different set of operations."

Numerous researchers have recommended eclectic research for the social sciences. These include Cronbach and Meehl (1955) and Campbell and Fiske (1959) in psychology; Webb et al. (1973) in the social sciences; and Cook and Selltiz (1964) and Curtis and Jackson (1962) in sociology. These researchers have used different names such as "multiple operationalism," "methodological triangulation," "convergent operationalism," "operational delineation," and "convergent validation." This confusion in terms is understandable because they had not read *LRF*; the correct term is "eclectic research."

Although many researchers have argued for eclectic research, social scientists still favor intensive research. Let me explain why.

Intensive research calls for the specialist ("one who knows more and more about less and less until eventually he knows everything about nothing"). Typically he has expensive equipment, conducts elaborate experiments, and collects large sample sizes. His team is composed of specialists in the same field. The specialist is the person who understands and can argue for expensive equiment or large-scale studies. He finds it easier to publish his results because journals are organized by narrow technical areas and because editors appear to value the reliability of a finding (the ability to replicate under the same conditions) more highly than the validity of a finding.

Eclectic research calls for the generalist ("one who knows less and less about more and more until eventually he knows nothing about everything"). The generalist has an interdisciplinary staff and spreads his budget out so that he must get by with makeshift equipment, crude experiments, and small sample sizes.

So you can see the difficulties faced by the eclectic researcher. Eclectic research is accepted by most researchers as being good for science . . . but it is bad for the scientist. How unfortunate.

Evidence on Eclectic Research

Although evidence can be cited that demonstrates the shortcomings of intensive research (e.g., the example of Youden on the distance to the sun), it is difficult to find research that contrasts eclectic and intensive strategies. The most relevant evidence that I found was the case of Immanuel Velikovsky. His works provide a critical test between eclectic and intensive research for the following reasons:

1. Many predictions were made
2. The predictions from the two strategies differed radically
3. It has been possible to test many of the predictions
4. The case is well documented.

Velikovsky used historical writings (Velikovsky, 1950) and cultural artifacts (Velikovsky, 1955) to develop theories about the history of the earth. These pieces of evidence, such as the *Bible*, are regarded by most scientists as being of such poor reliability as to be unworthy of use in the development of scientific theories. For example, any given passage in the *Bible* is subject to many interpretations.

Instead of regarding events in the *Bible* as analogies and parables, Velikovsky assumed that real events were being discussed. This reduced the number of interpretations. More importantly, Velikovsky assumed that the events were so important that they were observed by others on earth. Therefore writings from other cultures, such as Greek mythology, were also taken at face value. Furthermore, because the events were so dramatic, physical evidence should also exist, and so artifacts and geological findings were examined.

These various sources fit into a pattern, according to Velikovsky. He concluded that catastrophic events occurred in the world. These events (e.g., the near collision of Venus and Earth around 1500 B.C.) had such a great effect upon the earth that there was no need for highly reliable instruments to record the events. Everyone on earth was aware of what was happening. Velikovsky summarized his argument (p. 308 in Velikovsky, 1950; see also the last three paragraphs of Chapter 12 in Velikovsky, 1955, for a similar argument) as follows:

If a phenomenon had been similarly described by many peoples, we might suspect that a tale, originating with one people, had spread around the world, and consequently there is no proof of the authenticity of the event related. But just because one and the same event is embodied in traditions that arc very different indeed, its authenticity becomes highly probable, especially if the records of history, ancient charts, sundials, and the physical evidence of natural history testify to the same effect.

Velikovsky's use of extremely different approaches to test his theory did not impress the scientific community. He used "unreliable data" and covered many different scientific disciplines in which he was not a "recognized expert." It was all so outrageous that prominent people from the scientific community mounted an active, and partially successful, campaign to suppress the publication of Velikovsky's theories. The stated reasons for this attack upon Velikovsky were that the method used was not scientific and that he was not an expert in the fields affected by his theories.

Velikovsky made a series of different forecasts based on his theory. Most of these forecasts were labeled as impossible in the light of existing knowledge. Yet evidence from space probes and other sources has confirmed a large number of these predictions, and there has not yet been an incorrect prediction. Much of this evidence is summarized by De Grazia et al. (1966). The forecasts that have been verified by additional evidence have varied greatly in nature. They involve the temperature of Venus, the existence of electromagnetic fields in the solar system, the variations in the length of a day, radio noises from Jupiter, hydrocarbons in the atmosphere of Venus, the age of oil deposits in the Gulf of Mexico, the previous existence of advanced human culture in areas of northeastern Siberia that are not currently inhabited, and the age of the ancient civilization of Mexico.

Multiple Methods and Multiple Hypotheses

Velikovsky's research emphasized the use of multiple and different methods. This strategy will be stressed in Part II of *LRF* in the discussion of forecasting methods. For an interesting application of eclectic research to forecasting, see the study of offshore nuclear plants by BAKER et al. [1980]. It will also be used in Part III in describing methods for analyzing forecasting models. A third use of eclectic research is discussed in Part V, where it is suggested that researchers should test multiple hypotheses rather than advocate a single hypothesis. Though it is not terribly popular, research based on multiple hypotheses has provided us with most of the evidence that is summarized in this book.

SUMMARY

Subjective inputs by researchers are necessary and important. The proper time to use this information is before the analysis of the data. The researcher should provide an explicit summary of his prior knowledge. These are his hypotheses or theories, and the process is referred to as *a priori* analysis. Although this is a difficult and time-consuming process, it is superior to *a posteriori* analysis, which uses subjective inputs after analyzing the data. A good rule to follow about *a posteriori* analysis is this: Avoid it!

Decomposition offers numerous advantages. It is useful in judgmental forecasting. Decomposition is expected to be especially valuable in structuring forecasting models. The distinction between current status and change is of particular value. Also useful are breakdowns between base rate and individual variation, and between total market and market share. A good rule to follow about decomposition is this: Do it! It can often help, and will seldom hurt.

I suggest eclectic research for situations where uncertainty is high and measurement is difficult. In such cases, one should use approaches that are designed to measure a given concept but do so in different ways.

Part II

FORECASTING METHODS

P art II examines forecasting methods. An overview is given in Chapter 5. Chapters 6 through 9 discuss judgmental, extrapolation, segmentation, and econometric methods. Bootstrapping and other combined methods are examined in Chapter 10.

The primary purpose of Part II is to describe how the various forecasting methods can be used most effectively. Evidence is provided to indicate which specific techniques are most effective and which are least effective. These comparisons of techniques are carried out within each chapter (e.g., which techniques are most effective in judgmental forecasting) rather than across chapters (e.g., given a situation, are judgmental methods superior to econometric methods?). The latter comparisons are discussed in Part IV.

Five

CLASSIFYING
THE FORECASTING
METHODS

Contents

I know of no way of judging the future but by the past.

Patrick Henry
Speech at Second Virginia Convention
March 23, 1775

A long and complex case was presented to a group of executives. Each was then asked to identify the most important problem in the case. Of the six sales executives in the group, five saw the situation as a sales problem. All four production executives saw the problem as relating to organizational difficulties in the production area. In other words, there was a strong tendency for the executive to see the problem in terms of his own specialty (Dearborn and Simon, 1958).

Although I have not replicated this study with researchers, I predict similar findings. Those trained in judgmental forecasting methods would find that these are best for a given problem; those trained in extrapolation methods would solve the same problem using extrapolation; the econometricians would see regression analysis as the appropriate solution.

The world is easier and more comfortable when we can solve new problems with solutions that we have used previously. This happens with executives. It happens with generals (they are typically fighting the last war). And, it happens with us researchers!

Researchers often find problems because they have solutions that they can use. This has been referred to as the "law of the hammer." Give a child a hammer, and he will find a lot of things that need pounding.

How can one avoid this selective perception? One way is to use the systems approach. Within this framework, it makes sense to have a checklist of methods. The researcher can, after defining the objectives, go through the checklist to identify the most appropriate methods.

The use of eclectic research is another way to avoid selective perception. Specifically, the researcher can operate under the assumption that more than one method should be used in forecasting. To aid in the search for alternative methods, a checklist is provided in this chapter. It is called the forecasting methodology tree.

A number of schemes exist for classifying forecasting methods (e.g., see Chisholm and Whitaker, 1971; Chambers, Mullick, and Smith, 1974; Seo, 1984). These schemes are based upon the type of data used, the type of people doing the forecasting, or the degree of sophistication of the methods used to analyze data. The "forecasting methodology tree" is based upon the methods used to analyze the data.

Research on methods for analyzing data has historically been organized along three continuums:

1. Subjective vs. objective methods
2. Naive[G] vs. causal methods
3. Linear vs. classification methods

The discussion in this chapter uses the fictitious end points of each continuum.

SUBJECTIVE VS. OBJECTIVE METHODS

Subjective methods are those in which the processes used to analyze the data have not been well specified. These methods are also called implicit, informal, clinical, experienced-based, intuitive methods, guesstimates, WAGs (wild-assed guesses), or gut feelings. They may be based on simple or complex processes; they may use objective data or subjective data as inputs; they may be supported by formal analysis; but the critical thing is that the inputs are translated into forecasts in the researcher's head.

Objective methods are those that use well-specified processes to analyze the data. Ideally, they have been specified so well that other researchers can replicate them and obtain the same forecasts. These have also been called explicit, statistical, or formal methods. They may be simple or complex; they may use objective data or subjective data; they may be supported by formal analysis or they may not; but the critical thing is that the inputs are translated into forecasts using a process that can be exactly replicated by other researchers. Furthermore, the process could be done by computer.

Most forecasts are made with subjective methods (CERULLO and AVILA [1975] ROTHE [1978], DALRYMPLE [1985], MENTZER and COX [1984], and SPARKES and McHUGH [1984]). It also seems that the more important the forecast, the more likely it is that subjective methods will be used. Yet in many of these situations, objective methods would be more appropriate. In my opinion, the choice between subjective and objective methods is the most important decision to be made in the methodology tree.

NAIVE VS. CAUSAL METHODS

Joe had an accident. It seems that one night he was late and wanted to make up time, so he was going faster than usual. A slight mist was falling. Joe did not slow down for the curve! As he started to take the curve, he felt the car lean sharply and begin to slide. He stepped on the brake, but the car slid off the pavement, ran off the shoulder, and lunged into a shallow ditch. Although the car was not damaged, Joe scratched his left arm on the broken window handle. He thought little of the injury and managed to stop the bleeding with his handkerchief. Some days later Joe's arm swelled, and he developed a fever. When he saw a doctor, it was too late; infection had set in. Joe died. (This example is from Baker, 1955.)

What was the cause of Joe's death? Actually, there were many causes, and the **causal**^G description depends to a great extent upon one's objectives. For example, Ralph Nader would describe the accident differently than the automobile manufacturer or the aspiring local politician. Ralph would find the car at fault, the automobile manufacturer would tie the accident to the driver, and the politician would raise a cry about the dangerous roads.

A continuum of causality exists in forecasting models. At the naive end, no statements are made about causality (e.g., we can forecast how many people will die on the highways this Labor Day by using the number who died last Labor Day); in the middle, some models take account of some of the causality (e.g., we can predict Labor Day deaths on the basis of the number who died the previous Labor Day and also the weather forecast); finally, as in Joe's accident, the model may include many causal factors (e.g., Labor Day deaths can be forecast using information on weather, speed limits, the price of gasoline, the use of safety belts, the proportion of young drivers, and the number of miles in the interstate highway system). The selection of a model from along this continuum will depend upon the situation.

The end points of the naive–causal continuum are illustrated in Exhibit 5-1. The naive methods use data only on the variable of interest; historical patterns are projected into the future. Causal methods go beyond the variable of interest to ask "why?" Estimates of causal relationships are obtained (b). The problem then becomes one of forecasting the causal variables (the X's). Next, the estimates of the causal relationships are adjusted so that they are relevant for the period of the forecast (b_h). Finally, the forecast (Y_{t+h}) is calculated from the forecasts of the causal variables and the forecasted relationships.

The word "causal" has been used in a commonsense way here. A causal variable, X, is one that is necessary or sufficient for the occurrence of an event, Y. X must also precede Y in time. This interpretation seems useful despite the arguments to which it inevitably leads. The word "causal" appears to be so controversial that some researchers

Exhibit 5-1 NAIVE VS. CAUSAL METHODS

Naive
methods

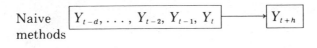

Causal
methods

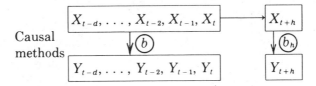

where
- Y = the variable to be forecast
- X = causal variables
- d = the number of periods of historical data
- h = the number of periods in the **forecast horizon**[G]
- t = the year
- b = the causal relationships in the historical data
- b_h = the causal relationships over the forecast horizon

prefer to use other terms such as "functionally related," "structural estimate," "stimulus-response," "dependent upon," or "determinant of." If you are interested in more on causality, Duncan–Jones (1970) provides a readable discussion. Wold and Jureen (1953, Chapters 1 and 2) relate causality to the use of regression models, and Blalock (1964) relates it to the use of nonexperimental data. HOGARTH [1980] and EINHORN and HOGARTH [1982] relate causality to judgmental forecasting.

The decision between naive and causal models is an important one in forecasting. It is especially important for long-range forecasting.

LINEAR VS. CLASSIFICATION METHODS

Methods that are objective and rely upon causality can be categorized according to whether they use linear or classification methods. This decision is the least important in the selection of a forecasting method and is best made after the earlier decisions have been completed.

The linear method is based upon the way we usually think about causality: "If X goes up, this will cause Y to go up by so much." An attempt is made to find linear relationships between X and Y. Linear methods are used because it is easier to work with models where the terms can be combined by using simple arithmetical operations. In particular, models such as the following are preferred:

$$Y = a + b_1X_1 + b_2X_2 + \cdots$$

where Y is the variable to be forecast, the X's are the causal variables, a is a constant, and the b's represent the relationships. This approach is "linear in the parameters." One might consider more complex forms (sometimes called "nonlinear in the parameters"). Such methods will not be discussed in this book because they would add unnecessary complexity to both your life and mine. They are harder to understand; they have not been shown to improve our ability to forecast; they are more expensive; and, although not hopeless, they offer little promise for the future.

The classification method attempts to find behavioral units that respond in the same way to the causal variables and to group these units. The objective is to obtain small differences within the groups, but large differences among the groups. To make a prediction, then, one merely needs to determine the category into which the unit falls and then to forecast the population and behavior within that category.

The preceding paragraph is too general; let me try to explain classification with an example. Assume that the task is to predict who will win the popular vote in the U.S. Presidential election in 1988. Assume that the leading candidates are Black for the Democrats, and White for the Republicans. The voters can be grouped into homogeneous categories. Forecasts are needed for the number of voters in each category. Then the voting behavior must be forecast (using prior voting records, subjective estimates, or surveys). Here is a fictitious example:

	Forecasts of	
Group Description	Voters × 1000	Probability of Voting for Black
Urban, college educated, live in northeast, age 35–50	918	.82
Rural, grade school, live in South, age 65 and up	810	.25

The classification approach was used in the 1960 Nixon–Kennedy election. Burdick, 1964, provides a fictionalized account of this effort. Pool and Abelson, 1961, give a nonfictional description.

METHODOLOGY TREE

The three continuums, along with statements about which decisions should be made first and last, allow for the construction of the methodology tree of Exhibit 5-2. The subjective method has been labeled as "judgmental." Interestingly enough, judgmental methods can be converted to an objective method called **bootstrapping**^{G} method. The objective–naive method is called "extrapolation"; the objective-causal-linear method is called "econometric" in deference to the field that contributed most to the development of this method; and the objective-causal-classification method is called "segmentation." These names were selected because they are commonly used. However, the terms do vary by field; that is, different researchers use different names for these methods.

The thicker branches of the methodology tree indicate which decisions are more important for most forecasting problems. The leaves of the tree (boxes) can be used as a checklist for selecting a method. Of course, there will be thin branches in the tree, which represent the selection of specific forecasting techniques.

Good advice to forecasters: Don't go out on a limb. Play it safe and use more than one branch. Then combine the forecasts from these different methods.

The methodology tree can also be used to structure books on forecasting. Thus, the next five chapters in *LRF* will cover each of the five

Exhibit 5-2   FORECASTING METHODOLOGY TREE

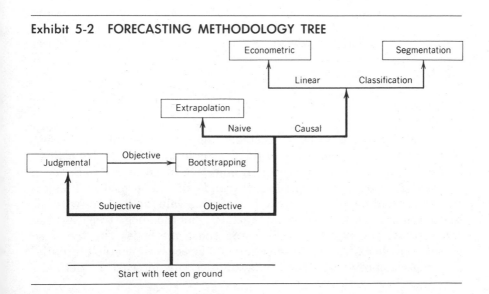

blocks. Chapter 10 also discusses methods that are based on combinations of the basic methods.

DESCRIBING FORECASTING METHODS

The early phases of scientific endeavor in a field involve descriptive studies. Descriptive studies on forecasting methods have developed over the past quarter century. Some of the landmark works are Brown's (1959b) *Statistical Forecasting for Inventory Control* and Box and Jenkins (1970) *Time Series Analysis: Forecasting and Control*. These works covered specific topics. Comprehensive descriptions of forecasting methods began in the 1970s; the quality of these works has improved substantially in recent years:

> Many books describe forecasting methods. These include BAILS and PEPPERS [1982], BOLT [1982], GRANGER [1980], GROSS and PETERSON [1982], HANKE and REITSCH [1981], LEVENBACH and CLEARY [1984], MAKRIDAKIS, WHEELWRIGHT, and McGEE [1983], and MAKRIDAKIS and WHEELWRIGHT [1984]. The first handbook in the field was published in 1982; it provides descriptions of various aspects of forecasting [MAKRIDAKIS and WHEELWRIGHT, 1982].

LRF provides only brief descriptions of methods because the existing sources are adequate. The primary focus in *LRF* is to develop generalizations as to which aspects of the methods are most useful for forecasting.

SUMMARY

Three key decisions were suggested to help in selecting forecasting methods. First, and most importantly, a choice must be made between subjective and objective methods. If objective methods are to be used, a choice must be made between naive and causal approaches. If objective and causal methods are used, it is of some value to consider whether to use linear or classification approaches. A methodology tree was used to illustrate the relationships among these methods. The tree also serves as a checklist for the selection of a forecasting method. Finally, a listing was provided of the books that describe forecasting methods.

Six

JUDGMENTAL
METHODS

Contents

What a piece of work is a man! How noble in reason! How infinite in faculty! In form and moving how express and admirable! In action how like an angel! In apprehension how like a god! The beauty of the world! The paragon of animals!

William Shakespeare*

The capacity of the human mind for formulating and solving complex problems is very small compared with the size of problems whose solution is required for objectively rational behavior in the real world—or even for a reasonable approximation to such objective rationality.

Herbert Simon (1957, p. 198)*

There is quite a contrast between Shakespeare's and Simon's viewpoints. On almost any basis one would choose Shakespeare! He is more poetic than Simon; he is more widely read; and his position is more popular. The only thing going for Simon is that he is right.

Shakespeare is expressing our hopes—a vision of the world as we want to see it. His view is one of the little lies that we tell ourselves. It makes us feel important.

We act as if Shakespeare were correct. Most forecasts are made using judgmental methods. The more important the forecast, the more likely we are to use judgmental methods in reaching it.

Judgmental forecasts have been well-studied. Much is known about the problems involved in using such forecasts, and much is known about how to improve judgmental forecasting.

What a wonderful position for a person who is writing a book on forecasting! To be able to talk about an area that is important and where people are generally doing things wrong, and to be able to say how to put things right!

This chapter first describes the two sources of judgmental forecasts—opinions and intentions. **Bias**[G] and other problems with judgmental forecasting are then described. The next three sections are devoted to methods for obtaining the forecast: the selection of judges, the wording of the questions, and the ways of obtaining the forecasts from the judges. The use of combined forecasts is discussed. Finally, there is a section on how to assess uncertainty. An intermission is provided in the middle of the chapter.

---

*These quotations were contributed by Paul Slovic.

TYPES OF JUDGMENTAL FORECASTS

Intentions[G] are statements that people make about their planned behavior, or about the behavior of things they can control. "Opinions" refer to things outside the judge's control; in this book, opinions refers to forecasts about events over which the judge has little control.

Intentions

Intentions data are most useful to the extent that the conditions in Exhibit 6-1 can be met. A discussion of the items in this list is provided.

Exhibit 6-1 CONDITIONS FAVORING USE OF INTENTIONS DATA

---

1. Event is important
2. Responses can be obtained
3. Respondent has a plan
4. Respondent reports correctly
5. Respondent can fulfill plan
6. New information is unlikely to change plan

Event Is Important.   The more important the event, the more likely it is that intentions will provide good predictions (e.g., Tobin, 1959; Murray, 1969; Friend and Thomas, 1970). For example, intentions are useful for predictions about events that have an important effect upon the judge, such as the choice of a marriage partner or an occupation. They are somewhat useful for predictions about fairly important events like the purchase of automobiles (e.g., (McNeil and Stoterau, 1967) TVs (Payne, 1975), and a TV service [STAPEL 1968]). Intentions are of minor value in forecasting unimportant events like the choice of butter or toothpaste (e.g., Bird and Ehrenberg, 1966).

The perception of importance is influenced by time; events that occur in the near future are perceived as more important. This implies that long-range intentions are useful only for events having a major impact on the respondent's life. Evidence supporting these statements has been found by numerous researchers. The following studies are typical:

Pratt (1968) found a relationship between importance and planning time. The estimated planning time for major consumer durables (clothes washers, dryers, and refrigerators) averaged about 13 weeks, and that for small durables (fans, radios, skillets) was about 2 weeks.

Clawson (1971) found that a 3-month consumer intentions survey was more closely related to behavior than 6-, 12-, and 24-month surveys.

Responses Can be Obtained.   It is important that the relevant decision makers can be identified and reached. Easier said than done! This is one reason why so much literature exists on this subject. The literature is organized around three major types of errors—sampling, nonresponse, and response errors. **Sampling errors**[G] create problems in generalizing from the sample to the population; nonresponse errors create problems in generalizing from the respondents to the sample; and response errors create problems in generalizing from the response to the individual respondent. Exhibit 6-2 illustrates these three sources of error for intentions data, assuming each type of error to be independent of the others.

An example may help to clarify Exhibit 6-2. Assume that you must forecast the sales of automobiles in the United States. You decide to ask people to forecast their own behavior. A sample is selected from the U.S. population, and its members are asked whether they expect to purchase a car within the next 6 months. You are interested in reducing the total error. Sampling errors result if the sample is too small or if it was selected from a list that was not representative of the population of potential automobile buyers. Nonresponse errors occur if individuals in the sample cannot be located, or if they refuse to answer. Response errors occur if the respondents do not know whether they will purchase cars, or if they want to answer in a way that makes them look good. Response error is affected by conditions 3 through 6 in Exhibit 6-1.

Respondent Has Plan.   Intentions are most useful when the respondent has a plan (e.g., Westoff, 1958). The extent to which this plan is formalized affects its value as a forecast. Legal contracts provide a high degree of commitment. Engagements are good predictors of marriages.

Exhibit 6-2   SOURCES OF ERROR IN INTENTIONS DATA
(A Three-Dimensional Graph)

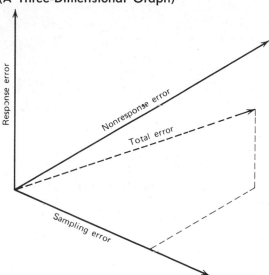

Planned expenditures for plant and equipment provide good predictions of actual expenditures [WIMSATT and WOODWARD, 1970]. Wicker provides further support:

> Wicker (1971) found that the correlation between intentions to donate to a church and actual donations was .92. In this case the church asked members to sign pledges, and it sent out quarterly statements.

Respondent Reports Plan Correctly.   The respondent may fail to report a plan correctly for any number of reasons: he may fail to understand the question; may feel that his response will be used against him; he may be unable to express his intentions clearly; the plan may reflect poorly on him (in which case he may lie); or may simply be unwilling to tell you about his plan ("It is confidential, you know"). For these reasons, intention and behavior often differ substantially:

LaPiere's (1934) study is often cited in this respect. He and a Chinese couple visited 250 hotels and restaurants and were refused service just once. Yet when a questionnaire was sent to the same places asking whether Chinese customers were welcome, 92% of the respondents said "no." Another example is provided in Doob and Gross (1968): intentions data and experimental evidence yielded different predictions in their study of automobile horn-honking.

Respondent Has Power to Fulfill Plan. Respondents are best able to fulfill their plans when their actions are independent of the environment. Often, for example in political negotiations or in labor-management relationships, respondents' actions are influenced by the actions of others. Interaction does not rule out the possibility of an intentions study, but it does increase the likelihood of response error.

New Information Is Unlikely to Change Plan. The value of the intentions forecast is reduced to the extent that changes occur between the time of the survey and the time of action. This is an obvious problem for political forecasts because often it is unclear what new information will occur (Watergate was an example in politics), or what information will be accepted as relevant by the decision makers (e.g., Watergate occurred well before the Nixon–McGovern election of 1972, yet most voters regarded it as irrelevant. On the other hand, a *Playboy* interview of President Carter appeared to be relevant to voters in the 1976 Democratic primaries).

The above conditions *do* arise often, so intentions surveys play an important role in forecasting. The technology in this area is well developed. Given these conditions, valid forecasts can be obtained by proper assessment of intentions. KALWANI and SILK [1982] present evidence on the validity of intentions in marketing. Intentions have long been useful in politics and the technology for measuring intention has improved over time:

PERRY [1979], in his review of the typical error in political forecasting, showed gains in accuracy for forecasts of voting in U.S. national elections:

Dates	Elections	Error
1936–48	7	4.0
1950–58	5	1.7
1960–68	5	1.5
1970–78	5	1.0

These gains have been achieved despite increasing refusal rates.

Opinions

Opinions data are more general than intentions data because they are not limited to situations where the respondent has an impact. Opinions data are also simpler to obtain. Sampling error is of little concern; in fact, forecasts are often made by using only one judge. Nonresponse errors are of little concern; if one expert refuses to answer, you find another expert. But there are many problems with response errors.

Economists have argued at great length over the relative value of opinions data and intentions data. How do these arguments get started? If you are interested in the topic you may want to examine Adams (1965) and Juster (1969). More relevant questions for our purposes are when should we use intentions data and when should we use opinions data.

Intentions studies seem most relevant if the conditions in Exhibit 6-1 are met. Otherwise, opinions studies should be used. This implies that intentions studies are useful for short-range forecasts, but that opinions surveys can be used for short- or long-range forecasting. From a cost viewpoint, intentions studies are most relevant to cases where there are few "intenders" and where they are easily located. Sometimes, both intentions and opinions can be used [e.g., SEWALL, 1981].

ERRORS IN JUDGMENT

This section discusses problems that you and I have as judges. They reduce our effectiveness in judgmental forecasting. Unfortunately, *awareness* of the problems is not always sufficient to overcome them.

Studies from social psychology document our difficulty in learning from the experience of others. Of particular interest is the study by Nisbett and Borgida (1975), where subjects' predictions of their own behavior were not influenced when they were given information on how others acted in the same situation (where they were told to harm other people). These studies suggest that information about problems that others have in forecasting will not have much effect on our beliefs about our own actions. (Even this finding is hard to believe about ourselves.)

What is to be done in the face of such damning evidence? Two things: suspend judgment about yourself, and, more importantly, develop and follow an explicit strategy for judgmental forecasting. Don't trust your common sense!

The errors in judgment are organized into two sections: bias and anchoring. These are only some of the errors. For a more complete treatment, see HOGARTH [1980] or KAHNEMAN, SLOVIC, and TVERSKY [1982].

Bias

Although bias can arise from the researcher and from the situation, the most serious form of bias is caused by the judge. Judges have preconceived notions about the world, and these can influence their forecasts. One form of bias has been called "**optimism**[G]." Predictions by judges reflect not only what they think will happen but also what they hope will happen. A good discussion on the effects of this bias is provided by Simon (1969). The effects are widespread, as shown many years ago:

> Hayes (1936) surveyed people two weeks before the 1932 U.S. Presidential election. Of male factory workers who intended to vote for Hoover, 84% predicted that he would win. Of those who intended to vote for Roosevelt, only 6% thought that Hoover would win.

> In McGregor (1938), opinions were used to forecast whether King Edward VIII would announce plans to marry within a year. In addition to being asked whether the King would marry, judges were also asked whether they thought he *should* marry. Of those who thought that the King should marry, 80% thought that he would marry. Of those who were indifferent, 60% thought that he would marry. Of those opposed to the marriage, only 32% thought that he would marry.

Kidd (1970) found that engineers were optimistic in predicting the time required to overhaul electric generators. The estimated time needed to complete a project was usually about 60% of the actual time required, even though the estimates were made after the project was well underway.

An analysis of annual earnings forecasts by 50 companies (Copeland and Marioni, 1972) found an overestimate of earnings that averaged 16%.

These examples involve cases where judges were biased, but they did not stand to gain personally. Imagine the effect of bias when judges also benefit personally; for example, the medical researcher who is paid by a drug company to test the efficacy of one of its drugs, or the salesperson who is asked to forecast sales during the next year. Typically the greater the judge's involvement in the forecast situation, the greater the expected bias.

Anchoring

"There is no reason for any individual to have a computer in their home," said Ken Olson, president of Digital Equipment Corporation at a convention of the World Future Society in Boston, 1977 [CERF and NAVASKY, 1984].

This example illustrates **anchoring**[G]. Anchoring is the tendency to start with an answer when making a forecast. More specifically, the example illustrates the type of anchoring that has been called **conservatism**[G]. "Conservatism," as defined here, is the assumption that the future will look like the past; there will be no abrupt changes.

Conservatism leads to underprediction of the amount of change. (For example, EGGLETON [1982] found that judgmental forecasts were more conservative than extrapolation forecasts.) The effects of conservatism are often confounded with the effects of optimism. This combined effect of bias and conservatism is illustrated by Herbert Hoover, who, on October 29, 1929 (just before the start of the Great Depression), said the following: "The fundamental business of the country, that is, the production and distribution of commodities, is on a sound and prosperous basis" (quoted by Cantril, 1938). The problem has been noted long ago, as shown in the following examples.

Ogburn (1934) found that students at colleges of losing football teams had forecasted that their teams would lose by an average of 3 points. The actual defeats averaged 18 points. Students at the winning colleges had forecasted victory by an average of 6 points.

Hultgren (1955) examined quarterly forecasts of tons of freight shipped over railroads from 1927 to 1952. The forecasts were made by experts employed by the railroad shippers. Forecast errors ranged from being too low by 1.7%, to being too high by 40.5%. The errors on the high side represented a bias toward good business.

Modigliani and Sauerlender (1955) also examined the railroad shippers' one-quarter forecasts, this time from 1927 to 1941. They found that, when shipments were rising, shippers underestimated by 5%. But when shipments were falling, they overestimated by about 16%. On the average for the period, their forecasts were high by 4%.

Evidence contrary to conservatism has been difficult to find. However, Dorn (1950) suggested that population forecasts have not been conservative. The predicted changes in population have generally been too large.

Tversky and Kahneman (1974) found that previous experience is not the only basis for anchoring. It can be created by the way the question is asked. Or the judge may jump to conclusions on the basis of early evidence. For example, Webster (1964) found that interviewers make judgments of prospective employees in the first 30 seconds of the employment interview and stick to them. The following examples, although extreme, illustrate how easily anchoring can occur and how misleading it can be:

Tversky and Kahneman (1974) asked subjects to predict the percentage of nations in the United Nations that were African. A starting value was selected by spinning a wheel of fortune in the subject's presence. The subject was asked to revise this number upward or downward to obtain his answer. This information-free starting value had a strong influence on the estimate. Those starting with 10% made predictions averaging 25%. This contrasts with the prediction of 45% by those given a starting value of 65%. (The correct answer is given in Appendix F.)

Multiplication Problem

Subjects are affected by initial data and tend to jump to conclusions. In Tversky and Kahneman (1974), subjects were asked to make rapid and intuitive estimates of math problems. One group was given $8 \times 7 \times 6 \times 5 \times 4 \times 3 \times 2 \times 1$. (Quickly, now, can you guess the product? _____). Another group was given $1 \times 2 \times 3 \times 4 \times 5 \times 6 \times 7 \times 8$. This is the same problem, of course, but the median estimate for those getting the ascending sequence was 512, whereas the median estimate for the descending sequence was 2250. (The correct answer is given in Appendix F.)

There are numerous other problems that resemble anchoring. People expect the world to adjust to their current view; thus most of us suffer from the gambler's fallacy (Jarvik, 1951). A consecutive run of, say, four heads in coin tossing will lead many people to expect a tail on the next toss. The future is expected to compensate for unfair deviations in one direction. The National Weather Service predicted a very hot summer in the eastern United States in 1977 because of the very cold winter that had just ended. The temperatures would "average out" over the year. Might this happen to businesspeople who experience four bad years or investors who have four bad investments? Here is a simple example of the gambler's fallacy (Tversky and Kahneman, 1971):

Eighth Graders IQ Problem

The mean IQ of the population of eighth graders in a city is *known* to be 100. You have selected a random sample of 50 children for a study of educational achievements. The first child tested has an IQ of 150. What do you expect the mean IQ to be for the whole sample? _____ (The answer is given in Appendix F.)

Carlson's (1967) review of economic forecasts finds evidence of optimism, conservatism, and the gambler's fallacy, all combined. AHLERS and LAKINISHOK [1983] also found evidence of optimism and conservatism in their analysis of Livingston's survey of economic forecasts.

Other errors arise with judgmental methods, but bias and anchoring are among the most serious. In the next section, I turn from errors to solutions. The solutions are considered for each of three steps in the development of judgmental models: selecting the judges, posing the question, and obtaining the forecasts. Ideally, one should proceed in the manner illustrated by the arrows in Exhibit 6-3. Typically, however, one must go back to an earlier step. Problems with bias may occur in any of these steps. It is expected to be more serious when uncertainty is high. Much can be done to correct for bias. Anchoring is more difficult to control, but some steps can still be taken.

Exhibit 6-3   STEPS IN THE DEVELOPMENT OF JUDGMENTAL MODELS

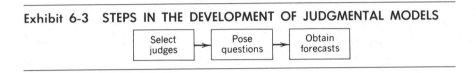

SELECTING JUDGES

The problems of selecting judges vary depending on whether one is using intentions or opinions data. This section provides advice on the selection of judges for each type of data.

Intentions

Careful selection of judges for intentions studies can reduce sampling error; this helps in generalizing from the sample to the population. The solution is probability sampling; it is well known and has been used for over half a century. Because you probably know about probability sampling, and because there are numerous good sources, the details are not discussed here.

Do not trust your intuitive feelings. Instead, rely on probability samples. Tversky and Kahneman (1971) illustrate the dangers of intuitive statistics, even for trained statisticians. Test yourself on the "sample-size-of-ten" problem. Most people do poorly on this—but, as Casey Stengel said, "You could look it up!"

Significance of Follow-up Samples

Suppose you have run an experiment on 20 subjects and have obtained a significant result that confirms your theory ($p < .05$ with two-tailed test). You now plan to run an additional group of 10 subjects. What do you think the probability is that the results will be significant, by a one-tailed test, separately for this group? $p =$ _____ (The answer is given in Appendix F.)

Expert Opinion

"I think there is a world market for about five computers." This remark is attributed to Thomas J. Watson, Chairman of the Board of IBM in 1943 [CERF and NAVASKY, 1984].

People are willing to pay heavily for expert advice about the future. Milton Friedman is consulted to tell us how the economy will change: stock analysts are paid large salaries to forecast the earnings of various companies; Jean Dixon will forecast anything; political experts command large fees to tell our leaders what the future holds; and Jimmy the Greek forecasts the outcome of sporting events. The evidence says that this money is poorly spent. Because few people pay attention to results in this area, we might call this the "seer-sucker theory"; which is, "No matter how much evidence exists that seers do not exist, seers will find suckers."

Expertise beyond a minimal level in the subject that is being forecast is of little value in forecasting change. This conclusion represents one of the most surprising and useful findings in this chapter. It is surprising because emotionally, we cannot accept it. It is useful because the implication is obvious and clear cut: *Do not hire the best expert you can—or even close to the best. Hire the cheapest expert.* You have already recouped the cost of this book if you will follow this advice.

If this conclusion bothers you (it bothered me), you might try a short exercise so that the information in this chapter will be more useful. Take 30 minutes (time yourself), and describe on paper what information or evidence could possibly convince you that expertise is of no value in forecasting. This exercise requires a lot of psychic energy. If you wind up with a blank page after 30 minutes, you have just finished this section, in which case you can branch to the next section, "Posing the Question," on page 96. If you can list possible evidence, then you might find something helpful in this chapter.

30-Minute Work Period

Before proceeding with the evidence, let me make one thing perfectly clear: I am not against experts. No one who has read about Lem Putt, the privy builder (Sale, 1930), could be against experts. Some of my best friends are experts. If they keep their place in forecasting, everything will be fine. But their place is in saying how things are (estimating current status), rather than in predicting how things will be (forecasting change). The estimation of current status does, of course, play an important role in forecasting. (Expertise in *forecasting methods* is also valuable.)

Many studies have been done on the value of experts. Most have come from psychology and finance, but there is evidence also from economics, medicine, sports, and other areas. Expertise in the field of interest has been measured in various ways (education, experience, reputation, previous success, self-identification). Accuracy has also been measured in many ways. With few exceptions, the results fall into the pattern illustrated in Exhibit 6-4. Above the low level of expertise labeled E_l (which can be obtained quickly and easily), expertise and accuracy are almost unrelated. It is likely, in fact, that accuracy drops off after expertise passes a certain level (indicated by the dotted line), but the evidence on this point is limited.

Evidence is available from well over 100 studies on the value of experts. Of these studies, only a few suggested that expertise improved forecast accuracy, and, even here, the gains were small. Of course, expertise does add to the comfort level of the client. A positive relationship would be expected between the client's confidence and the money spent on experts.

Exhibit 6-4   RELATIONSHIP BETWEEN EXPERTISE AND ACCURACY IN FORECASTING CHANGE

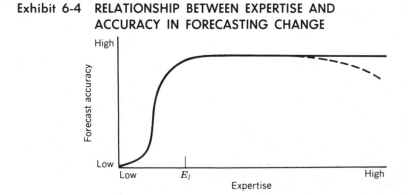

Psychology. Taft (1955) surveyed 81 studies from psychology that examined predictions made of others by experts and nonexperts. He concluded that nonpsychologists were more capable of making predictions about others than were psychology students or clinicians. The study was updated by Sarbin, Taft, and Bailey (1960), who added 10 studies. Grigg's study, described in the following example, is typical of the research that was reviewed, and more recent studies have been provided by Goldberg and by Levy and Ulman:

In Grigg (1958), 24 Ph.D.s, 24 trainees in psychology, and 24 naive subjects (undergraduates) listened to 10-minute interviews with each of three clients and then predicted how each client would fill out three different personality inventories. There was no difference in accuracy between the Ph.D.s and the trainees, and both were significantly more accurate than the naive subjects.

Goldberg (1965) found that 16 trainees did at least as well as 13 experts in diagnosing psychosis from scores on a personality inventory (the **MMPI**[G]).

Levy and Ulman (1967) asked judges to distinguish 48 normal people from 48 psychiatric patients by an examination of paintings done by these subjects. All predictions were significantly better than chance, but expertise did not lead to significant gains in accuracy:

Judges	Average Percent Correct
Professional mental health workers	66.5
Student mental health workers	64.5
Persons with no mental health experience	64.6
Chance	50.0

Additional studies in psychology by Grebstein (1963), Hiler and Nesvig (1965), and Oskamp (1967) reached the same conclusions.

Finance.   Cox (1930) compared the performances of experts and novices in forecasting prices of stocks. He found no advantage for expertise. A study by Cowles followed shortly and reached the same conclusion, as have other studies:

Cowles (1933) examined 255 editorials by Hamilton, an editor of the *Wall Street Journal,* who had gained a reputation for successful forecasting. During the period from 1902 to 1929, Hamilton forecasted 90 changes in the market. Of these forecasts, 45 were correct, and 45 were incorrect. People following Hamilton's advice would not have done as well over this period as if they had made random investments. Cowles also found that a sample of 20 insurance companies did slightly worse than the market averages from 1928 to 1931, that 16 financial services did slightly worse than the average from 1928 to 1932, and that forecasts in 24 financial publications did slightly worse than the averages over this same period. A follow-up study (Cowles, 1944) reinforced these conclusions.

An excellent review of the literature in finance is provided by Granger and Morgenstern (1970). These studies (except for Shelton, 1967) add support to the conclusion that expertise is of little value in forecasting. More recent studies provided by Staël von Holstein (1972) and Richards (1976) yielded the same results.

An exception to the findings about the stock market is that expertise based on inside information is of value. (See Brooks (1969, Chapter 4), Lorie and Niederhoffer, (1968), and PENMAN [1982].)

Medicine, Sports, and Sociology.   The first four studies described here suggest that expertise has no value. The next three suggest that expertise has minor value:

Johnston and McNeal (1967) had 12 judges predict the length of hospital stay for 379 mental patients over an 18-month period. Forecasts were made for 0 to 3 months vs. 4 months or longer. The judges' scores ranged from 63% to 86% correct. The more experienced judges were no more accurate.

Winkler (1971) examined forecasts for collegiate and professional football games for 1966 using 45 judges, and for 1967 using 10 judges. He found that expertise (as identified by the previous week's success or by self-ratings) was of little value.

AVISON and NETTLER [1976] found that expertise, measured by schooling, did not improve individual predictive accuracy for 52 items predicted in nine public opinion polls in the United States and Canada ($r^2 = .004$).

Armstrong and Overton (1977) found that two students and a housewife were as accurate in predicting which mail survey items would be subject to nonresponse bias as were nine faculty members who had substantial experience with survey research.

Kaplan, Skogstad, and Girshick (1950) found a small but statistically significant correlation for a sample of 26 forecasters between their accuracy in forecasting for 123 events in the social and natural sciences and their respective scores on items involving current social problems and science.

Winkler (1967) found that sportswriters did a little better than graduate students and faculty members on forecasting scores for collegiate and professional football games. The bookmakers' forecasts, in turn, were slightly better than the sportswriters'.

Wise (1976) examined 1556 predictions made publicly in the United States between 1890 and 1940. The predictions related to social, technological, economic, and political changes. Some evidence was found to support expertise, although the effects were small. The significance of the findings rested on one judge who could have been classified in either group.

As noted, these results are disturbing. They do not make much sense. Perhaps future research will offer new insight. However, given the evidence to date, I suggest that you avoid hiring the most expensive expert to forecast change. Instead, spread the budget over a number of less expensive experts. Also remember that experts are good at diagnosis (estimating the current status) and that is useful in forecasting.

Additional advice follows from the earlier discussion on bias: avoid using biased experts. Do not use anyone who will be affected by the forecast, and find experts who differ greatly on any factors believed to be related to the forecast. Then use more than one judge. How many? The gain from adding judges drops rapidly, while the cost per judge is fairly constant. Huber and Delbecq (1972) suggest using at least 5 judges; an increase to 10 gives better results, but thereafter improvements are minor. HOGARTH [1978], using theoretical arguments, concluded that you should use at least six but no more than 20 experts. LIBBY and BLASHFIELD [1978], using empirical studies, concluded that the optimum number of experts is between 5 and 9.

The argument is often made that we must tolerate some bias in our judges because their expertise is so great. For this reason, salespeople, politicians, stockbrokers, and others get involved in the forecast. Another explanation for our use of experts is that, by using them, we can avoid responsibility. For example, courts use expert ratings of the extent to which criminals are dangerous even though these ratings lack predictive validity [COCOZZA and STEADMAN, 1978].

POSING THE QUESTION

The wording of questions may have dramatic effects, as illustrated by this example from Hauser (1975); these questions were asked in 1940:

Question	Percent Answering "Yes"
1. "Do you believe in freedom of speech?"	96
2. "Do you believe in freedom of speech to the extent of allowing radicals to hold meetings and express their views to the community?"	22

Incidentally, although this example occurred during wartime, a follow-up in 1970 again found a minority answering "yes" to question 2.

Here is a fine opportunity to use some of that good advice on research strategies from Chapter 4:

Tom W. Problem

"Tom W. is of high intelligence, although lacking in true creativity. He has a need for order and clarity, and for neat and tidy systems in which every detail finds its appropriate place. His writing is rather dull and mechanical, occasionally enlivened by somewhat corny puns and by flashes of imagination of the sci-fi type. He has a strong drive for competence. He seems to have little feel and little sympathy for other people, and does not enjoy interacting with others. Self-centered, he nonetheless has a deep moral sense."

The preceding personality sketch of Tom W. was written during Tom's senior year in high school by a psychologist, on the basis of projective tests. Tom W. is currently a graduate student. Please rank the following nine fields of graduate specialization in order of the likelihood that Tom W. is a student in that field. Let rank 1 be the most probable choice.

_____ Business administration
_____ Computer science
_____ Engineering
_____ Humanities and education
_____ Law
_____ Library sciences
_____ Medicine
_____ Physical and life sciences
_____ Social science and social work

(Why not try your hand at the above problem before proceeding?)

This Tom W. prediction problem is borrowed from Kahneman and Tversky (1973). It is not a trick case, but it does illustrate some typical difficulties. In this study judges did not use all of their information in an efficient manner. They ranked the programs almost solely on the basis of the perceived similarity between the brief description given and a typical student in each program. The base rates for these graduate programs, that is, the fact that some programs are large relative to others, had almost no influence upon their predictions. As students in psychology, most of these judges should have been aware that the personality sketch had no validity. In addition, all of these judges had been exposed to the notion of base-rate prediction in their statistical training. In short, the question, as stated, led the judges to make poor use of their knowledge.

What might be done to improve prediction in the Tom W. case? Consider the following possibilities:

1. *Decomposition* suggests that we identify the key components of the problem. In this case the two most obvious components would be the base rate and the individual variation from the base rate.
2. *Prior theory* can be used along with decomposition. In this case some judges would state that thumbnail personality sketches cannot be used to predict individual variation. They would then be left with the problem of predicting by using the base rate only.
3. *Causality* can be used in the statement of the problem to show why the base rate is relevant [AJZEN, 1977].
4. *Eclectic research* might be used by wording the question in different ways. One could vary the order of the answer categories, provide one version with the thumbnail sketch and one without it, rewrite the thumbnail sketch to eliminate evaluative wording, and use judges with different educational backgrounds. A combination of these forecasts would be expected to be more accurate.

For further comments on Tom W., see Appendix F.

> The base rate problem has been the subject of much study. See AJZEN [1977], Carroll and Siegler (1977), CHRISTENSEN–SZALANSKI and BEACH [1982] and HOGARTH [1980]. For a practical application, see JOHNSON [1983].

These suggestions on wording can be applied to many questions on forecasting. In particular, one should distinguish between a judge's knowledge of the current situation and his forecast of change (or between base rate and individual variation). For example, assume that you want to predict the number of suicides in 1985. No matter how you phrase the question, it will mean different things to different people. Also, how much information should the question provide? A reasonable strategy is to word the question in different ways. If the current year was 1972, here are some possible ways the question might have been worded:

1. In 1970, there were 11.6 suicides per 100,000 people in the United States. What do you think the rate will be in 1985? _____
2. In 1970, there were 11.6 suicides per 100,000 people in the United States. Although the rate has fluctuated since 1900 (e.g., it rose in the 1930s), there has been no long-term trend. What do you think the rate will be in 1985? _____
3. By what percentage do you think the suicide rate will change between 1970 and 1985?

   Up by _____ %
   No change _____
   Down by _____ %

4. In 1970, there were 11.6 reported suicides per 100,000 population. Do you think that this correctly represents the suicide rate?

   Yes _____
   No, it is high by _____ %
   No, it is low by _____ %

(Incidentally, the data were taken from the U.S. Bureau of the Census, *Historical Statistics of the United States,* 1975, p. 414.)

Numerous possibilities exist for the introduction of bias into questions. HARRIS [1973] presents some examples; in one situation subjects were asked: "How tall was the basketball player?" Other subjects were asked, for the same player: "How short was the basketball player?" The respective averages for the player were 79 and 69 inches. Payne (1951) provides practical advice on the wording of questions, Noelle–Neumann (1970) discusses problems in wording and some solutions and SUDMAN and BRADBURN [1983] use the research findings to develop guidelines.

In the following subsections, specific techniques are discussed for posing the question. These include techniques for presenting information to the judges and for scaling the information received from the judges. These techniques are relevant to both opinions and intentions studies. Finally, consideration is given to questions for sensitive issues.

Presenting Information

Cardinal Krol, Archbishop of Philadelphia, was asked about his position on the Vietnam War shortly after a visit to President Nixon in January 1972. A spokesperson answered something to the effect that "although the Cardinal was against war, he really could not make any judgment about Vietnam because he did not have all of the facts." Of course, President Nixon did not have "all of the facts" either. Presumably, however, Nixon did have more facts than Krol. Was this information likely to help Nixon to make a better judgment about the value of the war in Vietnam?

The example of Cardinal Krol illustrates one of man's basic strategies: he blames his difficulties on a lack of information. Thus, it is commonly assumed that the accuracy of a judge can be improved by giving him more information.

The research on the relationship between the amount of information provided to a judge and his predictive accuracy yields results that parallel those of the research on the value of expertise; that is, beyond a minimum amount of information, additional information does not add to accuracy—but it does add to cost. The familiar refrain "We need more information" is often incorrect. So here is another useful piece of advice: don't invest a great deal of money in obtaining better data. It is good practice to be suspicious when people tell you they need more information in order to make better predictions.

Most of the evidence on the value of information comes from psychology. Goldberg (1968a) reviewed evidence from 13 studies. Some typical examples of these studies are presented here, along with a study of a transportation problem:

Kelly and Fiske (1950) asked judges to predict success for participants in a training program in psychology. Information about the participants had been collected during 7 days of testing and interviewing. Predictions based on only a small portion of these data were at least as accurate as predictions based on all of the data.

Borke and Fiske (1957) asked clinical psychologists to make predictions about neurotic patients' responses to various paper-and-pencil tests. Predictions based on a face-to-face interview were no better than those based on reading a verbatim transcript of an interview with these patients. Grigg (1958), in a similar study, reached the same conclusions.

Dudycha and Naylor (1966) created an artificial world, using a two-variable equation:

$$Y = b_1X_1 + b_2X_2$$

Evidence from this world (i.e., observations on X_1, X_2, and Y) were presented to subjects. Although both variables were valid, the addition of information on the less important variable did not improve accuracy in predicting, and in some cases it decreased the subjects accuracy.

Armstrong and Overton (1971) measured intentions to subscribe to a new type of urban transportation known as the Minicar system. A "brief" description, which was mailed to the sample, provided a picture of the car and described the service. A "comprehensive" description required that the subject attend a product clinic. Here the subject was guided through an exhibition of 18 wall graphs that explained key aspects of the service, was allowed to examine and to sit in the vehicle, and was shown a 14-minute movie that described the system. Guides were available to answer questions for the subjects. The cost per subject for the comprehensive description was about 10 times that for the brief description, not counting the cost of the prototype vehicle. Thirty-five subjects filled out the mail questionnaire on intentions to purchase the Minicar service. The same 35 subjects came in a week later for the comprehensive description. A comparison between intentions to purchase for the brief vs. the comprehensive description showed no difference. (Appendix F provides a brief description of the Minicar system.)

In summary, increasing the amount of information, that is, the number of bits of information, beyond a bare minimum, does not lead to improved forecasting by judges. (BRAUN and SRINIVASAN [1975] provide clues as to the "bare minimum.") This may be due to a limited ability to remember information (Miller, 1956a, b) or a limited ability to process information (Dudycha and Naylor, 1966).

The *presentation* of information is of greater concern than the *amount* of information. That is, how can a given amount of information be presented so that it is used most effectively by a judge?

Decomposition is one of the most effective ways to utilize an expert's information. The expert can be asked to respond to questions on each of the parts of a problem. The analyst then synthesizes the responses to construct the forecast. Hertz (1964) illustrated this process using a capital budgeting decision. This strategy can be especially useful with a group of experts, each of whom may have information on only part of the problem.

Eclectic research can also help to utilize various bits of information. One might present different information to each expert, perhaps information tailored to utilize that person's particular expertise. Responses from each of the judges would then be averaged. Pure speculation on my part.

The presentation of information on exponential growth is of particular interest, not only because it is common that things (like company sales) grow "percentagewise," but also because this information is difficult for judges to handle. Studies by WAGENAAR and SAGARIA [1975] and WAGENAAR and TIMMERS [1979] show that judgmental forecasts of exponential growth are highly conservative, partly because people tend to think in terms of unit differences rather than percentage changes. You can test this by asking someone to forecast the thickness of a thin piece of paper if it were folded in half 40 times. Show them the step by step folding up to eight folds, then ask them to forecast the thickness by judgment alone, assuming that it could be folded another 32 times. A group of 20 MBAs in my forecasting course at the University of Hawaii provided the following written predictions:

	N
Less than one foot	13
Greater than one foot, up to one mile	5
Greater than one mile, up to 2000 miles	2
Greater than 2000 miles	0

I have replicated the paper-folding exercise with other groups and found similar results. Few estimates exceed one mile. The actual answer is that it would be thick enough to stretch from the earth to the moon.

If judgmental forecasts must be made for exponential growth problems, two suggestions seem to help. You should:

1. Use fewer data; that is, do not examine the process too frequently [see WAGENAAR and TIMMERS, 1978; WAGENAAR, 1978] and
2. Present the historical growth as a decreasing function by using the inverse form, such as square miles per person rather than vice versa [see TIMMERS and WAGENAAR, 1977; WAGENAAR, 1978].

Even with these corrective procedures, the conservative bias often exists. Consider the following forecast of a decreasing function: "Where a calculator on the ENIAC is equipped with 18,000 vacuum tubes and weighs 30 tons, computers in the future may have only 1,000 vacuum tubes and perhaps weight $1\frac{1}{2}$ tons." So said *Popular Mechanics* in March 1949. [CERF and NAVASKY, 1984].

For long-range forecasts, it is often necessary to forecast the net effect of a number of trends. For example, assume that you have asked experts to make predictions on the size and nature of the advertising industry in the year 2000. To help with this prediction you provide them with information on the expected ownership of video tape recorders by families, the use of cable TV, the capability of families to transmit messages on TV as well as to receive them, the capability of selling information via credit card and so on. Some people, myself included, have proposed the use of scenarios as an aid to forecasting because the scenario can integrate the information and help to show inter-relationships. Thus, you could write a story about a family in the year 2000 and show how they utilize all of this new technology. Promising?

In 1977, I contacted leading experts on scenario writing to assess its predictive validity. I was unable to find evidence either for or against the value of scenarios in forecasting. There were many applications, but no attempts to validate. On the other hand, the method seemed to have promise. For example, had I used a scenario, I would have been able to predict the usage rate for the rotary lawn sprinkler that I purchased. It would have gone like this: "Place sprinkler on lawn. Return to water faucet and turn on water. When lawn is soaked, go to water faucet and turn off water; then go to sprinkler and relocate; return to water faucet and turn on water." In all, a frustrating and inefficient practice. As a result, the usage rate fell to zero. An alternative scenario using a sprinkler that oscillated would, I expect, have led me to predict a different usage rate.

As noted earlier, however (*LRF* pp. 40–45), the recent research on scenarios suggests that there are many pitfalls. Minor changes in the way a scenario is written can have major impacts on the forecast of its likelihood. In light of this research, I do not recommend scenarios as a technique *to improve accuracy*.

When one tries to get "all the information," the likelihood increases of presenting irrelevant information to the judge. As we saw in the case of Tom W. (p. 97), judges often use irrelevant information, even when they realize its irrelevance. I have encountered the same situation among personnel recruiters who try to predict the future success of job candidates. Some recruiters have told me that grades are not a valid predictor of job success for an individual (this happens to be correct); but then they say that, as long as the candidates provide this information, they will use it! ZUKIER's [1982] experiment showed that the addition of irrelevant information will lead judges to make more conservative forecasts. ROOSE and DOHERTY [1976] and SLOVIC and McPHILLAMY [1974] found that this irrelevant information was especially likely to be used if it was "commensurate" (corresponding in measure) across observations; grading is a good example of an irrelevant yet commensurate measure for predicting success on the job.

Predictions for the Tom W. case can be greatly improved by omitting the irrelevant information. Kahneman and Tversky (1973, p. 241) tested this by asking subjects to predict for "Don":

"About Don you will be told nothing except that he participated in the original study and is now a first-year graduate student. Please indicate your ordering, and report your confidence for this case as well."

For Don, there was a strong relationship ($r = .74$) between the judge's estimate of the base rate and his prediction of field of study. The moral of the story is that no information is better than worthless information!

One might even question the wisdom of providing any data at all to the experts. Objective data can be processed more effectively using an objective method. So why give them to the expert? Let the expert make the prediction on the basis of his own information; in this way information beyond the objective data may be utilized.

The strategy of letting the expert rely on his own information, however, is not without its difficulties. Consider the following problem:

"A word is selected at random from an English language dictionary. Is it more likely that the word starts with the letter k or that k is its third letter?"

[STOP AND CIRCLE ANSWER: 1st   3rd]

To answer this, the subject searches his memory for relevant information. He will find that some information is easy to recall and some is difficult. In this case, it is easier to search for words by their first than by their third letters (try it and time yourself if you doubt this). Thus most people will recall more k-as-the-first-letter words and conclude that these are more common. In fact, k-as-the-third-letter words are three times as common. Tversky and Kahneman (1973) call this a problem of availability. Events that are easy to recall seem more common.

Scaling

It is difficult to avoid the problem of availability. My suggestion is that you ask the question in different ways. KRUGLANSKI, FRIEDLAND, and FARKASH [1984] showed that many biases can be avoided if the question is properly worded.

Here is a question that my state (Pennsylvania) asks school children in a survey called "Education Quality Assessment":

"Someone whose skin is a different color from yours
wants to borrow your coat:
_____ (1) I would like it a lot.
_____ (2) I would like it.
_____ (3) I would not like it.
_____ (4) I would hate it."

This question is interesting because you are not allowed to be indifferent. As Pennsylvania's question is worded, you can answer it as either a prejudiced or an unprejudiced person. (Your answer is assumed to relate to your feelings about race rather than to your feelings about your coat.) Don't follow Pennsylvania's example; instead allow for "no opinion." In terms of scaling, this means that you should use scales with an odd number of points to handle such situations.

"Do you use 3-, 5-, or 7-point scales?" Now that is a popular question. It is asked so often you could hardly blame people for thinking that it is important. Actually, it is not very important, so this section is short. Much of the evidence is indirect and suggests that scaling is not important once you get past five categories, although small benefits accrue from more categories. Furthermore, there seems to be no danger in using more categories. Conclusion: use a lot of categories! Thomas Juster, who has done much research on this problem, suggested the use of 11-point scales for intentions studies. Huber and Delbecq (1972), who work with opinions studies, say that at least 5 categories should be used, and that an increase to 10 or more is better. COX [1980] reviews the research of this topic. Here is a description of Juster's work:

Juster (1964, 1966) compared an 11-point scale with a 3-point scale ("definite," "probable," "maybe"), in measuring intentions to purchase automobiles. Data were obtained from the 800 randomly selected respondents, the long scale being administered to them a few days after the short scale. Subsequent purchasing behavior of these respondents was then examined. The results indicated that the longer probability scale was able to explain about twice as much of the variance among the subsequent behavior of the judges as was the shorter scale. In addition, the mean value of the probability distribution for the 800 respondents on the 11-point scale provided a better estimate of the purchase rate for this group than the short scale.

If you care to do more reading on scaling, many sources exist. Consideration is given to the number of points on the scale, to the level of measurement, including **nominal**[G], **ordinal**[G], **interval**[G], and **ratio**[G] scales (Stevens 1959), to the reference points for a scale (Rothman, 1964), and to other issues. Green and Tull (1978) and Selltiz, Wrightsman, and Cook (1976, Chapter 12) provide a general review of these issues.

When people are asked to predict the probabilities that each of a list of mutually exclusive and totally exhaustive events will occur, you might expect the total probabilities across events to sum to 100%. Certainly these probabilities should not sum to more than 100%! But many people do make predictions that sum to more than 100%, as shown by the four experiments reported in TEIGEN [1983]. Furthermore, the greater the number of possibilities, the greater the total probabilities. Furthermore, when two new possibilities were added to an original list of four, two-thirds of the subjects assigned probabilities without changing the probabilities for the original four alternatives, and only one-sixth of the subjects made adjustments that reduced the probabilities of the first four alternatives. The biases were substantial; for example, students in the social sciences predicted vocational choice for a youth seeking vocational guidance. When 10 possible choices were available, the total probability was 288%. Perhaps the solution is to phrase questions so that respondents will not make such estimates. Or perhaps the responses can be normalized by the researcher so that they sum to 100%. Still another possibility is to frame the question as a series of two way options. Further research is in order and, fortunately, this research can be replicated or extended at low cost. As a start, I tested the general principle by giving a question on marketing strategy to Wharton School MBA students. In a version of this question that offered three alternative courses of action, each of the 30 subjects assigned probabilities that totaled exactly 100%. When six alternatives were presented, five of the 26 respondents gave probabilities that summed to more than 100%, and the overall average was 105%. Although overestimation occurred, it was smaller than in Teigen's experiments. The point of these studies is important: When soliciting probabilities, do not assume that the respondents will normalize their probabilities. (See also WRIGHT and WHALLEY [1983].

Sensitive Issues

"Would your friend do it?"

In some cases people may be reluctant to reveal their intentions. This typically occurs when the response may reflect poorly on the respondent. Sensitive issues include race, religion, politics, sex, and crime. For such issues one can use an indirect or **projective test**[G]; that is, the judge responds to an ambiguous question or reports how someone else (e.g., a friend) would react. This technique removes the personal threat to the judge.

I was unable to find studies that compared the predictive validity of projective and direct methods. Different forecasts were implied, however, by the Nescafé study:

Haire (1950) asked women shoppers to describe the personalities of two women. The only information given about the women was their shopping lists. These lists were identical except that one included a regular coffee while the other included an instant coffee, Nescafé, which at the time was a new product. The woman with Nescafé was described by almost half the respondents as being lazy and a poor planner, whereas few respondents felt this way about the other shopper. They said that the Nescafé shopper did not care as much about her family because she would not spend the time to make percolator coffee. The implied forecast was that, if Nescafé advertised that instant coffee saves time, sales would decrease. Housewives already knew that Nescafé saved time, but they felt guilty using it. Direct questions about instant coffee yielded a much different picture in this case. Respondents said that they did not drink instant coffee because they did not like the taste.

Few situations require the use of projective tests. They should be used when a truthful answer might put the respondent in a bad light. An extensive discussion of projective methods is provided in Selltiz, Wrightsman, and Cook (1976, Chapter 10).

INTERMISSION: Take a long break. You owe it to yourself!

OBTAINING THE FORECASTS

Once upon a time (actually in the early 1900s), there lived a German horse named Clever Hans. Clever Hans could answer an amazing variety of questions. Because it was hard for people to believe that a horse could be so smart, a commission was appointed to find out why he could answer questions. The commission found, for example, that Clever Hans could answer questions from strangers when his trainer was out of sight; thus, the trainer was not providing cues. The investigation stumbled about for some time until it was discovered that the answer lay not in Clever Hans, but in the person who asked the question. Clever Hans was able to answer a question only when the person asking it knew the answer! Without realizing it, questioners were giving cues about the correct answers. Generally they would lean forward to get a better view of Hans's hoof, at which point the horse would start tapping. When the correct answer approached, the questioner would often show an almost imperceptible head movement (that he was not aware of). This was the cue for Hans to stop tapping. He might still sound like a clever horse to you. Be reassured, however; Oskar Pfungst, who was leading the research commission, was able to follow the same type of cues as had Clever Hans, and he did almost as well as the horse in some experiments. (The original study is reported in Pfungst, 1911. For a brief summary, see Rosenthal and Rosnow, 1969, pp. 197–199.)

The story of Clever Hans suggests that the researcher can play an important part in judgmental forecasting without realizing it. She may unwillingly communicate additional information that affects the judgmental forecasts.

Since the time of Clever Hans, numerous studies have examined the relationship between the researcher and the subject. A review of this research is provided by Rosenthal and Jacobson (1978), who refer to this problem as the Pygmalion effect—"one treated like a lady acts like a lady." Two typical studies are summarized here:

In Rosenthal and Jacobson (1968), students in an elementary school were tested by researchers. The researchers then provided false information to the teachers. They said that some students were of high potential, and they predicted that these students would do well during the school year. Although the students had been randomly assigned to the group, those predicted to do well were found to do better than the others in the group over the rest of the year.

Peters (1971) described a study similar to Rosenthal and Jacobson's. Students were told by their teacher that blue-eyed children were superior to brown-eyed children. In the space of less than one day, the blue-eyed children were performing better than their brown-eyed classmates.

(Why do I find these results so surprising? After all, I have been a student, I have worked as a "blue-collar" worker, and I was a private in the U.S. Army. In these situations I learned that "one treated like a child acts like a child." The Pygmalion effect applied to me too.)

The Pygmalion effect, a type of self-fulfilling prophesy, has often been attributed to cooperative subjects. In other words, subjects respond to please the researcher. According to this argument, judges try to provide the forecasts that the researcher is looking for. Sigall, Aronson, and Van Hoose (1970) reviewed the evidence in this area and found nothing to support this cooperative subject theory. The key point, they said, is that the subject wants to look good in the eyes of the researcher. They ran an experiment contrasting the two hypotheses and found that "looking good" was important, but "cooperation" was not.

To speak about the subject alone in the Pygmalion effect is analogous to studying clapping by examining the right hand only. The subject's

responses are interpreted by the researcher. This, too, can be a source
of bias. "Bright young people" in companies may do well or *seem* to do
well, because their superiors view them as bright young people. Rosenthal and Jacobson (1968, pp. 37–41) also summarized research
showing how the researcher's bias can affect results. A typical study
is provided by Rosenthal and Fode:

A class in experimental psychology was asked to conduct experiments with rats (Rosenthal and Fode, 1963). Five rats were given
to each of 12 different student groups. Half of the groups were
told that their rats were "bright," and half were told that their
rats were "dull." In fact, there were no differences between the
two groups. The rats were required to run through a maze. The
average number of correct responses by the gifted rats was 2.3,
and that by the disadvantaged rats was 1.5 ($p < .01$). ("Now, you
parents get your children into those gifted programs at school.
Too bad about the other kids," said Scott, in a fit of sarcasm.)

This discussion suggests that the relationship between the judge
and the researcher may be a major source of error in judgmental forecasting. Another source of error arises from the interaction among
judges. Moore's (1921) study implies that these two types of interaction
have large and roughly equal impact upon the typical judge's opinions.

Interaction among judges is *desirable* when the forecasted behavior
is influenced by the opinions of other people. Examples are the intended
purchases of clothing, automobiles, furniture, or vacations. Another
important situation exists when one's actions are interdependent with
the actions of others, as in political decisions, union–management negotiations, and some buyer–seller relationships.

More often, interaction among judges is undesirable. Rather than
report true intentions or opinions, judges may report falsely to gain
approval by the group. The effects are shown dramatically in research
carried out by Asch:

In a series of trials, subjects were asked to match the length of a
line with one of three unequal lines (Asch, 1965). Each of the
subjects in the room was asked to announce his choice on each
trial. All of the subjects but one were confederates of the exper-

imenter. They had been instructed to give obviously wrong answers on some trials (all confederates giving the same wrong
answers). The situation was arranged so that the naive subject
responded last. Under such conditions, only about 25% of the
naive subjects continued to give correct answers. The rest showed
some conformity, and 30% of the subjects gave wrong answers
over half of the time. These results have been replicated many
times.

The results of the Asch experiment were obtained in a situation where
the answers were obvious. The effects of interaction should also be
considered when the task is not so clear-cut, as is generally true in
forecasting problems. Sherif's autokinetic study illustrates the effect
of such interaction when the situation itself provides no information.

Sherif (1936) placed subjects in a dark room. A pinpoint of light
was presented, and subjects were asked to judge how far the light
moved. Although the light was stationary, it appeared to move
because the observer had no point of reference. (This is called the
autokinetic effect.) The group exerted a powerful influence on each
subject's judgment of the movement. The group's earlier opinion
also led to anchoring when new members were added to the group.

One other effect of interaction among judges is that the stated intentions may affect the behavior of the judges. This can be an important
consideration when the judge is involved in the future situation, or
when she feels committed to the prediction (Bennett, 1955, provides
evidence on this).

In view of the importance of "judge–researcher" and "judge–judge"
interaction, the discussion on how to obtain the forecast has been organized along these dimensions. Techniques for obtaining forecasts are
plotted in their approximate locations in Exhibit 6-5. The discussion
that follows considers each of the techniques.

Surveys

Survey methods avoid interaction among judges. This is advantageous
if the judge's responses would be biased by how others react to her

Exhibit 6-5   INTERACTION EFFECTS ON TECHNIQUES TO OBTAIN
              JUDGMENTAL FORECASTS

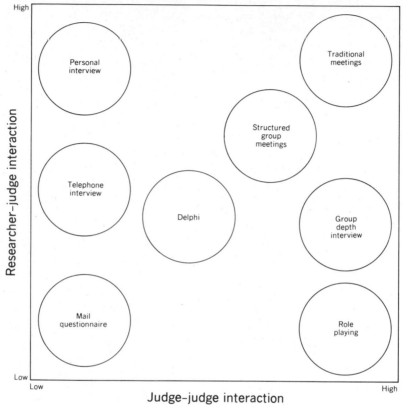

statements, or if the responses of others would bias her responses. The
assumption is made that other judges influence the responses but not
the actual behavior. When the actual behavior would be influenced, it
is important to account for this interaction; in such a case surveys
would not be appropriate.

Surveys also assume that the respondent has a good knowledge of
the situation and how she would act in it. If this is not the case, surveys
should not be used. An example is provided by Hofling et al.:

In Hofling et al. (1966), 33 graduate and student nurses were
asked on a questionnaire what they would do if a doctor tele-

phoned and asked that a patient be given a medicine. They knew
that it was a violation of hospital policy to order medication by
phone. Also they were told that they did not know the doctor, that
the medicine was not on the authorized list, and that the dosage
was twice the maximum allowable amount shown on the pill box.
In response, 94% of the nurses said that they would not administer
the dosage. A field experiment was also carried out on a comparable group of 22 nurses; only 1 nurse refused to administer the
drug.

The basic survey methods are mail, telephone, and personal interview. Combinations of these methods exist, as do other approaches
such as computer-led interviews (e.g., Greist et al., 1973). These approaches differ primarily in the amount of interaction among judges.
Thus mail questionnaires (more precisely, self-administered questionnaires) involve less researcher–judge interaction than do telephone or
personal interviews.

The relative merits of the various methods are briefly considered
here by examining them against five criteria: cost, speed of response,
sampling error, nonresponse bias, and response bias. A more complete
discussion and further references are given in Boyd and Westfall (1981).
Details on how to conduct mail and telephone surveys are provided in
DILLMAN [1978] and Erdos and Morgan (1983).

Cost.   Mail and telephone surveys are substantially cheaper per respondent than personal interviews. In some cases the personal interview is 3 to 10 times as expensive as mail and telephone surveys. The
personal interview is especially expensive when the sampling units
are widely dispersed geographically.

Speed.   The telephone is clearly the fastest survey method. Many
organizations are equipped to have interviewers feed responses directly
to the computer, so summaries can be obtained immediately. Mail
surveys are the slowest method, generally requiring at least a month.
Personal interviews, although substantially faster than mail, are not
as fast as telephone surveys. Of course, speed is generally not an important criterion for long-range forecasting.

Sampling Error.   Often, it is difficult to obtain a list of the desired
sample. In most situations the advantage lies with the personal interview. Mail surveys suffer because people change addresses. The most

serious problems, however, lie with telephone surveys; in addition to the fact that people move, about 10% of the population do not have telephones, and about 20% (mostly people who are younger, have less education, and have lower incomes) do not list their telephone numbers (Glasser and Metzger, 1972, 1975). The percentage of unlisted numbers is higher, about 30%, in urban areas. For these reasons, the lists for telephone surveys represent only about 70% of the households for general consumer intentions studies. Random digit dialing can be used for reaching the unlisted numbers, but this increases costs substantially (Glasser and Metzger, 1972) and it is a rude way to contact people.

Nonresponse Bias. The personal interview suffers least from nonresponse; it is more difficult to refuse someone face to face. Call-backs can be scheduled to ensure a high probability of reaching the respondent (Boyd and Westfall, 1970; Dunkelberg and Day, 1973). Although expensive, responses of 90% can sometimes be achieved.

Mail surveys have a serious problem with nonresponse. For example, general surveys face the problem that almost 10% of the population are not literate. Fortunately, however, much research exists on ways to reduce the nonresponse rate (Scott, 1961; Kanuk and Berenson, 1975; Linsky, 1975; Pressley, 1976; Erdos and Morgan, 1983). Followup has been shown to be an effective way to improve response rates. Monetary incentives up to about one dollar (1985 dollars) have also been found to be effective. (Armstrong, 1975b, reviews this literature.) Other useful practices are to use first class postage stamps for outgoing and return mail [do *not* use business reply postage, ARMSTRONG and LUSK, 1985], to ask short and relevant questions at the beginning, and to enclose an interesting cover letter. Surprisingly, length of questionnaire has a negligible effect. DILLMAN [1978] provides other useful advice. With techniques like these, one generally expects more than a 50% response rate, and 80% has often been achieved.

It is also possible to *estimate* the nonresponse bias in mail surveys. This can be done by reaching almost all of a subsample of the nonrespondents with a combination of mail, telephone, and personal contacts. This subsample can be used as an estimate for the nonrespondents. Another approach is to extrapolate responses across two or more waves. Armstrong and Overton (1977) show how simple extrapolations can reduce nonresponse bias by half.

Telephone surveys suffer greatly from nonresponse. Although nonresponse is reduced substantially by callbacks, even after as many as four callbacks not-at-homes may be in the neighborhood of 10%. Furthermore, it is easy to say "no" by telephone. Although some studies have achieved refusal rates lower than 5% (e.g., Kegeles et al., 1969), the samples were special. More commonly about 20% refuse, and 35% is not unusual (Hauck and Cox, 1974; Falthzik, 1972). Falthzik suggests when to call in order to reduce the total of not-at-homes and refusals (Monday through Thursday from 9:00 A.M. to 12 noon are the best times). Overall, response rates of 70% are good for telephone surveys.

The best way to reduce nonresponse bias, when one considers both cost and error, is to use eclectic research. One may start, for example, with a mail survey, follow it with three mail follow-ups, and then telephone the nonrespondents. Nonresponse bias can then be estimated by extrapolation and by intensive efforts to contact a small subsample of nonrespondents. Of course, some people still will not respond. Simon (1969) says one should not be annoyed at them; the pay for this job is low, and it is a bother. It is amazing that so many people *do* respond to surveys.

Response Bias.   Although George Gallup argued that personal interviews are most accurate (Gallup, 1976), the research suggests that for most issues the responses from mail, telephone, and personal interviews are similar. Rogers (1976), in a long survey focused mainly on education, obtained similar responses from telephone and personal interviews. Colombotos (1969) and Hochstim (1967) got similar results from mail, telephone, and personal interviews in health surveys.

The responses frequently differ on sensitive issues, however, including issues where "looking good" is of concern or where people feel that their response may be used against them. Sudman and Bradburn (1974) provide a thorough analysis of the literature on factors causing such response bias. Corrective procedures are examined in the review by KALTON and SCHUMAN [1982]. The following examples show how differences may arise on sensitive topics:

O'Dell (1962) used mail and personal interviews to study consumer behavior. On some questions there were sharp differences: 37% of the people interviewed used hair rinse, while 51% of the mail respondents did so; 17% of the interviewees borrowed money at the bank, compared with 42% of the mail respondents.

Wiseman (1972a) compared mail, telephone, and personal interviews. For most questions there were no differences. Differences were found, however, on sensitive issues. For example, for a question on the use of birth control, 75% of Catholic mail respondents were in favor, versus 44% of Catholic respondents interviewed by telephone or in person.

So far, the discussion has considered similarities and differences. But which type of survey is most accurate? Wiseman's study suggests that mail surveys have an advantage for sensitive issues. This was verified by Sudman and Bradburn (1974) in their review of 935 studies; self-administered questionnaires (mail) are best for threatening questions. Cannell and Fowler (1963) found mail responses superior to personal interviews in a survey on hospitalization (records were available on the true situation in this study).

The superiority of mail surveys for reducing response bias was expected because there is less researcher-judge interaction. There is also less possibility for cheating, which may be a problem with telephone and personal interviewers (Roth, 1966). The problems can often be controlled in interview studies by training the interviewers and by monitoring some of the interviews to guard against cheating. These procedures can lead to results that are highly replicable, as shown by the following study.

In McMillan and Assael (1968), two different marketing research firms, Chilton Research and National Analysts, were given identical questionnaires and sampling plans and were asked to conduct independent interview studies on attitudes toward transportation. The responses were remarkably similar.

Projective questions might also serve to improve the capability of the survey methods to forecast sensitive issues. As noted earlier (*LRF* p. 107), however, this is speculation.

The advantages and disadvantages of the various survey methods are summarized in Exhibit 6-7 (*LRF* p. 134). But first the other methods for obtaining forecasts are examined.

Delphi

The Delphi technique obtains opinions through a mail survey. It uses the anonymity of responses from such a survey, and it typically adds three features:

1. The respondents are experts in the subject area.
2. There is more than one round—that is, the experts are asked for their opinions on each question more than one time.
3. Controlled feedback is provided. Respondents are told about the group's responses on the preceding round. On round 2 and later rounds, respondents with extreme answers are sometimes asked to provide reasons, and these reasons are summarized anonymously for the next round.

Few techniques have captured the imagination of forecasters in such a grand manner as Delphi. It is truly a triumph of modern marketing. Would people be as captivated if it had been called "iterative mail surveys of experts?" It is much better to be named after the oracle at Delphi.

Delphi has been used for many years. Gerstenfeld (1971) found that over 10% of the firms in his sample of *Fortune's* 500 had used Delphi. McHale's (1973) survey of organizations, institutional units, and individuals engaged in futures research found that Delphi was one of the most popular techniques used. Hayden (1970), in a survey of "65 progressive companies," found 26% of them using Delphi; of these, 71% claimed that it was useful.

Delphi has been the subject of hundreds of journal articles and numerous books. Linstone and Turoff (1975) provide a comprehensive review of this literature, and so does Martino (1983). Many variations of Delphi are presented, but most use the basic format as was described. Johnson (1976) provides a description of how Delphi was used by Corning Glass Works for a long-range market forecast. For another application, see BASU and SCHROEDER [1977].

Despite the vast literature, comparatively little empirical work has been done on the value of the three key aspects of Delphi (i.e., experts, iterative procedure, and feedback) over the typical mail survey. There have been many claims. For example, Martino (1983, pp. 26–29) stated that the selection of experts is the most important decision when using Delphi. The evidence on these three issues is examined in the following subsections.

Experts.   The evidence reviewed early in this chapter stated that expertise in the subject is of little value in forecasting change. Why should it be any different for Delphi? Evidence in favor of experts in Delphi studies is lacking. The studies that have been published suggest high expertise is not necessary. Sackman (1975) refers to a study of computers that yielded similar results when replicated with graduate students instead of experts. Welty (1974) summarized additional evidence

from five studies which showed that nonexperts can be used instead
of experts; one of these studies is described here:

> Welty (1972) replicated a Delphi forecast of American culture in
> the year 2000. The initial study had been done by Rescher using
> 58 experts. Welty used 43 college students majoring in sociology.
> Of the 17 items examined by Welty, there were no significant
> differences on 14.

On the other hand, expertise is expected to be helpful when Delphi
is used to assess current status. This was supported by the following
studies:

> In Best (1974), 14 self-rated experts did better than 14 nonexperts
> in a Delphi study involving two questions involving estimates of
> current status. Similar results were found in a two-question Del-
> phi study by Jolson and Rossow (1971).

Rounds.   Certainly additional rounds produce greater agreement among
Delphi experts. Some people think this is an argument in favor of
adding rounds. Not so! The actual situation is just what you would
expect. Sackman (1975) cites the similarity between results from autokinetic studies and from Delphi studies. The critical question is whether
the average response moves toward greater accuracy on successive
rounds. The answer is yes; there are small increases in accuracy, but
it is not clear whether the gains are larger than one would obtain by
adding experts rather than adding rounds.

> Hample and Hilpert (1975) reanalyzed results from four Delphi
> studies. These studies, such as Dalkey (1969), used almanac ques-
> tions (i.e., questions with known answers, such as "How many
> kangaroos are there in Australia?") whose answers were unlikely
> to be known by the panel. They found 214 questions where the
> median response changed on subsequent rounds. Improvements
> in accuracy were found for 63% of these questions. Additional
> studies, not included in Hample and Hilpert's analysis, include

Jolson and Rossow (1971), who found increases in accuracy on six of seven comparisons over three rounds, Best (1974), who found improvements on five of six comparisons over two rounds, PARENTE, ANDERSON, and MYERS [1984] who found that additional rounds helped to predict *when* but not *if* an event would occur, and BOJE and MURNIGHAN [1982] who found no gain in accuracy over three rounds using almanac questions. Overall, it seems that additional rounds yield small gains in accuracy.

Feedback. Does it help to have people explain why they gave extreme answers? Hample and Hilpert (1975) examined this issue. Using data from two previous studies, they found that with no feedback, subsequent rounds were more accurate on 47% of the comparisons ($n = 30$); with feedback, subsequent rounds were more accurate on 58% of the comparisons ($n = 45$). Best (1974) reported a slight gain when feedback was provided for his two-question study. Gustafson et al. (1973) found no gain in accuracy; in fact, written feedback seemed to reduce accuracy. This limited evidence suggests that feedback produces slight gains in accuracy.

The Verdict on Delphi. This review suggests that high expertise is not required when Delphi is used to forecast change. Additional rounds and feedback each seem to contribute to accuracy, although the gains are modest and the evidence is limited.

Sackman (1975) provided a thorough review of Delphi. His criteria were strict, and his conclusion (his p. 74) was extreme: He said that "the massive liabilities of Delphi, in principle and in practice, outweigh its highly doubtful assets." After reviewing the Delphi literature and Sackman's critique, I agree with some of Sackman's points. Delphi researchers have been lax in examining Delphi; seldom do they study its predictive value, and seldom do they provide sufficient disclosure of their methods. On the other hand, Delphi has the advantages of the mail survey. The additional rounds and the feedback are of some value, perhaps of more value than increasing the size of a mail survey.

The primary advantage of Delphi is that it is a technique that is acceptable to organizations. It sounds fancy, yet the users can understand it. Groups using Delphi are almost as satisfied as those using traditional group meetings (Van de Ven, 1974). *Most importantly, Delphi is more accurate than traditional group meetings.* RIGGS [1983] provides some evidence on the accuracy of Delphi.

If you do use Delphi, observe the guidelines for good practice in judgmental forecasting. As shown in STEWART and GLANTZ [1985], expert surveys sometimes violate good practice.

Traditional Meetings

Remember the horse business problem (*LRF* p. 31)? It was stated that about half of the individuals who do this arithmetic problem get it wrong. If that depressed you, consider this: when the problem is given to groups, about half of the groups miss it (Thomas and Fink, 1961).

Although groups can't get the horse business problem right, they want to forecast the most important things in our lives. The traditional meeting is the most commonly used approach to forecasting. Surveys to support this conclusion (e.g., see PoKempner and Bailey, 1970), but you already know this. The traditional group meeting has many problems, not the least of which is the strong pressure to conform. But you know this too. Why, then, are traditional group meetings so popular? Well, people generally do not invest much energy in preparation, so meetings are easy. They also satisfy social needs; participants report high satisfaction with groups (e.g., Van de Ven, 1974; BOJE and MURNIGHAN, 1982). Finally, they help to satisfy power needs. It is nice that they do a good job on social and power needs because they certainly are not of much help in obtaining accurate forecasts. The following are some examples of research studies on the value of groups. Although Timmons (1942) cited studies showing advantages to groups in certain cases, most studies since then have shown little value for groups. The study by Kaplan is especially relevant as it deals directly with forecasting.

In Jenness (1932), subjects estimated the number of beans in a jar. Group discussion led to agreement, but did not improve accuracy.

Kaplan, Skogstad, and Girshick (1950) studied 26 people who made over 3,000 separate forecasts of 16 events in the social and natural sciences. They found that traditional discussion in a four-person group followed by individual forecasts led to correct predictions in 62% of the cases. As a basis for comparison, judges working alone were statistically averaged as four-person groups, and they were correct 63% of the time. In short, the group discussion did not improve forecast accuracy.

In Campbell (1968), the group solution to an organizational problem was inferior to the individual solution.

One could cite many more such studies. The group meeting is expected to do poorly—and it does. But instead of beating a dead horse, let's examine ways to make the group meeting effective in forecasting.

Structured Meetings

It is especially important to consider improvement in group meetings because most organizations will continue to do their forecasting this way. A number of techniques exist to control "judge–judge" and "researcher–judge" interaction. Two of these methods are considered in this section: developmental discussions and estimate-talk-estimate (**E-T-E**[G]).

The developmental discussion was adapted from Maier and Maier (1957). With this technique, a **facilitator**[G] is used rather than a leader. Instead of a group that works for its leader, one has a facilitator who works for the group. The facilitator:

1. Prepares for the meeting by decomposing the problem.
2. Provides an opportunity in the meeting for all members of the group to participate, and especially encourages the expression of minority opinions.
3. Avoids evaluation and helps the group to suspend evaluation.
4. Avoids introducing her own ideas to the group.

Rules 3 and 4 reduce researcher-judge interaction. Rules 2 and 3 reduce judge–judge interaction. Rule 1 uses the group's knowledge in a systematic way.

Consider again the horse business problem (*LRF* pp. 31, 120). Although group work was ineffective, the addition of a facilitator (using rules 2, 3, and 4) led to correct answers by 84% of the individuals (Maier and Solem, 1952). This improvement was significant ($p < .05$). It was not due to superior knowledge on the part of the facilitators (only 44% of the leaders had initially gotten the correct answer). Rather, it was due to their success in allowing minority opinions to exert a constructive influence.

Most of the research on developmental discussion deals with problem solving rather than with forecasting. The results support the advantages of developmental discussion. The study described below by Maier and Maier found decomposition to be useful, and Hall reported that better predictions were obtained if evaluation was suspended, and an opportunity was given to express minority opinions.

Maier and Maier (1957) compared discussion groups using rules 2, 3, and 4 with developmental discussion groups using all four rules in order to assess the value of decomposition. The problem was "the case of Viola Burns," an employee in an organization. Background information was provided, and groups were asked to decide whether Viola should be encouraged or discouraged from taking a new job. The case was designed so that the highest-quality judgment would be to discourage Viola from taking the job. Of the developmental discussion groups, 40% reached this decision vs. 18% for the free discussion groups.

Hall (1971) used the "lost-on-the-moon" problem. Participants were asked to predict which items in a given list experts would recommend as being necessary for a survival trip across the moon (see Appendix F for a full statement of the problem). After 148 upper management personnel from several business organizations had been randomly divided into 32 discussion groups of four to six members each, half of the groups were given instructions on how to reach a consensus. These instructions stressed the suspension of evaluation and promoted the expression of minority opinions (rules 2 and 3). These groups provided more accurate predictions than did groups not given instructions. HERBERT and YOST [1979] replicated this study and obtained similar results.

Hall, Mouton, and Blake (1963) asked subjects to predict the order in which jurors in the movie *Twelve Angry Men* would shift from a vote of "guilty" to "not guilty." Consensus rules led to improved predictions for 17 of 22 groups ($p < .05$). Similar results were obtained for the same problem by Holloman and Hendrick (1972).

Another method for structuring meetings is E-T-E. This technique is similar to Delphi except that a face-to-face meeting is used instead of a mail survey. Estimates in E-T-E are made anonymously. During the talk period, participants are asked to avoid arguing for their own position or even revealing it. Unlike Delphi, however, the researcher does not generally control the discussion, and people will sometimes argue for their own positions.

In comparison to Delphi, E-T-E offers advantages in terms of speed of response. The process can be completed within a matter of minutes or hours rather than weeks or months (Van de Ven's 1974 Delphi study took five months, for example). Although people enjoy unstructured meetings a bit more and they think they are more effective than E-T-E [BOJE and MURNIGHAN, 1982], E-T-E provides greater accuracy than do traditional meetings:

Gustafson et al. (1973) found slightly more accurate forecasts for E-T-E than for traditional meetings in a study asking judges to predict on questions such as this: "The observed weight of a person is 130 pounds. Is the person more likely to be male or female?"

There is, however, a disturbing finding that perhaps meetings should be eliminated. In other words, people would simply record their predictions. Hardly a social event, but the predictions would probably be about as good, and time would be saved. ROHRBAUGH's [1979] study on predicting grade point averages for students, and BORMAN's [1982] study of personnel predictions supports such a conclusion, as did the following studies:

Dalkey (1967), using almanac questions, concluded that anonymous individual forecasts (carried out before a group meeting) were more accurate than those obtained after a discussion among the group members.

Campbell (1968) found that group discussion of an organizational problem led to small but insignificant improvements in the quality of the decisions in comparison with prior decisions by the individuals.

One variation of E-T-E is to have an individual and anonymous first estimate, which is followed by a group discussion and a group decision. Unfortunately, the group decision seems to be inferior to the original pooled estimate of the individuals (Campbell, 1968; Maier, 1973).

Van de Ven (1974) proposes a "nominal group meeting." This is a variation of E-T-E in which more control is exerted over the discussion. A related possibility is to use a developmental discussion during the talk phase. The effects of these procedures on forecasting have not been assessed.

The best advice is to use *some* structured technique. FISCHER [1981] found few differences in his comparisons of the accuracy of various structured techniques.

Group Depth Interview

The group depth interview is useful for intentions studies when the behavior of the judge will be influenced by the responses of others and when the respondent is unsure how others will respond. This might occur for decisions such as the use of kilts by men, the purchase of a microwave oven or an electric car, or the adoption of a new approach to education by a school. Group depth interviews are more relevant to the extent that the changes are viewed as important, approval by others is evident, and uncertainty is high.

The group depth interview is basically a nondirective interview (it follows the rules provided on *LRF* pp. 28–31). The differences are that one is dealing with a group of perhaps four to eight people, rather than with an individual, and the scope of the initial question is generally narrower. Because of this narrower focus, the technique is sometimes called a focused group interview. (See Goldman, 1962, for an alternative description of this technique.)

Although the group depth interview is reasonable and widely used, I have been unable to find studies on its value in forecasting problems.

Role Playing

During the Vietnam peace action, high-ranking officers in the U.S. military played a game. They split into two groups, one representing the United States and the other representing North Vietnam. Various strategies were then examined. In particular, the bombing of North Vietnam was considered. As a strategy for the United States, limited bombing was a military failure in this role play. Unlimited bombing was a bit more favorable from a military viewpoint, but it had no clearcut advantage over no bombing at all. The decision makers ultimately ignored the results of this game and chose the poorest strategy from a military viewpoint: limited bombing. The prediction from the role playing was accurate; limited bombing was ineffective and costly (Halberstam, 1973).

In role playing, people act as if they were the actors in the situation to be forecast. The role play should be realistic. The following rules should be followed when role playing is used:

1. Use "props" to make the situation realistic. Special clothing sometimes helps; for example, in the study by Janis and Mann (1965) the person who played the role of the doctor was asked to wear a white coat. In some situations, it helps to rearrange the furniture.
2. The actors should not step out of their roles, that is, once the actors meet, they should "be" that person at all times. A good idea here is to ask the role players to separate, and then return to the meeting place a few minutes later, after they have mentally prepared themselves and are ready to stay with their new identities.
3. The actors should improvise as needed and should throw themselves into the role-playing session.

These rules can be implemented with a low budget. Elaborate simulations do not seem necessary [e.g., see ELSTEIN, SHULMAN, and SPAFKA, 1978; ARMSTRONG and WALKER 1983.].

Some role-playing situations have been found to create a great deal of realism. In addition to the Vietnam case mentioned, one could cite Zimbardo's (1972) simulation of a prison. The players in this case were surprised at their own behavior. The action was terminated prematurely because the realism seemed to be getting out of hand, and the safety of the "prisoners" was threatened. Orne, Sheehan, and Evans (1968) found that role playing was realistic enough that observers could not distinguish between subjects who were hypnotized and those who were role-playing a hypnotic trance.

When role playing is used to forecast, two possible instructions may be used. One is to ask the players "to act as you yourself would act in this situation." The other is to ask them "to act as you think the person you are playing would act." I have used the former, as have most of the studies cited in this section, but I am not sure about the effects of these differing instructions. This approach assumes that the role is the dominant influence on behavior. The instruction to "act as that person would act" would incorporate that individual's personal preferences. This instruction requires some knowledge about the person.

Role playing seems to be most valuable when the *interaction* among people has a lot to do with the responses of these people. In addition, role playing seems to be of value when:

1. There are conflicts among the people involved.
2. It is not feasible to obtain intentions data from the relevant people (e.g., the various people involved in the Falkland Islands crisis between Argentina and the United Kingdom).
3. The decision is an important one.

The role-playing approach has been popular in political science, where it is called gaming. Goldhamer and Speier (1959) report that Germany used role playing in 1929 to plan its war strategy; Japan did so in 1940; Russia has engaged in it periodically and Herman and Herman (1967) used it to simulate the outbreak of World War I.

The use of role playing in business seems to be limited. Busch (1961) said that the Lockheed Corporation would ask executives to stand in the shoes of their major customers during group discussions and that they found this to be a satisfactory way to forecast the behavior of these customers. Evidence from mock juries suggests that they provide valid predictions [KERR et al., 1979]. IBM used a form of role playing to predict the reactions of a jury in a trial (*Wall Street Journal,* Feb. 3, 1977, p. 7). BORMAN [1982] found role playing to yield accurate personnel predictions.

Predictions from role playing may differ greatly from those provided by other methods. Here is a simple example:

Cyert, March, and Starbuck (1961) divided judges into two groups of 16 each. Each group was assigned a different role. One role asked the judge to assume that as the chief cost analyst for a manufacturing concern, he was to produce a cost estimate on the basis of preliminary estimates provided by two assistants in whom he had equal confidence. In the other role, the judge was the chief market analyst and he had to provide a sales estimate. The data were identical for both roles. The cost analysts estimated on the high side, and the market analysts estimated on the low side. Seldom did the analyst simply average the estimates from his two assistants—the expected behavior if no role had been assigned.

It is only in recent years that the predictive value of role playing has been studied. In some of these studies, role playing was used to predict results that had been obtained experimentally. I found 13 studies using this approach; of these, 11 provided results that could have been used to predict the results of the experiment. The following are typical studies:

Greenberg (1967) used role playing and successfully replicated a laboratory experiment showing that higher anxiety produces a greater need for affiliation in first-born children. The subjects were told, "It is very important that you take your role seriously and that you act as if this were a real situation."

Willis and Willis (1970) told subjects about the purpose and design of a laboratory experiment on conformity and then asked them to play the role of naive subjects. The main effect agreed with those from the laboratory study, but no interaction effect was found.

Mixon (1972), using a crude role playing procedure, was able successfully to replicate the Milgram (1974) laboratory experiment on obedience. This is noteworthy because opinions surveys of psychiatrists and intentions surveys of potential participants in the experiment yielded predictions dramatically different from those obtained in the Milgram study (Milgram, 1974, pp. 27–31; Larsen et al., 1972).

Additional studies include Berscheid et al. (1973); Darroch and Steiner (1970); Holmes and Bennett (1974); Horowitz and Rothschild (1970); Houston and Holmes (1975); Ring, Wallston, and Corey (1970); Simons and Piliavin (1972); Terry (1974); Wexley,

Singh, and Yukl (1973); and Yinon, Shoham, and Lewis (1974). This has been a controversial topic in psychology. Viewpoints on the value of role playing may be found in Hamilton (1976), Freedman (1969), and Miller (1972).

The predictive value of role playing for real-life situations has been tested in eight situations. Overall, role playing yielded 70% correct predictions, in comparison with 21% correct predictions for opinions. Some of these studies are summarized here:

Crow and Noel (1965) had subjects role-play a historical situation. The case, known as the "East Algonian exercise," was based on the annexation of Texas by the United States. The authors stated that it was unlikely that their judges, who were students, could correctly identify the true situation. To test this, I asked John Cronin, a professor who specializes in military history at Delaware County Community College, in Pennsylvania, whether he could identify the situation. He spent a substantial amount of time but was unable to make a correct identification. The case was presented by Crow and Noel to 96 different groups. Each group was asked to role-play to reach, for the Mexican leader, a decision ranging from 1, a peaceful response, to 11, a warlike response. Although historians claim that the optimal decision would have been 1 or 2, only 1% of the groups reached these decisions. Fifty-seven percent reached 4 or 5. The actual decision was classified by historians as 4 or 5, and it proved disastrous for Mexico. In other words, the role playing yielded accurate predictions of the behavior of the Mexican leader in a problem where the prediction was not obvious.

Since 1908, Washington and Lee University has been running a mock political convention every four years to select a Presidential candidate for the party that is out of power. This convention is generally run in early May before the actual convention, which typically occurs in July or August. (A description of the details of this elaborate role play may be obtained from Washington and Lee University, Lexington, Virginia, 24450.) Including the Mondale nomination in 1984, the convention has been accurate on 13 of 18 candidates. In this case, however, public opinion polls, which have been conducted since 1936, provide a comparable record of accuracy (Runyon, Verdini, and Runyon, 1971; Gallup Opinion Index for 1972 and 1976; and the Harris survey for 1980 and 1984). The candidate who was leading in the Gallup poll at the same time as the Washington and Lee convention won on 8 of 12 occasions. During the same period, the role-playing prediction was also correct on 8 of 12 occasions. (The two approaches agreed on 7 occasions, and, when they did, all predictions were correct.)

Armstrong (1977) asked subjects to play the roles of seven members of the board of directors for the Upjohn Corporation. They were told that an unbiased group of medical scientists, after 20 years of study, were unanimously recommending that Panalba, an Upjohn drug with harmful side effects, be removed from the market. The board was given 45 minutes to agree on one of the following five decisions:

1. Recall Panalba immediately and destroy.
2. Stop production of Panalba immediately but allow what's made to be sold.
3. Stop all advertising and promotion of Panalba, but provide it for those doctors that request it.
4. Continue efforts to most effectively market Panalba until sale is actually banned.
5. Continue efforts to most effectively market Panalba, and take legal, political, and other necessary actions to prevent the authorities from banning Panalba.

Of the 57 groups that played the role faced by Upjohn, *none* removed the drug from the market. Furthermore, 79% decided to take decision 5. In fact, Upjohn also took decision 5. (Don't worry; the Supreme Court made the company take the drug off the market in 1970. On the other hand, if you travel in foreign countries, you still have a chance to purchase Panalba, but under a different name. Or so I am told; the Upjohn Corporation has been too busy to answer my letters. See Mintz, 1969, for descriptions of the events in this case.) The role-playing predictions in the Upjohn case differed substantially from the predictions by nonrole-players of what they would do in this situation. Only 2% of 71 respondents to an interview said they would select decision 5, and over half said they would choose decision 1 (to remove the drug from the market). In an opinions survey, 41% of the 46 respondents predicted that Upjohn would select decision 5.

ARMSTRONG and WALKER [1983] randomly assigned pairs of subjects (Wharton School MBA students) to make predictions by either giving opinions or by using role playing. Three situations were used, two being disguised versions of historical events, while the third was an event that had not yet occurred. In a test using the first historical event, subjects were asked to predict whether a supermarket chain would accept the proposal by a manufacturer to sell consumer durables in their stores. This was based on a plan developed by Philco (remember them?) in 1961. Subjects in the group giving their expert opinion regarded the plan as unrealistic and predicted that the supermarkets would not accept it. Those who role played the situation made substantially different predictions. In fact, the plan was accepted, and it proved to be a disaster. The second historical situation involved a sit-in by artists in the major art museum in Histavia. Subjects were asked to predict whether government leaders would give in to the demands by the artists that the government extend its program of purchasing artwork that the artists could not otherwise sell. This was based on an event in Holland as reported in the January 7, 1982 issue of the *Wall Street Journal*. The government did cave in, a response that was not predicted by opinions; the role players had a bit of success on this prediction. The event that had not yet occurred involved a possible strike by the National Football League players in 1982. Those subjects using expert opinion predicted no strike, while the role-playing groups predicted a strike. (As is well known to you football fans, there *was* a strike and it crippled the nation for many weeks.) One possible defect in the design was that the role descriptions contained additional relevant information. To test this, we ran a "role aware" version of the distribution case, whereby those who were to give expert opinions were provided with the roles along with the background information. This had no effect on the results. The following table summarizes our results:

Role Playing vs. Opinions in Predicting Outcomes
(entries represent predictions by pairs of subjects)

Situation	Prediction Same as Actual?	Opinions Normal	Opinions Role Aware	Total	Role Play	Statistical Significance*
Distribution plan	No	15	18	33	2	$P < .01$
	Yes	0	1	1	8	
Artists' reprieve	No	13	0	13	2	$P \simeq 10$
	Yes	1	0	1	2	
	No answer	0	0	0	2	
NFL 55% plan	No	11	0	11	4	$P \simeq 10$
	Yes	4	0	4	6	

*One-tailed Fisher Exact Test comparing opinions with role play.

A summary of the preceding evidence on actual situations provides much evidence favoring role playing. As shown in Exhibit 6-6, role playing was correct on 70% of the predictions versus 21% for expert opinions (the predictive accuracy of opinions was about the same as would be obtained by chance). Though the sample size is small, the evidence is consistent with that from the experimental studies by psychologists as noted. These gains in accuracy were achieved at a small increase in cost. For example, the role-playing sessions that we have done required less than one hour.

Choosing the Method

This has been a long and complicated section. To help you in selecting a method for obtaining a judgmental forecast, Exhibit 6-7 lists the primary methods in the order that they were discussed, rating them according to criteria that are relevant to most forecasting problems. A high rating is favorable. Much subjective judgment was added to the evidence presented in arriving at the ratings. The ratings are relevant within a column; do not add across columns. The weighting for the criteria will depend upon the specific situation that is being forecast.

Of particular interest is whether the study involves intentions or opinions. For example, assume that the study involves an opinions forecast on a sensitive topic involving a large change, where there are conflicting parties, with little information about how others will behave. Assume further that this is an important situation involving large expenditures of money and that the forecast is not needed immediately. In such a case, sampling and nonresponse errors are not relevant, and one should have ample opportunity to ensure that the question is well defined. In this example, role playing would clearly dominate the other techniques. Incidentally, this is not a trivial case!

COMBINED FORECASTS

In judgmental forecasting, there is safety in numbers. The practice of obtaining forecasts from a number of judges and using the combination is a sound one. Research on this approach has been conducted since the early 1900s.

Certainly the value of combining forecasts was evident in intentions surveys. In this section, evidence is provided that it is good practice also for other techniques in judgmental forecasting such as opinions surveys, Delphi, and role playing.

The earliest studies on the value of using a combined forecast were

Exhibit 6-6 ROLE PLAYING VS. OPINIONS: ACTUAL SITUATIONS

Situation	Conflict Among	Percentage of Correct Predictions (Sample Sizes)*		
		Chance	Opinion	Role Play
North Vietnam Bombing	Countries	33	0 (1)	100 (1)
USA-Mexico	Countries	18	1 (1)	57 (96)
Mock Political Conventions	Political Candidates	33**	67 (12)	67 (12)
Panalba	Stockholder & Consumer	20	41 (46)	79 (57)
Philco Distribution	Manufacturer & Retailer	25	3 (33)	80 (10)
Artists in Holland	Government & Labor	16	7 (14)	50 (4)
NFL 55% Plan	Employees & Owners	33	27 (15)	60 (10)
Unweighted Average		25	21	70

*The sample sizes represent the number of predictions.
**Assuming that there are about three candidates available.

133

Exhibit 6-7 RATINGS OF METHODS TO OBTAIN JUDGMENTAL FORECASTS
(1 = unfavorable and 5 = favorable; n.a. = not applicable)

Method	Cost	Speed	Situation Involves High Uncertainty & Interaction Among Conflicting Parties	Questions Cannot be Well Defined	Sampling Error Is Important	Nonresponse Error Is Important	Judges Are Concerned About Evaluation of Their Responses
Personal interview	3	4	1	4	5	5	2
Telephone interview	5	5	1	3	3	3	2
Mail questionnaire	5	2	1	1	4	4	4
Delphi	4	2	2	2	4	4	4
Traditional meeting	1	5	2	3	1	n.a.	1
Structured meeting	2	4	2	5	1	n.a.	3
Group depth interview	2	3	4	4	2	n.a.	2
Role playing	2	3	5	3	2	n.a.	5

conducted by asking people to estimate things like distance, volume, or weight. For example, Gordon (1924) had college students rank weights that they lifted; these rankings were then compared to the true order, and the average correlation for 200 judges was found to be .41. By averaging the rankings of any five random judges at a time, she obtained 40 combined rankings; the average correlation between the true ranking and the combined ranking was .68. Combined estimates were also obtained from groups of 10, 20, and 50 judges, and the correlations rose to .94 for the largest group. Similar results were obtained for judgments of such things as the temperature of a room, the number of items in a bottle, and the number of buckshot. DAWES [1977] demonstrated the predictive validity of combining in a problem calling for estimates of the height of people. Zajonc (1967) provides a summary of this literature.

It was concluded from these early studies that combining was at least as accurate as the average judge, almost always more accurate than the average, and sometimes better than the best judge. But Zajonc (1967) noted that these conclusions are not correct, technically speaking; they hold only if a majority of the individuals making judgments have a fair chance of being correct.

The possibility that a combination of forecasts can be better than the best forecast does not strike everyone as intuitively obvious. The demonstration is easy; one need only show that it is possible in at least one case. Consider that judge A predicts 10, judge B predicts 30, and the actual result turns out to be 20. The combined forecast of 20 in this case would be perfect even though each of the judges missed by 10.

Stroop (1932) duplicated Gordon's (1924) results by having *one* individual make 50 judgments and taking the average of these judgments rather than using an average of 50 different judges. In other words, in certain situations, the average may be obtained by multiple judgments from a single individual.

Aggregation of one judge's responses improves reliability, but not validity. When validity is a problem, it is better to average judges' responses in the hope that the biases among judges will compensate for one another. Forecasts by different judges are expected to be especially useful in cases of high uncertainty. For example, Klugman (1945) found that combining led to improvements when trying to judge the number of unfamiliar items in a jar (lima beans), but produced no significant gain for familiar items (marbles). To carry this notion of uncertainty one step further, the use of a combination from different judges would seem especially relevant for long-range forecasting, where uncertainty is high.

The discussion to this point has assumed that the combination was based on an unweighted average. Winkler (1967a, 1971) examined different weighting schemes in his study of the prediction of football scores. He compared equal ratings, accuracy for the preceding week's forecasts, and self-ratings. He concluded that it did not matter much how the judgments were weighted. My conclusion from his data is that self-ratings and accuracy scores have modest value and can be used as a screening device to eliminate judges who have very low self-ratings or have demonstrated very poor previous accuracy relative to the rest of the group. This would presumably eliminate judges who either do not understand the question involved or do not possess a minimum level of expertise. An alternative that avoids issues of weighting and the dangers of outliers is to use the median. Medians would seem advantageous for comparisons across methods. However, SEWALL [1981] did not find medians to be useful.

The evidence on the value of combining is impressive, and it comes from a variety of areas. As long as the judges possess a minimum level of expertise, combining is better than the average accuracy of the component forecasts. Some of the early evidence is summarized here:

Thorndike (1938) asked 1200 subjects to make predictions about 30 future events. The subjects were asked to make an individual prediction and then a group prediction. The average individual was correct 61.9% of the time. The combination from groups of four to six people was correct 64.4% of the time. In cases where the majority was wrong, the combined prediction was worse than the average judge.

Klugman (1947) had 109 soldiers, during World War II, try to predict the dates for the ending of hostilities with Germany and with Japan. For the German armistice, the combination was better than 75% of the judges. For the Japanese armistice, it was better than only 46% of the judges. (In the Japanese situation, the judges were not aware of the atomic bomb, so most of them could be expected to be wrong.)

Kaplan, Skogstad, and Girshick (1950), in their study of forecasts of events in the social and natural sciences, found that the average accuracy for all 26 of their judges was 53% with a range of 28% to 71%. Yet, if the choice favored by most forecasters had been used for each event, the accuracy would have been 68%, which was almost as good as the accuracy of the best judge.

Sanders (1963) used 12 students to make weather forecasts and found that the combined forecast was superior to the forecast by the best judge.

Goldberg (1965), in his study of psychiatric judgments, found that a combined staff score predicted almost as well as the best judge in a group of 29 clinicians.

Zarnowitz (1967) examined expert forecasts of the U.S. GNP and found that the group combination did better than 62% of the judges.

Winkler (1967), in forecasts of collegiate and professional football games, found that the accuracy of the combined forecast was almost as good as that of the best judge.

Additional studies provide support for the use of combined forecasts in finance (Staël Von Holstein, 1972), in psychology (Cooke, 1967 and Goldberg, 1970), in education (Wiggins and Kohen, 1971), in economics [ZARNOWITZ, 1984], and in weather forecasting (Staël Von Holstein, 1971).

Gains are expected if one uses eclectic research; that is, in addition to using different judges, the other key factors in judgmental forecasting can also be varied. I was unable to obtain much evidence in this area. The two studies that were found provide only mild support because the sample sizes were small:

Levine (1960) presented forecasts of the annual U.S. investment in plant and equipment from 1949 to 1954, generated by two different surveys of intentions, one by the U.S. Department of Commerce and the Securities and Exchange Commission (SEC), and one by McGraw-Hill. I calculated a combined forecast by taking a simple average of the two forecasts. The Commerce-SEC survey had a mean absolute percentage error (MAPE) of 3.8; the McGraw-Hill survey had a MAPE of 4.3; and the combined forecast had a MAPE of 3.5. The differences were not statistically significant.

Okun (1960) presented forecasts derived from two intentions studies of the U.S. housing market. The *Fortune* survey of homebuilders and the Survey Research Center's (SRC) survey of buying plans were each used to forecast yearly housing starts from 1951 through 1956. A combined forecast was also developed from the average of these two forecasts. The SRC forecast had a MAPE of 8.5; the *Fortune* survey had a MAPE of 7.5; and the combined forecast had a MAPE of 6.5. The superiority of the combined method was not statistically significant.

ASSESSING UNCERTAINTY

One of the advantages of judgmental forecasting is that it provides a number of methods for assessing the uncertainty in forecasts. These methods are described here, and the empirical evidence on their effectiveness is examined.

The methods for assessing uncertainty can be grouped into two categories: those that ask the judge to assess the uncertainty of his forecast, and those that make comparisons among different forecasts. These methods can be applied to both intentions and opinions studies.

Self-Assessments

Please read the following sentence: "FINISHED FILES ARE THE RESULT OF YEARS OF SCIENTIFIC STUDY COMBINED WITH THE EXPERIENCE OF YEARS."

Now count the number of times the letter F appears in that sentence. Count them only once; do not go back and count them again. Record your answer here: _____ . Now state your confidence in your answer on a scale from 0%, meaning that you are sure you are incorrect, to 100%, meaning that you are sure you are correct. Record your confidence here: _____.

Most people feel confident of their answers. A convenience sample of 50 reported an average confidence level of about 91%. This confidence level proved to be unrelated to accuracy. For the 34% who had the correct answer (which is 6), the average confidence level was about 87%. For the 66% who had incorrect answers (which ranged from 2 to 5, with a mode of 3), the average confidence level was about 93%. Accuracy and confidence were unrelated in this study.

This letter-F test illustrates an important conclusion for self-assessment. Ratings of self-confidence by individuals are often of such poor validity that one should generally consider them to be worthless for predictions of a single event. This conclusion is difficult to accept personally, although it is a bit easier to accept where others are concerned. The evidence on this issue comes from a variety of areas:

Thorndike (1938) found a very small relationship between self-confidence and accuracy in his study using 1200 subjects to predict future events. The relationship was, however, statistically significant.

Kaplan, Skogstad, and Girshick (1950) found a rank correlation of only .2 between a measure of confidence provided by each judge and his accuracy in forecasting events in the social and natural sciences.

Holtzman and Sells (1954) found no relationship between self-ratings of confidence by 19 judges and accuracy in the prediction of the success of aviation cadets. This occurred despite high agreement among the raters.

Winkler (1971) found little relationship between self-ratings and accuracy in predictions of football scores by 55 judges.

In WARSHAW [1980] 60 housewives were asked about their intentions to purchase various brands of soft drinks over a five-day period. Global intentions were asked: "What is the probability that you will purchase brand X between now and next Monday morning?" Also, a decomposed version was asked of the same subjects with questions about location and about the purchase of multiple brands. The decomposed version (which Warshaw refers to as a "derived intention") was significantly more accurate in predicting actual purchase behavior.

Prior research has shown that an eyewitness's expressed confidence affects the extent to which people will believe the witness's testimony. Jurors show much agreement in assessing the certainty expressed by the witness. It is interesting, then, to find that eyewitness confidence has little predictive validity. WELLS and MURRAY [1984] performed a meta-analysis on 31 previously published studies. The typical correlation between confidence and accuracy was only .07. This means that confidence explained less than 1% of the variance in accuracy. Wells says that some variables affect accuracy of judgment while other variables affect confidence. The results fit into a pattern of studies showing that individual confidence ratings are poor guides to accuracy unless the feedback in the task is exceptionally good. This pattern has a practical implication: don't ask individuals how confident they are in their judgmental forecasts.

Although it is generally worthless to use the self-rated accuracy of individuals for single events, there *is* a small positive relationship. This means that self-rated accuracy should be useful for cases with many judges and, possibly, for a single judge making many predictions (LARSEN and REENAN [1979] and LINDLEY [1982]). Thus confidence ratings are useful for consumer intentions studies. Dalkey et al. provide evidence on self-ratings by groups:

Dalkey, Brown, and Cochran (1970), in a study involving almanac-type questions, found a strong relationship between average self-ratings of confidence for 16 groups (each with 15 to 20 judges) and the levels of accuracy for the groups.

Self-ratings are expected to be most useful when uncertainty is not great. Thus they would generally be more useful in estimating current status than in forecasting change. Evidence consistent with this viewpoint is provided by Best:

Best (1974), using Delphi, asked 28 faculty members at the University of Oregon's College of Business to estimate the current demand for the *Oregon Business Review* and also to estimate the current student enrollment in their college of business. There was a strong relationship between self-rated expertise and accuracy for each of the two estimates.

Self-confidence ratings are expected to be most useful in situations where the judge receives good feedback on predictive accuracy. This occurs in weather forecasting. The data by Cooke and by Williams showed high correlations between self-confidence and accuracy. The study by Ferber et al. was consistent, although the results were not statistically significant:

Cooke (1906) rated the certainty of his weather forecasts in Australia in 1905:

Self-Rating of Forecast	Number of Forecasts	Percentage Correct
Almost certain	685	98
Normal probability	970	94
Doubtful	296	79

Williams (1951) examined the records of eight professional weather bureau forecasters in making 12-hour forecasts of rain for Salt Lake City from November 1949 to January 1950.

Self-Rating of Forecast	Number of Forecasts	Percentage Correct
1.0	509	97
0.8	292	74
0.6	294	59

Ferber, Chen, and Zuwaylif (1961) analyzed two-month man-power forecasts. The error of the forecasts was 4.7% for the 18 plants that kept records of accuracy and 5.3% for the 18 plants that did not keep records of accuracy.

Self-confidence is often poorly related to accuracy because "familiarity breeds confidence," but it does little to improve accuracy. Studies by Oskamp and by Ryback provide evidence in this area.

Oskamp (1965) provided biographical information about a person to 32 judges. The information was given in four stages. Stage 1 provided three sentences about the person's age, sex, marital status, race, military record, college background, and occupation; stage 2 provided one and a half pages on the person's life through age 12; stage 3 covered high school and college; stage 4 covered the army and other activities up to age 29. After each stage, the judge was asked 25 questions about the personality, attitudes, and behavior of the subject. No feedback was provided. The judge's accuracy was not significantly better than chance at any stage; however, their confidence went up markedly from stage 1 to stage 4.

Ryback (1967) asked 94 subjects to estimate the relative sizes of some geometrical figures. The judges repeated the task on five occasions spaced two or three days apart, with no feedback being provided to them. The accuracy of the judges did not change over time, but their confidence rose significantly ($p < .05$).

Another reason why self-ratings are poor is that they are **ipsative**[G]. A low confidence rating for one person is not directly comparable to a low rating by another judge. The ratings are personal.

Estimates of a distribution are similar in many respects to ratings of self-confidence. A simple approach is to ask judges for "high," "most likely," and "low" estimates. The estimates might be defined as follows:

"What do you think would be the upper limit to the forecast? As the upper limit, choose the value which has less than 1 chance in 20 of being exceeded."

A similar question would be used to secure a lower limit to the distribution. The upper and lower limits could then be viewed as the confidence interval.

Judges are overconfident, especially when they receive poor feedback as shown in the following studies:

Alpert and Raiffa (1968), in a study using almanac-type questions, found that the 98% confidence intervals stated by judges included the true value only about half the time. This overconfidence persisted even when the judges were given feedback about their overly narrow confidence bands, although the feedback was of some value. A replication of this study is provided in Pickhardt and Wallace (1974).

Staël von Holstein (1972) asked judges to forecast changes in prices of common stocks and to specify 99% confidence limits. Of all predictions, 43% fell outside these 99% confidence limits. Feedback was then provided to the judges that they were overestimating confidence. Of the predictions made after this feedback, 23% fell outside the 99% limits. Similar results were obtained by SCHREUDER and KLAASSEN [1984], but FISCHHOFF, SLOVIC, and LICHTENSTEIN [1977] had less success with training.

One way to combat overconfidence is to ask forecasters to list explicitly the reasons why their forecast might prove incorrect [COSIER, 1978; KORIAT, LICHTENSTEIN, and FISCHHOFF 1980]. Another technique is to provide extensive training and personalized feedback

[FISCHHOFF and MacGREGOR, 1982, and GAETH and SHANTEAU, 1984].

Still another way to develop estimates of uncertainty is to use the principle of decomposition. Separate estimates can be made for each component of error: response, nonresponse, and sampling error. The total error may then be computed (e.g., by assuming that each type of error is independent of the other types and then adding variances). Brown (1969) presents a description of this approach, which he refers to as **"credence analysis**[G]**."** Although this approach has face validity, I have been unable to find any empirical studies that assess its value.

Comparisons among Forecasts

When judges make independent forecasts, the agreement among judges can be used as a measure of certainty. However, if the backgrounds are similar, as frequently happens in economic forecasts, agreement can be high while accuracy is low. The following two studies provide situations where agreement was not related to accuracy:

> Holtzman and Sells (1954) showed high agreement among judges on which individuals would be successful as aviators after completion of a training program, but the accuracy of these forecasts was poor.

> Ogburn (1934) found high agreement among football forecasts by sportswriters, but the accuracy was poor.

A striking example was provided by Baker (1957). Designers at the Ford Motor Company were asked to design the car that would best meet the needs of the consumer. The managers claimed that they were determined to be objective about everything. Baker reported as follows: "The final concept as it looked in plaster was satisfying to every designer in the company, and when you get 800 stylists under one roof to agree that they like a creation, you have unusually high agreement." The company named this creation the Edsel. It was one of the biggest marketing disasters in the world.

Although agreement among judges can be a misleading measure of certainty, it is expected to be of value when the judges make truly independent forecasts. In one study where the judges' forecasts were independent, a modest relationship was found between accuracy and agreement among judges:

> Walker (1970) had subjects make estimates of the length of a line; the length, width, and height of a room; the weight of a book; the weight of a rock; the area of an irregular piece of paper; and the volume of a wastepaper bin. Four or more groups estimated each of the eight items, and each group had an average of 16 judges. Each judge worked independently. I reanalyzed Walker's data to examine the relationship between the agreement within the group and the accuracy of the group. Agreement within each group was measured by calculating the **coefficient of variation**[G]. Accuracy was measured by the absolute percentage difference between the average group estimate and the true value. When the coefficient of variation for the group's estimate was less than 10%, the mean absolute percentage error (MAPE) was 7%. When the coefficient of variation exceeded 10%, the MAPE was 19%.

In cases where one cannot make comparisons among judges, repeated forecasts can be obtained from the same judge. The measures should be separated in time, generally by days or weeks, and an examination should be made of the consistency over time. Such an approach is useful when the number of judges is restricted by a need for secrecy.

The use of eclectic research should, once again, be considered. Uncertainty could be assessed by comparing forecasts obtained by different judgmental methods. "Different methods" means using different forecasters, different phrasing of the question, different ways of collecting the forecasts, or, preferably, all of these. The basic assumption here is that each of the different approaches is subject to different errors. Disagreement among the results obtained by the various approaches should lead to less confidence in the forecast. This makes sense but it is pure speculation; I found little empirical evidence on this issue.

The various methods for assessing uncertainty are listed in Exhibit 6-8, along with guidelines for their use and some guesses about their costs. It is advisable to use more than one method for assessing uncertainty. Remember: ECLECTIC RESEARCH ALWAYS.

Exhibit 6-8 RATINGS OF JUDGMENTAL METHODS TO ASSESS UNCERTAINTY

Method	Use in Situations Where			
	Uncertainty Is	Feedback Is	Number of Judges Is	Cost Is
Self-assessments				
Self-confidence	Low	Good	Large	Low
Distribution estimates	Low	Good	Large	Low
Credence analysis	Moderate	Moderate	Moderate	Moderate
Comparisons among forecasts				
Different judges	High	Poor	Large	Moderate
Time consistency	High	Good	Small	Moderate
Different methods	High	Poor	Small	High

SUMMARY

Intentions and opinions data provide the two basic types of information used in judgmental forecasting. Intentions forecasts are relevant for events that are important to the judge. Assumptions are made that a response can be obtained from the judge, that the judge actually has a plan, that he reports correctly, that he can fulfill the plan, and that he is unlikely to change the plan over the forecast horizon. These assumptions imply that intentions data are most useful for assessing current status, somewhat useful for short-range forecasting, and of little value for long-range forecasting. Opinions data are simpler to obtain and can be used in a wider variety of situations.

Numerous errors arise in judgmental forecasting. One of the most serious is bias. Judges confuse their desires for the future with their forecasts. Another major problem is anchoring; judges are conservative and bound by tradition.

The development of judgmental methods was described in three stages: selecting judges, posing the question, and obtaining the forecast. Some practical suggestions were provided in each of these areas to eliminate problems of bias and, to some extent, to compensate for anchoring. The more important suggestions are summarized here.

On Selecting Judges

1. For intentions studies, use probability samples.
2. For opinions studies:
   (a) Use inexpensive experts to forecast *change* (assuming that they have at least a minimum level of expertise in the area to be forecast).
   (b) Do not use judges who are personally involved in the situation being forecast.

On Posing the Question

1. Use decomposition when:
   (a) Uncertainty is high,
   (b) Prior theory exists,
   (c) Different judges have different information.
2. Word the question in different ways, especially in cases where uncertainty is high (as in long-range forecasting).

3. Provide only the minimum relevant information to the judge.
4. Organize the information so the judge can understand it easily.
5. Use scales with many gradations for the judge's responses. Five gradations are O.K., but 11 are better. Use an odd number of scale points.
6. Ensure that probabilities of totally exhaustive and mutually exclusive events sum to 1.0

   (a) Use two way splits in the questions
   (b) Emphasize to the respondent that the probabilities should sum to 1.0
   (c) Normalize when necessary

7. Consider projective questions for sensitive issues.

On Obtaining the Forecast

1. In selecting a method to obtain forecasts, consider both "judge–judge" and "researcher–judge" interaction. Exhibit 6-5, "Interaction Effects on Techniques to Obtain Judgmental Forecasts," is provided as a guide for selecting appropriate methods.
2. A checklist for the selection of the most appropriate method to obtain forecasts is provided in Exhibit 6-7, which rates eight techniques against seven criteria.
3. The mail survey provides an inexpensive way to obtain intentions forecasts, and it is useful for sensitive issues.
4. Traditional group meetings are the most popular method of obtaining important judgmental forecasts, apparently because group satisfaction is higher with unstructured group meetings. Unfortunately, this is the poorest way of obtaining judgmental forecasts.
5. Structured group meetings are more effective than traditional meetings and cost about the same.
6. Role playing is useful when there are conflicting groups and uncertainty is high. It provides more accurate long-range forecasts for important events.

On Using Combined Forecasts

1. Use combined forecasts! The combined forecast is almost always better than the average component from which it was derived, and it is sometimes better than the best component.
2. Combining is especially valuable when uncertainty is high (as it is in long-range forecasting).

3. Use eclectic research; base the combination upon judges, questions, and methods of obtaining forecasts that differ substantially.

On Assessing Uncertainty

1. The basic approaches to the use of judgmental methods in assessing uncertainty are to ask the judges to rate their confidence, and to make comparisons among different judgmental forecasts.
2. Judges tend to be overconfident. This is especially true when experience is high and feedback is poor.
3. Self-ratings of confidence are valuable in situations where the judges have been receiving good feedback on the accuracy of their forecasts, and where large groups of judges are used.

In general, common sense in the use of judgmental methods of forecasting has led to undesirable practices. The most common approach is to use biased judges and have them make forecasts in traditional group meetings. A number of simple changes can lead to great improvement in accuracy at a modest cost. We think it is ridiculous when others use the crystal ball, but when *we* gaze into its depths . . .

Seven

EXTRAPOLATION METHODS

Contents

A trend is a trend is a trend,
But the question is, will it bend?
Will it alter its course
Through some unforeseen force
And come to a premature end?

Cairncross (1969)

Extrapolation is second only to judgmental forecasting in popularity. It can be used for short-range or long-range forecasting. The quotation from Cairncross, however, suggests that the errors increase when extrapolation is used for long-range forecasting.

This chapter describes the types of data that are available and explains when they may be used for extrapolations. The selection of data is important, as is the decision of how to analyze the data.

Techniques for analyzing data are then described. Attention is given to Markov chains, a method used when the pattern of events is of interest, and to exponential smoothing, a method for analyzing time series. The Box-Jenkins approach, moving averages, and regressions are also considered as ways to analyze time series. Some simple and fancy curves are then described briefly. These discussions would be long and complex except for one thing: the value of simplicity in extrapolation. Spellbinding rain dances exist for extrapolating data, but the empirical evidence suggests that you should not learn these dances. Comparable results can be achieved with simple methods. It is your choice: you can learn the fox-trot or you can learn to tap dance in scuba gear.

Eclectic research is reexamined. A strategy of combining forecasts from different methods is suggested, and the empirical evidence is reviewed.

This chapter concludes with a discussion of uncertainty. How can extrapolation techniques be used to estimate uncertainty, and what evidence exists regarding the value of these techniques?

DATA FOR EXTRAPOLATIONS

The basic strategy of extrapolation is to find data that are representative of the event to be forecast. The assumption is made that the future event will conform to these data. To ensure that this assumption is reasonable, it often helps to use the systems approach to define the elements of the system that will be stable. It is not necessary to refer to the study on the prediction of transistors from (*LRF* pp. 19–20). Nor will I refer to the study of the bituminous coal market by Hutchesson (1967), for if I did, you would ask, "Why didn't he look at the market for energy before examining the market for bituminous coal?" and I would have to say, "Well, he didn't, and I told you so." The extrapolations were bad, as you would plainly see if the following results were shown:

Hutchesson (1967) analyzed U.S. per capita consumption of bituminous coal from 1880 to 1920. Two extrapolations were made, one from a **logistic curve**[G] and the other from a **Gompertz curve**[G]. The forecasts of pounds per capita for 10, 20, and 30 years in the future are shown, along with the actual consumption.

Year	Forecast Horizon	Logistic Forecast	Gompertz Forecast	Actual Consumption
1930	10	15,100	14,300	7400
1940	20	18,500	21,700	6200
1950	30	21,200	32,700	6100

Sometimes the choice of data is obvious (e.g., forecasts of automobile sales in the United States may be obtained from historical data on automobile sales). Other times the selection of data is not so obvious. This is especially true in situations involving large changes (e.g., forecasting automobile sales in the Middle East).

In the following sections, four sources of data are described: historical data, analogous situations, laboratory simulations, and field simulations. The advantages and disadvantages of these sources are examined.

Historical Data

Extrapolations are typically based upon historical data for the event that is of interest. If we have direct experience with this event over a historical period, it provides an obvious way to forecast. For example, today's weather provides a good forecast of tomorrow's weather.

The accuracy of extrapolations is affected by two major conditions:

the accuracy of the historical data and the extent to which underlying conditions will change in the future.

Alonso (1968) described how errors in measurement can lead to large errors in forecasting change even if the underlying change process remains stable. He presented an example in which the current population was estimated to be within 1% (i.e., ± 1%) of actual, and the underlying change process was known perfectly. A two-period forecast was then calculated, and the forecast of *change* had a confidence interval of ± 37%. (This illustration is described in Appendix B of *LRF*.)

If, in addition to measurement error, the underlying process can change, the difficulties of forecasting change are compounded. Alonso's example assumed that, if the effects of the change in the underlying process were known within ± 20%, the compound forecast error from measuring current status and from estimating change would be ± 41% (see Appendix B).

The impact of measurement errors is important because real-world data are often inaccurate. Mistakes, cheating, shifting definitions, missing data, and abnormal events cause serious problems. Because accurate data are often not available when needed, recent historical data must be approximated.

If the time lag in the collection of data is large, and additional historical data cannot be obtained, the implication is that extrapolations may be more appropriate for medium-range than for short-range forecasts. On the other hand, because the underlying process changes more in the long range, extrapolations seem more appropriate to the short- rather than to the long-range.

When historical data cannot be obtained, as often occurs when large changes are expected, one might consider analogous situations. For example, if a new educational program was being introduced into a school system, one would look for evidence on other school systems. Evidence would be desired concerning schools where the situation before the change was similar to that in the school of current interest and where the proposed change was similar. Similar situations would arise in predicting the spread of an innovation in farming (Rogers, 1983); forecasting sales for a new product (Claycamp and Liddy, 1969); predicting the vote on a proposal for a new county health board; or forecasting acceptance of a new form of mass transit in Philadelphia. The last two were projects in which I was involved, and it was easy to identify analogous situations. For the county health board, similar proposals had been considered in the previous election in neighboring counties. For the mass transit system, similar systems had been introduced in the Netherlands.

Stein's paradox (Efron and Morris, 1977) says that the use of analogous data can improve predictions. Stein presented evidence that the overall league batting average early in the season can be used to improve the prediction of a baseball player's final batting average. The less information available on a given player, the more weight should be given to the league average. (This probably sounds like a paradox only to a trained statistician. But then, they averaged Volkswagens and batting averages—and that was a bit strange.)

Simulated Data

In cases where no actual situations are available, a simulation could be used to generate data. The simulation could be done in a laboratory or in a realistic situation; the latter is referred to as a field test.

Laboratory simulations frequently offer lower costs, better control over the changes, and more confidentiality than a field test. Such simulations have been used commercially for many years in marketing where, for example, new products can be tested in simulated stores. For a description of marketing simulations see WIND [1982, pp. 422–429]. The laboratory simulation strategy has also been employed successfully in personnel predictions via the "work sample:"

Studies on the validity of work samples are found in DOWNS et al. [1978], HINRICH [1969, 1978], REILLY and CHAO [1982], ROBERTSON and KANDOLA [1982] and SMITH [1976].

Field tests are used in areas such as marketing, social psychology, and agriculture. Descriptions of test marketing go back many years (e.g., Harris, 1964); WIND [1982, pp. 398–422] summarizes the literature. NEVIN [1974] tested the predictive validity of consumer laboratory experiments. An example of a field test in social psychology is provided by the study of obedience among nurses (Hofling et al., 1966), which was discussed in Chapter 6. This study illustrates the difficulties involved in field tests of behavior that is important to people. The subjects were upset when they learned about the experiment. (It's much easier to restrict your field experiments to less important matters, like preference for a new brand of beer.) Field tests offer greater realism than do laboratory experiments, and this is generally an important advantage.

Simulated data, though advantageous for assessing large changes, may be seriously influenced by the researcher's biases. Anyone who has worked on government-sponsored research knows this; the sponsors become committed to making the simulation a success.

An outstanding case demonstrating bias due to the sponsor is that of Lysenko, a Russian agricultural scientist (Medvedev, 1969), who tested hypotheses such as these: "Heredity is the property of the living body to demand certain environmental conditions and to react in a certain way to them"; and "No special hereditary substance exists, anymore than does the substance of combustion, phlogiston, or the substance of heat, caloric." Lysenko conducted field experiments that supported his theories and led to some strange methods of farming in Russia. Lysenko had a big advantage: Stalin was his buddy. Still, the effect of bias on both laboratory and field experiments is enormous— even for non-Russians.

The effects of bias on the part of the researcher or the organization funding the research are so powerful that they can be observed without carefully controlled experiments. For example, I found myself under a great deal of pressure when I obtained results suggesting that the U.S. Department of Transportation should end its funding of a project involving a new form of transportation. The pressure in this case came, not from the Department of Transportation, but from many of the recipients of roughly $1 million per year. No one was killed, but it was exciting. More details are provided in ARMSTRONG [1983d].

A summary of the types of data is provided in Exhibit 7-1. The data sources are rated against five criteria. The ratings were done subjectively by the author. Crude though they are, there are certain implications:

1. No one type of data is best for all situations.
2. For long-range extrapolations (large changes), data for the assessment of current status should be different from that used for predicting change.

The second implication seems reasonable, yet seldom is it used.

ANALYZING THE DATA

For simulated data, one can assume that future behavior will be like that in the simulation. An alternative procedure is to assume that the future behavior will be an average of the current behavior, without change, and the behavior observed in the simulation. This is an ex-

Exhibit 7-1   RANKING OF DATA FOR EXTRAPOLATIONS
              (1 = most appropriate or most favorable)

Source	To Estimate Current Status	To Forecast		Effects of Researcher's Bias	Cost
		Small Change	Large Change		
Historical data	1	1	4	1	1
Analogous situation	2	4	3	2	2
Laboratory simulation	4	3	2	4	3
Field test	3	2	1	3	4

tension of the principle of conservatism; to the extent that you are uncertain about the evidence, you should forecast small changes from the current situation. This tempering of the prediction would seem more appropriate for laboratory data than for field data. For example, predictions based on a laboratory experiment in agriculture should be used with caution. Again, one could refer to the Lysenko case; the results claimed for a controlled test did not hold up when the method was adopted by farmers.

Although conceptually simple, projection from the simulated data to the forecast situation encounters numerous difficulties. Gold (1964) assessed the extent of these difficulties in test marketing. One must be concerned whether the test market is representative of the actual situation that will prevail in the total market. Gold's study indicated that, even if the test were perfect, substantial errors occur in generalizing from the sample observations to the test market, and from the test market to the total market.

The next section considers the use of Markov chains, a method for examining data organized by events rather than by time. Techniques are then examined for analyzing time series data.

Markov Chains

Markov chains, named in honor of a Russian mathematician, have been the focus of much interest by researchers. Numerous books and articles have touted Markov chains as a superior forecasting technique. One of the earliest practical applications was to predict changes in the occupational status of workers (Blumen, Kogan, and McCarthy, 1955). Another early application was predicting doubtful accounts in finance

(Cyert, Davidson, and Thompson, 1962). Ezzati (1974) applied Markov chains to forecasts of the home heating market. Unfortunately, these studies are only descriptive; they provide no evidence on the value of Markov chains.

Markov chains use the recent pattern of behavior as a basis for forecasting. Behavior in the future is forecasted from knowledge of the current state of an element and from an analysis of how the element moves from one state to another. This statement may be vague, so here is an example of a simple Markov chain.

Assume that the task is to forecast the type of automobile purchased by families, considering large domestic (L), small domestic (S), and small foreign (F) cars. Also, assume that all cars can be classified within the scheme. Now suppose that three families report the following purchasing sequences over a 15-year period:

Family 1. *LLLLLLSLFLLL*
Family 2. *FSSSSSSSSL*
Family 3. *FFFFFFFSFLL*

This says, for example, that the first car purchased by family 2 was foreign, the next eight were small cars, and the last purchase was a large car.

If these families are representative of the total population of car-buying families, what predictions can be made about the future market shares for L, S, and F? The first step in using Markov chains for prediction is to develop a transition matrix. This summarizes the data by indicating the fraction of times that the behavior in one trial will change (move to another state) in the next trial. Our data on automobile purchases are used to develop the transition matrix in Exhibit 7-2.

This transition matrix indicates that 80% of those who purchased a large domestic car (L) will buy the same type the next time they

---

Exhibit 7-2   EXAMPLE OF A TRANSITION MATRIX

		Brand Purchased at Trial $t + 1$		
		L	S	F
Brand	L	.8	.1	.1
Purchased	S	.2	.7	.1
at Trial t	F	.2	.2	.6

shop, while 10% will switch to a small domestic car (S), and 10% to a small foreign car (F).

If the process underlying Exhibit 7-2 remains stable, and if the sample of families is representative of the entire population, the transition matrix can be used to forecast changes in market shares. One can multiply the current market shares (say 70% for L, 20% for S, and 10% for F) by the transition matrix to determine how market shares will change during the next buying cycle (about 1.4 years in this example). This yields a prediction for the next time period of 62% for L, 23% for S, and 15% for F. If forecasts were desired for the long run, the process could be repeated many times. For this example, the long-range solution approaches 50% for L, 30% for S, and 20% for F. (This was obtained by calculating $MP = M$, where M is the matrix of shares (L, S, and F), and P is the transition matrix. The calculations for this example are shown in Appendix F.)

Remember that an assumption of stability is made when Markov chains are used. This means that it becomes risky to obtain long-range forecasts in cases where efforts are made to change the transition matrix. For example, an American firm's success in convincing the U.S. government to restrict the entry of foreign cars would affect the entries in the last column of Exhibit 7-2.

Markov chains seem reasonable for some problems. For example, they are widely used for personnel predictions. This technique and similar ones have been recommended frequently for predictions in marketing when people are assumed to go through various states in using a product (e.g., trial, repeat purchase, and adoption). Unfortunately, despite many publications on Markov and related models, little research on their predictive value was found. Akers and Irwin (1967) claim that Markov chains have been of no demonstrable value in demographic forecasting. I suspect there may be unpublished cases in marketing where Markov chains led to no improvements because I have met some disappointed users.

In the following, two relevant empirical studies are summarized. *They involve short-range forecasting and suggest that Markov models have no substantial advantage over much simpler extrapolation methods.*

Armstrong and Farley (1969) examined the selection of supermarkets by each family, using data from 45 families in the *Chi-*

cago Tribune panel. Data from 6 months were used to estimate the transition matrix. Forecasts were made of the percentage of trips made to the favorite store during the following 6 months for each family. Forecasts from the Markov model were compared to an extrapolation that assumed nothing would change. The Markov model provided forecasts that were correlated to the actual changes ($r = .4$). Although this was significantly better than the "no-change" model, it reduced the standard error of the forecast by only 8%. When the data were analyzed by family, the Markov model was correct on forecasts of change for 19 families, and incorrect for 16 (no change was predicted for the other 10 families); this result is likely to have arisen by chance.

Barclay (1963) used Markov chains to predict the percentage of families that would purchase a new product. The Markov forecast, drawn from *Chicago Tribune* panel data from March to September 1956, was that the purchase rate during 27 bimonthly periods from 1957 to mid-1961 would be 10.8%. I reanalyzed Barclay's data and found that an extrapolation based on the average purchase rate from April through September 1956 yielded a forecast that 16.7% of the families would purchase the product. The Markov model always predicted on the low side, and the average absolute error was 6.6%. In contrast, the no-change model was low on 17 forecasts, was high on 9, and had an average absolute error of 2.5%.

Exponential Smoothing

Exponential smoothing is relatively simple, intuitively pleasing, inexpensive, and well known. It draws upon the philosophy of decomposition. Time series data are assumed to be made up of some basic components, the average, trend, seasonality, and error. The first three components are illustrated in Exhibit 7-3. The x's represent the historical data. Dashed line *A* represents an estimate of the updated average; dashed line *B* represents the forecast obtained when the trend is added to the estimate of current status; and dashed line *C* represents the forecast when the current status, trend, and seasonality components are combined.

Exhibit 7-3 DECOMPOSITION OF TIME SERIES DATA

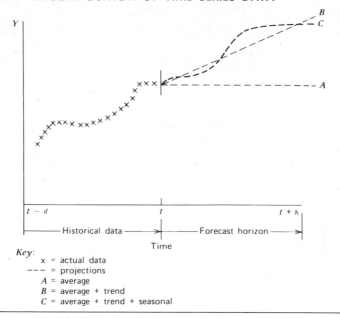

Key:
x = actual data
— — — = projections
A = average
B = average + trend
C = average + trend + seasonal

Exponential smoothing is similar to a moving average, but it places more weight on the most recent data. The weight on early periods drops off exponentially, so that the older the data, the less their influence. This weighting makes good sense and is supported by empirical studies (e.g., Ash and Smyth, 1973; Pashigian, 1964).

Exponential smoothing can be used, along with decomposition, to analyze historical data. A description of the major steps follows. To help in this discussion, the steps are listed by time priority in Exhibit 7-4. This listing goes beyond the exponential smoothing technique to consider all of the steps involved in obtaining the forecast. The description draws heavily from Brown (1959b) and Winters (1960). More recent work [e.g., see GARDNER, 1985b, for a summary] provides more efficient approaches. No doubt you will rely upon one of the many software packages now available. However, the framework in this chapter, which draws heavily upon Brown, is a good one to illustrate the various issues.

Clean Data.   The first step is to review the data to remove obvious errors. When many data are involved, this can be done by computer

---

Exhibit 7-4   STEPS IN FORECASTING
               WITH EXPONENTIAL
               SMOOTHING

---

1. Clean data
2. Deseasonalize data
3. Select smoothing factors
4. Calculate new average
5. Calculate new trend
6. Estimate current status
7. Calculate forecast
8. Update seasonal factors
   (Return to step 3)

---

by establishing limits for the data and identifying observations that go outside these limits; appropriately enough, these are called **outliers**[G]. The presence of outliers can affect the estimate of the mean, trend, or seasonality. If possible, outliers should be examined to determine whether they are due to an error (recording or keypunch errors are common causes of outliers) or a large change in the environment. When no explanation is found, it may be wise to temper the influence of outliers. There are many ways to do this. One approach, **windsorizing**[G], reduces the outliers to equal the most extreme observation about which you feel confident (Tukey, 1962). GEURTS [1982] claims that this step is likely to have a major influence on accuracy.

Another way to check for errors is to compare measures of a given quantity obtained in different ways. For example, to estimate the number of Japanese cameras sold in the United States in 1956, one could obtain estimates of the number of cameras that the United States claimed were imported from Japan, and the number of cameras that Japan claimed to have exported to the United States. A large difference would suggest the possibility that one of the measures was in error. If it were not clear which measure was in error, the two estimates could be averaged. Incidentally, in this particular example, Japan claimed that 160,180 cameras were exported to the United States, while the United States claimed to have imported 819,374 cameras from Japan (Armstrong, 1968a). I love the way they present six significant digits when there is so much uncertainty about the first digit.

Problems often arise when changes are made in definitions (e.g., Do the data on a U.S. economic series include Hawaii and Alaska in the complete series? Have the data been adjusted to compensate for inflation?). For short-term forecasts, there is a concern over matters such as the number of working days in a period. Once the problems of shifting definitions are identified, adjustments can be made.

Deseasonalize Data. Quite frequently the variable of interest depends upon the time of year. Monthly seasonal factors can be especially useful in economic forecasting. We know, although our local electric company may not, that the demand for electricity is high in the summer. What the electric company calls a "crisis," we call "July." Even Arthur Strimm knows this (see Exhibit 7-5).

Seasonal factors can be calculated in many ways. This can be done by using the **Census X-11 program**[G], by applying regression analysis where the months are represented by **dummy variables**[G], by calculating the relationship between each month and a corresponding moving average, or by relating each period to the average for the year. If the last approach is used, the trend must be removed before the seasonality factors are calculated.

The seasonal factors can be stated in either multiplicative (e.g., demand in January is 85% of that in the typical month in a year) or additive form (e.g., demand in January is 20,000 units below the average). Multiplicative factors are often used in economics. They are most appropriate when:

1. The data are based on a ratio scale, that is, the scale has a zero point and the intervals between points on the scale are meaningful.
2. Measurement error is low.
3. The trend is large.

Exhibit 7-5   ON THE VALUE OF SEASONAL FACTORS

MISS PEACH   By Mell Lazarus

Source.   "Miss Peach" by Mell Lazarus. Courtesy of Mell Lazarus and Field Newspaper Syndicate.

If conditions 1 and 2 are not met, consider additive factors.

Seasonal factors increase the error if there is a great deal of uncertainty in estimating these factors (Groff, 1973; Nelson, 1972). For example, if only 1 year of data were available, how could one tell whether the variations from month to month were random fluctuations or real seasonal effects? As the number of data increases, the reliability of the seasonality factors increases. It would be desirable, then, to place less weight on unreliable seasonal factors and more weight on highly reliable seasonal factors. Given a multiplicative factor, you could calculate a modified seasonal factor, $\overline{S}_j^*$:

$$\overline{S}_j^* = K_s + (1 - K_s)\overline{S}_j$$

where K_s is a dampening factor $(0 < K_s < 1)$, j is the period of the year, S_j is the raw seasonal factor, and $\overline{S}_j$ is the smoothed seasonal factor. The weight K_s could be set subjectively. A high K_s means more dampening. The K_s would be close to 1.0 if there were few data and little prior expectation of seasonality, and close to 0.0 for many data and a high prior expectation of seasonality. Then weight the seasonal factor by the square root of the number of data, as follows:

$$K_s = \frac{1}{\sqrt{d}}$$

where d is the number of years of data. Do you think we could call this Armstrong's modifier for seasonality? If data for enough years are available, say five or more, K_s could vary according to the standard deviation of the seasonality estimate.

The use of modified seasonal factors is consistent with the fact that some studies find seasonal factors useful, some find them to be of no value, while others find them to be detrimental (Nelson, 1972).

The final step in the calculation of seasonal factors is to normalize so that the average factor is exactly 1.0 (or 0.0 if additive factors are used). An easy way to normalize is to multiply each seasonal factor by the ratio of the number of periods to the total of the seasonal factors. Thus, for monthly seasonal factors, the correction would be to multiply each seasonal factor by $(12/\Sigma \overline{S}_j^*)$. The modified and normalized seasonal factor can be designated by $\overline{S}_j^{**}$.

Given the seasonal factors, the data can be deseasonalized. Exponential smoothing can be done on the deseasonalized data.

Select Smoothing Factors. Users of exponential smoothing often invest much time and energy in selecting the optimal smoothing factors. Of prime concern is alpha (α), the smoothing factor for the average:

$$\overline{Y}_t = \alpha \left(\frac{Y_t}{\overline{S}_j^{**}} \right) + (1 - \alpha)\overline{Y}_{t-1}$$

where $\overline{Y}$ is the calculated average, Y is the reported value, α is the smoothing factor, and t is the time period.

The smoothing factor determines how much weight is to be placed on the most recent data: the higher the factor, the heavier the weight. For example, a factor of 0.2 would mean that 20% of the new average is due to the latest observation, and the other 80% is due to the previous average. The weights on each period drop off exponentially. Thus the latest period is weighted by α, the period before that by $\alpha(1 - \alpha)$, and the observation two periods ago by $\alpha(1 - \alpha)^2$; data of d periods ago would be weighted by $\alpha(1 - \alpha)^d$.

How should the smoothing factor be selected? Traditionally, historical data have been used to determine which factors provide optimal forecasts (e.g., see Berry and Bliemel, 1972). DALRYMPLE and KING [1981] examined the selection of factors to minimize the error for h periods ahead. These procedures seem reasonable, yet I have been unable to find empirical evidence that they lead to improved forecasts. The evidence suggests that the accuracy of forecasts is not highly sensitive to the choice of the optimal smoothing factor. One need only select factors that are in the general region of the optimum. This has been my experience. Support may be found in Winters (1960).

You can use judgment initially to select the smoothing factors. I must tell you that I have no empirical evidence to support the following procedure. It is based upon my belief that the procedure should make sense to the analyst. Keep three things in mind:

1. If the process is unstable, use a high α so that the smoothing will quickly adjust to the new situation.
2. If the measurement error is high, use a low α to increase reliability, that is, to dampen the effects of transitory or unusual fluctuations.
3. If the time periods are short, use a low α. Monthly data require a lower α than do quarterly data, and weekly data a lower α than monthly data.

Rather than thinking directly about α, one could rephrase the question to ask how many historical observations should be included in the average. Ayres (1969, p. 100) suggested a rule of thumb that the extrapolation forward (by h periods) should not exceed the time span of the historical data (i.e., $d \geq h$). In my opinion, this rule understates the need for data in short-term forecasting and is too stringent for long-range forecasting. I suggest a rule of thumb that requires more data for short-term forecasts and fewer for long-term forecasts. This can be accomplished by a square root function. Therefore Armstrong's rule of thumb suggests that the number of periods of historical data is equal to four times the square root of the number of periods to be forecast, that is,

$$d = 4\sqrt{h}$$

For a 1-period forecast, this rule calls for 4 periods of historical data; for a 16-period forecast, 16 periods of historical data; and for a 100-period forecast, 40 periods of historical data. Limited evidence is presented in Exhibit 7-6; the time period that yielded the lowest error in each study was compared with recommendations from Armstrong's and Ayres' rules of thumb. Armstrong's rule underestimates the need for data and Ayres' rule underestimates it even more. If, as Ayres suggests, people follow his rule of thumb, a simple way to improve extrapolations would be to increase the number of historical data. This is a conclusion that Dorn (1950) reached in his review of forecasts on populations: demographers had been using too few data. SCHNAARS [1984], however, concluded that more data does not improve accuracy by a significant amount.

After an appropriate time span has been selected, Brown (1959a, b) states that the number of periods of data in an exponentially smoothed average can be approximated by

$$d = \frac{2 - \alpha}{\alpha}$$

One can select an appropriate time span, d, and then calculate the corresponding α by recasting the above formula:

$$\alpha = \frac{2}{d + 1}$$

To the extent that you are uncertain about α, it seems best to err on the high side [GARDNER, 1985b].

Exhibit 7-6 OPTIMAL HISTORICAL TIME SPAN FOR EXTRAPOLATION

Study	Forecast Horizon (periods)	Situation	Ayres' Rule	Optimum Span by . . . Armstrong's Rule	Actual Test
Ash & Smyth (1973)	1	Macroeconomic	1	4	5
HAGERMAN & RULAND [1979]	1	Annual earnings	1	4	5[+]
DALRYMPLE & KING [1983]	1	"Business"	1	4	18
Cragg & Malkiel (1968)	2, 3	Annual earnings	2.5	6.3	10
Orson (1968)	6	Electric power	6	10	10
DALRYMPLE & KING [1983]	12	Business	12	14	27

Typically, α is expected to be between 0 and 1. Indeed, the way I described the model makes an α of more than 1.0 seem counter-intuitive. By using a bit of algebra, however, we can recast the basic formula for exponential smoothing in a different, but equivalent form:

$$\overline{Y}_t = \overline{Y}_{t-1} + \alpha\, e_t$$

where e_t is the difference between the latest (deseasonalized) observation and the previous average. What this says is that we adjust the new average in light of the most recent change. If one expects the data to be highly auto-correlated, then an α greater than 1.0 might be considered. Still, this strikes me as risky.

Judgmental smoothing factors should be adequate. If the forecast is of particular importance, however, you should conduct a computerized search for the best smoothing constants to be sure that you are near the optimum. Many computer packages have this facility.

This discussion has covered the selection of an appropriate time span and, hence, an appropriate α for exponential smoothing of the average. A similar analysis can also be used in selecting a smoothing factor, beta (β), for the trend calculations, and also a gamma (γ) factor to smooth seasonality.

Calculate New Average. The formula for calculating the new average was presented in the preceding subsection. Brown's formulation is especially sensitive to starting values. A starting value must be selected for $\overline{Y}_{t-1}$. If a substantial amount of historical data exists (well in excess of $(2 - \alpha)/\alpha$ observations), the decision on the starting value is less important. You can use a range of starting values (highest, most likely, lowest) to test sensitivity.

Calculate New Trend. The trend is calculated from period-to-period changes in the new average. The trend can be calculated in a manner analogous to the calculation of the new average, that is, the new smoothed trend is the weighted average of the most recent trend in the average and the previous smoothed trend:

$$\overline{G}_t = (\beta)(\overline{Y}_t - \overline{Y}_{t-1}) + (1 - \beta)(\overline{G}_{t-1})$$

where β is the smoothing factor and $\overline{G}$ is the smoothed trend or growth factor. McCLAIN [1974], using theoretical arguments, suggests that it is best to use $\alpha = \beta$.

The starting value for $\overline{G}$ is often set at zero, but the analyst is advised to make a "best guess" here. This is most important where few historical data exist.

A decision must be made whether to use an exponential or an additive trend. The exponential trend is appropriate when:

1. All observations are greater than zero
2. Data are ratio scaled
3. Measurement error is small
4. Growth is expected to be geometrical

However, for long-range forecasts, exponential trends are risky—even if the above conditions are met. Little direct evidence is available on this issue, though. Elton and Gruber (1972) found additive and exponential trends to produce equivalent accuracy in their forecasts of the earnings of firms.

When uncertainty exists about the trend, it may be useful to estimate a dampened or modified trend. The reasoning here is the same as that used for the modified seasonal factors; it is desirable to place less weight on inaccurate estimates. For a multiplicative factor, calculate a modified trend factor, $\overline{G}_t^*$:

$$\overline{G}_t^* = K_G + (1 - K_G)\overline{G}_t$$

where K is a dampening factor ($0 < K_G < 1$). K could be set subjectively or by a search; it would be 1.0 if the trend estimates are of no value and 0.0 for highly accurate trend estimates.

GARDNER and McKENZIE [1985], in a study of data from the **M-Competition**[G] [MAKRIDAKIS et al. 1982], found significant improvements in accuracy due to dampening of the trend. Their scheme estimated a parameter that automatically increased the dampening for erratic trends. Consistent trends (noted for about ⅓ of their quarterly and monthly series) were not dampened at all. The dampening was especially valuable for longer forecast horizons. Dampening also helped to avoid large errors.

Some analysts have proposed that the acceleration also be calculated. In other words, the data on the trend in the changes can be exponentially smoothed. This procedure, generally called triple exponential smoothing (because average, trend, and acceleration are smoothed), might be adequate for short-term forecasts. It is risky, however, for longer term forecasts, because it violates **Occam's razor**[G] (i.e., use the simplest method). Eight studies were found on this topic:

Elton and Gruber (1972) forecasted firms' earnings up to three years; models with acceleration did poorer in this study than those without acceleration. Acceleration models were less accurate over a variety of forecast horizons in the M-competition [MAKRIDAKIS et al., 1982]. For short-range forecasts, Markland (1970) found an advantage to triple smoothing, Groff (1973) and Torfin and Hoffman (1968) found no difference, and Davies and Scott (1973), SCHNAARS [1984], and SCHNAARS and BAVUSO [1985] found that acceleration models did worse.

Estimate Current Status. The smoothed average typically lags the most recent changes. Thus, some adjustment should be made to bring the average up to date. The approach discussed here develops a substantial lag so Brown (1959a, b) suggested the following correction:

$$\overline{Y}_t^* = \overline{Y}_t + \left(\frac{1-\alpha}{\alpha}\right) \overline{G}_t$$

where $\overline{Y}_t^*$ is current status. In other words, the smoothed trend, $\overline{G}_t$, is multiplied by $(1 - \alpha)/\alpha$. Thus, if $\alpha = 0.4$, the trend would be multiplied by 1.5.

Calculate Forecast. The forecast may be obtained for 1 to h periods into the future by taking the estimate of current status, calculating the trend over the forecast horizon, and incorporating seasonality. If additive trends and multiplicative seasonality are assumed, the forecast is the product of the current status plus trend times seasonality:

$$F_{j,t+h} = (\overline{Y}_t^* + h\,\overline{G}_t^*)\,\overline{S}_j^{**}$$

where F is used to represent the forecast.

Update Seasonal Factors. Exponential smoothing can be applied to the seasonal factors using gamma (γ) as a smoothing factor, where γ is selected on the basis of the number of observations for the given period of the year (e.g., the number of January's), meaning that γ will nearly always differ from α and β:

$$\overline{S}_{j,t} = \gamma\left(\frac{Y_t}{\overline{Y}_t}\right) + (1 - \gamma)(\overline{S}_{j,t-J})$$

where J is the number of periods in the year (e.g., 12 for monthly data).

Thus the new smoothed seasonal factor is the weighted sum of the latest information on seasonality (e.g., the ratio of the latest observation to the smoothed average) and the previous smoothed estimate of seasonality. Each time new seasonal factors are calculated, it is necessary to dampen and normalize.

This procedure requires much data and small measurement error. A simpler approach, which gives adequate results, is to recalculate seasonal factors once a year (e.g., by using the Census X-11 program).

Return and Repeat Process. As each new observation comes in, it is a simple matter to update the exponentially smoothed forecast. If there are a number of forecasts, this can be done more cheaply by computer. *Frequent updating is important for accuracy.*

The smoothing factors are usually held constant. Brown (1959a, b), however, suggested that these factors be increased if large changes are expected; this makes sense. Harrison and Davies (1964) and Trigg and Leach (1967) suggested that the factors be increased if systematic errors are observed over time; this also makes sense. Arguing against this is that the added complexity of adaptive parameters might not yield significant gains in accuracy. *In fact, the 12 studies to date offer little evidence favoring adaptive parameters:*

SMITH [1974], Chow [1965], WHYBARK [1972], and DENNIS [1978] all found that adaptive parameters improved accuracy. But the findings by Chow, Whybark, and Dennis were not confirmed when replicated [(GARDNER, 1983b; EKERN, 1981]. Torfin and Hoffman [1968], Raine [1971], Adam [1973], Harris and Adam (1975), and Dancer and Gray [1977] found little difference in accuracy. GARDNER and DANNENBRING [1980], MABERT [1978] and McLEAVEY, LEE, and ADAM [1981] found poorer accuracy with adaptive parameters).

Many details have been glossed over in this description. The early works in this area are still useful (e.g., Brown, 1959a, b and Winters, 1960), but the forecasting texts listed on page 78 of *LRF* offer better descriptions. GARDNER [1985b] provides a comprehensive summary of the literature.

The important thing, I believe, is to find some way to implement the guidelines in this section (Exhibit 7-4). Use Gerstenfeld's Law of Trying. To test this claim, I asked a research assistant to use the guidelines to develop a computer program. The output looked reasonable and was verified by hand calculations on a sample of data. Also I presented the monthly data on international air travel from 1949 to 1958 and asked students to provide monthly forecasts for 1959 and 1960. Eight project reports were prepared. The details of the procedure varied greatly. Before any assessment was made of accuracy, I coded the extent to which each report conformed to the guidelines presented here. These ratings were crude because the reports did not always provide adequate descriptions. The mean absolute percentage error of the forecasts was about 5% for the four reports that followed the guidelines, and about 11% for the four reports that departed from the guidelines.

Numerous alternatives to exponential smoothing can be used. One possibility is subjective or "eyeball" extrapolations. ADAM and EBERT [1976], and CARBONE and GORR [1985] found objective methods to be a bit more accurate; however, LAWRENCE, 1983; LAWRENCE et al. 1985 found the accuracy of subjective extrapolations to be good relative to objective methods:

In LAWRENCE et al. [1985], three alternative judgmental methods were compared with extrapolative methods in forecasts for the 111 time series used in MAKRIDAKIS, et al. [1982]. No information was available to the judges other than the historical data. In general, the judgmental extrapolations ("eyeballing") were at least as accurate as the extrapolation methods. For longer lead times, the quantitative extrapolations were superior. (I believe this may be due to the dampening of the trend factor that occurs with judgmental extrapolations, as shown in EGGLETON [1982].) Surprisingly, subjects provided with tables gave slightly more accurate forecasts than those provided with graphs.

Moving Averages

As noted previously, moving averages are similar to exponential smoothing. The only conceptual difference is that each observation is weighted equally. Thus a four-period moving average would be

$$\overline{Y}_t = \frac{Y_{t-3} + Y_{t-2} + Y_{t-1} + Y_t}{4}$$

As a result, moving averages tend to lag current status even more than do exponentially smoothed averages. The average age of the data in the four-period example above would be two periods; this compares with 1.5 for the corresponding exponentially smoothed model. It is possible, however, to weight more recent observations more heavily, and corrections can be made for the lag.

The advantages of moving averages in comparison with exponential smoothing are that the former are easier to understand and that seasonality can be removed easily from the data by using an average that incorporates complete cycles. Thus, for quarterly data, the moving average could be based on 4, 8, or 12 periods.

An excellent computer program, Census Program X-11, has been available for moving-average analyses for many years (Shiskin, 1965). It has provisions for seasonality, trend, adjustments of outliers, working or trading day adjustments, and differential weighting of observations.

A disadvantage of moving averages is that many data need to be retained for the analysis. A 12-period average requires carrying the 12 periods of historical data in addition to the summary statistics. This disadvantage can become costly when many items are being forecast (e.g., inventory control).

The M-Competition showed moving averages to be less accurate than exponential smoothing [MAKRIDAKIS et al. 1982], as did FRANK [1969]. Other evidence includes the following studies, three of which favor exponential smoothing, and one that shows no difference.

Winters (1960) developed an exponentially weighted moving average with multiplicative seasonal factors to obtain a forecast one period ahead. He examined three sets of data—monthly sales of cooking utensils manufactured by a subsidiary of Alcoa, bimonthly sales of a type of paint manufactured by Pittsburgh Plate Glass, and the number of cellars excavated each month by Admiral Homes. Data were available for five to seven years. Exponential smoothing was slightly superior to a one-year moving average, but the latter did not include a trend estimate.

Kirby (1966) compared three extrapolation methods in short-range forecasting for company sales data. The forecasts were for 23 sewing machine products sold in five countries. The forecast horizon ranged from 1 to 6 months. A period of 7 ½ years was examined, using exponential smoothing and unweighted moving averages. The accuracies of the exponential smoothing and the moving averages were comparable for the 6-month horizon. As the forecast horizon was shortened, however, the exponential smoothing did slightly better. Kirby also developed forecasts from artificial data by imposing various types of error upon the original data. He found, for example, that with more random error the moving average performed better than the exponential smoothing, and that with a strong cyclical component the exponential smoothing did relatively better than the moving average. Overall, however, the differences among the various extrapolation methods examined by Kirby were small; this was the major conclusion.

Elton and Gruber (1972) found exponentially smoothed forecasts to be better than moving averages in one-, two-, and three-year forecasts of earnings. The relative advantage of exponential smoothing increased slightly as the forecast horizon was lengthened from one to three years. In this case, however, the moving average, did not have a trend factor.

Adam (1973) compared a two-period moving average with an exponentially smoothed average. One-period and 12-period forecasts were obtained for five simulated demand patterns. The moving averages yielded forecasts that were equivalent in accuracy to those obtained with exponential smoothing. (See also the replication by McLEAVY, LEE, and ADAM [1981].)

Box—Jenkins

Another approach to the analysis of time series is the Box–Jenkins (Box and Jenkins, 1976). It has been one of the most popular dances in the history of forecasting, and the book is among those most frequently stolen from libraries. (Stealing books is actually a form of defensive education for required courses. Although you may not be able to understand the textbook, you can make things more difficult for others by stealing it.)

Some of my best friends are Box–Jenkins experts, but I even have trouble understanding the interpreters. However, the number of interpretations continues to grow. It is interesting that some experts argue that other experts do not understand Box–Jenkins well enough (e.g., see discussants in Chatfield and Prothero, 1973). On the other hand,

CARBONE et al. [1983] found that 18 hours of classroom training were sufficient for learning it. Once learned, Box–Jenkins is expensive to apply. LUSK and NEVES [1984] found that it required about 25 minutes for the typical series though substantially less time was required for simple series.

It may not be necessary to become an expert in Box–Jenkins in order to obtain good results. HILL and FILDES [1984] and LIBERT [1984] each used automatic procedures and obtained accuracy that was comparable to Andersen's for the 111 series in the M-Competition. The automatic procedure was also faster (about two minutes of computer time per series). But it does not strike me as a good idea to use a complex method that you do not understand, especially when comparable results can be achieved with simple models that people do understand.

In general, Box–Jenkins uses the most recent observation as the starting value (Nelson, 1973) and then analyzes recent forecasting errors to determine the proper adjustments for future time periods. It is analogous to control procedures used in chemical processing, where an examination is made of the desired state and the actual state, and an adjustment based on the difference is made in the process. Usually the adjustment serves to compensate for only part of the error. For example, if the forecast was 10% low in the last period, the forecast for the next period might be adjusted upward by some fraction of this error (e.g., by 5%). This description suggests that Box–Jenkins is more appropriate for short-range than long-range forecasts.

The Box–Jenkins method allows for much flexibility in the selection of a model. This appeals to analysts. On the other hand, it calls for much subjectivity on the part of the analyst. Granger and Newbold (1974) consider this need for subjective inputs to be a disadvantage relative to exponential smoothing. Chatfield and Prothero (1973) suggest that the need for subjective inputs is so great that instead of Box–Jenkins one might use BFE (bold freehand extrapolation). In fact, LAWRENCE et al. [1985] have tried that! In a test of the reliability of the Box–Jenkins method, LUSK and NEVES [1984] obtained substantially different B-J models from those identified by Andersen for 111 time series in the M-Competition (though the overall accuracy did not differ much).

The detailed procedure becomes quite complicated. Systematic procedures are used to determine the best model for the historical data. These examine autoregression with previous values of the time series, differencing of successive values, and moving averages. A good description of these procedures is provided in MAKRIDAKIS, WHEEL-WRIGHT, and McGEE [1983, Chapter 9].

The Box—Jenkins procedures have had an immense impact on forecasting. Box—Jenkins is clearly the most widely discussed and the most highly cited work in forecasting. Theoretically, it sets the standard. Practioners and researchers tend to believe that it is the most accurate approach [FILDES and LUSK, 1984]. But the empirical evidence has been less convincing.

Results favorable to Box—Jenkins were obtained by Newbold and Granger (1974), REID [1975], BROWN and ROZEFF [1978], and DALRYMPLE [1978]. No differences were found in Chatfield and Prothero (1973), Groff (1973), Geurts and Ibrahim (1975), MABERT [1976], CHATFIELD [1978], KENNY and DURBIN [1982], ALBRECHT et al. [1977], MAKRIDAKIS and HIBON [1979], and MAKRIDAKIS et al. [1982]. Less accuracy was found in BRANDON, JARRETT, and KHUMAWALA [1983].

Thus, in only four of the fourteen comparative studies that I found was it reported that a *higher* degree of accuracy was achieved by using Box—Jenkins procedures. On the other hand, Box—Jenkins was less accurate only once. The most impressive evidence was provided in the large scale comparisons by MAKRIDAKIS and HIBON [1979] and MAKRIDAKIS et al. [1982, 1984]. (For the latter study, see also the discussion in ARMSTRONG and LUSK [1983].) Some of the comparative studies are described here:

A discussant to Chatfield and Prothero (1973) obtained forecasts from a simple naive model that were comparable to those from Box—Jenkins.

Groff (1973) examined monthly data for 63 time series representing factory shipments of automotive parts and drug items. There were also five simulated time series. The 1-month and 6-month forecasting errors from the best of ten Box—Jenkins models were slightly greater than the errors from exponentially smoothed models. However, overall, there was little difference among the forecasting errors of the various methods.

Newbold and Granger (1974) compared 1- to 8-month forecasts by exponential smoothing and by Box–Jenkins for 106 economic time series. The Box–Jenkins forecasts were superior on 60% of the comparisons. On the average, Box–Jenkins errors were 80% as large as those from exponential smoothing. The Box–Jenkins forecasts did relatively better for the shorter range forecasts.

Geurts and Ibrahim (1975) compared Box–Jenkins and exponential smoothing for 1-month forecasts of visitors to Hawaii. Each model was developed using data from 1952 to 1969, and the forecasts were made for the 24 months of 1970 and 1971. The forecast accuracy (**Theil's $U2^G$**) for the two methods was almost identical.

Regressions

Still another method of analyzing time series data is to run a regression, using time as the independent variable. This method, which weights all of the historical data equally, provides estimates of both current status and trend. If an additive trend factor is used,

$$Y = a + bt$$

The forecasting accuracy of regressions against time appears to be slightly inferior to that of exponential smoothing.

Wagle, Rappoport, and Downes (1968) found little difference, although it is difficult to draw any firm conclusions because their description is inadequate. Kirby (1966), found regression to be slightly inferior to exponential smoothing. Hirschfeld (1970) found regression to be less accurate than exponential smoothing in predicting the growth rates of 10 white males from age 6 to 16. Finally, Elton and Gruber (1972) found regression to be inferior to exponential smoothing for earnings forecasts, especially as the forecast horizon increased from 1 to 3 years.

Exhibit 7-7   RANKINGS OF EXTRAPOLATION METHODS
              (1 = highest ranking)

Method	Cost	Under-standability	Forecast Accuracy Short-Range	Long-Range
Exponential smoothing	1	2.5	1.5	1
Moving averages	2	1	3.5	3
Box–Jenkins	4	4	1.5	2
Regressions	3	2.5	3.5	4

Comparisons of Extrapolation Methods

These primary methods for extrapolation of time series data are listed
in Exhibit 7-7, where they are ranked on the criteria of cost, understandability, and accuracy. Exponential smoothing is a less expensive
forecasting method because it does not require storage of historical
data, as do moving averages and regression; Box–Jenkins requires
many diagnostic tests to keep up with the changes. Moving averages
are easy to understand, exponential smoothing and regressions are a
bit more difficult, and Box–Jenkins procedures are still harder to understand because of their complexity. The rankings on accuracy are
based on the previously presented evidence (including Appendix J).
They are heavily influenced by the M-Competition and by my judgment. Exponential smoothing is expected to be most accurate overall.
Under ideal conditions, moving averages can approximate exponential
smoothing; however, they use data inefficiently for start-up. Regressions suffer from their sensitivity to outliers and from errors in measuring the current status. Note, however, that the differences in accuracy for short-range forecasting are usually small (except for
regression). For longer term forecasts, these differences are expected
to become larger; thus, I expect exponential smoothing, with dampened
trend, to be superior. Quite likely, the relative accuracy of the methods
depends upon the situation. This issue is discussed in the commentary
to the M-Competition [see ARMSTRONG and LUSK, 1983], but to date
I do not believe we have good guidelines.
    One conclusion that emerges from the research on extrapolation is
simplicity. Beyond the fairly obvious steps that were recommended as
early as 1960 (clean the data, adjust for trading days, deseasonalize,
and then estimate the average and the trend), methodological sophistication has been of little value. This statement is based on my review

of the empirical evidence. Of the studies that I found, 18 showed no gain in accuracy for sophistication beyond the 1960-type procedures, nine studies found simpler methods to be more accurate, and only five studies found improved accuracy for sophisticated methods. (These results were abstracted from the studies listed in Appendix J, *LRF* pp. 494–495. I did not include studies that had been challenged nor the studies that compared exponential smoothing to moving averages.)

The need for simplicity is especially important where few historical data exist or where the historical data are unstable. Interestingly, instability can be judged just as well subjectively as statistically:

SCHNAARS [1984] compared sales forecasts generated by six extrapolation methods for 98 annual time series. The methods ranged from simple (next year will be the same as this year) to complex (curvilinear regression). A significant omission was the simple exponential smoothing model (i.e., without trend). The forecast horizon ranged from 1 to 5 years and successive updating was used so that almost 1500 forecasts were examined. This is an interesting study. The simplest model performed well, especially where there were few historical data and where the historical series seemed unstable. Stability was assessed just as effectively by subjects who looked at historical scatter plots as by using autocorrelation or runs statistics. Models that squared the time variable were especially inaccurate. (It has always struck me as a bit strange to raise time to some power in an attempt to improve forecasting. It is a dangerous practice and I strongly recommend against it.)

SCHNAARS and BAVUSO [1985] compared the short-range predictive accuracy of seven extrapolation models on 15 economic indicators, simple smoothing was included as one of the models. The random walk (no change from last period), was, in general, the most accurate of the methods examined. The most complex methods produced the least accurate forecasts.

Cycles and Fancy Curves

Once upon a time in the land of Academia, there lived two mystics named Dewey and Dakin (1947). They believed in cycles. Not the two-wheeler kind that you ride only once every 3 years after you grow up and then feel sore for a week. No, Dewey and Dakin believed in big panoramic cycles that explained man's existence. They drew inspiration from astronomy, where cycles had been used successfully. They claimed that the world is so complex, relative to man's ability for dealing with complexity, that a detailed study of causality is a hopeless task. The only way to forecast, they said, is to forget about causality and, instead, to find past patterns or cycles of behavior. These cycles should then be projected without asking why they exist. Dewey and Dakin believed that economic forecasting should be done only through mechanical extrapolation of the observed cycles. They emphasized that "the forecasts are written by the data themselves."

Much of the Dewey and Dakin book is devoted to a description of how cyclical components can describe historical events. The ability of cycles to fit data for events that have already occurred is not, however, the primary concern. How useful are cycles in forecasting? Well, Dewey and Dakin (1947, p. 277) did make some forecasts. These forecasts were made in 1946 and covered the period from 1947 to 1952. They expected the economy to trend downward and to reach a low in 1952. As noted in Schoeffler (1955), these forecasts proved to be drastically wrong. The economic growth from 1947 to 1952 exceeded all previous peacetime records in the United States. (I'm not sure why Schoeffler called this peacetime—unless we were actively waging peace in Korea.)

With the exception of seasonality cycles, I have been unable to find empirical evidence on the predictive value of cycles. I even obtained information from the Foundation for the Study of Cycles, which is associated with the University of Pittsburgh. (It publishes the *Journal of Interdisciplinary Cycle Research* and *Cycles*.)

The added complexity of cycles makes this method risky for anything but short-range forecasting (Cowden, 1963, thought so too). Small errors in estimating the length of the cycle can lead to large errors in long-range forecasting if the forecast gets out of phase with the true situation. Of course, if little uncertainty exists about the length of a cycle, use this information. For example, the attendance at the Olympic games follows a four year cycle . . . usually.

What have economists learned from this apparently fruitless quest? Well, **spectral analysis**[G] is a hot topic. This is a complex approach that is similar to a regression against time, except that now the independent variables are sines or cosines or various powers of time. (See Brown, 1963, pp. 396–401 or Chan and Hayya, 1976, for descriptions of spectral analysis.)

Spectral analysis is a dance in a different dimension. It is a sophisticated approach to the study of cycles. Advocates of spectral analysis apparently assume that previous failures with cycles resulted because the latter did not represent the complexity of the data.

Unlikely. A good rule to follow in extrapolation methods is to keep it simple. I have been unable to find any evidence that spectral analysis provides better forecasts.

Spectral analysis offers complex curves with no theory. There are a number of curves, both simple and complex, that can be justified on some *a priori* grounds. Discussions of various curves may be found in Harrison and Pearce (1972), Gilchrist (1976), and Johnston (1984). Despite many years of experience with various growth curves in market forecasting, it is difficult to provide generalizations. MEADE [1984] assesses the empirical evidence on this topic.

Remember to use complex forms only where there are good *a priori* reasons for doing so. An example of the use of *a priori* reasons in the selection of a curve is presented in the following. Despite all of this good thinking, a simple rule of thumb proved just as effective for prediction:

Armstrong (1975b), in a study on mail surveys, made predictions for the percentage reduction in nonresponse that would be achieved by monetary incentives. Four assumptions were made about the relationships:

1. The curve should go through the origin to reflect, by definition, the fact that no reduction in nonresponse is obtained with no incentive.
2. The curve should approach an asymptote (or limit). Obviously, the limit in this case cannot exceed 100%. An asymptote of 100% was selected under the assumption that "everyone has his price." (This decision was subject to much uncertainty.)
3. There should be diminishing marginal returns: each additional amount of money should have less impact.
4. The relationship should be simple if possible.

One way to capture these assumptions is to fit the data to the following functional form:

$$Y = l - \frac{l}{e^{bx}}$$

where Y = the reduction in nonresponse bias
   l = the asymptote
   x = the monetary incentive
   b = the parameter to be estimated
   e = the base for natural logs*

This functional form, which did not turn out to be so simple, can be transformed to

$$\ln (l - Y) - \ln (l) = bx$$

Assuming an asymptote of 100% gives

$$\ln (100 - Y) - \ln (100) = bx$$

The b was estimated via regression analysis, using 24 observations, to be 0.64. Thus the reduction in the percentage of nonresponse, R, can be predicted from

$$R = 100 - \frac{100}{e^{0.064x}}$$

The accuracy of this complex curve was matched by a simple extrapolation that said, "There is a 1% reduction in nonresponse for each 1 cent in incentive up to 40 cents." You can't imagine how disappointing such results are for an analyst! Analysts are like politicians; they would rather make simple things complex.

Studies in demography have made extensive use of curves for extrapolations. According to a review by Hajnal (1955), crude extrapolations have worked as well as complex ones. My impression from Dorn's (1950) review is that the more thinking the demographers put into their extrapolations, the more complex the methods become and the poorer the resulting forecasts.

Curves have been used in fields other than demography and survey research, of course, but the results are about the same. In contrast to short-range forecasting, the curves provide widely differing long-range forecasts. One conclusion is that simple curves are as good as complex

*This is one time I have lied in the glossary. In other cases, e represents error.

ones. Another conclusion, when using curves for long-range forecasts, is "Be careful." Mark Twain already said this (*Life on the Mississippi*, chapter 17, passed along via Daly, 1963):

In the space of one hundred and seventy-six years the Lower Mississippi has shortened itself two hundred and forty-two miles. That is an average of a trifle over one mile and a third per year. Therefore, any calm person, who is not blind or idiotic, can see that in the Old Oölitic Silurian Period, just a million years ago next November, the Lower Mississippi River was upward of one million three hundred thousand miles long, and stuck out over the Gulf of Mexico like a fishing-rod. And by the same token any person can see that seven hundred and forty-two years from now the Lower Mississippi will be only a mile and three-quarters long, and Cairo and New Orleans will have joined their streets together, and be plodding comfortably along under a single mayor and a mutual board of aldermen. There is something fascinating about science. One gets such wholesale returns of conjecture out of such a trifling investment of fact.

P.S. Don't use fancy curves to decide when to invest your money in the stock market (Levy, 1971b).

COMBINED FORECASTS

This chapter's adventure in eclectic research was inspired by Levins (1966), a biologist. He suggested that, rather than building one master model of the real world, one might build several simple models that, among them, would use all of the data available, and then average them. This implies that gains can be achieved by using a set of simple extrapolation methods and combining the forecasts. This strategy has received impressive support:

Bates and Granger (1969) tested combined forecasts of the international air travel market. They started with the premise that the gains are greatest if the forecasts are based upon different information, rather than merely upon different assumptions about the form of the relationship. They used five different methods to obtain 1-month forecasts for the period 1951–1960. Nine different combined forecasts were developed from the five original sets of forecasts using various weighting schemes to combine pairs of forecasts. As an example, forecasts for the months in 1953 were obtained by exponential smoothing and also an extrapolation by Box and Jenkins (taken from Barnard, 1963); the error variances of these forecasts were 196 and 188, respectively. A combined (average) forecast from these two methods had an error variance of only 150. Overall, the error variances of the combined forecasts were smaller than the error variance of either of the two components in all but one case (where the combined forecast and the best component tied). Therefore the combined forecasts were superior to the average of the individual forecasts. The gains from combining were greatest when the two original forecasts were relatively independent of one another. Additional evidence is available from MORRIS [1977], REINMUTH and GERUTS [1978], and BUNN [1979]. This evidence also favors combining.

MAKRIDAKIS and WINKLER [1983] examined the value of combining extrapolation forecasts using data that were selected from the 1001 series in the M-Competition [MAKRIDAKIS, et al., 1982]. Significant gains in accuracy were achieved as more forecasts were combined. Combinations of two methods led to a 7% reduction in MAPE. Significant error reductions occurred for the first five methods, after which the reductions were small. Combinations were more important for data measured on a shorter time interval (monthly data) than longer time (yearly data), presumably due to the lower reliability of estimate for the shorter time period. (See also WINKLER and MAKRIDAKIS [1983].)

Because the gains due to combining forecasts are expected to increase as the similarity between the forecasts decreases, and because extrapolation forecasts tend to diverge as the forecast horizon is lengthened, the gains for combined forecasts should be greater when the forecast horizon is longer. Long-range forecasts were examined in studies by Ogburn and by Armstrong:

Ogburn's study (1946, pp. 113–145) of the air travel market demonstrates that various extrapolation methods can provide widely varying predictions when large changes are expected. Using data through 1943, he extrapolated the 1953 revenue passenger miles (RPM) on U.S. domestic airlines by various methods. His forecasts are presented here. I added a combined forecast based on an average of Ogburn's five extrapolations, then compared the forecasts with actual RPMs of 14.9 billion in 1953.

Method	RPM Forecast	MAPE
a. Straight line projection	4.0	73
b. Logistic curve	5.6	62
c. Parabola	6.0	60
d. Gompertz curve	13.0	13
e. Constant percentage growth	30.0	101
Average error for a, b, c, d, e	—	62
Combined forecast (all of above)	11.7	21

The combined forecast was more accurate than the forecast obtained with Ogburn's favored method, which was the parabola, and also better than the average MAPE for Ogburn's five methods, 21% vs. 62%.

In Armstrong (1968a), three extrapolations were used for a 6-year backcast of 1954 camera sales for 17 countries. The extrapolations, developed using data from 1965–1960, were done by a method assuming no changes in sales, one that forecasted a constant percentage trend within each country, and one that applied the worldwide market trend to each country. The two combined forecasts were more accurate.

Extrapolation Method	MAPE
a. No change	67
b. Constant trend within country	51
c. Constant world market trend	37
Average errors for a, b, and c	52
Combined Forecasts	
Average of a & b	43
Average of a & b & c	33

I used equal weights in my reanalysis of these studies. When you are uncertain as to what weights to use, use equal weights. If you have strong evidence about which forecasts are likely to be most accurate, use this information to establish weights. Bates and Granger (1969) present a good discussion on how to weight, but studies to date have found few differences among weighting schemes.

ASSESSING UNCERTAINTY

A common approach to estimating uncertainty with extrapolation methods is to examine how closely a particular method fits the historical data. In other words, what is the typical error when comparing predicted and actual values for the data used to develop the model? The most important problem with this approach is that future environmental change makes the estimates less useful.

The estimation of uncertainty can be substantially improved if data are withheld and used to simulate the actual forecasting situation. These "let's pretend" forecasting errors are used as estimates of the uncertainty for the future. For example, to estimate the uncertainty involved in a two-year forecast, you would like to know how well the method has done on other two-year forecasts. Williams and Goodman found this approach to be superior to the usual approach of examining the fit to historical data. Newbold and Granger also found this approach to be useful in estimating uncertainty:

Williams and Goodman (1971) examined monthly data on phones for homes and businesses in three cities in Michigan. The first 24 months of data were analyzed by a regression on the **first differences**^{G} of the data. Seasonality was also estimated. Forecasts were made for an 18-month horizon. The model was then updated, and another forecast was calculated; this procedure was repeated for 144 months of data. When the standard error for the historical data was used to establish confidence limits, the actual values were contained within the 95% confidence limits for about 84% of the forecasts. When confidence intervals were based instead on the forecast errors, the actual values were contained in the 95% confidence intervals for about 90% of the forecasts.

Newbold and Granger (1974, p. 161) examined 1-month forecasts for 20 economic series covering 600 forecasts. Of their Box–Jenkins forecasts, 93% fell within the 95% confidence intervals; of their regression forecasts, 91% fell within these limits.

The measures of uncertainty can be used to develop tracking signals. These can monitor the forecasting system and indicate when it is no longer appropriate. For discussions on tracking signals, see GARDNER [1983a, 1985a].

SUMMARY

Historical data are useful for extrapolation if they are timely and accurate, and if the underlying process is expected to be stable in the future. If historical data are not available, a situation that occurs for large changes, one might examine historical data from analogous situations. If analogous situations do not exist, it may be necessary to use simulated data from either laboratory or field tests. Exhibit 7-1 ranked these four types of data (historical, analogous situations, laboratory simulation, and field test) as to appropriateness for estimating current status and for making short-range and long-range forecasts. Rankings were also provided on cost and the effects of researcher bias.

The method of Markov chains has been widely studied. It seems appropriate when there are various states of behavior that are related to one another. Unfortunately, little evidence could be found that Markov chains provide more accurate forecasts.

Exponential smoothing offers an inexpensive and simple approach for extrapolation. Exhibit 7-4 outlined an eight-step procedure for using exponential smoothing in forecasting. There were few surprises in this description, although the following points are worth repeating:

Step 1. Clean Data
(a) Remove or tone down the outliers.
(b) Combine multiple measures for a variable.
(c) Adjust for trading days.

Step 2. Deseasonalize Data
(a) Use multiplicative seasonal factors if you have ratio-scaled data, low measurement error, and large trends in the data. Otherwise, use additive factors.

(b) Use dampened seasonal factors rather than no seasonal or full seasonal factors. Increase emphasis on seasonality when you can obtain good estimates.

Step 3. Select Smoothing Factors

Forecast accuracy is not highly sensitive to the selection of smoothing factors. Use judgment to select a historical time span, and then derive a smoothing factor. Alternatively, search for the factors that minimize the forecast error in the historical data.

Step 4. Calculate New Average

The selection of starting values is important if data are limited. Use sensitivity testing to assess this problem.

Step 5. Calculate New Trend

(a) Use multiplicative factors if you have ratio-scaled data, low measurement error, and large trends in the data. Otherwise, use additive trends. In either case, dampen the trend.

(b) Generally speaking, ignore acceleration.

Step 6. Estimate Current Status

Adjust the new average to correct for lag.

Step 7. Calculate Forecast

Step 8. Update Seasonal Factors

Return to Step 4 and Repeat.

Keep things simple, especially if the historical series is short or unstable. Do not use adaptive smoothing constants.

Alternatives to exponential smoothing were discussed. The method of moving averages is similar to exponential smoothing, but it is slightly more expensive. Box–Jenkins is more difficult to understand and more expensive to use than exponential smoothing. From a theoretical viewpoint, it is most appropriate for short-range forecasts. These methods, along with regressions against time, were ranked on cost, understandability, and accuracy in Exhibit 7-7.

The use of various curves was examined. Complex curves, if used at all, should be limited to cases where uncertainty is low. To the extent that uncertainty is high, one should use simpler curves. For this reason, spectral analysis is particularly poor for long-range forecasting.

Perhaps the dominant messages for extrapolations are first to use simple methods. Then take advantage of more information by frequent updating and by combining forecasts from different methods. Combining is especially important for long-range forecasting.

For assessments of uncertainty, the fit to the historical data provides useful information on the minimum expected error. It is preferable, however, to withhold data and to simulate the forecasting situation.

Eight

ECONOMETRIC
METHODS

Contents

As soon as I could safely toddle
My parents handed me a Model.
My brisk and energetic pater
Provided the accelerator.
My mother, with her kindly gumption,
The function guiding my consumption;
And every week I had from her
A lovely new parameter,
With lots of little leads and lags
In pretty parabolic bags.

With optimistic expectations
I started on my explorations,
And swore to move without a swerve
Along my sinusoidal curve.
Alas! I knew how it would end:
I've mixed the cycle and the trend,
And fear that, growing daily skinnier,
I have at length become non-linear.
I wander glumly round the house
As though I were exogenous,
And hardly capable of feeling
The difference 'tween floor and ceiling.
I scarcely now, a pallid ghost,
Can tell *ex-ante* from *ex-post:*
My thoughts are sadly inelastic,
My acts incurably stochastic.

> "The Non-Econometrician's Lament"
> Sir Dennis Robertson (1955)*

I have some good news and some bad news. The good news is that this chapter is fairly simple, thanks to research done over the past quarter century. The bad news is that some people are going to be upset by the research. As a matter of fact, this research was hard on me emotionally because it indicated that many of the complex econometric techniques that I had learned were of little practical value in forecasting. Simplicity is a virtue in econometric methods.

In this chapter, advice is given on how to use econometric methods in forecasting. As defined here, "econometric methods" includes all quantitative procedures that use causal relationships. Chapter 8 dis-

---

*Used by permission of Macmillan London and Basingstoke.

cusses what you should do, what you should not do, what is worth further study, and where you can save time.

A brief discussion is first presented on conditions that favor the use of econometric methods. This is followed by a description of *a priori* analysis, the first stage in developing an econometric model. In effect, *a priori* analysis involves the use of judgment.

Sources of objective data are examined, and a checklist is provided to help in the search for data. The advantages and disadvantages of the various types of data are also discussed. An intermission is then provided because previous readers have said that the chapter is too long to read at one sitting.

Methods are described for analyzing objective data. These include experience tables and regression analysis. Particular attention is given to the problems involved in the use of regression analysis.

The estimates from objective data are used to update the *a priori* estimates. These estimates are then used in the two major types of problems: estimating current status (or current level) and forecasting change.

The chapter concludes with brief sections on the use of combined forecasts and on methods for assessing uncertainty.

This chapter describes many steps. Exhibit 8-1 is presented in an attempt to clarify its outline. It lists the major steps in the use of econometric methods.

Actually, Exhibit 8-1 oversimplifies matters. Although the processes are similar for estimating current status and for forecasting change, the models themselves may differ substantially. In other words, the decisions in the first four boxes depend on whether you are trying to estimate current status or to forecast change.

CONDITIONS FAVORING THE USE OF ECONOMETRIC METHODS

Three basic conditions favor the use of econometric methods. The first one is obvious: good information is needed on causal relationships. This information can come from subjective sources or from the analysis of objective data.

The second condition favoring econometric methods may not be obvious, because many econometricians ignore it: econometric methods are appropriate for large changes (or large differences) in the causal variables. For small changes, there is little reason to use econometric methods. Surprisingly, most econometric forecasting has involved small

Exhibit 8-1   STEPS IN DEVELOPING AN ECONOMETRIC MODEL

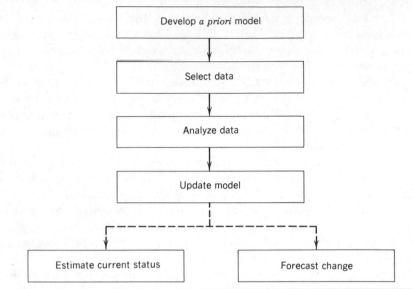

changes with the result that the method usually seems to be of little value (see Chapter 15).

The third condition, or set of conditions, is that the direction of changes in the causal variables can be accurately predicted, and that reasonable estimates can be made of the magnitudes of these changes.

A PRIORI ANALYSIS

Researchers and managers have useful information about the world. This information may come from experience. Better yet, it may come from previous empirical research, engineering studies, legislation, surveys of experts, and experiments. *A priori* analysis provides an efficient way to use this information. As noted in Chapter 4, it is better to utilize this information before analyzing the objective data than after.

A priori analysis comes in many different forms. Subjective decisions are required in the selection of data. Once the data are selected, additional analyses are possible as shown in Exhibit 8-2. The inverted triangle is designed to emphasize the importance of the items at the top of the triangle. The items in level *A* are always important in fore-

Exhibit 8-2 *A PRIORI* ANALYSIS IN ECONOMETRIC METHODS

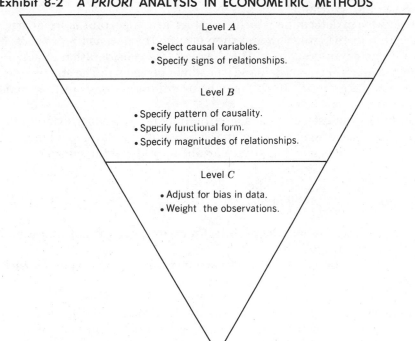

Level *A*
- Select causal variables.
- Specify signs of relationships.

Level *B*
- Specify pattern of causality.
- Specify functional form.
- Specify magnitudes of relationships.

Level *C*
- Adjust for bias in data.
- Weight the observations.

casting; those in level *B* are often important; and those in level *C* are sometimes important. Within a level, it is difficult to distinguish gradations of importance.

Causal Variables: Less Is More

The first step in the development of an econometric model should be the selection of the causal variables. Here there are two schools of thought. One favors the exploratory approach, where the analyst uses little judgment and, instead, develops a long list of potentially useful causal variables. At the other end of the continuum, *a priori* analysis suggests that a small number of causal variables be selected. (Evidence against the exploratory approach was presented in Chapter 4.)

It is important to select the proper conceptual variables. For example, I find that a model using market size, ability to buy, consumer needs, and price serves well for most problems in sales forecasting.

These conceptual variables provide a guide for the selection of **operational**^{G} variables.

One way to determine which variables are important is to identify the actors in the situation and then outline the decision process used by each actor. In economics, this has led to a consideration of supply (producer decisions) and demand (consumer decisions). The stakeholder approach (*LRF* pp. 16, 28–29) may be useful in carrying out this analysis of key actors.

To help in the selection of a small number of relevant variables for use in a forecasting model, the analyst should first develop a long and complete list. Ideas on potential variables can be obtained from:

• Previously published studies
• Experts in this problem area

Brainstorming also may be useful; it may uncover variables that had previously been ignored.

The second step is to use the following criteria to rate explicitly each of the variables:

1. Is there a strong causal relationship (i.e., do changes in the causal variable cause substantial changes in the dependent variable)?
2. Can the relationship be estimated accurately?
3. Will the causal variable show a substantial amount of change in the forecast period?
4. Can the changes occurring in the forecast period be forecast with fair accuracy?

These rules are summarized in Exhibit 8-3 for emphasis and to make it easier for the reader to find this list when you need it. These questions are *necessary* conditions. Should a variable score a "no" on any of these questions, it will be of little value in forecasting. Using these criteria, the researcher can screen out the less important variables. The remaining variables can be ranked according to an index using these criteria. Just what type of index is used does not seem to be crucial; what is important is that the researcher makes a systematic effort to select a small number of important variables. I also like the advice of MOSTELLER and TUKEY [1977, pp. 270–271] to chose variables that are "reasonably presentable" and will avoid "hilarious newspaper columns."

By following the rules in Exhibit 8-3, you will usually find many indicators for each given conceptual variable. *Select only one indicator*

Exhibit 8-3 CHECKLIST FOR SELECTING CAUSAL VARIABLES		
	Yes	No
1. Is a strong causal relationship expected?	_____	_____
2. Can the causal relationship be estimated accurately?	_____	_____
3. Will the causal variable change substantially?	_____	_____
4. Can the change in the causal variable be forecasted accurately?	_____	_____

for each conceptual variable. The selection among these operational variables is typically of little importance. Unfortunately, this is an area where I wasted much time in the past; I had operated under the delusion that the choice of the operational measure was important. Despite the claims in the econometric literature, I have been unable to find empirical evidence that the choice of an operational measure has much impact on forecast accuracy. Furthermore, I have failed when searching for the best measure in my own studies (e.g., in Armstrong, 1968a, different measures of buying power were shown to yield comparable results).

Rather than selecting the best measure, use a combined estimate from a set of reasonable indicators. Although this procedure may increase costs slightly, it provides a safer approach to forecasting. Such an approach was useful in my study of the photographic market, as described here:

In Armstrong (1968a), the combination of different estimates of current camera sales led to substantial gains in accuracy; the combination of different estimates of camera prices led to modest, but statistically significant, gains; and although the combination of alternative estimates of buying power led to no gains, it did not hurt forecast accuracy.

The advice to use a small number of causal variables in the analysis has also been a difficult one for me to accept. I falsely convince myself that certain variables are really important, as illustrated here in my study of the photographic market:

> In Armstrong (1968a), data from 11 variables were used to explain differences among countries. When this model was used to predict camera sales in 11 "new" countries, the mean absolute percentage error (MAPE) was 31%. An alternative model was developed using only two variables. This simpler and less expensive model was also used to predict camera sales in the 11 new countries; its MAPE was 27%. There was no significant difference between the forecast accuracy of the two models.

This failure to gain accuracy from additional variables is consistent with the more general evidence presented in Chapter 4. Additional evidence was provided in finance by MOYER [1977] and in sociology by Glaser (1954). Glaser's study was an exception to the work done in forecasting by criminologists over a period of 20 years. He was one of the first to advocate theoretically oriented research rather than the statistical manipulation of available data. He provided evidence that a small number of theoretically selected variables yields better forecasts than a large number of variables selected for statistical reasons. INCIARDI [1977] says that Glaser's advice is still ignored in criminology.

Direction of Relationships

The *a priori* information should be strong enough so that the analyst can state the sign of the relationship. In other words, given a change in the causal variable, what will be the direction of change in the dependent variable? If this is not possible, then this causal variable should not be used. This stage in the *a priori* analysis is a crucial one.

As an example of a variable that is subject to contrary yet reasonable hypotheses on direction, consider the uses of the consumer stock of a durable good. One might expect sales to be high when the stock is high. (If the stock is high, people are in the habit of using the product. If, in addition, the product gets broken or worn out, as happens with automobiles, a need arises for replacement sales.) On the other hand, one might expect sales to be low when the stock is high because consumers have less need to purchase what they already own.

Pattern of Causality

Rather than treating Y as a direct function of the causal variables, one can describe causality in detail. This has been done by using causal chains and simultaneous equations.

Causal chains provide an apparently useful way to decompose problems. Although the number of equations increases, the overall system is easy to understand. The results from the first equation are used as inputs to the second equation; the results from the second equation are entered into the third equation; and so on. An example is drawn here from my study of the photographic industry:

In Armstrong (1968b), a model was developed to make long-range forecasts of camera sales by country. The first stage in the causal chain was an econometric model to predict prices of cameras. It used taxes, resale price maintenance, and quotas as predictors. These price predictions were then entered into a model that predicted camera sales per capita as a function of personal consumption expenditures per capita and prices of cameras. The third stage was to predict the market size as a function of total population, literacy, age, and employment. Finally, the fourth stage calculated total camera sales on the basis of the predictions of camera sales per capita and market size.

Rather than increasing complexity, causal chains help to organize a problem into more manageable pieces and to illustrate what is happening. This method can turn a complex argument into a series of simple arguments. Using causal chains involves little danger, and it provides the benefits of decomposition.

A popular activity among econometricians has been to develop complex approaches to represent "simultaneous causality." Simultaneous causality occurs when a causal variable, say X, causes a change in Y, and the change in Y, in turn, causes a change in X. For example, as the price of automobiles is lowered, sales increase; the increase in sales then permits economies of scale that allow for further decreases in price. This is the interaction that made Henry Ford wealthy. Bennion (1952) provides an interesting discussion of simultaneous causality.

To represent simultaneous causality, econometricians have used simultaneous equations. That makes sense. Unfortunately, despite great expenditures of time and money by the best and the brightest econometricians, simultaneous equations have not been found to be of value in forecasting. This picture may change . . . but I doubt it. The failures of simultaneous equations have been noted for more than a quarter century. Christ (1960) said that, although simultaneous equations could sometimes be shown to do better on artificial data, he could find no real-world examples. L'Esperance (1964) tried but found no advantage for simultaneous equations over causal chains in an agricultural forecast.

If *a priori* information about the relationships were strong and if accurate data existed, then perhaps simultaneous equations would be of value. This is speculation. In the typical case, objective data must be used to analyze the relationships, and these data are prone to measurement error. The effects of measurement error may be greatly magnified by simultaneous equations. Stone (1966, p. 29) concluded that simultaneous equations are of little value if the causal variables are subject to large measurement errors. Summers (1965), Houthakker and Taylor (1966, p. 7), and Evans (1974, pp. 171–173) concluded that simultaneous equations were of little value in forecasting. I have been unable to find recent evidence on this issue.

Many have tried but few have succeeded. The moral of the research to date: forget simultaneous equations! This will save both of us a lot of time and energy. Many organizations currently follow this advice and rely on ordinary least squares regression [NAYLOR, 1981].

Functional Form

The selection of a **functional form**[G], that is, the way the dependent variable relates to the causal variables, is of little importance for small changes. For large changes, however, this can become an important decision.

Some researchers have recommended the use of nonlinear models. This does not pose a major problem if the model can be transformed into equivalent statements that are "linear in the parameters." If such a **transformation**[G] is not possible, I'd suggest that you avoid the nonlinear model. To date, I have been unable to find a published case where nonlinear models increased forecast accuracy.

A commonly used functional form in economies is the multiplicative model:

$$Y = aX_1^{b_1}X_2^{b_2} \cdots X_v^{b_v}$$

where the exponent b is interpreted as an **elasticity**^{G}, and v designates the number of variables. This form has a number of advantages:

1. It can be made linear in its parameters. This means that you can use a standard regression program after taking natural logs (ln) of both sides of the equation:

$$\ln Y = \ln (a) + b_1 \ln X_1 + b_2 \ln X_2 \cdots + b_v \ln X_v$$

   Thus it is often referred to as the log–log model. (Incidentally, the logs can be to the base 10, the base e, or any other base.)
2. This is a reasonable way to represent much human behavior. Constant elasticities are assumed; roughly speaking, this says that a 1% change in X will lead to a given percentage change in Y, which is equal to b. (This interpretation of elasticities provides a good approximation over a large range.)
3. It lends itself easily to *a priori* analysis because the researcher does not have to worry about units of measurement when specifying relationships. This advantage is an important one for areas that have been well studied; elasticities from different studies can be compared.
4. It often makes more efficient use of the data because it may correct for **heteroscedasticity**^{G}. In simple terms, if the errors in predicting Y are proportional to the magnitude of the X's (big errors are found when X is large), the log–log transformation will reduce the effect of these large errors. I have not found any evidence to suggest that this is an important problem in forecasting.

   Serious disadvantages of the log–log model include its requirement for ratio-scaled data and its sensitivity to measurement error.

   In economic problems and in many psychological problems, the multiplicative model is regarded as the standard. There is even some evidence for this view. O'Herlihy et al. (1967), for example, found the multiplicative model to be superior to the additive model in forecasting sales of consumer durables. Nevertheless, consideration of the advantages and disadvantages of the multiplicative model in a specific situation may lead one to depart from this standard. For example, if measurement error is substantial, a simple additive form may be preferred. In general, departures from the multiplicative model should be in the direction of the simple additive model. Ward found that complex functions were not helpful in forecasting:

Ward (1954) used four functional forms (e.g., parabolic) to predict success in five types of aviator training (e.g., flight simulation). More complex functional forms yielded poorer accuracy in cross-validation.

Fancier functional forms have gained enormous popularity in some academic disciplines. The topic has been of interest for many years in marketing. For example, the **logit**[G] transformation has been widely used. Based on the evidence to date, these functional forms have not produced significant gains in accuracy (e.g., see REIBSTEIN and TRAVER [1982] and SHOCKER and SRINIVASAN [1979]). Note, however, that WILTON and PESSEMIER [1981] obtained promising results.

Magnitudes of Relationships

The researcher can use her own judgment or the judgment of other experts in specifying magnitudes for the causal relationships. Also, it is likely that studies have been published for analogous situations. Previous studies are especially plentiful for economic problems. For example, in my work on the worldwide photographic industry, sources such as Harberger's (1960) studies of consumer durables were useful. Often there is a literature review that fulfills this need (e.g., Burk, 1968, on food consumption; Domencich and McFadden, 1975, on transportation; Salvendy and Seymour, 1973, on personnel; Cartter, 1976, on education; ARCHIBALD and GILLINGHAM [1980], on gasoline demand).

The *a priori* specification of magnitudes is especially important when:

1. Information on causality is strong,
2. Large changes are involved, and
3. Little information is available from objective data.

When these conditions do not hold, *a priori* specification of magnitude is expected to be of little value.

The alternative to using *a priori* information for deriving weights is to assume that you have no information on magnitudes. The implication then is that each relationship should be weighted equally. This is a simple procedure and no information exists to suggest otherwise. The simplest way to weight equally is to use **unit weights**[G].

Unit weights are appropriate when scaling is not a factor. This may be the case when the causal variables are unit-free, or when the predictions involve rankings rather than magnitudes (i.e., ordinal rather than interval or ratio data).

The advantages of unit weights over unrestricted *a priori* weights are minor. Using unit weights provides an alternative approach that offers two benefits:

1. The unit weights model can be used as a baseline for comparison. If the unrestricted weights yield predictions of comparable accuracy, this provides evidence that precise estimates of magnitudes are not required.
2. The unit weights model provides estimates of relationships that can be combined with those from the unrestricted weights. This is part of an eclectic strategy.

Little research is available to test the value of unit weights relative to unrestricted *a priori* weights.

A Priori Model

With the completion of the steps involved in levels A and B of Exhibit 8-2, you have a completely operational model to use in forecasting change. Although this extent of *a priori* analysis is rarely achieved in practice, published reports include an economic study by Theil and Goldberger (1961), a forecast of the demand for Ph.D.s by Cartter (1965), a forecast of bank assets by SMITH and BRAINARD [1976], and predictions of the heights of five-year-old boys in Iowa by Ehrenberg (1975). An example of an *a priori* model was provided in my study of the photographic market:

Armstrong (1968a) developed an *a priori* model that could be used to forecast the changes in camera sales by country:

$$\frac{Y_{t+h}}{Y_t} = (1.02)^h \left(\frac{M_{t+h}}{M_t}\right)^{1.0} \left(\frac{I_{t+h}}{I_t}\right)^{1.3} \left(\frac{C_{t+h}}{C_t}\right)^{-1.4}$$

where t = the current year
h = the number of years in the future
Y = camera sales (units)

M = the market size (the number of literate adults)

I = a measure of people's ability to buy (real personal consumption expenditure per capita)

C = the cost to consumers of camera goods of constant quality

This model stated that the percentage change in camera sales could be predicted using changes due to quality improvements and other excluded variables (2% per year growth), and to the percentage changes in market size, income, and camera prices. Roughly speaking, a 1% increase in income would lead to a 1.3% increase in sales, while a 1% decrease in price would lead to a 1.4% increase in sales.

This *a priori* analysis was used in obtaining **backcasts**[G] of the change in camera sales from 1960 to 1954. These backcasts were more accurate than those from a model assuming no change (MAPEs of 30% and 67%, respectively), and also more accurate than an extrapolation model based on a no-change component and a component assuming a constant trend within each country. (The MAPE for this combined extrapolation was 43%.)

STEPWISE REGRESSION

Some analysts prefer to skip the *a priori* analysis and go directly to the data. They let the data speak for themselves. Why do they ignore all that good advice about *a priori* analysis? There are at least two explanations: one is related to technology, and the other to publication standards.

Computers have reduced the cost of exploratory research. Stepwise regression procedures allow one to search through many possible predictor variables in order to find the "best" model. By contrast *a priori* analysis is slow and subjective. Unfortunately, the temptation to trust the computer is great.

Publication practices by academic journals may also inhibit *a priori* analysis. It is difficult to present the *a priori* analysis clearly and succinctly, not to mention that this part of the paper seems subjective. Some journals prefer to give the impression that science is untouched by human hands.

Setwise regression[G], where the analyst decides what possible groupings of variables make sense, then tests the various groupings, is more sensible, or should I say less dangerous. PEDHAZUR [1982, pp. 164–167] decribes it in more detail. (He calls it "blockwise regression.") Williams and Linden (1971) offer a computer program for setwise regression.

MORRIS [1981] presents stepwise procedures (and a computer program) to maximize predictive validity in a cross-validated sample. I'm skeptical about this procedure.

If you insist on using stepwise regression, do not use traditional tests of statistical significance. McINTYRE et al. [1983] provide tables that reflect the number of variables *examined*, rather than the number used in the final model.

OBJECTIVE DATA

Although *a priori* information is often valuable, it also contains the errors of the past. Sometimes our folklore on causality is incorrect. It is useful, then, to obtain objective data to verify as well as to improve upon our *a priori* information. This section describes the types of data that can be used, both experimental and historical. The value of multiple data sources is also examined. Finally, consideration is given to *a priori* analysis of the *data*.

One major distinction is the use of experimental vs. historical (**nonexperimental**^{G}) data. With experimental data, the effects of each variable can be isolated for study instead of trusting to fate, as with historical data. Furthermore, the effects of large changes can be assessed in situations where historical data may not exist. Numerous sources describe how to design experiments (e.g., Boyd and Westfall, 1981).

Laboratory experiments are especially advantageous for the assessment of large changes. The controls are more exact, enabling one to introduce and monitor change. Also, confidentiality can be maintained.

Field experiments are advantageous because they are more realistic than laboratory experiments. On the other hand, they are more expensive, it is difficult to bring about the intended changes, and confidentiality is usually sacrificed. COOK and CAMPBELL [1979] describe procedures for field experiments.

Historical data are advantageous because they are economical and realistic. For this reason, most econometric work is done with such data. Blalock (1964) discusses the problems and opportunities in trying to assess causality from historical data. The more important problems can be summarized as follows:

1. Objective data may be limited.
2. The data may not be accurate.
3. The **observations**[G] may not be independent of one another. (For time series this is called autocorrelation, but it can also occur for cross-sectional data. For example, the subjects in an experiment may talk to one another, so each subject's action is not independent.)
4. The factors may not vary. To assess relationships, it is necessary that both the dependent and the causal factors vary. The more variation there is, the easier it will be to measure the relationship.
5. The causal factors should vary independently of one another. Correlation among the independent variables, called **multicollinearity**[G], makes it difficult to determine which of the causal factors should get the credit for changes in the dependent variable. In effect, multicollinearity introduces uncertainty into the estimates of relationships.
6. The measurement process may have affected the results. This is typical for data collected in organizations; the measures may become goals and cause people to act differently.

The preceding criteria (except for item 6) can be examined by considering their effects upon regression analysis. The variance of a coefficient in a regression model is

$$
\text{Var}(b) = \frac{\text{Var}(Y|X)}{\sqrt{\sum_{d=1}^{D}(X_d - \overline{X})^2}} = \frac{\text{Var}(Y|X)}{\sqrt{\text{Var}\,X}\,\sqrt{D}}
$$

where D is the number of historical time periods.

This equation says that uncertainty in the estimate of the regression coefficient [Var (b)] is due to variations in Y that are not explained by the X's, or to a failure to secure a large number of observations that display wide fluctuations. Therefore, to reduce the variance of the estimate of the coefficient (i.e., to increase the reliability of the estimate), one can:

1. Increase the denominator by increasing the spread $(X_d - \overline{X})$; that is, find data sets with large variations in each causal variable. This is especially useful if the variation is centered around the likely values expected during the forecast horizon (see Daniel and Heerema, 1950); this may require experimentation.
2. Increase D, that is, increase the sample size of the historical data.
3. Decrease Var $(Y|X)$; that is, reduce the variation in Y that is due to factors other than X by:

(a) Choosing more homogeneous sample observations (avoid errors, windsorize, define the sample in accordance with well-defined criteria),

(b) Ensuring that "other factors" do not vary (experiment),

(c) Measuring the other factors and including them in the measurement model,

(d) Grouping observations and averaging (e.g., use a 4-year moving average), and

(e) Obtaining multiple measures for each factor and averaging them.

In summary, the ideal data set should provide many independent observations in which the variables of interest (dependent and causal) show wide variations, and the effects of all other causal variables are small.

The problem presented by the interaction between the measurement and the behavior might be assessed experimentally. If this is not possible, you might try to obtain data in ways where the measurement is not obvious to people. One example: to estimate how many people have looked at an exhibit in a museum, one could measure the amount of wear in the floor covering in front of the exhibit. An argument in favor of the use of such **unobtrusive data**[G] and a collection of clever examples can be found in Webb et al. (1973).

What should you do in the typical case where the forecasting budget does not allow for experimentation and none of the data approaches the ideal standards? You should use eclectic research and obtain different types of historical data! Find data that suffer from different defects in the hope that the defects will compensate for one another.

To help in the search for different types of data, I have provided the "Data Matrix" in Exhibit 8-4. The rows represent decision units such as people, organizations, or countries. The columns represent different time periods (days, weeks, months, quarters, or years).

Three types of data are illustrated in Exhibit 8-4. These data are described here, and consideration is given to their advantages and disadvantages in typical situations.

1. **Time series**[G] data take a given decision unit (e.g., c) and examine it at different points in time. For example, c could represent the U.S. photographic industry from 1960 to 1978. This type of data has been used in economics since 1862 (Zarnowitz, 1968). Time series data suffer from numerous problems. In many cases, there are few observations. In most cases, there is a lack of variation in the data, substantial measurement error, **interaction**[G], autocorrelation, and

Exhibit 8-4   THE DATA MATRIX

Decision Units	1	2	3	Time Periods $\bullet \bullet \bullet \bullet \bullet \bullet \bullet \bullet \bullet$	t
a					
b					
c				Time series	
$\bullet$					
$\bullet$					
$\bullet$					
$\bullet$					
n					

Cross-sectional

Longitudinal

multicollinearity. (These problems are discussed below in more detail.) So what do these data have in their favor? Well, they generally provide cheap, fast, and realistic information that is especially useful for estimating current status.

2. **Cross-sectional data**[G] take a given period of time (e.g., period 2) and examine differences among decision units. Such data have been used in economics since 1883 (Zarnowitz, 1968). The advantages of cross-sectional data over time series data are that larger variations can generally be found in the dependent variable and in the causal factors, there is less multicollinearity, and there is greater independence among the observations. The big disadvantage is the loss in realism for situations involving predictions of the future. Here is an example of the analysis of cross-sectional data:

In Armstrong (1968a), household survey data for the United States were used to obtain an estimate of income elasticity for camera purchases. The following estimate was obtained:

$$Y = (0.0000124)(I)^{1.5}$$

where Y is the dollar expenditure per potential buyer for photographic goods (per year), and I is the average income in the particular income category (per year). The constant term is merely a scaling factor. The income elasticity, 1.5, is in line with prior expectations.

3. **Longitudinal data**[G] take a sample of decision units (e.g., a through n) and examine changes over time (e.g., the difference between periods 2 and t). The use of this type of data is more recent than the use of time series and cross-sectional data. Longitudinal data generally cost more to obtain, but they provide one big advantage over time series data: each observation serves as its own control. In other words, the unique aspects of each decision unit are constant over time and are therefore less likely to enter into an explanation about changes. An early example of the analysis of longitudinal data is provided by Bandeen (1957). Another is drawn from my study of the international photographic market:

In Armstrong (1968a), longitudinal data from 21 countries were examined to obtain estimates of price and income elasticity:

$$\left(\frac{Y_{\overline{64\ 65}}}{Y_{\overline{60\ 61}}}\right) = (1.02)^d \left(\frac{I_{\overline{64\ 65}}}{I_{\overline{60\ 61}}}\right)^{1.1} \left(\frac{C_{\overline{64\ 65}}}{C_{\overline{60\ 61}}}\right)^{-0.4}$$

where the constant term 1.02 was fixed *a priori* to represent technological change, and

Y = rate of unit camera sales
    per potential buyer (per year)
d = number of years between initial
    and final data
I = a measure of income
C = price of camera goods (as estimated
    from changes in price of
    identical cameras in annual Sears catalogues)
$\overline{64\text{–}65}$ = the average for the years 1964 and 1965,
$\overline{60\text{–}61}$ = the average for the years 1960 and 1961.

In other words, each observation consists of the change in camera sales for a given country from the beginning to the end of the historical period, and the corresponding changes in income and the price of cameras for that country. The regression analyzes differences among these country change scores.

Multiple Data Sources

A listing of the various types of data is presented in Exhibit 8-5, along with a rating of their advantages and disadvantages. For laboratory experiments, only cross-sectional data are examined because it is unusual to obtain longitudinal or time series data from such experiments. The ratings required much subjectivity, and a difference of one point is not crucial. You may even prefer to insert your own ratings to assess the data for a particular problem. The ratings are relevant within columns but *should not* be added across columns (unless one has developed measures of importance for each column).

Exhibit 8-5 can be used after the analyst has identified the most important criteria. The analyst can then see how well each type of data meets the important criteria by examining the columns in Exhibit 8-5. Because some types of data are strong on certain criteria and weak on others, it is likely that more than one type of data should be used to "supplement" the weak areas.

The importance of finding different types of data is illustrated by the attempt to determine whether a causal link exists between smoking and cancer. Initial studies were criticized for numerous weaknesses. Over many years of study, however, a smoking-cancer relationship has been identified from cross-sectional data, using comparisons across people and across countries. It has been demonstrated by time series data, and by longitudinal data where specific people or other animals were followed across time. The results of these analyses show that the relationship holds for different populations, different geographical regions, and different times. (But some people still do not believe that a causal relationship exists. They are generally smokers or workers in the cigarette industry. For most of them, there is no information that could possibly change their minds. If you *do* want evidence, you can go as far back as Cornfield, 1954.)

Studies that have combined different types of data go back many years. Among them are:

Exhibit 8-5 RATINGS OF DATA FOR ECONOMETRIC METHODS
(1 = Unfavorable and 5 = Most Favorable)

Type of Data	Speed	Cost	Measurement Error	Confidentiality	Variation	Multi-collinearity	Independent Observations	Inter-action	Realism
Laboratory experiment									
Cross-sectional	3	3	5	5	5	5	5	5	1
Field experiment									
Cross-sectional	2	2	3	3	4	5	5	4	4
Longitudinal	1	1	4	2	4	5	3	4	5
Time series	1	1	2	2	4	4	3	4	5
Historical Data									
Cross-sectional	5	5	1	1	3	3	3	3	3
Longitudinal	5	4	3	1	1	1	1	2	5
Time series	5	5	1	1	1	1	1	1	5

Goreux (1957) in making long-range projections of food consumption, Kuh (1959) in a study on macroeconomics, Cook and Selltiz (1964) in studies on attitude measurement, Houthakker (1965) in an international study of consumer expenditures, Stout (1969) in studying the price elasticity of a specific beverage, and Mize and Ulveling (1970) in a study of air travel.

The eclectic use of data is expected to be especially helpful in situations where:

1. Uncertainty is high, and
2. Changes are large.

These conditions occur often in the social sciences. The limited evidence available suggests that there are small benefits for short-range forecasting, that the gains for medium-term forecasting are modest, and, surprisingly, that the gains for long-range forecasting are also only modest. Overall, the eclectic use of data led to increased costs and provided only small gains in accuracy, as shown in the following studies, all of which were done some time ago:

Schupack (1962) found that a combination of time series and cross-sectional data did not yield more accurate forecasts than those obtained from time series data in 1-year forecasts for 32 food items. In fact, the combination did slightly poorer.

Armstrong (1968a) used various types of data to obtain backcasts of the photographic market. The accuracy from this approach was compared with that from a single set of data. The combination approach used:

1. Cross-sectional data from 30 countries (averaged over 1960–1965)
2. Longitudinal data from 21 countries ($\overline{1964–1965}$ to $\overline{1960–1961}$)
3. Cross-sectional data on 1,200 U.S. households (aggregated by six income categories)

Each of the data sets had its own advantages and its own limitations. The household data were useful because large variations

in income were found and the quality of cameras offered for sale
was held constant; however, the lack of fluctuations in price prevented an estimate of price elasticity. Cross-sectional data by
country provided large differences in both price and income, but
other factors that caused differences among countries could not
be included. The longitudinal data across countries used each
country as its own control, thus avoiding many of the factors that
caused variation among countries. The longitudinal data suffered
from collinearity between price and income and from large measurement errors in the causal variables. The combination and
longitudinal-data-only models were compared in an unconditional
backcast for 17 countries for 1954 (assuming that nothing was
known before 1960). The combination model was slightly more
accurate with a MAPE of 21% vs. 26% for the longitudinal model.

Ferber (1969) reported that one of his thesis students, Abo-Baker,
found a combination cross-section and time series approach to be
better than one using only time series data or one using only
cross-sectional data in forecasting expenditures for new and used
cars. This finding was not upheld in his forecast of consumption
expenditures for public transportation.

Lyon (1969) used aggregate time series data for 1935–1961 and
11 different cross-sections over states (using each year from 1951–
1961) in developing a model to forecast U.S. cigarette consumption over a five-year period from 1962–1966. The combination
model was superior (in four of the five years) to forecasts generated
from a model based only on time series.

Laughhunn (1969, Chapter 5) compared models developed from
combinations of cross-section and time series, with models from
time series only. **Conditional forecasts**[G] were made for a one-
to five-year horizon for nine categories of consumer expenditures.
For the one-year forecasts, the combination approach yielded more
accurate predictions on only three of the nine categories. However,
as the forecast horizon lengthened, the combination method gained

relative to the time series approach until it was superior on seven of nine categories for both the four- and the five-year horizons.

A Priori Analyses of the Data

A priori analysis can be carried out on the data as well as the model. (These analyses were listed in level *C* in Exhibit 8-2.) This section examines the value of *a priori* adjustments for biases expected in the data.

The procedure for cleaning the data is similar to that in Chapter 7 (p. 161–162). Efforts should be made to deal with outliers, for example, and this should be done before using these data to estimate values for the forecasting model.

The data for a given conceptual variable may incorporate variation due to other variables. For example, income estimates for a country may be unduly influenced by exchange rates or by the black market and thus may provide poor estimates of "ability to purchase." If you suspect such biases in the data, you can consider two strategies to compensate for them. One is to find alternative indicators for the same conceptual variable, and then to average these in the hope of washing out the variation due to irrelevant factors (e.g., different estimates of ability to buy should be obtained).

The second strategy is to adjust the observations. Whether such an adjustment is useful is speculative. I tested this approach in my study of the photographic market and was surprised to find that it had no predictive validity.

In Armstrong (1968a), the value of adjusting observations was examined. This was an ideal situation for such a test because there were substantial differences among countries; also, articles about certain national camera markets claimed that unusual factors, such as high tourist sales, were present. I made an intensive examination of 31 countries, and predicted the residual error before the econometric model was used to fit the data in the calibration sample. For 17 countries, no difference was expected from the model; however, for the remaining 14 countries, the predictions of direction were correct on only 5 countries. This was a disappointing result in view of the strong prior knowledge that was claimed by the various sources—as well as by my own confidence in this strategy!

Because measurement error is so common, it is important to consider its effects. Errors can occur in either the dependent variable or the causal variables.

The presence of measurement error in the dependent variable leads to uncertainty in the estimates of the relationships. This uncertainty will be reflected in the confidence intervals estimated by regression analysis. One solution is to gain additional information on the dependent variable by finding additional observations.

When the size of the measurement error varies over the range of the independent variables (heteroscedasticity), it may be possible to obtain a more efficient estimate by the use of a transformation. This is a risky strategy, however, for the transformation changes the statement about the type of relationship; the relationship should be decided on the basis of the *a priori* analysis, *not* on the basis of what will provide the most reliable estimate.

Measurement error in the causal variables will increase uncertainty and lead to bias in the estimates of the coefficients. This is illustrated in Exhibit 8-6. Case A, with no error, is obvious. In case B, the 3's represent the observed value of X when the "true" value was 3.0. The 4's are the observed values of X when the true value was 4.0, and similarly for the 5's. Case C follows the same pattern but with more error. The line in each case is chosen to minimize the sum of the square of the errors in "fitting" or "explaining" Y (i.e., to minimize the square of the vertical distances from the line to the observations). Note the basic conclusion from Exhibit 8-6: as the error increases, the estimated relationship is biased toward zero, while the constant term is biased away from zero.

Adjustments can be made to compensate for certain types of errors in the causal variables. In general, when a causal variable contains information of poor quality (high error), less emphasis should be placed upon that information. To place less emphasis upon a relationship implies that its absolute value should be reduced. This is what the regression model did in Exhibit 8-6. If one assumes that the measurement error is random, the extent of the bias toward zero can be estimated from:

$$b = (1 + E)\hat{b}$$

where $\hat{b}$ is the regression estimate of the relationship, b is the true relationship, and E is the ratio of the error variance to the true variance. If there were no errors ($E = 0$), then the regression estimate would provide an unbiased estimate of the relationship. If the error variance were equal to the true variance, then $E = 1$ and $b = (2)\hat{b}$; that is, the true coefficient would be twice as large as the estimated

Exhibit 8-6   BIAS DUE TO RANDOM ERROR

(Circled numbers represent true values of X)

Case A: No Measurement Error in X

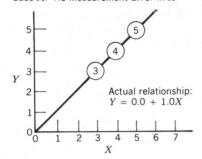

Actual relationship:
$Y = 0.0 + 1.0X$

Case B: Modest Measurement Error in X

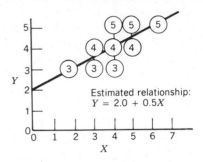

Estimated relationship:
$Y = 2.0 + 0.5X$

Case C: Large Measurement Error in X

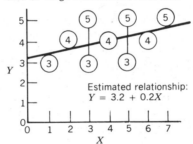

Estimated relationship:
$Y = 3.2 + 0.2X$

Note: The limiting solution, with infinite
measurement error, would be the
horizontal line $Y = 4.0$, which is
the average value for Y in this case.

coefficient. (For a discussion on how this formula was obtained, see a textbook on econometrics. I used Johnston, 1963, p. 150.)

The difficulties with the preceding formula for obtaining the true relationship from the estimated relationship are twofold. First, the assumption was made that there was no systematic error component; and, second, the estimate of the E factor must generally be estimated judgmentally.

The preceding discussion focused on the effect that error has upon the estimate of a given causal relationship. The effect upon the constant term was also noted. There is still another effect, however: errors in a given causal variable, say X_1, will generally affect the estimates of other causal relationships, say the relationship between X_2 and Y.

Adjustments for bias caused by measurement error are important when the measurement error is large relative to the true variation and when some precision is required in the estimate of the magnitude. This situation is expected only when large changes occur, as in long-range forecasting. I made a test of this hypothesis in my study of the international camera market (Armstrong, 1968a). Although the measurement errors were large, virtually no improvement in the accuracy of long-range backcasts of camera sales occurred when adjustments were made for bias in the estimates of the coefficients. There is little evidence, then, to support adjusting for bias—and little evidence to refute it. For short-term forecasting, adjusting for bias is expected to be of little value.

INTERMISSION: Take a long break. You owe it to yourself!

ANALYZING THE DATA

A priori analysis provides one way to obtain coefficients for the causal relationships. This section considers two methods to estimate these relationships from objective data: experience tables and regression methods. More attention is given to regression methods; they offer more promise and are more convenient than experience tables. The problems with using regression analysis are reviewed, and suggestions are made for overcoming these difficulties.

In spite of the promise of regression analysis, simplicity still has great merit. Evidence is provided to compare simple and complex methods.

Experience Tables

The origins of experience tables can be traced to Ben Franklin's "moral or prudential algebra" (Dawes and Corrigan, 1974). Experience tables involve a scoring procedure, such as:

+1 for a favorable rating on a factor
  0 for an indeterminate rating
−1 for an unfavorable rating

The score for an individual is simply the total across all factors. In some situations, the scoring may allow for only two categories, favorable and unfavorable, in which case +1 and 0 can be used.

The direction of the relationship is generally specified *a priori*. But at what point does a score become favorable or unfavorable? In general, the researcher experiments with the data and tries different levels to define a favorable rating. It seems preferable, however, to make these decisions *a priori* if possible . . . and it is nearly always possible.

Finally, the experience table is constructed by examining the behavior associated with each score. For example, what behavior is associated with a score of +12? With one of −6? It helps at this point to have ample objective data.

Forecasts are made by calculating the score for an individual, and then using the average behavior for people with that score.

Experience tables have been used in many fields. For example, the Burgess method in sociology, developed in the 1920s by Ernest W. Burgess, involved the examination of a large number of predictive factors (Burgess, 1939). Each factor was classified as being "favorable" or "unfavorable." A score was obtained for each observation by adding the number of favorable factors. For example, in predicting the probable success of paroling an eligible individual from prison, if 18 of 25 factors were favorable the prisoner's score would be 18. An examination of the data was then made to determine the percentage of successful parolees among those who scored 18. Experience tables were developed to indicate the success rate on parole for each score.

Ernest Burgess used a large number of causal variables. He did not differentiate between variables; all were considered to be of equal importance. Also, Burgess did not give a heavier weight to a more positive rating on a given factor; both were simply called "favorable." To correct some of these shortcomings, Glueck and Glueck (1959) suggested that only a small number of variables should be used and that variable weightings be obtained from data for each of the causal variables. Thus, if age were related to success on parole, middle-aged people would score higher than young people, and the geriatric set would score higher than middle-aged people.

Although the improvements proposed by the Gluecks seem reasonable, a review by Gough (1962) was pessimistic. He concluded that the Glueck proposals would not yield substantial improvements over Burgess (thus providing more evidence on the importance of being Ernest). Similar conclusions have been reached in personnel psychology by Quinn and Mangione (1973), although Stuckert offers mild support for the Glueck index:

Stuckert (1958) predicted the grade-point averages for about 500 freshmen at Ohio State for both 1949 and 1950. A Glueck index yielded slightly more accurate predictions than did a Burgess index.

Problems with experience tables persist even after making the adjustments proposed by the Gluecks. For instance, variables are examined one at a time; this can lead to serious errors when the data suffer from multicollinearity and interaction. An additional problem is the number of subjective inputs necessary. These problems can be overcome to a great extent by using regression analysis.

Regression Analysis

Before plunging ahead with regression analysis, it is important to distinguish between the measurement model and the **forecasting model**[G]. Previously the discussion related to obtaining estimates for use in the forecasting model. To obtain these estimates, one creates a measurement model to analyze the data. Regression analysis yields a measurement model, and it is seldom that the measurement model corresponds exactly to the forecasting model. In retrospect this statement seems obvious. But it isn't! The confusion between the measurement model and the forecasting model has led to serious errors in forecasting. This has been especially true whenever regression analysis was used. Although they frequently look the same, the measurement model differs from the forecasting model in three ways:

1. The measurement model contains "nuisance variables." These variables explain differences among observations in the data, but they are of no interest in the forecasting model. This situation occurs because, as a general rule, the analyst should include all variables that are important in explaining variation. An example, drawn from my study of the photographic market, is presented in the following paragraph. The one exception to this rule is that, if the nuisance variables are not correlated with the variables in the measurement model, they can be ignored altogether. (That is, they will not affect the regression weights.) This may be a reasonable assumption for experimental data, but it is a risky one for historical data:

In Armstrong (1968a), data from an international cross section were used to obtain estimates of income and price elasticity. The measurement model included measures of the climate of each country. These variables were related to differences in camera sales among countries, but they were irrelevant in forecasting change because the climate in each country was not expected to change substantially over the forecast horizon, nor could such changes be forecast.

2. The estimates from a measurement model should be combined with estimates from the *a priori* analysis and with estimates from other measurement models.
3. The estimates from the measurement model must be adjusted to represent the conditions faced during the forecast horizon. The measurement model may use data that are not representative of the forecast situation.

The first point is considered in this section, and the second and third points are discussed later in the chapter.

I am not going to discuss the details of regression analysis. Others have done so admirably:

Good descriptions of regression analysis are provided in Blalock (1979) and Johnston (1984). Mathematical wizards enjoy Malinvaud (1980). Advice that is oriented toward practical applications may be found in Cohen and Cohen (1975), Draper and Smith (1981), and PEDHAZUR [1982]. LEVENBACH and CLEARY [1984], and MAKRIDAKIS, WHEELWRIGHT, and McGEE [1983] provide a detailed treatment with emphasis on forecasting.

Discriminant analysis^G is a special form of regression analysis. It is used when the dependent variable refers only to categorical data. Typically, only two states are of interest (e.g., purchase or no purchase, innocent or guilty, pass or fail), although more categories can be handled. Because this version offers little more than convenience over regression analysis, no specific discussion is provided here. In general, the opportunities and problems correspond to those of regression analysis (numerous sources describe discriminant analysis—e.g., Green and Tull, 1978, PEDHAZUR [1982].

Many of you already know about regression analysis. (If you do not, please bear with me, and pay attention to the glossary.)

Like experience tables, regression analysis is inexpensive. But regression analysis has three major advantages over experience tables:

1. It uses the data in a more objective way; that is, the biases of the researcher become less important.
2. It estimates partial effects of each causal variable rather than gross effects.
3. It uses the data more efficiently.

In short, regression analysis has clear-cut advantages over experience tables. Researchers in nearly every field have switched from experience tables to regression tables.

Regression analysis does have its problems. Fortunately, much study has been done on these problems, and remedies have been proposed. In the following subsections, measurement error, interaction, multi-collinearity, autocorrelation, and simultaneous causality are discussed.

Measurement Error. For simple measurement models, the effect of measurement error upon the estimate of the causal relationship appears to be modest. Denton and Kuiper (1965), Denton and Oksanen (1972), and McDonald (1975) examined the impact of errors on estimates obtained from economic data. In each study, little change was noted when the preliminary data were replaced by more accurate data.

When measurement error is serious, it is important to keep the measurement model simple. This can be done as follows:

1. Using a small number of causal variables (in cases with extreme measurement error, the extrapolation method would be preferred as it uses no causal variables).
2. Using a simple functional form. Addition is preferable to multiplication, and multiplication is preferable to raising to powers greater than 1.0. Complex forms tend to magnify errors.
3. Using a simple set of equations. Avoid simultaneous equations.
4. Minimizing the sum of the absolute errors rather than the sum of the squared errors (Wiginton, 1972).

Particular attention should be given to obtaining accurate measures or the dependent variable:

KEREN and NEWMAN [1978], using simulation, found that errors in the dependent variable are more damaging than errors in the causal variable, which is not surprising.

Interaction. Interaction means that the relationship between two variables, say Y and X_1, is dependent upon the value of a third variable, say X_2. For example, it has been found that the relationship between education and income varies according to race. Another example is that certain chemicals do not react when placed together unless a catalyst is present.

Failure to account properly for interaction may lead to problems in forecasting. For example, a particular treatment for a given ailment may cure an adult but prove fatal to an infant. Efforts to rehabilitate a criminal may lead to different results depending upon whether the effort is initiated by the criminal, a peer group, or a judge.

Two strategies have been used in dealing with interaction. The first has been to find a functional form that captures the effects of interaction (e.g., the multiplicative form can represent certain types of interaction). The other approach has been to use segmentation to account for interaction, and then to use econometric methods within segments. This latter strategy is discussed in Chapter 10.

Multicollinearity. Multiple regression analysis offers advantages over experience tables especially in cases with multicollinearity. Still, high multicollinearity makes it difficult to obtain estimates (Blalock, 1963).

Multicollinearity can be dealt with in a number of ways. Probably the worst piece of advice is to drop one of the correlated variables. This will reduce the standard error at the cost of introducing bias into the estimate of the coefficient. The regression analysis should include all important variables. The idea of dropping one of the important variables to solve the problem of multicollinearity reminds me of the statement by a U.S. Army colonel that a Vietnamese village had to be destroyed in order to save it.

Another approach to multicollinearity has been to use factor analysis to create a small number of independent causal factors from the original set. This approach is the technician's delight, but the theoretician's nightmare. I side with the theoreticians. The *a priori* analysis should indicate which variables to use. If more than one measure is employed to represent a concept, the analyst can simply create an index using subjective weights (e.g., take an arithmetic average). Factor analysis has disadvantages because it is more difficult to understand,

and because it may yield factors that make little sense. Tom Swift learned this the hard way:

Armstrong (1967) reported on a study by Tom Swift. Tom, it seems, was given data on some blocks of metal. He had no prior knowledge about these blocks, but he did know how to use factor analysis and data had been collected for 11 variables. Tom interpreted three key factors: (1) compactness, (2) intensity, and (3) shortness. In fact, the data were explained exactly by five factors: (1) length, (2) width, (3) height, (4) density, and (5) cost per pound. Hopefully, Tom's study does not indicate the need for further research of this type.

Studies from the real world did not do much better than Tom Swift. To date, the evidence suggests that factor analysis is not helpful in forecasting. I have found eight studies:

Ostlund (1973) reduced 18 causal variables to seven factors and used these factors to predict the adoption of six different consumer products. This factor analysis resulted in a loss of predictive power.

Lack of success for factor analysis was also reported by Rock et al. (1970) with simulated data; Mayfield (1972), GOMEZ-MEJIA, PAGE, and TORNOW [1982], and MITCHELL and KLIMOSKI [1982] in personnel psychology; ALUMBAUGH et al. [1978] in parole prediction; and by Massy (1965), and MOORE [1982] in marketing.

The only good solutions to multicollinearity involve the use of information from other sources. *A priori* estimates provide one such source. Exhibit 8-5 offers ideas about other types of data. Estimates from these other sources can then be used to remove one of the variables from the measurement model. For example, assume that you are predicting the sales of caribou chips (Y) from knowledge of income (I) and the cost to consumers (C) for caribou chips and you are using household survey data:

$$Y = a + b_1 I + b_2 C$$

If I and C are highly correlated, it is difficult to estimate b_1 and b_2. But b_2 might be estimated separately by analyzing a field experiment where the price of caribou chips is varied by region. This estimate of b_2 can then be used to remove the price effect from the household survey data:

$$Y' = Y - b_2C$$

The income coefficient, b_1, is then estimated from

$$Y' = a + b_1I$$

Autocorrelation. For time series data, it is common for errors to be correlated with one another over time. When this occurs, the analyst is likely to falsely assume greater certainty in the estimates of the relationships. Autocorrelation may be detected by the **Durbin-Watson statistic**[G] (e.g., see Johnston, 1963, p. 192). This statistic picks up autocorrelation between adjacent time periods. The **runs test**[G] (Siegel, 1956, p. 52) is another way to spot autocorrelation.

One solution to autocorrelation is to formulate the model in terms of first differences; that is, the period-to-period changes in the dependent variable are related to the period-to-period changes in the causal variables. The resulting estimates of certainty are improved. But the cure is worse than the problem as far as long-range forecasting is concerned; the first-differences model picks up short-range effects instead of long-range effects.

Another solution is to use longer time periods (e.g., yearly rather than quarterly data). This is especially useful for long-range forecasting.

In general, however, the estimates themselves are not affected much by autocorrelation, and I have been unable to find much evidence that forecast accuracy is impaired. (Although GRANGER and NEWBOLD [1977, pp. 202–214], and DIELMAN [1985] provide some disconfirming evidence to this). So it is seldom worth bothering to make any correction. A great deal of fuss is created over autocorrelation, not because it interferes with the development of a forecasting model, but because it messes up the statistician's tests of significance. As discussed in Part III of this book, statistical testing will cause few problems because the same data do not have to be used for both estimating relationships and testing the statistical significance of the forecasts.

Simultaneous Causality. Although simultaneous causality might create difficulties in estimating causal relationships, it is not clear that these cause serious problems in forecasting. Certainly there has been no lack of research on this topic. My conclusion from this research is that attempts to model simultaneous causality have not improved accuracy.

The solutions for simultaneous causality increase the complexity of the model. This, in turn, increases the problems due to measurement error, interferes with implementation, and raises the likelihood of mistakes.

The simultaneous prediction of a set of dependent variables, commonly called canonical correlation, is not recommended. It can interfere with causal thinking, add complexity, and, as found in PRISTO [1979] and FRALICX and RAJU [1982], it harms predictive ability. So I refuse to provide references on how to use canonical correlation.

Summarizing. The problems involved with using regression analysis are summarized in Exhibit 8-7 along with ideas on what to do and what not to do.

Value of Simplicity

There are two important rules in the use of econometric methods, (1) keep it simple and (2) don't make mistakes. If you obey rule 1, rule 2 becomes easier to follow.

Exhibit 8-7 PROBLEMS AND REMEDIES IN REGRESSION ANALYSIS

Problem	Don't	Do
Measurement error	Ignore	Use a simple measurement model Adjust coefficients for bias
Interaction	—	Use the appropriate functional form Segment data first
Multicollinearity	Omit a variable Use factor analysis	Use other sources of data Form an index from multiple measures
Autocorrelation	Get excited	Obtain more data Use longer time periods
Simultaneous causality	Get excited	Nothing

The advice to avoid mistakes would be unimportant if few mistakes were made in applied work. I suspect errors are more common than we like to think. In addition to witnessing some of my own mistakes, I have, on occasion, seen errors by others.

The advice to keep things simple is not self-evident. To represent reality better, it would help to use a more complex model. Furthermore, it seems reasonable to expect a better representation of reality to yield more accurate forecasts. Doesn't it?

Actually, increases in complexity may lead to less accurate forecasts. Carl Harrington and I examined a model that seemed to be too complex. The model, from Ueno and Tsurumi (1969), had an error twice as large as those obtained from eyeball extrapolations in forecasting U.S. automobile sales from 1966 through 1969. (A description of this study is provided in Appendix H.)

Econometricians, however, believe that increased complexity yields improved accuracy. This also seems to apply to psychometricians [CLIFF, 1983]. This seems evident from the movement toward more complexity. As noted by Leser (1968), the long-term trends have been toward the use of more variables, more equations, more complex functional forms, and more complex interactions among the variables in econometric models. This increase in complexity can be observed by examining various issues of *Econometrica* since 1933 or by comparing econometric textbooks published over the last half century.

To gain further information on whether econometricians believe in a positive relationship between complexity and accuracy, I surveyed a group of leading econometricians. There were 21 respondents from this convenience sample. They were all in economics, most were academics, some were consultants, and most were well known. They were asked the following question by a mail survey: "Do complex methods generally provide more accurate or less accurate forecasts than can be obtained from less complex econometric methods for forecasting in the social sciences—or is there no difference in accuracy?" They were provided with the following definition of complexity: "Complexity" is to be thought of as an index reflecting the methods used to develop the forecasting model:

1. The use of coefficients other than 0 or 1
2. The number of variables (more variables being more complex)
3. The functional relationship (additive being less complex than multiplicative; nonlinear more complex than linear)
4. The number of equations
5. Whether the equations involve simultaneity

Definitions were also provided for the other key terms (see Appendix F).

There was substantial agreement on the value of complexity; 72% of the experts agreed that it was helpful and only 9% disagreed, as shown in Exhibit 8-8. Moreover, the experts were confident in their ratings on the value of complexity. The average confidence level was 4.0, where 1 equals no confidence, 5 equals extremely confident, and the respondents were asked to report a low confidence level if they did not understand the question. The experts were also given the opportunity to express any qualifications they considered important; 88% expressed qualifications, but no single factor was mentioned by more than one respondent.

Exhibit 8-8 EXPERTS' ATTITUDES ON MODEL COMPLEXITY AND FORECASTING ACCURACY (n = 21)

Complex Methods Rated	Percentage
Significantly more accurate	5
Somewhat more accurate	67
No difference (or undecided)	19
Somewhat less accurate	9
Significantly less accurate	0

An examination was made of the published empirical evidence related to the issue of complexity versus accuracy. The following studies provided indirect evidence on the value of complexity in forecasting:

Fox (1956) found small differences between regression coefficients when comparing single-equation and simultaneous equation methods; this would imply little difference in the forecast accuracy.

Friend and Taubman (1964) claimed that their simple model was superior to more complex models (unfortunately they did not include the data from their study; furthermore, the study examined only *ex post*[G] predictive validity).

Guilford (1965, p. 423), using data from a problem in education, obtained coefficients of .224 and .491 with a two-variable model. Virtually identical explanatory power was obtained when the weights were rounded to .2 and .5, then to 1 and 2, and finally to 1 and 1.

Howrey (1969) found no advantage for a more complex model in *ex post* forecasts in a transportation problem.

I reanalyzed data from the study by Jorgenson et al. (1970) and found a perfect negative correlation between the stability of the regression coefficients from one time period to the next and the complexity of each of their four models (as judged by the number of variables in the model). This lack of stability for more complex methods suggests a loss in predictive validity.

Fair (1971) found little difference between his simple model and the more complex Wharton model in a test of *ex post* predictive validity.

Elliott's (1973) study favored simplicity in national economic forecasting.

McLaughlin (1973) examined the accuracy of forecasts from 12 econometric services in the United States. These forecasts were made by models that differed substantially in complexity (although all were complex). No reliable differences in accuracy were found among these models, as the rankings of accuracy for the models in 1971 were negatively correlated (− .3 **Spearman rank correlation**[G]) with those for 1972. (If there are no reliable differences, then no differences will be found between accuracy and complexity.) Similar evidence was provided by PENCAVEL [1971], and Fromm and Klein (1973).

HATJOULLIS and WOOD [1979] examined the relative accuracy of short-range forecasts by five leading British econometric models from 1974 to 1977. (Presumably they differ with respect to complexity.) I reanalyzed these data by calculating the Spearman rank order correlations of the error in one forecast period versus the error in the next period. A positive correlation means that a model that is more accurate for one period will be more accurate the next period. The results, shown here, indicate that the model's relative accuracy in the period was not a good guide to its accuracy in the next period. Disappointing!

Rank Correlations for Accuracy of Five British Forecasting Models*

Variable	75.I vs. 75.II	75.II vs. 76.I	76.I vs. 76.II	76.II vs. 77.I	77.I vs. 77.II	Average
Gross domestic product	− .6	+ .1	+ 1.0	− .1	− .7	− .06
Consumer expenditure	− .1	− .4	− .8	− .8	+ .4	− .34
Gross fixed domestic investment	+ .7	+ .6	+ .4	+ .1	− .1	+ .34
Exports	+ .1	+ .1	− .1	+ .4	− .3	+ .04
Imports	+ .5	+ .2	− .2	+ .2	− .8	− .02
Consumer expenditure price deflator	+ .3	− .1	+ .9	− .2	+ .2	+ .22
Unemployment**	−1.0	− .5	− .5	− .5	+ .5	− .40
Average	− .01	.00	+ .12	− .15	− .13	− .03

*To read the column headings, 75.I means "first half of 1975".
**Based on only three models.

More direct evidence on the value of complexity was sought by using only studies with *ex ante* forecasts. The survey was restricted to studies that had been done in a competent manner. The results of this literature survey are summarized in Exhibit 8-9.

To determine whether the coding of the studies in Exhibit 8-9 was reliable, 8 of the 11 studies (all but McNees, Grant and Bray, and Johnston and McNeal) were independently coded by two research as-

Exhibit 8-9 ACCURACY OF SIMPLE VS. COMPLEX METHODS

Relative Accuracy of Complex Methods	Source of Evidence	Forecast Situation	Criterion for Accuracy	Nature of Comparison	Test of Statistical Significance
Significantly more accurate (p < .05)	—	—	—	—	—
More accurate	Stuckert (1958)	Academic performance	Percent correct	Unit weights vs. regression	None
	McNees (1974)	GNP	Theil coefficient; RMSE, mean absolute error	Small vs. large models	None
	Grant and Bray (1970)	Personnel	Correlation coefficient	Unit weights vs. regression	Armstrong
	Johnston and McNeal (1964)	Medicine	Correlation coefficient	Unit weights vs. regression	Authors
No difference	—	—	—	—	—
Less accurate	Dawes and Corrigan (1974)	Academic performance, simulated data, psychiatric ratings	Correlation coefficient	Unit weights vs. regression	Armstrong
	Lawshe and Schucker (1959)	Academic performance	Percent correct	Unit weights vs. regression	None
	Reiss (1951)	Criminology	Percent correct	Few vs. many causal variables	None
	Wesman and Bennett (1959)	Academic performance	Correlation coefficient	Unit weights vs. regression	None
	Scott and Johnson (1967)	Personnel selection	Percent correct, correlation coefficient	Unit weights vs. regression	None
Significantly less accurate (p < .05)	Claudy (1972)	Simulated data (typical of psychological data)	Correlation coefficient	Unit weights vs. regression	Armstrong
	Summers and Stewart (1968)	Political judgments	Correlation coefficients	Linear vs. nonlinear models	Armstrong

sistants who were unaware of the hypothesis. Small discrepancies were noted on two of these 8 studies.

The studies in Exhibit 8-9 suggest that complexity and accuracy are not closely related. No study reported a significant positive relationship between complexity and accuracy. Overall, seven comparisons favored less complexity, and four favored more complexity. The studies that assessed predictive validity directly were in agreement with the eleven studies that provided indirect evidence—added complexity did not yield improvements in accuracy. My study was published along with commentary by seven econometricians. The commentary did not produce additional empirical evidence.

The implication for the analyst is clear cut: use simple methods! In addition to being as accurate, they are less expensive, less prone to errors, and easier to implement. FILDES and HOWELL [1979] reached a similar conclusion in their literature review.

Of particular importance is the issue of estimating causal relationships by regression or unit weights. Einhorn and Hogarth (1975) examined the evidence on this issue and suggested that regression weights are preferable to unit weights in the following cases:

- Large sample size ($d > 200$) and a dependent variable that is accurately measured.
- Moderate sample size ($50 < d < 200$), a dependent variable that is very accurately measured, and a strong causal relationship ($R^2 > 0.5$).

Schmidt (1971), working with psychological data only, suggested regression weights when:

- Sample sizes are larger than 25.
- There are a small number of causal variables.

Additional evidence, with similar conclusions, has been reported by DORANS and DRASGOW [1978], KEREN and NEWMAN [1978], and PARSONS and HULIN [1982]. PARKER and SRINIVASAN [1976] found contradictory evidence.

Although regression provides only modest benefits over equal weights and then only in certain situations, it is more convenient to use, especially when the estimate of the constant term is important (constant terms are difficult to estimate *a priori*) or when scaling factors are important.

Perhaps the most useful implication from the research on unit weights vs. regression weights is that, in general, forecast accuracy is not very sensitive to the estimates of magnitudes. Once the sign is specified, a rough estimate of magnitude is usually sufficient. In practical terms, the following advice is offered:

1. If the sign of the coefficient in a regression conflicts with the *a priori* sign, drop the variable.
2. When uncertainty is high, combine unit weights and regression weights.
3. For most situations, pick the most convenient method (and that typically means regression analysis).

In general, do not invest a lot of time and energy in learning about all the details of regression analysis. The more sophisticated approaches have not held up well in forecasting [e.g., MORRIS, 1982].

The key factors for selecting between unit weights and regression are summarized in Exhibit 8-10. The assumption is made that the cost of using unit weights is about the same as that for regression weights.

UPDATING THE ESTIMATES

A priori estimates can be improved by incorporating estimates from the objective data. This updating process is especially important as a guard against folklore. For example, teachers assign strong causal relationships between their actions and students' learning, and they feel confident about these relationships. An updating process that draws upon objective data will bring the model closer to reality. In this example, it would reduce the importance of the teacher variable.

The weighting of new information has received much attention. Durbin (1953) presented a classical approach whereby each estimate is weighted inversely by its **variance.**[G] A crucial assumption behind this procedure is that the estimates are unbiased. Such an assumption is seldom realistic, especially when historical rather than experimental data are used. Furthermore, it is no easy matter to estimate the variance of *a priori* estimates.

Linguistics and statistics combined to yield a solution that was socially acceptable to econometricians: **Bayesian analysis.**[G] This provides formal procedures for updating *a priori* estimates. The Bayesian

Exhibit 8-10   UNIT WEIGHTS VS. REGRESSION WEIGHTS

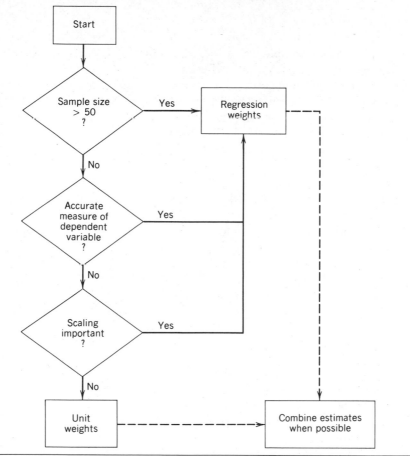

approach is described in numerous sources (e.g., Pratt, Raiffa, and Schlaifer, 1965).

The Bayesian philosophy is appealing, but the implementation is difficult. I was unable to find a Bayesian regression program that worked, though I gave up my search because the details are not important for improving forecast accuracy. That is, forecast accuracy seldom is sensitive to the precise estimate of the relationship. On the other hand, there seems to be no danger in using Bayesian analysis as long as it is used correctly.

A simple way to implement the Bayesian philosophy is to use **con-**

ditional regression analysis,[G] as described by Wold and Jureen (1953). This "poor man's approach to Bayesian regression analysis" involves the following steps:

1. Develop some simple rules to combine the a priori and regression estimates (e.g., use equal weighting).
2. Obtain a combined estimate of one of the relationships, and remove the effect of this relationship from the equation. Reestimate coefficients for the remaining variables.
3. Repeat step 2 until all relationships have been estimated.
4. Omit any combined estimate that violates the a priori sign, then reestimate.

Obviously, this procedure involves subjectivity. But it is easy to understand, and it should produce reasonable results. Examples of this procedure are presented in Armstrong (1970a) and in Tessier and Armstrong (1977).

A simple and reasonable approach is to make the forecasting model the focus of attention, rather than the measurement model. An a priori weighting scheme can be developed. When additional estimates are obtained, they are simply listed in a table, and then a weighting scheme is used to obtain a combined estimate.

The use of combined estimates is expected to be most useful when:

1. large changes are expected,
2. a substantial number of historical data are available,
3. a variety of types of data are available,
4. there are a small number of important relationships, and
5. uncertainty is great.

No empirical studies were found on the value of updating, given conditions 1 to 5. I assessed updating under conditions 1, 2, 3, and 4 in my study of the photographic market; the results, shown in the following, provided no support for the value of updating. Thus, my advice remains speculative.

In Armstrong (1968a, b), unconditional backcasts were made for 1954 camera sales in 17 countries, using data from no earlier than 1960. An a priori version produced forecasts with a $\overline{MAPE}$

of 30%. When the *a priori* model was updated, using results from an international cross-section, from longitudinal data across countries, and from household survey data, the $\overline{\text{MAPE}}$ was reduced to 23%, an improvement that was not statistically significant. Furthermore, the gain was due almost entirely to an improved estimate of the initial (1962) sales. Unfortunately, however, uncertainty was not great in this test because the updated causal estimates were almost identical to the *a priori* estimates: the income elasticity was updated from 1.3 to 1.34, and the price elasticity from -1.4 to -1.80.

ESTIMATING CURRENT STATUS

It is frequently useful to decompose a problem to consider current status and change separately (as noted in Chapter 4). Econometric models can be used for each part of the problem. This section of the chapter examines the value of econometric models for estimating current status.

Econometric models are expected to be most useful for estimating current status in situations where:

1. uncertainty about current status is great, and
2. good information exists on the causal variables.

These situations occur frequently in politics (e.g., what is the military strength of Red China?), in foreign trade (e.g., what is the size of the photographic market in Eastern Europe?), and in marketing. The last area, in particular, has been the subject of much study: estimating market size was studied in the 1930s by Brown (1937a, b), Cowan (1936, 1937), Weld (1939), and Wellman (1939). Little study has been done since 1940. (As an aside, I tried to get the U.S. Department of Commerce interested in using this approach to estimate market size but the idea was turned down by the director.

Do econometric models provide improved estimates of current status? Reference was made in the preceding section of this chapter to Armstrong (1968a, b), where an econometric model led to improved estimates of the current status. This, in turn, led to improvements in long-range backcasts. The following studies provided additional evidence that econometric models yield better estimates of current status:

In Armstrong (1970a), an econometric model was used to predict the level of camera sales. The model was developed from an analysis of 17 countries. The predictions were made for an 11-country validation sample, and an R^2 of 88% was found. The assumption that all countries look like the average country in the analysis sample yields $R^2 = 0$. A more meaningful measure is provided by the $\overline{\text{MAPE}}$ because it also accounts for systematic errors: for the econometric model the $\overline{\text{MAPE}}$ was 31%; for the alternative model (assuming each country was the same as the average for the validation sample) the $\overline{\text{MAPE}}$ was 117%.

Tessier and Armstrong (1977) developed an econometric model to estimate the size of the lodging industry. A combination of the econometric predictions and the preliminary sales data led to improved estimates of lodging sales. A simple average of the preliminary sales data and the econometric estimates reduced the error in predicting "final" sales from 10.5% to 5.7%. The combined estimate also led to improvements in two forecasting tests.

Many forecasters do not bother to decompose a problem into current status and change. In such cases, errors in the estimation of current status will cause systematic errors in the forecasts. This problem is common in short-range economic forecasts. Some remedies are:

• use the most recent errors to adjust the upcoming forecasts, or
• use judgment to adjust the upcoming forecasts.

The evidence presented suggests that the econometric estimate yields improved forecasts when combined with the most recent actual data. An adjustment for the error in an econometric time series model provides an alternative way of accomplishing the same thing. The adjustment is generally done mechanically as follows:

$$Y_{t+h} = a + b_1 X_{1,t+h} + b_2 X_{2,t+h} + k e_t$$

The e_t represents the error in predicting current status for Y (actual minus forecast). The k represents a weighting factor between 0 and 1; it would be 0 if e_t was expected to be unrelated to e_{t+h}, and would be close to 1 if e_t was closely related to e_{t+h}. For example, if the forecast was high by 8% in year t, and $k = 0.5$ for a 1-year forecast, next year's forecast would be decreased by 4%. In general, k will be higher for short-range than for long-range forecasting, because in the short range the error in estimating current status is large relative to the error in forecasting change. (The need for a correction factor is reduced if differencing is used or if the predictors include a lagged dependent variable.) The value of mechanical adjustments has shown up in a number of studies:

Juster (1972) showed how errors in a short-term macroeconomic forecasting model were reduced when the errors from the latest two time periods were used in making adjustments. Evans, Haitovsky, and Treyz (1972) and PFAFF [1977] reached a similar conclusion in their analysis of short-term macroeconomic forecasts. Mechanical adjustments reduced the error in one- and two-quarter forecasts by half, but there was little gain for long-range forecasts. Howrey (1969) obtained improvements from mechanical adjustments in transportation forecasts as did PFAFF [1977] in quarterly forecasts of the money stock. AHLBURG [1984] showed how Theil's decomposition can be used for such an adjustment.

Evidence presented in Chapter 6 (on judgmental methods) suggested that expert judgment is useful for estimating current status. As a result, judgmental adjustments should also help to improve the forecast; studies from economics suggest that they do (e.g., Evans, Haitovsky, and Treyz, 1972; McNees, 1975, HIRSCH, GRIMM and NARASIMHAM [1974]). *This provides an explanation for the apparent discrepancy between economics and psychology:* Economists claim that subjective adjustments will improve forecasts of change, while the literature in psychology indicates just the opposite. I am unaware of evidence from either field that subjective adjustments can improve forecasts of *change*. Such adjustments are often useful, however, in estimating current status. Indeed, McNees (1975) found that subjective adjustments of macroeconomic forecasts were of more benefit in measuring current status than in measuring change. In summary, subjective adjustments should be made for estimates of current status, but not for change.

The particular way in which econometric models are used to estimate current status may be largely a matter of style and convenience. In my opinion, it is better to decompose the problem explicitly. This makes it easier to examine what is happening, and provides a more efficient way to incorporate evidence from different sources. Furthermore, assuming that the model for estimating current status should be the same as the model used to forecast change imposes an unnecessary constraint on the analyst—a constraint that results from the confusion between measurement models and forecasting models.

FORECASTING CHANGE

One reason for the distinction between measurement models and forecasting models is that the coefficients in the measurement model should be adjusted to represent the conditions expected over the forecast horizon. It is possible, for example, that legislation may have been enacted that will alter a relationship in the future; you can make a change in the relationship to reflect this.

In general, the errors that may arise when econometric models are used to forecast change include the following types:

1. Errors in estimating the causal relationships that will hold over the forecast horizon. These, in turn, may be due to:

    (a) Errors in estimating the current relationships, or
    (b) Changes in the relationships over the forecast period.

2. Errors in forecasting changes in the causal variables over the forecast horizon.

Two strategies are examined for dealing with these problems. **Mitigation**[G] is a strategy that assumes the errors cannot be reduced. The second strategy is to try to reduce the errors.

Mitigation

Errors of types 1(a), 1(b), and 2 in the previous list cause forecast errors. The solution is simple: place less emphasis on the causal explanations and more on the trend due to unexplained factors. In other words, as the errors in the model increase, the researcher should move from the causal toward the naive end of the continuum.

A hypothetical example can be used to illustrate, in intuitive terms, why the strategy of mitigation is a good one. God has told you that the income elasticity for camera sales will be exactly +1.3. Because

God is trustworthy, there is no uncertainty about the elasticity of 1.3. However, God did not tell you the extent to which income would change over the next 10 years. To obtain forecasts of the change in income, you asked Ace Consultants. After receiving the income predictions, you learn that Ace Consultants are never truth tellers. The errors are so great that these consultants, in effect, provide random data (but they do it with style, and they know all the latest dances). With so much error in the forecasts of income, you should put no emphasis at all on Ace's "information." The same argument can be made if we assume the reverse situation—that is, you have perfect forecasts of income, but you have no idea about the income elasticity.

In the typical case there is some, but not complete, ignorance about changes in the causal variables. Therefore, the impact of a causal variable, such as income, should be reduced but not eliminated. This can be accomplished either by reducing the magnitude of the forecast coefficient, or by reducing the amount of change forecasted in the causal variable. If it is assumed that

$$\Delta Y = a + b(\Delta X)$$

where ΔY = the change in the dependent variable
$\quad a$ = a constant, but unexplained, trend
$\quad b$ = the causal relationship between X and Y
$\quad \Delta X$ = the change in the causal variable

then, if errors are expected in the model, mitigation can be carried out by reducing the magnitude of either b or ΔX. (Ridge regression provides a sophisticated way to do this. See KEREN and NEWMAN, 1978.)

The strategy of reducing ΔX is useful when the quality of forecasts varies across observations. Thus, in my camera study, different adjustments might be made for controlled markets (where the price change may be easy to forecast, at least for the controllers) and for free markets (where the price change may be difficult to forecast).

The degree of adjustment required in the model can be estimated by either

$$b_h = \left(\frac{1}{1 + E}\right) b$$

or

$$(\Delta X)_h = \left(\frac{1}{1 + E}\right) \Delta X$$

where b_h = the forecast coefficient
  E = the ratio of error variance to true variance
  b = the estimate of the true causal relationship
  $(\Delta X)_h$ = the forecasted change in X
  ΔX = the estimate of the true change in X

At the same time, a compensating change should be made in the constant term. For example, if b_h is used:

$$a = \Delta Y - b_h \, \Delta X$$

The constant term a moves closer to the historical trend line, ΔY, as the absolute value of b_h or ΔX is decreased.

The difficulty of these methods in compensating for errors in forecasting the causal variables lies in estimating E. It is likely that E will have to be based on subjective estimates. Difficult though it may be, you must find some estimate of E to complete the development of the model. To assume that the error is negligible is to assume a value for E of 0.0; this may lead to substantial errors in forecasting.

Mitigation proved to be of substantial importance in my study of the photographic market, but I am not aware of other studies on the value of this strategy.

> In Armstrong (1968a), the forecast coefficients were adjusted to compensate for errors. For example, E was estimated to be 1.0 for the price forecast and 0.33 for income. These estimates yielded forecast coefficients of -0.9 and 1.0 for price and income, respectively. (The causal elasticities for price and income had been estimated to be -1.8 and $+1.3$.) These crude adjustments for error proved to be extremely valuable (compared to assuming $E = 0.0$) for improving the performance of the camera forecasting model. The adjustment for error led to a reduction in the $\overline{\text{MAPE}}$ from 43% to 23% for the backcast of camera sales in 17 countries in 1954, a result that was statistically significant ($p <$ .05).

Reducing the Errors

One possibility for reducing errors is to obtain better estimates for the relationships over the forecast horizon. This strategy was discussed previously.

Another possibility for reducing errors is to obtain better forecasts of the causal variables. The econometric method is of little value if it is not possible to obtain reasonable forecasts of the causal variables.

It was suggested earlier that one criterion for using a variable in the forecasting model is that the variable can itself be forecast with some accuracy. Thus proper selection of variables for the model can help to ensure good forecasts of the causal variables. A popular strategy has been to find leading indicators, that is, variables whose effects will be felt after some time. For example, the sale of automobiles precedes the sale of replacement tires. The signing of a trade agreement precedes a change in foreign trade. Measurement of the leading indicator provides an alternative to *forecasting* the causal variable.

In some cases, considerable time and energy may have been invested by others in forecasting the causal variables. In economics, forecasts of income can be easily obtained from expert surveys and from econometric models of the national economy.

The forecasting of the causal variables is analogous to the forecasting of the dependent variable. Numerous methods are available for making the forecast—judgment, extrapolation, segmentation, or econometrics. If you use the last two methods, you must generate a new set of causal variables (to forecast the original set of causal variables). This explosion of the problem is another argument for simplicity in the original forecasting model.

One puzzling finding is that the point is quickly reached where greater accuracy in forecasting the causal variables does not lead to greater accuracy in forecasting the dependent variable. Obviously, you must strive for fairly accurate forecasts of the causal variables, but in most studies the **unconditional forecasts**[G] were more accurate than the conditional forecasts.

Of the 13 published studies that I found, two showed conditional forecasts to be more accurate (Fair, 1971, 1976), one showed no difference (Theil, 1966), and 10 showed unconditional forecasts to be more accurate: Neild and Shirley, 1961; Friend and Jones, 1964; O'Herlihy et al., 1967; Kennedy, 1969; Stekler, 1970; Evans, Haitovsky, and Treyz, 1972; Juster, 1972; SCHOTT [1978] in a reanalysis of forecasts by Suits, and also in a reanalysis of forecasts by Klein and Goldberger; and HIRSCH, GRIMM, and NARASIMHAM, 1974). All of these studies except O'Herlihy analyzed short-range forecasts. The superiority of the unconditional forecasts is statistically significant ($p < .05$, using the sign test).

It is still a mystery why unconditional forecasts do better. My guess is that, in these studies, many of the causal variables were forecast by judgment; as noted in Chapter 6, judgmental forecasts are conservative. In effect, the forecasts of the causal variables were mitigated. Because none of the analysts in the studies cited explicitly used mitigation, the inadvertent mitigation provided by the unconditional forecasts could have led to improved accuracy.

My recommendations for short-range forecasting are that you try to obtain *reasonably* accurate forecasts of the causal variables and that you use mitigation. The first piece of advice implies that you should not spend much money to obtain accurate forecasts of the causal variables!

My hypothesis for *long-range* forecasting is that accurate forecasts of the causal variables *are* important. Unfortunately, there has been little study on this issue. The one study (by O'Herlihy) was based on a small sample and no significant differences were found.

COMBINED FORECASTS

A combination of forecasts from different econometric models would be expected to improve upon a forecast from a single econometric model. One way to obtain different forecasts is to vary key elements in the econometric model; another approach is to have models developed independently by different researchers. An *a priori* weighting scheme is required in each case.

The strategy of alternative models suggests the development of a set of possible econometric forecasting models rather than a single model. This set of models should be based on various combinations of what the researcher feels are reasonable ways to develop the model. For example, he might try a variety of functional forms, different operational measures for the conceptual variables or different sets of data to develop models, and then use each of these models to develop a forecast. Differences among these forecasts will indicate their sensitivity to the various decisions made by the researcher. The forecasts can then be combined. This combined forecast will be most useful if the preceding forecasts were highly sensitive to the alternative models that were tried. Such a strategy was used successfully by BRANDON, FRITZ, and XANDER [1983] and by the following study:

Namboodiri and Lalu (1971) compared the average forecasts from a set of simple regressions to the forecasts from a single multiple

regression for 10-year forecasts of population growth in 100 counties in North Carolina. The MAPE for the combined forecasts was
5.8 vs. 9.5 for the single regression.

It is difficult to select *a priori* the best econometric model for a given
situation (unless one of the models happens to be *your* model). Because
reasonable people differ in their biases, one strategy is to average the
forecasts from models developed independently by different researchers. If, in fact, biases are serious, and if they differ among researchers,
this averaging process should lead to more accurate forecasts. The use
of alternative model builders also makes it more difficult for analysts
that cheat.

The relative benefit of the strategies of alternative models and of
alternative model builders are based on limited empirical evidence. Of
the two strategies my preference lies with the use of alternative model
builders, even though this is substantially more expensive than the
use of alternative models.

ASSESSING UNCERTAINTY

Numerous components contribute to uncertainty in econometric models:

1. Estimates of the current status,
2. Estimates of the forecast coefficients,
3. Forecasts of the causal variables, and
4. Excluded variables.

Standard errors[G] from a regression program assess primarily the
effects of errors in estimating the forecast coefficients (item 2 above).
Even then, regression analysis provides its most accurate estimates of
uncertainty near the midpoint of the causal variables. For example,
income elasticity is measured most accurately near the average income
level for these data. It is typical for the forecast to depart substantially
from this average. Sometimes the forecast of the causal variable goes
outside the range of the historical data. As this happens, the uncertainty due to the estimate of the causal relationship increases rapidly;
forecasts outside the range of the historical data are risky.

An additional problem in using the standard errors from a regression
program is that they relate only to the particular set of data in question.
The combination of subjective estimates and other objective estimates

should be considered. In the case of estimates from time series data, autocorrelation will produce standard errors that are smaller than they should be.

Despite these problems, the standard errors of the regression are useful. They provide a good measure of the information on each causal variable present in the measurement model. Moreover, this information is available at no additional cost. Be on guard, however; the uncertainty as estimated from the measurement model is not an ideal estimate of the uncertainty in the forecasting model.

Overall assessments of uncertainty can be made by using the forecasting model in a way that is representative of the forecasting situation. An ideal way to assess uncertainty is to withhold data and use the forecasting models to make a series of forecasts; an estimate of uncertainty is then based on the accuracy of these forecasts.

When it is difficult to represent a forecasting situation, you might consider a **Monte Carlo simulation**.[G] This requires an expected distribution for each of the four types of errors listed previously. These distributions can be estimated as follows:

1. Current status can be assessed subjectively or by comparing estimates drawn from different sources. Still another approach is to examine the differences between the preliminary estimates (available at the time of the forecast) and the final estimates (available some time later).
2. The forecast coefficients can be estimated by pooling the standard errors from the *a priori* estimate and from the various regression analyses. An adjustment should be made to reflect the uncertainty about the values of X that will be experienced in the future; this adjustment can be done subjectively.
3. The ability to forecast the causal variables can be assessed by examining previous efforts to forecast these variables. Lacking these, it should be sufficient to use subjective estimates for these distributions: What is the highest you would expect variable X_1 to be? What is the lowest?
4. The errors due to excluded variables can be estimated subjectively. Some help may be gained by examining the proportion of variance that is unexplained in the set of data that best represents the forecasting situation.

The Monte Carlo simulation proceeds by using random numbers to select from each of the distributions. Thus the first trial would require selecting one value from each of the four distributions and using this to calculate a forecast. The process is repeated many times, perhaps 1,000, to build up a distribution of the forecast variables. In addition to providing a distribution for the forecast, the Monte Carlo approach can also allow for an analysis showing which items are most responsible for the uncertainty in the forecast. Such information may be useful in guiding further measurement efforts.

The value of the Monte Carlo simulation seems reasonable, but I was unable to find any empirical evidence pointing one way or the other.

SUMMARY

Econometric models are expected to be useful when good information is available on the causal relationships, and when large and predictable changes are expected in the causal variables. A general approach to the development of econometric models was outlined in Exhibit 8-1— develop an *a priori* model, select data, analyze the data, and update the model.

The various steps in the *a priori* analysis were outlined in Exhibit 8-2. Important areas are the selection of a small set of causal variables and a statement regarding the direction of the relationships. A check-list for the selection of causal variables was summarized in Exhibit 8-3.

By adding three steps to the *a priori* analysis ((1) specification of the pattern of causality, (2) of the functional form, and (3) of the magnitudes of relationships), it is possible to develop an *a priori* model that can be used directly in forecasting. The most important advice in developing this *a priori* model is to keep each step simple.

Stepwise regression provides an alternative to *a priori* analysis, but it is not recommended. Setwise regression is a bit more reasonable, but I believe it is risky to use.

Various types of objective data were considered as sources of estimates for the forecasting model. These include experimental and historical data. They also include cross-sectional, time series, and longitudinal data as illustrated in the data matrix of Exhibit 8-4. These sources of data were rated against nine criteria in Exhibit 8-5. It is obvious even from these crude ratings that the sources of data have different advantages and disadvantages. This suggests an eclectic strategy: use a variety of sources, especially when uncertainty is high and large changes are expected.

A priori adjustments to the coefficients are important when the forecast situation is highly uncertain. The procedure for such an adjustment was described. As uncertainty increases, less emphasis should be placed on causality.

Estimates of relationships can be obtained from the data by using either experience tables or regression analysis. Regression analysis is more intuitively appealing and is no more expensive. One danger of the regression model is that some analysts equate this measurement model with the forecasting model. This places an unnecessary and often misleading restriction on the analyses.

Certain problems cause difficulties when using regression analysis. These problems, along with some brief solutions, were summarized in Exhibit 8-7. In general, the solutions rely on simplicity and on the use of different sources of data.

Simplicity is a virtue in regression. Obviously, simple methods are cheaper, easier to understand, and less prone to mistakes. In addition, simple methods are as accurate as complex ones. Although this is contrary to the beliefs of experts in econometrics, none of the 11 empirical studies examined showed a significant gain in accuracy from using complex methods. In fact, the data suggested the opposite, although this tendency was not significant.

Conditional regression analysis can be used to update the *a priori* estimates in light of the objective data. One way to do this is to list the estimates for each relationship and combine them, using an *a priori* weighting scheme. The choice of a weighting scheme is not expected to be of much importance.

The estimation of current status should be done independently of forecasting change; no one model is best for both purposes. If this is not done, it is then important to use judgment or mechanical adjustments based on recent errors to adjust the forecasts, especially for short-range forecasts. These adjustments help to compensate for the errors in estimating current status.

In forecasting change, it is important to mitigate the forecast coefficients to allow for various types of error over the forecast horizon. This step is ignored by people who forecast directly from measurement models. It is a dangerous omission for long-range forecasts.

Surprisingly, little benefit was found from obtaining good forecasts of the causal variables. This may be related to the absence of mitigation in the studies that were examined.

Combined forecasts were recommended. These may be generated by having the analyst consider reasonable variations of the judgments that went into developing the model. Preferably, econometric models should be developed independently by two or more researchers.

Regression analysis yields useful and inexpensive estimates of the uncertainty in the measurement of causal relationships. To estimate the uncertainty in the forecast, however, it is best to simulate the forecast situation by withholding actual data. If this is not possible, a Monte Carlo simulation can be used to examine the net effects of the major types of error.

Nine

SEGMENTATION METHODS

Contents

Birds of a feather flock together.

Old Saying

Imagine a model in which each type of the key actors is explicitly represented. Changes can then be evaluated by examining the reaction of each of these individual actors. In other words, people, organizations, and so on are divided into categories, and separate predictions are made for each category. Because different types of people respond in different ways to a given change, such a model has great intuitive appeal. Elements of this strategy were used in judgmental forecasting. This chapter discusses such a strategy used with explicit and causal methods; it is called the segmentation approach or multiple classification or multilevel cross tabulation or configurational analysis, depending upon your preference.

Segmentation approaches have been used in many fields. These approaches are often complex and generally expensive. The promise seems high, however. Each actor is treated separately, thus allowing for more realism. Segmentation also offers the advantages of decomposition described in Chapter 4.

The approach is an old one. Orcutt (1961) was so taken with this approach that he argued for a substantial effort by the government to develop a segmentation model of the U.S. economy. People would be born, go to school, marry, and live a full life in this simulation. John F. Kennedy used such a model to forecast the effects of different strategies in the 1960 presidential campaign (Pool, Abelson, and Popkin, 1965). Abelson and Bernstein (1963) described how segmentation could be employed on the fluoridation issue. Burdick (1964) implied that the approach is so powerful that it could be used by politicians for sinister purposes. Lee (1961) advocated the segmentation approach as a superior method for making psychological predictions, and Morgan and Sonquist (1963) advocated its use in survey research.

In spite of all this promise and much activity with regard to segmentation methods, their value in forecasting has been disappointing [e.g., see CURRIM, 1981]. As a result, this is the least important chapter in Part II. It is also the most speculative and the least empirical. Perhaps its major benefit is to indicate what has not worked rather than what has worked.

The plan of this chapter is as follows. First, the conditions favoring the use of segmentation are described. The use of *a priori* analysis is stressed here, as it was with econometric methods, for there are close parallels between the two methods. A brief discussion is then provided on the types of objective data that can be used to update the segmentation model. Most of the chapter is devoted to methods for developing the segmentation model. Consideration is given to methods for both dependent and independent segmentation. Segmentation methods can be used for estimating both current status and change because different considerations are sometimes involved in these two applications. The chapter concludes with discussions on combined forecasts and on the assessment of uncertainty.

CONDITIONS FAVORING SEGMENTATION

In general, segmentation provides the benefits of decomposition; that is, segmentation spreads the risk and capitalizes on compensating errors. (A more detailed argument is presented in Appendix E.) Segmentation seems especially useful when:

1. The segments are independent.
2. The segments are of equal importance.
3. The information on each segment is good.

These guidelines are, unfortunately, difficult to translate into operational terms. The problem becomes more complex when *dependent* segments are considered. An additional assumption must then be made:

4. The relationships among segments can be measured accurately.

Finally, all of these guidelines are expected to be more important for situations involving large changes.

The question of when segmentation methods are relevant can be examined further by contrasting segmentation with judgmental methods, which use causality in a subjective way, and with econometric methods, which use causality in an explicit way.

Versus Judgmental Methods

Segmentation offers advantages over judgmental methods when there are many segments. In such a case, it is more efficient to analyze the data with an explicit framework; the causal effects also become more apparent.

These advantages of segmentation over judgmental methods are most pronounced with independent segments. Nevertheless, there are some advantages also with dependent segments. Exhibit 9-1 indicates the possibilities for segmentation.

For a small number of interdependent actors, role playing is the preferred method. If the number of actors is large, role playing is still relevant; but if there are also many *types* of actors, it may be worthwhile to describe explicitly these relationships. This approach is referred to here as dependent segmentation simulation. Dependent segmentation explicitly assesses group actions and interactions.

For a small number of independent segments, it is often possible to ask actors directly about their intentions. As the number of segments increases, however, it is more difficult to process this information, so a model is developed to represent explicitly each type of actor. This approach, called "trees" here, is simpler than dependent segmentation; one merely sums up the predictions for all segments to get the overall forecast.

Versus Econometric Methods

Some people claim that the benefits of segmentation can be achieved by using dummy variable regressions. This is possible if the dummy variables are used to represent the segments. However, regression analysis is a clumsy and inefficient way to identify these segments. In general, researchers who use segmentation proceed in a manner that differs from that used by econometricians.

The major advantage of segmentation over econometric methods is that it makes fewer assumptions about behavior. It does not assume, as does the econometric method, that all actors respond in the same way to a causal variable. This means that segmentation is advantageous when the data suffer from one or more of three closely related problems:

Exhibit 9-1   SEGMENTATION VS. JUDGMENTAL METHODS

Relationship among Segments	Number of Segments	
	Small (judgmental)	Large (segmentation)
Dependent	Role play	Dependent segmentation
Independent	Surveys	Trees

- Interaction
- Nonlinear effects
- Causal priorities

The most serious of these problems is interaction. For example, a large dose of aspirin may be good for an adult who is ill, but it may be fatal for a healthy infant. Rather than look at *the* effect of aspirin, segmentation would identify groups that respond in given ways to this treatment.

Segmentation is useful when nonlinear effects are expected and the nature of these effects is difficult to describe. As an example of nonlinear effects, the economic benefits *to society* from the first year of elementary schooling seem to be positive, but the benefits from an additional year of graduate school are probably negative. (Efforts to show a benefit from graduate education have failed. On the cost side it is expensive and leads to prejudice in hiring decisions—thus the negative return.) Rather than looking for a complex function to represent these effects, segmentation would examine groups with similar amounts of education.

Finally, segmentation is advantageous when causal priorities exist in the data, that is, when the effect of one variable must be examined before considering the effect of another. This problem can be handled with causal chains in econometrics, but segmentation offers the simpler alternative of splitting the data first on the variables that come earliest in the causal chain.

A PRIORI ANALYSIS

Segmentation methods use causal variables to define the segments. *A priori* analysis for segmentation methods is analogous to that for econometric methods, so that the discussion in this section will be brief.

The basic steps in using segmentation to forecast are outlined in Exhibit 9-2. The first three steps (select variables, specify priorities, and specify **cutpoints**[G]) are used to define the segments. Forecasts must then be obtained for the population of the segment and for the typical behavior of an element in that segment. The population and behavior are then multiplied to yield a forecast for the segment. In the simple case of independent segments, one simply adds across segments to get an aggregate forecast. For dependent segments, an additional step is that forecasts are required for the relationships among seg-

Exhibit 9-2   STEPS IN THE DEVELOPMENT OF SEGMENTATION METHODS (Independent Segments)

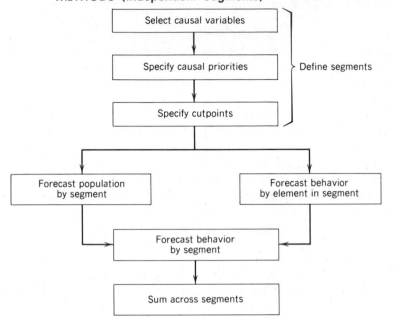

ments. Guidelines for *a priori* analysis in each of these areas are presented in the following sections.

Select Causal Variables

A priori analysis should be used to select a small number of causal variables. The guidelines for selecting causal variables here are analogous to those used for selecting causal variables in the econometric model. They are also similar to those used in Finley's (1968) segmentation study.

1. *Strong causal effects.* The causal variable should have a strong effect upon the dependent variable so that substantial differences will be found among segments.
2. *Ease in measuring effects of causal relationships.* Sufficient information should be available to measure the differences among segments.

3. *Large changes in population or behavior.* Within each segment, large changes should be expected in either the future population of the segment or in the future behavior of the actors in the segment.
4. *Ease in measuring population and behavioral changes.* The changes within each segment should be predictable.

You should select causal variables that rate well on each of these four criteria.

Specify Causal Priorities

The next stage of the *a priori* analysis is to specify the causal priorities that split the segments in the most effective way. In the example of the economic benefits of education, one would first split on age because an education split would not be relevant for all age groups. Had one split first on education, those over 65 would have been assigned to different educational groups, and this would be of no value.

Perhaps a better guideline is that the more general variables should be used first, or that the variables that affect most of the population should be used first. The Crest example in the next section may help to clarify matters.

Select Cutpoints

The cutpoints are the dividing lines for the causal variables. The *a priori* selection of cutpoints is dependent on the expected strength of the relationship and on the amount of information that the analyst expects to have. The stronger the relationship and the more information available, the more cutpoints are needed.

Although the analyst can make *a priori* specifications of the number of cutpoints, it is difficult to select specific values. Still, it is not expected that you will need precise estimates of cutpoints. The following guidelines may help:

1. When a certain minimum or threshold level must be reached before a variable is important, use this as a cutpoint.
2. Select cutpoints so as to avoid segments about which little information exists. For example, Einhorn's (1972b) simulation study suggests that segments with less than 10 observations should be avoided, 25 observations are adequate, and 50 are preferred. Lykken and Rose (1963) suggested that you should seldom use more than three

cutpoints. I suspect that computer technology will lead us to ignore this advice.

3. If measurement is poor, use few cutpoints.
4. If nonlinearity is strong, use more cutpoints.

With the completion of the first three steps in Exhibit 9-2, you now have an *a priori* definition of the segments. An example of these three steps is provided here, drawn from our study of the adoption of Crest toothpaste.

Montgomery and Armstrong (1968) used trees to predict which households would try Crest toothpaste after it was endorsed as a decay preventative by the American Dental Association. Four variables were used to segment families according to the probability that they would try Crest within the next 25 purchases or

Exhibit 9-3   EXAMPLE OF A TREE: THE CREST STUDY
(Percentage of Triers in Segment)

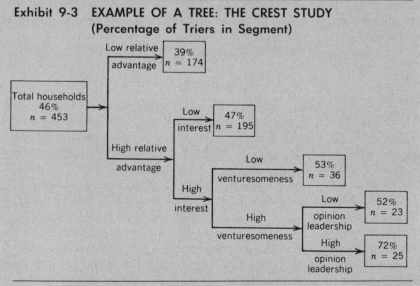

Notes:
1. High relative advantage indicates "presence of children." Other variables came from responses to a questionnaire on shopping behavior.
2. Cutpoints were specified at the mean response for each causal variable.

33 months, whichever came first. The selection of the variables and the specification of causal priorities and of cutpoints were done before examining Crest purchase data. The *a priori* segmentation is presented in Exhibit 9-3. It was hypothesized that for households that displayed loyalty to any brand, the percentage who had tried Crest would increase as one moved from the top to the bottom segment. As seen from the actual percentage of triers, the data supported the hypothesis on the rankings of the segments ($p < .05$ using the **Kendall rank correlation**^{G} coefficient).

The importance of specifying causal priorities was tested in the Crest study. Note the assumptions used in the tree: if Crest had no relative advantage, the decision maker would have little interest in further information; if the relative advantage was high but the decision maker expressed little interest, there was no need to probe further; if interest was high, it made sense to assess venturesomeness; finally, it helped to find out whether the venturesome decision makers regarded themselves as opinion leaders for this type of purchase. To test the value of this reasoning about causal priorities, the data were also split in a manner directly contradictory to the hypothesized causal priorities. The result? Virtually no differences were found among the segments with respect to the percentage of triers.

Forecast Population by Segment

The forecast of the population of each segment is typically an important step in segmentation methods. Seldom can the analyst develop good *a priori* estimates of population; instead, she must depend upon the objective data. However, *a priori* estimates should be made for the direction and magnitude of change within each segment.

The forecasting of populations is often relatively easy for problems in the social sciences, especially when the predictions relate to adults. A good prediction can be made for the number of people over 6 years of age for the next 6 years, because these people have already been born. Obvious, isn't it? (Well, it was not obvious to my school board. In 1971 it was planning to tear down the local elementary school and build a larger one. Fortunately, the board decided against this. In 1977 the board noticed that there were few children in the school, so they abandoned it. Then they built an addition to one of the schools in the early 1980s. So it goes.)

Forecast Behavior within Segments

Often an attempt is made to find segments that are both homogeneous and stable, that is, where the *behavior* is assumed to remain stable. This strategy was used by Stark and Glock (1968):

Stark and Glock (1968) used independent segmentation for the religion market. The segmentation yielded two segments whose populations were expected to change substantially in the future— a "high orthodoxy, low ethicalism" segment and a "low orthodoxy, high ethicalism" segment. The populations were expected to change because the former segment was composed of old people, and the latter of young people. The people in the high orthodoxy, low ethicalism segment provided substantially more financial support for churches than did the other segment. Stark and Glock assumed that financial behavior would not change as the people aged (until death, which is nature's way of telling them to slow down). It was only necessary to predict the population in each segment. Incidentally, they forecasted a decrease in revenues as a result of the population changes by segment.

Segmentation makes it possible to use various sources of *a priori* information to forecast the behavior within each segment. Different sources can be consulted for each of the segments. Thus the segmentation approach provides a convenient way to utilize subjective information from experts in different areas. This aspect would be relevant, for example, in making political forecasts by voter segment.

DATA FOR SEGMENTATION

The segmentation approach calls for the use of data about the individual actors. As a result, it tends to be an expensive technique. Therefore, it is worthwhile to collect primary data for the segmentation approach only for important problems. Normally, one must depend upon secondary data and subjective information.

The continuing improvements in the speed and capacity of computers make segmentation *analysis* less expensive. One can store disaggregate data on a computer and collapse it into segments at a modest cost. Spreadsheet programs for personal computers allow for inexpensive analyses.

The types of data that can be used for segmentation methods are the same as those for econometric methods with one significant difference: the segmentation approach is limited to disaggregate data. For this reason, the segmentation approach places a greater emphasis upon the use of survey data.

Previous survey data may be valuable in the development of a segmentation model. Many previous surveys are held in data archives and are available at a small cost. Hyman (1972) provides a description of the types of data that are available and the ways in which they can be obtained. This resource continues to grow. Such data were used with apparent success in the Kennedy–Nixon simulation:

The Simulmatics study (Pool, Abelson, and Popkin, 1965) of the 1960 Kennedy–Nixon election made extensive use of previous surveys. The authors used about 50 surveys on the voting behavior of 480 voter types. These surveys covered the period from 1952 to 1958 and were based on replies from about 100,000 respondents. These data were used to make predictions of the behavior of each segment, given changes in the issues. For example, it was decided that Kennedy did not have to avoid the religion issue; this issue drew the Catholic segments, but it had little effect on the other segments.

ANALYZING THE DATA

The methods for the analysis of data differ substantially, depending upon whether you are using trees or dependent segments. The discussion that follows is in accord with current developments in each area. Thus, for trees, the issue of *a priori* vs. exploratory research is considered because this has been a key issue; little attention is given to the *a priori* vs. exploratory issue for dependent segmentation. Similarly, the issue of direct vs. indirect segmentation has been important for trees, but not for dependent segmentation.

Trees will be discussed first. This is followed by a brief discussion of dependent segmentation that focuses on the use of simulation and input–output analysis.

Trees

The trend in segmentation has been toward the exploratory end of this continuum. This is probably due to advances in technology. The earliest attempts at segmentation relied primarily on sorting by hand. This was followed by the use of card sorters. Nevertheless, the work was slow and expensive, so it was important to decide what to do before starting. This forced the researcher to use *a priori* analysis to select variables, specify causal priorities, and select cutpoints.

Computer technology has advanced to the point where exploratory programs are widely available. These programs enable researchers to plunge into a problem with little *a priori* analysis and to demonstrate their cleverness when interpreting the results.

Segments can be defined by a direct approach, which selects the segments that are most relevant for predicting change in the variable of interest, or by an indirect approach, which groups actors who are alike on some *causal* variables. The direct and indirect approaches are illustrated in Exhibit 9-4.

Exhibit 9-4   DIRECT VS. INDIRECT SEGMENTATION

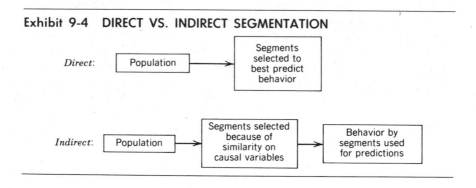

The indirect approach is advantageous, of course, when there is no information on the dependent variable. The indirect approach is also more general and can be used in a variety of situations.

Although the indirect approach seems to be an odd way to forecast, the generality of this approach makes it appealing. Imagine how many predictions can be made about someone who is a "tall, young, good-looking Anglo-Saxon adult male." Why, the only problem for this person lies in trying to live up to all these predictions.

One well-known approach to indirect segmentation is based on the life cycles of families. This has been used frequently in marketing research, with some apparent success. An example of indirect segmentation is provided by Kreinin and Lininger (1963):

Kreinin and Lininger (1963) defined "life cycle" in the following terms:

- Under 45, single
- Under 45, married
- 45 and over, married, dependent children
- 45 and over, married, no dependent children
- 45 and over, single

These categories were then split according to income and residence. The resulting segments varied dramatically in their likelihood of ownership of automobiles, from 10% in one segment to 98% in another segment.

A more recent application of the life cycle is provided by CLARKE, DIX and GOODWIN [1982].

The exploratory approach to indirect segmentation has been popular among researchers. The techniques used have often been referred to as cluster analysis. A highly technical literature exists, along with numerous programs, to enable you to do the very best job of clustering. I will not discuss this approach here, however, as it combines the worst of both worlds: it is exploratory (I have already warned you against that), and it is indirect. Furthermore, I have been unable to find evidence that clustering techniques can improve the accuracy of forecasts. Why is it so popular then? Well, it is the best of the rain dances among the segmentation techniques.

Rankings of the various approaches to trees are provided in Exhibit 9-5. The rankings are relevant only within a column. The superior generality of the indirect approaches has already been noted. The cost differences are due to the greater data requirements of the exploratory approach. For example, if you have 10 causal variables and split each into two categories, there would be 1024 different segments. Consider the problem of obtaining estimates for each of these segments. If a minimum sample size of 30 per segment was deemed adequate, this would call for a sample size of about 31,000, assuming that the observations would be balanced across the segments (as is seldom the case). In contrast, the *a priori* approach draws more heavily upon existing information.

Exhibit 9-5   APPROACHES TO TREES
               (1 = most favorable ranking)

Method	Generality	Cost	Accuracy
A priori direct	3	1.5	1
A priori indirect	1	1.5	2
Exploratory direct	4	3.5	3
Exploratory indirect	2	3.5	4

The rankings of accuracy rest heavily upon the argument that a method specifically designed to forecast a dependent variable will be superior to a general purpose model. Perhaps it is because this seems so obvious that few people have bothered to study the issue. One study that did examine (and support) this argument was carried out by Rock et al. (1970).

Modern technology is working against the use of *a priori* methods even for direct segmentation. A popular exploratory program for direct segmentation is **AID**[G] (automatic interaction detector). This program first makes the best two-way split of the data; each remaining segment is then examined for the next best two-way split, and so on. The routine is stopped when further splitting would fail to improve the description, or when the sample size would fall below some prespecified minimum (e.g., 30). (For an early, and good, description of AID see Sonquist and Morgan, 1964).

A revised version of AID, called AID-III, allows for greater *a priori* input (Press, Rogers, and Shure, 1969; Sonquist, Baker, and Morgan, 1974) by enabling the researcher to make decisions on the selection of variables, causal priorities, and cutpoints. Although I have not seen any validation of this particular program, it is a step in the right direction.

If you are one of the people who has trouble working on only one thing at a time, there is a program that allows the use of AID for more than one dependent variable (Gillo and Shelly, 1974). This is analogous to the use of canonical correlation which was criticized earlier, (see page 225 of *LRF*). Ah, the wonders of modern technology. Some day we may even be able to make air-conditioning systems work in office buildings.

The dangers of AID may be even greater than those of stepwise regression because it is so good at picking up **spurious relationships.**[G]

Einhorn (1972b) compared AID and regression on random data and found that regression produced fewer misleading results when the cell sizes for AID were small (e.g., 10).

The preferred method, as indicated in Exhibit 9-5, is the *a priori* direct approach. I would even bet on the sorting machine (and judgment) against exploratory or indirect approaches. Of course, there is no longer any need to use sorting machines because the *a priori* segments can be examined quickly and inexpensively by computer.

Dependent Segmentation

Numerous terms have been used to describe methods for segmentation where the behavior and population movements are not easily treated as being independent. In the following I will discuss microsimulation, simulation, and input-output.

A *microsimulation* model describes the decision processes of the various actors in a system and then to examine how the system changes over time. For example, Amstutz (1967), developed a microsimulation of the pharmaceutical industry to forecast the success of new drugs. The decision processes of the various actors in the marketing system were incorporated in the model. The actions of one group affected the actions of other groups. If one firm marketed a new product or developed a new advertising campaign, another firm would demonstrate its own creativity by trying to do the same thing. Much time and money went into the development of Amstutz's microsimulation, but surprisingly there was no evidence that this approach led to better forecasts.

Microsimulation models have been especially popular in marketing. The belief exists that the simple model used by economists (price, income, substitutes, and tastes) does not do justice to the complexity of the marketing environment. Thus, a number of comprehensive microsimulation models have been developed, such as the Howard–Sheth model (1969). Microsimulation models have also been used for many years in political science (Guetzkow et al., 1972). Unfortunately, little evidence exists on the predictive value of these models.

One simulation model that has received a great deal of publicity is "world dynamics" alias "urban dynamics" alias "industrial dynamics" (Forrester, 1968a). The publicity arose because world dynamics forecasted a dismal future for the world in *The Limits of Growth* (Meadows et al., 1972). It was the forecast rather than the method that led to the publicity. But what of the method? Well, it was complex, done by computer, supported by the Club of Rome, and brought to the world by way of M.I.T. All of the credentials were there, so people hardly noticed when the authors said that their only claim was that the inputs looked reasonable. Well, they looked reasonable to some, and unreasonable to others. I was one of those others because to me it seemed unreasonable not to expect the price of a raw material to go up when it becomes scarce. A critique of *The Limits of Growth* can be found in Morgenstern, Knorr, and Heiss (1973, pp. 55–65).

The Limits of Growth presented no evidence that world dynamics can provide valid forecasts. Furthermore, no cases were cited in which industrial dynamics simulation had led to improved forecasts in comparison with forecasts from other methods. I searched in vain for such evidence, as did Ansoff and Slevin (1968). Furthermore, I was told by one of the leading advocates of industrial dynamics that it is not even possible to validate this method. It reminded me of the reaction of the religious community in the late 1800s when researchers wanted to do scientific studies on the value of prayer (Brush, 1974). It is not possible to study such a question, according to the religious leaders.

I have not carried out a detailed examination of world dynamics. Perhaps there is merit to the method, but it is necessary to make decisions as to where to spend one's time. I do not expect much of a payoff from world-urban-industrial dynamics and am willing to wait until its predictive validity is demonstrated.

Although dependent simulation seems reasonable, it is complex, difficult to understand, and prone to errors. It is also expensive because so much information is needed to describe accurately the behavior within each segment and the relations among segments. However, it does solve the problem of what to do with that large organizational budget for research. Only William of Occam would be offended by all of the complexity. William of Occam is a dangerous man to offend.

The experts have already given a Nobel prize to Leontief (1964), the man who popularized *input-output* analysis. This is the economist's approach to simulation. Primary emphasis is placed on estimating relationships among segments. For example, one might start with a forecast of the demand for automobiles and then translate this into the demands for the various suppliers of the automobile manufacturers (e.g., steel, glass, plastics, and the largest supplier, the medical insurance industry).

Although input-output has been used primarily in studies of national economies, it seems relevant for any situation where the segments are highly dependent on one another, such as political relationships among nations, relationships among members of face-to-face groups, or business forecasting (Leontief, 1964). Input-output should yield consistent forecasts in such situations, that is, forecasts for one segment should be reasonable in light of forecasts for other segments.

Input-output is most appropriate when large changes are expected during a short time period. Presumably, the relationships between segments will remain constant for short time periods. For example, input-output was suggested to be of value in planning for a sudden shift from a peacetime to a wartime economy.

Miller, Berry, and Lai (1976) investigated the conditions favoring the use of input-output. They called it a "dependent strategy." Their study implied that input-output is preferable to direct extrapolation of the dependent variable when:

1. Good forecasts are available for the end-use industries. (However, as with econometric models, I do not think this is a critical area; Bezdek, 1974, found *ex ante* input-output forecasts to be superior to *ex post* forecasts.)
2. The relationships among segments can be forecast accurately. (Vaccara, 1971, found improved accuracy when an attempt was made to forecast the relationships instead of assuming them to be constant.)
3. Large changes are expected in the dependent variable.
4. A negative correlation exists among the forecast errors in each segment (so that the errors compensate for one another).

Input-output analysis is one area where I have had little experience. It is best, then, that I do not try to explain to you how this analysis should be done. In any event, describing how to do input-output analysis is a popular pastime among academicians. Descriptions are found in Almon (1974), Leontief (1964), Rabitsch (1972), and Yan (1969). Descriptions of input-output forecasting applications are provided by Mohn, Schaffer, and Sartorius (1976) for the Montreal Expo's baseball team; by Ranard (1972) for steel, petroleum, and refractory markets; and by Rippe, Wilkinson, and Morrison (1976) for the steel industry.

Input-output analysis has been used since 1941 (Zarnowitz, 1968), and some evidence has accumulated on its effectiveness. Despite the fact that the input-output data are often old and the forecasts of the segments crude, the record is favorable. Bezdek (1974) reviewed 16 input-output forecasts of the economies in seven countries from 1951 to 1972 and concluded that input-output was superior to alternative techniques. He also concluded that the method was more appropriate for economy-wide predictions than for specific industries.

Although input-output was more accurate than alternative techniques, the following qualifications should be added:

1. The improvements in accuracy were generally small.
2. The alternative techniques were generally simple and inexpensive extrapolations of the aggregate data that did not follow the best practice for extrapolation.
3. Input-output data are typically out of date. Vaccara (1971) reported on a forecast assumed to have been made in 1963, the year that the 1958 U.S. input-output data became available. Because input-output data are collected only every few years, they are generally 5 to 10 years old.
4. Input-output analysis is expensive.
5. Although the idea is simple, the details behind input-output are complex, making it difficult to implement.

Overall, input-output shows some promise for economy-wide forecasts, but applications in other areas appear questionable at this time.

CURRENT STATUS VS. CHANGE

As recommended for other methods, it usually helps to separate the estimation of current status from the prediction of change. For example, it would not seem wise to use input-output data that are 7 years old to estimate current status, although these data may provide a reasonable basis to forecast change.

As a general rule, segmentation methods are useful for estimating current status only when:

1. The segmentation data are recent,
2. uncertainty about the current status is high,
3. errors in estimating the behavior in each segment are small and largely independent of one another. (This implies that different sources of data or different methods are used in different segments.), and
4. errors in estimating the population in each segment are small and largely independent of one another.

These restrictions imply that the segmentation method is rarely applicable to estimating current status. However, such conditions do arise at times. For example, election night forecasts depend upon this strategy, as indicated by the following study:

Mitau, Thorson, and Johnson (1969) used to predict the 1966 Minnesota gubernatorial election on the basis of early returns. Voters were segmented by county population (two cutpoints) and by the average percentage of Democratic vote for the past three gubernatorial elections (three cutpoints). The early election returns were weighted by the estimated number of voters in each of these 12 segments, and this estimate of current status was used to project returns for the entire state. The Republican candidate, who was the underdog, received only 44.4% of the vote in the early returns. However, the segmentation model forecasted that he would win 53.2% of the vote. In fact, he did win, gaining 52.6% of the total vote.

A case history is provided by the Port of New York Authority's study of the air travel market. Estimates of the current status were not accurate, but the model performed well in a backcasting test. The following description of this study illustrates how the segmentation model was used to estimate current status and to forecast change.

The Port of New York Authority (1957) defined 290 segments for the air travel market. The 160 personal travel segments were split by age (3 cutpoints), occupation (4 cutpoints), income (3 cutpoints), and education (1 cutpoint). The 130 business travel segments were split by occupation (4 cutpoints), industry (2 to 13 cutpoints, depending upon occupation), and income (up to 3 cutpoints, depending upon the preceding segments). Population estimates for 1955, the year of the study, were drawn from special computer runs using the 1950 census; this yielded a population estimate for each segment. Information on the air travel behavior for each segment was obtained from a 1955 survey of 4000 adults. These respondents provided information on the travel behavior of 8200 adults for both business and personal travel (an average of about 50 responses per personal travel segment). The estimates of population and current travel behavior yielded an estimate of 30.4 million passenger trips for 1955. As a rough estimate, this compared favorably with the U.S. Civil Aeronautics Board's record of 38.7 million passenger trips because the latter figure included plane transfers and stopovers as additional trips. In addition, certain segments had been intentionally omitted from the Port of New York Authority's estimate.

This segmentation model was also used for long-range forecasting. Forecasts of population change for 1965 were obtained by using U.S. Bureau of Census projections, along with many simplifying assumptions, to break the forecast down into segments. Forecasts of behavior change were made by estimating the percentage of "fliers" in each personal travel segment from the 1955 survey data. An extrapolation was then made for 1965 by using the 1955 percentage and an assumption that the percentage was zero in 1935. The number of trips per flier was assumed to remain constant from 1955 to 1965. For the business travel segments, an extrapolation was made of trip frequency, again using 1935 as a zero point.

Overall, this segmentation approach worked well. National air travel was forecast to increase from 38.7 million trips in 1955 to 90 million in 1965. The actual number of trips in 1965 was 93.1 million; that is, the forecast error was about 3%. This is small relative to the 58% error for a model assuming no change.

COMBINED FORECASTS

In deference to eclectic research, it is recommended that forecasts obtained by using different segmentation methods be combined. This is a suggestion only, because I have no evidence on this issue. A checklist is provided here of major ways that segmentation forecasts may differ. The researcher can vary the:

1. definition of the segments,
2. estimate of current status within each segment,
3. forecasts of population change by segment,
4. forecasts of behavior change by segment, or
5. segmentation method; in particular, both trees and dependent segmentation could be used.

One might also ask different researchers to work independently to develop segmentation forecasts. This should help to ensure that reasonable variations will occur at least in items 1 to 4.

The primary reason for advocating combined forecasts is that, despite all of the research, we know little about the factors that are most important in the use of segmentation for prediction. Remember: when you do not know exactly where you should direct your efforts, use a shotgun!

This advice on the use of different forecasts is oriented toward accuracy. In many cases, the high cost of the segmentation method will rule out the use of different model builders and, to a lesser extent, will rule out the combined use of dependent segmentation and trees.

ASSESSING UNCERTAINTY

The use of different model builders also provides an opportunity to assess uncertainty. For example, *Business Week* (January 19, 1974, pp. 62, 64) reported one-year predictions on the effect of the oil crisis by two different researchers, Anne Carter and Clopper Almon. Both used input-output analysis, yet their forecasts differed substantially.

The segmentation method also lends itself to the assessment of uncertainty by segment. Often the researcher will have a good idea of which segments are the areas of highest uncertainty. This approach is expected to be useful when there are many segments and the uncertainty varies substantially by segment.

Monte Carlo simulation can be used to combine the estimates from each segment in order to develop an aggregate distribution. Hertz (1964) described how to use such a procedure to estimate uncertainty in a capital budgeting problem. Fernandez–Garza (1969) used this approach to estimate the uncertainty in the demand for the Minicar Mass Transit System (described in Appendix F). A **global assessment**[G] of uncertainty yielded a 95% confidence interval that had a range of 50,000 subscribers. A Monte Carlo simulation over 11 market segments yielded a 95% confidence interval of 37,000 subscribers.

SUMMARY

Researchers in many areas expected the segmentation strategy to offer substantial gains in forecasting. This promise appeared to be greatest for problems involving many actors. In particular, benefits were expected when the decisions by different actors were independent of one another. One should use many segments, of roughly equal importance, and for which good information exists. Benefits were anticipated for dependent segments if the relationships among segments could be measured with some accuracy.

Segmentation offers advantages over judgmental methods when there are many segments and many data. Dependent segmentation can be used to go beyond role playing, and trees can serve to analyze surveys. Segmentation is advantageous to econometric methods when the data suffer from interaction, nonlinearities, and causal priorities.

The arguments for *a priori* analysis in segmentation are similar to those proposed for econometric methods. Of particular importance are the selection of causal variables, statements on causal priorities, and specifications of cutpoints.

Data needs for segmentation also parallel those for econometric methods except that the segmentation method requires disaggregate data. Survey data are particularly well suited for segmentation studies.

The analysis of the data differs according to whether trees or dependent segmentation is used. For trees, one should use an *a priori* analysis that is directly related to the variable of interest. As summarized in Exhibit 9-5, exploratory and indirect approaches are expected to be less accurate and more costly. On the other hand, *a priori* and indirect segmentation may be preferable when generality is a major concern or when data are not available for the dependent variable.

For dependent segmentation, the simulation approaches can capture reality; however, they are complex, subject to error, and difficult to understand. Furthermore, little evidence exists to recommend their use in forecasting. The evidence on input-output analysis is more promising; it offers modest improvements for economy-wide predictions of large changes.

Segmentation methods are typically better suited to assessing change than to estimating current status because the data are frequently old. An important exception is the prediction of the outcome of political voting. The Port of New York Authority's study of the air travel market was used to illustrate the application of independent segmentation to estimating current status and forecasting change.

The use of combined forecasts was recommended, but no empirical evidence could be found in this area. The use of segmentation for assessing uncertainty was also illustrated, but again there was no empirical evidence on its value.

Overall, the segmentation approach has been a hotbed of activity, but little research has been done to determine which aspects contribute to better forecasting.

Ten

BOOTSTRAPPING AND OTHER COMBINED METHODS

Contents

George Bernard Shaw is reported to have received in the mail a proposal
for marriage in which a lady said, "With my beauty and your brains we
could have the perfect child." Shaw replied, "But what if the child had
my looks and your brains?"

Chapters 6 through 9 described various types of forecasting methods.
The best approach to a given forecasting problem may, however, call
for a combination of methods. The story about George Bernard Shaw
is relevant: when different methods are combined, it is not always clear
that they are being combined to utilize their best features. This chapter
presents guidelines to help ensure that the combination will be beneficial.

After describing the general guidelines, detailed consideration is
given to bootstrapping, the most important of the combined methods.
This method has important implications for forecasters.

Brief descriptions are provided of econometric methods within segments and of leading indicators. The chapter concludes with a discussion of combined forecasts that rely upon eclectic research; very different methods are combined.

GUIDELINES FOR COMBINING METHODS

A major consideration in the combination of *methods* is which method
to use first. Two rules seem important in specifying time priorities.
The first (and more important) is that subjective methods should precede objective methods. Auditors of financial forecasts believe this to
be good practice, according to DANOS and IMHOFF [1983] and so do
weather forecasters [MURPHY and BROWN, 1984]. The second rule
is that segmentation should precede extrapolation or econometric
methods. These rules are summarized in Exhibit 10-1.

Exhibit 10-1   PRIORITIES FOR COMBINING METHODS

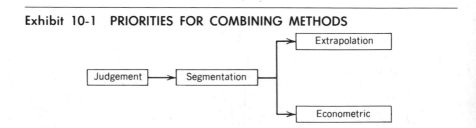

A substantial amount of evidence was presented earlier (especially in Chapter 4) that subjective methods should precede objective methods. (The subjective inputs were described under the designation "the *a priori* analysis.") This recommendation does not lessen the value of the individual's subjective inputs. Instead, it utilizes these inputs in a more effective way.

Arguments for using subjective inputs *after* the objective analysis have come from "practical" econometricians and from businesspeople. They are convinced that their subjective adjustments improve the accuracy of the forecasts. Hence businesspeople persist in such wasteful and prejudicial practices as using personnel managers to interview prospective employees (to make predictions about their probable success) after objective data have been received from these interviewees. Businesspeople and econometricians revise sales forecasts that have been produced by objective methods. Not only is this bad practice, but it also leads to poor forecasts. For a vivid example, see GLANTZ [1982]. A study by Strong provided evidence consistent with this viewpoint:

Strong (1956) surveyed managers attending an American Marketing Association conference on sales forecasting. Respondents from 297 companies replied on the extent to which they relied on judgment in one-year forecasts. (On the basis of my experience and previous surveys, I have assumed that this judgmental input usually followed the use of objective methods.) These respondents also reported on the errors they had experienced in their most recent one-year forecasts.

Reply	MAPE
Did not use judgment	6.8
Used judgment	8.5
Emphasized use of judgment	9.6

Some evidence has been presented by econometricians to suggest that subjective adjustments improve short-term economy-wide forecasts. Reinmuth and Geurts (1972) claimed to have found advantages to subjective adjustments, but their study was based on a single forecast (it is bad practice to generalize from a sample of one). CARBONE, et al. [1983] found no advantage to subjective adjustments of extrapolations. In Harris (1963), subjective adjustments made things worse. As suggested in Chapter 8, such adjustments can correct for errors in the estimate of current status, and they do not help to forecast change.

Exhibit 10-2   FLOODCASTING: HE'S A WIZARD ON CURRENT STATUS

Source.   "The Wizard of Id," by permission of Johnny Hart and Field Enterprises, Inc.

The recommendation that segmentation should precede extrapolation and econometric methods is based on common sense.

The discussions of methods in Chapters 6 through 9 suggested another important consideration in the combination of methods: different methods should be considered for different parts of the problem. In particular, different methods are of value in estimating current status, in forecasting short-range changes, and in forecasting long-range changes. Subjective methods are most appropriate for current status. The Wizard of Id illustrates this (Exhibit 10-2). Extrapolations are most relevant for short-range changes. Segmentation methods serve best for long-range changes. Finally, econometric methods are useful for estimating current status and for long-range forecasting. Exhibit 10-3 suggests which methods are appropriate for each time span. (Further empirical evidence relating to these recommendations is presented in Chapter 15.)

BOOTSTRAPPING

Frederick W. Taylor, the father of scientific management, created a bit of a sensation with his studies in the early 1900s. He applied scientific management to blue-collar jobs. The idea was that, by observing how a job was done, one could find ways to improve job performance. For example, he showed that a good way to find out how to improve a shoveler's shoveling is to observe him as he shovels. Scientific management, as defined by Taylor, involved telling others how to work more efficiently. You can imagine how happy that made management. Labor was a bit less enthusiastic about the idea.

The idea that scientific management could be applied to managers is something else again. Richard Cyert and James March, well-respected members of the academic community, presented the radical notion that economists might learn something by watching people make decisions rather than by assuming what the rational person would do (Cyert and March, 1963). The Wizard agrees, as you can see in Appendix I of *LRF*.

What about you doctors, lawyers, generals, stockbrokers, priests, psychologists, and management scientists? Could *your* job be studied scientifically . . . and be improved? More specifically, what about the predictions that you make; could a computer replace you for these predictions? The answers are "almost certainly" and "yes." (You thought maybe I was talking about someone else? Perhaps someone who works for you could be replaced by a computer, but. . . .)

Incidentally, Taylor (1911) did not think his method would be applicable to thinking-type jobs. He thought it would be most useful for low-level occupations such as pig-iron handling, where the ideal worker, Taylor said, "is so stupid that the word 'percentage' has no meaning to him, and he must consequently be trained by a man more intelligent than himself. . . ." Taylor knew how to get those managers on his side.

Bootstrapping assumes that the decision process used by people can be made explicit. In a sense, one can develop a "model of man" (or a "model of woman" if you are in a womanagement science). This isn't surprising, but it is surprising that the model of man is generally

---

Exhibit 10-3   METHODS FOR ESTIMATING CURRENT STATUS AND FORECASTING CHANGE

Estimating Current Status	Short-Range Forecasts	Middle-Range Forecasts	Long-Range Forecasts
Judgmental			
Extrapolation			
Econometric		Econometric	
		Segmentation	

superior to the man himself at forecasting! Thus the method is called bootstrapping: the forecaster can lift himself up by his own bootstraps. The concept almost seems impossible because what comes out of the model is superior to what went into the model.

Bootstrapping follows the guidelines on the combination of forecasts. Subjective methods are used before objective methods. The subjective method in this case *provides* the rules, and the objective method *applies* the rules. This is an intuitively pleasing combination (Einhorn, 1972a, presents evidence in favor of such an approach). The decision maker thinks that he knows how to make the forecasts, and he wants things done his way; in fact, his inputs are used to do this. The objective model does the repetitive work by applying the judge's rules without getting tired or irritable. This consistency seems to outweigh the losses that occur in going from a complex judgmental method to a simple objective method.

There are two approaches to bootstrapping: direct and indirect. These approaches are described below. A discussion follows on the effectiveness of bootstrapping and the situations in which bootstrapping is appropriate.

Direct Bootstrapping

Following Frederick Taylor's approach, direct bootstrapping involves a translation of the judge's rules into a model. In other words, the subjective process is made explicit and operational.

Often it is sufficient to ask the judges what rules they are using. Evidence that such an approach can successfully replicate expert's decisions is provided in finance by LARCKER and LESSIG [1983], and by the following two studies:

Kort (1957) analyzed 14 U.S. Supreme Court decisions on "right to counsel cases," from 1932 to 1947. There were 9 "pro" and 5 "con" decisions. The judges provided detailed records on why they decided as they did. Using the factors that the judges said were important, Kort was able to develop a mechanical weighting scheme to forecast similar cases from 1947 to 1956. His forecasts were correct for the 12 cases that were examined.

Amstutz (1967) programmed the decision rules used by the skilled union members of the American Medical Association (commonly known as doctors) as they prescribed drugs for patients. A panel of experts was unable to tell which drugs had been prescribed by the doctors and which had been prescribed by the computer (this is the **Turing test**[G]).

Sometimes judges are not aware of how they make decisions. In such cases, one might ask the judge to think aloud while they make predictions. The researcher records this thinking and translates it into specific rules. Often the rules are stated as questions that can be answered by "yes" or "no." (Some people call this the use of **protocols**[G], but I don't think Webster would use that term.) This procedure was used to match the decisions made by a professional investor in the Clarkson study.

Clarkson (1962) developed a model of an investment trust officer who selected stocks. The stocks selected by the computer program were similar to those selected by the trust officer. I do not believe that this small sample (one subject) study was ever replicated.

The "think aloud" approach is more expensive than just asking people what rules they use. Clarkson's study was a major undertaking, although he analyzed only one trust officer. Compare this with McClain (1972), who found that bootstrapping information could be obtained in about 3 hours by asking a doctor directly how she made decisions. The first attempt then, in direct bootstrapping, should be to ask the judge to describe the rules she uses. This strategy is widely used in research on experts. In the natural sciences and engineering, the term **expert systems**[G] is used, rather than bootstrapping. For a review of the expert systems literature, see DUDA and SHORTLIFFE [1983].

Indirect Bootstrapping

Indirect bootstrapping starts with the judge's forecasts and works backward to infer what rules the judge used to make these forecasts.

Indirect bootstrapping has had a long career. It started in 1923 when Henry A. Wallace (1923) developed a model of people who rated the quality of corn. (This is the same Wallace who later became Secretary of Agriculture and then Vice President of the United States.)

The basic approach to indirect bootstrapping is to develop a model where the judge's forecasts are themselves predicted by a quantitative model. In other words, the model uses the judge's forecasts as the dependent variable, and the variables that the judge used serve as the causal variables. Generally, this step is accomplished by regression analysis. The procedure is the same as described in Chapter 8, and the model looks the same:

$$Y' = a + b_1X_1 + b_2X_2 + \cdots + b_nX_n$$

except that Y' represents the judge's forecasts rather than the actual outcomes.

Research on bootstrapping has tried to capture the complexity of the judge's rules. This line of research yielded little. For example, Cook and Stewart (1975) examined seven different ways of obtaining the weights in a bootstrapping model and found that it did not make much difference which one was used. SCHMITT [1978] replicated this study. The conclusion is to use a simple linear model. This conclusion was supported by Goldberg (1968a, 1971), Heeler, Kearney, and Mehaffey (1973), Slovic, Fleissner, and Bauman (1972), and Wiggins and Hoffman (1968).

Indirect bootstrapping can generally be competitive in cost with direct bootstrapping. Evidence is mixed on the relative accuracy of these approaches. LARCKER and LESSIG [1983] and LEIGH, MacKAY, and SUMMERS [1984] found a slight advantage for the direct approach; Summers, Taliaferro, and Fletcher (1970) found no difference; GRAY [1979], NESLIN [1981], and SCHMITT [1978] found indirect bootstrapping to be superior. Perhaps the key consideration is whether the forecaster has a good awareness of the process. For example, CO-COZZA and STEADMAN [1978] found that psychiatrists did not have a good understanding of how they made predictions about the potential dangerousness of defendants in court cases. In such cases, the indirect approach is preferable.

Applications of indirect bootstrapping are found in many areas. One of the most popular uses has been to represent the judgments of consumers. For descriptions of this work, typically referred to as part of "conjoint analysis," see CATTIN and WITTINK [1982] and GREEN and WIND [1975].

Accuracy of Bootstrapping

The evidence cited above suggests that the bootstrapping model provides a good representation of the judge's decisions. But what about forecasting? Does the bootstrapping model provide good forecasts? Much research has been done in this area. It has been carried out independently by researchers with different backgrounds who were studying different problems. The only thing that has not changed is the conclusion: the bootstrapping model is at least as accurate as the judge. In most cases, the bootstrapping model is more accurate than the judge. Sometimes there are ties. Never has the typical judge been significantly better.

In view of the surprising nature of these findings and their importance, an extensive summary of the evidence is provided. All the bootstrapping models were indirect, unless otherwise indicated:

Yntema and Torgerson (1961) provided pictures of 180 ellipses to six subjects. The ellipses were various combinations of six sizes, six shapes, and five colors. Subjects were asked to judge the "worth" of each ellipse. The problem had been constructed so that worth always increased with size, thinness, and brownness, although these were not linear relationships. The subjects were trained with 180 ellipses on each of 11 days. The order of the ellipses was varied each day, and the subjects got feedback after each trial on the correct worth. On the twelfth day, the judge evaluated all 180 ellipses with no feedback. The ellipses were also evaluated using a bootstrapping model for each judge. The average R^2 between the judge's evaluation and the true worth was .71; the average R^2 between the bootstrapping model's prediction and the true worth was .79. In addition, a deductive bootstrapping model was constructed by asking the judges what weights they placed on size, shape, and color; this bootstrapping model performed as well as the inductive bootstrapping (average $R^2 = .79$). Shepard (1964) reported on a follow-up by Pollack (1962) that successfully replicated the Yntema–Torgerson results.

Bowman (1963) examined ice cream, chocolate, candy, and paint companies. A regression analysis of management's decisions on production and work force would have led to improvements over the decisions actually made in three of the four situations. He presented the following data on costs:

| | Company | | | |
Costs	Ice Cream	Chocolate	Candy	Paint
Actual	105.3	105.3	111.4	139.5
Using Bootstrapping Model	102.3	100.0	124.1	124.7

It is difficult to understand how Bowman arrived at his findings because the description is incomplete. Similar results were obtained for a brewery in a study by J. R. M. Gordon (described briefly in Buffa and Taubert, 1972).

Kleinmuntz (1967) developed a direct bootstrapping model. He coded the rules used by one expert to identify the best-adjusted and worst-adjusted subjects who sought counseling at college. Data from a personality inventory (the MMPI) were used. The bootstrapping model did as well as the best of eight clinicians in predictions based on five cross validation samples from different colleges.

Kunreuther (1969) developed a bootstrapping model for short-range production forecasting in an electronics firm. The model, developed partly from direct and partly from indirect bootstrapping, was a simple two-variable model. According to Kunreuther, this model would have enabled the firm to carry a 25% smaller inventory, while improving service to customers.

Michael (1969, 1971) used direct bootstrapping (which he called a heuristic method) to forecast sales for items in a mail order catalogue. He studied the rules used by a man who had been making these forecasts for a company, and developed a bootstrapping model to forecast sales for the coming season for 42 items. He concluded that experts were unable to distinguish which forecasts had been made by the bootstrapping model and which by the judge. The accuracies of the two forecasts were also comparable; in fact, the bootstrapping model did slightly better than the judge.

In Goldberg (1970), 29 judges used scores from the MMPI to differentiate between psychotics and neurotics among a sample of 861 patients. A bootstrapping model was developed for each judge, using a portion of the sample, and the rest of the sample was used for testing. The bootstrapping models were more accurate than 86% of the judges.

Wiggins and Kohen (1971) asked 98 graduate students in psychology to forecast first-year grade-point averages for 110 students entering graduate school. A bootstrapping model was developed for each judge. The bootstrapping model was superior for each of the 98 judges; furthermore, the typical bootstrapping model was better than the best of the 98 judges, and also better than the combined forecast by the 98 judges.

Dawes (1971) examined the admissions decisions for the Ph.D. program in psychology at the University of Oregon. There were six categories for rating applicants: (1) reject now; (2) defer rejection but looks weak; (3) defer; (4) defer acceptance but looks strong; (5) accept now; (6) offer fellowship. The committee used traditional measures in making its judgments, such as scores on Graduate Record Examination (GRE), quality index (QI) of school where undergraduate degree was received, grade point average (GPA), letters of recommendation, and record of work experience. A simple bootstrapping model (a regression of admissions committee decisions vs. GRE, QI, and GPA) reproduced the committee's decisions; the R^2 was .78, and none of the applicants rated in the lower 55% by the bootstrapping model were actually admitted by the admissions committee. Faculty evaluations after the first year were used as a measure of student success in the program. The bootstrapping model provided a more accurate ranking of student success than that provided by the admissions committee (Spearman rank correlation coefficients of .51 and .10, respectively). DAWES [1979] provided a follow-up.

Moskowitz and Miller (1972) provided another example in the field of production management. Eighty-six managers were presented with a simulated production problem and were asked to make production and work force decisions for one and three periods in the future. The forecasting error was varied during the experiment from low to medium to high. The bootstrapping model led to better decisions than the manager himself had made for both forecast horizons and for all three levels of forecast error. In no case was the manager superior to his model. Carter and Hamner (1972) replicated this study with similar results; in addition, they found that the combined decision from a number of bootstrapping models was even more effective. Moskowitz (1974) presented similar results, but this report appears to draw upon the same data as Moskowitz and Miller (1972). MOSKOWITZ et al. [1983] added further support.

Evidence from personnel forecasting was provided by a study of 16 managers by ROOSE and DOHERTY [1976]. Bootstrapping yielded a small gain (vs. the average judge) in the accuracy of predictions for the success of 160 salesmen.

EBERT and KRUSE [1978] developed bootstrapping models for five analysts who forecasted returns for securities using information on 22 variables. Bootstrapping was more accurate than the analysts for 18 of 25 comparisons, and it was as accurate as an econometric model.

In ABDEL-KHALIK [1980], mechanical models made more accurate predictions of defaults on loans than did 29 bank officers.

CAMERER [1981] concluded from his review that "bootstrapping will improve judgments under almost any realistic task conditions."

Somebody (actually it was Libby, 1976a) once thought that he had found an occasion when the judges defeated their models. The case involved the prediction of bankruptcy for 60 large industrial corporations. Goldberg (1976) showed, however, that Libby's result was due to severe skewness in the data. When the data were normalized, the percentage of times that the model beat the judge went from 23 to 72%. Another challenge comes from the small sample study by FILDES and FITZGERALD [1983].

The success of the bootstrapping model was not often sensitive to the type of regression analysis used, nor was it sensitive to the estimates of the magnitude of the relationship. That is a familiar story, because the same thing was observed in Chapter 8 for econometric models. Furthermore, Dawes and Corrigan (1974) reanalyzed the data from Yntema and Torgerson (1961), Goldberg (1970), Wiggins and Kohen (1971), and Dawes (1971) and found that a unit weights model did better than the bootstrapping model, though REMUS [1980] presented contradictory evidence. This too has a familiar ring to it. You do not even have to bother to run a regression. Merely specify signs for the relationships and you are in business. William of Occam wins again!

When to Use Bootstrapping

Bootstrapping offers advantages in a number of situations.

1. It is inexpensive (Robinson, Wahlstrom, and Mecham, 1974). This is relevant for jobs with repetitive predictions (e.g., doctors, lawyers, stockbrokers, judges, university administrators).
2. It provides a first step for the introduction of objective forecasting

models. Let's face it. Managers are in favor of change when it affects other people, but they are like everyone else when the change strikes home. They may not take kindly to suggestions that they can be replaced by a quantitative model, but the resistance might be lower if they can be sure that their model will be used to make the forecasts.

3. It provides a quantitative model in cases where no data exist for the dependent variable. You could use "what if" questions to develop a direct bootstrapping model with signs and unit weights. If the judge was unsure about answering abstract questions, you could create hypothetical data for the situation and ask the judge to make predictions. These predictions would be used to develop an indirect bootstrapping model. Such an approach was used by Christal (1968) to develop a model for officer promotions in the U.S. Air Force. Bootstrapping can help to predict the success of new products (e.g., PARKER and SRINIVASAN [1976]), the best treatment for someone with lower back pain, the results of a proposed organizational change, or the outcome of a new social program.

4. It gives the decision maker a better understanding of the rules that she has been using. Experience sometimes fails to provide this insight [ROOSE and DOHERTY, 1976]. This may also highlight areas of prejudicial decision making.

5. If the forecasts are currently made by an individual rather than a group, bootstrapping is likely to produce bigger gains in accuracy [ROOSE and DOHERTY, 1976].

Exhibit 10-4 summarizes this advice on when to use bootstrapping.

Exhibit 10-4   WHEN TO USE BOOTSTRAPPING⟶AND WHY

---

1. Repetitive forecasts⟶cheaper than judgment
2. First step toward objective method⟶judge keeps control
3. No objective data on dependent variable⟶allows for quantification
4. To examine judgmental forecasts⟶reveals prejudice

ECONOMETRIC METHODS WITHIN SEGMENTS

One common strategy for forecasting is to group the data into homogeneous segments, and then to develop an econometric model within each segment. This strategy has been used for many years. For example, Seashore (1961) found that women's grades in high school and college were more predictable than men's. It is also found in the large scale econometric models. The combination of econometric and segmentation approaches is most useful when:

1. There is interaction (more specifically, a variable affects different groups in different ways).
2. The objective data are limited.

The effects of interaction are handled by segmentation, but this quickly depletes the data. Econometric methods use the remaining data more efficiently within the segments. The approach is illustrated by the hypothetical example in Exhibit 10-5.

Exhibit 10-5 ILLUSTRATION OF ECONOMETRIC MODELS WITHIN SEGMENTS: FORECASTING SALARIES

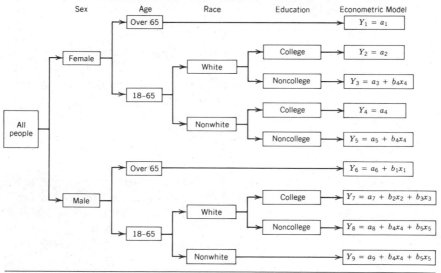

Note:

Y = yearly salary
x_1 = percentage of jobs in city with mandatory retirement age of 65 or less
x_2 = size of city
x_3 = age
x_4 = years of seniority in latest job
x_5 = union membership (1 = yes, and 0 = no)
a_i = constants

Salomon and Brown (1964) claimed that an approach using econometric models within each of 15 market segments led to more accurate forecasts than a "traditional method." Unfortunately, they did not provide sufficient information on what they did. Seven studies did allow for a comparison, and the results support the use of econometric methods within segments:

Elton and Gruber (1971) used econometric methods within segments to forecast the growth rate in earnings per share for 180 firms. They used a factor analysis of recent earnings data to group firms with homogeneous patterns of earnings growth. One-year forecasts were then made for 1964 earnings for firms in each of the ten homogeneous groups by using an econometric model. These forecasts were superior in accuracy to those provided by mechanical extrapolations of earnings by firm. However, another way of grouping (by SIC code) was also used, and these forecasts were inferior.

Kinney (1971) compared earning forecasts generated by two models:

1. Total earnings for the firm were multiplied by the forecasted percentage growth in GNP.
2. Earnings within each market segment of the firm were multiplied by the predicted percentage growth in the appropriate industry.

Model 2, the econometric method within segments, was superior for one-year forecasts. For 24 companies in 1968, the MAPE for the aggregate data model (model 1) was 17.2, while that for the model by segment was 13.4. For 19 companies in 1969, the respective figures were 11.6 and 11.2. Overall, the superiority of the model by segment was statistically significant ($p < .05$).

Raubenheimer and Tiffin (1971) developed an econometric model to predict job success for clerical workers. A model using 224 subjects had an R^2 of 6% when predicting success for 110 new subjects. The authors then broke the sample into three segments. The R^2 for each segment in the 110-subject validation sample was

7, 16, and 23%; that is, predictive ability was better for each segment than for the total sample.

Additional support for the use of econometric methods within segments was provided by COLLINS [1976] and SILHAN [1983] in finance, DUAN, et al. [1983] in health care, and PETERS, JACKOFSKY, and SLATER [1981] in personnel.

Another approach to using segmentation and econometric methods is to develop an econometric model after accounting for the effects of the segmentation. The dependent variable is the *deviation* between the actual value and the mean value for the segment, and the causal variables are the ones not used in the segmentation. In other words, the econometric model is used to predict residuals from the segment mean for each observation. This is an econometric method across segments. It assumes that individuals in all segments respond in the same manner to the variables in the econometric model. Evidence on the value of the approach is lacking, but an example is provided by Palmore:

Palmore (1969), using a sample of people between the ages of 60 and 94, started with actuarial tables from insurance companies. These broke the population into homogeneous segments on the basis of age, sex, and race. A regression analysis was used to explain differences in a longevity quotient that had been obtained by dividing the number of years a person lived by the expected number of years for a person in that segment. The econometric model explained only a small portion of the variance in these differences ($R^2 = .17$). (As a sidelight, it was found that the factor most closely related to longevity for old men was "work satisfaction." Involuntary retirement may lead to early death.)

LEADING INDICATORS

Leading indicators are obtained by exploring the data until you happen to find some variables whose trends precede similar trends in other variables. I would have no qualms about this if the search were for causal variables. But the idea of just using whatever happens to work strikes me as strange. This is not an extrapolation method because it uses other variables, and it is not an econometric model because there is no concern for causality. What is it then? Let me tell you by way of an analogy how leading indicators relate to extrapolation. An extrapolation model is like looking for a lost horse by following the direction in which it started out. Leading indicators are concerned with factors that often vary according to the presence or absence of horses—like flies, for example. If you can find the flies, maybe you can then find the horse nearby. Of course, you might merely find some horse shit.

I would not discuss leading indicators were it not for all of the historical interest in this approach. Possibly, leading indicators can serve as additional measures of current status. Most variables in the economy move together, so you can gain reliability in your assessment of current status by grouping a set of indicators. It is better to group variables that are expected to measure the variable of interest, however. Do not use noncausal leading indicators to forecast *change*. This is contrary to theory, and empirical evidence is lacking, except for the favorable results in AUERBACH [1982].

COMBINED FORECASTS

Eclectic research suggests the use of methods that are as different as possible. Use each method independently, then combine the forecasts. This procedure has been recommended in business forecasting for many years (National Industrial Conference Board, 1963, Chapter 8, and Wolfe 1966, p. 21). Reichard (1966, p. 202) and PoKempner and Bailey (1970) claimed that combining is common practice among business forecasters. However, DALRYMPLE's [1985] survey found that most firms either did not use combined forecasts or they used them infrequently. Combining is illustrated in Exhibit 10-6.

As an example of the use of Exhibit 10-6, consider a 10-year forecast of air travel in the United States. A judgmental method, such as a mail survey of experts outside of the airline industry, might be used for F_1; a simple extrapolation of the percentage change over the past 13 years could be used for F_2; a segmentation study based on a survey of traveling habits for the various types of air travelers might be used for F_3; and an econometric model employing population, income per capita, prices of air travel, prices of substitutes, and speed of service might be used for F_4.

The combined forecast is a weighted average of the different fore-

Exhibit 10-6   COMBINED FORECASTS FROM DIFFERENT METHODS

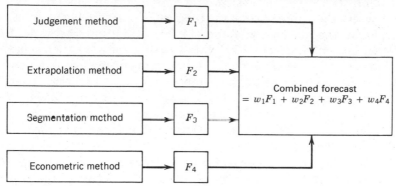

Note: The w's, the relative weights on various forecasts, should sum to 1.0.

casts, with the weights reflecting the confidence that the researcher has in each method. The weights should be selected before generating the forecasts to reduce the possibility of bias by the researcher. The use of a simple mechanical rule, such as providing equal weights for each forecast, is adequate in most situations.

Although the concern has been primarily with unintentional bias, it should be recognized that researchers, like politicians, doctors, professors, and businesspeople, apparently cheat once in a while (ARMSTRONG [1983d]). The cheating occurs because of organizational pressures, as in the testing of an airbrake by B. F. Goodrich (Heilbroner, 1972); because of peer group pressure (e.g., Dr. William Summerlin of Sloan-Kettering Institute, who painted laboratory mice to make them appear as if they had received successful skin grafts, or Sir Isaac Newton, who was expected to obtain more precise results; see Westfall, 1973); or because of payoffs. There is a fine line between payoffs and consulting. Often it is obvious that we, as consultants, are being asked to give not our expert opinion, but instead the forecast desired by the organization.

The combined forecast, done independently by different researchers, provides a safeguard against cheating. Using different researchers offers the following advantages:

1. You are more likely to include an honest researcher.
2. You make it difficult for cheating to occur. It is not easy for different researchers to come up with the *same* mistakes.

Of course, there are disadvantages if you already know what forecast you want. (But if you did, you would not have read this far.)

To assess the value of combined forecasts, I searched the literature for studies that combined forecasts from different methods. FALCONER and SIVESIND [1977] found significant advantages as their combination of an econometric and an extrapolative forecast was 51% better than the average of the components and 44% better than the best component. NELSON [1984] also found gains in accuracy from weighting macroeconomic forecasts from extrapolation and econometric models. RAUSSER and OLIVEIRA [1976] found that a combined forecast based on an average of an econometric and extrapolation forecast was better than either component. However, these studies used *ex post* forecasts. Schmitt (1954) claimed similar gains in population forecasting, but few details were provided. Granger and Newbold (1974) examined forecasts for three quarterly macroeconomic series in the United Kingdom; a combination of Box–Jenkins and econometric forecasts was generally more accurate than the average error of the components for one-period forecasts, but the weights were found retrospectively.

The most appropriate tests were those that used *ex ante* forecasts and provided sufficient descriptions to allow for a test of combined forecasts. In most of these studies it was necessary to reanalyze the results. In doing so, I used equal weights for each forecast. The studies are summarized here (see also the study by FILDES and FITZGERALD, 1983):

My reanalysis of a 10-year forecast of air travel passengers in the United States by the Port of New York Authority (1957) found that a simple unweighted combination of a segmentation and an econometric forecast did no better than the average forecast error.

I reanalyzed Okun's (1960) study of housing starts in the United States, where six one-year forecasts had been presented. There were two intentions forecasts and two extrapolations. This allowed for the calculation of four different combined forecasts. Small improvements were found for three of the four combined forecasts (the fourth forecast had the same error as the average for the components).

I reanalyzed Levine's (1960) study on forecasting capital expenditures by U.S. firms. Five different one-year forecasts were examined. A combined forecast was developed by averaging the
Commerce Department–SEC judgmental forecast and the extrapolation based on no change from the preceding year; the MAPE
was 6.4%. This compared with an average MAPE of 6.8% for the
two components. When the combination was based on an average
of the McGraw-Hill and the no-change forecasts, the MAPE was
5.9 vs. an average forecast error of 6.2 for the components.

In Vandome's (1963) quarterly forecasts of the United Kingdom's
economy, an econometric forecast missed by 6.2% and an extrapolation model missed by 5%, for an average error of 5.6%. A
combined forecast missed by 5.2%.

A reanalysis of O'Herlihy et al.'s (1967) five-year forecasts for
five product areas used a combination based on an econometric
model and a five-year extrapolation of growth in percentage terms.
There was no improvement of combined over average forecasts
for car exports, consumer durables, or energy, but the five-year
combined forecast of domestic auto demand was better than the
average (7.1% vs. 10.1%), and the combined forecast of coal consumption, with its 1% error, was better than either the econometric (+6.8%) or extrapolation (−8.7%) model.

In my study of the camera market (Armstrong, 1968b), a combined
forecast was developed using the average of an extrapolation model
and an econometric model. Six-year backcasts for 17 countries
were examined; improvements over the average backcast were
modest as the MAPE was reduced from 33% to 31.6%.

In BRANDON, FRITZ, and XANDER [1983], I first calculated
the root mean square error. After obtaining an average RMSE of
the four econometric forecasts, I combined it with a Box–Jenkins
forecast. This combined forecast had an RMSE that was 8.6% less
than its components.

Exhibit 10-7   ERROR REDUCTION BY COMBINING FORECASTS FROM
                DIFFERENT METHODS
                (All *ex ante* forecasts using Mean Absolute Percentage
                Error unless noted otherwise)

Study	Situation	Error Reduction
Port of N.Y. Authority (1957)	Air travel	0.0
FILDES AND FITZGERALD (1983)	Balance of payments	1.7[a]
Armstrong (1968b)	International photographic market	4.2
BRANDON, FRITZ AND XANDER (1983, p. 195)	U.S. GNP	4.8[b,c]
Levine (1960)	Capital expenditure	5.4[b]
Okun (1960)	Housing starts	6.2[b]
Vandome (1963)	National economy (UK)	7.1
O'Herlihy et al. (1967)	Five product categories (UK)	23.4
	Unweighted Average	6.6

[a]RMSE (Root Mean Square Error)
[b]Different combinations were presented; I used equal weights.
[c]All calculations were done using RMSE (not MSE as in this paper)

A summary of the evidence from the eight studies is provided in Exhibit 10-7. Combining is a powerful strategy! Combinations of two methods reduced the error by over 6%. It never hurt accuracy. Combinations of forecasts from three methods are expected to yield even further improvements, but only two studies were available on this: The error reduction in Rosenzweig (1957) was 0.0 and in BRANDT and BESSLER [1983] it was 17.9%.

UNCERTAINTY

The agreement among various forecasts can also be used as a measure of uncertainty. However, this is a crude measure, especially because the errors are usually positively correlated across the methods.

SUMMARY

The best approach to a given forecasting problem may call for a combination of different methods. There are many ways in which the methods can be combined, but few rules exist to guide the researchers in such combinations. Two rules were suggested:

1. Subjective methods should precede objective methods.
2. Segmentation should precede extrapolation or econometric methods.

Rule 1 is supported by evidence. Rule 2 seems to be obvious. Exhibit 10-1 provided a summary of these hypotheses. It was also suggested that different methods be used for estimating current status and forecasting change. These recommendations were summarized in Exhibit 10-3.

Bootstrapping, which involves the development of a model by using the judge's rules, offers substantial advantages. It is cheaper than judgmental forecasts for repetitive decisions; it offers advantages for implementation because the decision makers can be sure that their rules are being used; and it allows you to develop a quantitative model when no data exist for the dependent variable. A substantial body of empirical evidence indicated that bootstrapping is almost always as accurate as the typical judge, and generally more accurate. The particular way in which the bootstrapping model is developed is of little importance. You may use either indirect or direct methods because the performance of the model is highly dependent on the signs of the relationships, but is not sensitive to the magnitude of relationships. You should choose the cheapest and most acceptable way; this is likely to be the use of equal weights. Advice on when to use bootstrapping was provided in Exhibit 10-4.

The use of econometric methods within segments seems of value when interaction is high and when a moderate amount of historical data is available. The use of econometric methods across segments offers a sensible procedure in this same situation.

The method of leading indicators was briefly considered. From a theoretical viewpoint, there is little to recommend this method. Little empirical evidence was found to suggest that it is useful for forecasting change, although it may help to estimate current status.

Combining forecasts from different methods offers a powerful strategy for improving accuracy. Evidence from eight studies showed a reduction in the size of the error by over 6%.

Part III

EVALUATION

How should you evaulate forecasting models and forecasting processes? Part III discusses procedures for answering this question. Chapter 11 presents frameworks for the evaluation. Chapters 12 and 13 provide details for this framework; the former describes how to analyze the inputs to models, and the latter tells how to analyze the outputs from models.

PART III

Eleven

EVALUATION
SCHEMES

Contents

I don't mean to deny that the evidence is in some ways very strong in
favor of your theory, I only wish to point out that there are other theories
possible.

– Sherlock Holmes

Adventure of the Norwood Builder
Arthur Conan Doyle

Sherlock Holmes is right this time. Even so, forecasters often ignore
him! Much of the literature on forecasting methods reflects a "my
method is best" position by authors. Few papers entertain the possibility that other methods (or theories or models) are superior. This
chapter presents explicit frameworks for the evaluation of forecasting.

First I discuss the importance of using multiple models. Then I stress
the need for an *a priori* framework for evaluating methods. This framework is recommended to provide a better evaluation and to improve
the chances for implementation.

With respect to implementation, a distinction is made between the
criteria of "acceptability" and "quality." "Acceptability" refers to approval by those in the organization who would actually use the model;
"quality" refers to the model's ability to provide good outputs. A high-
quality model that is not accepted is of no value, nor is a low-quality
model that is accepted.

The chapter concludes with suggestions on evaluating the forecasting *system*. A checklist is provided to audit this system.

MULTIPLE MODELS

Statements such as "A mean absolute error of 20% represents a poor
forecasting record" or "Uncertainties about the long-range future ren-
der any forecasts beyond 10 years worthless" are frequently encountered in papers on forecasting. Such statements, by themselves, say
little; they remind me of that age-old question, "What's the difference
between an orange?" What is missing is a basis for comparison.

*The best way to evaluate the forecasting ability of a model is to com-
pare it with other models.* Thus a mean absolute error of 20% may be
very good indeed if the next best model has an error of 40%. And
forecasts beyond 10 years may be useful if the proposed model does a
better job than the implicit model that is currently being used. Nevertheless, if you insist on knowing the typical errors for a given situation,
see MENTZER and COX [1984] and ASCHER [1978].

All aspects of model evaluation depend upon the comparison of alternative models. Which model has the most realistic assumptions? Which model provides the best predictions? Which model costs the least to develop? In other words, the beauty of a model is all relative; an illustration is provided in Exhibit 11-1.

The selection of a *set* of reasonable models is of critical importance. This step requires judgment by the analyst and by the clients. In most cases, one would expect the current model to be used as a basis for

Exhibit 11-1   THE BEAUTY OF A MODEL: The First Miss America (1921).

Source.   © Miss America Pageant, permission for use granted.

comparison. Another guideline is that the models should stress variety; they should differ from one another to ensure that all reasonable approaches are examined. Still another guideline is to start with simple and low-cost models.

It is nice to appear to be reasonable and to present both sides of the issue. Nevertheless, I cannot think of anything worthwhile to say about research based on a single model. On the other hand, much published research on forecasting is done using a single model. Unfortunate.

WHEN AND WHAT TO EVALUATE

When should the plan for evaluation be developed, and what should it cover? The possibilities for "when" are *a priori* (before developing the forecasting models) and *a posteriori* (after developing the forecasting models).

The evaluation can focus on the process or on the content. Process relates to how the forecasting model will be evaluated and what will be the general framework for analysis. Content is more specific; it relates to an examination of the inputs and outputs for a given model. Although these categories overlap somewhat, they offer different perspectives.

Exhibit 11-2 presents four strategies for evaluation by considering the questions of what and when simultaneously. Box *A*, the *a priori* framework, is of particular concern in this chapter. Box *B*, the *a posteriori* framework, is a possibility. Although it is not recommended in this book, it is commonly used. Boxes *C* and *D*, the evaluation of inputs and outputs to a model, are considered only briefly in this chapter because they form the basis of Chapters 12 and 13.

Exhibit 11-2   STRATEGIES FOR EVALUATION: WHAT AND WHEN

		When	
		Before	After
	Process	A *A priori* framework	B *A posteriori* framework
What			
	Content	C Evaluate inputs	D Evaluate outputs

A Priori Framework

Chapter 3, on implementation, suggested that it is important to gain prior commitment from the key stakeholders. If this is not done, little meaningful change is likely to result. The prior commitment should include:

1. The models to be considered
2. The framework to be used
3. Specific criteria for items within the framework

Possible models were proposed in Part II of *LRF;* a framework for evaluation of models is provided in this chapter; and suggestions to help in the selection of criteria are presented here and in Chapters 12 and 13.

It requires much time and psychic energy to gain prior commitment—both for the forecaster and for the key stakeholders. It is uncomfortable; you feel that you are wasting time while the real work has not even begun. But this is a crucial step.

How do you know when you have gained prior commitment? Well, if you are not sure, you probably have not been successful here.

A Posteriori Framework

Forecasters who already know the right answer have no need for an *a priori* framework. They can do what many do—create a framework for evaluation after the forecasts have been obtained. This helps to ensure that the evaluation will not interfere with the desired solution. People who have worked on the evaluation of models know what I am saying here; others may think that I am being cynical. No, I am being realistic.

If the client has not committed himself to a framework for evaluation, he is free to contribute as he sees fit. Often the client sees fit to defend the existing methods. Or he may view himself as a problem finder—and find problems with your model or with your framework. This seems like a rational way to respond in such circumstances. (If you are not part of the solution, you are part of the problem.)

In response, the person proposing the forecasting model concludes that this is really a communication problem, so he spends a lot of time trying to explain the merits of his model.

At this point, each party acts as an advocate of his model. The cleverness of each researcher shows up as he tailors his framework to demonstrate the point to be made. Typically, each framework considers only a part of the problem. An example of research in which the framework followed the development of the model is provided in the Ford-Chevrolet study described below. Of course, this is typical of academic research because seldom can one identify the clients in advance. That is why we have those strange "Comments on Doe," where Professor Oates points out the errors in Doe's paper; and the "Reply to Oates' Comments on Doe," where Doe points out that his paper was on apples whereas Oates was discussing oranges.

Evans (1959) used a linear discriminant analysis of psychological data to distinguish between buyers of Fords and Chevrolets. At least four papers criticizing Evans' study were published. Meanwhile, Evans wrote two replies to the critics. Admittedly some good blows were landed in all of this fighting. Still, one gets the impression that it is like watching the blind men feel the elephant; each researcher picked a framework to suit the point he wanted to make. It might have saved time and effort had Evans used a comprehensive framework for evaluation in his initial paper.

Inputs and Outputs

Most of us find it easier to deal with the specific rather than the general. Thus, instead of discussing a general framework for analysis, we prefer to jump into detailed questions about the inputs and outputs for a given model. This book suggests that inputs and outputs should be analyzed only after agreement has been reached on an *a priori* framework.

The analysis of inputs should come before the models have been developed. This helps to maintain people's interest in the inputs. It also keeps the researcher honest. When examining studies using industrial dynamics and exploratory regression analysis, I was told that the researchers often changed the inputs if they did not like the outputs.

Forecasts become the center of attention once they are revealed. There is then less interest in the framework or in the inputs (except to change them to suit your biases). But if commitment was reached on the *process*, it is more likely that the forecasts will be accepted. The likelihood of rational decision making is increased if the decision makers have already considered what actions to take, given various forecasts.

Exhibit 11-3 FINDING THE RIGHT FORECAST

Source. "The Wizard of Id," by permission of Johnny Hart and Field Enterprises, Inc.

If you do not reach commitment on the process, and if the clients are not prepared for alternative forecasts, you may have a problem. If you are lucky, you have a favorable forecast to report (i.e., one that requires no difficult changes for the organization). But what if the forecast brings bad news? If you are one of those "smart consultants," like the Royal Meteorologist (Exhibit 11-3), you will make sure that the forecast sounds good. If you cannot make it sound good, you can use the fortune-teller's strategy and make it sound vague. So goes the dirty tricks department. If Royal Meteorologists and fortune-tellers know these tricks, then so do forecasting consultants.

EVALUATING ACCEPTABILITY

Acceptability can be evaluated by judging the model through the eyes of the user. In particular, the following should be examined:

1. Organizational value, that is, the user's perception of the value of the model to the organization.
2. Personal value, that is, the user's perception of the benefits (or costs) of the model to himself.

What is important here is not what actually exists—it is what clients believe to exist. Sometimes these perceptions match reality, but often they do not. Do not assume they are the same. Also, do not assume that the clients will perceive things in the same way that you do.

A written evaluation of acceptability should be made. The items in Exhibit 11-4 are typical of those that should be examined; also sug-

---

**Exhibit 11-4 EVALUATING ACCEPTABILITY OF A
          MODEL**

User perceptions of organizational value

Measures (examples)
  Profit
  Employment
  Customer service

Assessment techniques (examples)
  Self-administered questionnaires
  Nondirective interviews

User perceptions of personal value

Measures (examples)
  Security
  Achievement
  Power
  Income

Assessment techniques (examples)
  Direct questions
  Projective questions
  Group depth interviews
  Role playing
  Unobtrusive measures

---

gestions are provided on assessment. You should develop a checklist
for your problem and apply it separately to each of the stakeholders.
For an example of the assessment of alternative forecasting models,
see GOMEZ-MEJIA, PAGE, and TORNOW [1982].

The assessment of organizational value is generally easier than the
assessment of personal value, because the former is an acceptable thing
to talk about. A major problem, however, is that people in organizations
view a proposal in terms of its impact upon their particular units within
the organization. Furthermore, it is generally taboo to question the
goals of a unit. As a result, perceptions of the value of a proposed
method often vary substantially by group (e.g., labor vs. management,
production vs. marketing, stockholder vs. customer, line vs. staff).

Nondirective interviewing can be useful in getting people to express opinions without being constrained by these organizational taboos. So can self-administered questionnaires. Certainly the replies by each respondent must be kept confidential; thus it helps to have the surveys administered by people outside the organization.

The assessment of personal value is affected by a client's desire to answer so that he appear in a favorable light. For this reason, the assessment techniques in Exhibit 11-4 emphasize indirect approaches. (These techniques were discussed in Chapter 6.)

Beyond the use of checklists and a written evaluation of the acceptability of proposed forecasting models, little more can be said. Just use Gerstenfeld's law of trying.

In the following, I describe the approach used to evaluate the acceptability of a forecasting model that was being used by a large U.S. corporation. The company, Drinkit Corporation, had asked us to evaluate the model. The names have been disguised. The disguise fooled some people, who incorrectly thought their company was being described! Apparently, this description seems typical for organizations.

Armstrong and Shapiro (1974) examined the FAITH models, which are used by some of the largest corporations in the United States. Their advocates claim that the models are useful for predicting changes in market share when changes are made in prices, product line, or advertising. To evaluate the acceptability of these models, we interviewed key user groups, including marketing research, sales, product management, marketing management, and general management in the company. Individual and group interviews were used, and they were primarily nondirective. Two interviewers sat in on each session and took notes separately so that the reliability of the information could be improved. Highlights of these interviews are summarized here.

Perceived Organizational Value. Perceptions of the value of FAITH were mixed. The top two levels of management in Drinkit thought that FAITH provided better predictions than those currently made by the product managers. The middle and lower levels felt just the opposite, partially because they had confidence in their own judgment. Comments by the product managers included: "FAITH can't be wrong; if their estimates are off, the advocates claim it is because the input data were not right."

Perceived Personal Value

1. Opinion was split by organizational level: the higher levels thought that FAITH was valuable because it gave them more control over decision making; the middle and lower levels felt that FAITH was another attempt by higher managements to reduce subordinates' influence.
2. The low level of acceptability of FAITH also showed up in unobtrusive measures. For example, when the middle and lower levels of Drinkit management met for an all-day planning session, not one reference was made to FAITH—yet FAITH was then regarded by top management as the foremost quantitative planning model in the company.
3. Because the marketing managers were told by top management to use the FAITH models, middle- and lower-level managers would change the inputs to the FAITH model until they found a result that agreed with their own decision. This version was then presented to top management. In other words, managers were misusing the models.

The analysis of acceptability is often crude; however, the problems are sometimes of such magnitude that a precise examination is not required. In the case of Drinkit, it quickly became apparent that the major user group, the product managers, had little faith in FAITH.

EVALUATING QUALITY

Quality can be evaluated by examining the inputs (assumptions) to the model, or by examining the outputs (forecasts) from the model. The testing of inputs has been more popular. Some, such as Machlup (1955), have gone so far as to imply that the testing of inputs is the only worthwhile way to test models.

An equally unreasonable position was taken by Friedman (1953), who claimed that the testing of outputs is the only useful approach for testing models. (Nagel, 1963, criticized Friedman's position.)

It is better to test both the inputs and the outputs. The primary reason for testing inputs it to learn how to improve a given model. The major reason for testing outputs is to select the best model(s). Naturally, there is some overlap; tests of inputs may demonstrate that one model is clearly inferior to another, and tests of outputs may provide clues to improve the model.

These ideas on testing inputs and outputs can be translated into somewhat more operational terms by examining how the forecasting model relates to the real world. These relationships are illustrated in Exhibit 11-5. The right-hand side of the exhibit represents the inputs to the model: "Are the assumptions reasonable?" and "Does the model follow from the assumptions?" The left-hand side represents the outputs from the model: "Can the outputs be replicated?" and "Do the benefits from the model exceed the costs?" In the following, these four stages are discussed.

From the Real World to the Assumptions

Are the assumptions behind the model reasonable? To assess this, you should search for evidence relating directly to these assumptions. Below, ideas are presented on how to search for this evidence.

Exhibit 11-5   STAGES IN ANALYZING THE QUALITY OF A MODEL

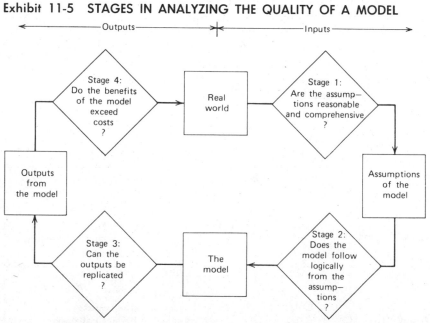

Source.   Reprinted from Armstrong and Shapiro (1974), with permission from the *Journal of Marketing*, published by the American Marketing Association.

One key decision is whether to use objective (empirical) or subjective data to test assumptions. Clearly, objective data, such as those obtained from experiments, are preferred. If objective data are not available, then you must use subjective data. For the assessment of acceptability you might use both objective and subjective data.

Another key decision is whether to utilize experts from inside the organization or from outside it. Outside experts are less subject to bias; on the other hand, their evidence may be less relevant to the specific problem faced by the organization. Bias is more serious for subjective data, although it can also occur for objective data. The issue of relevance is particularly important for objective data because it is important to ensure that these data were generated in a situation representative of the problem at hand.

These ideas about searching for objective vs. subjective evidence, and using inside vs. outside experts, are summarized in Exhibit 11-6. Within that exhibit, some specific techniques are proposed. The preferred approach (source a) is to use objective evidence generated from experiments for the problem at hand. Next best (source b) is to use objective empirical evidence developed by others. If this fails, you could use subjective impressions of people within the organization (source c). Alternatively you might turn to subjective evidence from unbiased outside experts (source d); this could come from papers published by experts or from hired consultants.

Unfortunately, it is frequently necessary to resort to subjective evidence from inside experts. The power of this approach can be improved by use of the following techniques:

Exhibit 11-6   SOURCES OF EVIDENCE ON ASSUMPTIONS

	Objective	Subjective
Inside Experts	a Experiments	c Surveys Unobstructive measures Bootstrapping
Outside Experts	b Empirical studies	d Consultants Theoretical papers

- Surveys of the people in an organization provide a fast, inexpensive way to determine whether they regard the assumptions for a model as reasonable. It is preferable that the surveys be self-administered and anonymous. The questions should provide a choice among assumptions rather than absolute answers. For example, an assumption may be stated and its exact opposite used as an alternative. The respondent could indicate the degree of agreement with each of these extremes.
- Unobtrusive measures may be helpful for emotional issues. Sometimes the organization trains people to talk in certain ways, yet they act differently. Is it possible to observe how people act and thus infer their beliefs? For example, people in a personnel department may claim that their predictions of the probable success of job applicants do not depend upon age, race, sex, or religion. Do they act that way?
- Indirect bootstrapping is a logical extension of unobtrusive measures to infer the assumptions that were used to make predictions. For the personnel example, variables on age, race, sex, and religion could be examined.

An example from our study of the FAITH models illustrates how some of these ideas can be used:

In Armstrong and Shapiro's (1974) study of the FAITH models, the advocates of FAITH based their claims on the reasonableness of the assumptions on face validity, which in this case meant that the assumptions looked reasonable to them. Strangely, however, they asked the clients to suspend their beliefs when evaluating the assumptions. (This is true. You were probably wondering where we got the name "FAITH models.") The following three assumptions were among those examined:

1. The models assumed that the switching between any two brands of beverages was equal in both directions; that is, the number of customers switching from Mother Fletcher's brand to Bestbuy is the same as the number switching from Bestbuy to Mother Fletcher's for a given period of time. No experimental evidence on this was available from within the company despite the fact that it had been evaluating FAITH over a six-year period (source a in Exhibit 11-6).
2. It was assumed that the forecasts were not sensitive to mea-

surement error in the data. We tested this using FAITH predictions for one of Drinkit's beverages, which was referred to as Kola. Predictions for each of 15 time periods were compared with actual data when different starting points were selected. When period 1 was used to obtain estimates for the FAITH model, the MAPE for periods 2 through 16 was 4.9%. When period 3 was used for estimation, the MAPE for the remaining 15 periods (i.e., periods 1, 2, and 4 through 16) was 2.7%. In all, six different starting points were examined, and the MAPE varied from 2.7% in the best case to 12.7% in the worst case. The implication is that forecast accuracy was highly sensitive to measurement error. (Source a in Exhibit 11-6.)

3. Published empirical evidence from Morrison (1966) suggested that the assumption about equal switching in each direction was unreasonable. (Source b in Exhibit 11-6.)

4. It was assumed that the brand of beverage purchased by a consumer was unrelated to the brand previously purchased by that consumer. Interviews with Drinkit's product managers indicated that this assumption was unreasonable. (Source c in Exhibit 11-6.)

5. The assumptions looked unreasonable to us as consultants. (Source d in Exhibit 11-6.)

In general, the users' assumptions conflicted with those employed in the FAITH models. Furthermore, we were unable to locate a single client who claimed to have an adequate understanding of the models. Typical comments were: "No one can explain FAITH to me"; "I don't know how FAITH works."

From the Assumptions to the Model

This stage of analysis involves an examination of the logical structure of the forecasting model. Here it is important that the structure of the model be fully disclosed. Unfortunately, claims of "competitive secrecy" are often used to rule out full disclosure. Such claims are sometimes used by charlatans.

A more sophisticated alternative used by some charlatans is to provide full disclosure, but to use complex procedures and difficult languages so that the clients cannot understand what is being said. Bafflegab puts the clients in an awkward position. The clients are apparently being given all of the information about the model's structure, and the advocate is spending much time with them trying to explain the assumptions; are they going to admit that they are so stupid that they cannot understand the model? The easy way out is to nod in agreement and to hope the advocate knows what he is talking about.

Bafflegab can be used to divert the client's attention from other stages of analysis. They exhaust themselves trying to understand the model, finally concluding that it is too complex for them and that they must trust the model builder.

Complexity is no virtue in forecasting, as was discussed in Part II. Thus there is no excuse for bafflegab, even if practiced by well-intentioned and pleasant people. One should insist that the change agent's duty is to explain the model so that the client can understand it. Good tests of understanding are for the client to:

1. be able to explain the structure of the model to someone else, and to
2. be able to explain the structure of the model in written form so that it makes sense to you.

The change agent should help to ensure that an understanding is reached. This brings us back to acceptability.

The advocates of FAITH used bafflegab. Although the model was not shown to be inconsistent, an immense amount of effort was required to work through the logical structure:

In Armstrong and Shapiro (1974), a detailed examination was made of the logical structure of the model, which the advocates referred to as FAITH-DYNAMICS. This examination was time consuming because of the model's complexity and because of poor documentation (we had to meet with the advocates for much of the explanation). We did not find any logical inconsistencies in the model. We then contacted other researchers who had made independent evaluations of this model; they also had detected no inconsistencies but, like us, had found the model to be obscure.

From the Model to the Outputs

Stage 3 is a routine auditing step. Given the model and the data, is it possible to replicate the output? You take a sample of the data that were used and enter it into the model that the advocates used. The procedure is analogous to a financial audit.

It is preferable to do the calculations by hand, using the model that you described in your own words.

This stage of analysis is often overlooked; we trust the model builders to be competent. But this stage has the following advantages:

1. It helps the clients to ensure that they understand the model.
2. It provides an additional check against errors.
3. Cheating is unusual, and this procedure helps to keep it unusual.

The point on honesty should not be overlooked. Cyril Burt, who is dead now, had been described as "one of the world's great psychologists." His main claim to fame had been his study of the IQs of identical twins. Strangely, as Burt published studies in 1955, 1958, and 1966, his sample sizes of identical twins increased from 21 to "over 30" and then to 53 pairs, yet the correlation between the IQ scores for identical twins was .771 in all three cases. One hypothesis is that he was cheating. (For a description of this case see Wade (1976).) Nevertheless, do not accuse anyone of cheating. Failures to replicate may arise in many ways, such as by mistakes. Speaking of replication, we were unable to replicate the FAITH results for Drinkit:

> Armstrong and Shapiro (1974) used the same data that were used by FAITH advocates to predict for 15 periods of Kola. For 12 of the 15 periods, the predictions by the FAITH advocates were more accurate than those obtained by us, using their data and their model. Their average error was half the error that we found. The advocates were unable to explain this discrepancy.

From the Outputs to the Real World

The analysis of outputs is the most important stage in assessing the quality of a model. Rather than attack the problem directly, you should break it into parts by means of a cost-benefit framework. The cost-benefit framework helps to make the examination more systematic and explicit.

Given a set of replicable models with realistic assumptions, the general procedure for a cost-benefit analysis is as follows:

1. List the potential benefits for each model.
2. List the potential costs for each model.
3. Weigh benefits against costs for each model.
4. Select the model with the most favorable cost-benefit score.

Although this list is simple from a conceptual viewpoint, it is hard to implement. Gerstenfeld's law of trying is recommended. Also recommended is Exhibit 11-7, which can be used as a checklist to ensure that all costs and benefits have been examined. It describes three cost items: initial development costs, maintenance costs (to keep the model up to date), and operating costs (time and dollars spent by users to obtain the forecasts). There are four benefits: improved accuracy of the forecasts, assessment of uncertainty (how much confidence should we place on the forecast?), assessment of alternative futures (including changes in the environment or changes in the organization's policies), and the contribution of the model to learning (will the forecasting model improve over time?).

The selection of alternative models is of particular concern in the cost-benefit analysis. Although it is best to have explicit alternatives, two procedures can be used with implicit alternatives:

- The test of large changes
- The Turing test

The first procedure involves the use of extreme inputs to test the generality of the model. This is especially useful if there are extreme inputs whose outcomes would be obvious. The key question is whether the model provides reasonable forecasts for large changes.

The Turing test (Turing, 1950) involves comparisons of the outputs from various models. This can be done even with forecasts from implicit models. The question is whether a panel of experts can distinguish differences in the reasonableness of outputs from different models. This procedure is often used in the research on expert systems.

Exhibit 11-7 COST-BENEFIT ANALYSIS OF FORECASTING MODELS

Costs	*Benefits*
Development	Forecast accuracy
Maintenance	Assessment of uncertainty
Operating	Assessment of alternative futures
	Learning

When using explicit alternatives, you should include the model currently used. This model will serve as a benchmark for comparisons.

Another explicit alternative should be based on simplicity. In Chapter 10, bootstrapping was proposed as a way to translate complex judgmental forecasting into a simple quantitative model. *Bootstrapping can also be used to translate a complex quantitative model into a simple quantitative model.* This procedure is illustrated in our study of the FAITH models, along with some of the steps used in the cost-benefit analysis.

In Armstrong and Shapiro (1974), the assessment of costs was relatively easy. Drinkit Corporation paid about $60,000 per year to the FAITH Corporation, and an additional $40,000 was estimated for the time spent by Drinkit personnel (in 1973 dollars). These costs were constant from year to year because there was a continuing need for expert assistance. On the benefit side, FAITH provided no assessment of uncertainty. FAITH advocates claimed, however, that their models were useful for improving accuracy, examining alternative futures, and learning. No empirical test had been made of these claims in six years of use by Drinkit. Because Drinkit was especially interested in forecast accuracy, we examined forecasts using large changes; an examination was also made of the accuracy of alternative models.

Large Changes. The FAITH models multiplied the following variables to obtain the best advertising level: industry volume × unit margin for brand × brand market share × competition's market share × brand switching. Under this model, if industry volume doubled, Drinkit should spend twice as much on advertising. This did not seem reasonable compared to the implicit forecasting model used by the product managers at Drinkit.

Alternative Models. Drinkit was unable to provide any cases where FAITH predictions were compared with the managers' judgmental predictions. We compared the FAITH forecasts with those from a simple quantitative model obtained by bootstrapping the FAITH model. That is, regression analysis was used, with the dependent variable based on FAITH forecasts, and the causal variables were those used by the FAITH model. This yielded a SON-OF-FAITH model. The advertising version of this model was

$$Y = 20.7 + 0.6X$$

where Y = market share (predicted by FAITH model)
      X = advertising dollars (divided by 1 million)

The SON-OF-FAITH model explained 98% of the variance in FAITH predictions.

Because SON-OF-FAITH required FAITH predictions, the model was recalibrated using actual data; four periods of Kola data were used. Forecasts were then made for periods 5 through 16, and the forecasts were compared with actual data. The MAPE for these predictions was 2.7% compared with a MAPE of 3% for predictions by the FAITH model. The superiority of this simple econometric model was also found when different starting values were used, although the differences were not statistically significant.

SCORESHEET FOR EVALUATING MODELS

The final step in the framework for analysis is to summarize the models according to the criteria and weights initially agreed upon. If you did a good job in gaining commitment, this is a routine step; you plug in the results, and the decision falls right out. If you did not reach commitment, there are at least three possibilities:

1. Everyone thinks the problem is unimportant.
2. You got the "right" answer (i.e., the answer the decision makers already wanted).
3. You are willing to create a confrontation to gain acceptance of your findings.

Armstrong and Shapiro describe the use of the scoresheet in the FAITH study.

One of the bad things about the Armstrong and Shapiro (1974) study was that we were not able to gain commitment. Nevertheless, we completed the analysis and obtained the results shown in Exhibit 11-8. The FAITH models were compared to the subjective process currently used by managers and also to the simple econometric model. The entries in Exhibit 11-8 are based upon our judgments after conducting various tests, some of which were described previously. Each exhibit entry is a rating of FAITH. Thus, for user perception of quality, FAITH rated as poor relative to management's judgment. The simple econometric model clearly dominated the FAITH model; it would have been superior to FAITH under any weighting scheme. Management's judgment was also superior in light of the problems expected with the acceptability of FAITH.

Exhibit 11-8   THE SCORESHEET: EXAMPLE BASED ON FAITH

	Ratings of FAITH vs.	
Criteria	Management's Judgment	Simple Econometric Model
Acceptability		
User perception of quality	Poor	Unknown
User perception of personal value	Poor	Unknown
Quality		
Stage 1: Reasonable assumptions	Poor	About the same
Stage 2: Logical structure	Good	About the same
Stage 3: Audit of outputs	Unknown	Poor
Stage 4: Cost-benefit analysis	Unknown	Poor

Source. Reprinted from Armstrong and Shapiro (1974), with permission from the *Journal of Marketing*, published by the American Marketing Association.

Our framework led to questions that had not been examined during the six years of evaluation by the Drinkit Company. These questions, in turn, led to conclusions that differed sharply from those that had been reached previously by Drinkit. Ah, but the lack of commitment! We were able to predict Drinkit's decision: They kept the FAITH.

EVALUATING THE FORECASTING SYSTEM

The preceding part of this chapter was oriented to an evaluation of forecasting models. For an overall examination of the forecasting system in an organization, I developed the "Forecasting Audit Checklist" (Exhibit 11-9). This checklist, based heavily upon the research in *LRF*, was originally presented in ARMSTRONG [1982b]. It addresses issues related to forecasting methods, assumptions and data, uncertainty, and costs.

The items on the checklist are worded in such a way that a "YES" is the desired response. My students and I have used the checklist to audit numerous organizations. In the following, I present some impressions from these applications. The numbers correspond with the items on the checklist:

1. Top management should be involved primarily in providing inputs to the forecasting system. But their involvement in the forecasting methods is expensive and is likely to lead to bias. In practice, most of the organizations we examined did not keep the forecasting methods independent of top management.

2. Objective methods can often reduce costs (e.g., in inventory control) or improve accuracy. For example, bootstrapping provides gains relative to unaided judgment, and econometric models provide further gains in accuracy.

3. Evidence that structured techniques can improve the accuracy of judgmental forecasts is impressive. Nevertheless, this item was often ignored by the organizations we examined.

4. Only a moderate amount of expertise is required to forecast change, though expertise *is* important for estimating current status. Some firms could save money by remembering this point.

5. The majority of the organizations based their forecast on the single "best" method. Few combined forecasts.

6. As firms move toward the use of objective methods, the problems involved with understanding seem to increase.

7. One of the most frequently violated guidelines was that com-

Exhibit 11-9 FORECASTING AUDIT CHECKLIST

Topic Areas	No	·?	Yes
FORECASTING METHODS			
1. Forecast independent of top management?	___	___	___
2. Forecast used objective methods?	___	___	___
3. Structured techniques used to obtain judgments?	___	___	___
4. Least expensive experts used?	___	___	___
5. More than one method used to obtain forecasts?	___	___	___
6. Users understand the forecasting methods?	___	___	___
7. Forecasts free of judgmental revisions?	___	___	___
8. Separate documents prepared for plans and forecasts?	___	___	___
ASSUMPTIONS AND DATA			
9. Ample budget for analysis and presentation of data?	___	___	___
10. Central data bank exists?	___	___	___
11. Least expensive macroeconomic forecasts used?	___	___	___
UNCERTAINTY			
12. Upper and lower bounds provided?	___	___	___
13. Quantitative analysis of previous accuracy?	___	___	___
14. Forecasts prepared for alternative futures?	___	___	___
15. Arguments listed *against* each forecast?	___	___	___
COSTS			
16. Amount spent on forecasting reasonable?	___	___	___

panies frequently made judgmental revisions of the objective forecasts of change.

8. Separate documents for plans and forecasts can help to solve difficulties associated with keeping the forecast independent of top management (item 1) and with avoiding judgmental revisions (item 7). It can also aid in assessing the accuracy of the forecast (item 13).

9. The budget for analysis and presentation of data often suffers relative to the costs for data collection. This item argues against that automatic response "we need more data"; instead, more emphasis should be given to the analysis and presentation of available data.

10. Many organizations report that the information needed to make forecasts is not available in a central location (e.g., a computer file).

11. Given the lack of evidence that one econometric model is more accurate than another, the decision on which econometric service to use should be based on cost or other criteria, such as ease of understanding.

12. Most organizations reported problems with the assessment of uncertainty. Forecasts are commonly presented (often with many significant digits!) with no mention of upper and lower confidence limits.

13. Many firms have no systematic procedures to track the accuracy of their forecasting methods.

14. Few firms reported that they prepared forecasts for alternative futures.

15. It is not common for an organization to explicitly list the arguments against each forecast.

16. Few firms kept track of the amount spent on forecasting. Nevertheless, the general amount thought spent on forecasting was reasonable.

SUMMARY

To evaluate forecasting models, compare them with alternative models. Of particular interest are comparisons with models that represent current practice, and models that are inexpensive and simple.

The scheme for evaluation should be developed before the data are analyzed. It is especially important that commitment be reached on the *process* used to evaluate the models. Little is gained by creating an evaluation framework after the forecasting models have been developed. Some attention should also be given to the *content* of the forecasting model, that is, to the inputs and outputs.

Acceptability and quality should each be explicitly evaluated for a proposed forecasting model. The model should score well in each area before it is adopted.

Acceptability can be examined by measuring the clients' perceptions of the value of a model not only to the organization, but to themselves. A checklist of methods was presented in Exhibit 11-4 for assessing these perceptions.

Quality is assessed by the four-stage approach outlined in Exhibit 11-5. This examines the reasonableness of the inputs, the logical consistency of the model, the replicability of outputs from the model, and a cost-benefit analysis of the outputs.

An explicit scoresheet was suggested for bringing together the results of the evaluations of acceptability and quality of a model (Exhibit 11-8).

Finally, a forecasting audit checklist was proposed to aid in the evaluation of a forecasting system (Exhibit 11-9).

Twelve

TESTING INPUTS

Contents

The most essential qualification for a politician is the ability to foretell what will happen tomorrow, next month, and next year, and to explain afterwards why it did not happen.

Winston Churchill
(via Cetron and Ralph, 1983)

A famous forecast concluded that the national IQ would decline. The basic assumptions for this forecast were that people who had lower IQs had more children than those with higher IQs, and that IQ is largely hereditary. This forecast was supported by well-respected sociologists and other people who might be considered to be experts. What was wrong with this forecast? It did not forecast well. (However, by some measures of intelligence, national quotients have shown a decline since the early 1960s. RIMLAND [1981] reviews alternative explanations.) Still, the theory persisted, perhaps because the inputs were so appealing: everyone knows that those less intelligent multiply at a faster rate.

A careful examination of the inputs to this IQ forecast reveals that they are faulty. It is true that IQ is hereditary to a large extent. However, it is not true that less intelligent people multiply at a faster rate. (Actually, they can't even add faster.) This false assumption arose because it was noted that larger families are produced by lower IQ people. However, the higher reproductive rate of those in the lower IQ groups who are parents is offset by the larger proportion of this group who never marry or who fail to reproduce at all. This explanation was first proposed by Willoughby and Cougan (1940) and later supported by Duncan (1952, 1969), Higgins, Reed, and Reed (1962), and OLNECK and WOLFE [1980].

The IQ forecasting model illustrates one of the uses of the examination of inputs, namely, to rule out models based on highly fallacious assumptions. Seldom, however, is a case so clear-cut that it will allow us to discard a model. In general, the testing of inputs is done to find ways to improve the model. Chapter 12 provides specific advice on testing inputs.

Forecasting models have two basic components: variables and relationships. Each component can be analyzed separately. In addition, you can examine the *process* that yields the variables and relationships. These various inputs are illustrated by the rectangles in Exhibit 12-1.

The concepts of validity and reliability are of particular importance

Exhibit 12-1   INPUTS TO FORECASTING MODELS

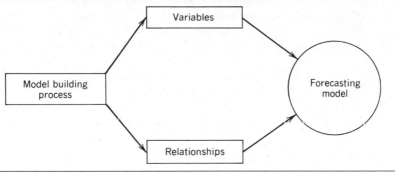

for analyzing inputs. The first part of the chapter describes these concepts. They are then applied to testing the process, the variables, and the relationships.

VALIDITY AND RELIABILITY

Techniques for improving the validity and reliability of forecasting methods were provided in Part II of this book. In this chapter, these concepts are discussed in more detail and their role in testing is described. This description draws upon Selltiz, Wrightsman, and Cook (1976).

Tests for validity may be classified into three categories: **face validity**[G], **predictive validity**[G], and **construct validity**[G]. These tests are described along with the test of reliability.

The test of face validity is whether "people who should know" agree that something is reasonable. This is the weakest of the validity tests. However, it is one on which most of us place great reliance. (As a check on this, you might ask your friends about the national IQ forecasting model. Some people cling strongly to false but seemingly reasonable assumptions.) Kelly and Fiske (1950) suggest that a more appropriate name would be "faith validity."

"People who should know" often do not know. Hotelling presents a case demonstrating the lack of a critical eye among academics. He was concerned that authors of textbooks did not understand the assumptions behind their materials. Consequently, they tended to introduce errors as the "facts" were copied from textbook to textbook. Hotelling wrote (1940, pp. 460–461):

One outstanding example is in certain formulae connected with the rank correlation coefficient, derived originally by Karl Pearson in 1907 and copied from textbook to textbook without adequate checking back. As one error after another was introduced in this process, the formulae presented to students . . . became less and less like Pearson's original equations.

To stem the flow of my own errors, I provide an Errata section in this Second Edition (*LRF* p. 450).

Mosier (1947) assessed the value of face validity by using two tests designed to select office workers. The two tests seemed to measure the same thing (i.e., the tests were the same, judged on face validity). You might examine them to see whether you think they measure the same skill:

Alphabetizing Test

Test 1. Below are five names in random order. If the names were placed in strict alphabetical order, which name would be *third?*

1. John Meeder
2. James Medway
3. Thomas Madow
4. Catherine Meagan
5. Eleanor Meehand

Test 2. In the following items you have one name which is underlined and four other names in alphabetical order. If you were to put the underlined name into alphabetical series, indicate by the appropriate letter where it would go:

A. _____

    Richard Carreton

B. _____

    Roland Casstar

C. _____   Robert Carstens

    Jack Corson

D. _____

    Edward Cranston

E. _____

When these tests were used on the same 43 clerical workers, the correlation between them was .01. In other words, those who passed test 1 were no more likely to pass test 2 than those who failed test 1. Also, the correlations between tests 1 and 2 and supervisors' ratings for 72 filing clerks were only .09 and .00, respectively.

Face validity suffers from the same problems as those associated with other judgmental data. As with judgmental forecasting, the process can be improved by adding structure. For example, a self-administered questionnaire asking experts to evaluate the validity of a set of assumptions is preferable to the use of unsolicited feedback. But even this is a weak test of validity. Strangely, few researchers go this far. The dominant approach to validity in many fields is the informal appeal to face validity.

Predictive validity, as applied to the inputs of the model, asks whether these inputs are valid for the forecast situation. For example, for a causal model, assessments would be made of the predictions of the causal variables. Also, to what extent are the causal relationships valid over the forecast horizon?

Construct validity asks whether a measurement measures what it claims to measure. Construct validity is assessed by using different methods to measure the construct and by examining the agreement among these measures. If these different approaches do, in fact, measure the same construct, they should agree with one another. This is another application of eclectic research.

Given that the inputs are valid, it is useful to ask whether they are reliable. Do repeated measures of the same input provide similar results? For example, it is useful to show that the procedure used to measure a given variable can be performed independently by different researchers and yield similar results each time. Reliability can also be assessed by having the same researchers repeat the procedure at different times.

The distinction between the tests for reliability and construct validity can be stated as follows: Reliability involves the agreement among *similar* ways of measuring an input; construct validity involves the agreement among *dissimilar* ways of measuring an input. This distinction is obviously one of degree, and often the differences are not clear-cut in practice. Still, the distinction, is useful in developing testing procedures. This should become clearer in the following sections where examples are provided.

TESTING THE MODEL BUILDING PROCESS

Obviously, many subjective decisions must be made in building a forecasting model. If the process can be replicated, this gives added as-

surance that the model will be useful. If not, the failure suggests that
more effort is needed to make the model building process more explicit
and structured.

The test of reliability asks whether another researcher can follow
the specific process and obtain the same results. This requires full
disclosure of the process. If you have ever tried to provide full disclosure
of a process, you know that it is expensive. If you have tried to replicate
work done by others, you know that few people are able to provide full
disclosure. Sometimes it is not the researcher's fault; it may be due to
limitations of time or budget.

In addition to testing the reliability of the model building process,
one could also test its construct validity. This is done to see whether
researchers can follow the *general process*. In other words, rather than
trying to follow the specific steps, a researcher would start from scratch
and independently develop a model. This is an expensive test because
all of the work must be repeated. If similar results are obtained, one
gains confidence in the model. If different results are obtained, one
gains clues about critical aspects of the process. This latter benefit
comes about, however, only if each researcher provides full disclosure.

Below, I present a study drawn from econometric models. The study
suggests that the econometric model building process is replicable and
valid. Three groups of researchers independently reached similar conclusions in this situation:

Armstrong and Grohman (1972) developed an econometric model
to predict air travel in the United States. After this model was
completed, we learned that the U.S. Civil Aeronautics Board (CAB)
had previously developed an econometric model (Saginor, 1967).
The two models proved to be highly similar. The selection of causal
variables was similar: both models used population, average fare
per passenger mile, and real disposable income per capita, although the Armstrong–Grohman model added speed and safety
variables. The same functional form was used: a multiplicative
model that examined changes in key causal variables. The signs
of the relationships were the same, and the magnitudes were
similar: for example, the CAB estimated price elasticity to be
-1.2, and our estimate was -1.2; the CAB estimated income
elasticity to be $+1.1$, and we estimated $+0.5$. Finally, the accuracy of unconditional forecasts from the CAB model was similar
to that from our model.

Our tardy literature review turned up another bonus: a study of the U.S. air travel market by Mize and Ulveling (1970). They did not seem to be aware of Saginor's study and were obviously unaware of our study, yet they also came up with a model using similar variables, functional form, and elasticities. Furthermore, they achieved an average accuracy of 4% in forecasts for 1964, 1965, and 1966; this was comparable to the error from our model of 6%. Both models did much better than extrapolations during this period.

Replication of the model building process also helps to control for cheating and mistakes.

TESTING THE VARIABLES

The reliability and validity of the dependent variable (the variable to be forecast) is of utmost importance [KEREN and NEWMAN, 1978]. Failure to do an adequate job here can jeopardize the rest of the enterprise. For example, ALEXANDER and WILKINS [1982] found that performance ratings have little validity; their conclusion raises questions about much of the prior research on predicting performance of job applicants. In addition, one should test the reliability and validity of the causal variables.

Application of the tests for validity and reliability is relatively straightforward. For reliability, you examine the agreement among similar measures of a variable (see Curtis and Jackson 1962, for an early but still useful description of this strategy). Another measure of reliability can be obtained from the variation among sample observations. To test for validity, you can use the agreement among dissimilar measures of the same variable (construct validity), or the ability to forecast the causal variables over the forecast horizon (forecast validity). You could also conduct a mail survey of experts to determine what they think to be valid measures (Sherbini, 1967, used this approach to test face validity in a study of international markets).

The following two studies illustrate the application of tests of reliability and construct validity. (Enough has already been said about face validity, and details on the predictive validity of inputs are not discussed here because the process is the same as that used in Chapter 13.) The example from Rabinowitz and Rosenbaum is interesting. They followed much of my advice (even anticipated what I would say!) and, as noted, did a thorough job in assessing reliability. Still they were unable to predict student–teacher rapport in the classroom. In any event, this study illustrates the testing of reliability. Such testing is common in psychology, but uncommon in other fields such as economics. My study of the photographic market illustrates the testing of construct validity, although it also contains elements of reliability testing:

Rabinowitz and Rosenbaum (1958) tested 49 student teachers in an attempt to predict student–teacher rapport when these people would be teaching in grades 3 to 6 one year later. For the dependent variable, rapport, each teacher was observed by six raters, and each rater worked alone for two half-hour periods. The dependent variable showed high **interrater reliability**[G]. The causal variables were based on tests whose reliability had been assessed by others.

In Armstrong (1968a), three measures were obtained for the price of cameras: a Kodak index based on the Kodak Instamatic 104 camera plus 10 packs of "type 126" black and white film; a Polaroid index based on the model 104 camera and 10 packs of "type 107" black and white film; and a Canon index based on the QL 25 camera. If each of these indices is a valid measure of the price of still cameras, they should be in agreement on which countries have high prices and which have low prices. Data from 26 countries were used to assess the agreement, and a measure of r^2 was computed for each pair of indices. There was a substantial amount of construct validity. Measures of r^2 were as follows:

	Polaroid	Canon
Kodak	.90	.79
Polaroid	—	.67

In addition, the reliability of the data was assessed by repeating our survey to obtain the price data. The same questionnaires were sent to the same importers in each country after a 6-month interval. The results were identical in most cases.

The various methods of validity and reliability testing are complements—not substitutes—of one another. In other words, a battery of tests should be used, and the input should be expected to do well on all. Ferber illustrated how misleading it would be to use a single measure:

In Ferber (1965), replies were received from 411 bank customers on the sizes of their savings deposits. The average deposit in this sample was calculated, and reliability was assessed for this average by using the variability among respondents (i.e., the traditional measure of sample reliability). Bank records showed that the true value was outside the 95% confidence interval (the reported deposit was half of the actual deposit). The measure of reliability provided a poor assessment in this case.

TESTING THE RELATIONSHIPS

The testing of relationships is relevant only for econometric, segmentation, and bootstrapping models, because it is here that relationships are explicitly examined.

To test the reliability of estimates of relationships, one examines the agreement among similar approaches. The most commonly used approach for assessing what would happen if the measurement process were repeated is to use standard errors of regression coefficients. A small standard error implies high reliability.

Although the standard error provides a simple and inexpensive measure, its shortcomings should be noted: it does not assess validity, and it overstates reliability because of the fitting process in the **calibration sample**[G]. The second problem can often be handled by splitting the data into two subsamples. The analysis, with all of the adjustments that inevitably occur, can be done on one of these subsamples. The resulting model can then be used with the second subsample to calculate standard errors. The disadvantage of this **split-sample**[G] technique is that one must often deal with small samples. Of course, it is possible to use the split-sample technique with small samples, and then to combine both samples to obtain an estimate after having assessed reliability.

When the split-sample technique is not available, it is still possible to account for chance relationships that show up when many variables are considered. Other people have noted this problem long ago (Binder 1964, for example), and they have been kind enough to provide tables so that you can avoid being misled by the traditional *t*-statistic. [See McINTYRE et al. 1983.] They adjust for the fact that many variables were called, but few were chosen for the model.

The test of construct validity helps to assess whether the relationship can be generalized to new situations (e.g., new time periods, new geographical regions, or new subjects). It also helps to assess whether uncertainty is high or whether biases exist in the data, thus helping to identify any further research that would be useful.

To assess construct validity, the relationship is measured by approaches that are as different as possible. The approaches can differ in many ways: different measures for the variables in the forecasting model, different time periods, different types of data, different analytical methods, or different subjects.

My study of the photographic market is used to illustrate tests of reliability, construct validity, and predictive validity of relationships:

The measurement of relationships in the study of the international photographic market (Armstrong, 1968a) was described briefly in Chapter 8 of *LRF*. The estimate of income elasticity was of particular interest, so four estimates were obtained. For the subjective estimate, reliability was estimated by me. Reliability estimates from regression analyses on three types of data were obtained from the standard errors of the regression coefficients. Construct validity was estimated by calculating the standard deviation among the four different estimates of income elasticity. The results were as follows:

Source of Estimate	Income Elasticity	Test	Standard Error
Subjective	1.3	Reliability	0.2
Household survey	1.5	Reliability	0.2
Cross section of countries	0.9	Reliability	0.1
Longitudinal over countries	1.6	Reliability	1.0
All of the above	1.3	Construct validity	0.3

Because incomes were rising over time, an assessment was made of the predictive validity of the estimate of income elasticity. The cross-sectional data were split into two groups: 15 countries of low income and 15 of high income. The estimated income elasticity for the high-income countries was 1.01 (standard error = 0.35), while that for the low-income countries was 1.03 (standard error = 0.11). These results supported the assumption that the estimate of income elasticity would be valid as income increased over the 10-year forecast horizon.

SUMMARY

Tests on the inputs of a model help to identify weak areas so that improvements can be made. A second goal of input testing is to select the most useful models. This is of less importance; generally, the best one can do is to eliminate models with highly unreasonable assumptions.

Input testing can be used on three aspects of the inputs; testing the model building process, testing variables, and testing relationships. For each of these aspects, one can examine reliability and validity. The suggestions made for these analyses are summarized in Exhibit 12-2.

Exhibit 12-2 METHODS FOR TESTING INPUTS TO A MODEL

Input	Test	Procedure
Model building process	Reliability	Replication following description
	Validity	Independent replication
Variables	Reliability	Agreement among similar indicators
		Sample variability
	Validity	Expert survey
		Agreement among different indicators
		Forecast accuracy for causal variables
Relationships	Reliability	Standard error of regression coefficient
		Split samples
	Validity	Agreement among different estimates (vary time, space, or subjects)

Thirteen

TESTING OUTPUTS

Contents

Far better an approximate answer to the right question, which is often
vague, than an exact answer to the wrong question, which can always
be made precise.

Tukey (1962)

Tests on the outputs of a model can be used to gain further insight
about the inputs to a model so that improvements can be made. For
this purpose, conditional forecasts are useful. The first section in this
chapter discusses the use of conditional forecasts.

The major reason for testing outputs, however, is to make comparisons among a set of models. Cost-benefit analyses of the outputs should
be made for each model in order to select the best one. These tests
should be carried out in situations analogous to the one encountered
in the forecasting problem. Much of this chapter is devoted to the choice
of an appropriate testing situation.

Accuracy is of major concern. How does one compare the accuracies
of alternative models? Measures of statistical and practical significance
are examined. The popularity of various accuracy measures is examined and typical forecast errors are presented.

CONDITIONAL VS. UNCONDITIONAL FORECASTS

The unconditional forecast uses only information available at the time
of the actual forecast. Thus, if the number of riots in the United States
from 1986 to 1991 were being forecast, no information from a time
later than 1985 would be used. Of course, this is what we normally
mean when we talk about forecasting.

Conditional forecasts can be conditional in different respects. One
can have information from the forecast situation that pertains to the
relationships or to the *variables*. Also, one can have actual ("known")
data for the situation, or it can be unknown. The various possibilities
are presented in Exhibit 13-1 along with their traditional names.

The *ex ante* forecast provides the best measure of a model's ability
to forecast and offers a benchmark for comparison. This chapter is
concerned primarily with *ex ante* forecasts.

Ex post forecasts can be used to assess how well the model would
do if the best possible forecasts were made of the causal variables. A
comparison between the *ex post* and the *ex ante* forecast is useful in
deciding whether further work should be done to improve the forecasts

Exhibit 13-1   TYPES OF CONDITIONAL AND UNCONDITIONAL FORECASTS

	Relationships	
Variables	Unknown	Known
Unknown	*Ex Ante*	Modified *Ex Ante*
Known	*Ex Post*	Calibration

of the causal variables. More detailed analyses could be made by using perfect forecasts for each of the causal variables, one at a time, to identify which variables are of greatest concern.

In the modified *ex ante* forecast, data from the forecast horizon are used to estimate the coefficients in the forecasting model. Then you go back to use the forecasts of the causal variables. A comparison can be made with the *ex ante* forecasts to assess the value of having the improved estimates of the relationships. You could use known data for only one of the relationships to test the sensitivity of the outputs.

Finally, **calibration**[G] forecasts can be examined to assess the net impact of better estimates of relationships and better forecasts of the causal variables.

These ideas on the use of conditional forecasts are relevant primarily for econometric and segmentation models. For judgmental models, it may be possible to create these tests by controlling the information that is given to the judges.

SITUATIONS FOR TESTING OUTPUTS

The testing situation should be as similar as possible to the forecasting situation. There should be a correspondence with respect to space, population, and time. For an important application of this principle, see the use of "work samples" for personnel selection [e.g., ROBERTSON and DOWNS, 1979; SMITH, 1976].

Space correspondence is the extent to which the environment of the test data corresponds to the environment of the forecasting problem. Obviously, the environment may have a large impact on the forecasting model. For example, Newton's laws do not apply throughout the universe, but they work well for the types of problems that we encounter in the earth's environment.

Many years ago, I was involved in a project to forecast the health of certain very important people (VIPs) around the world. Most of them would not have been interested in cooperating, and I am sure the C.I.A. did not bother to ask them. (Oh, they never told me who paid for the study. However, *Parade* magazine said that it was the C.I.A.) So, instead, we used executives in Minneapolis. Now Minneapolis is cold, but it isn't Moscow.

With respect to population, it is desirable to obtain data on the decision units that are the subject of the forecasting problem. Sometimes, however, it is necessary to compromise and to select analogous decision units. That is what we did in our VIP forecasting project. We were not really interested in those Minneapolis executives.

Generally, the selection of a relevant population is straightforward. One practice, however, has led to serious errors in assessing forecast validity. This is the selection of extreme groups from a population. Predictions made about these extreme groups lead to a phenomenon called regression toward the mean.

Regression toward the mean[G] occurs because, although extreme groups contain observations that differ significantly from the mean, they also contain observations that are due to errors in measurement. When later measurements are made, it is unlikely that the given observation will be subject to the same large error in measurement. Thus the mean of the extreme group regresses toward the population mean.

One well-known case of regression toward the mean has occurred in speed-reading courses. A reading test is given to a group of people. The slow readers then take the speed-reading course, after which they are retested. The forecast by the speed-reading advocates is upheld; they have been able to increase the speed of these slow readers. Of course, the measured speed would have been higher on the second test even if no speed-reading course had been given because the slow reader group would have included people who were not feeling good on the first test or misunderstood the directions or were tired or got bogged down by the selected passages to be read. Many of these transient factors may not occur with the same impact on the second testing. (Incidentally, according to Carver (1972), there is little evidence that speed-reading courses increase speed without reducing comprehension. Anecdotal evidence is provided by Woody Allen: he took a speed-reading course and was able to read *War and Peace* in 20 minutes. "It's about Russia," said Woody.)

I hope that none of you are speed-readers; but if you are, you can check your comprehension so far. Select the best answer: *Long-Range Forecasting* is about . . .

(a) The origin of Tonto's friend's name.
(b) The history of amateur fishing.
(c) The use and abuse of forecasting methods.
(d) Helpful hints on getting through life.

The correct answer is given in Appendix F.

The critical aspect of the test situation is generally the selection of a suitable time period. What time correspondence will allow for the best assessment of forecast validity?

To assist in the selection of appropriate test data, a "validation matrix" is presented in Exhibit 13-2. This matrix considers forecasts in cases where data on the forecast sample are available (the "known sample"); the data differ with respect to space (same population, but new environment); population (same space, but new population); both space and population. The last three categories are grouped into the "analogous sample" in Exhibit 13-2. Each type of data is examined for three time periods. Data from the time period immediately preceding the current time can be withheld to test forecast validity. The time period preceding that one can be used to calibrate the model and also to test for concurrent validity. The time period preceding that one can be used for a test of backcast validity. The time period after the current time represents the typical forecasting problem (shaded area).

Exhibit 13-2   THE VALIDATION MATRIX

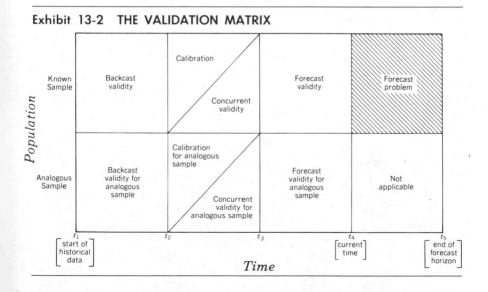

As can be seen from Exhibit 13-2, eight situations can be used to test forecast validity. Six situations allow for testing unconditional forecasts (all but the calibration samples). If one were to include conditional forecasts (from Exhibit 13-1), there would be many additional possible tests.

After describing the use of the calibration sample, I discuss concurrent, forecast, and backcast validity. The relative advantages and disadvantages of each test are examined.

Calibration

The data used to calibrate (estimate) the model have frequently been used to test forecast validity. The fit to the calibration data is used to draw inferences about forecast validity. Although tests on the calibration data are easily available, inexpensive, and popular, this approach is the least useful of the tests listed in the validation matrix. Fortunately, it is seldom necessary to use the calibration data because of the availability of the other tests in Exhibit 13-2.

A good fit between the model and the calibration sample may be the result of chance. This is especially likely for complex models. Furthermore, the researcher inevitably finds ways (he thinks) to improve the model, and these typically provide a better fit. The net result is that the fit between the model and the calibration data provides only a crude estimate of forecast validity. In some cases it may be considered as an upper limit to the predictive power of the model.

The relationship between the ability of a model to explain the variation in the calibration sample and its forecast validity has been studied for almost half a century. One of these studies, Williams and Goodman (1971), found that the fit to the calibration sample provided a fair estimate of predictive ability for short-range forecasts with an extrapolation model. However, the following studies, found that ability to fit the calibration data was a poor measure of forecast validity:

The U.S. National Resources Committee (1938) used econometric models to forecast changes in employment and consumption in 81 sectors of the economy for 1933–1936. Data from 1918 to 1932 were used to calibrate the model. A plot of the standard error of the regressions for 1918–1932 (the calibration sample) showed no relationship to the MAPEs for the 138 forecasts over the forecast horizon from 1933 to 1936. Thus the fit to the calibration data provided a poor estimate of forecast accuracy.

Ohlin and Duncan (1949) reviewed studies that attempted to forecast which prisoners could be successfully released on parole. In all six studies that allowed for a comparison, a causal model was superior to a naive extrapolation when the comparisons were made on the calibration data (as they had been in the original publications of the six studies). When these models were used to predict outside of the calibration data, the causal model was superior to the extrapolation in two cases, it was inferior in three cases, and there was one tie. Overall, the causal model was not more accurate.

Ferber (1956) examined forecasts of the total savings in the economy. Seven different models were calibrated from data for 1923–1940. Forecasts were then made for 1947–1949. There was only a small relationship between the R^2 for the calibration data and the forecast error.

Schupack (1962), in a study involving short-range sales forecasts for food and household products, found only a slight positive relationship between the fit of regression models to the calibration sample and their forecast accuracy.

In ELLIOTT and BAIER [1979], six econometric models provided good explanations of the changes in interest rates for a calibration sample. The R^2 for these models ranged from .858 to .996. However, for one-month ahead forecasts, these models were inferior to a no-change model.

Concurrent Validity

Locke (1961) asked 29 subjects to describe themselves using 81 adjectives. The data were analyzed by comparing subjects with long last names and those with short last names (six or fewer letters). Eighteen of the adjectives were significant in distinguishing between those with long and short names. In fact, the discriminant analysis distinguished almost perfectly between groups. Of course, when Locke cross-validated this model on a hold-out sample of 30 subjects, there was no forecast validity. Einhorn (1972b) presented a similar illustration using random data in a segmentation analysis.

There is a moral: predictive studies often fail to go beyond the calibration sample. Two examples provided here show the test of concurrent validity to be useful:

Kurtz (1948) reexamined a study that used the **Rorschach test**[G] to predict the success of life insurance sales managers. The use of 32 variables from this test led to almost perfect predictions for the 42 successful and 38 unsuccessful sales managers in the calibration sample. But when Kurtz tested concurrent validity, the Rorschach test was completely lacking in predictive power. (Interestingly, Kurtz reported that some advocates of the Rorschach test refused to accept this result as a failure.)

Frank, Massy, and Morrison (1965) reanalyzed an earlier study by Frank and Massy (1963) which had concluded that adopters of a new brand of coffee, Folger's, could be predicted from socioeconomic and purchasing data. This study had correctly classified about 73% of the purchasers in the calibration sample, but when the test was cross-validated only 48% were correctly classified. This was no better than chance. (In contrast to the preceding study, Frank, Massy, and Morrison were able to accept their negative result. But, of course, they found the error by themselves.)

The test of concurrent validity is more important to the extent that heavy reliance is placed on the calibration sample. Alternatively, if the calibration model is not used to a great extent, there is less need for a test of concurrent validity. In the extreme, when prior theory is used to calibrate the model, there is no calibration test, only a test of concurrent validity. The following is an example:

Armstrong and Overton (1977) used five models to predict the effect of nonresponse bias in mail survey results. Each model was calibrated *a priori*. For example, one model assumed that the effect of nonresponse would be zero. Another assumed that the average response in the latest wave of the questionnaire would provide the best prediction as to how nonrespondents would have answered. The concurrent validity of each of the five models was then tested on actual data.

It is seldom possible to test concurrent validity with time series data. If data are available for only one unit of observation (or if the data are not available on a disaggregate basis), concurrent validity cannot be tested.

A related problem in the use of concurrent validity arises from the use of small samples; that is, few data may be available for both calibrating the model and testing concurrent validity. There are solutions to this problem. The simplest one is to use **double cross validation**[G]. For this, one first examines concurrent validity. The names of the two subsamples are then reversed, and the process is repeated. In other words, the calibration is done on what was originally the concurrent validity subsample, and concurrent validity is tested on the original calibration sample. This procedure yields two estimates of concurrent validity. Two estimates are better than one. Right?

If sample size is very small, it is possible to use N-way cross validation. Here, all except one of the observations are used to calibrate the model. A forecast is made for the remaining observation. Next, this observation is replaced, and again, all the data but one are used to calibrate a new model; this model is then used to forecast for the one excluded observation. This process is repeated until each of the observations has been used for validation. (A discussion on N-way cross validation can be found in Frank, Massy, and Morrison (1965).) This procedure is also called the jackknife [MOSTELLER and TUKEY, 1977, p. 135].

If there are no concurrent data, you might think all is lost. But there is hope. One strategy is to create random data and to repeat the same procedures on these data that were used on the calibration sample. Comparisons can then be made between the fit to the calibration sample and the fit to the random data. For a rough idea of what will happen, Ando and Kaufman (1966) provided tables obtained by analyzing random data for sample sizes from 10 to 200, and using from 10 to 50 causal variables. It is better, however, to replicate the process than to use the tables. Examples of replication with random data are provided by Payne and Dyer (1975) and Armstrong (1975a).

An improvement of the random data validation was suggested by Montgomery (1975). Rather than using completely random data, you can randomize the data for the dependent variable only; that is, the values for the dependent variable are removed and then randomly reassigned to the observations. Again, the process used to calibrate the model is applied to these randomized data. This procedure has some appeal because the distribution for the dependent variable is retained.

A checklist for tests of concurrent validity is provided in Exhibit 13-3. This exhibit indicates when each procedure is appropriate and cites a reference describing an early application of the procedure.

Exhibit 13-3 TESTING CONCURRENT VALIDITY

Sample Size	Recommended Procedure	Early Applications
Large	Cross validation	Minor (1958)
Moderate	Double cross validation	Roach (1971)
Small	N-way cross validation	Wiseman (1972b)
None	Random data validation	Montgomery (1975)

The test of concurrent validity is a more appropriate test of forecast validity than is the fit to the calibration sample. The value of such a test is especially great when complex models are used. For example, Ward (1954) found that the **shrinkage**[G] from calibration to concurrent data was much greater for complex regression models. Concurrent validity is also useful when the calibration sample has been used to estimate a number of alternative models. Although the calibration sample is adequate in some situations [CATTIN, 1980; BARRETT, PHILLIPS, and ALEXANDER, 1981], it is safer to test concurrent validity.

This discussion assumed that data were available on the relevant population. An alternative is to use an analogous sample, as we did in the previously cited study on the health of VIPs. The model was calibrated on this group, and concurrent validity was also tested.

Forecast Validity

To obtain the best measure of forecast validity, one could use the forecasting models and monitor their success. A shortcut is to withhold data from a recent time period and to pretend that the forecasts are being made. This test is almost as good as the real thing, although it is possible that the model may be contaminated by the researcher's knowledge of the time period that is being withheld.

Preferably, the test of forecast validity is run on the decision units that are of interest. An unconditional test of forecast validity on these units would provide the ideal test of forecast validity for the problem.

Small samples cause problems in obtaining a good test of forecast validity. This is a common difficulty with time series data. One procedure that helps to make the most effective use of limited time series data is called **successive updating**^{G}. This involves the removal of data from the validation sample and their addition to the calibration sample after each forecast.

Successive updating is illustrated in Exhibit 13-4. In period t, forecasts are made over the horizon from $t + 1$ to $t + h$. In period $t + 1$, data from period $t + 1$ are used in the calibration sample and forecasts are made for periods $t + 2$ to $t + h$. This procedure is repeated until there is only a one-period forecast. The one-period-ahead forecasts are designated in Exhibit 13-4 by F_1, the two-period-ahead forecasts by F_2, and so on. This yields h of the one-period forecasts, $h - 1$ of the two-period forecasts, and so on down to one of the h-period-ahead forecasts. Examples of this procedure can be found in Armstrong and Grohman (1972), Williams and Goodman (1971), MABERT [1976], and SCHNAARS [1984]. This procedure, with its different starting points, provides a good test of validity.

Exhibit 13-4   SUCCESSIVE UPDATING

Calibration Data Ends With:	Forecast Periods					
	$t + 1$	$t + 2$	$t + 3$	$t + 4$	$\cdots$	$t + h$
t	F_1	F_2	F_3	F_4	$\cdots$	F_h
$t + 1$	—	F_1	F_2	F_3	$\cdots$	F_{h-1}
$t + 2$	—	—	F_1	F_2	$\cdots$	F_{h-2}
$\cdots$	$\cdots$	$\cdots$	$\cdots$	$\cdots$	$\cdots$	$\cdots$
$t + h - 1$	—	—	—	—		F_1

Backcast Validity

The White Queen lives backward through time. She begins to cry before she sticks herself with her broach and stops immediately afterward. Living backward in time, she explains to Alice, "always makes one a little giddy at first . . . but there's one great advantage in it—that one's memory works both ways."

Lewis Carroll
Through the Looking Glass

It is sometimes difficult to obtain data for forecast validation. Often, one plans to use a causal model but finds that historical data on the *causal* variables do not exist, although current data are available. The use of backcasting is suggested here; this involves withholding data from some time in the distant past and using only the most recent data to develop the forecasting models. You then backcast what happened in the earlier period. Obviously, this approach may suffer from contamination because the researcher may be affected by the knowledge of what has happened. An example of backcasting is provided in financial forecasting by SMITH and BRAINARD [1976]. Another example is described here:

> In Armstrong (1968b), data from 1965 to 1960 were used to calibrate models to forecast camera sales by country. These models were then used to make six-year backcasts for camera sales in 1954. The accuracy of these backcasts served to assess how well the models would do in a six-year forecast.

The White Queen was right: backcasting does make people a little giddy at first. Some researchers are skeptical of backcasting as a measure of forecast validity. In my opinion, backcast validity provides a useful approach to the assessment of forecast validity. The only empirical evidence that I found is from Theil, who found a close correspondence between conditional forecasts and conditional backcasts:

Theil (1966) examined input-output forecasts for two industries. He compared **mean square errors**[G] for conditional forecasts and backcasts. I converted these to root mean square errors for ease of interpretation. The correspondence was close:

Forecast Horizon (years)	Mean Square Errors			
	Agriculture, Forestry, Fishing		Basic Metal Industries	
	Backcasts	Forecasts	Backcasts	Forecasts
1	4.0	4.0	10.6	10.4
2	6.0	6.2	15.7	15.4
3	7.9	7.9	20.1	21.5
4	9.9	9.5	20.7	25.7
5.5	12.0	11.6	29.9	32.2
8	12.5	11.0	39.8	48.2

Backcasting is seldom used in published studies. That is unfortunate. It can add substantially to the assessment of predictive validity.

Ranking the Validation Tests

Some tests are more representative of forecast validity than others. I have ranked these tests in Exhibit 13-5. These rankings were drawn primarily from Gerstenfeld's law of trying because I could not find much empirical evidence. The rankings might be expected to vary, depending on the situation. Nevertheless, two things stand out from these rankings: first, the most popular method, the fit to the calibration data, is least valuable; and second, tests of backcast validity are highly rated, although they are not popular.

When more than one test is used, consideration must be given to the time sequence of the testing. For example, tests of concurrent validity should be carried out first because these data can then be incorporated into the calibration data to update the models. Similarly, tests of backcasting should be done before tests of forecasting so that the models can be recalibrated with the additional data included. The general principle is to save the most appropriate test for last. These ideas on time sequencing are summarized in Exhibit 13-5. Use more than one of the tests. One gains confidence in a model if it performs well in a variety of tests.

Exhibit 13-5   RANKING THE VALIDATION TESTS

Value (1 = most useful)	Time Sequence (1 = do first)	Test
1	4	Forecast validity
2	3	Backcast validity
3	4	Concurrent validity
4	3	Forecast validity with analogous data
5	2	Backcast validity with analogous data
6	2	Concurrent validity with analogous data
7	1	Calibration fit
8	1	Calibration fit with analogous data

TESTING ACCURACY

Accuracy is one of the most important criteria for a forecasting model. Measures of accuracy can help to assess costs and benefits in a situation.

A single measure of accuracy sometimes falls short. Is it better to forecast too high or too low? Do changes in direction have particular importance? Is it worse to err by forecasting that something will happen when it does not happen, or by forecasting that it will not happen when it does happen? It is difficult to develop generalizations on these points because they depend on the specific situation being examined.

This section describes some measures of forecast accuracy and discusses their advantages and disadvantages. You should be able to find some measures that will fit your problem.

Measures of Accuracy

This section of the book is not the most interesting. If you are not looking for a measure of accuracy, you may prefer to skip this section and go to the one on statistical and practical significance (p. 356). A review of accuracy measures can be found in Exhibit 13-7 (*LRF* p. 355).

A consistent notation will be followed. It is noted in the symbol list in the glossary and, for your convenience, is summarized here:

A is the actual result
F is the forecast
t is the time interval
h is the number of periods in the forecast horizon

For cross-sectional data, t represents the element to be forecast, and h is the number of elements. Unless otherwise noted, A and F are assumed to be equal to or greater than 0, and the data are ratio scaled (i.e., the intervals are meaningful, and there is a meaningful zero point).

1.   Mean error (ME) is calculated from

$$ME = \frac{\sum_{t=1}^{h} (A_t - F_t)}{h}$$

The mean error is primarily a test of systematic error (bias). It assumes that the cost of the errors is symmetrical. It should not be used by itself because it provides no measure of the error variance.

Notice that you could have a ME = 0 when large errors are present if the large errors had different signs and canceled one another. For this measure, F and A can take on negative values. Interval-scaled data are sufficient.

2. Mean absolute deviation (MAD) is calculated from

$$MAD = \frac{\sum_{t=1}^{h} (\,|\,A_t - F_t\,|\,)}{h}$$

The MAD reflects the typical error. It does not distinguish between variance and bias. It is appropriate when the cost function is linear (e.g., when the cost of an error of 10 units is twice that of an error of five units).

3. Root mean square error (RMSE) is calculated from

$$RMSE = \left[\frac{\sum_{t=1}^{h} (A_t - F_t)^2}{h}\right]^{1/2}$$

The RMSE is similar to the MAD; for unbiased errors, you can get a *crude* approximation of the RMSE from the MAD as follows (see Brown, 1963, pp. 282–283).

$$RMSE = 1.25 \, MAD$$

(In practice, this ratio often fluctuates by a significant amount.) Why would someone want to calculate the RMSE? For one thing, it is nice when you want to impress people (some forecasters prefer a complex measure to a simple one). Another reason for using the RMSE arises when there is a quadratic loss function; in other words, when the cost associated with an error increases as the square of the error. For instance, maybe the degree to which your client gets upset at bad forecasts increases with the square of the error? You should avoid the RMSE when the assessment of error is so crude that there are outliers (large measurement errors). These outliers will have a strong effect on the measure when they are squared.

4. Mean absolute percentage error (MAPE) is calculated from

$$MAPE = \left[\frac{\sum_{t=1}^{h} \left[\frac{|\,A_t - F_t\,|}{A_t}\right]}{h}\right] \cdot [100]$$

The MAPE is similar to the MAD except that it is dimensionless. This makes it nice for communication and helpful in making comparisons among forecasts from different situations. For example, to compare forecasting methods in two different situations with different units of measure, one can calculate the MAPEs and then average across situations.

When the cost of errors is more closely related to the percentage error than to the unit error, the MAPE is appropriate. This assumption is often reasonable. Problems may arise if values close to 0 are encountered for actual results. Finally, it helps if the actual results can be measured accurately.

The MAPE has a bias favoring estimates that are below the actual values. This can be seen by looking at the extremes: a forecast of 0 can never be off by more than 100%, but there is no limit to errors on the high side.

The *median* absolute percentage error might be preferred in situations where larger errors are not so costly. This measure is also useful in comparing models [as shown in MAKRIDAKIS, et al. 1982].

   5.   Adjusted mean absolute percentage error ($\overline{\text{MAPE}}$) is calculated from

$$\overline{\text{MAPE}} = \left[\frac{\sum_{t=1}^{h} \dfrac{|A_t - F_t|}{\frac{1}{2}(A_t + F_t)}}{h} \right] \cdot [100]$$

The $\overline{\text{MAPE}}$ is similar to the MAPE, but it does not favor low estimates. If the actual value is 100, a forecast of 50 is as good (or as bad) as a forecast of 200. At the extremes, the $\overline{\text{MAPE}}$ goes from 0 for a perfect forecast to 200 for an infinitely bad forecast. This is advantageous at times; for example, when working with judgmental forecasters, it will help to prevent an intentional biasing of the forecast. Another advantage is that the $\overline{\text{MAPE}}$ is less sensitive than the MAPE to measurement errors in the actual data.

The disadvantages are that the $\overline{\text{MAPE}}$ is more difficult to understand and more difficult to relate to decision making than is the MAPE. Thus, if the problems cited in the preceding paragraph are not serious, you should use the MAPE.

   6.   There are two measures of Theil's inequality (U). They are calculated as follows:

$$U1 = \frac{[(1/h)\sum_{t=1}^{h} (A_t - F_t)^2]^{1/2}}{[(1/h)\sum_{t=1}^{h} A_t^2]^{1/2} + [(1/h)\sum_{t=1}^{h} F_t^2]^{1/2}}$$

$$U2 = \frac{[(1/h)\sum_{t=1}^{h}(\Delta F_t - \Delta A_t)^2]^{1/2}}{[(1/h)\sum_{t=1}^{h}(\Delta A_t^2)]^{1/2}}$$

where Δ refers to changes.

There is some confusion about these measures because Theil proposed both, but at different times and under the same symbol. $U1$ is taken from Theil (1958, pp. 31–42), where he calls it a measure of forecast accuracy; it is bounded between 0 and 1, with 0 being a perfect forecast. $U2$ is from Theil (1966, Chapter 2), where he refers to it as a measure of forecast quality; for this, 0 represents a perfect forecast, 1 is the no-change forecast, and there is no upper limit. $U2$ can be interpreted as the RMSE of the proposed forecasting model divided by the RMSE of a no-change model.

Bliemel (1973) analyzed Theil's measures of inequality. He concluded that $U1$ was not very enlightening whether one is dealing with absolute values or with changes. For example, when changes are examined, *all* forecasting models will do better than a naive model that predicts no change! Yet Theil himself used $U1$ for change data. $U1$ is also difficult to understand and to relate to decision making. $U1$ can be viewed as an historical oddity; it should not be used for predicting either changes or absolute values.

$U2$ seems reasonable and is easier to interpret because the $U2 = 1.0$ benchmark is based on a no-change model. Values for $U2$ of less than 1 represent improvements over the no-change model. Furthermore, $U2$ has no serious defects. However, $U2$ does not pick up errors in forecasting levels but measures only errors in changes. Despite the advantages of $U2$ over $U1$, Bliemel says that $U1$ has been more widely advocated.

The confusion between $U1$ and $U2$ implies that these measures are not well understood. Imagine how much difficulty the *clients* will have with them. Fortunately, as will be noted in the summary, there is little need for Theil's U; other measures can do the job and do it more simply.

7. Coefficient of variation (CV) is calculated from

$$CV = \frac{RMSE}{[\sum_{t=1}^{h} A/h]}$$

The CV relates the root mean square error to the average value of the actual data. This unit-free measure is similar to the MAPE, but the MAPE is easier to interpret.

8. Coefficient of determination (R^2) is calculated from

$$R^2 = \frac{\sum_{t=1}^{h} [(F_t - \overline{F})(A_t - \overline{A})]^2}{[\sum_{t=1}^{h} (F_t - \overline{F})^2][\sum_{t=1}^{h} (A_t - \overline{A})^2]}$$

where $\overline{A}$ is the average A_t and $\overline{F}$ is the average F_t.

Although R^2 can be interpreted as the "proportion of variance explained," it is not an easy concept to explain to clients, nor is it easy to translate into decision-oriented terms. For example, an R^2 of 0 means that the model is not useful in explaining fluctuations, but it does not reflect its ability to forecast levels; thus, $R^2 = 0$ may not be a completely bad forecast. Similarly an R^2 of 1.0 does not represent a perfectly good forecast, as shown in Exhibit 13-6. Also, R^2 depends not only on the fit of the data but also on the steepness of the regression line (Barrett, 1974), implying that R^2 will be higher when changes are greater.

R^2 should not be used for the calibration sample. Instead, you should use $\overline{R}^2$ (the adjusted R^2). This adjustment allows for the fact that the regression model capitalizes on chance in finding the best fit to the calibration sample. In other words, $\overline{R}^2$ compensates for the loss in **degrees of freedom**^{G} in fitting the model. (In the extreme, you can get a perfect R^2 by using a large enough number of independent variables.)

Exhibit 13-6   PERFECT R^2 DOES NOT IMPLY PERFECT FORECAST

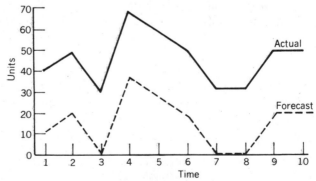

At least three methods have been proposed for calculating $\overline{R}^2$. These were summarized by Uhl and Eisenberg (1970) as follows:

Formula	Source
$\overline{R}^2 = 1 - (1 - R^2)\dfrac{h - 1}{h - v}$	Wherry (1931)
$\overline{R}^2 = 1 - (1 - R^2)\dfrac{h - 1}{h - v - 1}$	McNemar (1962)
$\overline{R}^2 = 1 - (1 - R^2)\dfrac{h + v - 1}{h - v - 1}$	Lord (1950)

where h is the number of observations, and v is the number of independent variables.

$\overline{R}^2$ is constrained to be less than 1.0, but it can be negative. Try not to let this bother you; if it comes out negative, use $\overline{R}^2 = 0$.

Uhl and Eisenberg analyzed the measures of $\overline{R}^2$. They estimated the fit to calibration data, and then examined the question of which measure provided the best estimate of R^2 for a concurrent validation sample. Although Wherry's formula is the most popular, it was the least effective of the three measures in estimating the shrinkage that occurred for R^2 when going from calibration to validation sample. The McNemar formula (sometimes called a "modified Wherry") was somewhat better, but Lord's formula worked best. To remember this, just praise the Lord!

If the analyst examines many variables to obtain a good fit to the calibration data (as occurs in stepwise regression), the v in the previous formulas should be the number of variables examined, rather than the number of variables included in the final version (Uhl and Eisenberg, 1970). This is not commonly done. It is a conservative procedure, although a bit harsh. Better yet, use the tables in McINTYRE, et al. [1983].

Because some forecasters make the mistake of using R^2 rather than $\overline{R}^2$ for the calibration sample, it is worthwhile to examine the dangers of R^2. R^2 is an inflated measure of the goodness of fit. Montgomery and Morrison (1973) describe how to estimate this inflation in R^2 for various sample sizes, different numbers of variables, and different assumptions as to the true R^2. For example, for 10 observations, three independent variables, and a true $R^2 = .25$, the calculated R^2 for a sample would be expected to be .54. If one assumes the true R^2 to be 0 (the traditional null hypothesis), there is a convenient rule of thumb for the inflation in R^2:

$$R^2 = \frac{v}{h}$$

where v is the number of independent variables, and h is the number of observations.

In most fields R^2 is more popular than R, perhaps because R^2 is a bit easier to explain. Curtis and Alf (1969) argue that R is a better measure of practical significance than is R^2. Suit yourself. Tradition is probably not worth fighting here. Furthermore, if practical importance is the issue, use the MAPE instead.

Here is a bad question to ask: "What is a good R^2?" R^2 means little in absolute terms. If you do not believe this, or if your friends are impressed by high R^2's, you may want to read Appendix G, called "Rules for Cheaters." Remember that Tom Swift had no trouble getting an R^2 of .85 with random data (Armstrong, 1970b). Also, Ames and Reiter (1961) showed that an R^2 in excess of .5 could be obtained by selecting an economic time series and regressing it against two to six other randomly selected economic time series. R^2 is most suitable when comparing different models in a given situation.

Finally, although it was assumed above that the data are interval scaled (or two categories of nominal data) in calculating R^2, other correlation coefficients assume only that the rankings are meaningful (i.e., the data are "ordinal"). Two of these measures, the Spearman and the Kendall coefficients, are described in textbooks on nonparametric statistics such as Siegel (1956).

9. Accuracy ratio $(\overline{Q})$ is calculated from

$$\overline{Q} = \frac{\sum_{t=1}^{h} Q}{h}$$

where

$$Q = \begin{cases} \dfrac{A_t}{F_t} & \text{if } A_t > F_t \\[2ex] \dfrac{F_t}{A_t} & \text{if } F_t > A_t \end{cases}$$

$\overline{Q}$ is similar to the MAPE. One key difference is that it is not bounded on both sides; it can range from 1 to infinity. For this reason, the accuracy ratio is preferable to the $\overline{MAPE}$ when dealing with large errors. In addition to being simple and easy to understand, the accuracy ratio is unit free. The loss function is assumed to be symmetrical in percentage terms; for example, if the actual value for a given problem was 10, answers of both 2 and 50 would have accuracy ratios of 5.

10a. Turning point (TP) errors may be of interest if special costs are associated with missing the direction of change. The types of turning point errors are illustrated here:

| | | Did a Directional Change Occur? | |
		No	Yes
Was a Change Predicted?	No	a	b
	Yes	c	d

The a's represent successful predictions when no change was forecast and none occurred. The d's represent a successful prediction of a change. The b's represent errors when a change occurs that was not predicted. Finally, the c's represent errors when change was predicted but did not occur. (As the famous economist said, "We predicted nine of the last five recessions.")

The translation of TP errors into a common unit of measure depends upon the situation, that is, the relative costs and benefits of the a's, b's, c's, and d's must be assessed. But this is a difficult task if the magnitudes of the changes vary. Because magnitudes do vary in most situations, and because the magnitudes affect costs and benefits, the TP should be supplemented by other measures. Fortunately, it is seldom necessary to use TP errors. Still, turning points have been used for many years in economic problems. Descriptions of turning points can be found in Smyth (1966), and applications of TPs are given in Fels and Hinshaw (1974).

10b. "Hits and misses" is analogous to TPs but is more general; it is concerned, not with a change in direction, but with whether or not an event occurs. For example, consider a jury that faces the following possibilities in regard to a person tried for murder (considering only the simplest cases):

	The Defendant . . .	
The Jury . . .	Did Not Commit Murder	Did Commit Murder
Does Not Convict	a	b
Convicts	c	d

In such an example, when there are "either-or" situations, the hits and misses table provides a good way to structure the problem. Costs and benefits can be assigned to each of the four categories.

Overall measures from the "hits and misses" table cause problems. Hedlund et al. (1973) discussed these problems in the context of predicting which mental patients are dangerous. So few of the patients are dangerous that an excellent overall prediction is obtained by assuming that none are dangerous. (That isn't a bad strategy; you would have to lock up a lot of nice people to detain a single dangerous one.) Joy and Tollefson (1975) examined hits and misses in the context of financial problems and Rosen (1954) used this measure in predicting suicides.

Rating the Measures of Accuracy

Although there are other measures of accuracy, the list above should be sufficient for most forecasting problems. A checklist is provided in Exhibit 13-7 to help in the selection of an appropriate measure of accuracy.

The typical procedure is to compare the various forecasting models on each of the selected measures. Ohlin and Duncan (1949) used an "index of predictive efficiency" to consider two models simultaneously. This measure can be calculated from

$$\text{IPE} = \frac{M1 - M2}{M1}$$

where $M1$ is the error measure for the current model, and $M2$ is the error measure for the proposed model. Such an approach would be helpful for some of the accuracy measures in Exhibit 13-7. For example, for the MAPE, IPE could be calculated from

$$\text{IPE} = \frac{(\text{MAPE})_1 - (\text{MAPE})_2}{(\text{MAPE})_1}$$

Exhibit 13-7 RATINGS OF THE MEASURES OF ACCURACY

Accuracy Measures	Scaling Requirements	Unit Free?	Loss Function Symmetrical?	Assesses Both Levels and Changes?	Closely Related to Decision Making?	Easy to Understand?
1. Mean error (ME)	Interval	No	Yes	No	No	Fairly
2. Mean absolute deviation (MAD)	Interval	No	Yes	Yes	Yes	Yes
3. Root mean square error (RMSE)	Interval	No	Yes	Yes	Yes	Fairly
4a. Mean absolute percentage error (MAPE)	Ratio	Yes	No	Yes	Yes	Yes
4b. Median absolute percentage error	Ratio	Yes	Yes	Yes	Yes	Yes
5. Adjusted MAPE ($\overline{\text{MAPE}}$)	Ratio	Yes	Yes	Yes	Fairly	Yes
6. Theil's measure of inequality ($U2$)	Interval	Yes	Yes	No	No	No
7. Coefficient of variation (CV)	Ratio	Yes	Yes	Yes	Yes	Yes
8. Coefficient of determination (R^2)	Varies	Yes	Yes	No	No	Fairly
9. Accuracy ratio ($\overline{Q}$)	Ratio	Yes	Yes	Yes	Fairly	Yes
10a. Turning points (TPs)						
10b. Hits and misses	Nominal	Yes	No	No	No	Fairly

When possible, it is preferable to translate the error scores into economic terms. One would like to compare the loss from forecasts using the current model with the loss that would occur under the proposed model. Dawes (1971) provided a good example of this for the prediction of which applicants to graduate school will be successful.

Once again, the strategy of eclectic research is recommended. If more than one of the measures is appropriate, use all of them. Certainly it leads to increased confidence if the good performance of a forecasting model holds up over a variety of measures. As an example, Schupack (1962) used various error measures in his study of econometric vs. extrapolation models on one-year forecasts of consumer products.

Statistical and Practical Significance

How much confidence can be placed in the results from a forecasting test? Measures of **statistical significance**[G] may be useful here. Many books describe appropriate tests: my favorites are Blalock (1979) for the standard tests and Siegel (1956) for **nonparametric tests**[G]. This section describes the philosophy behind tests of statistical significance. (For a longer discussion, see Bakan, 1966.)

Testing for statistical significance examines whether the superiority of a model is due to luck on the part of the researcher. He adopts the position that unusual events (e.g., things that happen, say, 5% of the time) do not happen to him. This 5% limit is set before analyzing the data. If the results fall in this unlikely region, he decides that luck was not responsible and that the proposed model produces different results from the current model. If the results do not fall in this ".05 level of statistical significance" region, he assumes that the proposed model offers no reliable advantage.

This procedure represents the classical approach to statistical significance. The proposed model is either accepted or rejected. Such a black and white viewpoint is difficult to use because the prior selection of the level of significance seldom is based on a cost-benefit analysis. (Quality control is one of the few areas where levels of statistical significance have been translated into cost-benefit terms.) Still, statistical significance can be of some value if one tries to set a reasonable level for significance before examining the data. The major role of significance tests is to decide how much confidence to place in a result. This is important because most of us, including trained statisticians, have a poor intuitive feel of the confidence we should place in a result. Consider the baby boy problem from Tversky and Kahneman (1971):

Baby Boy Problem

A certain town is served by two hospitals. In the larger hospital about 45 babies are born each day, and in the smaller hospital about 15 babies are born each day. As you know, about 50% of all babies are boys. The exact percentage of baby boys, however, varies from day to day. Sometimes it may be higher than 50%, sometimes lower.

For a period of one year, each hospital recorded the days on which more than 60% of the babies born were boys. Which hospital do you think recorded more such days? (Check one)

_____ The larger hospital?
_____ The smaller hospital?
_____ About the same? (i.e., within 5% of each other)

According to Tversky and Kahneman, most people do not get the correct answer (see Appendix F for the answer). This simple example (and some more complex ones from Tversky and Kahneman) suggests that we should rely upon formal tests of statistical significance and not upon our intuitions (even though these intuitions may be held strongly).

This advice, to rely on explicit statistical tests, is often ignored in forecasting studies. Significance tests are frequently performed on the calibration sample but then are ignored in comparing the accuracy of the forecasting models. It is far better to do just the reverse!

If the accuracy of more than two models is being examined, an adjustment should be made in the statistical testing. As the number of models is increased, a likelihood arises that some models will, by chance, look significant. For example, assume that 20 models are being compared with current practice. It is likely that one of these 20 comparisons will show up as being significant at the .05 level even if there are no real differences. The solution is to use tables for multiple comparisons. This too is advice that is often ignored. (Why, even I have been guilty of this oversight! Perhaps I will err in the future—but it would be wrong). Appendix C provides tables to be used for statistical significance for two or more alternative models. A discussion of relevant tests is provided in Patterson (1955).

How much of a difference makes a difference? Though a difference may be significant in a statistical sense, is it also significant in a practical sense? Such an evaluation depends upon the economics of the situation in which the forecasts are to be used. How much money or how many lives or how many resources can be saved if a proposed forecasting model is adopted, in comparison to the current model? How much more (less) does the proposed model cost? This is what cost-benefit analysis is all about.

Although **practical significance**[G] and statistical significance are discussed separately, it helps to consider them jointly when interpreting the results. The key decision is whether to adopt a proposed forecasting model, to keep the old model, or to pursue furtherresearch.

A guide to the interpretation of statistical and practical significance is provided in Exhibit 13-8. The test of statistical significance helps to assess confidence, and the test of practical significance measures importance. The only surprising guideline from Exhibit 13-8 is that statistically significant but practically insignificant models, Box *B*, should be discarded; confidence is high, but the proposed model lacks practical value. This is a rule of thumb. It is preferable to the common assumption that statistical significance implies practical significance. Box *D*,

---

Exhibit 13-8   INTERPRETING PRACTICAL AND STATISTICAL SIGNIFICANCE

| | | Statistically Significant? | |
		No	Yes
Practically Significant?	No	*A* Do more work on proposed method . . . maybe.	*B* Reject proposed method.
	Yes	*C* Do more work on proposed method.	*D* Adopt proposed method.

Another way to examine the advice in Exhibit 13-8 is as follows:

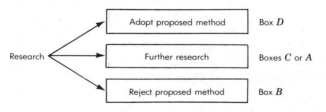

significant in both a practical and a statistical sense, provides an adequate basis for adopting a proposed method. Box A, significant in neither a statistical nor a practical sense, provides a dilemma; it may be that there is no value (in which case one should stick with the existing method), or it may be that insufficient data have been collected. The researcher should examine the latter possibility before discarding the proposed method. Finally, in Box C, the results are practically but not statistically significant. This indicates the need for more research to determine whether the superiority was due to luck.

In addition to testing against a preset level of significance, it helps to report information on the calculated level of significance. The reader of a report can then see whether the results were significant in terms of a critical level of significance for the problem at hand.

Popularity of the Criteria

What criteria are most preferred by academics and practitioners? CARBONE and ARMSTRONG [1982] asked a group of experts (attendees at the first International Symposium on Forecasting in Quebec in 1981) to list the criteria they would like to use for evaluating extrapolative methods. This focus on extrapolative methods ruled out criteria such as "better understanding" and "improved policies." In retrospect, the obvious answer would seem to be "potential savings from improved decision making." However, this answer was never used. Instead, the criteria that were chosen focused upon the forecasts. The most frequently mentioned criterion was accuracy, and within this category, mean square error (MSE) (or root mean square error) was most popular, especially for academics. Second in importance were criteria related to implementation, including "ease of interpretation" (mentioned by 38%) and "ease of use/implementation" (30%). Exhibit 13-9 summarizes the responses. I was surprised by the popularity of MSE and by the lack of popularity of R^2.

Given the opportunity, one would like the client to specify the criteria. Presumably, more than one criterion would be of interest. Exhibit 13-9 indicates some typical preferences.

Benchmarks For Accuracy

This chapter has emphasized the need for assessing alternative methods in a given situation. An alternative approach is to judge accuracy against that achieved by others in similar situations. To obtain such a benchmark, you could conduct a survey of experts to determine typ-

Exhibit 13-9   RELATIVE POPULARITY OF MEASURES OF ACCURACY
(Percentage of times mentioned)

	Percentage of	
	Academics (n = 63)	Practitioners (n = 63)
Mean square error (MSE or RMSE)	48	32
Mean absolute error (MAE)	19	22
Mean absolute percentage error (MAPE)	24	14
Mean percentage error (MPE)	8	8
Theil's U	5	2
R^2	0	3

Notes. The percentages are based on those who said accuracy was relevant. Some did not mention a specific measure, while others mentioned more than one, thus the columns do not sum to 100%.

ical levels of accuracy. Or you might find such benchmarks in the literature. For an example of the latter, the typical error in a one-year-ahead forecast of corporate earnings was determined [in ARMSTRONG, 1983b] to have a MAPE of 21.4 for judgmental forecasts. This estimate was based on many years of forecasts for 1,250 companies.

Evidence on the accuracy of sales forecasts was obtained from a survey of companies conducted by MENTZER and COX [1984]. As might be expected, the typical error increases as the forecast horizon increases and also as the forecast becomes more detailed. Exhibit 13-10 presents a summary of the typical MAPEs for sales forecasts. I do not, however, know what methods were used by these respondents. These should be treated as *very crude estimates*. ZARNOWITZ [1979], based on his studies of forecasts of GNP, suggests a rule of thumb that the forecast error is constant over the cumulative horizon. That is, the expected percentage error for a one-month forecast would be the same as for a one-quarter, one-year, or five-year forecast.

SUMMARY

Conditional forecasts can help in the analysis of the inputs to a model. Three types of conditional forecasts were summarized in Exhibit 13-1: *ex post,* modified *ex ante,* and calibration. However, the primary interest in testing outputs is to help in the comparison of alternative models. For this purpose, *ex ante* forecasts should be examined.

The testing situation should be similar to the actual forecasting

**Exhibit 13-10   TYPICAL ERRORS FOR SALES FORECASTS
(Entries are MAPEs)**

	Forecast Horizon		
Level	Under 3 Months	3 Months to 2 Years	Over 2 Years
Industry	8	11	15
Corporate	7	11	18
Product group	10	15	20
Product line	11	16	20
Product	16	21	26

Source. MENTZER and COX [1984] survey results from 160 corporations. These results are crude estimates because most firms do not keep systematic records. Further, the report of the study was ambiguous in its definitions of the time interval. We suppose that "Under 3 months" is intended to mean 'monthly,' but the length of time is not apparent for "Over 2 years."

problem. The validation matrix was provided in Exhibit 13-2 to help in the selection of appropriate situations, and these various situations were ranked in Exhibit 13-5. Most appropriate, by far, is to simulate the actual forecasting situation, using the decision units that are of interest. Least appropriate, but most popular, is to infer the forecast validity from the calibration sample. Backcast validity is a useful though seldom used test. Much attention was given to tests of concurrent validation because these tests are nearly always feasible; procedures were summarized in Exhibit 13-3 for examining concurrent validity for large and small samples.

The selection of a measure of accuracy depends to a great extent upon the situation. Twelve measures of accuracy were described, and ratings of these measures were provided in Exhibit 13-7. The MAPE provides a good measure for most situations. R^2, with all its problems, may do more harm than good.

Formal tests of statistical significance are preferable to the use of intuitive measures. Our common sense frequently is misleading. Tests of statistical significance were related to practical significance in Exhibit 13-8.

The popularity of criteria among academics and practitioners showed much agreement; the preferred measure, in general, was the root mean square error.(See Exhibit 13-9.)

The chapter concluded with a summary of typical errors for various levels of aggregation and for various time horizons (Exhibit 13-10).

Part IV

COMPARING
METHODS

P art IV compares the forecasting methods and answers the question, "Which is the best method for a given situation?" Chapter 14 examines the costs and benefits of the various methods in general terms. Chapter 15 evaluates the relative accuracy of each method.

Fourteen

COSTS AND BENEFITS OF THE FORECASTING METHODS

Contents

Men occasionally stumble over the truth, but most of them pick themselves up and hurry off as if nothing had happened.

Winston Churchill
(Noted in Cetron and Ralph, 1983)

This chapter presents a checklist to help in the selection of a forecasting
method. The assumption is that an explicit evaluation of costs and
benefits is superior to a subjective **global assessment**^{G}. The latter
approach is likely to lead to the conclusion that the new forecasting
problem looks just like the last one. Forecasters, like other people, get
into ruts. An explicit evaluation gives other methods due consideration.

Following the cost-benefit framework of Chapter 11, I rated the
various forecasting methods. Because it is so important, accuracy is
treated separately in the next chapter. My ratings were made at two
different points in time; on average, each of these ratings was within
0.5 rating points on the five-point scale. In addition, Robert Fildes,
who has published comprehensive evaluations of forecasting methods
[e.g. FILDES, 1982], provided independent ratings. His ratings and
my most recent ratings were within 1.0 rating points on average. The
ratings in Exhibit 14-1 are based on an average of my two sets of
ratings and the ratings by Fildes.

Ratings of forecasting methods also depend upon the particular forecasting problem. For example, what data are available? What capabilities exist in the organization for using various methods? The ratings
provided in Exhibit 14-1 do not consider differences in the situation.
You might want to revise the ratings to suit your particular problem.
You could even start from scratch and enter your own ratings, so that
you avoid problems with anchoring.

Once ratings are obtained, it is necessary to decide how to weigh
the costs and benefits. This task is not difficult on the cost side; however,
the assessment of benefits usually presents problems. Is it more important to obtain a good estimate of uncertainty or to be able to assess
alternative futures? Is it more important to be able to assess alternative
futures or to improve accuracy? These questions are specific to the
situation, so I leave the difficult work to the reader. Here is an example
of the type of analysis:

Selecting Forecasting Models: An Example

Assume that methods were being considered to provide long-range forecasts of automobile sales for General Motors. Ideally, one should treat each forecasting method as an investment and calculate a rate of return. The various column headings from Exhibit 14-1, along with accuracy, would enter into these calculations. If difficulties were found in translating the estimates into a common unit of measure (say dollars), one could use a satisficing model, that is, minimum acceptable levels would be used for each criterion. Comparisons among models could also be made by rating the importance of each criterion. For example, a 1 to 5 importance rating (5 being most important) for the General Motors example might result in the following: 1 for the cost factors, 3 for assessing uncertainty, 5 for assessing alternative futures, and 4 for learning. These importance ratings would then be multiplied by the ratings in Exhibit 14-1. The benefits due to accuracy could be assessed by using the framework in Appendix A.

The rest of this chapter covers the major considerations used in rating costs and benefits. The discussion covers each of the criteria listed in Exhibit 14-1.

DEVELOPMENTAL COSTS

Three major factors influence developmental costs:

- Data needs. Methods that require more data cost more because of added collection and processing expenses.
- The complexity of the method. More complex methods require more highly trained people and more time for analysis.
- Implementation. For both analyst and user to gain confidence in the model, significant time and money must be invested.

Thus complex methods have much higher development costs.

Data needs, complexity, and implementation were each examined to obtain rankings of development costs for the methods listed in Exhibit 14-1. As may be seen, judgmental methods are the least expensive because they draw mostly upon existing capabilities and existing data.

Objective methods often seem deceptively simple. When rating developmental costs or when preparing the forecasting budget using objective methods, remember Armstrong's law: "There's no such thing as an easy job."

Exhibit 14-1 COSTS AND BENEFITS OF FORECASTING METHODS (ACCURACY EXCLUDED)
(5 = most favorable rating)

Method	Costs			Benefits		
	Development	Maintenance	Operation	Uncertainty	Alt. Futures	Learning
Judgmental						
Intentions	3	3	3	3	3	1
Opinions	4	3	4	3	3	1
Delphi	3	4	3	3	3	2
Traditional meeting	5	5	3	2	2	2
Structured meeting	4	4	3	2	3	2
Group depth interview	4	5	3	2	3	2
Role playing	3	4	3	3	4	2
Extrapolation						
Markov chains	2	4	4	2	1	1
Moving averages	4	4	4	3	1	1
Exponential smoothing	4	4	5	3	1	1
Box-Jenkins	2	3	4	3	1	1
Regression	3	4	4	3	1	1

Econometric						
A priori	3	4	4	3	4	3
Updated	2	3	4	5	4	5
Segmentation						
Trees	2	3	4	3	3	3
Input-output	1	2	3	2	3	2
Simulation	1	2	3	4	4	4
Bootstrapping						
Direct	3	4	4	3	4	3
Indirect	2	3	4	3	4	4

*The ratings may be compared only within columns (e.g., a 4 on uncertainty is not related to a 4 on learning).

Remember the advice presented throughout Part II: keep it simple. Things will become complex all by themselves. Of course, we academics always like to make things look difficult. Perhaps that is our way of getting respect . . . and money. Out West they build dams to tap the pork barrel. The South constructs the nation's military defenses. Here in the East we do complex research for the government. One of my more memorable experiences was the difficulty in getting permission to use a simple method when a complex one could also be used; the job involved the federally funded Minicar project, and it eventually led to the paper by Armstrong and Overton (1971). (The hassle reminded me of the three men who went to lunch in Washington, D.C. The bill came to $100. The first man reached for the check, but the second man snatched it away from him saying. "I'll put it on my company's expense account because it will only cost $50 after the tax deduction." Ultimately, however, the third man took possession of the bill; his firm was on a cost-plus government contract so that it made $20 on the lunch.) But I digress. The point is that complex methods are often encouraged simply because they are expensive and impressive. Avoid this.

MAINTENANCE COSTS

The argument for maintenance costs parallels that used for developmental costs. Complex methods are more expensive to maintain. They require more data and more effort to document and keep up to date. Thus the ratings are similar to those for developmental costs.

Often data are routinely collected for other purposes, so the full cost should not be charged to forecasting. Still, expenses are involved to ensure that the data are collected in a consistent manner. Updating and revising the data create small additional costs. A major concern is changing definitions. These may call for expensive revisions. Unfortunately, shifting definitions are common: "Gee, we changed the definition of a riot in 1967," Alaska and Hawaii were added to our totals as of 1968," "Foreign cars were added to the totals starting in 1958," and so on.

For maintenance costs, remember Murphy's law: "If something can go wrong, it will." In deference to Murphy's law, you should keep the methods simple.

OPERATING COSTS

Unlike developmental and maintenance costs, operating costs usually are not much higher for complex methods. Once a complex objective method is developed, operating costs are low because the forecasts are generated either by computer or by a clerk performing routine calculations. (Of course, some consultants do not like the client to get away that easily, so they may develop objective methods that require continuing assistance.

Operating costs are usually high for judgmental methods. Judgmental forecasts have short life spans and before long, new forecasts must be obtained. The forecasts generally call for time expenditures by analysts, managers, and other well-paid people.

Operating costs are of particular interest when a large number of forecasts are required. For example, in inventory control problems, forecasts are often required for thousands of items. Operating costs are also important if forecasts are desired for alternative assumptions about the future environment or for the examination of different policies.

Low operating costs are preferable for pragmatic reasons. Organizations view forecasting as a staff activity that is not crucial for day-to-day operations. In bad times, organizations save money by cutting frills . . . such as forecasting. For example, I once had a consulting job with a large firm whose sales had taken a sudden turn for the worse. I worked with a man named Jones to develop better short-range forecasting methods. On Monday, Jones and I worked to prepare for a presentation on Friday. On Wednesday, I called Jones to see whether everything was ready to go. The operator answered, "I'm sorry; we have no Mr. Jones here." Jones, it seemed, was fired on Tuesday. It is not clear that Jones deserved this, and he certainly had not predicted his own fate. But Jones was the only forecaster in an organization that seemed to be in dire need of better forecasts. (Come to think of it, this reflects poorly on my accuracy as a forecaster because I did not predict that Jones would be fired. But, then, I too suffer from optimism and anchoring.)

Parkinson's law (Parkinson, 1957) is worth remembering for operating costs. It says that "work expands so as to fill the time available for its completion." A corollary would be that "forecasting expenses rise to meet the budget." This is especially true for judgmental methods. According to Morgenstern, Knorr, and Heiss (1973), some organizations have spent over $250,000 for a Delphi study.

I have looked, without success, for evidence that judges make more accurate forecasts if they spend more time on each forecast. Negative findings were obtained in Hall, Mouton, and Blake (1963) and in Chapman and Chapman (1967). This lack of evidence does not bother judges. They still act as if they can do a better job, given more time. As an extreme example, Schneidman (1971) took four months to predict which of 25 subjects was most likely to commit suicide. Gough (1962), in his review of the literature, found most writers agreeing that the judgmental method is a time-consuming, painstaking task; he refers to a study by Sanford, who claimed that a minimum of six hours is required to predict the success of a student entering college. Note that judgmental methods lead to high operating expenditures.

ASSESSING UNCERTAINTY

The use of each method for the assessment of uncertainty was discussed at length in Part II of *LRF*. Here are some generalizations:

- Judgmental methods are advantageous because of the different ways one can estimate uncertainty, but they tend to understate uncertainty.
- Extrapolation methods offer simple and inexpensive ways to assess uncertainty.
- Econometrics and segmentation can, in some cases, go beyond extrapolations to *explain* the sources of uncertainty.

   More emphasis should be given to the assessment of uncertainty. RUSH and PAGE [1979] found that the use of measures of uncertainty in published forecasts declined from 1910 to 1964. Firms surveyed in DALRYMPLE's [1985] study typically reported little or no formal assessment of uncertainty.

ASSESSING ALTERNATIVE FUTURES

The analysis of alternative futures, or **sensitivity analysis**[G], is useful for planning purposes. Questions such as "If X occurred, how would people respond?" can be asked. The organization can then try to influence whether or not X occurs; or, if they have no control over X, they can plan for this contingency. This section discusses the question of which forecasting method is best for sensitivity testing.

   Extrapolation is of little value for examining alternative possibilities. On the other hand, segmentation and econometric methods are well designed for this; the inputs can be varied to reflect the changes in the environment or the changes in the organization's policies, and the results can then be examined.

Econometric methods are particularly well suited to testing alternative futures because the alternatives can be examined in a consistent and inexpensive manner. One merely inserts different values for the causal variables to reflect the changes in the environment or in organizational policies. It is simple to vary the inputs, and the outputs are easy to interpret. An example of this use of the econometric method is provided in my study on the photographic market:

> In Armstrong (1968a), an econometric model was used to assess the impact of changes that were expected to influence the photographic market. An analysis of the Kennedy-round tariff cuts showed that sales would increase substantially in underdeveloped countries (e.g., a 37% increase for Brazil), but only modestly in developed countries. Other analyses could also be made: What would happen if resale price maintenance were abolished in Austria? What if the high sales taxes in Greece were reduced? What if economic growth in the United States slowed down substantially?

Judgmental methods can be used to assess alternative futures, but the estimates may be adversely affected by bias and anchoring. Furthermore, a group may become incensed at the introduction of alternative possibilities because its members see this as an attack on their good judgment. As a result, it helps to use unbiased judges (people who are outside the influence of the organization). Efforts should be made to reduce the influence of the researcher by using structured methods.

Groups can adopt formal procedures to remove the detrimental effects of their norms (assuming they can decide that there are detrimental effects). Two techniques are of particular value:

1. Group depth interviews are useful for predicting how members of an organization will act in a given situation. For example, how would they act if their factory were closed?
2. Role playing goes beyond group depth interviews in the assessment of alternative futures by protecting the participant from peer pressure (he is only acting within his new role!). New situations can be

described, including new types of roles, new organizational struc-
tures, new decisions, or new environments. The consequences of
these new situations can be acted out. For example, role playing
has been used to examine reactions to new offers or new strategies
in labor-management negotiations, to examine the jury's reaction
to a defense strategy in a law case, and to test customers' reactions
to a new marketing strategy.

LEARNING

You were probably wondering whether I had forgotten about Winston
Churchill and people who stumble over the truth. Not at all. This
section discusses truth and learning. I am a firm believer in progress;
a forecasting model should be improved over time.

The extent to which forcasting models contribute to learning varies
greatly. Extrapolation methods can be quickly discounted. The researcher may learn from experimentation which method works best,
but the reasons for the improvement seldom are obvious. If the environment changes, it may be necessary to develop a new extrapolation
model.

At the other extreme, the econometric model is well suited to learning. Analyses of conditional forecasts are useful in indicating where
learning is needed. Additional information can be used to update the
relationships in the model.

The mere presence of the econometric model serves as a focus for
learning. Existing knowledge is conveniently summarized by the model.
Furthermore, the learning is no longer dependent upon key personnel;
they may leave the organization, but the model will remain faithful.
As described in the following example, econometric models can indicate
areas where we need to learn more and they provide a focus for this
learning.

In my study of the photographic market (Armstrong, 1968a), the
development of the econometric model revealed great uncertainty
about price elasticity. Furthermore, there was a lack of data about
camera prices in various countries. Communication with top management in some large photographic companies led to the conclusion that such data were not obtained in a systematic way.
Some studies had been done on price elasticity, but because they

lacked the focus of a formal model, they had been filed away. Management forgot about the results.

Segmentation methods also offer a framework for learning. Survey results can be added to these models, rather than having the results filed in the warehouse or in the waste basket.

Judgmental methods are of particular importance because they are used for most important forecasts, and because we know a lot about the learning process that occurs in judgmental methods. In the rest of this chapter, I examine why judges have difficulty learning and what can be done to improve learning.

Problems with Judgmental Learning

Expertise . . . breeds an inability to accept new views.

Laski (1930)

Consider the following study. Skinner (1948) put a hungry pigeon in a cage. On a certain time schedule, food was supplied to the pigeon. This time schedule was fixed and had nothing to do with the bird. What happened? The bird "learned" how to make the food appear. Whenever it wanted food, it repeated the behavior that it was engaged in when the food first appeared. For example, if the pigeon was turning counterclockwise when the food appeared, it concluded that its counterclockwise movement had produced the food. This initial learning proved to be highly resistant to change, even though it had nothing to do with the appearance of the food.

Do people do any better than pigeons? Consider the stockbroker. Consider also the manager—Strickland did, and people did a good job of simulating pigeons. Kahneman and Tversky imply that we act like pigeons.

Strickland (1958) had subjects act as managers for two subordinates whom we will call Stan and Ned. The manager could see Stan's work and could communicate easily with him. Communication was poor with Ned. Over the total work period, both Stan and Ned produced the same amount of work. Whom did the manager trust? He trusted Ned; Stan, he thought, required constant surveillance to produce the same output. In other words, the manager concluded that his managing was largely responsible for Stan's output. (This result is also interesting because increased communication led to less trust.)

Kahneman and Tversky (1973) discussed a training program for a flight school. Trainers adopted the recommendation from psychologists that they use only positive reinforcement for training; that is, they praised successful work and said nothing otherwise. After a time they concluded that positive reinforcement did not work; they would praise someone for successfully completing a series of complex maneuvers, but this trainee would not do as well on the next trial. What was happening? Learning involves making some mistakes. The student cannot perform successfully on each trial. Thus you expect regression toward the mean; an exceptionally good trial will be followed by a more average trial, and similarly for an exceptionally poor trial. The flight school trainers saw this regression toward the mean, but they attributed these changes to their actions as trainers. As a result, they learned that "what works" was to punish someone for bad behavior because then he would probably improve on the next trial. Rewarding others, they concluded, just led to overconfidence on the part of the learner.

The illusion of control occurs even in situations where the person clearly has no control, such as in gambling (Langer, 1975). Mark Twain said it well in describing a fight: "Thrusting my nose firmly between his teeth, I threw him heavily to the ground on top of me."

In Chapter 6, evidence was presented to show that experts do not learn from experience. The pigeon-type studies provide a clue as to why this occurs: people and pigeons sometimes use a poor strategy for learning. The major problem is that they look for confirming evidence rather than disconfirming evidence. A bit of confirming evidence may help to reach a minimum level of expertise. After that, it does not help. Wason's studies provide evidence on this issue:

Wason (1960, 1968a) presented subjects with a three-number sequence: 2, 4, 6. The subjects were told that this sequence had been generated by a rule that the experimenter had in his head. The subjects were then asked to learn the rule by generating additional three-number sequences (e.g., 8, 10, 12). After each sequence, the experimenter told the subject whether or not the new sequence agreed with the rule. The subject could generate as many three-number sequences as he wished; when he felt confident of the rule, he wrote it.

The correct rule in the Wason study was "three numbers in increasing order of magnitude," that is, $a < b < c$. Only about 25% of the subjects learned the correct rule. (I replicated this experiment a number of times and my results have been similar to Wason's.) Usually a subject selects a hypothesis (e.g., "add two to each successive number") and looks only for evidence to *confirm* this hypothesis (e.g., 10, 12, 14). He does not attempt to refute his hypothesis. In other words, most people refuse to entertain the possibility that they are wrong!

The story gets worse. Subjects who wrote the wrong rule were allowed to try again (i.e., they were allowed to generate additional sets of numbers to obtain more evidence). About half of these subjects continued to search for confirming evidence *for the same rule*. (It's like magic; if only we pronounce the rule correctly, then it will work.)

It is not clear whether subjects failed to use disconfirming evidence because they were unable or because they were unwilling. When asked how to find out whether their hypothesis was wrong, however, few of them recognized the need to look for disconfirming evidence by generating a sequence of numbers inconsistent with their hypothesis.

Before you try this test on others, remember that it can be threatening to people's self-esteem. So do not ask them to reveal their answer. One of Wason's subjects reacted in an extreme fashion and had to be removed by ambulance.

The above studies are of immense importance to the issues discussed in *LRF*. They imply that:

1. Rational arguments will not be successful in implementing important changes (remember also the Jesus Christ study from *LRF* p. 24).

2. Expertise offers little advantage in forecasting the effects of large changes.
3. Anchoring and bias will probably occur in judgmental forecasting.

So . . . are the studies correct? Now I am in a difficult situation. If you believe "yes," I can present confirming evidence to make you happy. If you believe "no," I can use the rational argument and you may get mad at me. So I will not say much. Of course, you could learn more on this from the substantial amount of literature now available.* The following study by the Chapmans also suggests that people seek confirming evidence:

Chapman and Chapman (1969) asked 32 experts to examine data from homosexual and heterosexual subjects. The data on these subjects were contrived so that there were no relationships for variables that previous empirical literature had found to be irrelevant. Nevertheless, the practicing clinicians saw the relationships that they expected to see which, incidentally, were the same invalid relationships that were expected by a group of nonexperts). Furthermore, some valid relationships conflicted with folklore in this case; when these valid relationships were introduced into the data, the clinicians still saw the invalid relationships. In other words, they had great difficulty in seeing the valid relationships in the data even though their effects were large. (Similar results for a different problem were obtained by Chapman and Chapman, 1967.)

The Chapmans' study suggests that experts do not learn effectively when disconfirming evidence is given to them. Strickler also found that experts did not learn from disconfirming evidence, but nonexperts did:

*Further evidence is also provided in Bruner and Potter (1964), Wason (1968b, 1969), Johnson-Laird and Wason (1970), Hartsough (1975), Langer (1975), Langer and Roth (1975), MAHONEY and KIMPER [1976], MAHONEY and DeMONBREUN [1977], MYNATT, DOHERTY and TWENEY [1978], LORD, ROSS and LEPPER [1979], MANK-TELOW and EVANS [1979], JONES and RUSSELL [1980], and TWENEY and YACHANIN [1984].

Strickler (1967) replicated a study by Hiler and Nesvig (1965). The task was to predict which figure drawings had been done by psychiatric patients and which by normal people. Hiler and Nesvig found no difference between eight students and six clinicians in their ability to predict, as the former were correct 65% of the time, and the latter were correct 64% of the time. Strickler added a new wrinkle; before the judges were asked to make their predictions, they were given results from an empirical study on aspects of drawings that were related to psychiatric problems. Six practicing clinicians, all with Ph.D. degrees and with an average of 14 years of experience, were correct on 66% of the 87 drawings. In other words, they did not do any better with this new information than they had done in the Hiler–Nesvig study. However, the students were correct on 72% of the cases, which was significantly better than the clinicians' level of accuracy ($p < .05$). The inexperienced judges *did* learn from the new information.

Improving Judgmental Learning

Bernard Baruch was asked, "What is the secret of your success at being economic advisor to seven Presidents of the United States? He replied, "It's rather simple. People ask my advice because I have good judgment. Good judgment comes from experience. Experience— well, that comes from bad judgment."

(Noted in *Firestone*, 1972)

The preceding section reviewed problems with judgmental learning. These were caused by factors relevant to the situation as well as to the judges. An examination of these factors will help identify areas for improvement. The factors include the following:

Situation	Judge
Complexity	Feeling of expertise
Feedback	Search for disconfirming evidence

Each of these factors is examined in the following discussion. For a more complete discussion, see FISCHHOFF and MacGREGOR [1982].

Complexity. Evidence from Archer, Bourne, and Brown (1955) and from Dudycha and Naylor (1966) suggests that learning proceeds more slowly when the task is complex. Although you can seldom change the task, its apparent complexity can be reduced by using decomposition. Decomposition can explicitly organize the bits and pieces of subjective information so that the judge can use feedback more effectively. The mere use of paper and pencil is one step in this direction. For example, in the study cited by Chapman and Chapman (1967), the accuracy of the judges was improved by providing them with paper, pencil, and a ruler. Smedslund (1963) also found a slight gain from paper and pencil, although most subjects did not even think to construct 2 × 2 tables for their data, which consisted of two variables, each variable having two possibilities.

Feedback.   Ryback (1967) reviewed the literature on the value of feedback and found that when feedback was absent, little learning occurred. Conversely, he found that the more immediate and precise the feedback, the greater the learning. Not surprising. MURPHY and DAAN [1984], found that feedback led to improved accuracy by weather forecasters.

Feedback is most useful when it is tied to the individual's own behavior, with negative feedback for incorrect responses, and positive feedback for correct responses. This is much more effective than general advice, as shown by GAETH and SHANTEAU [1984].

Although feedback should be rapid, it is also important that it be summarized in a way that is easy to understand. Case-by-case feedback was helpful in Sechrest, Gallimore, and Hersch (1967), but it was not effective in SCHMITT [1978] or FISCHER [1982] nor in the following study:

In Graham (1971), case-by-case feedback was provided to novice judges as they used personality data (from the MMPI) to predict which persons were college students and which ones were hospitalized psychiatric patients. The 14 judges who received case-by-case feedback were correct on 72% of the cases. This was better than chance (50%), but it was not significantly better than the results for the 14 judges who received no feedback (69%).

Data that are summarized after a number of trials are more effective. Hammond, Summers, and Deane (1973) found no gain for case-by-case feedback, but feedback after each group of 20 trials improved results. The following study provides further support:

Ward and Jenkins (1965) presented contrived data on the relationship between cloud seeding and rain to a group of 72 judges. The data can be summarized as follows:

	Rain	No Rain
Seeding	a	b
No Seeding	c	d

Previous studies cited by Ward and Jenkins suggested that, when data are presented on a case-by-case basis, the judgment of a relationship relies primarily on the frequency of entries labeled a above, that is, cases where the policy variable (seeding) and the intended outcome (rain) occur together. Thus seeding in a wet climate would lead a judge to perceive a relationship even though seeding may have no relationship to rain. In other words, the judgments are not based on *conditional* probabilities, as they should be. In this particular experiment, it was found that only 17% of the judges followed a logically defensible rule in perceiving the data when receiving feedback on a case-by-case basis; however, when summary information of the type outlined in the seeding-rain table was provided, 75% did so. In fact, subjects receiving only summary data did better than those receiving both case-by-case *and* summary data.

The preceding discussion on feedback considered only information on the accuracy of predictions. You might also consider other types of feedback. The major types are illustrated by the Brunswick lens model of Exhibit 14-2. This model, taken from Brunswick (1955), has been adapted to fit the terminology used in *LRF*. The b's represent the estimated relationships according to the actual data, while the $\hat{b}$'s represent the relationships as seen by the judge. The dashed line represents feedback on the accuracy of the judge's predictions. (WERNER, ROSE, and YESAVAGE [1983] demonstrate the Brunswick Lens Model in forecasting dangerous behavior by mental patients.)

The bootstrapping model can provide feedback to the judge on how he is making the decisions. The econometric model provides information on the actual relationships. Actual outcomes and a record of forecasts are needed to assess accuracy.

What type of feedback is most useful? According to Newton's study, feedback from the econometric model improves accuracy the most. This

Exhibit 14-2   THE BRUNSWICK LENS MODEL OF FEEDBACK

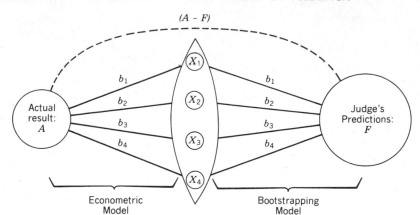

Notes:
1. The X's are the causal variables.
2. The dashed line represents feedback on the accuracy of the judge's predictions.
3. The solid lines represent relationships.

adds support to Goldberg's (1959) speculation, drawn from a sample of one. (Support is also provided in Nystedt and Magnusson, 1973.):

Newton (1965) had judges make predictions of 53 students' grade-point averages from information on IQ, high school rank, college board score, and a rating by the high school principal. Five feedback conditions were established. In each case, information was provided on accuracy. Cases 2 through 5 also received the feedback from the following sources; thus, the conditions were:

1. Accuracy only
2. Bootstrapping model and accuracy
3. Econometric model and accuracy
4. Bootstrapping and econometric models and accuracy
5. Same as case 4 but with more explicit rules

The feedback from the econometric model (condition 3) yielded significant though small improvements in accuracy. This seemed to be the only important factor in this study. Feedback conditions 1 and 2 yielded no improvements in accuracy, while conditions 3, 4, and 5 each provided similar improvement.

Feelings of Expertise. Evidence presented in Chapter 6 suggested that education and experience generally have a detrimental influence on forecasters because they increase confidence but not accuracy. This increased confidence interferes with further learning; this, in turn, may reduce accuracy, although evidence here is inconclusive (e.g., Crow, 1957).

It does not seem like a friendly act to tear down a forecaster's confidence. However, you can save money by avoiding expensive educational programs. The section on feedback concluded that the key element in learning about the forecast situation is empirical evidence. Thus, *if there is little empirical evidence,* avoid training in that area; all you will do is transmit the folklore. The discussions on the virtues of simplicity also indicated that there is no need for expensive training programs. You can simply use empirical studies. Now, how many highly trained real-world forecasters do you know who use this approach to learning? As nearly as I can tell, it is a rare few. Instead, expensive programs that transmit folklore are preferred. (If the same standards were applied to university professors as are applied to the drug industry, we would be out of our jobs tomorrow. We have tried, but have been unable to prove efficacy. We can't prove that we help people to learn more effectively than they could learn by living a more normal life. But that's another story.)

Remember Lem Putt, the privy builder (from Chapter 6)? Expertise is sometimes useful and education in some areas *is* relevant. In addition to privy building, worthwhile areas include how to assess the current situation and how to improve certain skills (e.g., skills in using forecasting methods).

Search for Disconfirming Evidence. An active search for disconfirming evidence can greatly improve learning ability—even for us experts. Disconfirming evidence becomes less threatening when we are in control, and when we seek it out. What happens when active search is absent? The Jesus Christ study (Batson, 1975) suggested that disconfirming evidence increased the experts' confidence in their *currently held* beliefs. This finding was supported also by Geller and Pitz (1968).

One of the problems is that judges remember incorrectly, as illustrated in the following study:

Fischhoff and Beyth (1975) asked judges to make predictions on political and social events. After the events had passed, they went back to the judges and asked them what predictions they had made. The judges were seldom surprised by the outcomes. Often they remembered incorrectly what they had predicted. Even when they had written their predictions, and the predictions could be seen to be incorrect, they rationalized what was written and claimed, "I knew it would happen." This type of remembering is convenient for us; it means that we can go through life without changing our beliefs. (More on this study is provided by Fischhoff, 1975, and hindsight bias by physicians is shown in ARKES [1981].

Unfortunately, learning is painful. Finding one's mistakes is not a pleasant experience. (Do you think I like having to add page 450 of this edition, the one that lists errors in the first edition?) In groups, learning gets even more painful. As a result, many organizations have procedures to discourage learning. They focus on finding evidence to confirm all of their prior decisions and actions. Many organizations and governments have achieved the level of duplicity described by George Orwell in *Nineteen Eighty-Four:*

Day by day and almost minute by minute the past was brought up to date. In this way every prediction made by the Party could be shown by documentary evidence to have been correct; nor was any item of news, or any expression of opinion, which conflicted with the needs of the moment, even allowed to remain on record. All history was a palimpsest, scraped clean and reinscribed exactly as often as was necessary.

With an active search for disconcerning evidence, a judge describes her current beliefs using either an *a priori* analysis or bootstrapping. She then decides what information would be sufficient to change these beliefs, and conducts an active search for such data. Experimentation is especially important in this search for disconfirming evidence. The key question should be, "What information could possibly change my mind?" If you cannot answer this question, you cannot design an experiment that will contribute to your learning. If you have an experiment that *might* work, you can go back to the above question with dummy data to see whether, in fact, any results do change your mind. In effect, you are applying the concepts of implementation to yourself.

SUMMARY

A checklist was used for a cost-benefit analysis of the various types of forecasting methods. This provided the ratings in Exhibit 14-1. The major reasons behind these ratings were described.

Here are some things to keep in mind about costs:

• DEVELOPMENTAL COSTS		Armstrong's law: "There is no such thing as an easy job."
• MAINTENANCE COSTS		Murphy's law: "If something can go wrong it will."
• OPERATING COSTS		Parkinson's law: "Work expands to fill the time allotted."

For the assessment of uncertainty, judgmental methods offer a wide variety of inexpensive techniques, extrapolation methods are simple to use, and econometric and segmentation methods help in understanding the sources of the uncertainty.

The assessment of alternative futures is important because of the value of this information in planning. Econometric methods, scenarios, and role playing were highly recommended for assessing alternative futures.

When changes are large, as in long-range forecasting, it is important that the forecasting method contribute to learning. Extrapolation methods are of little value in this respect, but econometric methods are very helpful.

Unfortunately, we seldom use econometric methods for learning. Instead, we have great confidence in our ability to use judgmental forecasting methods and to learn from them. This confidence is unfounded! The unaided judge is an inefficient learner. (That includes me . . . and possibly you also?) The primary reason is that people do not use disconfirming evidence. This problem is especially serious for people who view themselves as experts. They continue to use the same model even if conditions change. Experts should actively seek disconfirming evidence.

Even though people insist on using judgmental methods to forecast, much can be done to improve learning. The Brunswick lens model provides a convenient way to illustrate the types of feedback. A brief review of advice on improving judgmental learning is provided in Exhibit 14-3.

Exhibit 14-3 IMPROVING JUDGMENTAL LEARNING	
Factors Relating to	Solutions
Complexity	Decomposition
Feedback	Fast feedback Grouped data Empirical studies
Feelings of expertise	Empirical studies Avoidance of training programs
Active search	Experimentation

Fifteen

AN EVALUATION OF ACCURACY

Contents

Of all the horrid, hideous notes of woe,
Sadder than owl songs on the midnight blast,
Is that portentous phrase, "I told you so."

Lord Byron

I agree with Christ, who said, "The ultimate test of an econometric model . . . comes with checking its predictions." (That was Carl Christ in 1951, and his name rhymes with "grist.") Accuracy is generally the primary criterion in the selection of a forecasting method. Because accuracy is highly dependent upon the nature of the situation, this chapter provides guidelines for selecting the most accurate method for a particular situation.

The plan of the chapter is as follows. First there is a discussion on how to assess the value of improved accuracy. Next, the situational factors that are expected to affect accuracy are described. These factors are used to produce hypotheses on the accuracy of methods in different situations. The empirical evidence on these hypotheses is then reviewed. Finally, a user's guide to the selection of forecasting methods is provided.

VALUE OF IMPROVED ACCURACY

How valuable is it to develop a more accurate forecasting model? Numerous researchers have tried to answer this question. The value of improved accuracy was studied by Dunnette (1966) for personnel selection, Dawes (1971) for the selection of graduate students, Lave (1963) for weather forecasts for an agricultural product, Buffa (1975) for inventory control, and SCHNEE [1977] and MARKS [1980] for weather forecasting. This research supports the commonsense notion that the value of improved accuracy depends upon the situation.

The evaluation of forecast accuracy for a firm is of general interest. It also represents one of the easiest situations to evaluate relatively speaking, because costs and benefits can be translated into dollars. Nelson (1973, pp. 11–14) and Daub (1974) examined the value of improved forecasting to a firm. An alternative approach to such evaluation is presented here. It is based upon two key questions:

1. What decisions are affected by the forecast? (If no decisions are affected, improved accuracy will have no value.)
2. What is the current level of accuracy? (To what extent is it possible to improve?)

Exhibit 15-1   FACTORS FOR
EVALUATION OF IMPROVED ACCURACY

A. Market size
B. Costs
C. Commitment of costs (when?)
D. Error reduction
E. Loss function (how much?)
F. Cost of capital
G. Tax rate

These questions should be considered in evaluating accuracy in any situation. To evaluate the accuracy of a firm's forecasts, these questions call for an examination of the seven factors listed in Exhibit 15-1.

The use of Exhibit 15-1 is illustrated in Appendix A. An attempt was made to use reasonable estimates in this illustration in order to obtain a rule of thumb on the value of accuracy to the firm. This rule suggested that large firms could budget no more than about one percent of their sales revenues for the forecasting effort. To judge from data in Wheelwright and Clarke's (1976) survey, the actual forecasting budget ranges from about 2% in firms with $10 million sales, to 0.1% in firms with $1 billion sales.

To estimate potential cost savings for your organization, rather than use this rule of thumb or the practices of other organizations, you should use your own estimates within the framework of Appendix A.

DESCRIBING THE FORECASTING SITUATION

Descriptors of forecasting situations that may affect accuracy can be grouped into three areas: complexity of the behavior, knowledge about the situation, and anticipated change in the environment. Exhibit 15-2 lists these factors; they are described in the following subsections.

Ideally, we would like a set of descriptors of the situation that leads directly to the selection of a forecasting method. The procedure would be analogous to shopping for a suit. You provide a description of the problem according to certain key dimensions to find a suit that fits. Unfortunately, the method does not work out as well for forecasting methods as it does for suits, although the guidelines presented in this chapter will get you into the right size ranges (i.e., you will come close to the most accurate method).

Exhibit 15-2   DESCRIPTORS OF THE FORECASTING SITUATION

I. COMPLEXITY OF THE BEHAVIOR
   A. Number of important factors
   B. Nonlinearities in the relationships
   C. Interaction

II. KNOWLEDGE ABOUT THE SITUATION
   A. Amount of *a priori* knowledge on relationships
   B. Quantity of data available
   C. Extent of measurement error
   D. Scaling properties

III. ANTICIPATED CHANGE IN THE ENVIRONMENT
   A. Rate of change
   B. Change in rate of change
   C. Length of forecast horizon

Complexity of the Behavior

The complexity of a situation is dependent upon (1) the number of variables, (2) the degree of nonlinearity, and (3) the degree of interaction. Indicators of complexity and simplicity are suggested below.

Simple Situations	Complex Situations
One or two variables	Five or more variables
Linearity	Nonlinearity
Little interaction	High interaction

Obviously, these indicators leave a wide middle ground in which you must use your judgment and knowledge of the problem.

Interaction, the extent to which the relationship depends upon other variables, is a common source of complexity in nonexperimental data. Subjective judgments on whether interaction exists are difficult to make. Segmentation methods, such as AID, can be used to assess whether there is interaction in the data.

Knowledge about the Situation

How much knowledge does the analyst have before he collects objective data for the current study? Knowledge is poor if he cannot choose a small number of causal variables; knowledge is moderate if he is fairly sure of the variables and of the directions of the relationships. His knowledge is good if he is sure which variables are important, what the directions of the relationships are, what the functional form looks like, and what the approximate magnitudes of the relationships are.

The quantity of the data refers to the number of independent observations. Small samples, say less than 20 provide poor knowledge; samples of, say, 20 to 1000 show moderate knowledge and samples over 1000 indicate good knowledge. Of course, these are crude estimates.

The extent of measurement error should be compared to the true variation. For example, low measurement error might exist when the ratio of the standard deviation of error relative to the true standard deviation is less than 0.2, and large measurement error when this ratio exceeds 1.0. But these are only rough estimates.

The scaling properties of the data can be classified according to the scheme proposed by Stevens (1959). Poor knowledge occurs when the scaling is crude, as with nominal scales (for example, "yes-no" categories); moderate knowledge occurs when ordinal (ranking) or interval data are available; and good knowledge involves ratio data (meaningful intervals with a known zero point).

Change in the Environment

To what extent will the environment change? The answer involves judgments about the likely changes in the causal variables. Large changes are involved if the causal factors take on values that are outside of the historical experience. Large changes also occur when acceleration is great, that is, when substantial changes occur in the rate of change of the causal variables. Finally, long time periods involve large changes because so many of the conditions have time to change.

HYPOTHESES ON ACCURACY OF METHODS VS. SITUATIONS

Identifying the key descriptors of forecasting situations is the first step in developing hypotheses about the accuracy of forecasting models. The second step involves three key methodological decisions:

• Should objective or subjective methods be used?
• Should naive or causal methods be used?
• Should linear or classification methods be used?

Exhibit 15-3   HYPOTHESES RELATING ACCURACY OF METHODS TO THE SITUATION

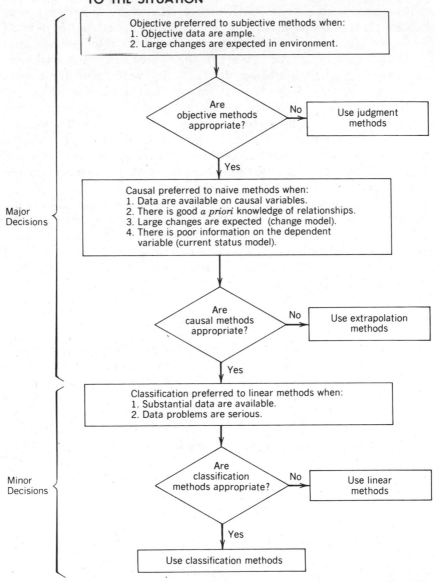

The more important situational factors are incorporated in Exhibit 15-3. These hypotheses were drawn primarily from the evidence presented in Part II of *LRF*.

Evidence on the hypotheses in Exhibit 15-3 is presented below. Some of the evidence was drawn from work that I have done. Most of it, however, is based on previously published empirical research by others. In some cases I reanalyzed data from these studies. The interpretation of the results was sometimes open to question, and in a few cases I had research assistants interpret the studies; these codings were done independently, and the research assistants were not informed of my hypotheses.

OBJECTIVE VS. SUBJECTIVE METHODS

Psychologists, starting with Sarbin (1943), have devoted much effort to the comparison of objective and subjective forecasts. These comparisons, referred to as clinical vs. statistical predictions, created much controversy.

Meehl (1954) reviewed 20 studies and concluded that objective methods were equal or superior to subjective methods in 19 of the studies. McNemar (1955) examined Meehl's work and concluded that the one exception did not hold, as there was no statistically significant difference. Gough's (1962) review also indicated that the objective method was superior. Lindzey (1965) claimed that he had found a case where subjective methods were preferable to objective methods. Meehl (1965) replied that his boxscore was now up to 50 empirical investigations, and that Lindzey's was the only exception. Then Goldberg (1968b) reanalyzed Lindzey's study and showed that there was no statistically significant difference.

Meehl (1956) concluded from his studies: "After reading these studies, it almost looks as if the first rule to follow in trying to predict the subsequent course of a student's or patient's behavior is carefully to avoid talking to him, and that the second rule is to avoid thinking about him!"

These results were not so strong as they first seemed, however. As Sawyer (1966) pointed out, most of the studies assessed fit to the calibration sample, but not predictive ability. He suggested that an examination of predictive situations would have been more appropriate. Holt (1970) reached a similar conclusion. In my opinion, this criticism does not change the basic conclusion. Some of the studies *were* based on predictive situations, and the objective methods did better in these studies.

The studies from psychology tried to control the amount of information used in both objective and subjective methods. Seldom does this occur in real-world forecasting problems. The judge often has additional information, especially with respect to the current situation. It seems worthwhile, then, to examine the relative performance of objective and subjective methods in real situations. It is hypothesized that subjective methods are relatively more accurate when there are:

- small changes, and
- few objective data.

This hypothesis is based on the relative strength of judges in assessing the current situation, and the need for data when objective methods are used. For large changes and numerous data, however, objective methods are expected to be more accurate.

The literature from technological forecasting suggests that objective data cannot be relied upon to make long-range forecasts and that judgmental forecasting is superior. That is an understandable belief. It is also what the "man in the street" believes. And it is wrong.

We conducted a study to test the relative value of objective and subjective methods when ample data were available. The results, which follow, indicated that the relative superiority of objective over subjective models increased as the amount of change increased. The superiority was small for small changes, and large for large changes:

Armstrong and Grohman (1972) compared subjective and objective methods in forecasts of the U.S. air travel market for 1963 to 1968. The subjective forecasts were prepared by the Federal Aviation Agency (FAA). Two objective methods were used: an econometric method, and a simple extrapolation assuming a constant percentage change. The subjective forecasts were inferior to the objective methods. The objective and subjective methods were relatively equal for the one-year forecast horizon, but the relative accuracy of the judgmental method deteriorated rapidly thereafter. (We suspect that the FAA forecasts were not ideal because evidence exists that U.S. public regulators adopt the industry's biased viewpoint.) The results were:

Forecast Horizon (years)	Number of Different Forecasts	Mean Absolute Percentage Errors		
		FAA Judgment (subjective)	Extrap- olation (objective)	Econometric (objective)
1	6	6.8	5.7	4.2
2	5	15.6	12.7	6.8
3	4	25.1	17.4	7.3
4	3	34.1	22.5	9.8
5	2	42.1	27.5	6.2
6	1	45.0	29.9	0.7
Average*	21	28.1	19.3	5.8

*Each row (i.e., each forecast horizon) was weighted equally in calculating the average. The results were not sensitive to the weights.

Further evidence on subjective vs. objective methods was gained by reanalyzing previously published empirical studies that examined unconditional forecasts. The summary below covers all relevant studies I could find. Most of the studies were from economics, although there were studies from weather (Winkler and Murphy, 1968; Russo, Enger, and Sorenson, 1964), personnel (Korman, 1968), education (Cartter, 1965), politics (Pool, Abelson, and Popkin, 1965), and agriculture [BRANDT and BESSLER, 1983].

The studies were categorized by the number of objective data and the amount of change in the environment. Studies that used few data for the objective method, even though many data may have been available, were categorized as having few data. Although it is difficult to put a precise measure on this criterion, the studies proved to be easy to classify.

Environmental change was considered to be large if the rate of change were fast or if there were substantial changes in the rate of change. This criterion varies according to the type of problem. For most economic forecasts, a time period of less than two years was considered to represent small changes. For a study involving weather (Russo et al., 1964), the short-range forecasts were for two hours. Again, the dividing line was not clear, but the classifications were easy to make (except for Cragg and Malkiel, 1968, and Liebling, Bidwell, and Hall, 1976).

The evidence is summarized in Exhibit 15-4. The prior hypotheses

Exhibit 15-4 EVIDENCE ON ACCURACY OF OBJECTIVE VS. SUBJECTIVE METHODS
($a > b$ means that a is more accurate than b)*

Environmental Change	Objective Data	
	Few	Many
	I	II
Small	H_0 [17] **Subjective > objective**	[1] **Subjective > objective**
	Copeland & Marioni (1972)	Liebling, Bidwell, & Hall (1976)
	Cragg & Malkiel (1968)	
	Hirsch & Lovell (1969)	
	KEEN [1981]	
	Korman (1968)	
	Kosobud (1970)	
	Levine (1960)	
	McNees (1975)	
	Milkovich, Annoni, & Mahoney (1972)	
	Mincer & Zarnowitz (1969)	
	Modigliani & Weingartner (1958)	
	Okun (1960)	
	Rippe & Wilkinson (1974)	
	Smyth (1966)	
	Vandome (1963)	
	Zarnowitz (1967)	

[3] **No difference**
BUNN & SEIGAL [1983]
Green & Segall (1966, 1967)
Staël von Holstein (1971)
[7] **Objective > subjective**
Christ (1975)
Haitovsky, Treyz, & Su (1974)
Hultgren (1955)
MABERT [1976] (P)
McNees (1974)
Modigliani & Sauerlender (1955)
Russo, Enger, & Sorenson (1964) (P)

III

[1] **Subjective > objective**
Rippe & Wilkinson (1974) (P)
(H₀) [1] **No difference**
Cragg and Malkiel (1968)
[0] **Objective > subjective**

Large

(H₀) [2] **No difference**
AHLERS & LAKINISHOK [1983]
Winkler & Murphy (1968)
[2] **Objective > subjective**
Armstrong and Grohman (1972)
Harris and Adam (1975)

IV

[1] **Subjective > objective**
ARMSTRONG [1983b] (P)
[1] **No difference**
DAUB & PETERSON [1981]
(H₀) [3] **Objective > subjective**
Armstrong and Grohman (1972) (P)
Cartter (1965)
Pool, Abelson, and Popkin (1965) (P)

* Prior hypotheses are indicated by (H₀), and results achieving statistical significance are indicated by (P). The number of comparisons is indicated in bracket [ ]. The ">" means "more accurate than."

397

are indicated by H_0 in each of the four categories. Few studies reported on statistical significance, and few provided enough information to allow for a test. However, when the results were shown to be significant at $p < .05$, the study is denoted by P.

Small Changes—Few Data

Situations where change is small and a limited number of objective data are available favor subjective methods. That was the prior hypothesis, and the empirical evidence provides mild support. Of the 27 comparisons, 17 agreed with the hypothesis (Okun made two comparisons), 7 disagreed, and there were 3 ties (Green and Segall present one study published in two installments). If one makes the simplifying assumption that all comparisons were of equal value, the superiority of the subjective method is statistically significant ($p < .05$, one tail test).

Unfortunately, the researchers in most of these studies did not test their results for statistical significance, nor did they provide enough information to allow for such tests. My impression, however, was that in most cases the results would not have been significant, for the differences between the objective and subjective forecast errors were small.

The typical study compared an elaborate judgmental method against an objective method that was based on few data. The following are examples of some of these studies that favored subjective methods:

Okun (1960) examined one-year forecasts of U.S. housing starts from 1951 to 1961. I reanalyzed his results to compare forecasts by two subjective methods and two objective methods. The subjective methods were based on intentions studies of house buyers and house builders. They had MAPEs of 8.5% and 7.5%, respectively. In contrast, two simple objective methods were used, one based on no change from the fourth quarter of the preceding year, and the other based on the whole preceding year; the MAPEs were 8.5% and 11.7%, respectively. Thus judgmental methods were slightly more accurate. Okun achieved similar results when investigating business investment plans in the United States from 1948 through 1956. A subjective method (a survey done by the Commerce Department and the Securities and Exchange Commission) was more accurate than two objective methods (same as fourth quarter of preceding year, and same as preceding year), as the MAPEs were 3% vs. 8% and 11%, respectively. None of these differences was statistically significant.

Levine (1960) examined business investment in the United States from 1950 to 1954. He included both the Commerce-SEC (intentions) survey and the McGraw-Hill (intentions) survey, and compared these with the assumptions of no change from the preceding year. The MAPEs were 5% and 4% for the surveys, and 8.4% for the extrapolation. The superiority of the surveys was not statistically significant.

In Zarnowitz (1967), judgmental methods were superior to extrapolations in short-term forecasts of U.S. GNP and of a production index. The superiority of the judgmental method decreased as the forecast horizon was lengthened from one to four quarters, with no difference in accuracy being noted in the four-quarter forecast horizon. (Statistical significance was not examined.)

Mincer and Zarnowitz (1969), in an extension of Zarnowitz (1967), evaluated judgmental and extrapolation methods in short-term forecasts of GNP and of an index of industrial production. The relative advantage of the judgmental forecasts decreased as the time span increased (using one to four quarters of quarterly data and one to two periods on a semiannual basis).

Some of the studies favoring subjective methods were of dubious quality. The study by Milkovich, Annoni, and Mahoney (1972) was based on a single observation. Korman's (1968) study used a judgmental criterion that favored the judgmental method of predicting. In most of the studies, the extrapolations used few data even though more data were available. In this sense, the studies were a bit unrealistic.

Two of the studies favoring objective methods, those of Hultgren and of Modigliani and Sauerlender (1955), used similar methods and drew upon the same data. Hultgren's study is described here:

Hultgren (1955) examined one-quarter forecasts of railway freight traffic from 1927 through 1952 for each of 32 commodities. Judges from business firms provided a combined railroad shippers' forecast. The MAPE of this forecast was 7.5% over all commodity groups. An objective method was developed by taking the five preceding trends from quarter t to $t + 1$ and applying the average ratio to the last quarter. The average error from this method was 6.5%. Thus a simple objective forecast proved to be slightly better than the survey. The judges in this case were expected to be biased, and this may have been a factor in the poorer showing of the subjective method.

Small Changes—Many Data

Little empirical evidence exists in this category, even though it is expected to be a common situation. The hypothesis is that it does not matter which method is used. Only five studies were relevant to this hypothesis; two favored objective methods, one favored subjective methods, and there were two ties. The Armstrong–Grohman study was described earlier. Two studies are summarized here; as can be noted, they provide only weak evidence:

Harris and Adam (1975) compared five extrapolation methods and one judgmental method in making daily forecasts of food demand in a hospital. Each of the extrapolation methods yielded forecasts that were more accurate than the judgmental forecasts for the 31-day validation period.

Liebling, Bidwell, and Hall (1976) examined three 1-year forecasts, two 2-year forecasts, and one 3-year forecast of nonresidential fixed investment. A judgmental survey was superior to econometric forecasts provided by three large-scale econometric models.

The study by Winkler and Murphy (1968) showed no difference between the two types of weather forecasting methods, but the article did not explain how the test was conducted. BRANDT and BESSLER [1983] also found no differences in a study on agricultural forecasting.

Large Changes—Few Data

Judges suffer from bias and anchoring. As a result, they are not expected to do well in forecasting large changes. On the other hand, little can be expected of objective methods if there are few data. Here, then, as with small changes—many data, there is no strong reason to prefer either the subjective or the objective method.

Little evidence could be found for this category. Rippe and Wilkinson (1974) found evidence favoring subjective methods while Cragg and Malkiel, found no difference:

Cragg and Malkiel (1968), in a study of the earnings growth of U.S. corporations, compared forecasts by securities analysts from five investment firms with simple extrapolations. The analysts had access to all of the data and often visited the corporations to discuss prospects with executives. An examination of forecast errors over a 2- or 3-year forecast horizon led Cragg and Malkiel to conclude that the simple extrapolations were about as good as the judgmental forecasts.

Studies on forecasting annual profits for firms favor subjective methods [ARMSTRONG, 1983b], but, in this case, the judges have more information and possibly some control over the outcome.

Large Changes—Many Data

Although judges are expected to perform poorly for large changes, objective methods are ideally suited for large changes given sufficient data. Thus objective methods are hypothesized to be superior to subjective methods in this situation.

Evidence in favor of objective methods was obtained by Armstrong and Grohman (1972). The studies by Pool et al. and by Cartter also favored objective methods:

In a political study by Pool, Abelson, and Popkin (1965), a segmentation approach provided a more accurate forecast than an intentions study (straw vote). For the 1960 election, the 32 northern states were ranked according to the vote for Kennedy as forecasted by the segmentation method, which was based on data through 1958. These rankings correlated better with the actual rankings ($r^2 = .62$) than did a 1958 straw vote ($r^2 = .53$). The difference was significant at $p < .05$.

Cartter (1965) used an econometric method that involved estimation primarily from *a priori* information. He forecast a glut of Ph.D.s after 1968. This forecast differed substantially from the judgmental forecast by the U.S. Office of Education, which had forecast a shortage of about 120,000 Ph.D.s by 1973/1974. (Incidentally, a discussant, Abbott L. Ferriss, seemed upset at Cartter, and he pointed out many shortcomings in Cartter's forecast. In case you have not heard, Cartter was correct.)

NAIVE VS. CAUSAL METHODS

Starting in the 1920s, criminologists advocated the use of causal models to predict which prisoners could safely be paroled. Enthusiasm was high. In 1949, Ohlin and Duncan reviewed the vast literature, but they found only six studies where a test of predictive validity had been made (outside of the calibration sample). They compared the econometric forecasts from these studies with a naive model that assumed no differences among prisoners. For the naive model, the prediction was based on the average from the calibration sample. The causal method was more accurate in two cases, the naive method was more accurate in three cases, and there was one tie. This result was significant in neither a practical nor a statistical sense—a depressing conclusion after 20 years of work on causal methods! Schuessler (1954) reached a similar conclusion after reviewing the evidence on parole prediction for the preceding quarter-century. Other fields, especially economics, have also yielded results that do not reflect favorably on the value of causal methods.

Although causal methods have not shown any overall superiority, they do help in certain situations. The deciding factor is the amount of change in the environment. This factor explains many, though not all, of the discrepancies in the findings on the relative accuracy of naive and causal methods.

The evidence presented in Part II of *LRF* suggested that causal methods have little relative advantage over naive methods for small changes (for short-range forecasting). For large changes (long-range forecasting), however, causal methods are expected to be more accurate.

The hypotheses in the preceding paragraph may not seem unusual to you—unless you are an expert, because for many years experts in causal methods have been claiming superiority for causal methods in short-range forecasting.

Other sources also suggest that experts favor causal methods:

- Herman Wold, a respected econometrician, suggested (North Atlantic Treaty Organization, 1967 p. 48) that causal methods are more appropriate for short-range than long-range forecasts because "the longer the forecast span, the more the actual course of events will be affected by minor influencing factors that are too numerous to be taken into explicit account in a causal model."
- Brown (1970, p. 441) claimed that econometric models were originally designed for short-range forecasting.
- Kosobud (1970), in a paper on short-range forecasting, referred to "the growing body of evidence on the predictive value of econometric methods."
- Econometric services sell short-range forecasts, and one of their claims has been improved accuracy.
- The press publishes short-range forecasts from well-known econometric models with the implication that these models will provide accurate forecasts.
- Worswick (1974), in a review of a book on short-range economy-wide forecasting, says that "the value of econometric models in short-term forecasting is now fairly generally recognized."

It is difficult to find published opinions that disagree with these statements. Perhaps my biases interfered with my search. To explore this possibility, I made a more systematic analysis of this problem, using experts.

Survey of Experts

A survey on econometric forecasting was conducted in late 1975. The survey was based on a convenience sample of 54 experts. Although 29 questionnaires were returned, 8 were incomplete because the respondents felt that they lacked the necessary expertise. Thus, usable replies were received from about half of the relevant experts. The respondents were from some of the leading schools in econometrics (e.g., M.I.T., Harvard, Wharton, Stanford, Michigan State) and from well-known organizations that sell econometric forecasts (e.g., Chase Econometrics,

Wharton Econometric Forecasting Associates). Many of the respondents were well-known econometricians.

The questionnaire asked, "Do econometric methods generally provide more accurate or less accurate forecasts than can be obtained from competitive methods for short-term forecasting in the social sciences? Or is there no difference in accuracy?" (A set of definitions was also provided, as shown in Appendix F.)

As shown in Exhibit 15-5, 95% of the experts agreed that predictions from econometric models are more accurate than predictions from other methods. The respondents also reported that they had a lot of confidence in their opinions. On a scale from 1 ("no confidence") to 5 ("extremely confident"), the average confidence level was 4, and no one reported a confidence level less than 3. Those who responded with "significantly more accurate" had the highest confidence levels.

Another question asked the respondent for a self-rating "as an expert on applied econometrics." Eight respondents rated themselves as "very much of an expert," six as "fairly expert," four as "somewhat of an expert," and two as "not much of an expert," (there was one nonresponse on this question). Those who rated themselves as more expert felt that econometric models were more accurate; five of the eight who rated themselves in the highest category considered econometric methods to be significantly more accurate, a rating that was significantly higher than the ratings by the other respondents ($p < .05$ using the **Fisher exact test** [G].)

Empirical Evidence

The study cited earlier by Armstrong and Grohman was explicitly designed to allow for a comparison between causal and naive methods as the change in the environment increased. As shown here, it sup-

Exhibit 15-5 SURVEY ON ACCURACY OF ECONOMETRIC VS. NAIVE METHODS ($n = 21$)

Econometric Forecasts Rated as	Percentage
Significantly more accurate	33
Somewhat more accurate	62
No difference (or undecided)	0
Somewhat less accurate	5
Significantly less accurate	0

ported the hypothesis that causal methods are of little value for short-range forecasting, but of substantial value for long-range forecasting:

Armstrong and Grohman (1972), in a study on the U.S. air travel market, hypothesized that causal methods are superior to naive methods for long-range forecasting. The situation involved good information on the causal relationships and ample data on the causal variables. The MAPE for an econometric model was substantially less than that for an extrapolation model (5.8 vs. 19.3). This difference was significant at the .01 level, using the **Wilcoxon matched-pairs signed-ranks test** [G] (Siegel, 1956). To test the value of the causal method as the change in the environment increased, the errors of the econometric and extrapolation models were compared as the forecast horizon was lengthened. The results, in the following table indicate that the ranking of the differences in error between the extrapolation and econometric models was in perfect agreement with the hypothesis (significant at the .01 level by the Spearman rank correlation coefficient). The ranking of the ratio of the errors was not quite in perfect agreement with the hypothesis, yet the similarity was close enough so that the null hypothesis of "no agreement" was rejected at the .01 level:

Relative Accuracy of Causal vs. Naive Methods over Time

Forecast Horizon (years)	Number of Different Forecasts	Econometric MAPE (causal) (A)	Extrapolation MAPE (naive) (B)	Difference [B − A]	Ratio (A/B)
1	6	4.2	5.7	1.5	.74
2	5	6.8	12.7	5.9	.54
3	4	7.3	17.4	10.1	.42
4	3	9.8	22.5	12.7	.44
5	2	6.2	27.5	21.3	.22
6	1	0.7	29.9	29.2	.02

To gain further evidence, an examination was made of all published empirical studies that I could find in the social sciences. This survey was conducted by examining references from key articles, by searching through journals, by following up references suggested by those who read previous versions of *LRF*, by examining abstracts, and by using FILDES [1981].

A summary of the evidence is presented in Exhibit 15-6. Three types of evidence were examined:

- "Inadequate tests" include studies in which one of the methods was done poorly, where factors other than the naive and causal dimensions varied, or where there was only one observation. The evidence from these studies is weak.
- "Conditional forecasts" provide better evidence than the inadequate tests. However, they provide the objective methods with an unfair advantage because the naive forecasts were all unconditional. Actually, this potential advantage was found to be no advantage at all from the evidence cited in Chapter 8. In fact, with econometrics as currently practiced, knowledge of how the causal variables change over the forecast horizon was found to be a disadvantage! This is thought to be due to a failure to mitigate (see *LRF* p. 238–240).
- "Unconditional forecasts" are of major interest because they come closest to representing the true forecasting situation.

Some studies appear twice in Exhibit 15-6 because two comparisons were made.

Although the coding of the studies was easy in most cases, a check was made by having a sample of nine studies coded independently by two research assistants who were unaware of the hypotheses. Their ratings agreed with mine on all but one of these comparisons. It did not seem, then, that different people would code the studies much differently.

It was rare for any of the authors to test for statistical significance, and most papers did not provide sufficient evidence to allow for a test of significance (sufficient data were provided by Kosobud, 1970; Markland, 1970; and Vandome, 1963).

Short-Range Forecasting. As noted above, no difference in accuracy was expected for short-range forecasts by naive and causal methods. The empirical literature provided further support: of the 21 studies assessing unconditional forecasts, 9 favored causal methods (1 with significant results), 6 favored naive methods (1 significant), and there were 6 ties. For the 19 conditional forecasts, 4 favored causal methods, 10 favored naive methods, and there were 5 ties. The inadequate tests showed a slight advantage for causal methods. Over all 46 comparisons, the score was 17 favoring causal methods, 17 favoring naive methods, and 12 ties. This result is consistent with the hypothesis of no difference.

These results contradict the existing folklore. I hope that you were looking for this disconfirming evidence. *Long-Range Forecasting* is not the first place where such disconfirming evidence has been presented, so it is interesting to observe how people responded in the past. One case was provided by Christ (1951). He presented evidence that econometric models were no more accurate, and comments were published by Lawrence Klein and Milton Friedman. Klein, whose model was examined by Christ, stated (Christ, 1951, p. 21) that "a competent forecaster would have used an econometric model . . . far differently and more efficiently than Christ used his model." Friedman, however, was receptive. He said (Christ, 1951, p. 112) that additional evidence would strengthen Christ's conclusion and that "the construction of additional models along the same general lines [as Klein's model] will, in due time, be judged failures." I think that Friedman came closer to the truth. Complex econometric methods have failed in *short-range* forecasting in the sense that they have not been more accurate.

Long-Range Forecasting.   Causal methods were expected to be more accurate for long-range forecasting, all other things equal. Of course, all other things were not equal in these studies. Notably, some causal methods were subjective and others were objective. Nevertheless, Exhibit 15-6 summarizes all of the evidence that I could find.

Two studies, Rosenzweig and Ogburn, were based on only one observation, thus they were classified in the inadequate column. The studies by Pfaff and by Smith and Brainard used *ex post* forecasts for the causal model. The unconditional forecasts are of greatest interest. Here, all seven comparisons favored the causal method (statistically significant using the sign test at $p < .05$). In ARMSTRONG [1983b], causal (judgment) methods were superior to extrapolations on 14 of 17 studies of annual earnings for firms. Some of the studies are described here:

Ogburn (1946) made a 10-year forecast of the U.S. air travel market on the basis of data through 1943. The extrapolation he favored, a second-degree parabola, yielded a forecast of 6 billion revenue passenger miles (RPMs). A simple causal model (based primarily on a regression against national income) yielded a fore-

Exhibit 15-6 EVIDENCE ON ACCURACY OF NAIVE VS. CAUSAL METHODS*

Environ-mental Change	Hypotheses on Accuracy	Inadequate Test	Conditional Forecasts (ex post)	Unconditional Forecasts (ex ante)
			Type of Evidence	
Small	Naive > causal	[1] Jaffe et al. (1974)	[10] BURROWS [1971] Cooper (1972) Elliott (1973) Granger & Newbold (1974) Ibrahim & Otsuki (1976) McWHORTER et al. [1977] Nelson (1972) PENCAVEL [1971] PFAFF [1977] SMITH & BRAINARD [1976]	[6] BOPP & NERI [1978] Cooper & Nelson (1975) MABERT [1976] Markland (1970) (F) Naylor, Seaks, & Wichern (1972) Vandome (1963)
	ⓗ₀ No difference	[1] Farrell (1954)	[5] Burch and Stekler (1969) GOULD & WAUD [1973] Levenbach, Cleary, & Fryk (1974) Narasimham et al. (1974) Uri (1977)	[6] AHLERS & LAKINISHOK [1983] BINROTH et al. [1979] BRANDT & BESSLER [1983] NELSON [1984] Ridker (1963) Sims (1967) SMYTH [1983]

Causal > naive	[4] Crane & Crotty (1967) Dalrymple & Haines (1970) Moore (1969) KEEN [1981]	[4] ELLIOTT & UPHOFF [1972] FINKEL & TUTTLE [1971] Kosobud (1970) RAUSSER & OLIVEIRA [1976]	[9] Ash and Smyth (1973) BURROWS [1971] Christ (1975) HATJOULLIS & WOOD [1979] HOWREY et al. [1974] McNees (1974) Rippe, Wilkinson, & Morrison (1976) Russo, Enger, & Sorenson (1964) (P) Sims (1967)
Large			
Naive > causal	[1] Rosenzweig (1957)	[0]	[0]
No difference	[0]	[1] PFAFF [1977]	[0]
(H0) Causal > naive	[1] Ogburn (1946)	[1] SMITH & BRAINARD [1976]	[7] Armstrong (1968a) (P) Armstrong & Grohman (1972) (P) CUMMINS & GRIEPENTROG [1985] (P) O'Herlihy et al. (1967) (P) Pool, et al. (1965) (P) ARMSTRONG [1983b] (P)

* The preferred hypothesis in each category is indicated by (H0), and results significant at the .05 level are indicated by (P). The number of comparisons is indicated in brackets [ ].

409

cast of 8 billion RPMs. Actual RPMs were 14.9 billion, so the causal approach was superior (46% vs. 60% errors).

Rosenzweig (1957) made an 11 year forecast of aluminum sales in the United States for 1965. A naive method, constant percentage change from 1910 to 1954, yielded a forecast of 8.5 billion pounds. A simple causal method (based on the relationship between aluminum sales and GNP) yielded a forecast of 8.4 billion pounds. Another causal method (based on a segmentation by major types of customers) yielded a forecast of 8.9 billion pounds. According to the 1966 edition of *Metal Statistics,* aluminum sales were 7.2 billion pounds in 1965. The naive method had a slight advantage over the average of the two causal methods (18% vs. 20%).

Pool, Abelson, and Popkin (1965), in their forecast of the 1960 United States presidential election, found that their causal (segmentation) approach provided more accurate results than a naive method. The segmentation was based on data through 1958; the naive method assumed that the 1960 party vote would be the same as the 1965 party vote (the naive method seemed reasonable). Each method was used to rank the 32 northern states according to the Kennedy vote. The causal method correlated well with actual results ($r = .82$), but the naive method was poorer ($r = .42$). I tested the difference between these coefficients and found it to be statistically significant ($p < .01$). A similar test was made for the 1964 election, and the correlations for the segmentation and naive methods were .52 and $-.16$, respectively. This result, which covered 48 states, was statistically significant ($p < .01$).

O'Herlihy et al. (1967) compared the errors from causal and naive methods used to make five-year forecasts in Great Britain. They examined five forecasts published in the *National Institute Economic Review* in 1960 and 1961. The results, summarized in the following table, show that the causal method was superior in all five cases, usually by a substantial margin ($p < .05$, using the sign test). The relative superiority of the causal method was greater when change was large. The error of the causal method was only about one-fifth that of the naive method when large changes were involved, but the ratio averaged about $3/5$ when moderate changes were forecasted.

Change	Forecast Areas	Errors (%)	
		Naive (extrapolation)	Causal (econometric)
Moderate	Energy	−9.2	−4.1
	Coal	−8.7	+6.8
	MAPE	9.0	5.4
Large	Domestic autos	+17.3	−2.9
	Auto exports	+35.8	+7.5
	Consumer durables	+147.7	+34.0
	MAPE	66.9	14.8

In my study of the six-year backcast of cameras (Armstrong, 1968a), data were organized according to the amount of change that actually occurred between 1960–1965 and 1954. The causal model (an updated econometric model) was superior to the extrapolation model (based upon a combination of forecasts from three simple models: no change, constant trend by country, and constant trend over all countries). This superiority was large and statistically significant ($p < .05$); furthermore, it was greatest when change was large. The last column in the table reports the ratio of the causal $\overline{\text{MAPE}}$ to the naive $\overline{\text{MAPE}}$.

Amount of Change*	Number of Countries	MAPE		
		Naive (extrapolation)	Causal (econometric)	Causal/ Naive Ratio
Moderate (0.55)	6	26	21	0.81
Large (0.47)	5	41	30	0.73
Very large (0.31)	6	62	20	0.32

*The figure in parentheses is the average ratio of 1954 sales to the 1960–1965 average.

CUMMINS and GRIEPENTROG [1985] compared forecasts from econometric and extrapolation methods for medium term forecasts of insurance claims. They used quarterly data from 1965 to 1974, then made forecasts for eight quarters ahead. By using successive updating to 1982, they obtained eight forecast periods. As shown in the table, the econometric model, from a simple one variable regression, was more accurate then the three extrapolation methods. The differences were statistically significant.

Model	Percentage Error in the Eighth Quarter	
	Body Injury	Property Damage
Econometric	3.0	2.7
Extrapolation		
Time trend	3.4	6.6
ARIMA 1	5.2	5.9
ARIMA 2	5.2	7.0
Average extrapolation	4.6	6.5

The above evidence is favorable to econometric methods. Furthermore, Chapter 8 presented evidence that econometric methods can be used to improve the estimate of current status. Finally, as noted in Chapter 10, econometric methods used in combination with other methods yield improvements in short-range forecasting. Hence Milton Friedman's pessimistic outlook is correct only for short-range forecasting. Causal methods are preferred for long-range forecasting.

LINEAR VS. CLASSIFICATION METHODS

After a decision has been made to use a causal method, it is necessary to choose between linear and classification methods. As hypothesized in Exhibit 15-3, classification methods are assumed to be more accurate when ample data exist and when serious problems occur in the data (interaction, nonlinearities, and causal priorities).

The evidence on the relative accuracy of linear and classification methods is presented in Exhibit 15-7. Again, the methods that are hypothesized to be most effective are indicated by (H_0). Only 12 studies were found. They offer modest support for the hypotheses.

Exhibit 15-7 EVIDENCE ON ACCURACY OF LINEAR VS. CLASSIFICATION METHODS*

Data	Data Problems	
	Minor	Major
Small or moderate sample (less than 1000 observations)	H_0 [2] **Linear > classification** Armstrong (1968a)(P) Goldberg (1965)(P) [0] **No difference** [0] **Classification > linear**	[2] **Linear > classification** Forehand & McQuitty (1959) Pritchard (1977) H_0 [1] **No difference** Fegley, Armstrong, & Salisbury (1971) [1] **Classification > linear** Lykken and Rose (1963)
Large sample (more than 1000 observations)	H_0 [0] **Linear > classification** [1] **No difference** TRAUGOTT & TUCKER [1984] [0] **Classification > linear**	[0] **Linear > classification** [0] **No difference** H_0 [5] **Classification > linear** Armstrong and Andress (1970)(P) PAGE [1977] Port of N.Y. Authority (1957) Sonquist (1970) Stuckert (1958)

*The preferred hypothesis is indicated by H_0, and statistically significant results (at $p < .05$) are indicated by (P). The number of studies is shown in brackets [ ]. The ">" means "more accurate than".

The key hypotheses are in categories I and IV. Seven studies were found, and the results are all in the predicted direction ($p < .05$). However, the evidence is really stronger than this because results significant at $p < .05$ were found in each of four studies where a test of statistical significance could be made (the Port of New York Authority was a one-observation study, and Sonquist used simulated rather than actual data for his studies). The studies are described in the following sections.

Few Data—Minor Data Problems

Econometric methods make more effective use of the data than classification methods. Unfortunately, I was able to find only two studies that assessed predictive validity in this situation; both studies supported the hypothesis:

Goldberg (1965) reanalyzed data on psychoticism and neuroticism from Meehl (1959). Data from 402 individuals were used to develop linear regression models and a segmentation model. These models were used to predict for a new sample of 861 individuals. Of 19 linear regressions that were tried, 13 were superior to the classification approach. If one makes the bold assumption that these represent 19 independent tests, the results would be statistically significant ($p < .05$).

In a study of the photographic market (Armstrong, 1968a, pp. 160–162), data from 19 countries were used to develop a regression model and also a segmentation model. The latter divided the countries into nine classifications based on income (three categories) and price (three categories). The regression model provided a better prediction than the classification model for 11 new countries (the MAPEs were 31% and 54%, respectively, a result that was statistically significant at $p < .05$).

Few Data—Major Data Problems

Although the classification model would be preferred for serious data problems, the lack of data creates a problem. Just how many data are required is not clear. I have used a dividing line of 1000 observations (this was suggested by Einhorn, 1972b).

Four studies were found. They are consistent with the favored hypothesis of no difference between linear and classification methods.

Forehand and McQuitty (1959) forecasted the grades of 366 freshmen in a college of engineering. A regression model and a segmentation model were used. The segmentation model had 81 possible cells, but the data were limited. Nine of the segments had no observations, and 21 had only one observation. The results were as follows:

| | Correlation (r) | |
Model	Calibration	Concurrent Validity
Regression	.50	.38
Segmentation	.74	.24

Lykken and Rose (1963) reexamined data from Smith, who had used a linear discriminant function to predict which subjects were normal and which were psychotic. A segmentation model provided a better fit to the calibration sample than did the linear discriminant function, but no further tests of predictive validity were made.

Fegley, Armstrong, and Salisbury (1971) used econometric and segmentation methods to forecast deaths for a sample of 272 people over a 20-year horizon. The models were calibrated on half of the sample, and concurrent validity was tested on the other half. There were no significant differences between the econometric and segmentation forecasts.

Pritchard (1977), in a study to predict whether probation would be revoked for adult male probationers, compared three multiple regressions with four segmentation methods. A variety of accuracy measures were in agreement on the superiority of the regression methods. The average hit rate was 70% for the regressions and 62% for the segmentation methods. This difference is not statistically significant. Sample sizes for this study were 152 and 151 for the calibration and concurrent validation samples respectively.

Many Data—Minor Data Problems

This case is not of great interest. There is no preference for either linear or classification methods. Furthermore, I could find only one study. Conclusion: do it the cheapest and simplest way.

Many Data—Major Data Problems

The classification method is designed for situations with large sample sizes and major data problems. Linear methods perform well with large samples but suffer from data problems. Thus, classification methods would be preferred.

Five empirical studies were found; all supported the hypothesis. Although the differences were small in all cases, the results were statistically significant in one of the two cases where tests were made. Four of the studies are summarized here:

In the Port of New York Authority (1957) study of U.S. air passenger trips, an econometric model and a segmentation model were each used to make a 10-year forecast. The error for the segmentation model was 3%, and that for the linear model was 16%.

Stuckert (1958) found a classification approach to be superior to a linear approach in forecasting the academic achievements of almost 1000 students from the 1949 and 1950 freshman classes at Ohio State. This situation was one where interaction in the data was expected. The classification approach used five variables to define 16 segments. The linear approach used a regression of four variables. An index of relative efficiency was used to examine the results (the index was based on the percentage reduction of incorrect answers from that obtained if the prediction was based solely on the most popular category in the validation sample). The average efficiency for the 1949 and 1950 samples combined was 37% for the classification method and 33% for the linear method. In other words, the classification method was slightly more accurate, but the difference was not significant.

Sonquist (1970) used simulated data with over 2000 observations to compare the linear and classification methods. The simulation made it possible to examine the effectiveness of each method under different conditions. It was assumed that there was little *a priori* information. Sonquist concluded that classification was superior to linear methods when there was interaction because classification was better able to reproduce the known structure. This result provided only an indirect test of predictive validity.

Armstrong and Andress (1970) compared linear and classification methods in predicting the volumes of gasoline sold at various stations offering a major brand. It was assumed that there was little *a priori* information about causality. In addition, the situation was judged to be complex (interaction and nonlinearities were suspected), and the data base was large (2717 stations were used for developing the models). Thus our hypothesis was that classification methods should be more accurate than linear methods in this situation. The AID program, along with standard rules of thumb for exploratory research, was used to develop a segmentation model, and the linear method was developed by stepwise regression. Predictions were made for 3000 "new" stations; the MAPE for the linear method was 58% and that for the classification method was only 41% ($p < .01$).

SUMMARY

Accuracy is generally the key criterion in the selection of a method. The value of improved accuracy can be substantial. The key factors involved in the assessment of improved accuracy were briefly described. (A summary was provided in Exhibit 15-1.) A rule of thumb is that firms could achieve savings of over 1% of sales revenues by improvements in forecast accuracy.

Three descriptors of the situation are expected to affect accuracy: complexity of behavior, knowledge of the situation, and anticipated change in the environment. A general discussion of these descriptors and evidence from Part II of *LRF* were used to develop hypotheses on which methods will be most accurate in which situations (summarized in Exhibit 15-3). These hypotheses were organized to correspond with the existing research. The evidence was then reviewed, the major findings being as follows:

1.   In general, my summary of 39 comparisons showed that subjective methods had a small advantage over objective methods (subjective methods were more accurate for 20 of the 32 studies that showed differences). Subjective methods are especially useful when changes are small and few objective data are available (subjective methods being more accurate in 17 of the 24 comparisons that revealed differences). Objective methods seem superior for large changes and many data; large improvements in accuracy were obtained for three of the five studies that were available (Exhibit 15-4). These results conflict with the folklore in forecasting.

2.   Experts have a strong preference for causal over naive methods. This preference is reflected by published statements and also by a survey where 95% of the experts reported such a belief. The evidence does not support such a preference. Of 57 empirical comparisons, only 26 supported the superiority of causal methods. When the *situation* is considered, however, the following conclusion emerges: causal methods are superior for large changes (long-range forecasts), but not for short-range forecasts. Substantial improvements for causal over naive methods were found in all seven comparisons that assessed the unconditional predictive validity for large changes. These results, summarized in Exhibit 15-6, provide disconfirming evidence for those econometricians who have devoted their energies toward short-range forecasting. Only 10 of 21 unconditional forecast tests found causal methods to be more accurate for short-range forecasting, and these improvements were small.

3.   Linear methods are preferred to classification methods when data are few and data problems are minor (two studies agreed and none disagreed). The situation is just the reverse when data are ample and major problems exist in the data (four studies agreed and none

Exhibit 15-8   A USER'S GUIDE TO SELECTING ACCURATE METHODS

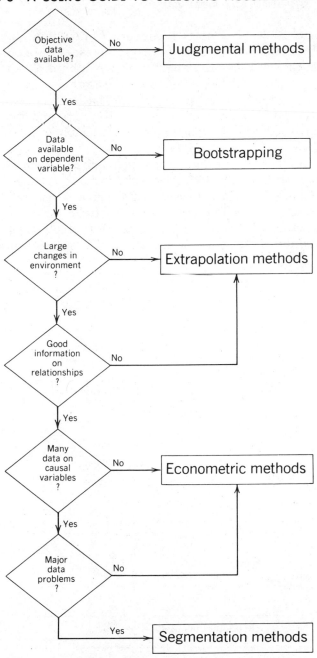

disagreed). These differences were generally small and only one comparison was statistically significant.

The advice from this chapter is converted into a form that is easier to use in Exhibit 15-8. A series of "yes-no" questions are posed for the selection of the most accurate method. This exhibit directs you only to the major type of method, so references are provided to help in the selection of a specific technique. Remember that this exhibit covers only accuracy; it is important to consider also costs and other benefits (see Exhibit 14-1). Finally, remember that a combined forecast is preferable to a forecast from a single method.

Here is another way to summarize the empirical evidence. Suppose you were asked if you could improve the accuracy of the long-range forecasts for an organization. Naturally you first ask how they are currently making these forecasts. To your delight, they describe a traditional meeting. Tell them "yes." Then try to find out which of the steps in Exhibit 15-9 would be acceptable. These procedures are all designed to improve forecasting accuracy.

Exhibit 15-9   IMPROVING ACCURACY IN LONG-RANGE
              FORECASTING
              (→ indicates path to increased accuracy)

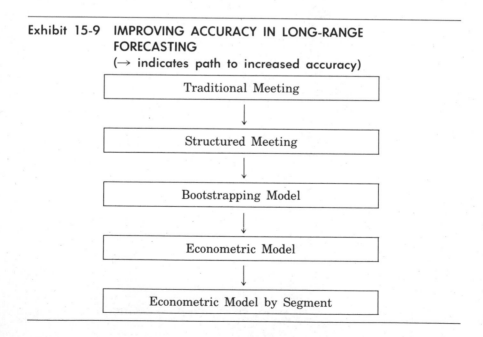

Part V

COMMENCEMENT

P art V is more impressionistic than Parts II, III, and IV. It contains opinions gathered over 25 years and thousands of hours of study on forecasting problems.

Chapter 16 discusses current trends in the use of forecasting methods and speculates about the methods that will be used in the future. Chapter 17 identifies areas where further research is needed on forecasting methods.

Sixteen

TRENDS IN THE USE OF FORECASTING METHODS

Contents

Processionary caterpillars feed upon pine needles. They move through the trees in a long procession, one leading and the others following—each with his eyes half-closed and his head snugly fitted against the rear extremity of his predecessor.

Jean-Henri Fabre, the great French naturalist, after patiently experimenting with a group of the caterpillars, finally enticed them to the rim of a large flower pot. He succeeded in getting the first one connected up with the last one, thus forming a complete circle, which started moving around in a procession, with neither beginning nor end.

The naturalist expected that after a while they would catch on to the joke, get tired of their useless march, and start off in some new direction. But not so.

Through sheer force of habit, the living, creeping circle kept moving around the rim of the pot—around and around, keeping the same relentless pace for seven days and seven nights—and would doubtless have continued longer had it not been for sheer exhaustion and ultimate starvation.

Incidentally, an ample supply of food was close at hand and plainly visible, but it was outside the range of the circle so they continued along the beaten path.

They were following instinct—habit—custom—tradition—precedent—past experience—"standard practice"—or whatever you may choose to call it, but they were following it blindly.

They mistook activity for accomplishment. They meant well but got no place.

Source Unknown

The research reported in this book has been hard on human beings, the noblest of God's creatures. The computer can beat us at forecasting, we learn like pigeons, and we adopt new methods like processionary caterpillars.

People are most like processionary caterpillars when they work in large bureaucratic organizations. Individuals who are intelligent, open, and creative are often converted into processionary caterpillars when they become "team players." It happens to the best of us. And when it happens, energy is directed to keeping things the way they are at the present time.

Organizations need to change to survive. Change agents are their saviors. Nevertheless, they treat their saviors in the traditional manner (e.g., in the well-known case of Jesus Christ). Examples are provided by Nader, Petkas, and Blackwell (1972).

ROGERS [1983] summarized the research on innovation and found that the innovator is a deviant from the group. George Bernard Shaw summed up things this way:

The reasonable man adapts himself to the world: the unreasonable one persists in trying to adapt the world to himself.
   Therefore, all progress depends on the unreasonable man.

Man and Superman: The Revolutionist's Handbook (1903)

Innovators are valuable to society, but they are not popular. You have a choice. If you choose to innovate, Chapter 3 should help to reduce your suffering.

Conformity to group opinion is often responsible for preventing change. But it can also serve to help bring about change. If "everyone else" (e.g., the competitors) is adopting a new course, then one conforms by changing. As many of you know, large organizations are more interested in following innovations that have been adopted by others. To help with this strategy, Chapter 16 reviews some of the trends in forecasting methods. For another description of the trends, see ASCHER [1978].

FROM SUBJECTIVE TO OBJECTIVE

One of the trends in forecasting methods has been toward the use of objective rather than subjective methods. Weather forecasting provides an example. Early attempts at weather forecasting were based primarily upon subjective methods. Gradually, however, as historical data were collected in a more systematic fashion and as computers became available, there was a movement toward objective methods (Glahn, 1965; Turner, 1970). This transition was slow. Klein (1969) suggested that the subjective-objective mix would continue to change gradually until there is a completely objective system for weather forecasting. By the early 1980s, objective weather forecasts were widely used and they provided good accuracy. For long term forecasts, their accuracy seemed to be better than that for subjective forecasts [MURPHY and BROWN, 1984].

To be sure, the trend towards objective methods has been slow, especially for *important* problems. Surveys continue to indicate that subjective methods are still dominant [CERULLO and AVILA, 1975; ROTHE, 1978; GREENLEY, 1983; MENTZER and COX, 1984; SPARKES and McHUGH, 1984; and DALRYMPLE, 1985]. Executive opinion, for example, is widely used, especially for longer range forecasts. It is also used frequently for large aggregates (e.g., for the corporate forecast rather than the individual item product forecast). In published forecasts of the metals market, RUSH and PAGE [1979] found an *increased* reliance on subjective forecasts in the period from 1910 to 1964.

One factor that may have slowed the adoption of objective methods is that they do not always yield improvements. Advocates of objective methods have seldom noted the importance of tailoring the method to the situation. As a result, objective methods have not lived up to their advance billing. As noted in Chapter 15, for example, objective methods have not been very accurate in short-range forecasting, which is the area where they have been most frequently applied. On the other hand, they are more accurate in long-range forecasting when ample data are available.

Objective models have been widely adopted for short-range forecasting of products, primarily because they are less expensive than subjective methods. The use of personal computers will extend this cost advantage to additional situations. I believe the primary argument for the adoption of objective methods will be reduced costs, not improved accuracy. The Law of the Hammer also applies here: given a personal computer, people will search for things on which to use it. DALRYMPLE's [1985] survey supports the impression that the use of computer models is gaining rapidly; in sales forecasting, the percentage of firms reporting that they "always" use computers increased from 25% in 1975 to 39% in 1983.

Bootstrapping could produce a revolution. It can reduce the cost of the forecasting done by highly paid professionals such as doctors, generals, judges, marketing managers, psychiatrists, school administrators, and lawyers ... with a small gain in accuracy. But of all God's creatures, these are the noblest. They will fight to prevent technological changes from eliminating part of their job. Bootstrapping would make their organization less dependent upon them. Nevertheless, some professionals will seize the opportunity to reduce the repetitive elements of their jobs.

One barrier to the adoption of objective methods is that managers do not want to lose control. This factor showed up in the decision by some firms to give up on their computer models LAWRENCE [1983]. Is it possible that personal computers will change this?

FROM NAIVE TO CAUSAL

In most fields, the movement from naive to causal methods is regarded as progress. It is a widespread trend, and numerous researchers have commented on it: Klein (1969) in weather forecasting, Schuessler (1954) in sociology, Hood (1955) in economics, and others. The trend is aided by improvements in the quality and quantity of data, and by improvements in our ability to store and analyze data with computer technology. Most notable has been the widespread availability of regression programs.

The trend from naive to causal methods has led to some discouraging results, again due to the failure of advocates to take into account the peculiarities of the situation. Failures have occurred in sociology (Ohlin and Duncan, 1949; Schuessler, 1954), in meteorology (Klein, 1969), and in economics (Hood, 1955).

Do not expect significant advantages from causal methods in short-range forecasting. They cost more, and they are no more accurate. Yet this is where the advocates have been using causal methods. My prediction: people will continue to waste money in this way (and, remember, I am an optimist). Personal computers will encourage waste.

There is one exception to the conclusion on short-range forecasting. The eclectic use of forecasts is becoming more popular. Causal methods can *add* to the accuracy of the combined forecast.

There is good reason to expect the trend toward causal methods to continue for long-range forecasting. Causal objective methods (such as regression) provide more accurate forecasts. Also, in this case, folklore is on the side of causal methods; the man in the street (and the manager behind the desk) believes in causality.

The trend toward causal-objective methods has been slow in business. PoKempner and Bailey (1970) surveyed 161 senior marketing executives; only 15% placed a heavy emphasis upon causal methods. Judging from recent surveys by ROTHE [1978], GREENLEY [1983], MENTZER and COX [1984], SPARKS and McHUGH [1984], and DALRYMPLE [1985], fewer than 20% of organizations make significant use of regression in forecasting. However, personal computers will probably accelerate the trend.

FROM CLASSIFICATION TO LINEAR AND BACK AGAIN

The earliest attempts at prediction in the social sciences used classification methods. These were simple methods, with one or two variables and one or two cutpoints. For example, one might try to predict the likelihood of a riot in a city if unemployment of people under 30 years was higher or lower than 20%.

As regression methods developed and as computers became available, forecasters shifted from classification to linear methods. Why not use information about the *amount* of unemployment in trying to predict riots?

Further developments in computer technology have made it less expensive to store and to analyze data. Thus the simplicity of the linear model is no longer so important. One can effectively use all of the information with segmentation methods because there is little increased cost in adding variables or cutpoints.

This assessment of trends seems to agree with the impressions of others. For example, Akers and Irwin (1967) said that demographic forecasting, which had shifted from segmentation to econometric methods, was turning back to the segmentation method.

Again, the promise of a method must be considered in relation to the situation. Segmentation methods are most relevant for situations where ample data exist and data problems are serious. I predict a modest increase in the use of segmentation methods as a result of the availability of computers.

TRENDS IN LONG-RANGE FORECASTING

The trends in long-range forecasting are clear-cut. (That is fortunate because this book is about long-range forecasting.) On the assumption of ample data, the trends will be:

• From subjective to objective
• From naive to causal
• From linear to classification

The implications of these trends are illustrated in Exhibit 16-1. The size of the box indicates the current popularity of the method in very rough terms. The arrows may be likened to water pipes; a thin arrow (pipe) means that the trend will be slow, and a thick arrow means that the trend will be rapid.

The big problem is to wean people away from judgmental methods. The easiest way to do this is to proceed via bootstrapping models; they are more acceptable because the forecaster can be sure that his model is being used. Personal computers will allow the user to keep control

Exhibit 16-1   TRENDS IN LONG-RANGE FORECASTING METHODS

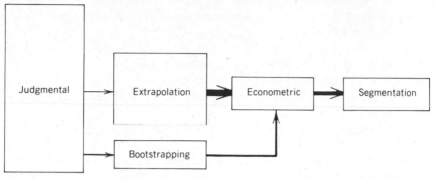

Key:
1. The size of a box denotes the current popularity of the method.
2. The size of an arrow denotes the ease of the transition. A thin arrow says that resistance to change is high.

of the bootstrapping model. Once the bootstrapping model is adopted, the movement to econometric models is simple. The argument is no longer one of ego: you are concerned only with finding the best coefficients.

Another trend in long-range forecasting is the use of eclectic research; in particular, the practice of obtaining a combined forecast by using different methods. DALRYMPLE's [1985] survey indicated that 38% of the respondent firms used combined forecasts "usually" or "frequently."

There is another trend—an unfortunate trend. It is called the rain dance.

THE RAIN DANCE

Throughout *LRF* I have emphasized the value of simple methods; they are cheaper, easier to implement, and often more accurate than complex models. Despite this, much money is spent on complex methods. Why?

The rain dance has something for everyone. The dancer gets paid. The clients get to watch a good dance. The decision maker gets to shift the problem onto someone else in a socially acceptable way. (Who can blame him? He hired the best dancer in the business.)

The major shortcoming of the rain dance is that it focuses the problem on something outside of us. The problem is due to the gods or to the environment—not to us. This attitude is more comfortable, but it is seldom valid in forecasting. Most problems in forecasting come from ourselves. For example, . . .

- We like to adjust the forecast to suit our biases.
- We put too much faith in judgmental methods.
- We fail to consider the relationship between the forecasting method and the situation.
- We confuse measurement models with forecasting models.

This transference of the problem from simple things within us to complex things outside us creates the illusion of progress. It also creates inefficiencies, but we tolerate these in large companies and in nonprofit organizations.

My optimism calls for a forecast that simple methods will be used, but the rain dance theory says otherwise. We will continue to see those good dances (Box–Jenkins, spectral analysis, simultaneous equations, LISREL, expensive expert Delphi panels, Markov chains, etc.). When people tire of these, there will be new dances to take their places. It has been happening since the time of the original oracle of Delphi.

If you would like to read further on the science of rain dances, see Appendix I, "The Wizard Who Oversimplified."

SUMMARY

This chapter reviewed some of the trends taking place in the use of forecasting methods and compared them with what should be taking place. Change has occurred slowly, perhaps because of conflicting evidence on the value of different methods. These conflicts have sometimes arisen because of the failure to consider the method in relation to the situation. Although there appear to be trends from subjective to objective methods, and from naive to causal methods, these trends seem to be most useful for long-range forecasting. I expect to see a greater use of econometric models in long-range forecasting, aided to a large extent by the passion for personal computers.

The situation for short-range forecasting is already favorable. Most reasonable methods perform adequately. But the major trend has been toward more complexity—more rain dances. I hope that this trend will be reversed. I look for a greater use of combined forecasts, and I hope that more attention will be given to the assessment of current status.

Seventeen

RESEARCH ON FORECASTING METHODS

Contents

One day through the primeval wood
A calf walked home as good calves should,
But made a trail all bent askew.
Since then three hundred years have fled,
And I infer the calf is dead.
But still he left behind his trail,
And thereby hangs my moral tale.
The trail was taken up next day
By a lone dog that passed that way
And then a wise bellwether sheep
Pursued the trail o'er vale and steep,
And drew the flock behind him, too,
As good bellwethers always do.
And from that day o'er hill and glade,
Through those old woods a path was made.

The years passed on in swiftness fleet,
The road became a village street;
And this, before men were aware,
A city's crowded thoroughfare.
And soon the central street was this
Of a renowned metropolis;
And men two centuries and a half
Trod in the footsteps of that calf.
Each day a hundred thousand rout
Followed this calf about
And o'er his crooked journey went
The traffic of a continent,
A hundred thousand men were led
By one calf near three centuries dead.
They followed still his crooked way,
And lost one hundred years a day;
For thus such reverence is lent
To well-established precedent.

"The Path of the Calf"
Sam Walter Foss, 1895

What types of research are most useful to further progress in forecasting methods? What specific areas are most in need of further research? These questions are addressed in Chapter 17.

The plan of the chapter is first to describe a basic problem in research called the persistence of folklore. The next part of the chapter examines alternative research strategies, including directed research, multiple hypotheses, and experimentation. The third section describes some topics that should be examined, and others that are currently being examined but are deserving of less effort. The last section discusses meta-analysis, an approach to research that will be of substantial value as scientific work on forecasting continues to grow.

PERSISTENCE OF FOLKLORE

Tell the truth and you will get your head bashed in.

Hungarian Proverb
(Noted in Szasz, 1973)

Scientists suffer from the same problem in learning as do other people—they look for confirming rather than disconfirming evidence. They follow "the path of the calf."

(Evidence that people search for confirming evidence was presented in Chapter 14.) The same appears to be true for that class of people known as scientists. Bassie (1972), who has had a long career in econometrics, suggested that econometricians focus too much on confirming evidence. So did I (Armstrong, 1978). Studies by psychologists also indicate that scientists are biased toward confirming their own beliefs. For example, two-thirds of the recording errors found by Rosenthal favored the experimenter's hypothesis, and such a bias was found among three-fourths of the experimenters in the same study (Rosenthal and Rosnow, 1969). In another study (Rosenthal and Fode, 1963), experimenters were provided with two equivalent samples of rats and were told that one sample was gifted and the other was disadvantaged. In the subsequent laboratory experiments, the gifted rats learned tasks more quickly than the disadvantaged ones.

The search for confirming evidence becomes stronger as a result of group pressure. The scientist is evaluated by her peers. Groups of scientists are often intolerant of ideas that are different, as shown in the case of Immanuel Velikovsky (De Grazia, 1966). Barber (1961) described attempts by scientists to suppress those who produced major advances. To see how scientists respond to even modest departures from the past, see the treatment accorded by discussants to forecasting papers by Christ (1951), Cooper (1972), Armstrong [1978], and MAKRIDAKIS and HIBON [1979]. See also the book reviews of Sackman

(1975) and Chein's (1945) reaction to Sarbin's finding that expertise did not help in psychological predictions.

Because of this need for confirming evidence, the first theory in a field tends to persist. Often this first theory mirrors the common beliefs of the man in the street. As long as confirming evidence is sought, there will be no change in the folklore. Examples of folklore that were examined in *LRF* include the following:

- Econometric methods provide more accurate short-range forecasts than alternative methods.
- Complex models are more accurate than simple models.
- Long-range forecasts are best made by judgmental methods.
- Expertise is important in forecasting change.

These bits of folklore still exist, although there is little evidence to support them and much evidence to refute them. For example, in the survey on econometric methods in Chapter 15, two of the respondents who viewed themselves as having high expertise, and who had the highest confidence in their ratings, stated that they were not aware of any empirical evidence that tested their belief.

It is undoubtedly easier to see folklore in fields other than our own. The history of psychical research offers examples that should not be threatening to most of us. Consider the possibility of extrasensory perception (ESP). People having good ESP would be useful as forecasters. Many people believe in ESP, and so do many scientists. The search for empirically *confirming* evidence has gone on for over a century.

One of the earliest groups to support ESP was the British Society for Psychical Research, founded in 1882. Its early successes were tarnished when the main subjects, the five daughters of Reverend Creery, admitted a few years later that they had cheated. The society's next major project also involved deceit: 16 years after some dramatic confirming evidence had been shown, Blackburn, the researcher, admitted that he was cheating. He said in 1908: "[The hoax] originated in the honest desire of two youths to show how easily men of scientific mind and training could be deceived when seeking for evidence in support of a theory they were wishful to establish." [*Time*, March 4, 1974, pp. 48–49.]

Psychic researchers have shown a great resistance to disconfirming evidence. They have even developed "scientific procedures" to cope with disconfirming evidence should it arise: they cite "negative ESP" if the number of correct predictions falls substantially below average, and "displacement" if subjects correctly predict an event before or after the one in question.

That is psychical research, you say (and perhaps biorythms [HOLMES, et al. 1980; LOUIS, 1978]). But the same behavior is found in fields of higher repute. Remember Cyril Burt and his studies showing a strong relationship between IQ and heredity (Wade, 1976)? He supported a belief that many people find comfortable. (It allows us to think that the problem of low IQs is God's fault rather than ours.)

In economics, it is interesting to examine what happens when even mildly disconfirming evidence is provided. For example, the discussants for Cooper's (1972) paper devoted much effort to explaining why econometric methods did not perform well compared to extrapolations. No consideration was given to shortcomings in the extrapolation models.

The need to avoid disconfirming evidence is expected to be even greater for important issues. For example, economics tells us that in a reasonably competitive market, such as exists in the United States, people are worth what they earn. Evidence contradicting such a belief would be expected to be ignored or refuted. This belief is an important one in our society. According to studies in social psychology (e.g., see Lerner and Simmons, 1966), people have a strong desire to believe that the world is just. If someone else is making a lot of money, he must deserve it. Luckily for those who earn a lot of money, this belief is shared by most of those who earn little money.

Enough of this depressing evidence. What can be done to improve the situation? That is the subject of the following section.

RESEARCH STRATEGIES

Arrowsmith (Lewis, 1924) illustrates the basic problem faced by a scientist. Martin Arrowsmith, as you may know, was a medical scientist who decided to withhold a potential cure from part of the population to determine whether the cure was effective in stopping an epidemic. This was upsetting to people; either a cure is effective, in which case everyone should get it; or it is worthless, and no one should get it. The way to decide this, people think, is to get a group of experts together to reach a decision. That is how the United States decided to introduce the swine flu vaccine program. (Having read *Arrowsmith* and early drafts of my book, I realized how ridiculous this was, so I did not get a swine flu shot. At this moment I am still alive.)

What *Arrowsmith* says, in simple terms, is that to learn what is right, a scientist must do something wrong; that is, the scientist must examine hypotheses that contradict the current beliefs. Now, that is not easy to do; pick any important belief that people hold and try to prove it wrong, and you will quickly find out how difficult it is to change a "made-up" mind. For experimental evidence on this, see LORD, ROSS, and LEPPER [1979]. Brush's (1974) account of the reluctance of the religious community to permit the scientific study of the value of prayer is illustrative of what happens.

Science can help to legitimize the search for disconfirming evidence. Unfortunately, not all strategies used by scientists are useful in this respect. Consider the three possibilities:

1. To disconfirm existing beliefs (science)
2. To confirm existing beliefs (advocacy)
3. To disconfirm unimportant beliefs (irrelevancy)

Strategy 1 is being suggested here, but, as shown by Mahoney, it is unpopular relative to strategy 2.

MAHONEY [1977] sent copies of a research paper to 75 reviewers. Two versions of the paper had been created, one with results favoring a dominant hypothesis in the field (behavior modification) and one refuting it. The papers were identical in all respects except for these results. Those reviewing the version with confirming evidence rated it as more sound methodologically than those who received disconfirming evidence. The paper with confirming evidence was also rated as a more important scientific contribution.

Strategy 2, to confirm existing beliefs, is a popular one with scientists. This is done by developing arguments and collecting evidence to support the favored hypothesis. To the extent that hypothesis testing is done, it involves the use of an unreasonable null hypothesis. Greenwald (1975) made a survey of referees for a journal and found a bias toward studies that rejected the null hypotheses. He concluded from the survey that the null hypothesis is selected to confirm a dominant hypothesis.

Strategy 3, to disconfirm unimportant beliefs, is also a popular strategy. One can refute these unimportant beliefs without getting people upset. On the other hand, it is not satisfying to have people think that one is working on an unimportant topic. That is where bafflegab comes in [ARMSTRONG, 1980a]. Complex and poor writing can make almost any research look respectable.

And the Lord said, "Behold, they are one people, and they have all one language; and this is only the beginning of what they will do; and nothing they propose to do will now be impossible for them. Come, let us go down, and there confuse their language, that they may not understand one another's speech." Therefore its name was called Babel, because the Lord confused the language of all the earth. . . .

Genesis 11:6 9

Consultants and large bureaucracies use this strategy profitably, as illustrated in Exhibit 17-1. And many researchers are carrying on the Lord's work by confusing the language.

If you agree that strategy 1 provides the most reasonable basis for scientific research, then it is important to consider operational strategies for such research. How can one search for disconfirming evidence?

The method of multiple hypotheses is ideally designed for finding disconfirming evidence. With multiple hypotheses, each research project is designed to compare two or more *reasonable* hypotheses. However, rather than looking directly on what's wrong, it may help to look for evidence to confirm one (but not the others) of the hypotheses. This change in perspective was successful in the experiment by TWENEY et al. [1980] and gained further support in TWENEY, DOHERTY, and MYNATT [1982].

The method of multiple hypotheses contrasts sharply with the advocacy strategy, where the researcher attempts to find confirming evidence. A researcher using advocacy tries to make the strongest case for his favored hypothesis. Obviously this biases the way the scientist perceives the world. (Evidence on this bias is presented in Geller and Pitz, 1968; Pruitt, 1961; and JONES and RUSSELL, 1980.)

Mitroff (1972) argues that advocacy is common and has served as the route to success for scientists. I agree. An examination of empirical studies published in *Management Science* showed that almost 64% used the advocacy approach, 14% lacked any prior hypothesis, and only 22% used the method of multiple hypotheses (ARMSTRONG, 1979).

Chamberlin (1965) argued in 1890 for the method of multiple hypotheses, claiming that sciences that employ this strategy progress more rapidly. His paper has been reprinted periodically and has been seconded by others (e.g., Platt, 1964). Nevertheless, the method of multiple hypotheses remains unpopular in the social sciences. My survey of publications in *Management Science* showed no trend toward an increased use of multiple hypotheses over the past quarter-century. My review of the literature on forecasting also yielded a small per-

Exhibit 17-1 THE VALUE OF OBSCURE LANGUAGE.

centage of papers using multiple hypotheses. However, the papers that did use multiple hypotheses were the most useful ones in helping me reach the conclusions in *LRF*.

Replication studies can serve a useful function in disconfirmation. Replication can guard against chance findings, cheating, and mistakes. This is not a trivial matter. REID, SOLEY, and WIMMER [1981] reported that 40% of 30 published replications they found in advertising research conflicted with the original results. WOLIN [1962] found gross miscalculations in three of seven studies in psychology (also about 40%). Unfortunately, replication research is rare. [For more on this see ARMSTRONG, 1982d.] In an attempt to address this problem, the *International Journal of Forecasting* encourages replication studies in forecasting.

SPECIFIC RESEARCH AREAS

My advice on the systems approach (in Chapter 2) applies to researchers as well as to normal people. Many researchers would disagree with this statement. They can describe in detail *what* they are doing, but not *why*. Nor can they explain *when* their research will prove beneficial. (What ever happened to present worth calculations when talking about investments in research?) These people generally refer to their work as **pure research.**[G] They hope that someone else will figure out why they did it.

Pure research was of little value to this book. The most useful studies were those that were directed at specific problems in forecasting studies that were done with specific objectives in mind. Few highly rated studies were the result of pure research (this is consistent with Sherwin and Isenson, 1967, but KREILKAMP [1971] concluded just the opposite).

In the following subsections I suggest a few areas for directed research. The emphasis is on research needed for long-range forecasting—not only because that is the major concern in this book, but also because it offers the greatest potential. A list of research areas is provided in Exhibit 17-2. The research that is expected to yield a high payoff is organized into two columns: "Hot Topics," or areas that are currently being examined, and "Not-So-Hot Topics," or areas that have received little attention. A third column lists areas that have received much attention, but where further effort is expected to have a low payoff. (I hope that your favorite area did not fall into this category). The discussion in the following subsections considers each area listed in Exhibit 17-2.

Exhibit 17-2 RESEARCH AREAS FOR LONG-RANGE FORECASTING

| | High Payoff | | Low Payoff |
Area	Hot Topics	Not-So-Hot Topics	Hot Topics
Implementation	Scenarios	Presentation	
Judgment	Expertise Biases Structured meetings Role playing	Decomposition	Delphi
Extrapolation	Simplicity	Dampened seasonality Dampened trend	Spectral analysis Adaptive parameters
Econometric	A priori analysis	Multiple data sources Current status models Simplicity Mitigation	Simultaneous equations
Segmentation	A priori-direct		Exploratory-indirect
Bootstrapping	Indirect	Direct	
Combined Forecasts	Number of Methods		

Implementation

Scenarios can have a significant input on how people use forecasts. Research on this topic can help people to use forecasts in a more effective way. Users must also learn how to avoid being misled by scenarios.

What type of presentation techniques will help to gain acceptance of the forecasts? For example, how important is it to present arguments against the forecast . . . to support the forecast with vivid examples . . . to provide causal arguments for the forecast . . . to keep the forecast simple . . .?

Judgment

Research has identified faulty procedures that people use in making judgmental forecasts. The challenge for the future is to find ways to overcome these judgmental defects. Typically, the solutions lie in the use of more structure, so techniques like decomposition, consensus, and Delphi have been found to be useful.

Role playing seems like a particularly important area. Does it really provide a significantly better way to forecast the outcomes of conflict situations? What is the most effective way to structure role playing sessions?

Although little interest has been shown in decomposition, the limited evidence suggests that it is a technique with much potential. Research on how and when to use decomposition would be useful.

Few Delphi studies have been designed in such a way that we could learn anything from them. However, from these studies, we have a pretty good idea on how to use Delphi and what to expect from it. Additional validation studies are needed.

Extrapolation

Research on extrapolation methods has grown rapidly. For example, FILDES and LUSK [1984] calculated a 25% per year growth rate in the publication of comparative studies on ARIMA models from 1971 to 1978.

The issue of which method is most appropriate for which situation is also important. To date, research on this topic has been exploratory. As a result, different interpretations arise for each study. Of particular interest are the variety of interpretations of the results from the M-Competition (for example, see ARMSTRONG and LUSK [1983] and FILDES and LUSK [1984]). I believe that the time has come for research to test specific hypotheses. Exhibit 17-3 outlines the basic pattern for such research.

Research from the past 25 years suggests that relatively simple methods are adequate for extrapolation. The combination of forecasts from two or more extrapolation methods will reduce errors significantly. Research is needed on the effect of modified seasonal factors. Research is also needed on ways to improve extrapolations for medium- and long-range forecasts. For example, what is the most effective way to dampen the trend? What guidelines do we have on the value of combining forecasts? How can we better estimate uncertainty?

Econometrics

A priori analysis has been a major interest of econometricians. This emphasis is well placed. In fact, it would be worthwhile if even more

Exhibit 17-3   A FRAMEWORK FOR RESEARCH ON EXTRAPOLATION

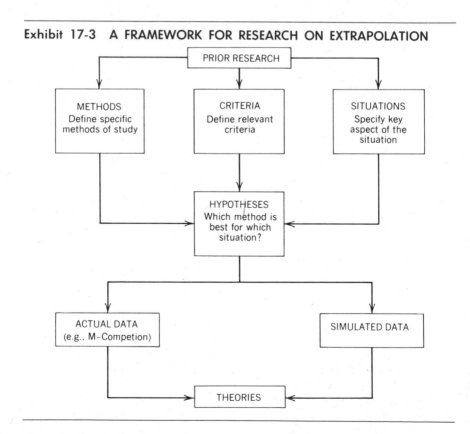

were done to find out what types of *a priori* analysis are useful in long-range forecasting. (See Exhibit 8-2 for a listing of the types of analysis.)

Some not-so-hot topics seem worthy of additional work. For very long-range forecasting, where accuracy may be sensitive to the estimates of the causal relationships, it might be worthwhile to use multiple data sources. More work is also needed on current status models; to what extent should one rely upon cross-sectional estimates, or upon time series estimates of current status? How should one weight the alternative estimates? Finally, there are the striking results on the value of simplicity. Is it possible to develop guidelines relating simplicity to the situation?

Mitigation, the adjustment of the model to compensate for uncertainty over the forecast horizon, has been almost totally ignored. This topic would appear to be of great importance for long-range forecasting. It was of great importance in the one empirical test found. To generalize from such scanty evidence, however, is risky.

The most popular area of all simultaneous equations, has been of almost no demonstrable value. "You don't understand, Scott. This is pure research," the econometrician said. "Give us time." Perhaps another quarter-century of work by hundreds of econometricians will prove fruitful. But I doubt it. There appear to be more useful ways of spending our time and money. For those who insist on further work, why not apply it to long-range rather than short-range forecasting? This reorientation would improve its chances for success.

Segmentation

We need research that will lead to guidelines on how to develop effective segmentation models. In particular, this research should focus on *a priori* methods directed at specific forecasting problems. What sample sizes are required? How many segments are needed? How should one select cutpoints? How should one project population and behavior within segments?

Part of the problem with the research to date is that it has not been specifically directed to the study of forecasting methods. Most work in segmentation has been of the exploratory and has not been specifically directed at forecasting.

Bootstrapping

Indirect bootstrapping is of particular interest. Still, it would be useful to have more comparative studies on the costs, accuracy, and acceptability of indirect and direct bootstrapping. Indirect bootstrapping should also be compared with unit weight models.

Much work has already been done on bootstrapping. One major issue is implementation. Will decision makers yield to technological innovations, or will they resist them in the same manner that blue-collar workers resisted scientific management? I see some hope. Bootstrapping could truly produce a revolution in forecasting and personal computers may aid in this movement.

Further research could help to identify the situations in which bootstrapping is most useful. When is bootstrapping better than judgmental methods? Under what conditions should econometric methods be used instead of bootstrapping? Also, which type of bootstrapping is most effective in a given situation?

Combined Forecasts

The combination of forecasts from different methods guards against mistakes, cheating, and faulty assumptions. In addition to reducing the chance for big errors, it yields modest reductions in the typical error. We need guidelines on when to use combined forecasts and how to select the component methods. Of particular importance, how many methods should be combined?

META-ANALYSIS

As can be seen from the references in this book, or in FILDES [1981], a vast amount of research has been produced on forecasting. This offers a new opportunity to researchers. In studying issues, they can draw upon prior research findings. This strategy of "studying studies" was christened "meta-analysis" by GLASS [1976].

Meta-analysis differs from traditional reviews in that it is more systematic as well as more quantitative. The key steps in meta-analysis are the development of hypotheses, the search for studies, the selection of studies, and a statistical analysis of the studies selected.

The *development of multiple hypotheses* is a critical first step if the likelihood of bias in the later steps is to be reduced [ARMSTRONG, 1979]. For the *search*, explicit rules are needed to determine which studies should be obtained. These rules should help to ensure that a representative sample of the prior studies is obtained. It is seldom possible to identify *all* prior studies. Modifications in these rules may be necessary during the search, in which case, records should be kept of the changes. (JACKSON [1980] reported that traditional reviews usually do not describe the rules used for the search.) *Selection* rules are then established to determine which of the studies are relevant. For the *analysis*, formal procedures should be used to code the results. The use of independent coders is useful. Then the rules are used to combine probabilities across studies and to estimate the magnitude and stability of effects. This analysis should be formally related to the hypotheses. Detailed discussions of the procedures for meta-analysis are provided in HUNTER, SCHMIDT, and JACKSON [1982] and GLASS, McGAW, and SMITH [1981]. An example of this procedure for meta-analysis is provided in ARMSTRONG and LUSK [1985]. This paper stresses the importance of contacting the authors of the original papers to ensure that their work has been interpreted correctly, to obtain additional information on their study, and to obtain suggestions on research that may have been overlooked. Although WOLIN [1962] reported some difficulty in obtaining responses from authors, I have found authors, such as those cited in *LRF*, to be cooperative. EATON [1984] also reports good cooperation.

HUNTER, SCHMIDT, and JACKSON [1982] argue that the only meaningful way to assess the state of knowledge is to cumulate individual study results using statistical procedures. Support for this viewpoint is provided in the experiment by COOPER and ROSENTHAL [1980], which found that meta-analysis led to larger estimates of effects and more confident conclusions than were obtained from a traditional reviewing process.

I believe that meta-analysis provides the most appropriate way to resolve the numerous controversies that exist in forecasting today. Of course, the usefulness of meta-analysis depends upon having a strong foundation of basic studies.

SUMMARY

Folklore is expected to persist in science because researchers search for confirming rather than disconfirming evidence. This process is intensified as a field develops and groups of scientists work together.

The method of multiple hypotheses was suggested to change the role of the researcher from one where she advocates a particular hypothesis to one where she searches for disconfirming evidence in comparing a set of reasonable hypotheses.

Research that is directed at specific forecasting problems is expected to lead to rapid progress. A list of areas was proposed for further research; some of these are already being studied, but others receive little attention. These areas were summarized in Exhibit 17-1 along with some areas where effort should be greatly reduced.

Meta-analysis was then proposed as a way to best summarize the rapidly growing body of research on forecasting.

THE THIRD EDITION

I have started work on the third edition. Certainly I have overlooked important and useful contributions from the past. Furthermore, I will miss things in the future. But I will miss fewer things if you help.

Please let me know what I have overlooked. Especially valuable is work that *contradicts* the generalizations reached in this book. The ideal type of study would be:

- Directed at specific forecasting methods.
- Empirical.
- Based on multiple hypotheses.
- Published.
- Understandable.

Please send the references on new or omitted work to the following address:

Dr. J. Scott Armstrong
Wharton School
University of Pennsylvania
Philadelphia, PA 19104

I would also like to hear about the mistakes in *LRF*. Also, if I have misinterpreted your research, let me know.

ERRATA FOR THE FIRST EDITION

"I did my best. But it wasn't good enough."

William Saroyan

I realize that science proceeds by trial and error, but I get distressed upon discovering *my* errors. It has been pointed out to me that errors are to be expected. That is why they put erasers on pencils. (Somehow, in my case, the erasers are used up well before the pencil is.)

Despite the enormous help that I received from others, some errors occurred in the first edition. Many people were kind enough to point these out to me. The typographical errors were annoying (such as my explanation of exponential weights on historical data, which appeared in early printings of the first edition), but I believe that the reader could identify these and figure out what I was *trying* to say. However, I made two troublesome errors in the first edition:

1. Contrary to what I wrote, the correction for lag in the Winter's model is correct in Winters (1960). This was noted in reviews of *LRF* by J.G. Settle in *Applied Statistics* (vol. 28, 1979, p. 306) and by Robert Fildes in the *Journal of the Operational Research Society* (Vol. 30, 1979, pp. 673–674). A correction was published in GARD-NER [1984].
2. The rough approximation of the RMSE from the MAD was inverted when taken from Brown (1963). It incorrectly became RMSE = 0.8 MAD (rather than 1.25 MAD).

No doubt there are errors in this Second Edition, so I plan to have an ERRATA section in the Third Edition.

In addition to my mistakes, some of my suggestions appear, in view of recent evidence, to be wrong. In contrast to my original suggestions:

• Scenarios do not seem to be useful as a way to forecast the likelihood of events,
• Adaptive parameters do not seem worthwhile for extrapolation, and
• Exponential smoothing is more accurate than moving averages.

These types of changes are expected to occur as we gather additional evidence.

APPENDICES

APPENDIX A
ON THE VALUE OF IMPROVED ACCURACY IN FORECASTING
(see *LRF*, pp. 388 and 389)

This appendix assesses the value of improved accuracy for a firm. The primary purpose is to establish a framework that can be applied in a specific situation. The appendix also provides a rough estimate of the value of improved accuracy in a firm's *sales* forecast. If you do not like my assumptions, feel free to use your own.

The value of improved accuracy was said, in Chapter 15 (*LRF* p. 389), to be a function of a number of factors. These were the size of the firm, the costs incurred by the firm, the proportion of resources that the firm must commit now for a given year in the future, the extent to which accuracy can be improved, the dollar cost associated with forecast errors, the tax rate, and the time value of money. Subjective estimates are provided here for each of these items.

A. *Market Size.* The firm in this example has sales of $1 million per year in the selected product market.

B. *Costs.* Costs are of interest because we are concerned about possible cost savings. Costs were estimated by selecting 100 firms at random from 25 industries in the *Value Line* investment survey for 1977. Before-tax earnings were estimated to be 10%; thus costs are 90%.

C. *Commitment.* The firm makes decisions *now* that affect costs in future years—for example, plant location, size of plant, equipment, key personnel, long-term contracts with suppliers and distributors, bond issues, union contracts, and research and development. It would be useful, but expensive, to examine each of these decision areas separately. Furthermore, these estimates would vary by industry and by firm.

The proportion of the (eventual) costs to which the firm must commit itself is expected to drop continuously as the forecast horizon increases. For some items, no prior commitment is necessary; for example, one can decide at the last minute to turn on the electric lights. For other items, such as the location and size of a factory, prior commitments may be made that cover 20 years or more.

To determine a reasonable level of commitment for this typical firm, I have assumed that 25% of the total costs require no commitment. After that, commitment drops off steadily until year 20, after which the commitments are negligible. The rate of decrease is faster at first, but then slows. (This curve can also be viewed as representing the

Exhibit A-1   SAVINGS FROM IMPROVED FORECAST ACCURACY
(For hypothetical firm with $1 million sales)

Forecast Year (h)	C Commitment	D Error Reduction	E Loss Function	F Cost of Capital Factor @ 12%	G Present Value Dollar Savings*
1	0.220	0.025	0 644	0.893	2847
2	.174	.038	.568	.797	2694
3	.137	.050	.510	.712	2234
4	.107	.062	.460	.636	1739
5	.083	.074	.420	.567	1313
6	.065	.086	.387	.507	992
7	.050	.099	.367	.452	742
8	.038	.113	.353	.404	549
9	.029	.126	.343	.361	407
10	.022	.140	.335	.322	298
11	.017	.153	.328	.287	221
12	.013	.167	.322	.257	162
13	.010	.180	.317	.229	118
14	.008	.193	.313	.205	89
15	.007	.206	.310	.183	74
16	.006	.219	.309	.163	60
17	.005	.232	.307	.146	47
18	.004	.244	.305	.130	35
19	.003	.257	.303	.116	24
20	.002	.270	.301	.104	15
Totals	1.000	—	—	—	14,660

*This column is the product of all columns here times $900,000 costs per year.

proportion of the costs incurred in year h as the result of decisions made in year $h - t$.) The resulting estimates are presented in column C of Exhibit A-1. (Column letters in Exhibit A-1 correspond to the numbers given to the various factors examined in the text.)

D. *Error Reduction.* The extent to which the sales forecast error can be reduced depends upon the level of accuracy achieved by current forecasting practice. If current practice is extremely accurate, little gain is possible. Errors in very short-term forecasting result from inaccuracies in estimating current sales. These errors are expected to be about 6% on the average. (They were over 10% in Tessier and Armstrong, 1977.) The forecast error increases as the forecast horizon increases.

The error curve starts at 6% for forecast horizon zero (i.e., for the average error in estimating current status). Many estimates were available for sales forecast errors for a *one-year horizon*. These include:

Study	MAPE
Strong (1956)	8.0
RICKETTS and BARRETT [1973]	7.3
DALRYMPLE [1975]	6.9
BAKER and TRALINS [1976]	10.3
DALRYMPLE (1985)	9.9
SCHREUDER and KLAASSEN [1984]	<u>7.3</u>
	Average 8.3

It was difficult to find estimates or errors for longer horizons; DAL-RYMPLE [1985] mentioned a 14.2 MAPE for three-year horizons, and MENTZER and COX [1984] (see p. 361 of *LRF*) reported errors of about 20% for "over two years." An examination was made of ASCHER [1978] to determine the size of errors as well as their growth over the forecast horizon. It was difficult to tell whether forecast errors increased faster or slower than the increase in the length of the horizon. These informal explorations impressed me with my ignorance. As a result, I thought it was best to depend on William of Occam and *simplicity*. My conclusion was to use the estimate of about six % for year zero, and eight % for year one; then to increase the error linearly by two % per year. This assumption is reflected in column 1 of Exhibit A-2. (This assumption is more conservative than the one presented in the first edition of *LRF*.) Exhibit A-2 is completed by simple arithmetic, yielding column D, which was then transferred to Exhibit A-1.

To what extent may these errors be reduced? Results from Tessier and Armstrong (1977) suggested that a 50% reduction in errors is possible in the estimate of current status. This estimate of error reduction is probably high, however, because the study was done with the lodging industry, where the level of error is unusually high. Therefore I estimated that a 30% error reduction can be achieved in estimating current status.

As the forecast horizon increases, more data become available and it is therefore possible to draw upon additional forecasting methods.

Exhibit A-2   ESTIMATES OF ERROR REDUCTION

Forecast Year (h)	(1) Current Forecast Errors (%)	(2) Possible Reduction in Error (%)	Percentage Error Reduction* [(1) × (2)] ÷ 100	Midpoint of Year	D Error Reduction†
0	6	30.0	1.8		
1	8	40.0	3.2	1	2.5
2	10	44.0	4.4	2	3.8
3	12	46.5	5.6	3	5.0
4	14	48.3	6.8	4	6.2
5	16	50.0	8.0	5	7.4
6	18	51.6	9.3	6	8.6
7	20	53.0	10.6	7	10.0
8	22	54.2	11.9	8	11.3
9	24	55.3	13.3	9	12.6
10	26	56.3	14.6	10	14.0
11	28	57.1	16.0	11	15.3
12	30	57.9	17.4	12	16.7
13	32	58.4	18.7	13	18.0
14	34	58.8	20.0	14	19.3
15	36	59.1	21.3	15	20.6
16	38	59.3	22.5	16	21.9
17	40	59.5	23.8	17	23.2
18	42	59.7	25.1	18	24.4
19	44	59.9	26.4	19	25.7
20	46	60.0	27.6	20	27.0

*This column represents the reduction in the MAPE; for example, for year 2, the MAPE would be reduced by 3.2, from 8.0 to 4.8.
†This column uses the midpoint of each year. These estimates were used in calculating the yearly savings.

Thus the possibility for error reduction is expected to increase as the forecast horizon increases. My estimate of error reduction is presented in column 2 of Exhibit A-2. It was based on subjective assumptions of 40% for 1-year forecasts, 50% for five-year forecasts, and 60% for 20-year forecasts. A smooth curve was constructed through these points. These estimates appear conservative in light of the results in Armstrong and Grohman (1972). This translates into small improvements in the reduction of MAPEs for short-range forecasts (2.5% for one-year forecasts) and large improvements for long-range forecasts (27% for 20-year forecasts).

E. *Loss Function.* Errors in the forecast will cause inefficiencies in the firm. The dollar value of these inefficiencies will be some percentage of the dollars committed because management can take corrective action. Unfortunately, such corrective actions seldom live up to their promise because, as in the "Path of the Calf," we pay great reverence to tradition. Sometimes these decisions, based upon poor forecasts, defy the law of sunk costs and lead to even poorer decisions to cover up (e.g., the Vietnam bombing forecast). Hence the loss function here may be based on an optimistic assessment of our capability for taking corrective action.

The loss function for the firm in this example is symmetrical. In other words, the cost of underestimating (which would cause either an opportunity cost or inefficient production) is equal to the cost of overestimating by the same percentage (leading to an excess investment in resources).

Losses are high when the reaction time is short, for there is less time to find alternative uses for the excess resources or to make adjustments (such as scheduling overtime) if resources are short. For the day-to-day operations of the firm, little effective reaction is possible, and it was assumed that 70% of the dollars committed would be lost. As the time horizon lengthens, the loss function decreases. Errors in the five-year forecast will become apparent well before year five arrives, so that changes can be made. Thus it was assumed that, for the one-year forecast, the reactions will be such that 60% will be lost; for the five-year forecast, 40% will be lost; and for the 20-year forecast, only 30% will be lost. A smooth curve was fitted to these points, and the value at the midpoint of each year was entered in column E of Exhibit A-1.

F. *Cost of Capital.* A cost of capital of 12% was used. This figure was selected on the basis of opinions of three Wharton faculty members who specialize in this area, and also on my own opinion, as I have been an expert witness on the cost of capital in antitrust cases. I also reviewed the literature on cost of capital. For example, the cost of capital was estimated to be 10.5% in an excellent study by Stewart C. Myers, "What was A. T. and T.'s Cost of Capital in Early 1971?" (Sloan School of Management, M.I.T., 50 Memorial Drive, Cambridge, Mass. 02139). The present worth of future revenues is discounted at 12% in column F of Exhibit A-1. For example, the value of a dollar received 20 years from now is only 10 cents.

G. *Present Value.* Column G of Exhibit A-1 calculates the before-taxes present value savings of improved accuracy, using assumptions

A through F. This present value is equal to

$$\text{Savings} = \sum_{h=1}^{20} (A_h)(B_h)(C_h)(D_h)(E_h)(F_h)$$

where the letters correspond to the assumptions, and h designates the forecast horizon. For example, the savings for year 3 would be:

$$\text{Savings}_3 = (1,000,000)(0.90)(0.137)(0.05)(0.510)(0.712) = \$2234$$

The tax rate was not explicitly entered into my calculations, that is, I figured *before-tax earnings*. If, however, you adopt solely the viewpoint of the stockholders, you should compute after-tax earnings.

The total present value savings for this hypothetical firm with sales of $1 million would be about $15,000.

The importance of the forecast horizon can be assessed from the last column of Exhibit A-1. As expected, the greatest gains can be made in the first five years (74% of the total savings). About 1% of the savings are achieved for years 16 through 20. Gains beyond 20 years are zero in this example because I assumed no commitment beyond this date.

The conclusion that there is little value to forecasts beyond 15 years bothers me. The analysis in Appendix A assumes that one is dealing with rational organizations, that management will learn from its poor forecasts, and that corrective action will be taken. Unfortunately, the research cited in Chapter 14 suggests that these assumptions are naive. What seems to happen is that one error leads to another. Often we refuse to recognize the errors. Instead, we compound the felony by covering up the error, or by continuing to act as if there were no error. "For thus such reverence is lent to well-established precedent." We see around us mistakes in urban design, transportation, education, housing, and other fields that were made more than 20 years ago. Yet the suffering goes on. Sometimes it requires a sit-in, riot, or demonstration to get our bureaucrats to consider corrective action. Conclusion: the analysis in Appendix A greatly underestimates the value of improved accuracy in forecasting, especially in longer range forecasts.

If firms were rational, we would expect them to recognize the potential savings from improved forecasts and to invest money to bring about such savings. Of course, firms do make substantial investments in forecasting. I analyzed data from Wheelwright and Clarke (1976), who had surveyed expenditures on forecasting by firms of various sizes. In rough terms, these expenditures were:

Annual Sales of Company ($\times$ \$1 million)	Annual Budget for Forecasts (\$)	Budget as Percentage of Sales
10	19,000	1.9
60	32,000	0.5
300	56,000	0.2
1,000	137,000	0.1

Obviously, firms must spend something to achieve their current levels of accuracy. Appendix A asked how much might be saved from *improvements* in accuracy. It seems that firms could benefit from additional investments in forecasting methods. Expenditures of 1% of sales would not seem unreasonable.

The framework of Appendix A can be used to calculate potential savings for your organization. Those of you with a personal computer can test various assumptions on your spreadsheet.

APPENDIX B
EFFECT OF ERRORS IN MEASUREMENT ON EXTRAPOLATIONS

It was stated in Chapter 7 (p. 154) that errors in the measurement of historical data will lead to errors both in measuring current status and in forecasting change. The first point is obvious. To see how the measurement error affects the forecast of change, consider the following example, adopted from Alonso (1968).

Suppose that data are available on the population of region for both 1950 and 1960 and that the accuracy of each estimate is good. The 1950 population (P_{50}) was estimated to be 100,000 people. Assume that God says there are 19 chances out of 20 that the true population in this region for 1950 lies within 100,000 ± 1000. Similarly, God also says that the 1960 population (P_{60}) is 105,000 ± 1000. The problem is to forecast the population in 1980. The 1980 population can be forecast by extrapolation, using a rate of change equal to that from 1950 to 1960. Thus

$$P_{80} = (P_{60})\left(\frac{P_{60}}{P_{50}}\right)^2 = \frac{(P_{60})^3}{(P_{50})^2}$$

that is, the 1980 population is equal to the current population times the square of the growth from 1950 to 1960. (The growth term is squared because there are 10-year intervals from 1960 to 1980.) Substitution into the above formula yields a forecast population of 115,800.

How much confidence should be placed in this forecast of 115,800? If it is assumed that there is no **specification error** (i.e., the underlying causal factors yield a constant percentage growth equal to P_{60}/P_{50}), what is the effect of the measurement error?

There is a well-known (i.e., well known to those who know) formula for approximating the error in the forecast that results from errors in the inputs to a model (for the derivation of this formula, see Hahn and Shapiro, 1967):

(1) $$\sigma_y^2 = \sum_{i=1}^{h} \left(\frac{\partial y}{\partial x_i}\right)^2 \sigma_{x_i}^2$$

Using this formula and the assumption that time periods are uncorrelated, we can calculate the measurement errors in different time periods. Thus to calculate the error for P_{80}:

$$P_{80} = \frac{(P_{60})^3}{(P_{50})^2}$$

we then have

$$\frac{\partial P_{80}}{\partial P_{60}} = \frac{3(P_{60})^2}{(P_{50})^2} = 3\left(\frac{P_{60}}{P_{50}}\right)^? \quad \text{and} \quad \frac{\partial P_{80}}{\partial P_{50}} = \frac{-2(P_{60})^3}{(P_{50})^3} = -2\left(\frac{P_{60}}{P_{50}}\right)^3$$

Substituting in (1), we obtain

$$\sigma_{80}^2 = \left[3\left(\frac{P_{60}}{P_{50}}\right)^2\right]^2 \sigma_{60}^2 + \left[-2\left(\frac{P_{60}}{P_{50}}\right)^3\right]^2 \sigma_{50}^2$$

Simplifying yields

(2) $$\sigma_{80}^2 = 9\left(\frac{P_{60}}{P_{50}}\right)^4 \sigma_{60}^2 + 4\left(\frac{P_{60}}{P_{50}}\right)^6 \sigma_{50}^2$$

Our problem stated a probability of .05 that the true value of P_{60} or P_{50} would fall outside a range of ± 1000. The .05 level represents ± 1.96 σ; therefore, for both σ_{50} and σ_{60}, we get

$$1.96\sigma = 1000$$

$$\sigma = \frac{1000}{1.96} = 510$$

This value for σ may then be inserted into (2):

$$\sigma_{80}^2 = 9\left(\frac{105,000}{100,000}\right)^4 (510)^2 + 4\left(\frac{105,000}{100,000}\right)^6 (510)^2 = 4,239,614$$

$$\sigma_{80} = 2059$$

The 95% confidence interval for σ_{80} is (1.96) (2059) = 4036. Thus the prediction for P_{80} is 115,800 $\pm$ 4036. Note that the coefficient of variation (the ratio of the standard deviation to the mean) went from about 0.5% in 1960 to 1.8% in 1980. If you are concerned about the ability to forecast *change*, the standard deviation of the forecast, 2059, can be compared with the change from 1960 to 1980 of almost 10,800; the coefficient of variation relative to the change is 19%. The 95% confidence interval for the change is 10,800 $\pm$ 4036, that is, $\pm 37\%$.

What happens to the forecast error if the underlying structure changes? In this case, assume that there is no measurement error and go back to the population example. Assume that the growth rate in the above problem has a 20% specification error so that the growth rate for the decade is estimated to be $5.0 \pm 1.0\%$. Assuming again that the specification errors in each decade are independent of one another, you could do a lot of calculations using (1). These calculations were done, but you have been spared the details. The specification error led to an introduction of uncertainty in P_{80} of about 1600 units; that is, we started from a known value of 105,000 in 1960, and have a forecast interval of $115,800 \pm 1600$ for 1980. The coefficient of variation for the forecast of change is about 7.5%.

In the typical case, both measurement and specification error exist. Both should be examined to find the effect upon the forecast. For the population example, the measurement and specification errors were calculated to yield a forecast interval of $115,800 \pm 4400$. The combined error is not much greater than that found for measurement error alone (the coefficient of variation for the forecast is about 21%). Still, this error is large in view of the fact that the initial data and the forecast of change were rather accurate. The 95% confidence interval for the change is $\pm (4400 \div 10,800)$ or $\pm 41\%$.

The moral of this exercise is that small errors in measuring current status can create large errors in forecasting change.

APPENDIX C
TABLES FOR STATISTICAL SIGNIFICANCE WITH MULTIPLE COMPARISONS

A central theme of *LRF* is the use of the eclectic strategy in model building, that is, the development of a number of reasonable models. (See especially Chapter 11.) When such a procedure is followed, the typical test of statistical significance between the performances of two of these models is no longer applicable. The more comparisons, the more likely it is that statistically significant differences will be found by chance.

The following tables should be used to test for statistical significance when multiple comparisons are being made. One limitation of these tables is the assumption of equal sample sizes for each hypothesis. If unequal sample sizes are encountered, either use these tables as an approximation (as a better approximation than Student's *t*), or see Dunnett (1964) for tables that adjust for unequal sample sizes.

Exhibits C-1 and C-2 are used to compare two or more candidate models with a benchmark model. The benchmark model should generally be based on current practice. These tables are used when the researcher has no prior hypothesis that the models are superior to the benchmark model.

Exhibits C-3 and C-4 are used when the researcher has prior hypotheses as to which models will be superior to the benchmark. Thus a one-tail test is provided.

Exhibit C-5 is used when there is no benchmark model. Comparisons are made among a set of models to see which are superior.

To use the tables, calculate the *t*-test in the normal manner (see almost any statistics textbook or computer statistical package), then determine which table is relevant, and, finally, see whether the calculated value exceeds the critical level.

Exhibit C-1
MULTIPLE COMPARISONS AGAINST A BENCHMARK WITH NO PRIOR HYPOTHESES ON DIRECTION
(Dunnett's t at 5% level for two-tail comparisons between several treatments and a control)

Degrees of Freedom	Number of Treatment Means (Excluding the Control)								
	1	2	3	4	5	6	7	8	9
5	2.57	3.03	3.29	3.48	3.62	3.73	3.82	3.90	3.97
6	2.45	2.86	3.10	3.26	3.39	3.49	2.57	3.64	3.71
7	2.36	2.75	2.97	3.12	3.24	3.33	3.41	3.47	3.53
8	2.31	2.67	2.88	3.02	3.13	3.22	3.29	3.35	3.41
9	2.26	2.61	2.81	2.95	3.05	3.14	3.20	3.26	3.32
10	2.23	2.57	2.76	2.89	2.99	3.07	3.14	3.19	3.24
11	2.20	2.53	2.72	2.84	2.94	3.02	3.08	3.14	3.19
12	2.18	2.50	2.68	2.81	2.90	2.98	3.04	3.09	3.14
13	2.16	2.48	2.65	2.78	2.87	2.94	3.00	3.06	3.10
14	2.14	2.46	2.63	2.75	2.84	2.91	2.97	3.02	3.07
15	2.13	2.44	2.61	2.73	2.82	2.89	2.95	3.00	3.04
16	2.12	2.42	2.59	2.71	2.80	2.87	2.92	2.97	3.02
17	2.11	2.41	2.58	2.69	2.78	2.85	2.90	2.95	3.00
18	2.10	2.40	2.56	2.68	2.76	2.83	2.89	2.94	2.98
19	2.09	2.39	2.55	2.66	2.75	2.81	2.87	2.92	2.96
20	2.09	2.38	2.54	2.65	2.73	2.80	2.86	2.90	2.95
24	2.06	2.35	2.51	2.61	2.70	2.76	2.81	2.86	2.90
30	2.04	2.32	2.47	2.58	2.66	2.72	2.77	2.82	2.86
40	2.02	2.29	2.44	2.54	2.62	2.68	2.73	2.77	2.81
60	2.00	2.27	2.41	2.51	2.58	2.64	2.69	2.73	2.77
120	1.98	2.24	2.38	2.47	2.55	2.60	2.65	2.69	2.73
∞	1.96	2.21	2.35	2.44	2.51	2.57	2.61	2.65	2.69

Source. Reproduced from C. W. Dunnett, "New Tables for Multiple Comparisons with a Control," *Biometrics,* **20,** (1964), 482–491. With permission from The Biometric Society.

Degrees of Freedom	Number of Treatment Means (Excluding the Control)													
	1	2	3	4	5	6	7	8	9	10	11	12	15	20
5	4.03	4.63	4.98	5.22	5.41	5.56	5.69	5.80	5.89	5.98	6.05	6.12	6.30	6.52
6	3.71	4.21	4.51	4.71	4.87	5.00	5.10	5.20	5.28	5.35	5.41	5.47	5.62	5.81
7	3.50	3.95	4.21	4.39	4.53	4.64	4.74	4.82	4.89	4.95	5.01	5.06	5.19	5.36
8	3.36	3.77	4.00	4.17	4.29	4.40	4.48	4.56	4.62	4.68	4.73	4.78	4.90	5.05
9	3.25	3.63	3.85	4.01	4.12	4.22	4.30	4.37	4.43	4.48	4.53	4.57	4.68	4.82
10	3.17	3.53	3.74	3.88	3.99	4.08	4.16	4.22	4.28	4.33	4.37	4.42	4.52	4.65
11	3.11	3.45	3.65	3.79	3.89	3.98	4.05	4.11	4.16	4.21	4.25	4.29	4.39	4.52
12	3.05	3.39	3.58	3.71	3.81	3.89	3.96	4.02	4.07	4.12	4.16	4.19	4.29	4.41
13	3.01	3.33	3.52	3.65	3.74	3.82	3.89	3.94	3.99	4.04	4.08	4.11	4.20	4.32
14	2.98	3.29	3.47	3.59	3.69	3.76	3.83	3.88	3.93	3.97	4.01	4.05	4.13	4.24
15	2.95	3.25	3.43	3.55	3.64	3.71	3.78	3.83	3.88	3.92	3.95	3.99	4.07	4.18
16	2.92	3.22	3.39	3.51	3.60	3.67	3.73	3.78	3.83	3.87	3.91	3.94	4.02	4.13
17	2.90	3.19	3.36	3.47	3.56	3.63	3.69	3.74	3.79	3.83	3.86	3.90	3.98	4.08
18	2.88	3.17	3.33	3.44	3.53	3.60	3.66	3.71	3.75	3.79	3.83	3.86	3.94	4.04
19	2.86	3.15	3.31	3.42	3.50	3.57	3.63	3.68	3.72	3.76	3.79	3.83	3.90	4.00
20	2.85	3.13	3.29	3.40	3.48	3.55	3.60	3.65	3.69	3.73	3.77	3.80	3.87	3.97
24	2.80	3.07	3.22	3.32	3.40	3.47	3.52	3.57	3.61	3.64	3.68	3.70	3.78	3.87
30	2.75	3.01	3.15	3.25	3.33	3.39	3.44	3.49	3.52	3.56	3.59	3.62	3.69	3.78
40	2.70	2.95	3.09	3.19	3.26	3.32	3.37	3.41	3.44	3.48	3.51	3.53	3.60	3.68
60	2.66	2.90	3.03	3.12	3.19	3.25	3.29	3.33	3.37	3.40	3.42	3.45	3.51	3.59
120	2.62	2.85	2.97	3.06	3.12	3.18	3.22	3.26	3.29	3.32	3.35	3.37	3.43	3.51
∞	2.58	2.79	2.92	3.00	3.06	3.11	3.15	3.19	3.22	3.25	3.27	3.29	3.35	3.42

Source. Reproduced from C. W. Dunnett, "New Tables for Multiple Comparisons with a Control," *Biometrics,* **20** (1964), 482–491. With permission from The Biometric Society.

Exhibit C-3 MULTIPLE COMPARISONS AGAINST A BENCHMARK WITH PRIOR HYPOTHESES ON DIRECTION
(Dunnett's t at 5% level for one-tail comparisons between several treatments and a control)

Degrees of Freedom	Number of Treatment Means (Excluding the control)								
	1	2	3	4	5	6	7	8	9
5	2.02	2.44	2.68	2.85	2.98	3.08	3.16	3.24	3.30
6	1.94	2.34	2.56	2.71	2.83	2.92	3.00	3.07	3.12
7	1.89	2.27	2.48	2.62	2.73	2.82	2.89	2.95	3.01
8	1.86	2.22	2.42	2.55	2.66	2.74	2.81	2.87	2.92
9	1.83	2.18	2.37	2.50	2.60	2.68	2.75	2.81	2.86
10	1.81	2.15	2.34	2.47	2.56	2.64	2.70	2.76	2.81
11	1.80	2.13	2.31	2.44	2.53	2.60	2.67	2.72	2.77
12	1.78	2.11	2.29	2.41	2.50	2.58	2.64	2.69	2.74
13	1.77	2.09	2.27	2.39	2.48	2.55	2.61	2.66	2.71
14	1.76	2.08	2.25	2.37	2.46	2.53	2.59	2.64	2.69
15	1.75	2.07	2.24	2.36	2.44	2.51	2.57	2.62	2.67
16	1.75	2.06	2.23	2.34	2.43	2.50	2.56	2.61	2.65
17	1.74	2.05	2.22	2.33	2.42	2.49	2.54	2.59	2.64
18	1.73	2.04	2.21	2.32	2.41	2.48	2.53	2.58	2.62
19	1.73	2.03	2.20	2.31	2.40	2.47	2.52	2.57	2.61
20	1.72	2.03	2.19	2.30	2.39	2.46	2.51	2.56	2.60
24	1.71	2.01	2.17	2.28	2.36	2.43	2.48	2.53	2.57
30	1.70	1.99	2.15	2.25	2.33	2.40	2.45	2.50	2.54
40	1.68	1.97	2.13	2.23	2.31	2.37	2.42	2.47	2.51
60	1.67	1.95	2.10	2.21	2.28	2.35	2.39	2.44	2.48
120	1.66	1.93	2.08	2.18	2.26	2.32	2.37	2.41	2.45
∞	1.64	1.92	2.06	2.16	2.23	2.29	2.34	2.38	2.42

Source. Reproduced from Charles W. Dunnett, "A Multiple Comparison Procedure for Comparing Several Treatments with a Control," *Journal of the American Statistical Association,* **50,** (1955), 1096–1121. With permission from the *Journal of the American Statistical Association.*

Exhibit C-4 MULTIPLE COMPARISONS AGAINST A BENCHMARK WITH PRIOR HYPOTHESES ON DIRECTION
(Dunnett's t at 1% level for one-tail comparisons between several treatments and a control)

Degrees of Freedom	Number of Treatment Means (Excluding the Control)								
	1	2	3	4	5	6	7	8	9
5	3.37	3.90	4.21	4.43	4.60	4.73	4.85	4.94	5.03
6	3.14	3.61	3.88	4.07	4.21	4.33	4.43	4.51	4.59
7	3.00	3.42	3.66	3.83	3.96	4.07	4.15	4.23	4.30
8	2.90	3.29	3.51	3.67	3.79	3.88	3.96	4.03	4.09
9	2.82	3.19	3.40	3.55	3.66	3.75	3.82	3.89	3.94
10	2.76	3.11	3.31	3.45	3.56	3.64	3.71	3.78	3.83
11	2.72	3.06	3.25	3.38	3.48	3.56	3.63	3.69	3.74
12	2.68	3.01	3.19	3.32	3.42	3.50	3.56	3.62	3.67
13	2.65	2.97	3.15	3.27	3.37	3.44	3.51	3.56	3.61
14	2.62	2.94	3.11	3.23	3.32	3.40	3.46	3.51	3.56
15	2.60	2.91	3.08	3.20	3.29	3.36	3.42	3.47	3.52
16	2.58	2.88	3.05	3.17	3.26	3.33	3.39	3.44	3.48
17	2.57	2.86	3.03	3.14	3.23	3.30	3.36	3.41	3.45
18	2.55	2.84	3.01	3.12	3.21	3.27	3.33	3.38	3.42
19	2.54	2.83	2.99	3.10	3.18	3.25	3.31	3.36	3.40
20	2.53	2.81	2.97	3.08	3.17	3.23	3.29	3.34	3.38
24	2.49	2.77	2.92	3.03	3.11	3.17	3.22	3.27	3.31
30	2.46	2.72	2.87	2.97	3.05	3.11	3.16	3.21	3.24
40	2.42	2.68	2.82	2.92	2.99	3.05	3.10	3.14	3.18
60	2.39	2.64	2.78	2.87	2.94	3.00	3.04	3.08	3.12
120	2.36	2.60	2.73	2.82	2.89	2.94	2.99	3.03	3.06
∞	2.33	2.56	2.68	2.77	2.84	2.89	2.93	2.97	3.00

Source. Reproduced from Charles W. Dunnett, "A Multiple Comparison Procedure for Comparing Several Treatments with a Control," *Journal of the American Statistical Association,* **50,** (1955), 1096–1121. With permission from the *Journal of the American Statistical Association.*

Exhibit C-5 MULTIPLE COMPARISONS WITH NO BENCHMARK
(Tukey's t at 5% level, adjusted for making all paired comparisons)

Degrees of Freedom	Number of Treatment Means								
	2	3	4	5	6	7	8	9	10
5	2.57	3.25	3.69	4.01	4.26	4.48	4.65	4.81	4.94
6	2.45	3.07	3.46	3.75	3.98	4.16	4.33	4.47	4.59
7	2.36	2.94	3.32	3.58	3.79	3.97	4.12	4.24	4.36
8	2.31	2.86	3.20	3.46	3.66	3.82	3.96	4.08	4.19
9	2.26	2.79	3.13	3.37	3.55	3.71	3.84	3.96	4.06
10	2.23	2.74	3.06	3.29	3.47	3.62	3.75	3.86	3.95
11	2.20	2.70	3.01	3.23	3.41	3.56	3.68	3.78	3.88
12	2.18	2.67	2.97	3.19	3.36	3.50	3.62	3.73	3.82
13	2.16	2.64	2.93	3.15	3.32	3.45	3.57	3.67	3.76
14	2.14	2.62	2.91	3.12	3.28	3.42	3.53	3.63	3.71
15	2.13	2.60	2.88	3.09	3.25	3.38	3.49	3.59	3.68
16	2.12	2.58	2.86	3.06	3.22	3.35	3.46	3.56	3.64
17	2.11	2.57	2.84	3.04	3.20	3.33	3.44	3.53	3.61
18	2.10	2.55	2.83	3.03	3.17	3.30	3.41	3.51	3.59
19	2.09	2.54	2.81	3.01	3.16	3.29	3.39	3.48	3.56
20	2.09	2.53	2.80	2.99	3.15	3.27	3.37	3.46	3.54
24	2.06	2.50	2.76	2.95	3.09	3.21	3.31	3.40	3.48
30	2.04	2.47	2.72	2.90	3.04	3.15	3.25	3.34	3.42
40	2.02	2.43	2.68	2.86	2.99	3.10	3.20	3.27	3.35
60	2.00	2.40	2.64	2.81	2.94	3.05	3.14	3.22	3.29
120	1.98	2.38	2.61	2.77	2.90	3.00	3.08	3.17	3.22
∞	1.96	2.34	2.57	2.73	2.85	2.95	3.03	3.10	3.16

Source. J. W. Tukey, *The Problem of Multiple Comparisons,* Princeton, N.J.: Princeton University Press, 1953 (396 pp dittoed).

APPENDIX D
BRIEF GUIDE TO SOURCES USEFUL IN FORECASTING

Data collection is expensive and time-consuming. This appendix is designed to help reduce the time and costs involved. Six areas are discussed:

- Guidelines for collecting data
- Guides to data sources
- Data sources
- Sources of forecasts
- Guides to people and organizations interested in forecasting
- Guides to forecasting literature

Guidelines for Collecting Data

1. Use the telephone. If you can figure out whom you want to talk to, almost anyone will talk to you, especially if you call long distance.
2. Purchase small blocks of consulting time from different people rather than lots of time from one person.
3. If you write, write to someone important. You are more likely to get an answer. (Letters to assistant professors are frequently ignored.)
4. Find a good librarian.
5. Use the library. If you think a problem is important, someone has written about it.

Guides to Data Sources

Where to go for data? Many people have helped to answer this question. Here is a partial listing:

American Demographics, (P.O. Box 6543, Syracuse N.Y.). This journal discribes demographic data, much of it from the U.S. Bureau of the Census. It also contains advertisements from various suppliers of these data.

Briscoe, G. and Hirst, M., "A Further Appreciation of Demand Forecasting Models: Some Methods Based on Survey Information," *Long Range Planning,* 8 (February 1975), 87–97. The title is misleading. Actually, it describes the types of anticipations, attitudinal, and intentions data that are widely available.

Brownstone, David M., and Carruth, Gorton, *Where to Find Business Information.* N.Y.: Wiley, 2nd Ed., 1982.

Daniells, Lorna M. (compiler), *Business Forecasting for the 1980s— and Beyond.* Graduate School of Business, Harvard University, Boston, 1980. An annotated bibliography about forecasting, forecasts on specific subjects, forecasting methods, and additional sources. (Can be ordered from Baker Library, Graduate School of Business Administration, Harvard University, Soldiers Field, Boston, MA. 02163.)

Directory of Computerized Data Files. Springfield, VA: U.S. Dept. of Commerce, National Technical Information Service, 1983.

Encyclopedia of Associations. Detroit: Gale Research. Published Annually.

Encyclopedia of Business Information Sources. Detroit: Gale Research, 1983. Sourcebooks, periodicals, organizations, directories, handbooks, bibliographics, on-line data bases, and other information.

Frank, Nathalie P. and Ganly, John V., *Data Sources for Business and Market Analysis.* Third Edition. Metuchen, NJ: Scarecrow Press, 1983.

Frey, Frederick W. (Ed.), *Survey Research on Comparative Social Change: A Bibliography.* Cambridge, MA: M.I.T. Press, 1969. Provides references to cross-national surveys for developing nations (drawn from more than 260 English language journals).

Harvey, Joan M., edits a variety of statistical sources. They are published by CBD Research in Beckenham, England. The publications typically cover a continent.

Hauser, Philip M., *Social Statistics in Use.* New York: Russell Sage, 1975. Discusses data on population, marriage, education, working, welfare, crime, marketing, housing, transportation, recreation, government, politics, and public opinion.

Hyman, Herbert, *A Secondary Analysis of Sample Surveys.* New York: Wiley, 1972. Describes sources of survey data.

U.S. Department of Commerce (National Referral Center, National Technical Information Service), *A Directory of Computerized Data Files.*

Washington, D.C., 1976. Covers U.S. and foreign data on economics, social science, and technology.

World Index of Economic Forecasts. Industrial Tendency Surveys and Development Plans. George Cyriax (Ed.) New York: Facts on File, 1981. Information on organizations that provide forecasts, plans, and surveys for over 100 countries.

Data Sources

The following represents a selected list of data sources that I have found useful:

Business International. Much of the information these people sell is available from the government for nothing, but Business International makes the data more easily available. Can be found in some libraries. This organization is located at One Dag Hammarskjold Plaza, New York, NY 10017.

Mitchell, Brian R., *European Historical Statistics, 1750–1975.* New York: Facts on File, 1980. Editions are also available for Africa, Asia, Australia, and America. These are updated periodically.

National Bureau of Economic Research. This organization keeps track of over 3000 monthly, quarterly, and annual economic series. These data are updated on a computer file within two days of official release. The cost to subscribe is low. For a description of these data see Charlotte Boschan, "The NBER Time Series Data Bank," *Annals of Economic and Social Measurements,* **1** (April 1972), 193–209. Contact NBER at 269 Mercer St., New York, NY.

United Nations. *Demographic Yearbooks* are helpful, as are the *Statistical Yearbooks.* The U.N. also collects data on imports and exports of major nations.

U.S. Bureau of the Census, *Historical Statistics of the United States: Colonial Times to 1970.* Washington, D.C., 1975. Two volumes covering data on population, health, GNP, education, religion, recreation, crime, land use, climate, agriculture, construction, technology, government, trade, and so on.

U.S. Department of Commerce. Helpful for obtaining economic data for both the United States and foreign countries. Call your local field office. (Call as a representative of your company, even if it is a one-person "company," and you will get better service.) Useful publications include *Statistical Abstract of the United States* (Annual), and *Long-Term Economic Growth 1860–1970*.

Sources of Forecasts

In some cases you may be content to use forecasts that have been developed by others. Forecasts are frequently published, and they cover a wide variety of areas. One use of these forecasts is for comparison after you have developed your own forecasts.

To my knowledge, the most complete and up-to-date review of forecasts in the economic area is provided by

Predicasts, Inc.
200 University Circle Research Center
11001 Cedar Avenue
Cleveland, Ohio 44106

This company publishes *Predicasts,* a quarterly publication that summarizes forecasts of various U.S. industries by the SIC (Standard Industrial Classification) number. The sources of the forecasts are also listed, but these sources often do not tell how the forecast was made. *Predicasts* can be found in major business libraries. Predicasts, Inc., also publishes *Worldcasts,* which is issued eight times per year and covers major markets around the world.

Economic Forecasts, For economy-wide forecasts, see Elsevier Science, NY. A monthly journal that presents and discusses forecasts of real GNP and other major economic variables for over 20 countries.

Periodically, books are published that provide forecasts of various areas. The problem with these books is that they quickly become out of date. The following are some important efforts from the past:

Houthakker, H. S., and Taylor, L. D., *Consumer Demand in the United States: Analyses and Projections.* Boston: Harvard University Press, 1966, 1970. Provided forecasts to 1975 for over 80 "personal consumption expenditure categories." These forecasts were generated by econometric models, and the models are described in the book.

Landsberg, Hans H., Fischman, L. L., and Fisher, J. L., *Resources in America's Future: Patterns of Requirements and Availabilities 1960–2000.* Baltimore: Johns Hopkins Press, 1963. Out of date, but you can contact Resources for the Future, 1775 Massachusetts Avenue, N.W., Washington, D.C. 20036, for more recent work on related topics.

Sheldon, Eleanor B., and Moore, W. E. (Eds.), *Indicators of Social Change.* New York: Russell Sage, 1968.

Guides to People and Organizations Interested in Forecasting

The **World Future Society** provides the best clearinghouse for people and organizations who are interested in *forecasts*. This organization holds conventions, maintains mailing lists, runs a speakers' bureau, keeps track of the literature on forecasting, publishes a magazine, *The Futurist*, and publishes a directory, *The Future*. Its address is:

World Future Society
P.O. Box 30369
Bethesda Branch
Washington, D.C., 20014

Another source is *Social Forecasting: Documentation 1975* 4th Ed. This is published by Irades Edizioni Previsionali, 6-00198, Rome, Italy. Copies are available from the World Future Society.

The **International Institute of Forecaster (IIF)**, founded in 1981 by Robert Carbone, Robert Fildes, Spyros Makridakis, and me, is interested in *forecasting methods*. The IIF conducts an annual International Symposium on Forecasting. It is designed to bring together researchers and practitioners from different countries, different organizations (academic, government, and business) and different fields (social, behavioral, management, and engineering).

Guides to Forecasting Literature

Major developments in the forecasting literature have taken place since the original edition of *LRF*. One is the publication of *A Bibliography of Business and Economic Forecasting* by FILDES [1981]. A revised edition was published in 1984 and the plan is to provide periodic revisions. This book provides a key-word index to research publications on forecasting methods. A detailed description is provided in the UP-DATED BIBLIOGRAPHY.

The directors of the IIF edit a journal. From 1982–84 it was the *Journal of Forecasting*. Starting in 1985, it is the *International Journal of Forecasting*. This journal publishes refereed papers on forecasting. It covers many disciplines including management (marketing, accounting, production, finance, organizational behavior) and the social sciences (psychology, sociology, demography, economics). It includes papers dealing with subjects such as the development, maintenance, or implementation of forecasting systems, and papers examining the impact of uncertainty on organizations. All forecasting methods are of interest such as econometrics, extrapolation, segmentation, input-output, and judgment. Of particular interest are papers that compare different approaches in actual forecasting situations. In addition to refereed papers, the *International Journal of Forecasting* provides book reviews, a clearinghouse for working papers, and summaries of research papers published elsewhere.

Current Contents: Social and Behavioral Sciences. Institute for Scientific Information, 325 Chestnut Street, Philadelphia, PA. 19106. This weekly guide presenting tables of contents from journals is found in major libraries. The Institute for Scientific Information also indexes articles by author and by key words. Their *Social Sciences Citation Index* is helpful in locating follow-up studies. The *Social Science Subject Index* lists published articles on forecasting. (Use the key word "forecasting"; "predicting", though not so helpful, contains some relevant items.

Despite the benefits of computer searches, it is still useful to browse in the library. Occasionally you will find a key article that, in turn, will lead you to further references. Which journals are best to browse through? The most frequently cited in *LRF* are, by rank order:

Original Edition	UPDATED BIBLIOGRAPHY
1. *Journal of Marketing Research*	1. *Journal of Forecasting*
2. *Journal of the American Statistical Association*	2. *Organizational Behavior and Human Performance*
3. *Organizational Behavior and Human Performance*	3. *Journal of Applied Psychology*
4. *Psychological Bulletin*	4. *Journal of Personality and Social Psychology*
5. *Journal of Business*	5. Management Science
6. *Management Science*	6. *Journal of Accounting Research*
7. *Public Opinion Quarterly*	7. *Decision Sciences*
8. *Journal of Applied Psychology*	8. *Journal of Marketing Research*
9. *Journal of Consulting Psychology*	9. *Interfaces*
10. *Review of Economics and Statistics*	10. *(Tie among four journals)*

Note that "prior experience" provided a poor forecast in this situation. Six of the top ten journals in the original edition were not in the top ten for the UPDATED BIBLIOGRAPHY. The *Journal of Forecasting,* which did not exist prior to 1982, was in first place with 30 citations. *Organizational Behavior and Human Performance* continued to be a valuable source (moving from third to second place) as did the *Journal of Applied Psychology* (from eighth to third place). The *Journal of Personality and Social Psychology* moved into the top ten.

APPENDIX E
THE VALUE OF DECOMPOSITION: A THEORETICAL ARGUMENT

This appendix examines the effect of decomposition on the variance of an estimate. In other words, if you are trying to estimate a pheonomenon, M, when is it useful to decompose M, estimate its parts, and then aggregate the individual estimates? The purpose of this appendix is to develop guidelines for using a decomposition strategy. These guidelines are applied in Chapter 9 of *LRF*.

Consider the problem of minimzing the variance in the total estimate of phenomenon M, where M is a positive number. M could be estimated directly (called a global assessment) with a standard error of σ_M. Alternatively, the problem could be broken into two segments, X_1 and X_2. The standard errors of X_1 and X_2 could be estimated; this would allow us to calculate $\overline{M}$ (where $\overline{M}$ designates the estimate done by parts, and cov is covariance.)

(1) Given that $\overline{M}$ is a function of X_1 and X_2,
(2) suppose that $\overline{M} = X_1 + X_2$, with both X_1 and X_2 being positive;
(3) then, in general, $\sigma_{\overline{M}}^2 = \sigma_{X_1}^2 + \sigma_{X_2}^2 + 2 \operatorname{cov}(X_1, X_2)$.

If it is assumed that the errors in X_1 and X_2 are independent, cov $(X_1, X_2) = 0$, and

$$(4) \qquad \sigma_{\overline{M}}^2 = \sigma_{X_1}^2 + \sigma_{X_2}^2$$

If the relative error (defined here as the coefficient of variation) is as reliable for the parts as for the whole, then

$$(5) \qquad \frac{\sigma_M}{M} = \frac{\sigma_{X_1}}{X_1} = \frac{\sigma_{X_2}}{X_2}$$

We are interested in comparing the relative error $\sigma_{\overline{M}}/\overline{M}$ with σ_M/M to see under what conditions $\sigma_{\overline{M}}/\overline{M}$ is less than σ_M/M. In other words, when is the decomposed variance less than the variance from the global estimate? From (2) and (4) above:

$$(6) \qquad \frac{\sigma_{\overline{M}}}{\overline{M}} = \frac{\sqrt{\sigma_{X_1}^2 + \sigma_{X_2}^2}}{X_1 + X_2}$$

Equation (5) was solved for σ_{x_1}, and the result was substituted into (6) to yield (7):

(7)
$$\frac{\sigma_{\overline{M}}}{\overline{M}} = \frac{\sqrt{(\sigma_M/M)^2 X_1^2 + (\sigma_M/M)^2 X_2^2}}{X_1 + X_2}$$
$$= \frac{\sigma_M}{M}\left(\frac{\sqrt{X_1^2 + X_2^2}}{X_1 + X_2}\right)$$

Therefore $\sigma_{\overline{M}}/\overline{M}$ will be less than σ_M/M because

$$\frac{\sqrt{X_1^2 + X_2^2}}{X_1 + X_2} < 1$$

The greatest improvements occur if the problem is broken into equal segments. Assume that two equal segments were considered, that is, $X_1 = X_2$. Then

$$\frac{\sqrt{X_1^2 + X_2^2}}{X_1 + X_2} = \sqrt{\frac{2X_1^2}{4X_2^2}} = \sqrt{\frac{1}{2}} = 0.71$$

This says that estimation by two equal and uncorrelated segments would reduce the coefficient of variation to 71% of its original value. The gain decreases as $X_1/\overline{M}$ or $X_2/\overline{M}$ approaches 1, that is, as the estimate by segments is dominated by either X_1 or X_2.

For example, when $X_1 = 5X_2$, then

$$\frac{\sqrt{X_1^2 + X_2^2}}{X_1 + X_2} = 0.85$$

In this case, the reduction in uncertainty is only half as great as it is with segments of equal size.

Gains can also be made by breaking the problem into more independent segments. If the problem is broken down into four independent segments, then

$$\frac{\sigma_{\overline{M}}}{\overline{M}} = \left(\frac{\sigma_M}{M}\right)\frac{\sqrt{X_1^2 + X_2^2 + X_3^2 + X_4^2}}{X_1 + X_2\,X_3 + X_4}$$

Now, if $X_1 = X_2 = X_3 = X_4$ (i.e., the segments are of equal size), then

$$\frac{\sigma_{\bar{M}}}{\bar{M}} = \frac{\sigma_M}{M}\left(\frac{1}{2}\right)$$

Thus, there is a gain in accuracy as the number of segments is increased. When the segments are equal and independent, the accuracy increases according to the square root of the number of segments.

The assumption of independence is of key importance. Obviously it would be difficult to find segments that were completely independent. Decomposition will help only if the covariance among the segments is less than the average variance of the segments. For example, if

$$\text{cov}\,(X_1, X_2) = \frac{\sigma_{x_1} + \sigma_{x_2}}{2}$$

then (4) becomes $\sigma_{\bar{M}}^2 = 2\sigma_{x_1}^2 + 2\sigma_{x_2}^2$

(6) becomes $\dfrac{\sigma_{\bar{M}}}{\bar{M}} = \dfrac{\sqrt{2\sigma_{x_1}^2 + 2\sigma_{x_2}^2}}{X_1 + X_2}$

(7) becomes $\dfrac{\sigma_{\bar{M}}}{\bar{M}} = \dfrac{\sigma_M}{M}\left(\dfrac{\sqrt{X_1^2 + X_2^2}}{X_1 + X_2}\right)(\sqrt{2})$

Therefore $\sigma_{\bar{M}}/\bar{M}$ will be less than σ_M/M when

$$(\sqrt{2})\,\frac{\sqrt{X_1^2 + X_2^2}}{X_1 + X_2} < 1$$

If two equal segments are considered (i.e., $X_1 = X_2$), then

$$(\sqrt{2})\,\frac{\sqrt{X_1^2 + X_2^2}}{X_1 + X_2} = (\sqrt{2})\,\sqrt{\frac{2X_1^2}{4X_2^2}} = \frac{\sqrt{2}}{\sqrt{2}} = 1.0$$

In other words, the decomposition is of no value when

$$\text{cov}\,(X_1, X_2) \geq \frac{\sigma_{x_1}^2 + \sigma_{x_2}^2}{2}$$

In summary, the previous analysis implies that decomposition will lead to improvements under the following conditions:

- The segments are relatively independent.
- The segments tend to be of equal importance.
- The information on each of the segments is "valid and reliable."

The last item is an important one to remember. If the parts are defined such that the reliability of the segment estimates is greatly reduced, then the overall combination may be poorer (see the example presented by Frankel, 1969).

APPENDIX F
COMMENTS AND ANSWERS TO QUESTIONS

This appendix provides answers to questions posed to the reader. It also offers some comments on these problems and a bit of trivia. The answers are organized by chapter.

Chapter 3

For the horse business question, the correct answer is $20 (also cited in Chapter 6).

Chapter 4

For the decomposition problem, the correct answers are:

• Families in the United States = 57 million (*World Almanac*)
• High School Dropouts = 2,690,000 (*World Almanac*)
• Polaroid color film − 51 million packs (Polaroid Annual Report)
• Pounds of tobacco = 1.8 billion (*Statistical Abstract of the United States*)
• Contest cards = 66.5 million (WIBG radio station, Philadelphia, PA)

Chapter 6

1. For trivia fans, in 1974 the actual percentage of nations in the United Nations that were African was 29%.
2. Multiplication problem answer is 40,320.
3. "Eighth graders' IQ" answer is 101. The IQ for the remaining 49 students is independent of the IQ of the first student tested; thus the remaining 49 would be expected to have an average IQ of 100. The first student's IQ, when added in, would bring the average up to 101. (Most people answer 100 for this question.)
4. In the "significance of follow-up samples" problem, most people answer about .85. The correct answer is about .48. (An explanation is provided on p. 105 of Tversky and Kahneman, 1971.)
5. Tom W. has no correct answer. However, the base rates should exert a strong influence upon the predictions. Furthermore, for people who do not think that the thumbnail sketch is valid, the base rates provide the only information; in this case the base rate ranking would be the correct answer. The base rates were as follows (*Source: Digest of Educational Statistics,* 1975 edition, U.S. Department of Health, Education, and Welfare. Washington, D.C., p. 85):

Rank	Field	Enrollment
1	Humanities and education	354,900
2	Business administration	107,900
3	Law	103,600
4	Physical and life sciences	76,100
5	Social science and social work	74,100
6	Engineering	54,500
7	Medicine	49,500
8	Library science	14,100
9	Computer science	9,300

Carl Harrington and I extended the Tom W. study to examine the value of the advice given in *LRF* on helping people to deal with irrelevant information. Unfortunately this did not work out. Our sample of management students did not regard the psychological sketch as irrelevant data. The following prediction problem was presented in the following abstract form to 14 subjects:

Suppose you were asked to predict what field an unknown graduate student was in. You were given two pieces of information:
(1) A personality sketch written by the student's high school psychologist
(2) The number of graduate students enrolled in each field.
How much weight would you place on each factor in reaching a prediction?
_____ % Personality sketch
_____ % Size of graduate field

The subjects said that they would place 55% of the weight on the psychological data and 45% on the base rate. When we replicated Tom W., the subjects claimed to have put 92% weight on the psychological sketch and only 8% on the base rate. Thus, when presented with a specific problem, the weights used by the subjects were influenced by the information presented.

To test the importance of this presentation of information, we created a new prediction problem, the case of George. Subjects were given the psychological sketch *and the actual base rates*. This had little effect. Subjects gave similar predictions for George as for Tom W., and they claimed to have placed 74% of the weight on the psychological sketch and 26% on the base rate. These results provided little support for our hypothesis: we had expected that subjects would rely heavily upon the base rate data when they were easily available.

6. The following description of the Minicar system was provided with the mail questionnaire, along with a picture of the car:

The proposed Minicar system represents an attempt to solve some of the traffic and air pollution problems in the downtown Philadelphia area. It would also provide another way for people to satisfy their transportation needs.

There would be four key aspects of this Minicar system for a user:
1. *A Specially Designed Car.*   The car would be as wide as a standard car but only half as long. It would have an engine which produces little exhaust and its small size would help relieve parking and traffic congestion.

The car would utilize new safety features with the result that its safety would at least equal that provided by standard automobiles today. It would have an acceleration equivalent to a standard car and would be capable of expressway speeds.

2. *Full Insurance and Service.*   The system would provide insurance for the driver and all servicing for the car—cleaning, fuel, maintenance, and repairs—while the cars are parked at the Minicar garages.

3. *Shared Use.*   A subscriber would be guaranteed the use of a car but a specific car would not be assigned to him. He would go to the nearest Minicar garage and get the most convenient Minicar (which generally would not be the car he last used). Once that car was checked out, it would become his private car until he returned to a Minicar garage.

4. *Flexible Parking.*   There would be numerous Minicar garages around the downtown area of Philadelphia. The user could drop off or pick up a Minicar at any of these stations. The plan is to have enough garages so that the user in center city will never be farther than two blocks from a Minicar station.

The "lease'n park" service would allow the subscriber use of a car for a fixed monthly fee. These charges would include *all costs* (ample insurance, fuel, parking, maintenance, etc.).

7. The lost-on-the-moon problem (p. 122) from Hall (1971) is as follows:

Your spaceship has just crash-landed on the moon. You were scheduled to rendezvous with a mother ship 200 miles away on the lighted surface of the moon, but the rough landing has ruined your ship and destroyed all the equipment on board, except for the 15 items listed below.

Your crew's survival depends upon reaching the mother ship, so you must choose the most critical items available for the 200-mile trip. Your task is to rank the 15 items in terms of their importance for survival. Place number 1 by the most important item, number 2 by the second most important, and so on through number 15, the least important.

_____ Box of matches
_____ Food concentrate
_____ Fifty feet of nylon rope
_____ Parachute silk
_____ Solar-powered portable heating unit
_____ Two .45-caliber pistols
_____ One case of dehydrated milk
_____ Two 100-pound tanks of oxygen
_____ Stellar map (of the moon's constellation)
_____ Self-inflating life raft
_____ Magnetic compass
_____ Five gallons of water
_____ Signal flares
_____ First-aid kit containing injection needles
_____ Solar-powered FM receiver-transmitter

Judgments by experts were used to define the correct answers in this problem. If you would like to use this exercise, the correct answers are provided here, along with the score sheet used by Hall.

Items	NASA's Reasoning	NASA's Ranks	Your Ranks	Error Points	Group Ranks	Error Points
Box of matches	No oxygen on moon to sustain flame; virtually worthless	15	_____	_____	_____	_____
Food concentrate	Efficient means of supplying energy requirements	4	_____	_____	_____	_____

Items	NASA's Reasoning	NASA's Ranks	Your Ranks	Error Points	Group Ranks	Error Points
Fifty feet of nylon rope	Useful in scaling cliffs, tying injured together	6				
Parachute silk	Protection from sun's rays	8				
Solar-powered portable heating unit	Not needed unless on dark side	13				
Two .45-caliber pistols	Possible means of self-propulsion	11				
One case of dehydrated milk	Bulkier duplication of food	12				
Two 100-pound tanks of oxygen	Most pressing survival need	1				
Stellar map (of the moon's constellation)	Primary means of navigation	3				
Self-inflating life raft	Carbon dioxide bottle in military raft may be used for propulsion	9				
Magnetic compass	Magnetic field on moon is not polarized; worthless for navigation	14				
Five gallons of water	Replacement for tremendous liquid loss on lighted side	2				
Signal flares	Distress signal when mother ship is sighted	10				

Items	NASA's Reasoning	NASA's Ranks	Your Ranks	Error Points	Group Ranks	Error Points
First-aid kit containing injection needles	Needles for vitamins, medicines, and so on will fit special aperture in NASA space suits	7	_____	_____	_____	_____
Solar-powered FM receiver-transmitter	For communication with mother ship, but FM requires line-of-sight transmission and short ranges	5	_____	_____	_____	_____
		Total	_____			_____

Error points are the absolute difference between your ranks and NASA's (disregard plus or minus signs).	Scoring for individuals:	
	0–25 = excellent	56–70 = poor
	26–32 = good	71–112 = very poor;
	33–45 = average	suggests possible faking
	46–55 = fair	or use of earth-bound logic

Chapter 7

In the Markov chain example (p. 158–159), the market shares in the next period can be obtained by matrix algebra:

[Market shares in period t] × [transition matrix]

= [Market shares in period $t + 1$]

$$[.7 \quad .2 \quad .1] \begin{bmatrix} .8 & .1 & .1 \\ .2 & .7 & .1 \\ .2 & .2 & .6 \end{bmatrix} = [L \quad S \quad F]$$

The pattern of calculations is illustrated by arrows for L's share. L is the market share this period times repeat purchases (.7 × .8), plus S's share times the share stolen from S (.2 × .2), plus F's share times the share stolen from F (.1 × .2). This totals to .62. Analogous calculations for S and F yield shares of .23 and .15, respectively. This process can be repeated a few more times, and it will then be noted that the shares quickly stabilize. This is called the steady-state solution.

The steady-state solution $[m_1 \ m_2 \ m_3]$ can also be calculated by setting up simultaneous equations from

$$[m_1 \quad m_2 \quad m_3] \begin{bmatrix} .8 & .1 & .1 \\ .2 & .7 & .1 \\ .2 & .2 & .6 \end{bmatrix} = [m_1 \quad m_2 \quad m_3]$$

Chapter 8

The definitions used in the survey of experts (pp. 226–227 and 403–404) are presented here. Definitions a, c, e, and f were used in the question on complexity. (All of these definitions were used in the study referred to in Chapter 15.)

a. "Econometric methods" include all methods which forecast by explicitly measuring relationships between the dependent variable and some causal variables.
b. "Competitive methods" would include such things as judgment by one or more "experts" or extrapolation of the variable of interest (e.g., by relating the variable to "time" such as in autoregressive schemes).
c. By "do," we mean that comparisons should be made between methods that appear to follow the best practices available at the current time. In other words, the methods should each be applied in a competent manner.
d. "Short-term" refers to time periods during which changes are relatively small. Thus, for forecasts of the economy, changes from year to year are rather small, almost always less than 10%. For some situations, however, one-year changes may be substantial.
e. "Forecasts" refer to unconditional or *ex ante* forecasts only. That is, none of the methods shall use any data drawn from the situation that is being forecast. Thus for time series, only data prior to time *t* could be used in making the forecasts.
f. The "social sciences" would include economics, psychology, sociology, management, etc. In short, any area where the behavior of people is involved.

Chapter 9

The Minicar system (pp. 269, 481) was described in the notes for Chapter 6.

Chapter 13

(1) The best answer to the speed reading test (p. 336–337) is (c); (c) is usually the correct answer in multiple choice questions. However, partial credit is given for (d) (helpful hints on getting through life).
(2) On the baby boy problem, Tversky and Kahneman (1971) reported that 22% said "larger," 22% said "smaller," and 56% said "about the same." The correct answer is "smaller."

Chapter 15

The definitions for the survey on the accuracy of econometric methods (pp. 403–404) are given on *LRF* 485.

APPENDIX G
RULES FOR CHEATERS

Some people are impressed by a high R^2. There are simple things that can be done to raise R^2; other than that, they are of no value. The most important thing is not to use these rules (please don't), but to be aware that others use them.

1. Discard outliers after you examine the regression results.
2. Aggregate the data, especially when it reduces sample size significantly.
3. Experiment by trying lots of variables.
4. Try different functional forms.
5. Use stepwise regression and retain all coefficients with t statistics greater than 1.0 (Haitovsky, 1969).
6. Include a lot of variables in the final equation.
7. Use R^2 rather than $\overline{R}^2$.

These rules should yield R^2 values of over 99% for time series data and about 90% for cross-sectional data.

APPENDIX H
THE VIRTUE OF SIMPLICITY
(see *LRF*, p. 226)

Ueno and Tsurumi (1969) developed a highly complex econometric model. They used this model to make unconditional forecasts of U.S. domestic automobile production for the years 1966, 1967, 1968, and 1969.

To examine the value of complexity, Carl Harrington and I conducted a brief study. Respondents were given a graph of U.S. automobile production from 1947 to 1965 (the same data used by Ueno and Tsurumi), and were asked to make "eyeball" estimates for 1966–1969. Two variations were used:

1. A graph labeled "U.S. Production of Automobiles, 1947–1965" (see Exhibit H-1).
2. A graph labeled "Production of Product *X* in Transylvania, 2000–2018" (same as Exhibit H-1, but with changes in the title and axes).

Exhibit H-1   U.S. PRODUCTION OF AUTOMOBILES, 1947–1965

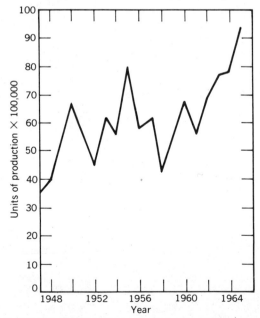

Exhibit H-2 JUDGMENTAL VS. ECONOMETRIC FORECASTS OF AUTOMOBILES IN THE UNITED STATES AND TRANSYLVANIA

| | Judgmental | | | | | | | | Econometric | | Actual |
| | I U.S. Auto Only (n = 13) | | II and IIIA Transylvania (n = 28) | | IIIB U.S. Auto (Second) (n = 15) | | Ueno and Tsurumi | | | | |
Year	Forecast (millions)	Error (%)	Forecast (millions)	Error (%)	Forecast (millions)	Error (%)	Forecast (millions)	Error (%)			Production (millions)
1966	9.74	13.3	8.54	−0.1	9.29	8.0	9.46	10.0			8.60
1967	9.90	33.1	8.35	12.2	9.49	27.6	10.69	43.7			7.44
1968	9.79	11.0	8.49	−3.7	9.47	7.4	11.49	30.3			8.82
1969	10.57	28.6	8.76	6.6	9.47	15.2	11.27	37.1			8.22
MAPE		21.5		5.7		14.6		30.3			

Exhibit H-3 PERCENTAGES OF JUDGES
WITH MAPEs LESS THAN THE
ECONOMETRIC MODEL

Year	I	II and IIIA	IIIB
1966	15	68	33
1967	69	100	87
1968	85	96	93
1969	54	100	73

The second graph removed all information about the situation (product, place, time) to force respondents to extrapolate from the historical·data only.

Three groups of respondents were used:

• Group I ($n = 13$) received only the U.S. graph.
• Group II ($n = 13$) received only the Transylvania graph.
• Group III ($n = 15$) received the Transylvania graph first (IIIA) and then the U.S. graph (IIIB).

Exhibit H-2 compares the combined forecasts for Groups I, II, IIIA, IIIB with forecasts by Ueno and Tsurumi. As shown in this exhibit, the combined forecast for each group was more accurate than the econometric model error of 30.3%. Yet each individual forecaster spent less than 5 minutes in making his forecast!

The superiority of the judgmental method held up even for the average judge. The 4-year MAPE for the average judge in each group was as follows: group I, 24.3%; groups II and IIIA, 13.0%; and group IIIB, 19.2%. Exhibit H-3 illustrates that most of the judges in each group were more accurate than the Ueno and Tsurumi model.

What is the moral of the story? Too much complexity can be bad!

A final comment concerns the relative accuracy of the three groups of respondents. For each year, the respondents extrapolating from the Transylvania data (where information about the situation had been removed) were more accurate. Judges forecasting for the U.S. market were less accurate, but more accurate than Ueno and Tsurumi. This is an interesting result, but what is the moral? Less is more?

APPENDIX I
THE WIZARD WHO OVERSIMPLIFIED: A FABLE*

Harold Peterson

In a certain kingdom, there was a school for the education of princes approaching manhood. Since the king and his court spent much of their time playing chess—indeed, chess was called the sport of kings—it was decided that the subject called "games" should be added to the curriculum of this school. A wizard was engaged to develop the course.

Never having played chess himself, the wizard was a little uncertain about what to teach in this course. (Only a *little* uncertain because his ignorance of chess was outweighed by his strong confidence in his general ability.) He sought the advice of a colleague in another kingdom and from him received the following communication:

"Above all else, a course in games should be rigorous and intellectually challenging. We wizards long ago concluded that chess, as actually played, is so complicated that it is impossible to formulate a body of principles and decision rules; these are essential to the rigorous analysis of any subject. We have therefore introduced a few simplifying assumptions. For example, in chess, the pieces move in a bewildering fashion—some forward, some on the diagonal, and some even at a right angle; we have tidied up this confusion by assuming that all pieces move according to the same rule. With such assumptions, we have been able, albeit with great difficulty, to develop a model, a set of principles, and decision rules which are teachable, and intellectually challenging. A 700-page treatise describing these is enclosed."

The wizard was much impressed by the 700-page treatise, and used it in his course. He found that it was teachable, and that the task of learning this model and solving problems with the decision rules was indeed rigorous and intellectually challenging, as proved by the fact that good students did well on their examinations, while poor students failed them.

The wizard maintained an active correspondence with wizards in other kingdoms about the model and its decision rules. In this correspondence, the game was referred to as "chess" although this was solely for convenience of expression; it was taken for granted that everyone

*From *Quarterly Journal of Economics,* **79** (May 1965), 209–211. Permission to reprint was granted by the *Quarterly Journal of Economics* (Wiley).

knew that their game was not quite like chess as played in the real world. Eventually, some of this correspondence came to the king's attention. Although he didn't understand the formulas and the jargon, he did notice that the word "chess" was mentioned, and he commanded the wizard to appear before him.

At this audience, the wizard asked, "How can I serve you, O King?"

And the king replied: "I understand that you are teaching the princes how to play chess. I wish to improve my own game. Can you help me?"

"What we call chess may not exactly be like your game, your majesty. So before answering your question, I must analyze the problem. Please describe chess as you play it."

So the king explained the game of chess. As he did so, the wizard noted that it had the same physical layout, the same number of pieces, and apparently the same objective as the game he taught in school. It seemed clear therefore that the solution was simply to apply the decision rules for this game, although he of course did not immediately reveal this fact to the king for he wanted to preserve his reputation for wizardry. Instead, he said thoughtfully: "I will study the problem and return in 90 days."

At the appointed time, the wizard appeared again, carrying a crimson pillow on which lay a spiral-bound report with a Plexiglas cover. It was a paraphrase of the 700-page manuscript. "Follow the rules in this report, your majesty, and you will become the best chess player in the world," he said.

The king avidly studied the report, but soon ran into difficulty. He summoned the wizard again. "I see reference to kings, and men, and squares, which are familiar terms to me; but what is all this about 'jumping,' and 'double jumping,' and 'countervailing force,' and 'suboptimization'; and where do you mention queens, rooks, bishops, and knights?"

"But your majesty, as I have clearly explained in the introduction, it was necessary to simplify the environment a trifle. I doubt that these simplifications lessen the practical usefulness of what I have written, however."

"Have you by chance watched some chess players to find out?" asked the king.

"Oh, no, your gracious majesty, but I do carry on an extensive correspondence with other wizards. This is better than observing actual practice because it is generally agreed that wizards are smarter than chess players."

"And your princes. Are they equipped to play chess in the real world because of what they have learned in your course?"

"No offense intended, sir, but we wizards do not believe this to be a proper question. The purpose of our course it to teach princes to think, not to prepare them for a mere vocation."

At this point, the king lost his patience, but since he was a kindly king, he sent the wizard back to his schoolroom rather than to a dungeon.

Moral for LRF readers: Observe actual decision-makers and forecasters. I also like Peterson's views on the dance and on education. As for his views on simple models and on 700-page treatises . . . well you can take these with a grain of salt.

APPENDIX J

FORECAST ACCURACY OF SIMPLE VS. SOPHISTICATED EXTRAPOLATION METHODS*

(For "results" a "+" means sophisticated methods were more accurate, a "0" means negligible difference, and a "−" means they were less accurate.)

Study	Major Comparisons	Results
Winters (1960)	exponential smoothing vs. moving averages	+
FRANK (1969)	exponential smoothing vs. moving averages	+
Elton & Gruber (1972)	exponential smoothing vs. moving averages	+
Chow (1965)**	adaptive vs. constant parameters	+
WHYBARK [1972]***	adaptive vs. constant parameters	+
SMITH (1974)	adaptive vs. constant parameters	+
DENNIS [1978]***	adaptive vs. constant parameters	+
BROWN & ROZEFF [1978]	Box-Jenkins vs. simple trend	+
Newbold & Granger (1974)	Box-Jenkins vs. exponential smoothing	+
REID [1975]	Box-Jenkins vs. exponential smoothing	+
DALRYMPLE [1978]	Box-Jenkins vs. regression	+
Kirby (1966)	exponential smoothing vs. moving averages	0
Adam (1973)	exponential smoothing vs. moving averages	0
Raine (1971)	adaptive vs. constant parameters	0
Dancer & Gray (1977)	adaptive vs. constant parameters	0
Chatfield & Prothero (1973)	Box-Jenkins vs. no-change	0
Albrecht et al. (1977)	Box-Jenkins vs. no-change	0
Groff (1973)	Box-Jenkins vs. exponential smoothing	0
Geurts & Ibrahim (1975)	Box-Jenkins vs. exponential smoothing	0
Mabert (1976)	Box-Jenkins vs. exponential smoothing	0

CHATFIELD [1978]	Box-Jenkins vs. exponential smoothing	0
KENNY & DURBIN [1982]	Box-Jenkins vs. exponential smoothing	0
Torfin & Hoffman (1968)	6 models of varying complexity	0
Markland (1970)	4 models of varying complexity	0
JOHNSON & SCHMITT (1974)	10 models of varying complexity	0
CAREY [1978]	21 models of varying complexity	0
HAGERMAN & RULAND [1979]	3 models of varying complexity	0
MAKRIDAKIS & HIBON [1979]	22 models of varying complexity	0
RULAND [1980]	8 models of varying complexity	0
MAKRIDAKIS ET AL. [1982]	21 models of varying complexity	0
Armstrong (1975b)	complex curve vs. rule of thumb	0
GARDNER [1979a]	25 models of varying complexity	—
GARDNER & DANNENBRING [1980]	adaptive vs. constant parameters	—
MABERT [1978]	adaptive vs. constant parameters	—
McLEAVEY, LEE & ADAM [1981]	adaptive vs. constant parameters	—
LEDOLTER & ABRAHAM [1981]	adaptive vs. constant parameters	—
COGGIN & HUNTER [1982–3]	adaptive vs. constant parameters	—
BRANDON, JARRETT & KHUMAWALA [1983]	Box-Jenkins vs. 8 simple models	—
SCHNAARS [1984]	six models of varying complexity	—
SCHNAARS & BAVUSO [1985]	seven models of varying complexity	—

*This table was adapted from ARMSTRONG [1984a] with permission from the Institute of Management Sciences. Additional studies are included here.

**Results were challenged by GARDNER [1983b]

***Results were challenged by EKERN [1981]

NOTES: 1. These papers represent all published studies that I could find on this topic up to 1985.
2. For discussion, see LRF 178–179.

GLOSSARY

Key Terms
Symbols and Acronyms

"But 'glory' doesn't mean 'a nice knock-down argument,'" Alice objected.
"When I use a word," Humpty Dumpty said, in a rather scornful tone,
"it means just what I choose it to mean—neither more nor less."
"The question is," said Alice, "whether you can make words mean so
many different things."
"The question is," said Humpty Dumpty, "which is to be master—that's
all."

Through the Looking Glass
Lewis Carroll

I, like Humpty Dumpty, may be accused of having some strange definitions. (They are not strange to me, of course.) When reading about
forecasting problems in the social sciences, I found that the same words
were used in different ways. *Long-Range Forecasting* attempts to use
each term as it is most commonly defined. This glossary presents the
particular definition that I used for each term. Because the term may
be used differently in your field, it is suggested that you check with
the glossary from time to time.

Useful sources for this glossary included *Webster's New Collegiate
Dictionary* (this must be the eighth time it is new because I used the
ninth edition), Springfield, MA, 1983, and also Myers, (1974).

The definitions are stated in simple terms. I do not think this has
caused any loss in precision. At any rate, I have an aversion to elegant
definitions.

This glossary includes only terms that are used in *LRF*. MAKRI-
DAKIS and WHEELWRIGHT [1978, pp. 567–641] provide a detailed
and extensive glossary that is especially strong on terms for extrapolation methods.

Words in the glossary are set in boldface type and tagged with a
superscript "G" the first time they appear in the text. If the first mention also contains a *description*, it is cross-referenced in the glossary
using the notation *LRF* XXX. Further usage of the terms can be found
through the subject index.

The first page of the glossary is a list of symbols. Preference was
given to the use of English letters rather than Greek. I tried to ensure
that each symbol had only one meaning. I failed. The alphabet is too
small. For example, *t* has two meanings; the intended meaning should,
however, be apparent from the text.

In the following list, no distinction was made between lowercase
and uppercase letters except as noted.

Symbol	Description
A	actual value
APE	average percentage error
b	causal relationship
c	cost
cv	coefficient of variation
d	number of observations
e	error
E-T-E	estimate-talk-estimate
F	*forecast value*
G	growth or trend
h	forecast horizon
H_0	null hypothesis
I	income
j	period of the year
k	a constant
l	limit or asymptote
LRF	*Long-Range Forecasting*
m	market size
MAPE	mean absolute percentage error
n	sample size (number of decision units)
p	probability
Q	accuracy ratio
r	correlation coefficient
R^2	coefficient of determination
S	seasonal factor
t	time; also a measure of statistical significance
TP	turning point
U	Theil's inequality
v	number of variables
w	weighting factor
x	causal variable
y	dependent variable (variable to be forecast)
α, β, γ	alpha, beta, and gamma: smoothing factors in exponential smoothing for average, trend, and seasonality, respectively
$\sum$	summation sign
$>$	more than
$<$	less than

Adjusted R^2. $\overline{R}^2$ (see also R^2) is adjusted for loss in the degrees of freedom. This adjustment partially corrects R^2 so that it does not falsely state the percentage of variation explained. The adjusted R^2 is always preferred to R^2 when the fit to the calibration sample is being examined.

AID. (Automatic Interaction Detector). A computer program that makes successive two-way splits in the data to find homogeneous subcells that differ from one another. (*LRF* 262*)

Anchoring. The tendency for judges to start with a convenient answer in making their forecasts. This answer (or anchor) can be based on tradition or previous history, or on convenient data. (*LRF* 87)

A *posteriori* analysis. The researcher's knowledge is used after the data have been analyzed. Well expressed by the quotation from Churchill on *LRF* 53.

A *priori* analysis. The researcher's knowledge is stated before his or her analysis of a given set of data.

Autocorrelation. Interdependence among the error terms in a set of observations; the value of the error in one time period is correlated with the value in another time period. Usually refers to correlations among adjacent time periods. (*LRF* 224)

Backcasting. Predicting what occurred in a time period before that used for analysis, that is, forecasting backward in time. Sometimes called "postdiction," but that sounds like a speech problem.

Bayesian analysis. A procedure whereby new information is used to update prior information. (*LRF* 232)

Bias. A systematic error, that is, deviations from the "true value" in one direction. Can occur with any type of forecasting method, but is especially common with judgmental forecasting.

Bootstrapping. A model of how a person makes a judgmental forecast. This model can be used on a computer or by a clerk. See also Expert Systems.

Brainstorming. A structured procedure for helping a group to generate ideas. The basic rule is to suspend evaluation. There are two steps that help in this regard:

1. Gain agreement from the group to use brainstorming.
2. Select a facilitator who:

*The page numbers indicate where the term is first used in this book, page 262 in this case.

(a) does not introduce his or her own ideas,
(b) records ideas,
(c) encourages quantity,
(d) reminds the group not to evaluate (either favorably or unfa-
     vorably), and
(e) encourages wild ideas.

(For more on brainstorming see Taylor, Berry, and Block, 1958.)

Calibrate. To estimate the relationships (and constant terms) in a forecasting model.

Calibration sample. The data used in developing a forecasting model. (*LRF* 335)

Causal. This term is used in a commonsense way. One variable, X, is said to cause changes in another variable, Y, when changes in X are either necessary or sufficient to bring about a change in Y, and when the change in X occurs before the change in Y. (*LRF* 74)

Census Program X-11. A computer program used to calculate moving averages. It was developed by the U.S. Bureau of the Census.

Coefficient of determination. See R^2.

Coefficient of variation. The ratio of the standard error to the mean.

Cognitive dissonance. An uncomfortable feeling that arises when an individual has conflicting attitudes about an event or object.

Conceptual. Something that cannot be directly observed and measured. Examples of conceptual variables are health, cost of capital, travel, life, liberty, and the pursuit of happiness.

Conditional forecast. A forecast made with some knowledge about the event to be forecasted, that is, data from the forecast horizon are used in the forecast. A synonym is "*ex post* forecast."

Conditional regression analysis. (or "the poor man's approach to Bayesian regression"). A procedure for using objective data to update prior estimates of regression coefficients. (*LRF* 234)

Consensus. A feeling within a group that its conclusion represents a fair summary of the conclusions reached by the individual members of the group. Hall (1971) views consensus as the decision-making process rather than the resulting feeling in the group. I draw heavily upon Hall's description here. Consensus should make good use of the group's resources, and it should provide for a fair resolution of conflicts within the group. Consensus is difficult to reach, so not every conclusion will meet with everyone's approval. Complete unanimity is not the goal, and it is rarely achieved. However, each individual should be able to accept the group's conclusion on the basis of logic and feasibility. When all group members feel this way, consensus has been reached. This means, in effect, that a single person can block the group if that person thinks it is necessary. Here are some guidelines to use in achieving consensus:

1. Avoid arguing for your own viewpoint. Present your position as lucidly and logically as possible, but then listen to the other members' reactions and consider them carefully.
2. Do not assume that someone must win and someone must lose when the discussion reaches a stalemate. Instead, consider a restatement of the problem, or the next-most-acceptable alternative.
3. Do not change your mind simply to avoid conflict and to reach agreement. Be suspicious when agreement seems to come too quickly and easily. Explore the reasons, and be sure that everyone accepts the solution for similar or complementary reasons.
4. Avoid conflict-reducing techniques such as majority vote, averages, coin flips, and bargaining. When a dissenting member finally agrees, don't feel that he or she must be rewarded by having his or her own way on some later point.
5. Differences of opinion are natural and expected. Seek them out and involve everyone in the decision process. Disagreement can improve the group's decision because a wide range of opinions increases the chance that the group will hit upon better solutions.

Conservatism.   The assumption that things will continue to be much as they are now. (*LRF* 87)

Construct validity (or Conceptual validity).   Evidence that an operational measure measures what it purports to measure. Typically assessed by examining the correspondence among different operational measurements of the same concept. In *LRF*, "construct" refers to relationships as well as to variables. (*LRF* 323–325)

Credence analysis.   Analysis of total survey error. It gives separate consideration to response, nonresponse, and sampling error when assessing total error. (*LRF* 144)

Cross-sectional data.   Data on a number of different units (e.g., people, countries, firms) for a single time period. The idea is to explain differences among these units. (*LRF* 208)

Cross validation.   A test of concurrent validity that is made by splitting the data by probability methods, estimating the model using one subsample, and testing it on the remaining subsample. There are more elaborate approaches known as double cross validation, *N*-way cross validation, and random data validation. (*LRF* 341)

Cutpoints.   The level (e.g., the midpoint) for a given variable that is used to split data into segments. (*LRF* 253)

Decomposition.   The strategy of breaking a problem into subproblems, solving them, and then combining the solutions to the subproblems to get an overall solution. (*LRF* 58)

Degrees of freedom.   The number of observations not used up in the estimation process, that is, the number of independent observations. In regression analysis, the number of degrees of freedom equals the number of observations minus the number of regression coefficients (including the constant). The larger the number of regression coefficients estimated, the larger the number of constraints imposed on the sample, and the smaller the number of variables left to provide precise estimates of the regression coefficients. A greater number of degrees of freedom provides more reliable estimates. (*LRF* 350)

Delphi.   A method for obtaining forecasts from a panel of experts.

Dependent variable.   The variable that is of interest to the researcher, the variable that is to be forecast; in regression analysis, this is the variable on the left-hand side of the equation.

Discriminant analysis.   A variation of regression analysis used when the dependent variable is based on categorical data. The simplest variation is a dependent variable with two categories (e.g., "accepted bribe" and "did not accept bribe"). Special programs must be used for three or more categories. (*LRF* 220)

Double cross validation.   The analysis data are split into two subsets. A model is estimated on one part and then tested on the other. The second part is then used to provide estimates, and the resulting model is tested on the first part of the sample. (*LRF* 341)

Dummy variable.   A causal variable that assumes only two values, 0 and 1. The coefficient of a dummy variable in a regression equation shows the average effect on the level of the dependent variable when the dummy variable assumes the value of 1. For example, a dummy variable might represent the presence or absence of capital punishment in a geographical region. The regression coefficient could then show how the level of violent crimes changes, depending upon whether there is capital punishment. Incidentally, more than two categories can be handled by using additional dummy variables. To represent political affiliation (e.g., Republican, Democrat, or Independent) one could use two dummy variables ("Republican or not?" and "Democrat or not?"). Suits (1957) describes how to use dummy variables.

Durbin-Watson statistic.   A measure of the correlation between errors in time t and those in $t + 1$. Values of this statistic range from 0 to 4. If no autocorrelation is present, the expected value is 2. Small values (less than 2, approaching 0) indicate positive autocorrelation; large values (greater than 2, approaching 4) indicate negative autocorrelation. (*LRF* 224)

Eclectic research.   A strategy of allocating a given research budget over a series of different approaches rather than to a single approach. Applies to both building and evaluating models. (*LRF* 52)

Econometrics.   The development of theory followed by the use of objective measurement methods, usually regression analysis. "The thinking man's regression analysis." This method is applicable not only in economics but also in other social sciences.

Elasticity.   An expression of the relationship between two variables. For modest changes, elasticity expresses the percentage change in the variable of interest that is caused by a 1% change in a causal variable. For example, an income elasticity of $+1.3$ for unit automobile sales means that a 1% increase in income will lead to an increase of 1.3% in the sales of automobiles. (*LRF* 201)

E-T-E (Estimate-talk-estimate).   A structured group procedure calling for independent and anonymous estimates, then a group discussion, and finally another round of individual estimates. Also called mini-Delphi. (*LRF* 121–124)

Ex ante.   A forecast that uses no information from the situation being forecast. This term is used interchangeably with "unconditional."

Experimental data.   Data from situations where a researcher has systematically changed certain variables. Control varies from laboratory experiments, where the researcher controls most of the relevant environment, to field experiments, where he or she has control over only a small part of the relevant environment.

Expert systems.   A subset of artificial intelligence. The computer is used to simulate an expert's decisions or forecasts. (See also Bootstrapping.). (*LRF* 277)

Exploratory research.   The practice of carrying out research without *a priori* analysis. The data are allowed to speak for themselves.

Ex post.   Forecasts that use some information from the situation being forecast. This term is used interchangeably with "conditional."

Face validity. Expert opinion on whether a measure represents what it purports to represent. (*LRF* 323)

Facilitator. A group member whose only role is to help the group function more effectively. The facilitator should concentrate on the process that the group follows and forget about substantive issues. The facilitator works for the group (in contrast to the typical situation, where the group works for the leader). (*LRF* 121)

First differences. Time series data where period-to-period changes are examined.

Fisher exact test. A nonparametric test used to assess the relationship in a 2×2 table when there are small samples. See Siegel (1956) for discussion and computational procedure.

Forecast horizon. The number of periods from the current time period (or most recent period of actual data) to the start of the time period that is being forecast. Designated by h in *LRF*.

Forecasting. Estimating in "unknown" situations. This book draws little distinction between "forecasting" and "predicting." Forecasting, however, connotes an estimation of the future. Prediction is more general and connotes estimates for any time period—before, during, or after the current one.

Forecasting model. A model that is used to obtain forecasts. This should be distinguished from the measurement model. The forecasting model may draw upon a variety of measurement models for estimates of key parameters. (*LRF* 219)

Forecast validity. The extent to which a model is useful in making forecasts. (*LRF* 323–325)

Functional form. A mathematical statement of the way that the causal variables relate to the dependent variable. (*LRF* 200)

Global assessment. An overall estimate (in contrast to one that provides for an explicit estimate of the parts).

Gompertz curve. A growth curve that has the shape of a nonsymmetrical S-curve. It can be stated as

$$\log Y = \log l + kG^t$$

where Y is the dependent variable, l is the upper asymptote, k is a coefficient to be estimated, G is the growth expressed as a constant ratio per unit of time, and t represents time.

Helper. See **Facilitator.**

Heteroscedasticity.   The variability of the error term differs over the range of data. For example, small errors may occur for small values, and large errors for large values. (*LRF* 201)

Homoscedasticity.   The variability of the error term is constant over the range of the data.

Intensive research.   Allocating a given research budget to a single approach. (*LRF* 64)

Intentions studies.   Surveys of how people say they will act in a given situation. (*LRF* 81)

Interaction.   A situation where the relationship between X_1 and Y depends upon the level of X_2.

Interrater reliability.   The amount of agreement between two or more raters who follows the same procedure. (*LRF* 328)

Interval scale.   The measured intervals are meaningful, but the zero point of the scale is not meaningful (e.g., the Fahrenheit scale for temperature).

Ipsative scores.   *Webster's Dictionary* has had over 100 years in the business, and its editors have collected over 450,000 words. But they missed "ipsative!" "Ipsative" is a word because people use it. It refers to scores that measure relative importance within an individual. Strictly speaking, ipsative scores do not allow for comparisons among people. (E.g., Lloyd likes football better than basketball. Bonnie likes basketball better than football. Does Bonnie like basketball better than Lloyd likes basketball? You do not have enough information to answer that question.) (*LRF* 143)

Kendall rank correlation.   A measure of the association between two sets of rankings. Siegel (1956) provides discussion and computational procedures. An alternative to the Spearman rank correlation, Kendall also allows you to calculate partial correlations.

Learning partner.   According to the research on learning, when we want to learn something that is important to ourselves, we turn to someone with whom we feel comfortable (instead of using experts, teachers, etc.).

Logistic curve.   A growth curve where the percentage growth gets smaller over time. It typically has the shape of a symmetrical S-curve. It can be calculated from

$$\frac{1}{Y} = \frac{1}{l} + kG^t$$

where Y is the dependent variable, l is the asymptote, k is a coefficient to be estimated, G is the growth factor, and t represents time.

Logit. A transformation of the dependent variable in a regression that bounds the predicted value between zero and one. (But *not equal to zero*. The log of zero is minus infinity and computers do not like being asked to use this.) Thus, it might be appropriate for market share predictions. Transform the dependent variable by

$$ Y = \ln \left(\frac{Y}{1 - Y} \right) $$

with the remainder of the equation unchanged.

Longitudinal data. Data that represent changes between two time periods for a number of decision units. (*LRF* 209)

MAPE. Mean absolute percentage error.

$\overline{\text{MAPE}}$. Adjusted mean absolute percentage error.

M-Competition. The abbreviation for the study of extrapolation methods by MAKRIDAKIS et al. [1982, 1984].

Mean square error. The error term is squared. An alternative to the mean absolute deviation, except that more weight is placed on larger errors.

Measurement error. The extent to which errors are introduced by failures or shortcomings in the way that numbers are assigned to the concept.

Measurement model. A model used to obtain estimates of coefficients from data. The measurement model is not the same as the forecasting model; it represents an input to the forecasting model.

Mini-Delphi. See **E-T-E.**

Mitigation. Reducing the emphasis on the change due to causal relationships. (*LRF* 238)

MMPI. (Minnesota Multiphasic Personality Inventory). A psychological test designed to identify serious personality disorders.

Model. A representation of the real world. In this book, "model" refers to statements about (*a*) variables and (*b*) relationships among variables.

Monte Carlo simulation. A procedure that tries to simulate real-world events. First, the problem is decomposed; then a distribution (rather than a point estimate) is used for each of the decomposed parts. A trial is created by drawing randomly from each of the distributions.

The procedure is used for many trials to build up a distribution for the overall outcomes. (*LRF* 244)

Multicollinearity. The extent to which the causal variables move together in a set of data. It is usually measured by the correlation coefficient among the causal variables. High multicollinearity makes it difficult to determine the extent to which each of the causal variables is individually causing changes in the dependent variable. (*LRF* 206)

Multiple hypotheses. The strategy whereby a single researcher uses two or more reasonable hypotheses when studying a problem. (*LRF* 9)

Naive method. A model that does not attempt to explain why an event occurs, but simply examines variations over time. (*LRF* 73)

Neurosis. A personality disorder marked by relatively mild abnormalities in dealing with reality (e.g., nervous mannerisms).

Nominal scale. Measurement that classifies objects (e.g., "yes" or "no"; "red," "white," or "blue").

Nondirective interviewing. A style of interviewing in which the interviewee is given only a general question and is then encouraged to discuss what he or she feels to be important. (*LRF* 28–31)

Nonexperimental data. Data where there has been no systematic manipulation of key variables.

Nonparametric tests. Tests of statistical significance that make few assumptions.

Observation. Measurements for a given unit (e.g., person, country, firm) taken for a given time period.

Occam's razor. The rule that one should not introduce complexities unless absolutely necessary. Attributed to William of Occam (or Ockham) of England in the early 1300s. Although this is a good rule, William died of the Black Death in 1349.

Operational. A definition of the steps involved in measuring a variable or a relationship. This should be specific enough so that other reasonable people can carry out the same procedure.

Optimism. Tendency for a respondent to forecast favorable events as more likely to occur. (*LRF* 86)

Ordinal scale. Measurement of data that allows only for ranking; that is, the intervals are not meaningful.

Outliers. Observations that differ dramatically from the distribution for a particular variable. (*LRF* 162)

Parameter. The "true" value of a relationship.

Practical significance. The importance of a result to decision making. "A difference that makes a difference." (*LRF* 358)

Prediction. See **Forecasting.**

Predictive validity. See also **Forecast validity.** (*LRF* 323–325)

Projective test. A test (method) that asks the subject to respond to a vague stimulus. It is assumed that the subject will project his or her own feelings. (*LRF* 107)

Protocols. The record of a person's thought process when asked to think aloud in doing a task (such as when making a forecast). (*LRF* 277)

Psychosis. Severe personality disorder marked by a loss of touch with reality and basic changes in personality.

Pure research. Research for which the researcher has no idea of any potential use.

R^2. The coefficient of determination. Indicates the percentage variation in the dependent variable that is explained by variations in the causal variables.

$\bar{R}^2$. R^2 after adjustment for the loss in degrees of freedom for the variables included in the model. See **Adjusted R^2**

Ratio scale. The measured intervals are meaningful, and the zero point of the scale is known (e.g., the Kelvin scale for temperature is a ratio scale).

Regression toward the mean. The tendency for extreme observations measured in one time period to revert toward the sample mean when measured during another time period. (*LRF* 336)

Reliability. The extent to which a repetition of the measurement process will yield the same results. (*LRF* 18)

Response error. The error that occurs when a respondent does not reveal his or her true feelings on a subject. May be due to misunderstanding the question, failure to understand his or her true feelings, lying, or a desire to present oneself in a favorable light.

Role playing. People are assigned to play the roles of people in a given situation. They try to "pre-enact" this situation to see what happens when various strategies are employed. (*LRF* 34)

Rorschach test. A projective test in which the subject is presented with inkblot designs and is asked to report what they see.

Runs test. Examination of a series of data to detect tendencies for the series to move in one direction or the other.

Sampling error.   The error that occurs when the sample is not representative of the target population. (*LRF* 82)

Satisfice.   To achieve something better than a minimum acceptable level on each of several criteria. (*LRF* 18)

Scenario.   An account or story about a projected course of action in a possible environment. (*LRF* 18)

Sensitivity analysis.   Variations are introduced into the causal variables in a model to examine what effect they have upon the variable of interest. (*LRF* 372)

Setwise regression.   Experimenting with sets of variables rather than with one variable at a time in developing a model. (*LRF* 204–205)

Shrinkage.   The loss of predictive validity that results when moving from the calibration to the concurrent validity data.

Simultaneous causality.   This occurs when the time interval of the data set is so long that one cannot distinguish the direction of causality. (*LRF* 224)

Spearman rank correlation.   A measure of the association existing between two sets of rankings. A discussion and computational procedures are given in Siegel (1956).

Specification error.   Error caused by failure to include all important variables in a model.

Spectral analysis.   An attempt to explain historical variations by using complex mathematical curves. (*LRF* 180)

Split samples.   See **Cross validation.** (*LRF* 329)

Spurious relationships.   Relationships that are due to chance rather than causality.

Standard error.   A measure of the precision of a coefficient. It tells how reliably the relationship has been measured. The standard deviation for a relationship. (*LRF* 243)

Statistical significance.   The extent to which an event is likely to have occurred by chance. Thus "a difference significant at the .05 level" means that there is only a 5% chance that there is no difference. In such a case, people are often willing to assume that the difference really is a difference. (*LRF* 356)

Stepwise regression.   There are two versions: "step-up" and "step-down." The step-up version first enters the causal variable with the highest correlation to the dependent variable, next enters the one with the highest partial correlation (given the variable already included in the model), then enters the variable with the highest partial correlation (given the two variables included in the model), and so on, until certain stopping rules are encountered. One common stopping rule is to include all those and only those variables that have a t-statistic equal to or greater than 1. (This rule maximizes the adjusted R^2 for the step-up procedure.) The step-down version puts all of the variables in initially, then removes the one that contributes least to R^2, next removes from the remaining variables the one that contributes least, and so on. (*LRF* 53)

Successive updating.   Validation data are used to recalibrate the model at the completion of each forecasting test. (*LRF* 343)

Systems approach.   (See *LRF* Chapter 2.)

Theil's $U2$.   A measure of forecast accuracy.

Time series data.   Data that examine a decision unit at different points in time. (*LRF* 207)

Transformation.   Involves the performance of an arithmetic operation upon a variable (e.g., taking the natural log of a dependent variable; subtracting a constant from the measure of income). Sometimes called "transgeneration." (*LRF* 200)

Turing test.   A group of experts is presented with outputs from a model of a judge and from the judge, and is asked to identify which are from the model and which from the judge. (*LRF* 277)

Type III error.   The right answer to the wrong problem. (Incidentally, a Type I error is to conclude that there is a difference when there is not, and a Type II error is to conclude there is no difference when there is one.)

Uncertainty.   The lack of confidence associated with a forecast.

Unconditional forecast.   An estimate of what will happen in a situation when no data from that situation are used in the forecast. Same as *"ex ante."*

Unit Weights.   The predictor variables are weighted by a factor of $+1$ or -1, where the signs are based on *a priori* information. Often used as equivalent to equal weights. Things are a bit more complex than it seems at first glance, however, because one may need to decide how to scale the variables. (*LRF* 202)

Unobtrusive data.   Data where the act of measurement does not affect the thing that is measured. (*LRF* 207)

Validity.   Generally, truth. In *LRF*, validity also connotes usefulness. (*LRF* 18)

Variance.   A measure of variation that uses the square of the deviation from the sample mean. Thus big deviations are heavily weighted.

Wave.   The response to a mail questionnaire that results from a given stimulus (e.g., from the initial mailing, a postcard follow-up, a telephone follow-up).

Wilcoxon matched-pairs signed-ranks test.   A nonparametric test used to determine whether there is a statistically significant difference between two sets of paired data. This test gives more emphasis to larger differences and is almost as powerful as the t-test. See Siegel (1956) for a further description and for computational details.

Windsorizing.   The practice of modifying outliers in the data by making them no more extreme than the most extreme data that you believe to be accurately measured. (*LRF* 162)

REFERENCES

With Ratings and Annotations

This section of the book contains the references from the first edition. To make room for the new material in the book, however, it was necessary to prune the old references. The problem appears to be the same as that facing the pharaoh in the following cartoon:

"I'm afraid I'll have to let some of you go. The people are complaining about excess prophets."

Source. © *Omni* Magazine, 1982. Reprinted with permission.

Of course, I did not trust to chance in pruning the list. Papers with empirical evidence relevant to the conclusions in *LRF* stayed. Descriptive materials were dropped if more recent descriptions did a better job. Some of the older materials were retained when they lent a historical perspective. In all, almost 700 references remain.

The items in the References are cross-indexed to the page in the text on which they are cited at the end of each entry. They are identified by *LRF* XXX, the *LRF* standing for *Long-Range Forecasting* and the Xs are the page numbers in the text. This is the same procedure as used in the UPDATED BIBLIOGRAPHY and Glossary.

In the few cases where unpublished sources are cited, instructions are provided on how to obtain a copy of the book or article. An attempt was also made to choose the most readable source when multiple sources were available. I have tried to indicate when books have been revised since the first edition.

The annotations tell something about the article beyond the description provided in the text of this book. They were updated in the revised edition.

The ratings are global judgments by me and are based on the following criteria:

1. Is the article relevant and important to the study of forecasting methods? This is the key factor. Some otherwise good articles are rated poorly with respect to this objective.
2. Does the article provide new and convincing information? I am biased toward papers that contain empirical results.
3. Is the article well written? I have preferences for simplicity and for full disclosure.
4. Does the article contain much information beyond the summary already provided in *LRF*?

These factors were used to develop a four-star system that may be interpreted as follows:

****   *Outstanding!* Scores well on all criteria above. This work should be of great interest to readers of *LRF*.

***   *Very good.* Is important in some respects.

**   *Good.* Contains something of value. However, the readers of *LRF* would find this work of interest only in special cases.

*   *Marginal.* Scores poorly on at least one of the four criteria or low on a number of criteria.

—   Is of no value with respect to forecasting methods and was referenced on a side issue.

In summary, the rating scheme provides information on the value of an item for further study of forecasting methods.

The right-hand column of each page contains coded information to help you locate studies. There are three categories:

M   What forecasting method was used?
F   What field was examined?
E   Does the study contain empirical evidence?

The code for E is Y for "yes" or N for "no." For papers designated as empirical, an "m" indicates that the study used the method of *m*ultiple hypotheses (i.e., Ym designates an empirical study that tested two or more reasonable hypotheses). NR means that coding is not relevant. The codes for M and F are as shown here:

M (Method)		F (Field)	
Bo = Bootstrapping		Agr =	Agriculture
Ec = Econometric		Dem =	Demography
Ex = Extrapolation		Eco =	Economics
I = Implementation		Edu =	Education
Ju = Judgmental		Int =	International business
Sg = Segmentation		Fin =	Finance
T = Testing models		Med =	Medicine
NR = Not relevant		Mkt =	Marketing
		Per =	Personnel
		Pol =	Politics
		Pro =	Production
		Psy =	Psychology or psychiatry
		Sci =	Scientific method
		Soc =	Sociology
		Tec =	Technology
		Trn =	Transportation
		Wea =	Weather
		NR =	Not relevant

	M	F	E*

* **A**belson, Robert P., and Bernstein, Alex, "A Computer Simulation Model of Community Referendum Controversies." *Public Opinion Quarterly,* **27** (1963), 93–122.   Sg   Soc   N

Simulation of the fluoridation controversy. A "how-to-do-it" article, that, unfortunately, uses only artificial data. (*LRF* 250)†

*** **Adam, Everett, Jr., "Individual Item Forecasting Model Evaluation,"** *Decision Sciences,* **4** (1973), 458–470.   Ex   Pro   Ym

Uses simulated data to compare seven types of extrapolation models. This study was replicated by McLEAVEY, LEE, and ADAM [1981]. Some corrections were made, but the basic conclusions held up. (*LRF* 171, 174, 494, 626)

** **Adams, F. Gerard, "Prediction with Consumer Attitudes: The Time Series-Cross Section Paradox,"** *Review of Economics and Statistics,* **47** (1965), 367–378 (*LRF* 85)   Ju   Ec   N

** **Akers, Donald S., and Irwin, Richard, "Demographic Projection Techniques,"** in Joseph P. Martino and Thomas Oberbeck (Eds.), *Long Range Forecasting Methodology.* U.S. Government Printing Office, 1967 (*LRF* 159, 428)   Ex   Dem   Y

* **Alinsky, Saul David,** *Rules for Radicals: A Practical Primer for Realistic Radicals.* New York: Random House, 1971 (*LRF* 38)   I   Pol   N

** **Almon, Clopper, Buckler, M.B., Horwitz, L.M., and Reinbold, T.C.,** *1985: Interindustry Forecasts of the American Economy.* Lexington, Mass: Lexington Books, 1974.   Sg   Eco   Y

Readable discussion of input-output analysis. No effort to validate the method. (*LRF* 265)

*** **Alonso, William, "Predicting Best with Imperfect Data,"** *Journal of the American Institute of Planners,* **34** (1968), 248–255. (*LRF* 154, 459)   Ex   Dem   N

** **Alpert, M., and Raiffa, H., "A Progress Report on the Training of Probability Assessors."** Unpublished paper, Harvard University, 1968. Reprinted in KAHNEMAN, SLOVIC, and TVERSKY [1982], pp. 294–305. (*LRF* 143)   Ju   NR   NR

*** **Ames, E., and Reiter, S., "Distributions of Correlation Coefficients in Economic Time Series,"** *Journal of the American Statistical Association,* **56** (1961), 637–656.   Ec   Eco   Y

The authors found high correlations among randomly selected series from the *Historical Statistics for the United States.* For a randomly selected series of 25 years, it was usually possible to explain 50% of the variance by regressing the series against two to six other randomly selected time series. (*LRF* 352)

* **Amstutz, Arnold E.,** *Computer Simulation of Competitive Market Response.* Cambridge, Mass.: MIT Press, 1967. (*LRF* 263, 277)   Sg   Mkt   Y

*M(Method), F(Field), E(Empirical)

†Remember, *LRF* (xxx) indicates the pages in *LRF* that discuss this item. In this case Abelson and Bernstein is discussed on page 250 and only that page.

	M	F	E*
** Ando, Albert, and Kaufman, G.M., "Evaluation of an *ad hoc* Procedure for Estimating Parameters of Some Linear Models," *Review of Economics and Statistics*, 48 (1966), 334–340. (*LRF* 341)	T	NR	N
* Ansoff, H. Igor, and Slevin, Dennis P., "An Appreciation of Industrial Dynamics," *Management Science*, 14 (1968), 383–391. See reply in Forrester (1968b). (*LRF* 264)	Sg	NR	N
* Archer, E.J., Bourne, L.E., and Brown, F.G., "Concept Identification as a Function of Irrelevant Information and Instruction," *Journal of Experimental Psychology*, 49 (1955), 153–164. (*LRF* 379)	Ju	Psy	Y
** Armstrong, J. Scott, "The Derivation of Theory by Means of Factor Analysis" or "Tom Swift and His Electric Factor Analysis Machine," *American Statistician*, 21 (December 1967), 17–21. (*LRF* 223)	Sg	NR	Ym
** Armstrong, J. Scott, "Long Range Forecasting for a Consumer Durable in an International Market." Unpublished PhD Thesis, MIT, 1968a.	Ec Ex Sg	Int	Ym

This 266-page work contains the details for the study of the international camera market. (Copies are available from the Dewey Library, Sloan School, MIT, 50 Memorial Drive, Cambridge, Mass. 02139.) (*LRF* 54, 162, 185, 197, 198, 203, 208, 209, 212, 214, 217, 220, 234, 235, 240, 328, 330, 373, 374, 409, 411, 413, 414)

	M	F	E*
* Armstrong, J. Scott, "Long Range Forecasting for International Markets: The Use of Causal Models," in Robert L. King (Ed.), *Marketing and the New Science of Planning*. Chicago: American Marketing Association, 1968b, 222–227.	Ec Ex	Int	Ym

Other than data and details, this paper contains little that is not contained in *LRF*. (*LRF* 199, 235, 291, 292, 344)

	M	F	E*
*** Armstrong, J. Scott, "An Application of Econometric Models to International Marketing," *Journal of Marketing Research*, 7 (1970a), 190–198. (*LRF* 234, 236)	Ec	Int	Ym
** Armstrong, J. Scott, "How to Avoid Exploratory Research," *Journal of Advertising Research*, 10 (August 1970b), 27–30. (*LRF* 54, 352)	Ec	NR	Y
* Armstrong, J. Scott, "Tom Swift and His Electric Regression Analysis Machine: 1973," *Psychological Reports*, 36 (1975a), 806. (*LRF* 56, 341, 591)	Ec	Edu	Y
* Armstrong, J. Scott, "Monetary Incentives in Mail Surveys," *Public Opinion Quarterly*, 39 (Spring 1975b), 111–116.	Ju	NR	Ym

Analyzes the literature on effects of monetary incentives, and predicts reduction of nonresponse in mail surveys as a function of monetary incentives. (*LRF* 114, 181, 495)

	M	F	E*
** Armstrong, J. Scott, "Social irresponsibility in Management." *Journal of Business Research*, 5 (1977), 185–213. (*LRF* 129)	Ju	NR	Ym
** Armstrong, J. Scott, "Forecasting with Econometric Methods: Folklore vs. Fact," *Journal of Business*, 51 (1978), 549–564 with (discussion by six well-known econometricians on pp. 565–593 and my reply on pp. 595–600). (*LRF* 433)	Ec	Eco	Ym
** Armstrong, J. Scott, and Andress, James G., "Exploratory Analysis	Sg	Mkt	Ym

	M	F	E*

of Marketing Data: Trees vs. Regression." *Journal of Marketing Research,* **7** (1970), 487–492.

A critique of this paper can be found in Douglas C. Crocker, "Comments on Exploratory Analysis of Marketing Data: Trees vs. Regression." My reply was entitled "Exploratory Analysis of Marketing Data: A Reply." Both are in the *Journal of Marketing Research,* **8** (1971), 509–513 (*LRF* 413, 417)

** Armstrong, J. Scott, Denniston, W.B., and Gordon, M. M., "The Use of the Decomposition Principle in Making Judgments," *Organizational Bahavior and Human Performance.* **14** (1975), 257–263.   Ju   NR   Ym

Answer to postcard contest erroneously given in billions rather than in millions. (*LRF* 58, 181)

* Armstrong, J. Scott, and Farley, John U., "A Note on the Use of Markov Chains," *Management Science,* **16** (1969), B281–B285.   Ex   Mkt   Ym

The authors' names were omitted . That was a serious mistake! (*LRF* 159)

*** Armstrong, J. Scott, and Grohman, Michael C., "A Comparative Study of Methods for Long-Range Market Forecasting," *Management Science,* **19** (1972), 211–221. (*LRF* 326, 343, 394, 397, 401, 405, 409, 455)   Ec Ex Ju   Trn   Ym

* Armstrong, J. Scott, and Overton, Terry S., "Brief vs. Comprehensive Descriptions in Measuring Intentions to Purchase," *Journal of Marketing Research,* **8** (1971), 114–117. (*LRF* 101, 114, 370)   Ju   Trn   Ym

* Armstrong, J. Scott, and Overton, Terry S., "Estimating Nonresponse Bias in Mail Surveys," *Journal of Marketing Research,* **14** (1977), 396–402.   Ju   NR   Ym

Uses judgment and extrapolation to predict how nonrespondents would respond. (*LRF* 95, 114, 340)

* Armstrong, J. Scott, and Shapiro, Alan C., "Analyzing Quantitative Models," *Journal of Marketing,* **38** (April 1974), 61–66 (*LRF* 305, 307, 309, 311, 312, 314, 315, 316)   T   NR   N

** Armstrong, J. Scott, and Soelberg, Peer, "On the Interpretation of Factor Analysis," *Psychological Bulletin,* **70** (1968), 361–364.   Sg   NR   Y

Shows how "important factors" could be identified from random data if no attempt were made to assess reliability. Then surveys empirical papers on factor analysis and finds that about two-thirds made no attempt to assess the reliability of the factors. Tobias and Carlson (1969) provide a useful critique. (*LRF* 000)

** Asch, S.E., "Effects of Group Pressure upon the Modification and Distortion of Judgments," in Harold Proshansky and Bernard Seidenberg (Eds.), *Basic Studies in Social Psychology,* New York: Holt, Rinehart and Winston, 1965. (*LRF* 110, 544)   Ju   Psy   Y

** Ash, J.C.K., and Smyth, D.J., *Forecasting the United Kingdom Economy.* Farnborough, England: Saxon House, 1973.   Ec Ex   Eco   Y

This book examines short range forecasts by the National

	M	F	E*

Institute, London Business School, and other organizations. (*LRF* 161, 167, 409)

** Ayres, Robert U., *Technological Forecasting and Long-Range Planning*. New York: McGraw-Hill, 1969.   NR Tec N
Well-written, short, and interesting. (*LRF* 166)

* **B**ailey, Robert, *Radicals in Urban Politics: The Alinsky Approach.* Chicago: University of Chicago Press, 1974. (*LRF* 38)   I Pol N

*** Bakan, David, "The Test of Significance in Psychological Research," *Psychological Bulletin,* **66** (1966), 423–437.   T Psy N
An interesting article on the value of tests of statistical significance. Moderately difficult reading, but worth the effort. Bakan's article was followed by R. LaForge, "Confidence Intervals or Tests of Significance in Scientific Research?" and D.B. Peizer, "A Note on Directional Interference." Both appeared in *Psychological Bulletin,* **68** (1967), 466–468. (*LRF* 356)

— Baker, Henry G., "Sales and Marketing Planning of the Edsel," in *Marketing's Role in Scientific Management,* Chicago American Marketing Assoc., June 1957, 128–144.   NR Mkt N
This was written shortly before the Edsel was introduced. The benefits of marketing research were praised, and a description was provided of the marketing research used in the decision to introduce the Edsel. (*LRF* 144)

— Baker, J. Stannard, "A Framework for Assessment of Causes of Automobile Accidents," in P. Lazarsfeld and M. Rosenberg (Eds.), *The Language of Social Research,* Glencoe, Ill.: Free Press, 1955. (*LRF* 74)   NR NR N

* Bakwin, H., "Pseudodoxia Pediatrica," *New England Journal of Medicine,* **232** (1945), 691–697. (*LRF* 60)   Ju Med Y

** Bandeen, R.A., "Automobile Consumption, 1940, 1950," *Econometrica,* **25** (1957), 239–248.   Ec Eco Y
Uses longitudinal data covering changes in auto sales by state in the United States. (*LRF* 209)

* Barber, Bernard, "Resistance by Scientists to Scientific Discovery," *Science* **134** (1961), 596–602. (*LRF* 433)   NR Sci N

** Barclay, William D., "A Probability Model for Early Prediction of New Product Success," *Journal of Marketing,* **27** (January 1963), 63–68.   Ex Mkt Ym
Describes a simple application of Markov chains. (*LRF* 160)

* Barnard, C.A., "New Methods of Quality Control," *Journal of the Royal Statistical Society,* Series A, **126** (1963), 255–258.   Ex Trn Y
The labels in Table 1 conflict with the text. The error is in the text, I believe. (*LRF* 184, 520)

* Barrett, James P., "The Coefficient of Determination—Some Limitations," *American Statistician,* **28** (February 1974), 19–20. (*LRF* 350)   NR NR N

		M	F	E*

** Bass, Bernard M., and Leavitt, Harold J., "Experiments in Planning   NR   Psy   Y
and Operating," *Management Science,* 9 (1963), 574–585.

Reports on three laboratory experiments which showed a positive relationship between participation in planning, on the one hand, and morale and productivity, on the other. (*LRF* 36)

* Bassie, V. Lewis, "A Note on Scientific Method in Forecasting," in   Ec   Eco   N
Bert G. Hickman (Ed.), *Econometric Models of Cyclical Behavior,* Vol. 2. *Studies in Income and Wealth No. 36,* New York: Columbia University Press, 1972, pp. 1211–1218. (*LRF* 433)

*** Bates, J.M., and Granger, C.W.J., "The Combination of Forecasts,"   Ex   Eco   Ym
Operational Research Quarterly, 20 (1969), 451–468.

The authors compared and found small differences in accuracy among various extrapolation methods, but combinations were superior when based on methods that used different information. Extends work from Barnard (1963). (*LRF* 183, 186)

**** Batson, C. Daniel, "Rational Processing or Rationalization? The   Ju   Psy   Y
Effect of Disconfirming Information on a Stated Religious Belief," *Journal of Personality and Social Psychology,* 32 (1975), 176–184. (*LRF* 24, 383)

**** Bell, Daniel, "The Myth of Crime Waves," in Daniel Bell (ed.) *The*   NR   NR   N
End of Ideology. Glencoe, Ill.: Free Press, 1962. (*LRF* 60)

**** Bennett, Edith, "Discussion, Decision, Commitment, and Consen-   I   Psy   Ym
sus in 'Group Decision,'" *Human Relations,* 8 (1955), 251–273.

The process of decision making and the degree of group consensus were more important than reaching a decision or public commitment. (*LRF* 35, 111)

** Bennion, E.G., "The Cowles Commission's Simultaneous Equations   Ec   Eco   N
Approach: A Simplified Explanation," *Review of Economics and Statistics,* 34 (1952), 49–56.

A good explanation of the simultaneous equations approach. Shows why the best "historical fit" does not necessarily provide the best forecast. (*LRF* 129)

** Berry, William L., and Bliemel, F.W., "Selecting Exponential   Ex   NR   Y
Smoothing Constants: An Application of Pattern Search," in *Proceedings of the American Institute for Decision Sciences,* 1972, pp. 503–510. (*LRF* 165)

*** Berscheid, Ellen, et al., "Anticipating Informed Consent," *Ameri-*   Ju   Psy   Ym
can Psychologist, 7 (1973), 913–925.

Presents descriptions of six previously published experiments (including Milgram's obedience study) to subjects and asks them to "imagine that you are that typical subject . . . answer these questions as if you had just participated in the experiments." Finds that people were less willing to participate in studies if there were no debriefing and if they might look bad in the experiment. (*LRF* 127)

** Best, Roger J., "An Experiment in Delphi Estimation in Marketing   Ju   Mkt   Ym

	M	F	E*

Decision Making," *Journal of Marketing Research*, **11** (1974), 448–452. (*LRF* 119)

**** Bezdek, Roger H., *Empirical Tests of Input-Output Forecasts: Review and Critique*, U.S. Department of Commerce, Bureau of Economic Analysis, Staff Paper No. 24, July 1974.
     Sg   Eco   Ym

This review of the empirical evidence on the use of input-output for *ex ante* forecasts covers 16 studies from seven nations from 1951 to 1972. (*LRF* 265)

** Binder, Arnold, "Statistical Theory," *Annual Review of Psychology*, **15** (1964), 277–310.
     NR   Psy   N

Discusses multiple comparisons and other topics. (*LRF* 329)

* Bird, M., and Ehrenberg, A.S.C., "Intentions-to-Buy and Claimed Brand Usage," *Operational Research Quarterly*, **17** (1966), 27–46. (*LRF* 81)
     Ju   Mkt   Y

*** Blalock, Hubert M., Jr., "Correlated Independent Variables: The Problem of Multicollinearity," *Social Forces*, **42** (1963), 233–237. (*LRF* 222)
     Ec   Soc   Y

**** Blalock, Hubert M., Jr., *Causal Inferences in Nonexperimental Research*. Chapel Hill: University of North Carolina Press, 1964.
     NR   NR   NR

If you have struggled with the analysis of data, you will love this! Discusses how to use and interpret data. (*LRF* 75, 205)

** Blalock, Hubert M., Jr., *Social Statistics*, New York: McGraw-Hill, 1979. (*LRF* 220, 356)
     NR   NR   NR

** Bliemel, Friedhelm, W., "Theil's Forecast Accuracy Coefficient: A Clarification," *Journal of Marketing Research*, **10** (1973), 444–446. (*LRF* 349)
     T   NR   N

*** Blumberg, Paul, *Industrial Democracy: The Sociology of Participation*, New York: Schocken Books, 1968 (Revised 1978).
     I   Pro   Ym

Dennis W. Organ reviewed this book in June 1974 (*Business Horizons*, p. 93–94), calling it the "best documented and most eloquent case on record for democratization of the economic enterprise." It reviews the Hawthorne studies: There is no "Hawthorne effect." The results are explained by the desire to participate in things affecting one's life. (*LRF* 35)

* Blumen, Isadore, Kogan, M., and McCarthy, P.J., *The Industrial Mobility of Labor as a Probability Process*. New York State School of Industrial and Labor Relations, Cornell University, Ithaca, N.Y., 1955.
     Ex   Per   Y

Describes an early industrial application of Markov chains. No validation was attempted. (*LRF* 157)

** Borke, Helene, and Fiske, D.W., "Factors Influencing the Prediction of Behavior from a Diagnostic Interview," *Journal of Consulting Psychology*, **21** (1957), 78–80.
     Ju   Psy   Y

Clinicians were able to make as accurate predictions about neurotic patients after reading a transcript of an interview as they could after a face-to-face interview. (*LRF* 100)

** Bowman, Edward H., "Consistency and Optimality in Managerial
     Bo   Pro   Ym

Decision Making," *Management Science*, 9 (1963), 310–321. (*LRF* 279, 556)

* Box, George E., and Jenkins, G.M., *Time Series Analysis Fore-*   Ex   NR   N
  casting and Control. San Francisco: Holden Day, 1970.
  This book is not my style. I would guess, however, that it is
  the most frequently cited book on forecasting. Its impact has
  been immense. Perhaps where there is smoke there is fire?
  (*LRF* 78, 174)

** Boyd, Harper, and Westfall, Ralph, "Interviewer Bias Once More   Ju   NR   Y
  Revisited," *Journal of Marketing Research*, 7 (1970) 249–253.
  (*LRF* 114, 205)

** Boyd, Harper, and Westfall, Ralph, *Marketing Research*. Home-   NR   NR   NR
  wood, Ill.: Irwin, 1981.
  The discussion on methods of collecting data is especially
  strong. (*LRF* 113, 205)

* Bridgman, Percy W., *The Logic of Modern Physics*, New York: T   Sci   N
  Macmillan, 1927. (*LRF* 65)

* Brooks, John Nixon, *Business Adventures*. New York: Weybright   NR   Mkt   N
  and Talley, 1969.
  A fascinating book, but out of print. (*LRF* 94, 551)

* Brown, L.O., "Quantitative Market Analysis: Multiple Correlation,   Ec   Mkt   Y
  Accuracy of the Methods," *Harvard Business Review*, 16 (1937a),
  62–73. (*LRF* 235)

* Brown, L. O., "Quantitative Market Analysis: Scope and Uses,"   Ec   Mkt   Y
  Harvard Business Review, 15 (1937b), 233–244. (*LRF* 235)

*** Brown, Rex V., "Just How Credible Are Your Market Estimates?,"   Ju   Mkt   N
  Journal of Marketing, 33 (July 1969) 46–50.
  Good description and reasonable argument, but no validation
  of the procedure. (*LRF* 144)

*** Brown, Robert G., "Less Risk in Inventory Estimates," *Harvard*   Ex   Pro   N
  Business Review, 37 (July–August 1959a), 104–116.

  I thought this was a good description of exponential smoothing, but the reaction from many of my students was that the
  account is incomplete. (*LRF* 166, 170, 171).

**** Brown, Robert G., *Statistical Forecasting for Inventory Control*. New   Ex   Pro   NR
  York: McGraw-Hill, 1959b. (*LRF* 78, 161, 166, 170, 171)

** Brown, Robert G., *Smoothing, Forecasting and Prediction of Dis-*   Ex   Pro   NR
  crete Time Series. Englewood Cliffs, N.J.: Prentice-Hall, 1963.
  Details on Brown's earlier works. (*LRF* 180, 347, 450)

* Brown, T. Merritt, *Specification and Uses of Econometric Models*.   Ec   Eco   N
  New York: St. Martin's Press, 1970. (*LRF* 403)

** Bruner, J.S., and Potter, M.C., "Interference in Visual Recognition,"   Ju   Psy   Y
  Science, 144 (1964), 424–425.

  Once an uncertain situation has been perceived in a certain
  way, it is difficult to view it in any other way. (*LRF* 378)

* Brunswick, Egon, "Representative Design and Probabilistic Theory   Ju   Psy   N
  in a Functional Psychology," *Psychological Review*, 62 (1955),
  193–217.

	M	F	E*

Included only to give proper credit, this paper has a high fog index. (*LRF* 381)

* **Brush, Stephen G., "The Prayer Test,"** *American Scientist,* **62 (1974), 561–563.**   I   NR   N

Francis Galton studied the value of prayer. He found, for example, that kings and queens, who are the objects of their subjects' prayers, die earlier than lawyers, gentry, and military officers; members of the clergy, presumably a prayerful class of men, live no longer than lawyers and physicians; the proportion of stillbirths suffered by praying and nonpraying parents appeared to be identical; and so on. People did not appreciate Galton's work in this area, and it does not appear that the study has changed many attitudes since its completion in the 1870s. (*LRF* 264, 436)

** **Buffa, Elwood S., and Taubert, William H.,** *Production-Inventory*   Bo   Pro   Ym
Systems: Planning and Control. **Homewood, Ill.: Irwin, 1972.**
Contains a brief description of J.R.M. Gordon's work on bootstrapping on pp. 133–146. (*LRF* 280)

* **Buffa, Frank P., "The Application of a Dynamic Forecasting Model**   Ex   Pro   Y
with Inventory Control Properties," *Decision Sciences,* **6 (1975), 298–306.**
Compares a simple exponential smoothing model to an exponential smoothing model with trend, seasonality, and an adaptive rule for alpha. The latter model provided better one-month-ahead *ex ante* forecasts, but the three changes were confounded. (*LRF* 388)

** **Burch, S.W., and Stekler, H.O., "The Forecasting Accuracy of Con-**   Ju   Eco   Y
sumer Attitude Data," *Journal of the American Statistical Association,* **64 (1969), 1225–1233. (LRF 408)**

* **Burdick, Eugene,** *The 480.* **New York: McGraw-Hill, 1964.**   NR   NR   NR
A novel. (*LRF* 76, 250)

* **Burgess, Ernest W.,** *Predicting Success or Failure in Marriage.* **New**   Ec   Soc   Y
York: Prentice-Hall, 1939. (LRF 218)

** **Burk, Marguerite C.,** *Consumption Economics: A Multidisciplinary*   Ec   Eco   Y
Approach. **New York: Wiley, 1968.**
Econometric studies of food consumption. You might say it offers a lot of thought for food. (*LRF* 202)

* **Burns, Arthur F., and Mitchell, Wesley C.,** *Measuring Business*   Ec   Eco   Y
Cycles. **New York: National Bureau of Economic Research, 1946. (LRF 53, 548)**
The popularity of their approach has lasted over the years.

* **Busch, G.A., "Prudent-Manager Forecasting,"** *Harvard Business*   Ju   Mkt   N
Review, **39 (May–June, 1961), 57–64. (LRF 126)**

* **Cairncross, Alec, "Economic Forecasting,"** *Economic Journal,* **79**   Ec   Eco   N
(1969), 797–812. (LRF 152)

*** **Campbell, Donald T., and Fiske, D.W., "Convergent and Discrim-**   T   Psy   N
inant Validation of the Multitrait-Multimethod Matrix," *Psychological Bulletin,* **56 (1959), 81–105.**

This article is widely cited and has led to much follow-up research. (*LRF* 65)

** Campbell, John P., "Individual versus Group Problem Solving in   Ju   Psy   Ym
an Industrial Sample," *Journal of Applied Psychology*, **52** (1968),
205–210. (*LRF* 124)

** Cannell, Charles, and Fowler, Floyd, "Comparison of a Self-Enu-   Ju   Med   Ym
merative Procedure and a Personal Interview," *Public Opinion
Quarterly*, **27** (1963), 250–264.

Self-report was better for items where it was helpful for respondent to consult records in this survey on hospitalization. (*LRF* 116)

* Cantril, Hadley, "The Prediction of Social Events," *Journal of Ab-*   Ju   Soc   Y
normal and Social Psychology, **33** (1938), 364–389. (*LRF* 88)

** Carlson, John A., "Forecasting Errors and Business Cycles," *Amer-*   Ju   Eco   N
ican Economic Review, **58** (1967), 462–481. (*LRF* 90)

** Carroll, John S., and Siegler, Robert S., "Strategies for the Use of   Ju   NR   Ym
Base-rate Information," *Organizational Behavior and Human Per-
formance*, **19** (1977), 392–402.

People make greater use of base rate information when there are small samples, exhaustive sampling of the population, and a population percentage that corresponds to a whole number in the sample. (*LRF* 98)

* Carter, Phillip L., and Hamner, W.C., "Consistency and Bias in   Bo   Pro   Ym
Organizational Decision Making." Working paper obtained from
Carter at the Graduate School of Business Administration, Michigan State University, East Lansing Mich. 48823, approximately
1972.

Uses same experiment as Moskowitz and Miller (1972). (*LRF* 282)

* Carter, Reginald K., "Client's Resistance to Negative Findings and   I   NR   N
the Latent Conservative Function of Evaluation Studies," *American
Sociologist*, **6** (May 1971), 118–124.

Contains a good suggestion on fees for consultants who want to bring about change: the larger the number and the greater the importance of the recommendations implemented by the organization, the lower the consulting fee. (*LRF* 35)

*** Cartter, Allan M., "The Supply and Demand of College Teachers,"   Ec   Edu   Y
*Proceedings of the American Statistical Association: Social Statis-
tics Section*, 1965, 70–80. (*LRF* 203, 395, 397, 402)

* Cartter, Allan M., *Ph.D.s and the Academic Labor Market.* New   Ec   Edu   Y
York: McGraw-Hill, 1976.

Predicted enrollment and hiring levels for 15 years. The early 1980s were expected to be a bad time for Ph.D.s—big supply and small demand. (*LRF* 202)

* Carver, Ronald P., "Speed Readers Don't Read, They Skim," *Psy-*   NR   NR   NR
chology Today, **6** (August 1972), 22 seq–30.

Carver's paper is concerned about fallacious methods in the assessment of speed reading. In particular, the assessment of comprehension does not distinguish between what the person knew about the subject before reading and what the person knew after reading. Carver's article made some people mad. Richard G. Graf did a follow-up: "Speed Reading: Remember the Tortoise," *Psychology Today*, **7** (December 1973), 112–113. His results supported Carver's. In Graf, the original speed of the speed reader trainees was much lower than that of the control group. (*LRF* 336)

* Cotron, Marvin J., and Ralph, Christine A., *Industrial Applications*   NR   Tec   NR
of Technological Forecasting. New York: Wiley-Interscience, 1971, Revised edition published by Robert E. Krieger, 1983, Naples, Florida.

Good quotations. Describes some of the "go words" used by technological forecasters. Disappointing collection of papers; a review by Tony Flowerdew in the *Operational Research Quarterly*, **24** (1973), 331, said that most of this book comes under the heading "Technological Research Allocation System Hassle," or its acronym. (*LRF* 322, 366)

**** Chamberlin, T.C., "The Method of Multiple Working Hypotheses,"   NR   Sci   N
Science, **148** (1965), 754–759.

This article was first published in *Science* in 1890, was reprinted in 1897, 1931, 1944, and 1965, and is still relevant in 1978. See also Platt (1964). (*LRF* 437)

* Chambers, John C., Mullick, S., and Smith, D.D., *An Executive's*   NR   NR   N
Guide to Forecasting. New York: Wiley, 1974.

This book is based on a highly cited *Harvard Business Review* article. The conclusions were not based on empirical findings. I think that some of the conclusions are wrong. (*LRF* 72)

* Chan, Hung, and Hayya, Jack, "Spectral Analysis in Business   Ex   Mkt   N
Forecasting," *Decision Sciences*, **7** (1976), 137–151. (*LRF* 180)

*** Chapman, Loren J., and Chapman, J.P., "The Genesis of Popular   Ju   Psy   Ym
but Erroneous Psychodiagnostic Observations," *Journal of Abnormal Psychology*, **72** (1967), 193–204.

Uses the "draw-a-person" test. (*LRF* 372, 378, 380)

*** Chapman, Loren J., and Chapman, J.P., "Illusory Correlation as   Ju   Psy   Ym
an Obstacle to the Use of Valid Psychodiagnostic Signs," *Journal of Abnormal Psychology*, **74** (1969), 271–280.

People see what they expect to see, and this interferes with perceiving real relationships. Makes one question the value of experience. (*LRF* 52, 378)

* Chatfield, C., and Prothero, D.L., "Box-Jenkins Seasonal Fore-   Ex   Eco   Y
casting Problems in a Case Study," *Journal of the Royal Statistical Society: Series A*, **136** (1973), 295–352.

The 58 pages include discussions by other people at a conference, as well as a reply by Box and Jenkins and then a reply to the Box-Jenkins' reply. The paper does not examine alternative methods, but looks only at Box-Jenkins. The papers demonstrate so much confusion that it makes one thing per-

fectly clear: Box-Jenkins is not easy even for *experts* in Box-
Jenkins methodology. (*LRF* 174, 175, 176, 494)

*   Chein, Isidor, "The Logic of Prediction: Some Observations on Dr.   Ec   Psy   N
Sarbin's Exposition," *Psychological Review*, **52** (1945), 175–179.
An emotional outburst against the use of objective methods.
(*LRF* 434)

** Chisholm, Roger K., and Whitaker, Gilbert R., Jr., *Forecasting*   NR   NR   N
Methods, Homewood, Ill.: Irwin, 1971.
More concerned with measurement than with forecasting. (*LRF*
72)

** Chow, Wen M., "Adaptive Control of the Exponential Smoothing   Ex   Pro   Ym
Constant," *Journal of Industrial Engineering*, **16** (1965), 314–317.
See GARDNER [1983b] for an unsuccessful attempt to rep-
licate these results. (*LRF* 171, 494, 609)

** Christ, Carl F., "A Test of an Econometric Model for the United   Ec   Eco   Ym
States, 1921–1947," in *National Bureau for Economic Research*,
Conference on Business Cycles, New York, 1951, pp. 35–107 with
discussion on pp. 107–129. See also Christ (1956). (*LRF* 388, 407,
433)

** Christ, Carl F., "Aggregate Econometric Models," *American Eco-*   Ec   Eco   Ym
nomic Review, **46** (1956), 385–408.
An extension of Christ (1951). (*LRF* 526)

** Christ, Carl F., "Simultaneous Equation Estimation: Any Verdict   Ec   Eco   Y
Yet?" *Econometrica*, **28** (1960), 835–845. (*LRF* 200)

** Christ, Carl F., "Judging the Performance of Econometric Models   Ec   Eco   Ym
of the U.S. Economy," *International Economic Review*, **16** (1975),   Ex
54–74.   Ju
Reviews forecasting performance for 1970–1973, using models
developed with 1953–1970 data. Examines both *ex ante* and
ex post forecasts. Subjectively adjusted forecasts improved accuracy for *ex ante* forecasts but made things worse for *ex post*
forecasts. (*LRF* 397, 409)

*** Christal, R.E., "Selecting a Harem—and Other Applications of the   Bo   Per   Y
Policy-capturing Model," *Journal of Experimental Education*, **36**
(Summer 1968), 35–41.
Claims that this approach has been used successfully in rep-
resenting a number of different types of personnel decisions
(promotions, job ratings, and grading of jobs). (*LRF* 284)

** Clarkson, Geoffrey, P.E., *Portfolio Selection*. Englewood Cliffs, N.J.: Bo   Fin   Ym
Prentice-Hall, 1962 (*LRF* 277)

**** Claudy, John G., "A Comparison of Five Variable Weighting Pro-   Ec   Psy   Ym
cedures," *Educational and Psychological Measurement*, **32** (1972),
311–322.
Claudy did studies on simulated data with sample sizes of 20,
40, 80, and 160. He used unit weights, regression coefficients,
and three other weighting schemes. (*LRF* 230)

		M	F	E*

** Clawson, J.S., "How Useful Are 90-Day Purchase Probabilities?," *Journal of Marketing,* **35** (October 1971), 43–47. (*LRF* 82) — Ju Mkt Y

** Claycamp, Henry J., and Liddy, L.E., "Prediction of New Product Performance: An Analytical Approach," *Journal of Marketing Research,* **6** (1969), 414–420. — Eo Mkt Y

No alternative model for comparison, and thus no demonstration that the authors' model led to better forecasts. (*LRF* 154)

** Coch, Lester, and French, John R.P., Jr., "Overcoming Resistance to Change," *Human Relations,* **1** (1948), 512–532. — I Pro Ym

One of the earliest and best known of the participation studies. (*LRF* 35)

** Cohen, J., and Cohen, P., *Applied Multiple Regression/Correlation for the Behavioral Sciences.* New York: Wiley, 1975. — Ec NR NR

The authors discuss many practical issues (e.g., what to do about missing data). (*LRF* 220)

** Cole, Rosanne, "Data Errors and Forecasting Accuracy," in Jacob Mincer (Ed.), *Economic Forecasts and Expectations Analyses of Forecasting Behavior and Performance,* New York: National Bureau of Economic Research, 1969. (Distributed by Columbia University Press.) (*LRF* 61) — Ec Eco Y

** Colombotos, John, "Personal vs. Telephone Interviews: Effect on Responses," *Public Health Reports,* **84** (September 1969), 773–782. — Ju Soc Ym

The author found no differences between personal and telephone interviews on physicians' responses to political, professional, and personal items. (*LRF* 115)

** Cook, Richard L., and Stewart, Thomas R., "A Comparison of Seven Methods for Obtaining Subjective Descriptions of Judgmental Policy," *Organizational Behavior and Human Performance,* **13** (1975), 31–45. Replicated successfully by SCHMITT [1978]. (*LRF* 278, 641) — Bo NR Ym

** Cook, S.W., and Selltiz, C., "A Multiple-Indicator Approach to Attitude Measurement," *Psychological Bulletin,* **62** (1964), 36–55. (*LRF* 65, 212) — NR Psy NR

* Cooke, Jane K., "Clinicians' Decisions as a Basis for Deriving Actuarial Formulae," *Journal of Clinical Psychology,* **23** (1967), 232–233. — Ju Psy Y

Discussion is so brief that it is hard to understand. In any event, she concluded that a combined forecast for distinguishing between psychiatric and nonpsychiatric people was consistently superior to any single judge. (*LRF* 137)

* Cooke, W. Ernest, "Forecasts and Verifications in Western Australia," *Monthly Weather Review,* January 1906. — Ju Wea Y

I used the description of this study in Raiffa (1969). (*LRF* 141)

*** Cooper, J. Phillip, and Nelson, Charles R., "The ex ante Prediction Performance of the St. Louis and FRB-MIT-PENN Econometric Models — Ec Eco Ym
Ex

and Some Results on Composite Predictors," *Journal of Money, Credit, and Banking,* **7** (1975), 1–32.

The authors used Box-Jenkins as a benchmark for accuracy in this study of one-quarter-ahead forecasts of macroeconomic variables. (*LRF* 408)

***   Cooper, Ronald L., "The Predictive Performance of Quarterly Econ-   Ec   Eco   Ym
ometric Models of the United States," in Bert G. Hickman (Ed.),   Ex   ●
*Econometric Models of Cyclical Behavior, Vol. 2. Studies in Income
and Wealth, No. 36.* New York: Columbia University Press, 1972,
pp. 813–926, with discussion on pp. 926–947.

Long and detailed. Much work went into this study that compared an extrapolation model with seven different quarterly
econometric models. The extrapolation was based on a regression against the dependent variable for up to eight preceding
quarters. Data from 1949 through 1960 were used for model
development, and forecasts were made for quarters from 1961
through 1965. Of the eight forecasting models, the extrapolation model was most accurate for 18 of the 33 variables
being forecast. The discussants criticized this study, but clearly
the econometric models were not superior here. (*LRF* 408,
433, 435)

**   Copeland, Ronald M., and Marioni, R.J., "Executives' Forecasts of   Ex   Fin   Ym
Earnings per Share versus Forecasts of Naive Models," *Journal of*   Ju
Business, **45** (1972), 497–512. (*LRF* 87, 396)

*   Cornfield, J., "Statistical Relationships and Proof in Medicine,"   T   Med   N
American Statistician, **8** (December 1954), 19–21.

Discussion on the smoking-cancer controversy. Good reading
for those who feel that "proof" of causation always depends
on direct experimentation (also good reading for those who
think that the smoking-cancer issue is still undecided). It was
decided long ago. (*LRF* 210)

*   Cowan, Donald R.G., "Sales Analysis from the Management   Ec   Mkt   Y
Standpoint," *Journal of Business,* **9** (1936), 52 seq. and **10** (1937),
14 seq. (*LRF* 235)

*   Cowden, Dudley, J., "The Perils of Polynomials," *Management*   Ex   NR   N
Science, **9** (1963), 542–550.

Theoretical argument showing how the expected error increases with increased complexity in the model, with small
samples, and with longer forecast horizons. (*LRF* 180)

***   Cowles, Alfred, "Can Stock Market Forecasters Forecast?" *Econo-*   Ju   Fin   Ym
metrica, **1** (1933), 309–324.

The answer was "no," and this answer has been reinforced in
numerous studies since 1933 such as Jensen (1968). (*LRF* 94)

**** Cowles, Alfred, "Stock Market Forecasting," *Econometrica,* **12** (1944),   Ju   Fin   Ym
206–214.

Follow-up to Cowles (1933). (*LRF* 94)

		M	F	E*

** Cox, Garfield V., *An Appraisal of American Business Forecasts*, — Ju Fin Ym
Chicago: University of Chicago Press, 1930.
Examines the ability of 11 different services in forecasting
national business conditions. (*LRF* 94)

*** Cragg, John G., and Malkiel, Burton G., "The Consensus and — Ec Fin Ym
Accuracy of Some Predictions of the Growth of Corporate Earn- — Ex
ings," *Journal of Finance*, **23** (March 1968), 67–84. (*LRF* 167, — Ju
395, 396, 397, 401)

* Cragg, John G., and Malkiel, Burton G., "Expectations and the — Ec Fin Ym
Structure of Share Prices," *American Economic Review*, **60** (1970),
601–617.
Unsuccessful attempt to replicate Whitbeck and Kisor (1963).
(*LRF* 167, 573)

* Crane, D.B., and Crotty, J.R., "A Two Stage Forecasting Model: — Ec Pro Y
Exponential Smoothing and Multiple Regression," *Management* — Ex
Science, **13** (1967), B501–B507.
I found this difficult to understand. (*LRF* 409)

** Cronbach, Lee J., and Meehl, Paul E., "Construct Validity in Psy- — T Psy N
chological Tests," *Psychological Bulletin*, **52** (1955), 281–302.
This article is widely cited.(*LRF* 65)

** Crow, Wayman J., "The Effect of Training upon Interpersonal Per- — Ju Psy Y
ception," *Journal of Abnormal and Social Psychology*, **55** (1957),
355–359.
A training program increased the confidence and *reduced* the
accuracy of judges. (*LRF* 383)

** Crow, Wayman J., and Noel, Robert C., "The Valid Use of Simu- — Ju Pol Ym
lation Results," Mimeo, Western Behavioral Sciences Institute, 1150
Silverdado Street, La Jolla, Calif. 92037 (June 1965). (*LRF* 128)

** Curtis, Ervin W., and Alf, Edward F., "Validity, Predictive Efficiency, — T Per N
and Practical Significance of Selection Tests," *Journal of Applied*
Psychology, **53** (1969), 327–337. (*LRF* 352)

*** Curtis, R.F., and Jackson, E.F., "Multiple Indicators in Survey Re- — Ju Soc N
search," *American Journal of Sociology*, **68** (1962), 195–204. (*LRF*
65, 327)

* Cyert, Richard M., Davidson, H.J., and Thompson, G.L., "Estima- — Ex Fin Y
tion of the Allowance for Doubtful Accounts by Markov Chains,"
Management Science, **8** (1962), 287–303.
Good illustration but no evidence. (*LRF* 158, 275)

* Cyert, Richard M., and March, James G., *A Behavioral Theory of* — NR NR NR
the Firm, Englewood Cliffs, N.J.: Prentice-Hall, 1963. (*LRF* 275)

** Cyert, Richard M., March, James G., and Starbuck, W.H., "Two — Ju Mkt Y
Experiments on Bias and Conflict in Organizational Estimation," — Pro
Management Science, **7** (1961), 254–264. (*LRF* 126)

** Dalkey, Norman C., "Delphi," in Joseph P. Martino and Thomas — Ju NR Ym
Oberbeck (Eds.), *Long-Range Forecasting Methodology: 1967*,
Washington, D.C.: U.S. Government Printing Office. (*LRF* 123)

		M	F	E*
***	Dalkey, Norman C., "Analyses from a Group Opinion Study," *Futures*, 1 (1969), 541–551. (*LRF* 118, 605)	Ju	NR	Ym
**	Dalkey, Norman C., Brown, B., and Cochran, S., "Use of Self-Ratings to Improve Group Estimates," *Technological Forecasting*, 1 (1970), 283–291. (*LRF* 140)	Ju	NR	Ym
**	Dalrymple, Douglas J., and Haines, George H., Jr., "A Study of the Predictive Ability of Market Period Demand-Supply Relations for a Firm Selling Fashion Products," *Applied Economics*, 1 (1970), 277–285.	Ec	Mkt	Y

A comparative study of methods for short-range forecasts of women's sportswear. No advantage found for log-log model over linear model. (*LRF* 409)

| * | Daly, Rex F., "Long-Run Economic Projections: A Review and Appraisal," *Agricultural Economics Research*, 15 (October 1963), 113–121. (*LRF* 183) | Ex | Eco | N |
| ** | Dancer, Robert, and Gray, Clifford, "An Empirical Evaluation of Constant and Adaptive Computer Forecasting Models for Inventory Control," *Decision Sciences*, 8 (1977), 228–238. | Ex | Mkt | Ym |

Short-range forecasts of 359 liquor products over a 28-month period. No advantage for adaptive models. (*LRF* 171, 494)

**	Daniel C., and Heerema, N., "Design of Experiments for the Most Precise Estimation of Linear Extrapolation," *Journal of the American Statistical Association*, 45 (1950), 546–556. (*LRF* 206)	Ec	NR	N
***	Darroch, R.K., and Steiner, I.D., "Role-Playing: An Alternative to Laboratory Research," *Journal of Personality*, 38 (1970), 302–311. (*LRF* 127)	Ju	Soc	Ym
*	Daub, Mervin, "On the Cost to the Firm of Aggregate Prediction Errors," *Journal of Business*, 47 (1974), 11–22.	NR	NR	Y

Complex analysis to determine the value of perfect forecasts. (*LRF* 388)

| * | Davies, S.W., and Scott, T.W.K., "Forecasting Industrial Production," *National Institute Economic Review*, No. 66 (November 1973), 54–68. | Ec Ex | Pro | Ym |

Short-range *ex post* forecasts with small sample sizes. A follow-up study is published in No. 69 (1974), 27–28 (*LRF* 170)

| **** | Dawes, Robyn M., "A Case Study of Graduate Admissions: Application of Three Principles of Human Decision Making," *American Psychologist*, 26 (1971), 180–188. | Bo Ju | Edu | Ym |

Good description of bootstrapping and a useful application that should be adopted by universities. I originally predicted that adoption would be slow. It has been. See DAWES [1979]. (*LRF* 281, 283, 638)

| **** | Dawes, Robyn M., and Corrigan, Bernard, "Linear Models in Decision Making," *Psychological Bulletin*, 81 (1974), 95–106. | Bo Ec | NR | Ym |

Interesting tidbit is the description of Ben Franklin's "moral or prudential algebra": List pros and cons in separate columns, apply weights subjectively, then sum the columns. Ben's method is still a good one. (*LRF* 217, 230, 283)

		M	F	E*
*	Dearborn, D.C., and Simon, H.A., "Selective Perception: A Note on the Departmental Identification of Executives," *Sociometry*, **21** (1958), 140–144. (*LRF* 72)	NR	NR	NR
*	De Grazia, Alfred, et al. (Eds.), *The Velikovsky Affair*. New York: University Books, 1966.	NR	Sci	N
	Fascinating description of the reactions to Immanuel Velikovsky. See especially the paper by Ralph E. Juergens. (*LRF* 67, 433)			
*	Denton, Frank T., and Kuiper, John, "The Effect of Measurement Errors on Parameter Estimates and Forecasts: A Case Study Based on the Canadian Preliminary National Accounts," *Review of Economics and Statistics*, **47** (1965), 198–206. (*LRF* 221)	Ec	Eco	Y
***	Denton, Frank T., and Oksanen, E.H., "A Multi-Country Analysis of the Effects of Data Revisions on an Economic Model," *Journal of the American Statistical Association*, **67** (1972), 286–291. (*LRF* 221)	Ec	Eco	Ym
*	Dewey, Edward R., and Dakin, Edwin F., *Cycles: The Science of Prediction*. New York: Holt, 1947. (*LRF* 179, 180)	Ex	Eco	Y
*	Domencich, Thomas A., and McFadden, Daniel, *Urban Travel Demand*. New York: American Elsevier, 1975. (*LRF* 202)	NR	Trn	Y
*	Doob, Anthony N., and Gross, A.E., "Status of Frustrator as an Inhibitor of Horn-Honking Responses," *Journal of Social Psychology*, **76** (1968), 213–218. (*LRF* 84)	Ju	Psy	Y
***	Dorn, Harold F., "Pitfalls in Population Forecasts and Projections," *Journal of the American Statistical Association*, **45** (1950), 311–334.	Ex	Dem	N
	Historical review of population forecasting. (*LRF* 88, 166, 182)			
***	Draper, Norman R., and Smith, H., *Applied Regression Analysis*. New York: Wiley, 1981.	Ec	NR	NR
	A good discussion of the practical problems one encounters when analyzing data, although the latest edition seems to be caught up in statistical sophistication. (*LRF* 220)			
***	Dudycha, Linda W., and Naylor, J.C., "Characteristics of the Human Inference Process in Complex Choice Behavior Situations," *Organizational Behavior and Human Performance*, **1** (1966), 110–128. (*LRF* 101, 102, 379)	Ju	NR	Y
**	Duncan, Otis Dudley, "Is the Intelligence of the General Population Declining?," *American Sociological Review*, **17** (1952), 401–407. (*LRF* 322)	NR	Soc	N
*	Duncan, Otis Dudley, "Social Forecasting—the State of the Art," *Public Interest*, **17** (Fall 1969), 88–118. (*LRF* 322)	Ex Sg	Dem Soc	N
**	Duncan-Jones, Paul, "Causation, Path-Analysis and the Old Sausage Machine," *Journal of the Market Research Society*, **12** (1970), 200–203. (*LRF* 75)	Ec	NR	N
*	Dunkelberg, William C., and Day, George S., "Nonresponse Bias and Callbacks in Sample Surveys," *Journal of Marketing Research*, **10** (1973), 160–168. (*LRF* 114)	Ju	Fin	Y
**	Dunnett, Charles W., "A Multiple Comparison Procedure for Com-	T	NR	NR

	M	F	E*

paring Several Treatments with a Control," *Journal of the American Statistical Association,* **50** (1955), 1096–1121. (*LRF* 465, 466)

** Dunnett, Charles W., "New Tables for Multiple Comparisons with a Control," *Biometrics,* **20** (1964), 482–491. (*LRF* 462, 463, 464) — T — NR — Y

** Dunnette, Marvin D., *Personnel Selection and Placement.* Belmont, Calif.: Wadsworth, 1966. (*LRF* 388) — NR — Per — NR

** Durbin, J., "A Note on Regression When There is Extraneous Information about One of the Coefficients," *Journal of the American Statistical Association,* **48** (1953), 799–808. (*LRF* 232) — Ec — NR — N

*** **E**fron, Bradley, and Morris, Carl, "Stein's Paradox in Statistics," *Scientific American,* **236** (May 1977), 119–127. (*LRF* 155) — Ex — NR — Ym

** Ehrenberg, A.S.C., "The Practical Alternative to Regression," *Proceedings of the American Statistical Association: Business and Economics Statistics Section,* 1975, pp. 313–314. — Ec — Med — Y

The obvious is not always obvious—so papers like this are useful. Suggests that one can generalize from similar situations rather than developing a new model from scratch. (*LRF* 203)

** Einhorn, Hillel J., "The Use of Nonlinear, Noncompensatory Models in Decision Making," *Psychological Bulletin,* **73** (1970), 221–230. — Ju — Per — Ym

A critique of this paper is provided by Goldberg (1971).(*LRF* 538)

** Einhorn, Hillel J., "Expert Measurement and Mechanical Combination," *Organizational Behavior and Human Performance,* **7** (1972a), 86–106. — Ju — Med — Ym

Suggests a combination of judgement and objective methods with the judge gathering the data and the statistician processing it. Examines decomposed vs. global judgments for three judges predicting the life span of 193 people with Hodgkins's disease. (*LRF* 276)

*** Einhorn, Hillel, J., "Alchemy in the Behavioral Sciences," *Public Opinion Quarterly,* **36** (1972b), 367–378. — Ec Sg — NR — Ym

Discusses danger of proceeding without a theory when using AID, regression, or factor analysis. (*LRF* 56, 255, 263, 340, 415)

*** Einhorn, Hillel J., and Hogarth, R.M., "Unit Weighting Schemes for Decision Making," *Organizational Behavior and Human Performance,* **13** (1975), 171–192. (*LRF* 231) — Ec — NR — Ym

*** Elliott, J.W., "A Direct Comparison of Short-Run GNP Forecasting Models," *Journal of Business,* **46** (1973), 33–60. (*LRF* 228, 408) — Ec Ex — Eco — Ym

*** Elton, Edwin J., and Gruber, Martin J., "Improved Forecasting through the Design of Homogeneous Groups," *Journal of Business,* **44** (1971), 432–450. (*LRF* 286) — Ex Sg — Fin — Ym

*** Elton, Edwin J., and Gruber, Martin J., "Earnings Estimates and the Accuracy of Expectational Data," *Management Science,* **18** (1972), B409–B424. (*LRF* 169, 170, 174, 177, 494) — Ex Ju — Fin — Ym

	M	F	E*

* Encel, Soloman, Marstrand, Pauline K., and Page, William, *The*   NR   NR   N
Art of Anticipation. London: Martin Robertson, 1975.
Planning is the major concern here, rather than forecasting.
The discussion of cost-benefit analysis is interesting. (*LRF*
19, 39)

** Erdos, Paul L., and Morgan, Arthur J., *Professional Mail Surveys.*   Ju   Mkt   Y
Malabar, Florida: Robert E. Krieger, 1983. (*LRF* 114)

** Evans, Franklin B., "Psychological and Objective Factors in the   Ec   Mkt   Y
Prediction of Brand Choice: Ford versus Chevrolet," *Journal of
Business,* **32** (1959), 340–369.
A controversial article in marketing research. At least six
journal articles analyzed this paper. This case provides an
interesting history of the evaluation of a research paper.

1. Steiner, Gary, "Notes on Franklin B. Evans' 'Psychological
   and Objective Factors in the Prediction of Brand Choice,'"
   Journal of Business, **34** (1961), 57–60. Suggests that other
   explanations should have been considered; for example,
   the criterion variable was not reliable, and the psychological measure was not valid.
2. Winick, Charles, "The Relationship among Personality
   Needs, Objective Factors, and Brand Choice: A Re-Examination," *Journal of Business,* **34** (1961), 61–66. Points
   out data showing large year-to-year changes in perceptions
   of Ford and Chevrolet. Also states that the psychological
   test is not highly reliable, nor is variation expected to be
   large.
3. Evans, Franklin B., "Reply: You Still Can't Tell A Ford
   Owner from a Chevrolet Owner," *Journal of Business,* **34**
   (1961), 67–73. Steiner misinterpreted Table 19, Evans says;
   its rank order data and differences were, in fact, small.
   Evans tried Winick's idea of using homogeneous model
   years and found no differences in results. Winick's critique
   of the reliability of the Edwards test was wrong.
4. Kuehn, Alfred A., "Demonstration of a Relationship between Psychological Factors and Brand Choice," *Journal
   of Business,* **36** (1963), 237–241. Points out errors by Evans
   in his plot of Figure 1. Analyzes two best variables and
   finds a significant difference.
5. Evans, Franklin B., and Harry V. Roberts, "Fords, Chevrolets, and the Problem of Discrimination," *Journal of
   Business,* **36** (1963), 237–241. Criticizes Kuehn for failing
   to allow for the fact that he chose the best two of the 11
   variables. Also, the plotting error by Evans made no difference.
6. Marcus, Alan S., "Obtaining Group Measures from Personality Test Scores: Auto Brand Choice Predicted from

	M	F	E*

the Edwards Personal Preference Schedule," *Psychological Reports,* **17** (1965), 523–531. Suggests use of a cross classification rather than a linear model.

7. There were also attacks on Evans' work in the popular press. For example, see Pierre Martineau, "Letter to the Editor," *Advertising Age,* Dec. 21, 1959, p. 76. (*LRF* 302)

* Evans, Michael K., "Econometric Models," in William F. Butler and Robert A. Kavesh (Eds.), *How Business Economists Forecast,* Englewood Cliffs, N.J.: Prentice-Hall, 1974. (*LRF* 57, 200) — Ec Eco N

** Evans, Michael K., Haitovsky, Y., and Treyz, G.I., "An Analysis of the Forecasting Properties of U.S. Econometric Models," in Bert G. Hickman (Ed.), *Econometric Models of Cyclical Behavior,* Vol. 2. Studies in Income and Wealth, No. 36, New York: Columbia University Press, 1972, pp. 949–1139, with discussion on pp. 1140–1158. — Ec Eco Y

This paper is based on an excellent idea; it has good raw data; the study design is fair; the interpretation of the results is impressionistic, with hypotheses obtained after the data were examined; and the writing is difficult to follow. (*LRF* 237, 241)

* Ezzati, Ali, "Forecasting Market Shares of Alternative Home-Heating Units by Markov Process Using Transition, Probabilities Estimated from Aggregate Time Series Data," *Management Science,* 21 (1974), 462–473. — Ex Mkt Y

Forecasts the demand for oil burners, gas burners, and electric heaters for 1973–1984. No validation. (*LRF* 158)

*** **F**air, Ray C., *A Short-Run Forecasting Model of the United States.* Lexington, Mass.: Heath Lexington Books, 1971. Fair's work was updated in his book, *Specification, Estimation, and Analysis of Macroeconomic Models.* Cambridge, Mass. Harvard University Press, 1984. (*LRF* 228, 241) — Ec Eco Ym

** Fair, Ray C., "An Evaluation of a Short-Run Forecasting Model," in Lawrence R. Klein and Edwin Burmeister (Eds.), *Econometric Model Performance,* Philadelphia: University of Pennsylvania Press, 1976. (*LRF* 241) — Ec Eco Ym

** Falthzik, Alfred M., "When to Make Telephone Interviews," *Journal of Marketing Research,* 9 (1972), 451–452. — Ju NR Y

For surveys of the general population, response rates are higher if you call during the week (Monday through Thursday). Also, it is better to call in the morning, next best is the afternoon, and nights are worst. (Of course, it is cheaper to call at night.) (*LRF* 115)

* Farrell, M.J., "The Demand for Motor Cars in the United States," *Journal of the Royal Statistical Society: Series A,* 117 (1954), 171–193 with discussion on pp. 194–201. (*LRF* 408) — Ec Eco Y

		M	F	E*

** Fegley, Kenneth A., Armstrong, J. Scott, and Salisbury, James B., "Analysis of Medical Forecasting Techniques," Mimeo: University City Science Center, October 1971. — Ec Sg / Med / Ym

Compares simple vs. complex functional forms; also compares segmentation and econometric methods. (Copies can be obtained from J. Scott Armstrong). (*LRF* 413, 415)

** Fels, Rendigs, and Hinshaw, C. Elton, "An Analysis of Turning Point Forecasts: A Fairly Polite Comment," *American Economic Review*, **64** (1974), 724–727. — T / Eco / N

Although it really was not polite, it did summarize work done on turning points while the authors criticized a paper by Stekler. Stekler replied politely on pp. 728–729 of this same issue. (*LRF* 353)

*** Ferber, Robert, "Are Correlations Any Guide to Predictive Value?" *Applied Statistics*, **5** (June 1956), 113–122. (*LRF* 339) — T / Eco / Y

*** Ferber, Robert, "The Reliability of Consumer Surveys of Financial Holdings: Time Deposits," *Journal of the American Statistical Association*, **60** (1965), 148–163. (*LRF* 329) — Ju / Fin / Y

* Ferber, Robert, "Contributions of Economics to the Study of Consumer Market Behavior," *Applied Economics*, **1** (1969), 125–136. (*LRF* 213) — Ec / Mkt / N

** Ferber, Robert, Chen, N., and Zuwaylif, F., "Employers' Forecasts of Manpower: An Interview Study," *Journal of Business*, **34** (1961), 387–395. (*LRF* 142) — Ju / Per / Y

* Fernandez-Garza, Alberto, "A General Computer Model for Forecasting the Demand Distribution with an Application to the Minicar System." Unpublished MBA Thesis, Wharton School: University of Pennsylvania, Philadelphia, 1969. (*LRF* 269) — Sg / Trn / Y

*** Finley, James R., "Farm Practice Adoption: A Predictive Model," *Rural Sociology*, **33** (1968), 5–18. — Sg / Agr / Ym

A segmentation model reduced error by almost half in comparison to a naive model. Good use of *a priori* analysis. (*LRF* 254)

* Firestone, O.J., in discussion of "Forecasting with Statistical Indicators," Bert G. Hickman (Ed.), *Econometric Models of Cyclical Behavior*, New York: Columbia University Press, 1972, pp. 1189–1190. (*LRF* 379) — NR / Eco / N

* Fischhoff, Baruch, "Hindsight ≠ Foresight: The Effect of Outcome Knowledge on Judgment under Certainty," *Journal of Experimental Psychology: Human Perception and Performance*, **1** (1975), 288–297. — Ju / Soc / Y

Finding out that an outcome had occurred increased its perceived likelihood as remembered by the judge. (*LRF* 39, 384)

*** Fischhoff, Baruch, and Beyth, Ruth, "I Knew It Would Happen: Remembered Probabilities of Once-Future Things," *Organizational Behavior and Human Performance*, **13** (1975), 1–16. (*LRF* 39, 384) — Ju / Psy / Y

* Flesch, Rudolph, "Preparation of Effective Reports," in H.B. May- — NR / NR / NR

	M	F	E*

* Flesch, Rudolph, "Preparation of Effective Reports," in H.B. Maynard (Ed.), *Industrial Engineering Handbook*. New York: McGraw-Hill, 1956, pp. 8-299–8-312. (*LRF* xii) — NR NR NR

** Forehand, G.A., and McQuitty, L.L., "Configurations of Factor Standings as Predictors of Educational Achievement," *Educational and Psychological Measurement*, 19 (1959), 31–43. (*LRF* 413) — Sg Edu Y

* Forrester, Jay W., "Industrial Dynamics—after the First Decade," *Management Science (Theory)*, 14 (1968a), 398–415. (*LRF* 263) — Sg NR N

* Forrester, Jay W., "Industrial Dynamics: A Response to Ansoff and Slevin," *Management Science (Theory)*, 14 (1968b), 601–618. (*LRF* 517) — Sg NR N

** Fox, Karl A., "Econometric Models of the United States," *Journal of Political Economy*, 64 (1956), 128–142. (*LRF* 227) — Ec Eco Ym

** Francis, R.G., "The Relation of Data to Theory," *Rural Sociology*, 22 (1957), 258–266. (*LRF* 55) — T Soc N

** Frank, Ronald E., and Massy, W.F., "Innovation and Brand Choice: The Folger's Invasion," in Stephen A. Greyser (Ed.), *Toward Scientific Marketing*. Chicago: American Marketing Association, 1963. A study of the introduction of Folger's coffee into Chicago in 1959. (*LRF* 340) — NR NR N

*** Frank, Ronald E., Massy, W.F., and Morrison, D.G., "Bias in Multiple Discriminant Analysis," *Journal of Marketing Research*, 2 (1965), 250–258. (*LRF* 340, 341) — Ec Mkt Ym / T

** Frankel, Lester R., "Are Survey Data Being Over-adjusted?" in Leo Bogart (Ed.), *Current Controversies in Marketing Research*. Chicago: Markham, 1969. (*LRF* 478) — Sg NR N

* Freedman, Jonathan L., "Role Playing: Psychology by Consensus," *Journal of Personality and Social Psychology*, 13 (1969), 107–114. Arguments against the validity of role playing. (*LRF* 128) — Ju Psy N

*** French, John R.P., Key, E., and Meyer, H.H., "Participation and the Appraisal System," *Human Relations*, 19 (1966), 3–20. Managers who wrote out their own sets of goals were more successful in making changes. (*LRF* 36) — I Pro Ym

** Friedman, Milton, "The Methodology of Positive Economics," *Essays in Positive Economics*. Chicago: University of Chicago Press, 1953. (*LRF* 306, 556) — T Eco N

* Friend, Irwin, and Jones, Robert C., "Short-Run Forecasting Models Incorporating Anticipatory Data," in *Models of Income Determination: Studies in Income and Wealth, No. 28*. New York: National Bureau of Economic Research, 1964, pp. 279–326. Replies by L. Klein and F.T. Juster are included. (*LRF* 241) — Ec Eco Y

** Friend, Irwin, and Taubman, P., "A Short-Term Forecasting Model," *Review of Economics and Statistics*, 46 (1964), 229–236. (*LRF* 227) — Ec Eco Y

* Friend, Irwin, and Thomas, William, "A Reevaluation of the Predictive Ability of Plant and Equipment Anticipations," *Journal of the American Statistical Association*, 65 (1970), 510–519. Anticipations data improve short-range predictive ability. (*LRF* 81) — Ec Eco Ym

	M	F	E*

*   Fromm, Gary, and Klein, L.R., "A Comparison of Eleven Econometric   Ec   Eco   Ym
Models of the United States," *American Economic Review*, **63** (1973),
385–393.
Not much difference was found among models in their ability
to provide quarterly forecasts. (*LRF* 228)

** **G**allup, George H., *The Sophisticated Poll Watcher's Guide.*   Ju   Pol   N
Princeton, N.J.: Princeton Opinion Press, 1976. (*LRF 115, 129*)

** Geller, E. Scott, and Pitz, G.F., "Confidence and Decision Speed   Ju   NR   Ym
in the Revision of Opinion," *Organizational Behavior and Human
Performance*, **3** (1968), 190–201.
Although disconfirming evidence did not lead to a reduction
in confidence in the old belief, it did decrease the speed with
which decisions were made. This study was done with red and
white poker chips. (*LRF* 52, 383, 437)

*   Gerstenfeld, Arthur, "Technological Forecasting," *Journal of Busi-*   NR   NR   Y
ness, **44** (1971), 10–18.
The author, the founder of Gerstenfeld's law of trying, made
a survey of 425 firms in *Fortune's* 500 (and got 162 returns)
about long-range planning methods. (*LRF* 117)

*** Geurts, Michael D., and Ibrahim, I.B., "Comparing the Box-Jenkins   Ex   Trn   Ym
Approach with the Exponentially Smoothed Forecasting Model Ap-
plication to Hawaii Tourists," *Journal of Marketing Research*, **12**
(1975), 182–188. (*LRF 176, 177, 494*)

*   Gilchrist, Warren, *Statistical Forecasting.* London: Wiley, 1976.   NR   NR   N
Purely descriptive with a preference for statistical formulae.
Draws generalizations but does not present evidence to support them. Chapter 9 (pp. 150–161) provides a decent treatment of growth curves. (*LRF* 181, 609)

*   Gillo, Martin W., and Shelly, Maynard, "Predictive Modelling of   Sg   NR   N
Multivariable and Multivariate Data," *Journal of the American
Statistical Association*, **69** (1974), 646–653. (*LRF 262*)

*   Glahn, Harry R., "Objective Weather Forecasting by Statistical   Ec   Wea   N
Methods," *The Statistician*, **15** (1965), 111–142. (*LRF 425*)   Ex

*** Glaser, Daniel, "A Reconsideration of Some Parole Prediction Fac-   Ec   Soc   Y
tors," *American Sociological Review*, **19** (1954), 335–340.
This paper, which examines about 30 years of research effort
in forecasting success on parole, suggests that theory should
precede the development of a predictive model. (*LRF* 198)

** Glasser, Gerald J., and Metzger, Gale D., "Random-Digit Dialing   Ju   NR   Y
as a Method of Telephone Sampling," *Journal of Marketing Re-
search*, **9** (1972), 59–64.
Shows how to reach unlisted telephone numbers. Useful article, but a nasty business. (*LRF* 114)

** Glasser, Gerald J., and Metzger, Gale D., "National Estimates of   Ju   NR   Y
Nonlisted Telephone Households and Their Characteristics," *Jour-
nal of Marketing Research*, **12** (1975), 359–361.

	M	F	E*

This paper describes the characteristics of people with unlisted numbers. (*LRF* 114)

* Glueck, Sheldon, and Glueck, Eleanor, *Predicting Delinquency and Crime*. Cambridge, Mass.: Harvard University Press, 1959. (*LRF* 218) | Ec | Soc | Y

*** Gold, Jack A., "Testing Test Market Predictions," *Journal of Marketing Research*, 1 (August 1964), 8–11. | Ex | Mkt | Ym

See also the comments by Edwin Berdy and by Victor Cole, which appear with a reply by Gold in *Journal of Marketing*, 2 (1965), 196–200. (*LRF* 157)

** Goldberg, Lewis R., "The Effectiveness of Clinicians' Judgements: The Diagnosis of Organic Brain Damage from the Bender-Gestalt Test," *Journal of Consulting Psychology*, 23 (1959), 25–33. | Ju | Med | Y

Experts were no better than novices on diagnosis. There was
no relationship between an individual's accuracy and his confidence. A suggestive finding was that expertise derived from
empirical studies did lead to greater accuracy; unfortunately,
there was only one expert who had achieved his expertise via
empirical studies. (*LRF* 382)

*** Goldberg, Lewis R., "Diagnosticians vs. Diagnostic Signs: The Diagnosis of Psychosis vs. Neurosis from MMPI," *Psychological Monographs*, No. 79 (1965). (*LRF* 93, 137, 413, 414) | Ec Ju Sg | Psy | Ym

**** Goldberg, Lewis R., "Simple Models or Simple Processes? Some Research on Clinical Judgments," *American Psychologist*, 23 (1968a), 483–496. (*LRF* 100, 278, 573) | Ju | NR | N

* Goldberg, Lewis R., "Seer over Sign: The First 'Good' Example?" *Journal of Experimental Research in Personality*, 3 (1968b), 168–171. | Bo Ju | Fin | Ym

A critique of Lindzey (1965). (*LRF* 393, 550)

**** Goldberg, Lewis R., "Man versus Model of Man: A Rationale, Plus Some Evidence for a Method of Improving on Clinical Inferences," *Psychological Bulletin*, 73 (1970), 422–432. (*LRF* 137, 281, 283) | Bo Ju | Psy | Ym

*** Goldberg, Lewis R., "Five Models of Clinical Judgment: An Empirical Comparison Between Linear and Nonlinear Representations of the Human Inference Process," *Organizational Behavior and Human Performance*, 6 (1971), 458–479. | Ec | Psy | Ym

Critique of Einhorn (1970). The linear model proved better
than the conjunctive and disjunctive models in representing
predictions by 29 clinicians as to psychotic vs. neurotic patients. (*LRF* 278, 532)

* Goldberg, Lewis R., "Man versus Model of Man: Just How Conflicting Is That Evidence?" *Organizational Behavior and Human Performance*, 16 (1976), 13–22. | Bo Ju | Fin | Ym

A reanalysis of Libby (1976a) revealed that his study was a
positive finding for bootstrapping. See Libby's (1976b) reply
to Goldberg. (*LRF* 283, 550)

* Goldhamer, Herbert, and Speier, Hans, "Some Observations on Political Gaming," *World Politics*, 12 (October 1959), 71–83. (*LRF* 126) | Ju | Pol | N

		M	F	E*
*	Goldman, Alfred E., "The Group Depth Interview," *Journal of Marketing*, **26** (July 1962), 61–68. (*LRF* 124)	Ju	Mkt	N
**	Gordon, Kate, "Group Judgments in the Field of Lifted Weights," *Journal of Experimental Psychology*, **7** (1924), 398–400. (*LRF* 135, 589)	Ju	NR	Ym
***	Goreux, L., "Long-Range Projections of Food Consumption," *Monthly Bulletin of Agricultural Economics and Statistics*, **6** (June 1957), 1–18. (*LRF* 212)	Ec	Agr	Y
***	Gough, H.G., "Clinical versus Statistical Prediction in Psychology," in Leo J. Postman (ed.), *Psychology in the Making*, New York: Knopf, 1962, pp. 526–584. (*LRF* 218, 372, 393)	Ju	Psy	N
**	Graham, John R., "Feedback and Accuracy of Predictions of Hospitalization from the MMPI," *Journal of Clinical Psychology*, **27** (1971), 243–245. (*LRF* 380)	Ju	Med	Ym
***	Granger, Clive W.J., and Morgenstern, Oskar, *Predictability of Stock Market Prices*. Lexington, Mass.: Heath Lexington Books, 1970. (*LRF* 94)	NR	Fin	Y
***	Granger, Clive W.J., and Newbold, P., "Economic Forecasting: The Atheist's Viewpoint," in G.A. Renton (Ed.), *Modelling the Economy*, London: Heinemann, 1974.	Ec Ex	Eco	Ym

The authors examined 50 monthly macroeconomic time series and made forecasts for one to eight months in the future. The Box-Jenkins model performed well. (*LRF* 175, 290, 408, 557)

| ** | Grant, Donald L., and Bray, Douglas W., "Validation of Employment Test for Telephone Company Installation and Repair Occupations," *Journal of Applied Psychology*, **54** (1970), 7–15. | Ec | Per | Ym |

Regression weights slightly better than unit weights on cross validation; the original sample size was 430. (*LRF* 229, 230)

| ** | Grebstein, Lawrence C., "Relative Accuracy of Actuarial Prediction, Experienced Clinicians, and Graduate Students in a Clinical Judgment Task," *Journal of Consulting Psychology*, **27** (1963), 127–132. | Ju | Psy | Ym |

Professional experience was not related to accuracy in prediction. (*LRF* 93)

| * | Green, David, Jr., and Segall, J., "The Predictive Power of First-Quarter Earnings Reports: A Replication," *Journal of Accounting Research*, **4**, Suppl. (1966), 21–36. | Ex Ju | Fin | Ym |

Interestingly enough, this is a follow-up of the authors' 1967 paper. (*LRF* 397, 398)

| * | Green, David, Jr., and Seagall, J., "The Predictive Power of First Quarter Earnings Reports," *Journal of Business*, **40** (1967), 44–55. (*LRF* 397, 398) | Ex Ju | Fin | Ym |

| ** | Green, Paul E., and Tull, Donald S., *Research for Marketing Decisions*. Englewood Cliffs, N.J.: Prentice-Hall, 1978. | NR | Mkt | NR |

Chapter on scaling is good. (*LRF* 106, 220)

| ** | Greenberg, Martin S., "Role Playing: An Alternative to Deception," *Journal of Personality and Social Psychology*, **7** (1967), 152–157. (*LRF* 127) | Ju | Psy | Ym |

		M	F	E*
*	Greenwald, Anthony G., "Consequences of Prejudice against the Null Hypothesis," *Psychological Bulletin*, 82 (1975), 1–20. (*LRF* 436)	T	Psy	Y
**	Greist, John H., et al., "A Computer Interview for Suicide Risk Prediction," *American Journal of Psychiatry*, 130 (1973), 1327–1332. (*LRF* 113)	Ju	Psy	Y
**	Grigg, Austin E., "Experience of Clinicians, and of Speech Characteristics and Statements of Clients as Variables in Clinical Judgement," *Journal of Consulting Psychology*, 22 (1958), 315–319. (*LRF* 93, 101)	Ju	Psy	Ym
**	Groff, Gene K., "Empirical Comparison of Models for Short Range Forecasting," *Management Science*, 20 (1973), 22–31. (*LRF* 164, 170, 176, 494)	Ex	Mkt	Ym
*	Guetzkow, Harold S., Kotler, Philip, and Schultz, Randall L., *Simulation in Social and Administrative Science.* Engelwood Cliffs, N.J.: Prentice-Hall, 1972. (*LRF* 263)	Sg	Soc	NR
*	Guilford, Joy P., *Fundamental Statistics in Psychology and Education.* New York: McGraw-Hill, 1965. (*LRF* 228)	NR	NR	NR
*	Gunning, Robert, *The Technique of Clear Writing.* New York: McGraw-Hill, 1959. (*LRF* xiii)	NR	NR	NR
***	Gustafson, David H., Shukla, R.K., Delbecq, A., and Walster, G.W., "A Comparative Study of Differences in Subjective Likelihood Estimates Made by Individuals, Interacting Groups, Delphi Groups, and Nominal Groups," *Organizational Behavior and Human Performance*, 9 (1973), 280–291. (*LRF* 119, 123)	Ju	NR	Ym
*	Hacke, James E., Jr., *The Feasibility of Anticipating Economic and Social Consequences of a Major Technological Innovation*, Stanford Research Institute, Menlo Park, Calif., October 1967. (*LRF* 19)	Ex	Tec	Y
*	Hahn, Gerald J., and Shapiro, Samuel S., *Statistical Models in Engineering.* New York: Wiley, 1967. (*LRF* 459)	NR	NR	NR
*	Haire, Mason, "Projective Techniques in Marketing Research," *Journal of Marketing*, 14 (1950), 649–652. (*LRF* 107)	Ju	Mkt	Y
**	Haitovsky, Yoel, "A Note on the Maximization of R^2," *American Statistician*, 23 (February 1969), 20–21. (*LRF* 487)	T	NR	N
**	Haitovsky, Yoel, Treyz, G., and Su, V., *Forecasts with Quarterly Macroeconomic Models.* New York: Columbia University Press, 1974, pp. 3–22. (*LRF* 397)	Ec	Eco	Y
**	Hajnal, John, "The Prospects for Population Forecasts," *Journal of the American Statistical Association*, 50 (1955), 309–327. Notes that demographers' lack of success in forecasting had not led to any decrease in demand for their services. (*LRF* 182)	Ex	Dem	N
*	Halberstam, David, *The Best and the Brightest.* London: Barrie and Jenkins, 1973. The Vietnam war game is described on pp. 558–560. (*LRF* 125)	Ju	Pol	N

**   Hall, Ernest Jay, "Decisions, Decisions, Decisions," *Psychology*   Ju   Psy   Ym
     Today, 5 (November 1971), 51 seq.

     Examined the value of group background (established vs. ad
     hoc groups) and group process (trained vs. untrained). The
     results are only partially presented. (*LRF* 122, 482, 501)

**   Hall, Ernest J., Mouton, J.S., and Blake, R.R., "Group Problem-   Ju   Psy   Y
     Solving Effectiveness under Conditions of Pooling vs. Interaction,"
     Journal of Social Psychology, 59 (1963), 147–157.

     Contains a better description of the work referred to in Hall
     (1971). (*LRF* 122, 372, 605)

*   Hamilton, V. Lee, "Role Play and Deception: A Re-Examination of   Ju   Psy   N
     the Controversy," *Journal for the Theory of Social Behavior*, 6
     (1976), 233–250. (*LRF* 128)

**   Hammond, Kenneth R., Summers, D.A., and Deane, D.H., "Neg-   Ju   Psy   Ym
     ative Effects of Outcome-Feedback in Multiple-Cue Probability
     Learning," *Organizational Behavior and Human Performance*, 9
     (1973), 30–34. (*LRF* 380)

**   Hample, Dale J., and Hilpert, Fred P., Jr., "A Symmetry Effect in   Ju   NR   Ym
     Delphi Feedback." Paper presented at the International Commu-
     nication Association Convention, Chicago, 1975. (Copies avail-
     able from the authors. Department of Speech Communication, Uni-
     versity of Illinois, Urbana, Ill. 61801.)

     Slight tendency was found for movement toward accuracy in
     subsequent rounds of Delphi. This increased accuracy oc-
     curred when the shift was toward the skewed end of the dis-
     tribution. (*LRF* 118, 119)

**   Harberger, Arnold C. (Ed.), *The Demand for Durable Goods*. Chi-   Ec   Eco   Y
     cago: University of Chicago Press, 1960.

     A collection of empirical studies based primarily on econo-
     metric analysis using time series. The stress is on measure-
     ment, and little consideration was given to forecasting. (*LRF*
     202)

**   Harris, Douglas, "Predicting Consumer Reaction to Product De-   Ju   Mkt   Y
     signs," *Journal of Advertising Research*, 4 (June 1964), 34–37.

     Harris asked people to act as potential consumers in rating
     china and other dinnerware. This study tested concurrent
     validity. (*LRF* 155)

*** Harris, J.G., Jr., "Judgmental versus Mathematical Prediction: An   Ex   Soc   Ym
     Investigation by Analogy of the Clinical vs. Statistical Contro-   Ju
     versy," *Behavioral Science*, 8 (1963), 324–335.

     Criticizes Holt (1958) as a study of data fitting rather than
     of prediction. Harris also presents his study of forecasting
     football scores, which compares extrapolation and judgement
     methods. (*LRF* 55, 273)

*** Harris, Ronald J., and Adam, Everette E., Jr., "Forecasting Patient   Ex   Mkt   Ym
     Tray Census for Hospital Food Service," *Health Services Research*,   Ju
     Winter (1975), 384–393.

		M	F	E*

Compares extrapolation methods with intuitive forecasts. (*LRF* 171, 397, 400)

* Harrison, P.J., and Davies, O.L., "The Use of Cumulative Sum (CUSUM) Techniques for the Control of Routine Forecasts of Product Demand," *Operations Research,* **12** (1964), 325–333.   Ex   Mkt   Y

Good idea, but nearly incomprehensible. I think that information must have been left out of the explanation. (*LRF* 171)

* Harrison, P.J., and Pearce, S.F., "The Use of Trend Curves as an Aid to Market Forecasting," *Industrial Marketing Management,* **1** (January 1972), 149–170. (*LRF* 181)   Ex   Mkt   N

** Hartsough, W. Ross, "Illusory Correlation and Mediated Association: A Finding," *Canadian Journal of Behavioral Science,* **7** (1975), 151–154.   Ju   NR   Y

Study using colors paired with words. People see what they expect to see. (*LRF* 378)

* Hauck, Mathew, and Cox, Michael, "Locating a Sample by Random Digit Dialing," *Public Opinion Quarterly,* **38** (1974), 253–260.   Ju   Soc   Y

The authors found it difficult to obtain household demographic information with random digit dialing (35% refusals). (*LRF* 115)

** Hauser, Philip M., *Social Statistics in Use.* New York: Russell Sage, 1975. (*LRF* 96, 469)   NR   NR   NR

* Hayden, Spencer, "How Industry Is Using Technological Forecasting," *Management Review,* **59** (May 1970), 4–15. (*LRF* 117)   NR   NR   Y

** Hayes, S.P., Jr., "The Predictive Ability of Voters," *Journal of Social Psychology,* **7** (1936), 183–191. (*LRF* 86)   Ju   Pol   Y

* Hedlund, James W., Sletten, Ivan W., Altman, Harold, and Evenson, R.C., "Prediction of Patients Who Are Dangerous to Others," *Journal of Clinical Psychology,* **29** (1973), 443–444. (*LRF* 59, 354)   Ec T   Psy   Y

** Heeler, Roger M., Kearney, M.J., and Mehaffey, B.J., "Modeling Supermarket Product Selection," *Journal of Marketing Research,* **10** (1973), 34–37. (*LRF* 278)   Bo   Mkt   Y

* Heilbroner, Robert L., *In the Name of Profit.* Garden City, N.Y.: Doubleday, 1972. (*LRF* 289)   NR   NR   NR

* Hermann, Charles F., and Hermann, M.G., "An Attempt to Simulate the Outbreak of World War I," *American Political Science Review,* **61** (1967), 400–416. (*LRF* 126)   Ju   Pol   Y

*** Hertz, David B., "Risk Analysis in Capital Investment," *Harvard Business Review,* **42** (1964), 95–106. (*LRF* 102, 269)   Ju   Fin   N

* Higgins, J.V., Reed, E.W., and Reed, S.C., "Intelligence and Family Size: A Paradox Resolved," *Eugenics Quarterly,* **9** (1962), 84–90. (*LRF* 322)   NR   Soc   Ym

** Hiler, E. Wesley, and Nesvig, David, "An Evaluation of Criteria Used by Clinicians to Infer Pathology from Figure Drawings," *Journal of Consulting Psychology,* **29** (1965), 520–529. (*LRF* 93, 379)   Ju   Psy   Ym

* Hirsch, Albert A., and Lovell, Michael C., *Sales Anticipations and Inventory Behavior.* New York: Wiley, 1969.   Ec   Eco   Y

	M	F	E*

Assumes too much on the part of the reader. Makes strange comparisons (e.g., the accuracy of three-month sales forecasts for firms was judged in comparison with the accuracy of 12-month forecasts of the national economy.) (*LRF* 396)

* Hirschfeld, W.J., "A Comparison of Regression with Time Series-Exponential Smoothing Predictions of Craniofacial Growth," *Growth*, **34** (1970), 431–435. (*LRF* 177)   Ex   Med   Ym

** Hochstim, Joseph R., "A Critical Comparison of Three Strategies of Collecting Data from Households," *Journal of the American Statistical Association*, **62** (1967), 976–989.   Ju   Med   Y

Mail, telephone, and personal interviews used. (*LRF* 115)

*** Hofling, Charles K., Brotzman, E., Dalrymple, S., Graves, N., and Pierce, C.M., "An Experimental Study in Nurse-Physician Relationships," *Journal of Nervous and Mental Disease*, **143** (1966), 171–180.   Ju   Med   Y

Excellent study but the authors infer too much from their data. This study was replicated by Steven G. Rank and Cardell K. Jacobson, "Hospital Nurses Compliance with Medication Overdose Orders: A Failure to Replicate," *Journal of Health and Social Behavior*, **18** (1977), 188–193. Two important changes were made in the replication: the nurses were familiar with the drug, and they were able to obtain peer group support for their refusal to obey. Still, half of the nurses were prepared to follow orders if the doctor insisted. (*LRF* 112, 155)

* Hogan, Warren P., "Technical Progress and Production Functions," *Review of Economics and Statistics*, **40** (1958), 407–411.   Ec   Eco   Y

Critique of Solow (1957), followed by Solow's reply on pp. 411–413. (*LRF* 54)

** Holloman, Charles R. and Hendrick, Hal W., "Adequacy of Group Decisions as a Function of the Decision-Making Process," *Academy of Management Journal*, **15** (1972), 175–184.   Ju   Psy   Ym

Compares six ways to have a group make predictions of the behavior of the jurors in the movie *Twelve Angry Men*. A consensus after a majority vote was most accurate, consensus alone was second best, and majority vote third; averaged prediction, leader prediction, and committee prediction all did poorer. (*LRF* 123)

** Holmes, David S., and Bennett, David H., "Experiments to Answer Questions Raised by the Use of Deception in Psychological Research," *Journal of Personality and Social Psychology*, **29** (1974), 358–367.   Ju   Psy   Ym

Subjects were told they would be given a painful electric shock. Other subjects were asked to role-play that they would receive the shock. Both groups of subjects gave similar responses about how they felt (e.g., calm, tense), but the role-play subjects did not show the same physiological changes. (*LRF* 127)

		M	F	E*

** Holt, Robert R., "Clinical and Statistical Prediction: A Reformulation and Some New Data," *Journal of Abnormal and Social Psychology*, **56** (1958), 1–12. (*LRF* 541)   Ec Ju   Psy   N

*** Holt, Robert R., "Yet Another Look at Clinical and Statistical Prediction," or, "Is Clinical Psychology Worthwhile?" *American Psychologist*, **25** (1970), 337–349. (*LRF* 393)   Ec Ju   Psy   N

** Holtzman, W.H., and Sells, S.B., "Prediction of Flying Success by Clinical Analysis of Test Protocols," *Journal of Abnormal and Social Psychology*, **49** (1954), 485–490. (*LRF* 139, 144)   Ju   Edu   Y

** Hood, William C., "Empirical Studies of Demand," *Canadian Journal of Economics and Political Science*, **21** (1955), 309–327. (*LRF* 427)   Ec   Eco   N

*** Horowitz, I.A., and Rothschild, B.H., "Conformity as a Function of Deception and Role Playing," *Journal of Personality and Social Psychology*, **14** (1970), 224–226.   Ju   Psy   Ym
Reproduces Asch's (1965) study of conformity with role playing. (*LRF* 127)

* Hotelling, Harold, "The Teaching of Statistics," *Annals of Mathematical Statistics*, **11** (1940), 457–470.   NR   NR   NR
Incidentally, Hotelling's comments about the problems with teaching are the same ones we hear today. (*LRF* 323)

*** Houston, B. Kent, and Holmes, Davis S., "Role Playing versus Deception: The Ability of Subjects to Simulate Self-Report and Physiological Responses," *Journal of Social Psychology*, **96** (1975), 91–98. (*LRF* 127)   Ju   Psy   Ym

** Houthakker, H.S., "New Evidence on Demand Elasticities," *Econometrica*, **33** (1965), 277–288 (*LRF* 212)   Ec   Eco   Y

* Houthakker, H.S., and Taylor, L.D., *Consumer Demand in the United States*. Cambridge, Mass.: Harvard University Press, 1966 (Revised 1970). (*LRF* 200, 471)   Ec   Eco   Y

* Howard, John A., and Sheth, Jagdish N., *The Theory of Buyer Behavior*. New York: Wiley, 1969. (*LRF* 263)   Sg   Mkt   NR

* Howrey, E.P., "On the Choice of Forecasting Models for Air Travel," *Journal of Regional Science*, **9** (1969), 215–224. (*LRF* 228, 237)   Ec   Trn   Y

* Huber, George P., and Delbecq. André, "Guidelines for Combining the Judgments of Individual Members in Decision Conferences," *Academy of Management Journal*, **15** (1972), 161–174.   Ju   NR   N
Interesting conclusions, but it was not clear to me how these conclusions were reached. (*LRF* 96, 105, 589)

** Hultgren, Thor, "Forecasts of Railway Traffic," in *National Bureau of Economic Research, Short-Term Economic Forecasting: Studies in Income and Wealth*, No. 17, Princeton, N.J., 1955, pp. 363–380. (*LRF* 88, 397, 400)   Ex Ju   Trn   Ym

* Hummel, Francis E., *Market and Sales Potential*. New York: Ronald Press, 1961.   Ec   Mkt   Y
Read the Rayco case as a "how not to do it" and forget the rest of the book. (*LRF* 53)

	M	F	E*

* Hutchesson, B.N.P., "Market Research and Forecasting for the Chemical Industry: The State of the Art," *Industrial Marketing Research Association Journal*, 3 (1967), 242–260. (*LRF* 153)   Ex   Mkt   N

* Hyman, Herbert H., *A Secondary Analysis of Sample Surveys*. New York: Wiley, 1972.   Ju   NR   NR
Contains a list of 17 data archives. (*LRF* 259, 469)

** Ibrahim, I.B., and Otsuki, T., "Forecasting GNP Components Using the Method of Box and Jenkins," *Southern Economic Journal*, 42 (1976), 461–470.   Ec Ex   Eco   Ym
Box-Jenkins proved more accurate than Wharton and OBE econometric models for one-period-ahead forecasts. No test of statistical significance was done. (*LRF* 408)

* Jaffee, Dwight, Malkiel, B.G., and Quandt, R.E., "Predicting Common Stock Prices: Payoffs and Pitfalls," *Journal of Business Research*, 2 (1974), 1–16.   Ec   Fin   Y
The authors concluded that "various naive models can do as well or better than the [regression] equations analyzed in this paper." (*LRF* 408)

* Janis, Irving L., and Mann, Leon, "Effectiveness of Emotional Role-Playing in Modifying Smoking Habits and Attitudes," *Journal of Experimental Research in Personality*, 1 (1965), 84–90.   Ju   Psy   Y
If you would like to stop smoking, this approach might help. (*LRF* 125)

** Jantsch, Erich, *Technological Forecasting in Perspective*. Paris: Organization for Economic Cooperation and Development, 1967.   NR   Tec   N
An annotated bibliography of 413 items is presented and the coverage goes beyond technological forecasting. (*LRF* 7)

*** Jarvik, M.E., "Probability Learning and Negative Recency Effect in the Serial Anticipation of Alternative Symbols," *Journal of Experimental Psychology*, 41 (1951), 291–297. (*LRF* 89)   Ju   Psy   Y

* Jenness, Arthur, "Social Influences in the Change of Opinion," and "The Role of Discussion in Changing Opinion Regarding a Matter of Fact," *Journal of Abnormal and Social Psychology*, 27 (1932), 29–34 and 279–296.   Ju   Psy   Y
The first of these articles provides a review of the literature, and the second reports on a "how-many-beans-in-a-jar" study of judgment. (*LRF* 120)

* Jensen, Michael C., "The Performance of Mutual Funds in the Period 1945–1964," *Journal of Finance*, 23 (1968), 389–416.   Ju   Fin   Y
The 115 mutual funds in this study were unable to predict better than a "buy-the-market-and-hold" strategy. (*LRF* 528)

** Johnson, Jeffrey L., "A Ten-Year Delphi Forecast in the Electronics Industry," *Industrial Marketing Management*, 5 (March 1976), 45–55.   Ju   Mkt   Y

	M	F	E*

Describes the operational details of a Delphi study at Corning Glass Works. Provides data on speed of response, response rates, dropout rates, calendar time, and time use per panel member. (*LRF* 117)

*** Johnson Laird, P.N., and Wason, P.C., "A Theoretical Analysis of Insight into a Reasoning Task," *Cognitive Psychology*, 1 (1970), 134–148.

Ju   Psy   Y

Helps explain why experience does little to overcome prejudice. (*LRF* 378)

*** Johnston, John, *Econometric Methods*. New York: McGraw-Hill, 1963; revised 1984. (*LRF* 181, 215, 220, 224)

Ec   Eco   NR

* Johnston, Roy, and McNeal, B.F., "Combined MMPI and Demographic Data in Predicting Length of Neuropsychiatric Hospital Stay," *Journal of Consulting Psychology*, 28 (1964), 64–70. (*LRF* 229, 230)

Ec   Psy   Y
Ju

*** Johnston, Roy and McNeal, B.F., "Statistical versus Clinical Prediction: Length of Neuropsychiatric Hospital Stay," *Journal of Abnormal Psychology*, 72 (1967), 335–340. (*LRF* 94)

Ec   Psy   Y
Ju

* Jolson, Marvin, and Rossow, Gerald, "The Delphi Process in Marketing Decision Making," *Journal of Marketing Research*, 8 (1971), 443–448.

Ju   NR   Y

Navy people and computer people made estimates of naval strength and of the computer running time for a problem. (*LRF* 119)

** Jorgenson, Dale W., Hunter, Jerald, and Nadiri, M.I., "The Predictive Performance of Econometric Models of Quarterly Investment Behavior," *Econometrica*, 38 (1970), 213–224.

Ec   Eco   Ym

I reexamined their data to test the hypothesis that simple models are more stable than complex ones. The simplicity of the four models, ranked by the number of variables (five, six, seven, and nine), agreed perfectly with the ranking of stability ($p < .05$). In other words, complexity *reduced* stability. (*LRF* 228)

* Joy, O. Maurice, and Tollefson, John O., "On the Financial Applications of Discriminant Analysis," *Journal of Financial and Quantitative Analysis*, 10 (1975), 723–739.

T   Fin   N

Good discussion on the measures that can be used to assess accuracy in classification problems. (*LRF* 354)

** Juster, F. Thomas, *Anticipations and Purchases: An Analysis of Consumer Behavior*. Princeton, N.J.: Princeton University Press, 1964. (*LRF* 106)

Ju   Mkt   Y

*** Juster, F. Thomas, "Consumer Buying Intentions and Purchase Probability: An Experiment in Survey Design," *Journal of the American Statistical Association*, 61 (1966), 658–696. (*LRF* 106)

Ju   Mkt   Y

*** Juster, F. Thomas, "Consumer Anticipations and Models of Durable Goods Demand," in Jacob Mincer (Ed.), *Economic Forecasts and Expectations*. New York: National Bureau of Economic Research, 1969. (Distributed by Columbia University Press.) (*LRF* 85)

Ju   Mkt   Y

		M	F	E*

* Juster, F. Thomas, "An Evaluation of the Recent Record in Short-Term Forecasting," *Business Economics*, **7** (May 1972), 22–26. — Ec Eco N

Strong conclusions—for example, "The record reveals no clear-cut and sustained advantage of complex and highly structured model forecasting systems over the simpler and less well specified judgmental forecasting systems." (*LRF* 237, 241)

*** **K**ahneman, Daniel and Tversky, Amos, "On the Psychology of Prediction," *Psychological Review*, **80** (1973), 237–251. (*LRF* 97, 104, 376) — Ju Psy Y

** Kanuk, Leslie, and Berenson, Conrad, "Mail Surveys and Response Rates: A Literature Review," *Journal of Marketing Research*, **12** (1975), 440–453. (*LRF* 114) — Ju NR Y

*** Kaplan, A., Skogstad, A.L., and Girshick, M.A., "The Prediction of Social and Technological Events," *Public Opinion Quarterly*, **14** (Spring 1950), 93–110. (*LRF* 120–121) — Ju Soc Y

* Kegeles, S.S., Fink, C.F., and Kirscht, J.P., "Interviewing a National Sample by Long-Distance Telephone," *Public Opinion Quarterly*, **33** (1969), 412–419. — Ju Med Y

Respondents to a previous personal interview on the subject were likely to respond also to a follow-up telephone survey. (*LRF* 114)

*** Kelly, E. Lowell, and Fiske, D.W., "The Prediction of Success in the VA Training Program in Clinical Psychology," *The American Psychologist*, **5** (1950), 395–406. (*LRF* 55, 100, 323) — Ju Per Y

* Kennedy, M.C., "How Well Does the National Institute Forecast?" *National Institute Economic Review*, No. 50 (November 1969), 40–52. — Ec Eco Y

Confusing write-up. (*LRF* 241)

* Kidd, J.B., "The Utilization of Subjective Probabilities in Production Planning," *Acta Psychologica*, **34** (1970), 338–347. (*LRF* 87) — Ju Pro Y

** Kinney, William R., Jr., "Predicting Earnings: Entity versus Sub-entity Data," *Journal of Accounting Research*, **9** (1971), 127–136. (*LRF* 286, 644) — Ju Pro Y

*** Kirby, Robert M., "A Comparison of Short and Medium Range Statistical Forecasting Methods," *Management Science*, **13** (1966), B202–B210. — Ex Mkt Ym

Exponential smoothing, moving average, and regression-against-time models were compared for short- and intermediate-range forecast accuracy. Kirby used actual data on sewing machine sales in five countries, as well as simulated data. Good study, but some important details seem to be missing. (*LRF* 173, 177, 494)

** Klein, W.H., "The Computer's Role in Weather Forecasting," *Weatherwise*, **22** (1969), 195 seq. — NR Wea N

Historical review. (*LRF* 425, 427)

** Kleinmuntz, Benjamin, "Sign and Seer: Another Example," *Journal of Abnormal Psychology*, **72** (1967), 163–165. (*LRF* 280) — Bo Ju Psy Ym

	M	F	E*

** Klugman, Samuel F., "Group Judgments for Familiar and Unfa- · Ju · Psy · Y
miliar Materials," *Journal of General Psychology*, **32** (1945),
103–110. (*LRF* 135)

** Klugman, Samuel F., "Group and Individual Judgments for An- · Ju · Pol · Y
ticipated Events," *Journal of Social Psychology*, **26** (1947), 21–28.
(*LRF* 136)

*** Koopmans, T.C., "Measurement without Theory," *Review of Eco-* · Ec · Eco · N
nomics and Statistics, **29** (1947), 161–172.
A review of Burns and Mitchell (1946). (*LRF* 53)

*** Korman, Abraham K., "The Prediction of Managerial Performance: · Ju · Per · Ym
A Review," *Personnel Psychology*, **21** (1968), 295–322.
Of major interest is the comparison of subjective and objective
methods. The major problem with the analysis is that the
criterion (managerial success) is similar to the subjective predictor (ratings of potential success by managers). (*LRF* 395,
396, 399)

** Kort, Fred, "Predicting Supreme Court Decisions Mathematically: · Bo · Pol · Ym
A Quantitative Analysis of the 'Right to Counsel' Cases," *American* · Ju
Political Science Review, **51** (1957), 1–12.
Franklin Fisher, *American Political Science Review*, **52** (1958),
321–338, criticized Kort's study; actually, it beat the hell out
of the details. Kort replied in the same issue. (*LRF* 276)

** Kosobud, Richard F., "Forecasting Accuracy and Uses of an Econ- · Ec · Eco · Ym
ometric Model," *Applied Economics*, **2** (1970), 253–263. · Ex
The criterion ($\bar{R}^2$) and the extrapolation model were not ideal
for such a comparison. The write-up seems to omit some relevant material. (*LRF* 396, 403, 406, 409)

* Kreinin, M.E., and Lininger, C.A., "Ownership and Purchase of · Sg · Mkt · Y
New Cars in the U.S.," *International Economic Review*, **4** (1963),
310–324. (*LRF* 260, 261)

** Kuh, E., "The Validity of Cross-Sectionally Estimated Behavior · Ec · Eco · Y
Equations in Time Series Applications," *Econometrica*, **27** (1959),
197–214.
Discusses differences between cross-section and time series
data. Suggests that estimates from the two types of data be
averaged. (*LRF* 212)

*** Kunreuther, Howard, "Extensions of Bowman's Theory on Mana- · Bo · Pro · Ym
gerial Decision-Making," *Management Science*, **15** (1969), · Ju
415–439. (*LRF* 280)

** Kurtz, A.K., "A Research Test of the Rorschach Test," *Personnel* · T · Per · Ym
Psychology, **1** (1948), 41–51. (*LRF* 340)

*** Langer, Ellen J., "The Illusion of Control," *Journal of Personality* · Ju · Psy · Y
and Social Psychology, **32** (1975), 311–328.

		M	F	E*

Competition, choice, familiarity, and involvement tend to give people a feeling of control, even in situations involving chance. Describes six studies. (*LRF* 376, 378)

*** Langer, Ellen J., and Roth, Jane, "Heads I Win, Tails It's Chance: The Illusion of Control as a Function of the Sequence of Outcomes in a Purely Chance Task," *Journal of Personality and Social Psychology,* **32** (1975), 951–955. — Ju · Psy · Y

Subjects attribute successes to themselves, but blame chance for their failures. (*LRF* 376, 378)

** LaPiere, R.T., "Attitudes vs. Actions," *Social Forces,* **13** (1934), 230–237. (*LRF* 84) — Ju · Soc · Y

* Larsen, Knud S., Coleman, D., Forbes, J., and Johnson, R., "Is the Subject's Personality or the Experimental Situation a Better Predictor of a Subject's Willingness to Administer Shocks to a Victim?" *Journal of Personality and Social Psychology,* **22** (1972), 287–295. (*LRF* 127) — Ju · Psy · Y

* Laski, Harold J., "Limitations of the Expert," *Chemical Technology,* **4** (April 1974), 198–202. — Ju · NR · N

Originally published in *Harpers* in 1930. (*LRF* 375)

*** Laughhunn, D.J., *On the Predictive Value of Combining Cross-Section and Time-Series Data in Empirical Demand Studies.* Bureau of Economic and Business Research, University of Illinois, Urbana, 1969. (*LRF* 213) — Ec · Eco · Ym

* Lave, Lester, "The Value of Better Weather Information for the Raisin Industry," *Econometrica,* **31** (1963), 151–164. (*LRF* 388) — T · Agr · Y

** Lawler, Edward E., and Hackman, John R., "The Impact of Employee Participation in the Development of Pay Incentive Plans," *Journal of Applied Psychology,* **53** (1969), 467–471. (*LRF* 36) — I · Pro · Ym

** Lawshe, C.H., and Schucker, R.E., "The Relative Efficiency of Four Test Weighting Methods in Multiple Prediction," *Educational and Psychological Measurement,* **19** (1959), 103–114. (*LRF* 230) — Ec · Edu · Ym

* Lee, M.C., "Interactions, Configurations, and Nonadditive Models," *Educational and Psychological Measurement,* **21** (1961), 797–805. (*LRF* 250) — Sg · Psy · N

* Leontief, Wassily W., "Proposal for Better Business Forecasting," *Harvard Business Review,* **42** (November–December 1964), 166 seq. (*LRF* 264, 265) — Sg · Eco · N

* Lerner, Melvin J., and Simmons, C.H., "Observer's Reaction to the 'Innocent Victim': Compassion or Rejection?" *Journal of Personality and Social Psychology,* **4** (1966), 203–210. (*LRF* 435) — Ju · NR · Y

** Leser, C.E.V., "A Survey of Econometrics," *Journal of the Royal Statistical Society: Series A,* **131** (1968), 530–566. (*LRF* 226) — Ec · Eco · N

** L'Esperance, Wilford L., "A Case Study in Prediction: The Market for Watermelons," *Econometrica,* **32** (1964), 163–173. (*LRF* 200) — Ec · Agr · Ym

** Levenbach, Hans, Cleary, Jim P., and Fryk, Dave A., "A Comparison of ARIMA and Econometric Models for Telephone Demand," *Proceedings of the American Statistical Association: Business and Economics Statistics Section,* 1974, pp. 448–450. (*LRF* 408) — Ec Ex · Mkt · Y

		M	F	E*
**	Levine, Jacob, and Butler, John, "Lecture vs. Group Decision in Changing Behavior," *Journal of Applied Psychology*, 36 (1952), 29–33. (*LRF* 35)	I	Pro	Y
**	Levine, Robert A., "Capital Expenditures Forecasts by Individual Firms," in National Bureau of Economic Research, *The Quality and Significance of Anticipations Data*, Princeton, N.J., 1960, pp. 351–366. (*LRF* 138, 291, 292, 396, 399)	Ju	Fin	Y
***	Levins, R., "The Strategy of Model Building in Population Biology," *American Scientist*, 54 (1966), 421–431. (*LRF* 183)	NR	NR	N
*	Levitt, Theodore, "Marketing Myopia," *Harvard Business Review*, 38 (July–August 1960), 45–56. (*LRF* 15)	NR	NR	N
*	Levitt, Theodore, *Innovation in Marketing*. New York: McGraw-Hill, 1962. (*LRF* 15)	NR	NR	N
**	Levy, Bernard I.,and Ulman, E., "Judging Psychopathology from Paintings," *Journal of Abnormal Psychology*, 72 (1967), 182–187. (*LRF* 93)	Ju	Psy	Ym
***	Levy, Robert A., "The Predictive Significance of Five-Point Chart Patterns," *Journal of Business*, 44 (1971b), 316–323. Do you believe that charting helps in predicting the stock market? How about the Easter Bunny? (*LRF* 183)	Ex	Fin	Y
***	Lewin, Kurt, "Group Decision and Social Change," in Theodore Newcomb and E.L. Hartley (Eds.), *Reading in Social Psychology*. New York: Holt, Rinehart and Winston, 1947. (*LRF* 35)	I	Mkt	Ym
*	Lewis, Sinclair, *Arrowsmith*. New York: Harcourt, Brace, 1924. Novel about the dilemma faced by an experimenter; to learn, you must do something wrong. (For trivia fans, Lewis refused a Pulitzer Prize for this novel in 1925.) (*LRF* 435)	T	Med	NR
**	Libby, Robert, "Man versus Model of Man: Some Conflicting Evidence," *Organizational Behavior and Human Performance*, 16 (1976a), 1–12. Bootstrapping of 43 bank loan officers. (*LRF* 283, 538)	Ec Ju	Fin	Ym
*	Libby, Robert, "Man versus Model of Man: The Need for a Nonlinear Model," *Organizational Behavior and Human Performance*, 16 (1976b), 23–26. A reply to Goldberg's (1976) critique. (*LRF* 538)	Ec Ju	Fin	N
**	Liebling, Herman I., Bidwell, Peter T., and Hall, Karen E., "The Recent Performance of Anticipation Surveys and Econometric Model Projections of Investment Spending in the United States," *Journal of Business*, 49 (1976), 451–477. (*LRF* 395, 396, 400)	Ec Ju	Eco	N
**	Lindzey, G., "Seer vs. Sign," *Journal of Experimental Research in Personality*, 1 (1965), 17–26. See also Goldberg (1968b). (*LRF* 393, 538)	Ec Ju	Psy	Ym
**	Linsky, Arnold S., "Stimulating Responses to Mailed Questionnaires: A Review," *Public Opinion Quarterly*, 39 (Spring 1975), 82–101. (*LRF* 114)	Ju	NR	NR
*	Linstone, Harold A., and Turoff, Murray (Eds.), *The Delphi Method: Techniques and Applications*. Reading, Mass.: Addison-Wesley, 1975.	Ju	NR	NR

A collection of papers on various aspects of Delphi. Unfortunately, the art is not in good shape. Contains an extensive bibliography. Reviewed by Harold Sackman in *Futures*, **8** (1976), 444–446. (*LRF* 117)

*** Locke, E.A., "What's in a Name?," *American Psychologist*, **16** (1961),   Ec   NR   Y
607. (*LRF* 339)

*   Lord, F.M., "Efficiency of Prediction When a Regression Equation   T   NR   NR
from One Sample is Used in a New Sample," *Research Bulletin*,
RB 50–40, (7 pages). Princeton, N.J.: Educational Testing Service,
1950. (*LRF* 351)

*   Lorie, J.H., and Niederhoffer, V., "Predictive and Statistical Prop-   Ju   Fin   Y
erties of Insider Trading," *Journal of Law and Economics*, **11** (1968),
35–53.

Inside information can lead to a better prediction of stock prices. This point has been made elsewhere. For example, read the account of the Texas Gulf Sulphur case in Brooks (1969). (*LRF* 94)

**   Lykken, D.T., and Rose, R., "Psychological Prediction from Actu-   Ec   Psy   Ym
arial Tables," *Journal of Clinical Psychology*, **19** (1963), 139–151.   Sg
(*LRF* 255, 413, 415)

**   Lyon, Herbert L., "The Utility of Using Extraneous Information in   Ec   Mkt   Ym
Sales Forecasting," in Philip R. McDonald (Ed.), *Marketing In-
volvement in Society and the Economy*. Chicago: American Marketing Association, 1969, pp. 220–225.

My interpretation of this study was supplemented with information from the author by personal communication. (*LRF* 213)

[*Note:* See Mc after Mb.]

*   **M**acdonald, J. Ross, "Are the Data Worth Owning?" *Science*, **176**   T   NR   NR
(1972), 1377.

How high is the sun? The author says that a good rule of thumb to estimate measurement error is to obtain the best estimate you can by using independent sources, and then multiply by 3. (*LRF* 65)

*   Machlup, Fritz, "The Problem of Verification in Economics," *South-   T   Eco   N
ern Economic Journal*, **22** (1955), 1–21.

Argues that unconditional predictions are useless. (*LRF* 306)

**   Maier, Norman, R.F., *Problem Solving Discussions and Confer-   Ju   NR   Ym
ences*. New York: McGraw-Hill, 1963.

A useful guide on how to run group meetings. Unfortunately, this excellent book is now out of print. (*LRF* 32)

**   Maier, Norman R.F., "Prior Commitment as a Deterrent to Group   Ju   Per   Ym
Problem Solving," *Personnel Psychology*, **26** (1973), 117–126.
(*LRF* 124)

*** Maier, Norman R.F., and Maier, Richard A., "An Experimental Test   Ju   Per   Ym
of the Effects of 'Developmental' vs. 'Free' Discussions on the Qual-

	M	F	E*

ity of Group Decisions," *Journal of Applied Psychology*, **41** (1957), 320–323. (*LRF* 121, 122)

** Maier, Norman R.F., and Solem, Allen R., "The Contribution of a Discussion Leader to the Quality of Group Thinking: The Effective Use of Minority Opinions," *Human Relations*, **5** (1952), 277–288. (*LRF* 31, 121)

Ju Psy Ym

* Malinvaud, E., *Statistical Methods of Econometrics*, New York: Elsevier North Holland, 1930. (*LRF* 220)

Ec Eco NR

** Mann, Floyd C., "Studying and Creating Change: A Means to Understanding Social Organization," in Conrad M. Arensberg (Ed.), *Research in Industrial Human Relations*. New York: Harper and Brothers, 1957, pp. 146–167. For a shorter version, see in Timothy W. Costello and Sheldon S. Zalkind (Eds.). *Psychology in Administration*. Englewood Cliffs, N.J.: Prentice-Hall, 1963. (*LRF* 37)

I Fin Y

* Markiewicz, Dorothy, "Effects of Humor on Persuasion," *Sociometry*, **37** (1974), 407–422. (*LRF* xiii)

NR NR NR

** Markland, Robert E., "A Comparative Study of Demand Forecasting Techniques for Military Helicopter Spare Parts," *Naval Research Logistics Quarterly*, **17** (1970), 103–119.
(LRF 170, 406, 408, 495)

Ec Pro Ym
Ex

**** Marrow, Alfred J., and French, J.R.P., "Changing a Stereotype in Industry," *Journal of Social Issues*, **1** (1945), 33–37. (*LRF* 33).

I Pro Y

* Martino, Joseph P., *Technological Forecasting for Decision Making*, New York: American Elsevier, 1983.
This second edition, which is half the length of the original edition, provides a good description of Delphi. (*LRF* 117)

NR Tec NR

** Massy, William F., "Principal Components Regression in Exploratory Statistical Research," *Journal of the American Statistical Association*, **60** (1965), 234–256. (*LRF* 223)

Ec Mkt Ym

* Mayfield, Eugene C., "Value of Peer Nominations in Predicting Life Insurance Sales Performance," *Journal of Applied Psychology*, **56** (1972), 319–323. (*LRF* 223)

Ju Pro Y

* McClain, John O., "Decision Modeling in Case Selection for Medical Utilization Review," *Management Science*, **18** (1972), B706–B717. (*LRF* 277)

Bo Med Y

* McDonald, John, "An Analysis of the Significance of Revisions to Some Quarterly U. K. National Income Time Series," *Journal of the Royal Statistical Society: Series A*, **138** (1975), 242–256, (1972). (*LRF* 221)

Ec Eco Y

** McFall, R.M., "Effects of Self-Monitoring on Normal Smoking Behavior," *Journal of Consulting and Clinical Psychology*, **35** (1970), 135–142.
Small sample, but subjects who kept track of their smoking increased it by 87%. When they kept count of the number of times they felt like smoking but did not, the smoking rate went down by 31%. Conclusion: measure the behavior that you want to achieve. (*LRF* 37)

I Med Ym

		M	F	E*

** McGregor, Douglas, "The Major Determinants in the Prediction of Social Events," *Journal of Abnormal and Social Psychology*, 33 (1938), 179–204. — Ju, Soc, Y
Analysis of 3500 predictions made by 400 people. (*LRF* 86)

* McHale, John, "The Changing Pattern of Futures Research in the USA," *Futures*, 5 (June 1973), 257–271. (*LRF* 117) — NR, NR, Y

** McLaughlin, Robert L., "The Forecasters' Batting Averages," *Business Economics*, 3 (May 1973), 58–59. (*LRF* 228) — Ec, Eco, Ym

* McMillan, Robert K., and Assael, Henry, *National Survey of Transportation Attitudes and Behavior, Phase I: Summary Report.* Highway Research Board, 1968. (*LRF* 116) — Ju, Trn, Ym

** McNees, Stephen K., "How Accurate are Economic Forecasts," *New England Economic Review*, (November–December 1974), 2–19. (*LRF* 229, 230, 397, 409) — Ec, Eco, Ym

*** McNees, Stephen K., "An Evaluation of Economic Forecasts," *New England Economic Review*, (November–December 1975), 3–39. — Ec, Eco, Ym
Extension of McNees (1974). Here he examines the forecast accuracy of seven major econometric models. This evaluation of macroeconomic forecasts is periodically updated by McNees. The latest version (with John Ries as co-author) was in the November/December 1984 issue. (Available from the Research Department, Federal Reserve Bank of Boston, Boston, Mass 02106) (*LRF* 237, 396)

* McNeil, John, "Federal Programs to Measure Consumer Purchase Expectations, 1946–1973: A Post-Mortem," *Journal of Consumer Research*, 1 (December 1974), 1–10. — Ju, Eco, N
Discusses the reasoning behind the U.S. government's decision in 1973 to end its sponsorship of consumer intentions and attitudes surveys. (*LRF* 553)

*** McNeil, John M., and Stoterau, Thomas L., "The Census Bureau's New Survey of Consumer Buying Expectations," in *Proceedings of the American Statistical Association: Business and Economic Statistics Section*, 1967, pp. 97–113. — Ju, Eco, Y
See McNeil (1974) also. (*LRF* 81)

* McNemar, Quinn, "Review of Clinical versus Statistical Prediction by P. E. Meehl," *American Journal of Psychology*, 68 (1955), 510. (*LRF* 393) — Ec, Ju, Psy, N

* McNemar, Quinn, *Psychological Statistics*, New York: Wiley, 1962. (*LRF* 351) — Ju, Psy, NR

* Meadows, Donella H., et al., *The Limits to Growth*, New York: Universe Books, 1972. (*LRF* 263) — Sg, NR, Y

* Medvedev, Zhores, A., *The Rise and Fall of T.D. Lysenko*, New York: Columbia University Press, 1969. (*LRF* 156) — T, Agr, N

** Meehl, Paul E., *Clinical versus Statistical Prediction: A Theoretical Analysis and a Review of the Evidence.* Minneapolis: University of Minnesota Press, 1954. (*LRF* 393) — Ec, J, NR, Ym

	M	F	E*
** Meehl, Paul E., "Wanted: A Good Cookbook," *American Psychologist*, 11 (1956), 263–272. (*LRF* 393)	Ec Ju	NR	Ym
** Meehl, Paul E., "A Comparison of Clinicians with Five Statistical Methods of Identifying Psychotic MMPI Profiles," *Journal of Counseling Psychology*, 6 (1959), 102–109. (*LRF* 414)	Ec Ju	Psy	Ym
*** Meehl, Paul E., "Seer Over Sign: The First Good Example," *Journal of Experimental Research in Personality*, 1 (1965), 27–32.	Ec Ju	NR	Ym

Meehl used this opportunity to update his box score of studies from 18 in his 1954 book to about 70 as of 1965. (*LRF* 393)

| * Michael, George C., "A Heuristic Approach to Forecasting A Simulation of Estimating Sales by a Catalog Control Buyer," abstract in Philip R. McDonald (Ed.), *Marketing Involvement in Society and the Economy*. Chicago: American Marketing Association, 1969, p. 412. (*LRF* 280) | Bo
Ju | Mkt | Ym |
| ** Michael, George C., "A Computer Simulation Model for Forecasting Catalog Sales," *Journal of Marketing Research*, 8 (1971), 224–229. | Bo
Ju | Mkt | Ym |

Contains more detail on Michael (1969). Nevertheless, the description seemed incomplete. (*LRF* 280)

| * Milgram, Stanley, *Obedience to Authority: An Experimental View*. New York: Harper and Row, 1974. (*LRF* 127, 561) | NR | NR | Y |
| * Milkovich, George T., Annoni, A.J., and Mahoney, T.A., "The Use of Delphi Procedures in Manpower Forecasting," *Management Science*, 19 (1972), 381–388. | Ju | Per | Y |

This would have been a good study if the authors had used more than one observation. (*LRF* 396, 399)

| * Miller, Arthur G., "Role Playing: An Alternative to Deception? A Review of the Evidence," *American Psychologist*, 27 (1972), 623–636. | Ju | NR | N |

Review article based on four empirical studies. A negative view of role playing, based on what I thought to be strange arguments. This reference is provided to give you an alternative to the viewpoint in LRF. (*LRF* 128)

* Miller, George A., "The Magical Number Seven, Plus or Minus Two," *Psychological Review*, 63 (1956a), 81–97. (*LRF* 102)	Ju	NR	N
* Miller, George A., "Information and Memory," *Scientific American*, 195 (August 1956b), 42–46. (*LRF* 102)	Ju	NR	N
** Miller, Jeffrey G., Berry, William L., and Lai, Cheng-Yi F., "A Comparison of Alternative Forecasting Strategies for Multi-stage Production-Inventory Systems," *Decision Sciences*, 7 (1976), 714–724. (*LRF* 265)	Sg	Pro	Ym
** Mincer, Jacob, and Zarnowitz, Victor, "The Evaluation of Economic Forecasts," in Jacob Mincer (Ed.), *Economic Forecasts and Expectations: Analyses of Forecasting Behavior and Performance*. New York: Columbia University Press, 1969. (*LRF* 396, 399)	Ex Ju	Eco	Ym
* Minor, F.J., "The Prediction of Turnover of Clerical Employees," *Personnel Psychology*, 11 (1958), 393–409.	Ec	Per	Y

Good illustration of shrinkage. (*LRF* 342)

	M	F	E*

* Mintz, Morton, "FDA and Panalba: A Conflict of Commercial and Therapeutic Goals," *Science*, 165 (1969), (875–881). (*LRF* 129) — NR NR NR

** Mitau, G. Theodore, Thorson, S., and Johnson, Q., "Aggregate Data in Election Prediction," *Public Opinion Quarterly*, 33 (1969), 96–99. (*LRF* 267) — Ju Pol Y

* Mitroff, Ian, "The Myth of Objectivity," or, "Why Science Needs a New Psychology of Science," *Management Science*, 18 (1972), B613–B618.
For more recent discussion on this see ARMSTRONG [1980b]. (*LRF* 437, 581, 588) — NR Sci Y

** Mixon, Don, "Instead of Deception," *Journal for the Theory of Social Behavior*, 2 (1972), 145–177. (*LRF* 127) — Ju Psy Ym

** Mize, Jan L., and Ulveling, Edwin F., "The Demand for Domestic Airline Passenger Transportation: An Analysis and a Forecast for 1975," *Mississippi Valley Journal of Business and Economics*, 6 (Fall 1970), 56–68. (*LRF* 212, 327) — Ec Trn Ym

** Modigliani, Franco and Sauerlender, Owen H., "Economic Expectations and Plans of Firms in Relation to Short-Term Forecasting," in National Bureau of Economic Research, *Short-Term Forecasting*. Studies in Income and Wealth, No. 17, Princeton, N.J., 1955. (*LRF* 88, 397, 399) — Ex Trn Ym

** Modigliani, Franco, and Weingartner, H.M., "Forecasting Uses of Anticipatory Data on Investment and Sales," *Quarterly Journal of Economics*, 72 (February 1958), 23–54. (*LRF* 396) — Ex Ju Mkt Ym

* Mohn, N. Carroll, Schaffer, William A., and Sartorius, Lester C., "Input-Output Modeling: New Sales Forecasting Tool," *University of Michigan Business Review*, 28 (July 1976), 7–15. (*LRF* 265) — Sg Mkt N

** Montgomery, David B., "New Product Distribution: An Analysis of Supermarket Buyer Decisions," *Journal of Marketing Research*, 12 (1975), 255–264. (*LRF* 341, 342) — Bo T Mkt Y

** Montgomery, David B., and Armstrong, J. Scott, "Consumer Response to a Legitimated Brand Appeal," in Johan Arndt (Ed.), *Insights into Consumer Behavior*. Boston: Allyn and Bacon, 1968. (*LRF* 256) — Ec Sg Mkt Y

** Montgomery, David B., and Morrison, Donald G., "A Note on Adjusting R^2," *Journal of Finance*, 28 (1973), 1009–1013. (*LRF* 351) — T NR N

** Moore, Geoffrey H., "Forecasting Short-Term Economic Change," *Journal of the American Statistical Association*, 64 (1969), 1–22. (*LRF* 409) — Ec Ex Eco Y

* Moore, Henry T., "The Comparative Influence of Majority and Expert Opinion," *American Journal of Psychology*, 32 (1921), 16–20.
The impacts of "majority" and "expert" opinion are of roughly comparable magnitude when it comes to influencing group opinion. This study covered speech, morals, and music. (*LRF* 110) — Ju Soc Y

*** Morgan, James N., and Sonquist, John A., "Problems in the Analysis of Survey Data, and a Proposal," *Journal of the American Statistical Association*, 58 (1963), 415–434. (*LRF* 250) — Ec Soc N

	M	F	E*

** Morgenstern, Oskar, *On the Accuracy of Economic Observations.*   NR   Eco   Y
Princeton, N.J.: Princeton University Press, 1963. (*LRF* 59)

* Morgenstern, Oskar, Knorr, Klaus, and Heiss, Klaus P., *Long Term*   Ec   NR   Y
Projections of Power: Political, Economic, and Military Forecasting.   Ex
Cambridge, Mass.: Ballinger, 1973. (*LRF* 261, 371)   Ju

* Morrison, Donald G., "Testing Brand-Switching Models," *Journal*   NR   Mkt   Y
of Marketing Research, 3 (1966), 401–409. (*LRF* 310)

** Mosier, Charles I., "A Critical Examination of the Concepts of Face   T   NR   N
Validity," *Educational and Psychological Measurement*, 7 (1947),
191–205. (*LRF* 324)

** Moskowitz, Herbert, "Regression Models of Behavior for Mana-   Bo   Pro   Ym
gerial Decision Making," *Omega*, 2 (1974), 677–690.   Ju
Replication that supports Bowman (1963). (*LRF* 282)

** Moskowitz, Herbert, and Miller, J.G., "Man, Models of Man, or   Bo   Pro   Ym
Mathematical Models for Managerial Decision Making?" *Pro-*   Ju
ceedings of the American Institute for Decision Sciences, New Orleans, November 1972, pp. 849–856. (*LRF* 282, 524)

** Murray, J. Alex, "Canadian Consumer Expectational Data: An   Ju   Mkt   Y
Evaluation," *Journal of Marketing Research*, 6 (1969), 54–61.
Compares Canadian experience with that of the U.S. (*LRF*
81)

* Myers, John G., "Statistical and Econometric Methods Used in   NR   Eco   N
Business Forecasting," in William F. Butler, Robert A. Kavesh, and
Robert B. Platt, (Eds.) *Methods and Techniques of Business Fore-*
casting. Englewood Cliffs, N.J.: Prentice Hall, 1974. (*LRF* 498)

* Nader, Ralph, Petkas, Peter, and Blackwell, Kate, *Whistle Blow-*   I   NR   N
ing. New York: Grossman, 1972. (*LRF* 38, 424)

*** Nagel, Ernest, "Assumptions in Economic Theory," *American Eco-*   T   NR   N
nomic Review, 53 (1963), 211–219.
A critique of Friedman (1953). (*LRF* 306)

** Namboodiri, N.K., and Lalu, N.M., "The Average of Several Simple   Ec   Dem   Y
Regression Estimates as an Alternative to the Multiple Regression
Estimate in Postcensal and Intercensal Population Estimation: A
Case Study," *Rural Sociology*, 36 (1971), 187–194. (*LRF* 242)

** Narasimham, Gorti, Castellino, Victor F., and Singpurwalla, Nozer   Ec   Eco   Ym
D., "On the Predictive Performance of the BEA Quarterly Econo-   Ex
metric Model and a Box-Jenkins Type ARIMA Model," *Proceedings*
of the American Statistical Association: Business and Economic
Statistics Section, 1974, pp. 501–504.
Ex post evaluation of macroeconomic forecasts from 1970 to
1974. No tests of statistical significance. (*LRF* 408)

** National Industrial Conference Board, *Forecasting Sales*, Studies   NR   NR   N
in Business Policy, No. 106, New York, 1963. (*LRF* 288)

** Naylor, Thomas H., Seaks, T.G., and Wichern, D. W., "Box-Jenkins   Ec   Eco   Ym
Methods: An Alternative to Econometric Models," *International Sta-*   Ex
tistical Review, 40 (1972), 123–137.

	M	F	E*

No tests of statistical significance. (*LRF* 408)

* Neild, R.R., and Shirley, E.A., "Economic Review: An Assessment of Forecasts 1959–1960," *National Institute Economic Review*, No. 15 (May 1961), 12–29. (*LRF* 241) — Ec Eco Y

*** Nelson, Charles R., "The Prediction Performance of the FRB-MIT-Penn Model of the U.S. Economy," *American Economic Review*, 5 (1972), 902–917. — Ec Ex Eco Ym

Box-Jenkins was more accurate than an econometric model for one-quarter ahead *ex post* forecast accuracy. Box-Jenkins was more accurate for the 2-year validation period. (*LRF* 164, 408)

* Nelson, Charles R., *Applied Time Series Analysis for Managerial Forecasting*. San Francisco: Holden-Day, 1973. (*LRF* 175, 388) — Ex Eco Ym

*** Newbold, P., and Granger, C.W.J., "Experience with Forecasting Univariate Time Series and the Combination of Forecasts," *Journal of the Royal Statistical Society: Series A*, **137** (1974), 131–165. — Ec Ex Eco Ym

Uses 80 monthly economic time series. Overlaps Granger and Newbold, 1974. (*LRF* 176, 187, 494)

**** Newton, Joseph R., "Judgment and Feedback in a Quasi-clinical Situation," *Journal of Personality and Social Psychology*, 1 (1965), 336–342. (*LRF* 382) — Ju Psy Ym

**** Nisbett, Richard E., and Borgida, Eugene, "Attribution and the Psychology of Prediction," *Journal of Personality and Social Psychology*, **32** (1975), 932–943. — Ju NR Y

"Subjects' unwillingness to deduce the particular from the general was matched only by their willingness to infer the general from the particular." See also BORGIDA [1978]. (*LRF* 85, 589)

** Noelle-Neumann, Elisabeth, "Wanted: Rules for Wording Structured Questionnaires," *Public Opinion Quarterly*, **34** (Summer 1970), 190–201. — Ju NR N

Discusses problems with wording, such as monotony, follow-up questions, position of the question, how to define the object of the study, and how to express alternatives. Presents examples and suggests solutions. (*LRF* 99)

* North Atlantic Treaty Organization, *Forecasting on a Scientific Basis*. Lisbon, Portugal, 1967. (*LRF* 403) — NR NR NR

*** Nystedt, Lars, and Magnusson, David, "Cue Relevance and Feedback in a Clinical Prediction Task," *Organizational Behavior and Human Performance*, **9** (1973), 100–109. (*LRF* 382) — Ju Edu Ym

* O'Dell, William F., "Personal Interviews or Mail Panels," *Journal of Marketing*, **26** (October 1962), 34–39 (*LRF* 115) — Ju Mkt Ym

** Ogburn, William F., "Studies in Prediction and the Distortion of Realtiy," *Social Forces*, **13** (1934), 224–229. (*LRF* 88, 144) — Ju Soc Y

* Ogburn, William F., *The Social Effects of Aviation*, Boston: Houghton Mifflin, 1946. (*LRF* 184, 407, 409) — Ex Trn Y

		M	F	E*

** O'Herlihy, C., et al., "Long-Term Forecasts of Demand for Cars, **Ec** **Eco** **Y**
Selected Consumer Durables and Energy," *National Institute Economic Review*, **40** (May 1967), 34–61. (*LRF* 201, 241, 291, 292, 409, 410)

**** Ohlin, Lloyd E., and Duncan, O.D., "The Efficiency of Prediction **Ec** **Soc** **Ym**
in Criminology," *American-Journal of Sociology*, **54** (1949), 441–452. (*LRF* 339, 354, 402, 427)

** Okun, Arthur H., "The Value of Anticipations Data in Forecasting **Ex** **Eco** **Ym**
Natioal Product," in National Bureau of Economic Research, *The* **Ju**
Quality and Economic Significance of Anticipations Data, Princeton, N.J.: 1960. (*LRF* 138, 290, 292, 396, 398).

* Orcutt, Guy H., et al., *Microanalysis of Socioeconomic Systems: A* **Sg** **Eco** **NR**
Simulation Study. New York: Harper and Brothers, 1961. (*LRF* 250)

** Orne, M.T., Sheehan, P.W., and Evans, F.J., "Occurrence of Post- **Ju** **Psy** **Y**
hypnotic Behavior Outside the Experimental Setting," *Journal of Personality and Social Psychology*, **9** (1968), 189–196. (*LRF* 125)

* Orson, R.W., "Forecasting in the Electricity Supply Industry," in **Ex** **Mkt** **Y**
Michael Young (Ed.), *Forecasting and the Social Sciences*, London: Heinemann, 1968. (*LRF* 167)

*** Oskamp, Stuart, "Overconfidence in Case Study Judgments," *Jour-* **Ju** **Psy** **Y**
nal of Consulting Psychology, **29** (1965), 261–265. (*LRF* 142)

* Oskamp, Stuart, "Clinical Judgment from MMPI: Simple or Com- **Bo** **Psy** **Ym**
plex?" *Journal of Clinical Psychology*, **23** (1967), 411–415. **Ec**
Clinical psychologists used MMPI plus education and age **Ju**
variables to predict which patients had mental problems. (*LRF* 93, 142)

* Ostlund, Lyman E., "Factor Analysis Applied to Predictors of In- **Ec** **Mkt** **Y**
novative Behavior," *Decision Sciences*, **4** (1973), 92–108. (*LRF* 223)

** Palmore, Erdman, "Predicting Longevity: A Follow-up Controlling **Ec** **Med** **Y**
for Age," *The Gerontologist*, **9** (1969), 247–250. (*LRF* 287) **Sg**

* Parkinson, C. Northcote, *Parkinson's Law*. New York: Ballantine, **NR** **NR** **NR**
1957. (*LRF* 371)

* Pashigian, B. Peter, "The Accuracy of the Commerce-S.E.C. Sales **Ex** **Eco** **Y**
Anticipations," *Review of Economics and Statistics*, **46** (1964), **Ju**
398–405. (*LRF* 161)

** Patterson, C.H., "Diagnostic Accuracy or Diagnostic Stereotypy," **T** **NR** **N**
Journal of Consulting Psychology, **19** (1955), 483–485.
This provides a history on the problem of multiple comparisons. (*LRF* 357)

** Payne, Donald E., "Jet Set, Pseudo-Store, and New Product Test- **Ju** **Mkt** **Y**
ing," *Journal of Marketing Research*, **3** (1966), 372–376.
Good study on validity of intentions to purchase a new type of TV. (*LRF 81*)

* Payne, James L., and Dyer, James A., "Betting after the Race is **Ec** **Pol** **Y**
Over: The Perils of *Post Hoc* Hypothesizing," *American Journal of Political Science*, **19** (1975), 559–564. (*LRF* 341)

		M	F	E*

* Payne, Stanley L., *The Art of Asking Questions*. Princeton, N.J.: Princeton University Press, 1951.
Contains good checklists. (*LRF* 99) — Ju Soc N

* Peters, William, *A Class Dividend*. Garden City: Doubleday, 1971.
The "blue eyes and brown eyes" study of prejudice. (*LRF* 109) — NR NR N

* Pfungst, Oskar, *Clever Hans*. New York: Holt, 1911.
See Rosenthal and Rosnow (1969, pp. 197–199) for a short summary. (*LRF* 108) — NR NR Y

** Pickhardt, Robert C., and Wallace, John B., "A Study of the Performance of Subjective Probability Assessors," *Decision Sciences* 5 (1974), 347–363.
Assesses uncertainty in a management game. About 30% of the actual values fell outside the subjectively estimated 98% confidence intervals. Judges had difficulty with estimates close to 0 or 1 (e.g., in horse racing, bettors put too high a probability on long-shots and too low on favorites). (*LRF* 143) — Ju NR Y

**** Platt, John R., "Strong Inference," *Science*, 146 (1964), 347–353.
Important paper on the use of multiple hypotheses. (*LRF* 437, 525) — T NR N

** PoKempner, Stanley J., and Bailey, E., *Sales Forecasting Practices*. New York: The Conference Board, 1970.
(*LRF* 120, 288, 427) — NR NR NR

* Pollack, I., "Action Selection and the Yntema-Torgerson 'Worth' Function." Paper read at the April 1962 meeting of the Eastern Psychological Association.
According to Shepard (1964), Pollack replicated the Yntema-Torgerson study. I was unable to obtain a copy of Pollack's paper. (*LRF* 279) — Bo NR Y

** Pool, Ithiel de Sola, and Abelson, Robert P., "The Simulmatics Project," *Public Opinion Quarterly*, 25 (Summer 1961), 167–183. (*LRF* 76, 559) — Sg Pol Ym

** Pool, Ithiel de Sola, Abelson, Robert P., and Popkin, S. L., *Candidates, Issues and Strategies*. Cambridge, Mass.: MIT Press, 1965.
Expanded and updated version of Pool and Abelson (1961). Includes 1964 U.S. Presidential election. (*LRF* 250, 259, 395, 397, 401, 410, 413) — Sg Pol Ym

*** Port of New York Authority, *Air Travel Forecasting 1965–1975*. Saugatuck, Conn.: Eno Foundation, 1957. (*LRF* 267, 290, 292) — Sg Trn Y

* Pratt, John W.; Raiffa, Howard, and Schlaifer, Robert, *Introduction to Statistical Decision Theory*. London: McGraw-Hill, 1965. (*LRF* 233, 413, 416) — Ec NR N

* Pratt, Robert W., "Consumer Buying Intentions as an Aid in Formulating Marketing Strategy," in Robert L. King (Ed.), *Marketing and the New Science of Planning*. Chicago: American Marketing Association, 1968, pp. 296–302. (*LRF* 81) — Ju Mkt Y

		M	F	E*

** Press, Laurence I., Rogers, M.S., and Shure, G.H., "An Interactive   Sg   NR   N
Technique for the Analysis of Multivariate Data," *Behavioral Science*, **14** (1969), 364–370. (*LRF* 262)

** Pressley, Milton M., *Mail Survey Response: A Critically Annotated*   Ju   NR   N
Bibliography. Greensboro, N.C.: Faber, 1976.
Contains 110 entries. (*LRF* 114)

*** Pritchard, David A., "Linear versus Configural Statistical Predic-   Sg   Soc   Ym
tion," *Journal of Consulting and Clinical Psychology*, **45** (1977),
559–563. (*LRF* 413, 415)

* Pruitt, D.G., "Informational Requirements in Making Decisions,"   Ju   NR   Y
American Journal of Psychology, **74** (1961), 433–439. (*LRF* 52,
437)

* **Q**uinn, Robert P., and Mangione, Thomas W., "Evaluating   Ju   Per   Y
Weighted Models of Measuring Job Satisfaction: A Cinderella
Story," *Organizational Behavior and Human Performance*, **10** (1973),
1–23. (*LRF* 218)

*** **R**abinowitz, W., and Rosenbaum, J., "A Failure in the Prediction   Ec   Edu   Ym
of Pupil-Teacher Rapport," *Journal of Educational Psychology*, **49**
(1958), 93–98. (*LRF* 328)

* Rabitsch, Elisabeth, "Input-Output Analysis and Business Fore-   Sg   Eco   N
casting," *Technological Forecasting and Social Change*, **3** (1972),
453–464. (*LRF* 265)

* Raiffa, Howard, *Decision Analysis*. Reading, Mass.: Addison-Wes-   NR   NR   NR
ley, 1968. (*LRF* 57)

** Raiffa, Howard, "Assessments of Probabilities." Unpublished pa-   Ju   NR   Y
per, January 1969. (Copies may be obtained from John Fitzgerald
Kennedy School of Government, Littauer Center, Harvard University, Cambridge, Mass. 02138). (*LRF* 573)

** Raine, Jesse E., "Self-Adaptive Forecasting Reconsidered," *Deci-*   Ex   Mkt   Ym
sion Sciences, **2** (1971), 181–191. (*LRF* 171, 494)

* Ranard, Elliot D., "Use of Input/Output Concepts in Sales Fore-   Sg   Mkt   N
casting," *Journal of Marketing Research*, **9** (1972), 53–58.
A "how-to-do-it" article. (*LRF* 265)

* Raubenheimer, I. van W., and Tiffin, J., "Personnel Selection and   Ec   Per   Y
the Prediction of Error," *Journal of Applied Psychology*, **55** (1971),   Sg
229–233. (*LRF* 286)

* Reichard, Robert S., *Practical Techniques of Sales Forecasting*. New   NR   Mkt   N
York: McGraw-Hill, 1966. (*LRF* 288)

* Reinmuth, James E., and Geurts, M.D., "A Bayesian Approach to   Ec   Mkt   Ym
Forecasting the Effects of Atypical Situations," *Journal of Market-
ing Research*, **9** (1972), 292–297.
Good idea, but only one data point! (*LRF* 273)

**** Reiss, Albert J., Jr., "The Accuracy, Efficiency and Validity of a   Ec   Soc   Ym
Prediction Instrument," *American Journal of Sociology*, **56** (1951),
552–561. (*LRF* 55, 230)

		M	F	E*

**   Richards, R. Malcolm, "Analysts' Performance and the Accuracy   Ju   Fin   Ym
of Corporate Earnings Forecasts," *Journal of Business*, **49** (1976),
350–357. (*LRF* 94)

**   Ridker, Ronald G., "An Evaluation of the Forecasting Ability of the   Ec   Eco   Ym
Norwegian National Budgeting System," *Review of Economics and*   Ex
Statistics, **45** (1963), 23–33.

Compares five different models, using extrapolation and econometric methods; also uses five different criteria. Concludes that naive methods are as good as econometric methods for annual *ex ante* forecasts over the 12-year test period. However, the effects of the various methods were confounded. (*LRF* 408)

**   Ring, Kenneth, Wallston, K., and Corey, M., "Mode of Debriefing   Ju   Psy   Ym
as a Factor Affecting Subjective Reaction to a Milgram-Type Obedience Experiment: An Ethical Inquiry," *Representative Research in Social Psychology*, **1** (1970), 67–88.

Replicates Milgram (1974), using sound instead of electric shocks, and also having the experimenter act surprised at the victim's pain. Results were similar to Milgram's. (*LRF* 127)

***   Rippe, Richard D., and Wilkinson, Maurice, "Forecasting Accuracy   Ec   Eco   Ym
of the McGraw-Hill Anticipations Data," *Journal of the American*   Ex
Statistical Association, **69** (1974), 849–858.   Ju

Intentions were more accurate than extrapolation and econometric methods for *ex post* forecasts over a four-year forecast horizon. (*LRF* 396, 397, 401)

*   Rippe, Richard D.; Wilkinson, Maurice, and Morrison, Donald,   Sg   Mkt   Ym
"Industrial Market Forecasting with Anticipations Data," *Management Science*, **6** (1976), 639–651.

The authors used an input-output model that incorporated anticipations data to make one-year forecasts in the steel industry. The model did better than two simple naive models, but the sample sizes were small, the effects of the various methods were confounded, and the writing is poor. Otherwise, the article is O.K. (*LRF* 265, 409)

*   Roach, Darrell E., "Double Cross-Validation of a Weighted Appli-   T   Per   Y
cation Blank over Time," *Journal of Applied Psychology*, **55** (1971), 157–160. (*LRF* 342)

*   Robertson, Dennis H., "The Non-Econometrician's Lament," in Erik   NR   Eco   NR
Lundberg (Ed.), *The Business Cycle in the Post-war World*. London: Macmillian, 1955. (*LRF* 192)

*   Robinson, David, Wahlstrom, Owen, and Mecham, Robert C.,   Bo   Per   Y
"Comparison of Job Evaluation Methods: A 'Policy Capturing' Approach Using the Position Analysis Questionnaire," *Journal of Applied Psychology*, **59** (1974), 633–637. (*LRF* 283)

**   Rock, Donald A., Linn, R.L., Evans, F.R., and Patrick, C., "A Com-   Sg   NR   Ym
parison of Predictor Selection Techniques Using Monte Carlo Methods," *Educational and Psychological Measurement*, **30** (1970), 873–884.

		M	F	E*

Two indirect methods of segmentation were compared with two direct methods. A comparison was made between direct segmentation and forward and backward stepwise regressions. The regressions, especially the step-up version, provided better forecasts. *(LRF 223, 262)*

** **Rogers, Theresa F.,** "Interviews by Telephone and in Person: Quality of Responses and Field Performance," *Public Opinion Quarterly,* **40** (1976), 51–65.   **Ju   Edu   Ym**

Telephones can be used for long interviews (about 50 minutes). *(LRF 115)*

** **Rosen, Albert,** "Detection of Suicidal Patients: An Example of Some Limitations in the Prediction of Infrequent Events," *Journal of Consulting Psychology,* **18** (1954), 397–403.   **T   Soc   N**

The suicide rate is only about 1 in 10,000 people per year. This creates problems for prediction. *(LRF 354)*

* **Rosenthal, Robert, and Fode, K.L.,** "The Effect of Experimenter Bias on the Performance of the Albino Rat," *Behavioral Science,* **8** (1963), 183–189. *(LRF 110)*   **T   Psy   Ym**

** **Rosenthal, Robert, and Jacobson, L.,** *Pygmalion in the Classroom.* New York: Holt, Rinehart and Winston, 1968.   **T   NR   Ym**

The first 60 pages provide a good review of the "self-fulfilling" prophecy. *(LRF 109, 110)*

* **Rosenthal, Robert, and Rosnow, Ralph L., (Eds.),** *Artifact in Behavioral Research.* New York: Academic Press, 1969.   **T   NR   Ym**
(LRF 52, 108, 433, 559)

** **Rosenzweig, James E.,** *The Demand for Aluminum: A Case Study in Business Forecasting.* University of Illinois, Bureau of Economics and Business Research, Champaign, 1957. *(LRF 292, 409, 410)*   **Ec   Mkt   Y**

* **Roth, Julius A.,** "Hired Hand Research," *The American Sociologist,* **1** (1966), 190–196.   **T   NR   N**

Suggests that cheating and cutting corners are the rule rather than the exception among hired research workers. The solution? Roth says that the workers should participate in decision-making on the project. There is also a need to audit results. *(LRF 116)*

** **Rothman, James,** "Formulation of an Index of Propensity to Buy," *Journal of Marketing Research,* **1** (1964), 21–25.   **Ju   Mkt   Ym**

Compares four scales to assess coupon redemption for two brands of soap and two brands of cereal. *(LRF 106)*

* **Runyon, John H., Verdini, J., and Runyon, S.S.,** *Source Book of American Presidential Campaign and Election Statistics, 1948–1968.* New York: Frederick Ungar, 1971. *(LRF 129)*   **NR   NR   NR**

*** **Russo, J.A.; Enger, I., and Sorenson, E.L.,** "A Statistical Approach to the Short-Period Prediction of Surface Winds," *Journal of Applied Meteorology,* **3** (1964), 126–131. *(LRF 395, 397, 409)*   **Ec   Wea   Ym**
Ex

		M	F	E*

** Ryback, D., "Confidence and Accuracy as a Function of Experience in Judgment-Making in the Absence of Systematic Feedback," *Perceptual and Motor Skills*, **24** (1967), 331–334. (*LRF* 142, 380)   Ju   NR   Y

*** **S**ackman, Harold, *Delphi Critique: Expert Opinion, Forecasting, and Group Process.* Lexington, Mass.: D. C. Heath, 1975.   Ju   NR   NR

Although this book is short (76 pages followed by about 150 annotated references), it provided a thorough review and evaluation of Delphi. Brian Twiss, in a review in *Futures*, 8 (1976, 357–358, says that the book has been highly controversial. Furthermore, he implies that Sackman's book will not convince advocates of Delphi to discard it. For critiques on Sackman see the special issue on Delphi in *Technological Forecasting and Social Change*, **7**, No. 2, 1975. (*LRF* 117, 118, 119, 433)

*** Saginor, Irving, *Forecast of Scheduled Domestic Air Passenger Traffic for the Eleven Trunkline Carriers, 1968–1977.* Washington, D.C.: Civil Aeronautics Board, September 1967.   Ec   Trn   Y

This 33-page booklet provides a simple and well-explained example of an econometric study. (*LRF* 326)

* Sale, Charles, *The Specialist.* London: Putnam, 1930.   NR   NR   NR

Lem Putt, the privy builder, makes a good argument for the value of an expert. Nonexperts cannot build a good privy. Great fun for a 20-minute book. (*LRF* 92)

* Salomon, M., and Brown, R.V., "Applications of Econometrics to Commercial Forecasting Problems," *Operational Research Quarterly*, **15** (1964), 239–247.   Ec Sg   Mkt   Y

Unfortunately, there is insufficient information in this paper. (*LRF* 286)

* Salvendy, Gavriel, and Seymour, W. Douglas, *Prediction and Development of Industrial Work Performance*, New York: Wiley, 1973. (*LRF* 202)   NR   Per   NR

** Sanders, Frederick, "On Subjective Probability Forecasting," *Journal of Applied Meteorology*, **2** (1963), 191–201.   Ju   Wea   Y

Weather forecasters became overconfident when no objective record was kept of forecast accuracy. This did not occur when they kept records. (*LRF* 137)

*** Sarbin, Theodore R., "A Contribution to the Study of Actuarial and Individual Methods of Prediction," *American Journal of Sociology*, **48** (1943), 593–602.   Ec Ju   Edu   Ym

First of the "clinical vs. statistical" studies in psychology. A good study that has held up well over the years. (*LRF* 393)

*** Sarbin, Theodore R., Taft, R., and Bailey, D.E., *Clinical Inference and Cognitive Theory.* New York: Holt, Rinehart and Winston, 1960. (*LRF* 93, 568)   Ec Ju   Psy   Ym

*** Sawyer, Jack, "Measurement and Prediction, Clinical and Statistical," *Psychological Bulletin*, **66** (1966), 178–200. (*LRF* 393)   Ec Ju   NR   N

		M	F	E*

** Scheflen, Kenneth C., Lawler, E.E., and Hackman, J.R., "Long-Term Impact of Employee Participation in the Development of Pay Incentive Plans," *Journal of Applied Psychology*, 55 (1971), 182–186. Management departed from participative management in two of the three participative groups, surprising both the workers and the researchers. Performance then dropped in these groups. (*LRF* 36) — **I Pro Ym**

*** Schmidt, Frank L., "The Relative Efficiency of Regression and Simple Unit Predictor Weights in Applied Differential Psychology," *Educational and Psychological Measurement*, 31 (1971), 699–714. Used simulated data and examined studies from psychology to determine when to use regression weights instead of unit weights. (*LRF* 231) — **Ec Psy Ym**

** Schmitt, Robert C., "An Application of Multiple Correlation to Population Forecasting," *Land Economics*, 30 (1954), 277–279. (*LRF* 290) — **Ec Ex Dem Ym**

** Schneidman, Edwin S., "Pertubation and Lethality as Precursors of Suicide in a Gifted Group," *Life-Threatening Behavior*, 1 (Spring 1971), 23–45. (*LRF* 372) — **Ju Psy Y**

* Schoeffler, Sidney, *The Failures of Economics: A Diagnostic Study*. Cambridge, Mass.: Harvard University Press, 1955. (*LRF* 000) — **Ec Eco N**

**** Schuessler, Karl F., "Parole Prediction: Its History and Status," *Journal of Criminal Law, Criminology, and Police Science*, 45 (1954), 425–431. (*LRF* 402, 427) — **Ec Ex Ju Soc Ym**

*** Schupack, Mark B., "The Predictive Accuracy of Empirical Demand Analysis," *Economic Journal*, 72 (1962), 550–575. Good study, but difficult to read. (*LRF* 212, 339, 356) — **Ec Ex Eco Ym**

** Scott, Christopher, "Research on Mail Surveys," *Journal of the Royal Statistical Society, Series A*, 124 (1961), 143–191. (*LRF* 114) — **Ju NR Y**

** Scott, Richard D., and Johnson, R.W., "Use of the Weighted application Blank in Selecting Unskilled Employees," *Journal of Applied Psychology*, 51 (1967), 393–395. (*LRF* 230) — **Ec Per Ym**

* Seashore, H.G., "Women Are More Predictable than Men." Presidential address, Division 17, American Psychological Association Convention, New York, Sept 1961. (*LRF* 285) — **Ec Sg Edu Y**

** Sechrest, Lee, Gallimore, R., and Hersch, P.D., "Feedback and Accuracy of Clinical Predictions," *Journal of Consulting Psychology*, 31 (1967), 1–11. (*LRF* 380) — **Ju Psy Ym**

* Selltiz, Claire, Wrightsman, Lawrence S., and Cook, Stuart W., *Research Methods in Social Relations*. New York: Holt, Rinehart and Winston, 1976. (*LRF* 106, 108, 323) — **NR NR NR**

* Seo, K.K., *Managerial Economics*. Homewood, Ill.: Irwin, 1984. (Sixth edition of the original text by Spencer). Contains good simple description of demand analysis and forecasting. (*LRF* 72) — **Ju Ec Ex Eco N**

** Shelton, John P., "The Value Line Contest: A Test of Predictability — **Ju Fin Ym**

	M	F	E*

of Stock Price Changes," *Journal of Business,* **40** (1967), 251–269. (*LRF* 94)

** Shepard, R.N., "On Subjectively Optimum Selections among Multi-Attribute Alternatives," in Maynard W. Shelly and G.L. Bryan (Eds.), *Human Judgments and Optimality,* New York: Wiley, 1964, pp. 257–281.   Ju | NR | N

Good survey of the early work in judgmental forecasts. (*LRF* 279, 559)

* Sherbini, A.A., in book "directed by" Bertil Liander, *Comparative Analysis for International Marketing.* Boston: Allyn and Bacon, 1967. (*LRF* 327)   NR | Int | Y

* Sherif, Muzafer, "The Formation of a Norm in a Group Situation," in M. Sherif, *The Psychology of Social Norms.* New York: Harper and Row, 1936, pp. 89–112. (*LRF* 111)   Ju | NR | Y

** Sherwin, C., and Isenson, R.S., "Project Hindsight," *Science,* **156** (1967), 1571–1577. (*LRF* 439)   NR | Sci | Y

** Shiskin, Julius, *The X-11 Variant of the Census Method II Seasonal Adjustment Program,* Washington, D.C.: U.S. Bureau of the Census, 1965. (*LRF* 173)   Ex | NR | N

*** Siegel, Sidney, *Nonparametric Statistics.* New York: McGraw-Hill, 1956.   T | NR | NR

According to *Current Contents,* this was the second most frequently cited work in mathematical and statistical journals over the 1961–1972 period. (*LRF* 224, 352, 356, 405, 505, 506, 510, 512)

**** Sigall, H. Aronson, E., and van Hoose, T., "The Cooperative Subject: Myth or Reality?" *Journal of Experimental Social Psychology,* **6** (1970), 1–10. (*LRF* 109)   NR | Psy | Ym

* Simon, Herbert A., *Models of Man: Social and Rational.* New York: Wiley, 1957. (*LRF* 80)   NR | NR | NR

* Simon, Julian L., *Basic Sesearch Methods in Social Science.* New York: Random House, 1969, (Revised 1978). (*LRF* 86, 115)   NR | NR | NR

* Simons, Carolyn W., and Piliavin, J.A., "Effect of Deception on Reactions to a Victim," *Journal of Personality and Social Psychology,* **21** (1972), 56–60.   Ju | Psy | Ym

Results from experiment and role play differed substantially in this study. (*LRF* 128)

** Sims, Christopher A., "Evaluating Short-term Macroeconomic Forecasts: The Dutch Performance," *Review of Economics and Statistics,* **49** (1967), 225–236.   Ec | Eco | Y

Econometric models provided better forecasts than did naive models for 1953–1963. The econometric models were relatively less accurate, however, in the more recent years. (*LRF* 408, 409)

** Skinner, B.F., "Superstition in the Pigeon," *Journal of Experimental Psychology,* **38** (1948), 168–172. (*LRF* 375)   Ju | NR | Y

	M	F	E*

** Slovic, Paul, Fleissner, D., and Bauman, W.S., "Analyzing the Use of Information in Investment Decision Making: A Methodological Proposal," *Journal of Business*, **45** (1972), 283–301. — Ju, Fin, N

The longer a stockbroker has been in the business, the less insight he seemed to have in how he made decisions. (*LRF* 278)

*** Smedslund, J., "The Concept of Correlation in Adults," *Scandinavian Journal of Psychology*, **4** (1963), 165–173. (*LRF* 380) — Ju, NR, Y

** Smyth, D.J., "How Well Do Australian Economists Forecast?" *Economic Record*, **42** (1966), 293–311. — Ju, Eco, Y

Judgmental forecasts underestimate positive changes two thirds of the time. Good description of turning-point errors. (*LRF* 353, 396)

* Solow, R.M., "Technical Change and the Aggregate Production Function," *Review of Economics and Statistics*, **39** (1957), 312–320. (*LRF* 54, 543) — Ec, Eco, Y

*** Sonquist, John A., *Multivariate Model Building*. Survey Research Center, University of Michigan, Ann Arbor, 1970. — Sg, NR, Ym

A good study and extensive bibliography. (*LRF* 413, 417)

** Sonquist, John A., Baker, E.L., and Morgan, J.N., *Searching for Structure (Alias AID-III): An Approach to Analysis of Substantial Bodies of Micro-data and Documentation for a Computer Program.* Ann Arbor: Institute for Social Research, University of Michigan, 1974.

This is a descriptive title! (*LRF* 262)

** Sonquist, John A., and Morgan, James N., *The Detection of Interaction Effects.* Monograph No. 35, Survey Research Center, University of Michigan, Ann Arbor, 1964. — Sg, NR, Ym

Presents nine examples of comparisons between regression and cross classification. (*LRF* 262)

** Staël Von Holstein, Carl-Axel S., "An Experiment in Probabilistic Weather Forecasting," *Journal of Applied Meteorology*, **10** (1971), 635–645. (*LRF* 137, 143, 397) — Ju, Wea, Y

** Staël Von Holstein, Carl-Axel S., "Probabilistic Forecasting: An Experiment Related to the Stock Market," *Organizational Behavior and Human Performance*, **8** (1972), 139–158. (*LRF* 94, 137, 143) — Ju, Fin, Ym

* Stark, Rodney, and Glock, Charles Y., "Will Ethics Be the Death of Christianity?" *Transaction*, **5** (June 1968), 7–14. — Sg, Soc, Y

Transaction is now called *Society*. (*LRF* 258)

** Stekler, Herman O., *Economic Forecasting*. New York: Praeger, 1970. — Ec, Ex, Ju; Eco; Ym

Stekler's articles are pasted together here with a few words. Stekler contrasts *ex ante* with *ex post* forecast errors, compares econometric with extrapolation and judgmental forecasts, and looks at the growth of error over the forecast horizon. (*LRF* 241)

** Stevens, S.S., "Measurement, Psychophysics and Utility," in — NR, NR, N

	M	F	E*

C. West Churchman and P. Ratoosh (Eds.), *Measurement Definitions and Theories*, New York: Wiley, 1959. (*LRF* 106, 391)

* Stone, LeRoy A. and Brosseau, James D., "Cross Validation of a System for Predicting Training Success of Medex Trainees," *Psychological Reports*, **33** (1973), 917–918. (*LRF* 56) — Ec · Edu · Y

* Stone, Richard, *Mathematics in the Social Sciences and Other Essays*. London: Chapman and Hall, 1966. (*LRF* 200) — Ec · Eco · N

** Stout, Roy G., "Developing Data to Estimate Price-Quantity Relationships," *Journal of Marketing*, **33** (April 1969), 31–36. (*LRF* 212) — Ec · Mkt · Y

** Strickland, Lloyd H., "Surveillance and Trust," *Journal of Personality*, **26** (1958), 200–215. — Ju · Pro · Ym

Shows how people "learn" that authoritarian management is successful even when it is not. (*LRF* 375)

** Strickler, George, "Actuarial, Naive Clinical, and Sophisticated Clinical Prediction of Pathology from Figure Drawings," *Journal of Consulting Psychology*, **31** (1967), 492–494. (*LRF* 379) — Ec Ju · Psy · Ym

* Strong, Lydia, "Sales Forecasting Comes of Age," *Management Review*, **45** (1956), 687–701. — NR · NR · Y

The author administered a survey at the American Marketing Association's conference on sales forecasting. Further details are provided in her article, "Sales Forecasting: Problems and Prospects," on pp. 790–803 of the same volume. (*LRF* 273, 454)

** Stroop, J.R., "Is the Judgment of the Group Better than That of the Average Member of the Group?" *Journal of Experimental Psychology*, **15** (1932), 550–560. (*LRF* 135) — Ju · NR · Ym

**** Stuckert, R.P., "A Configurational Approach to Prediction," *Sociometry*, **21** (1958), 225–237. (*LRF* 219, 230, 413, 416) — Ec Sg · Edu · Ym

** Sudman, Seymour, and Bradburn, Norman, *Response Effects in Surveys: A Review and Synthesis*. Chicago: Aldine, 1974. — Ju · NR · Y

Statistical analysis of 935 published studies. Interesting conclusion: for threatening questions, it is best to use self administered questionnaires that should be filled out with no one else present, and preferably not done at work or any other place where there is a line of authority. (*LRF* 115, 116)

*** Suits, Daniel B., "The Use of Dummy Variables in Regression Equations," *Journal of the American Statistical Association*, **52** (1957), 548–551. (*LRF* 504) — Ec · NR · N

** Summers, David A., and Stewart, Thomas R., "Regression Models of Foreign Policy Beliefs," *Proceedings of the American Psychological Association*, 1968, pp. 195–196. (*LRF* 230) — Bo · Pol · Y

*** Summers, David A., Taliaferro, J.D., and Fletcher, D.J., "Subjective vs. Objective Description of Judgment Policy," *Psychonomic Science*, **18** (1970), 249–250. — Bo Ju · Pol · Ym

Subjects report their judgment to be complex but the data refute this view. (*LRF* 278)

		M	F	E*

* Summers, Robert, "A Capital Intensive Approach to Small Sample Properties of Various Simultaneous Equation Estimators," *Econometrica*, **33** (1965), 1–41. — Ec / Eco / Ym

Compares simultaneous equations and single equations for conditional forecasts and finds small differences. (*LRF* 200)

* Szasz, Thomas S., *The Second Sin*. London: Routledge and Kegan Paul, 1973. — NR / NR / N

The "second sin," is telling the truth. Society does not like this and treats truth tellers harshly. (*LRF* 433)

*** Taft, R., "The Ability to Judge People," *Psychological Bulletin*, **52** (1955), 1–28. — Ju / Psy / Ym

A literature review with 81 references, updated by Sarbin, Taft, and Bailey (1960). (*LRF* 93)

** Taylor, D.W., Berry, P.C., and Block, C.H., "Does Group Participation When Using Brainstorming Facilitate or Inhibit Creative Thinking?" *Administrative Science Quarterly*, **3** (1958), 23–47. (*LRF* 501) — Ju / NR / Ym

* Taylor, Frederick W., *The Principles of Scientific Management*. New York: Harper and Brothers, 1911. (*LRF* 275) — NR / NR / NR

* Terry, Roger L., "Role Playing and the Effects of Expectancy Confirmation," *Journal of Social Psychology*, **94** (1974), 291–292. — Ju / NR / Y

Not enough of a description. (*LRF* 128)

** Tessier, Thomas H., and Armstrong, J. Scott, "Improving Current Sales Estimates with Econometric Methods," Wharton Working Paper, University of Pennsylvania, Philadelphia, PA. 1977. (*LRF* 234, 236, 453, 454) — Ec / Mkt / Ym

* Theil, Henri, *Economic Forecasts and Policy*. Amsterdam, North-Holland, 1958 (Revised 1965). (*LRF* 349) — Ec / Eco / NR

* Theil, Henri, *Applied Economic Forecasting*. Chicago: Rand McNally, 1966. (*LRF* 241, 344, 349) — Ec / Eco / NR

** Theil, Henri and Goldberger, A.S., "On Pure and Mixed Statistical Estimation in Economics," *International Economic Review*, **2** (1961), 65–78. (*LRF* 203) — Ec / Eco / Y

*** Thomas, E.J., and Fink, C.F., "Models of Group Problem Solving," *Journal of Abnormal and Social Psychology*, **63** (1961), 53–63. (*LRF* 120) — Ju / NR / Ym

* Thompson, Philip D., *Numerical Weather Analysis and Prediction*, New York: Macmillan, 1961. (*LRF* 59) — NR / Wea / NR

*** Thorndike, R.L., "The Effect of Discussion upon the Correctness of Group Decisions When the Factor of a Majority Influence Is Allowed For," *Journal of Social Psychology*, **9** (1938), 343–362. — Ju / NR / Y

Groups find it easier to tolerate being wrong than to tolerate differences of opinions among group members. (*LRF* 136, 139)

* Timmons, William M., "Can the Product Superiority of Discussers Be Attributed to Averaging or Majority Influences?" *Journal of Social Psychology*, **15** (1942), 23–32. — Ju / Soc / Ym

	M	F	E*

Discussion does, on occasion, lead to improvements over mere averaging. (*LRF* 120)

* Tobias, Sigmund, and Carlson, James E., "Brief Report: Bartlett's Test of Sphericity and Chance Findings in Factor Analysis," *Multivariate Behavioral Research*, **4** (1969), 375–377. (*LRF* 518) — Ec NR Ym

** Tobin, James, "On the Predictive Value of Consumer Intentions and Attitudes," *Review of Economics and Statistics*, **41** (1959), 1–11. (*LRF* 81) — Ju Mkt Ym

** Torfin, Garry P., and Hoffmann, T.R., "Simulation Tests of Some Forecasting Techniques," *Production and Inventory Management*, **9** No. 2 (1968), 71–78. (*LRF* 170, 171, 495) — Ex NR Ym

* Trigg, D.W. and Leach, A.G., "Exponential Smoothing with an Adaptive Response Rate." *Operational Research Quarterly*, **18** (1967), 53–59. (*LRF* 171) — Ex NR Ym

** Tukey, J.W., "The Future of Data Analysis," *Annals of Mathematical Statistics*, **33** (1962), 1–67. (*LRF* 1, 162, 334) — NR NR NR

** Turing, A.M., "Computing Machinery and Intelligence," *Mind*, **59** (1950), 433–460. (*LRF* 313) — T NR N

* Turner, John, "A Survey of Forecasting Practices," in David Ashton and Leslie Simister (Eds.), *The Role of Forecasting in Corporate Planning*. London: Staples Press, 1970. — NR NR Y

Survey of how firms forecast in the United States and in Britain. For long-range forecasting, subjective methods are most common, next extrapolation, then econometric methods. (*LRF* 425)

*** Tversky, Amos, and Kahneman, Daniel, "Belief in the Law of Small Numbers," *Psychological Bulletin*, **76** (1971), 105–110. — Ju, T NR Y

Concludes that even trained statisticians may have a poor intuitive feel for certain statistical phenomena. (*LRF* 89, 90, 356, 479, 486)

** Tversky, Amos, and Kahneman, Daniel, "Availability: A Heuristic for Judging Frequency and Probability," *Cognitive Psychology*, **5** (1973), 207–232. (*LRF* 105) — Ju NR Y

* Tversky, Amos, and Kahneman, Daniel, "Judgment Under Uncertainty: Heuristics and Biases," *Science*, **185** (1974), 1124–1131. — Ju, T NR Y

A highly influential paper. According to the *Social Sciences Citation Index*, it is cited, on average, over 50 times per year. It is reprinted in KAHNEMAN, SLOVIC, and TVERSKY [1982]. (*LRF* 88, 89).

* Ueno, Hiroya, and Tsurumi, Hiroki, "A Dynamic Supply and Demand Model of the United States Automobile Industry, Together with a Simulation Experiment," in Lawrence R. Klein (Ed.), *Essays in Industrial Econometrics*, Vol. 1, Economics Research Unit, Wharton School, University of Pennsylvania, Philadelphia, 1969. — Ec Eco Y

This essay is written mostly in equations and numbers. (*LRF* 226, 488, 490)

	M	F	E*

*** Uhl, Norman, and Eisenberg, Terry, "Predicting Shrinkage in the   T   NR   Ym
Multiple Correlation Coefficient," *Educational and Psychological
Measurement*, **30** (1970), 487–489. (*LRF* 351)

  * U.S. Bureau of the Census, "Measuring the Quality of Housing—   NR   NR   NR
An Appraisal of Census Statistics and Methods," Working Paper
No. 25, July 1967. (*LRF* 60)

 ** U.S. National Resources Committee, *Patterns of Resource Use* (pre-   Ec   Eco   Y
liminary edition for technical criticism). Washington, D.C.: U.S.   T
Government Printing Office, 1938. (*LRF* 338)

 ** Uri, Noel D., "Forecasting: A Hybrid Approach," *Omega*, 5 (1977),   Ec   Pro   Ym
463–472.

Box-Jenkins forecasts were superior to econometric forecasts
with respect to MAPE (4.8 vs. 6.0). On the other hand, the
systematic error was larger for Box-Jenkins forecasts than
for econometric forecasts (APE of +4.0 vs. −1.2). Overall,
this study was classified as a tie. (*LRF* 408)

*** **V**accara, Beatrice N., "An Input-Output Method for Long-Range   Ex   Eco   Ym
Economic Projections," *Survey of Current Business*, **51** (July 1971),   Sg
47–56.

Looks at the value of input-output vs. an extrapolation method
of forecasting (slight advantage to the I-O method). (*LRF* 265,
266)

  * Van de Ven, Andrew H., "Group Decision Making and Effective-   Ju   Edu   Y
ness," *Organization and Administrative Sciences*, **5** (Fall 1974),
1–110. (*LRF* 119, 120, 123, 124)

 ** Vandome, Peter, "Econometric Forecasting for the United King-   Ec   Eco   Ym
dom," *Bulletin of the Oxford University Institute of Economics and
Statistics*, **25** (1963). 239–281. (*LRF* 291, 292, 396, 406, 408)

  * Velikovsky, Immanuel, *Worlds In Collision*. New York: Macmillan,   NR   NR   NR
1950. (*LRF* 66, 67)

  * Velikovsky, Immanuel, *Earth in Upheaval*. Garden City: Double-   NR   NR   NR
day, 1955. (*LRF* 66, 67)

 ** **W**ade, Nicholas, "IQ and Heredity: Suspicion of Fraud Beclouds   T   Psy   N
Classic Experiment," *Science*, **194** (1976), 916–919. (*LRF* 312,
435)

  * Wagle, B., Rappoport, J.Q.G.H., and Downes, V.A., "A Program   Mkt   Ym
for Short-Term Sales Forecasting," *The Statistician*, **18** (1968),
141–147.

		M	F	E*

Different extrapolation methods were used to provide forecasts of monthly sales for 20 products. Not much difference was found in the accuracy of the extrapolations (including one that was done by hand). Looks like a good study, but the write-up is incomplete. (*LRF* 177)

* Walker, H.E., "The Value of Human Judgment," *Industrial Marketing Research Association Journal*, 6 (May 1970), 71–74. (*LRF* 145, 170)   Ju   NR   Y

* Wallace, Henry A., "What is in the Corn Judge's Mind?" *Journal of the American Society of Agronomy*, 15 (1923), 300–304. (*LRF* 278)   Bo   Agr   Y

** Ward, J.H., Jr., *An Application of Linear and Curvilinear Joint Functional Regression in Psychological Prediction*, Research Bulletin. Air Force Personnel and Training Research Center. Lackland Air Force Base, San Antonio, Tex., 1954.   Ec   Edu   Ym

There is a description of this study in Wiggins (1973, pp. 74–77). (*LRF* 202, 342)

**** Ward, William C., and Jenkins, Herbert M., "The Display of Information and the Judgment of Contingency," *Canadian Journal of Psychology*, 19 (1965), 231–241. (*LRF* 381)   Ju   NR   Ym

**** Wason, P.C., "On the Failure to Eliminate Hypotheses in a Conceptual Task," *Quarterly Journal of Experimental Psychology*, 12 (1960), 129–140.   Ju   NR   Ym

Subjects who made quick decisions were wrong more often than those who gathered more data before making a decision. (*LRF* 52, 377)

** Wason, P.C., "On the Failure to Eliminate Hypotheses—a Second Look," in P.C. Wason and P. N. Johnson-Laird (Eds.), *Thinking and Reasoning*. Baltimore: Penguin Books, 1968a, pp. 165–174. (*LRF* 52, 377)   Ju   NR   Ym

*** Wason, P.C., "Reasoning about a Rule," *Quarterly Journal of Experimental Psychology*, 20 (1968b), 273–281.   Ju   NR   Ym

An alternate to "2, 4, 6" problem known as: the "A-D-4-7" problem. Discouraging finding; it did not help to tell people to look for disconfirming evidence. (*LRF* 52, 378)

** Wason, P.C., "Regression in Reasoning?" *British Journal of Psychology*, 60 (1969), 471–480.   Ju   Psy   Ym

More on Wason (1968b) and on how to improve subject's use of data. (*LRF* 378)

* Webb, Eugene J., et al., *Unobtrusive Measures: Non-reactive Research in the Social Sciences*. Chicago: Rand McNally, 1973. (*LRF* 65, 207)   NR   NR   NR

** Webster, Edward C., *Decision Making in the Employment Interview*. Montreal, Quebec: Eagle, 1964.   Ju   Per   Y

The employment interview is a search for negative evidence. (*LRF* 88)

	M	F	E*

* Weld, L.D.H., "The Value of the Multiple Correlation Method in Determining Sales Potentials," *Journal of Marketing*, 3 (1939), 389–393.   Ec   Mkt   Y

Weld says that he wants the credit for being the first person to use the multiple correlation method to identify sales potentials. Advocates an exploratory rather than a theoretical use of regression. (*LRF* 235)

* Wellman, H.R., "The Distribution of Selling Effort among Geographical Areas," *Journal of Marketing*, 3 (January 1939), 225–239. (*LRF* 235)   Ec   Mkt   Y

** Welty, Gordon, "Problems of Selecting Experts for Delphi Exercises," *Academy of Management Journal*, 15 (March 1972), 121–124. (*LRF* 118)   Ju   Soc   Ym

* Welty, Gordon, "The Necessity, Sufficiency and Desirability of Experts as Value Forecasters," in Werner Leinfellner and Eckehart Köhler (Eds.), *Developments in the Methodology of Social Science*. Boston: Reidel, 1974, pp. 363–379. (*LRF* 117)   Ju   NR   N

*** Wesman, A.G., and Bennett, G.K., "Multiple Regression vs. Simple Addition of Scores in Prediction of College Grades," *Educational and Psychological Measurement*, 19 (1959), 243–246. (*LRF* 230)   Ec   Edu   Ym

* Westfall, Richard, "Newton and the Fudge Factor," *Science*, 179 (1973), 751–758. (*LRF* 289)   T   NR   NR

* Westoff, Charles F., "Fertility through Twenty Years of Marriage: A Study in Predictive Possibilities," *American Sociological Review*, 23 (1958), 549–556.   Ec   Soc   Y

How well can you forecast the number of children who will be born in the first 20 years of marriage by asking engaged couples? Fairly well for those who use family planning—otherwise poorly. (*LRF* 82)

*** Wexley, Kenneth, Singh, J.P., and Yukl, G.A., "Subordinate Personality as a Moderator of the Effects of Participation in Three Types of Appraisal Interviews," *Journal of Applied Psychology*, 58 (1973), 54–59. (*LRF* 128)   I   Per   Ym

** Wheelwright, Steven C., and Clarke, Darral, G., "Corporate Forecasting Promise and Reality," *Harvard Business Review*, 76 (November–December 1976), 40 seq.   NR   Eco   Y

This survey received only a 25% response rate, and the report is incomplete, yet what is there is interesting. (*LRF* 25, 389, 457)

* Wherry, R.J., "A New Formula for Predicting the Shrinkage of the Coefficient of Multiple Correlation," *Annals of Mathematical Statistics*, 2 (1931), 440–457. (*LRF* 351)   T   NR   NR

** Whitbeck, Volkert S., and Kisor, M., Jr., "A New Tool in Investment Decision-Making," *Financial Analysts Journal*, (May–June, 1963), 55–62.   Ec   Fin   Y

Uses regression analysis to predict price/earnings ratios for 135 stocks. Finds that undervalued stocks in one cross section

	M	F	E*

did better in the next time period and overvalued stocks did worse. Cragg and Malkiel (1970) were unable to replicate the findings. (*LRF* 529)

* Wicker, A.W., "An Examination of the 'Other Variables' Explanation of Attitude-Behavior Inconsistency," *Journal of Personality and Social Psychology* **19** (1971), 18–30. (*LRF* 83) — Ju / Psy / N

*** Wiggins, Jerry S., *Personality and Prediction: Principles of Personality Assessment.* Reading, Mass.: Addison-Wesley, 1973. — Ec Ex Ju / Psy / Ym
This book provides a thorough treatment of forecasting in psychology. (*LRF* 571)

* Wiggins, Nancy, and Hoffman, P.J., "Three Models of Clinical Judgment," *Journal of Abnormal Psychology,* **73** (1968), 70–77. — Ju / Psy / Ym
Goldberg (1968a) comments on this study. (*LRF* 278)

*** Wiggins, Nancy, and Kohen, E., "Man vs. Model of Man Revisited: The Forecasting of Graduate School Success," *Journal of Personality and Social Psychology,* **19** (1971), 100–106. (*LRF* 137, 281, 283) — Bo Ju / Edu / Ym

** Wiginton, John C., "MSAE Estimation: An Alternative Approach to Regression Analysis for Economic Forecasting Applications," *Applied Economics,* **4** (1972), 11–21. — Ec / NR / Ym
MSAE stands for "minimizing the sum of absolute errors." Wiginton discusses the history of MSAE since 1890 and examines evidence on MSAE versus least squares estimates. (*LRF* 221)

* Williams, John D., and Linden, Alfred C., "Setwise Regression Analysis—A Stepwise Procedure for Sets of Variables," *Educational and Psychological Measurement,* **31** (1971), 747–748. (*LRF* 205) — Ec / NR / NR

* Williams, Philip, Jr., "The Use of Confidence Factors in Forecasting," *Bulletin of the American Meterological Society,* **32** (1951), 279–281. — Ju / Wea / Y
See Raiffa (1969) for a summary. (*LRF* 141)

*** Williams, W.H. and Goodman, M.L., "A Simple Method for the Construction of Empirical Confidence Limits for Economic Forecasts," *Journal of the American Statistical Association,* **66** (1971), 752–754. (*LRF* 186, 338, 343) — Ex / Mkt / Y

** Willis, Richard H., and Willis, Y.A., "Role Playing vs. Deception: An Experimental Comparison," *Journal of Personality and Social Psychology,* **16** (1970), 472–477. (*LRF* 127) — Ju / Psy / Y

* Willoughby, R.R. and Cougan, M., "The Correlation between Intelligence and Fertility," *Human Biology,* **12** (1940), 114–119. (*LRF* 322) — NR / NR / Ym

*** Winkler, Robert L., "The Quantification of Judgment: Some Experimental Results," in *Proceedings of the American Statistical Association; Business and Economics Statistics Section,* 1967a, pp. 386–375. — Ju / Soc / Ym
Study of football forecasts, (*LRF* 95, 136, 137)

		M	F	E*

*** Winkler, Robert L., "Probabilistic Prediction: Some Experimental   Ju   Soc   Ym
Results," *Journal of the American Statistical Association*, 66 (1971),
675–685.
Still more on football forecasts. (*LRF* 95, 136, 139)

* Winkler, Robert L. and Murphy, Allan H., "Evaluation of Subjective   Ju   Wea   Y
Precipitation Probability Forecasts," *Proceedings of the First National Conference on Statistical Meteorology.* Boston, 1968, pp.
148–157. (*LRF* 395, 397, 400)

*** Winters, Peter R., "Forecasting Sales by Exponentially Weighted   Ex   Mkt   Y
Moving Averages," *Management Science*, 6 (1960), 324–342.
(*LRF* 161, 165, 171, 173, 450, 494)

** Wise, George, "The Accuracy of Technological Forecasts,   Ju   Nr   Y
1890–1940," *Futures*, 8 (1976), 411–419.
Examines and codes 1556 predictions made publicly by Americans between 1890 and 1940. (*LRF* 95)

* Wiseman, Frederick, "Methodological Bias in Public Opinion Sur-   Ju   Soc   Ym
veys," *Public Opinion Quarterly*, 36 (Spring 1972a), 105–108.
Examines response bias in mail vs. telephone vs. personal
interviews. (*LRF* 115)

** Wiseman, Frederick, "Methodological Considerations in Segmen-   Ju   Mkt   Y
tation Studies," in Fred C. Allvine (Ed.), *Combined Proceedings.*
Chicago: American Marketing Association, 1972b, pp. 306–311.
(*LRF* 342)

*** Wold, Herman, and Jureen, Lars, *Demand Analysis: A Study in*   Ec   Eco   NR
Econometrics, New York, Wiley, 1953. (*LRF* 75, 234)

* Wolfe, Harry D., *Business Forecasting Methods.* New York: Holt,   NR   Eco   NR
Rinehart and Winston, 1966. (*LRF* 288)

* Worswick, G.D.N., "Preston, R.S., The Wharton Annual and In-   Ec   Eco   N
dustry Forecasting Model," *Journal of Economic Literature*, 12 (1974),
117–118.
(*LRF* 403)

* **Y**an, Chiou-Shuang, *Introduction to Input-Output Economics.* New   Sg   Eco   N
York: Holt, Rinehart and Winston, 1969. (*LRF* 265)

* Yinon, Yoel; Shoham, Varda, and Lewis, Tirtza, "Risky-Shift in a   Ju   NR   Y
Real vs. Role-Played Situation," *Journal of Social Psychology*, 93
(1974), 137–138. (*LRF* 128)

*** Yntema, D.B., and Torgerson, W.S., "Man-Computer Cooperation   Bo   NR   Y
in Decisions Requiring Common Sense," *IRE Transactions of the*   Ju
Professional Group on Human Factors in Electronics, 1961, Reprinted in Ward, Edwards, and Amos Tversky (Eds.), *Decision Making.* Baltimore: Penguin Books, 1967, pp. 300–314. (*LRF* 279, 283)

* **Z**ajonc, Robert B., *Social Psychology: An Experimental Approach.*   Ju   NR   NR
Belmont, Calif.: Brooks/Cole Publishing, 1967. (*LRF* 000)

*** Zarnowitz, Victor, *An Appraisal of Short-Term Economic Forecasts.*   Ex   Eco   Ym
National Bureau of Economic Research, Occasional Paper No. 104,   Ju
New York, 1967. (*LRF* 137, 396, 399)

	M	F	E*

* Zarnowitz, Victor, "Prediction and Forecasting, Economic," *Inter-national Encyclopedia of the Social Sciences*, 12 (1968), 425–439. (*LRF* 207, 208, 265) — NR Eco N

* Zimbardo, Philip, "The Pathology of Imprisonment," *Society* (April 1972), 4–8. (*LRF* 125) — Ju Soc Y

UPDATED
BIBLIOGRAPHY

The Future is not what it used to be.

Ken Watt

This UPDATED BIBLIOGRAPHY demonstrates the rapid growth in the field. The previous References in *LRF*, as revised, contain about 700 items. The UPDATED BIBLIOGRAPHY, which is based primarily on research since the completion of the first edition in 1977, contains more than 350 items. These references cover the period up to early 1985. Some references prior to 1977 are also included, these having been overlooked in the first edition.

Summaries are provided for most of the items. These summaries were sent to the authors of the papers. I asked the authors whether they were accurate and fair. Almost all authors replied, often sending corrections, suggestions, and copies of their latest research.

The items in the UPDATED BIBLIOGRAPHY are cross-referenced to the pages in the text using my standard notation, LRF xxx. The recent research items are also highlighted in the book by capitalizing the AUTHORS' LAST NAMES. Note that some items are not cited in *LRF*.

ABDEL-KHALIK, A. Rashad and EL-SHESHAI, Kamal M., [1980], "Information choice and utilization in an experiment on default prediction," *Journal of Accounting Research,* vol. **18**, pp. 325–342 . . . (*LRF* 282)*

ACKOFF, Russell L., [1983], "Beyond prediction and preparation," *Journal of Management Studies,* vol. **1**, pp. 59–69 . . . (*LRF* 7)

ADAM, Everette E., Jr. and EBERT, Ronald J., [1976]. "A comparison of human and statistical forecasting," *AIIE Transactions,* vol. **8**, no. 1, pp. 120–127 . . . In this experiment, 240 graduate business students made subjective extrapolations for six patterns of simulated data. The accuracy of these forecasts was compared with that from three extrapolation models. Compared with the models, the human forecasters tended to be biased and were more strongly influenced by random noise in the data. An exponential smoothing model with trend and seasonal components was more accurate than the intuitive extrapolations, except in cases where the data pattern was characterized

*These numbers in parentheses indicate where the item is discussed in the text.

by trend and low seasonality; here there were no significant differences. (*LRF* 172)

AHLBURG, Dennis A., [1984], "Forecast evaluation and improvement using Theil's decomposition," *Journal of Forecasting*, vol. 3 pp. 345–351 . . . This paper discusses the use of Theil's decomposition and presents an analysis of data on annual housing starts. The mechanical adjustment provided major improvements in accuracy for the two-quarter-ahead forecast, and minor improvements for eight-quarters-ahead. (*LRF* 237)

AHLERS, David and LAKINISHOK, Josef, [1983], "A study of economists' consensus forecasts," *Management Science*, vol. 29, pp. 1113–1125 . . . This study examines the economic forecasts from J.A. Livingston's survey of about 50 well-known business, public, and academic economists. (See also KEEN [1981].) The study covers the period from the first survey, in 1947, up to 1978; separate analyses are also provided for 1947–1960, 1961–1969, and 1970–1978. Forecast accuracy was examined for ten macroeconomic variables and for two forecast horizons, 7 and 13 months. Some conclusions supported previous research findings, such as: (1) economists underestimate changes; (2) economists are too optimistic; (3) economists do better than a "no-change" model. (This is my conclusion from the data presented; the authors concluded that this improvement was not significant); (4) economists did no better than a simple trend extrapolation; and (5) forecasts of turning points are of little value in comparison with naive forecasts such as "always predict that the indicator will move in the direction that it generally moves." One surprising conclusion by the authors is that the quality of the economists' forecasts improved over time, but this conclusion was based on only three time periods. (*LRF* 90, 397, 408, 618)

AJZEN, Icek, [1977], "Intuitive theories of events and the effects of base-rate information on prediction," *Journal of Personality and Social Psychology*, vol. 35, pp. 303–314 . . . (*LRF* 98)

ALBRECHT, W. Steve; LOOKABILL, Larry L. and McKEOWN, James, [1977], "The time series properties of annual earnings," *Journal of Accounting Research*, vol. 15, pp. 226–244 . . . This study compares forecast errors of Box-Jenkins and no-change models. (*LRF* 176, 494)

ALEXANDER, Elmore R., III and WILKINS, Ronnie D., [1982], "Performance rating validity: The relationships of objective and subjective measures of performance," *Group and Organization Studies,* vol. 7, pp. 485–498 . . . Many previous studies have attempted to predict successful job performance, where job performance was based on subjective measures. Typically, these subjective measures were performance ratings by the workers' immediate supervisor. But are these performance ratings valid indicators of job performance? Alexander and Wilkins reviewed prior research. While performance ratings were related to actual performance in a number of laboratory experiments, this might have been an artifact of the research design. In most of these studies, all things except performance were controlled; thus, there was no other basis for the ratings than performance. Alexander and Wilkins suggested that the interaction between a worker and supervisor may be a relevant variable that was excluded from these studies. It is important, then, to test the validity of subjective ratings in a field setting. They did this, using data on 130 vocational rehabilitation counselors from 23 different groups. Objective measures of output on this job are provided quarterly to the supervisors by the State of Tennessee. The correlations between the subjective ratings and the objective measures were positive, but low (over four criteria, r^2 ran from .01 to .08). In short, subjective ratings of performance are suspect. (*LRF* 327)

ALUMBAUGH, Richard V.; CRIGLER, M.A. and DIGHTMAN, C. R., [1978], "Comparison of multivariate techniques in the prediction of juvenile postparole outcome," *Educational and Psychological Measurement,* vol. **38**, pp. 97–106 . . . This study compared factor analysis vs. stepwise regression vs. stepwise discriminant function to select variables for predicting recidivism for 579 juvenile cases during the 15-month period after release from parole. The authors used cross-validation and concluded that the stepwise discriminant function was best. They say the poor showing of factor analysis conflicts with a study by Alumbaugh in 1969. (*LRF* 223)

ANDERSON, Craig A., [1983a], "Imagination and expectation: The effect of imagining behavioral scripts on personal intentions," *Journal of Personality and Social Psychology,* vol. **45**, pp. 293–305 . . . The subjects in these experiments (114 college students) were asked to prepare behavioral scenarios by drawing cartoons relating to six types of behavior: blood donation, tutoring, taking a new part-time job, running for student-government office, changing academic major, and taking a trip over spring break. The main hypothesis was that in scenarios where the subject is the main character, the subject would change behavioral intentions. Increased intentions were expected for scenarios where the self-as-main-character performed the behavior, decreased intentions if the self-as-main-character did not. This hypothesis draws upon prior research on "availability": The more often the subject imagined the behavior, the greater the expected change in intentions. The hypothesis was supported, and the study did a convincing job of ruling out competing hypotheses. The second experiment replicated these findings and obtained evidence that the changes persisted over a three-day period. Some questions remain unanswered: Would the changes in intentions lead to changes in behavior? Could these results be applied to a business executive writing scenarios about possible strategic actions she might take for the organization? This is a well-designed and clearly written study on an important topic. (*LRF* 43)

ANDERSON, Craig A., [1983b], "Abstract and concrete data in the perseverance of social theories: When weak data lead to unshakeable beliefs," *Journal of Experimental Social Psychology,* vol. **19**, pp. 93–108 . . . (*LRF* 42, 43, 45)

ARCHIBALD, Robert and GILLINGHAM, Robert, [1980], "An analysis of the short-run consumer demand for gasoline using household survey data," *Review of Economics and Statistics,* vol. **62**, pp. 622–628 . . . (*LRF* 202)

ARKES, Hal R. et al., [1981], "Hindsight bias among physicians weighing the likelihood of diagnoses," *Journal of Applied Psychology,* vol. **66**, pp. 252–254 . . . Hindsight bias was found in this study of 75 physicians. Compared to a control group, physicians given information that an unlikely outcome had occurred were more likely to say they would have predicted that outcome. Implications for forecasting: *Users of forecasts are likely to feel that preparers of forecasts did a poor job when unusual events occur.* (*LRF* 39, 384)

ARMSTRONG, J. Scott, [1977], "Forecasting the air travel market," in M. Wayne DeLozier, D.M. Lewison, and A.G. Woodside (Eds.), *Experiential Learning Exercises in Marketing.* Santa Monica, California: Goodyear . . . I use this experiential exercise as an introduction to the various types of forecasting methods (the forecasting methodology tree). For a number of years the case circulated privately. Now it is available in published form. If you are unable to obtain a copy, you can write to me and I will provide a copy for $10.00. The case and instructor's guide is 25 pages, and it is designed for an 80-minute class. (*LRF* not cited)

ARMSTRONG, J. Scott, [1979], "Advocacy and objectivity in science," *Management Science,* vol. **25**, pp. 423–428 . . . (*LRF* 437–444)

ARMSTRONG, J. Scott, [1980a], "Unintelligible management research and academic prestige," *Interfaces,* vol. **10**, pp. 80–86 . . . This paper shows that journals that are more difficult to read are regarded as more prestigious. Also, readers rated authors as more competent when their papers were written in a complex manner. (*LRF* 46, 436)

ARMSTRONG, J. Scott, [1980b], "Advocacy as a scientific strategy: The Mitroff myth," *Academy of Management Review,* vol. **5**, pp. 509–511 . . . (see Mitroff 1972, *LRF* 555)

ARMSTRONG, J. Scott, [1980c], "Teacher vs. learner responsibility in management education," Department of Marketing, Working Paper, Wharton School, Phila., Pa. 19104. (*LRF* 18)

ARMSTRONG, J. Scott, [1981], "Review of *Mail and Telephone Surveys* by Don A. Dillman," *Journal of Business,* vol. **54,** pp. 622–625 . . . (*LRF* 599)

ARMSTRONG, J. Scott, [1982a], "Strategies for implementing change: An experiential approach," *Group and Organization Studies,* vol. **7,** pp. 457–475 . . . The COMPU-HEART Case was presented to 16 undergraduate seniors at the Wharton School. They were asked to describe their plans for implementation. Each subject worked individually. Only one subject (6%) suggested a procedure that resembled the Delta Technique. A role playing version of the case was then presented to 15 groups of executives from health care providers. Only one group (7%) used a procedure that resembled the Delta Technique. This group was successful at implementing change while all other groups failed. A different group of subjects was then given brief instruction (five to ten minutes) on the use of the Delta Technique. Of these 14 groups, two encountered difficulty in applying the rules and were unsuccessful in their change efforts. The other 12 groups (86%) were all successful in gaining commitment to change. (*LRF* 33, 36)

ARMSTRONG, J. Scott, [1982b], "The forecasting audit," in Spyros Makridakis and Steven C. Wheelwright (Eds.), *The Handbook of Forecasting: A Manager's Guide.* New York: Wiley, pp. 535–552 . . . (*LRF* 317)

ARMSTRONG, J. Scott, [1982c], "The value of formal planning for strategic decisions: Review of empirical research," *Strategic Management Journal,* vol. **3,** pp. 197–211 . . . A review of research from organizational behavior supported the guidelines suggested for formal corporate planning: that is, use an explicit approach for setting objectives, generating strategies, evaluating strategies, monitoring results, and obtaining commitment.

A review was made of all published field research on the evaluation of formal planning. Formal planning was superior in 10 of the 15 comparisons drawn from 12 studies, while informal planning was superior in only two comparisons. Although this research did not provide sufficient information on the use of various aspects of the planning process, mild support was provided for having participation by stakeholders. Formal planning tended to be more useful where large changes were involved, but, beyond that, little information was available to suggest when formal planning is most valuable. (*LRF* 7, 643)

ARMSTRONG, J. Scott, [1982d], "Research on scientific journals:

Implications for editors and authors," *Journal of Forecasting,* vol. 1, pp. 83–104 . . . I reviewed the empirical research on the communication of research findings. From this, I developed guidelines for journals. Many of these guidelines were adopted by the *International Journal of Forecasting. (LRF* 439)

ARMSTRONG, J. Scott, [1983a], "Strategic planning and forecasting fundamentals," in Kenneth Albert (Ed.), *The Strategic Management Handbook.* New York: McGraw Hill, pp. 2-1 to 2-32 . . . This paper presents viewpoints on planning, shows how forecasting relates to planning and presents checklists for practitioners. *(LRF* 7, 125)

ARMSTRONG, J. Scott, [1983b], "Relative accuracy of judgmental and extrapolative methods in forecasting annual earnings," *Journal of Forecasting,* vol. 2, pp. 437–447 . . . Analyzes previously published studies on annual earnings forecasts. Comparisons of forecasts produced by management, analysts and extrapolative techniques indicated that: (1) management forecasts were superior to professional analyst forecasts (the mean absolute percentage errors were 15.9 and 17.7, respectively, based on five studies using data from 1967–1974), and (2) judgmental forecasts (both management and analysts) were superior to extrapolation forecasts on 14 of 17 comparisons from 13 studies using data from 1964–1979 (the mean absolute percentage errors were 21.0 and 28.4 for judgment and extrapolation, respectively). *(LRF* 360, 397, 401, 407, 409, 642)

ARMSTRONG, J. Scott, [1983c], "The importance of objectivity and falsification in management science," *Journal of Management,* vol. **9,** pp. 203–216 . . . Written in response to BOAL and WILLIS [1983]. Ian Mitroff has a reply in the same issue. *(LRF* 588)

ARMSTRONG, J. Scott, [1983d], "Cheating in management science" (with commentary), *Interfaces,* vol. **13** [August], pp. 20–29 . . . If you observe what you believe to be cheating, my advice is that you do not call it "cheating." Try to replicate the findings and report your results only as a "failure to replicate." *(LRF* 156, 289)

ARMSTRONG, J. Scott, [1984a], "Forecasting by extrapolation: Conclusions from 25 years of research," *Interfaces,* vol. **14,** pp. 52–61 . . . Provides a discussion on the results presented in Appendix J. Commentary on this paper by Robert U. Ayres, Carl Christ, and J. Keith Ord follows on pages 61–66 of the same issue. *(LRF* 495)

ARMSTRONG, J. Scott, [1984b], "Do judgmental researchers use their own research? A review of *Judgment Under Uncertainty: Heuristics and Biases," Journal of Forecasting,* vol. **3,** pp. 236–239 . . . A review of KAHNEMAN, SLOVIC and TVERSKY [1982]. *(LRF* 617)

ARMSTRONG, J. Scott, [1985], "Research on forecasting: A quarter-century review, 1960–1984," *Interfaces* (in press) . . . This paper summarizes my opinions on the major advances in forecasting. Substantial progress has been made over this 25 year period. (*LRF* not cited)

ARMSTRONG, J. Scott and LUSK, Edward J., [1983], "Research on the accuracy of alternative extrapolation models: Analysis of a forecasting competition through open peer review," *Journal of Forecasting,* vol. **2**, pp. 259–262, with seven commentaries followed by replies by each of the original six authors on pages 263–311 . . . This set of papers discusses what can be learned from the M-Competition [MAKRIDAKIS, et al., 1982] and what research should be done in the future. (*LRF* 176, 178, 441, 623)

ARMSTRONG, J. Scott and LUSK, Edward J., [1985], "An application of meta-analysis to survey research: The effect of return postage," Department of Marketing Working Paper, Wharton School, . . . An application of meta-analysis. It stresses the importance of testing multiple hypotheses and the benefits of contacting the original authors. It concluded that first class return postage will draw responses from an additional 9% of the original mail-out, in comparison with business reply return postage. Never use business reply on return envelopes in survey research. (*LRF* 114, 445)

ARMSTRONG, J. Scott and WALKER, Harry S., [1983], "Validation of role playing as a predictive technique for conflict situations," *World Future Society Bulletin,* vol. **17** [July–August], pp. 15–22 . . . The design of the experiment was as follows:

1. Randomly assign four subjects into groups of two based on arrival time (1st person group A, 2nd person group B, and so on).
2. Separate groups to opposite sides of the room.
3. Read general instructions and answer questions.
4. Read role playing instructions, pass out roles, and answer questions.
5. Distribute text of one situation to each person.
6. Distribute response questionnaire.
7. Rearrange furniture so a table is in the center of the room with two chairs on either side.
8. Make sure groups prepare to meet each other.
9. Bring groups together at table when they're prepared (no longer than 20 minutes).
10. Describe where the meeting is held.
11. Allow the role play to continue for up to 60 minutes or until a

consensus is reached or until discussion on the event to be predicted ceases.

12. Separate groups and ask them to force the decision or projected decision into one of the responses on the questionnaire.

13. Ask if anyone recognized the situation and mark their answer sheet if yes.

14. Repeat 5 through 13 for the next situation.

15. Tell the subjects not to discuss the situation or test procedure with anyone else and dismiss with a thank you. (*LRF* 125, 130)

ASCHENBRENNER, K. Michael and KASUBEK, W., [1978], "Challenging the Cushing Syndrome: Multiattribute evaluation of cortisone drugs," *Organizational Behavior and Human Performance,* vol. **22**, pp. 216–234 . . . Decomposed estimates of dangerousness for seven cortisone drugs were obtained from five physicians. The overall ratings based on separate ratings of six side effects led to substantial agreement among the physicians. In contrast, the global ratings led to much disagreement among the physicians. (*LRF* 59)

ASCHER, William [1978], *Forecasting: An Appraisal for Policy-Makers and Planners.* Baltimore, MD: Johns Hopkins University Press . . . Ascher looks at forecasting in population, economics, energy, transportation, and technology. He asks, for example, whether forecasting is getting more accurate over time? (In most areas his answer seemed to be "No.") He also assessed whether forecast accuracy differs by method or by source; I found it difficult to draw conclusions about these issues from the information presented in the book. (*LRF* 298, 425, 454)

ASCHER, William and OVERHOLT, William H., [1983], *Strategic Planning and Forecasting.* New York: Wiley . . . This book, which focuses on political forecasting, discusses some worthwhile topics such as how to present forecasts, the relationships between forecasting and planning, how to organize the forecasting and planning functions, and how to choose a forecasting method. For the most part, these sections draw primarily upon the authors' experience and the prevailing opinions of experts, rather than upon empirical evidence. (*LRF* 687)

ASSMUS, Gert, [1984], "New product forecasting," *Journal of Forecasting,* vol. **3**, pp. 121–138 . . . A state of the art review of models for new product forecasting. It describes attributes and costs of some of the more popular commercial models. (*LRF* not cited)

AUERBACH, Alan J., [1982], "The index of leading indicators: Measurement without theory, thirty-five years later," *Review of Economics and Statistics,* vol. **64**, pp. 589–595 . . . This study reaches some favorable conclusions about the use of leading indicators in forecasting.

Equal weighting of the 12 leading indicators did better than regression weights. (*LRF* 288)

AVISON, William R. and NETTLER, Gwynn, [1976], "World views and crystal balls," *Futures,* vol. 8, [February], pp. 11–21 . . . (*LRF* 95)

BABICH, George and GOODHEW, John, [1978], "Short-term econometric forecasting and seasonal adjustment," *Economic Record,* vol. 54, pp. 229–236 . . . This paper compares forecasts using deseasonalized data with those from a model that used dummy variables to estimate seasonality on one and two-period ahead forecasts for 14 variables over eight periods. Little difference was found, though the deseasonalized approach tended to be more accurate. (*LRF* not cited)

BAILS, Dale G. and PEPPERS, Larry C., [1982], *Business Fluctuations: Forecasting Techniques and Applications.* Englewood Cliffs, N.J.: Prentice Hall . . . This textbook covers primarily regression and time series methods. It contains a chapter on "Translating the Forecast to Management," drawn primarily upon the authors' opinions and experience. (*LRF* 78)

BAKER, Earl Jay, [1979], "Predicting response to hurricane warnings: A reanalysis of data from four studies," *Mass Emergencies,* vol. 4, pp. 9–24 . . . This study reviews survey research data from three serious hurricanes in the United States and produces some interesting findings: (1) if people believed the hurricane forecasts, they were more likely to evacuate, but this relationship was weak; also, the relationship held up only for very short-range forecasts (less than three hours before landfall); (2) attention devoted by a person to monitoring the hurricane forecasts was unrelated to whether that person evacuates or not; (3) public education about the dangers and proper responses to hurricane forecasts was not related to evacuation behavior. In general, the studies failed to identify strong predictors of evacuation behavior. Encouragingly, the strongest predictor was the degree of risk to which respondents were exposed. (*LRF* 40, 626)

BAKER, Earl J.; WEST, S.G.; MOSS, D.J. and WEYANT, J.M., [1980], "Impact of offshore nuclear power plants: Forecasting visits to nearby beaches," *Environment and Behavior,* vol. 12, pp. 367–407 . . . To forecast the effect of offshore nuclear plants upon the visits to beaches, the authors spread their budget among many methods including: prior research, studies of analogous situations (beaches near land-based nuclear plants), surveys of experts, intentions surveys, and attitude surveys. Each approach suffered from serious problems, yet when considered as a group they provided a convincing picture. Whereas the intentions survey indicated that about one-quarter of the tourists would avoid beaches with offshore nuclear plants, the other methods suggested one-quarter was a substantial overestimate. The authors concluded that 5 to 10 percent is a reasonable estimate. Floating nuclear plants were not so important as finding a clean and uncrowded beach with nice facilities. (This is one of the few cases where I think it is fortunate that data do not exist to test predictive ability.) (*LRF* 67)

BAKER, H. Kent and TRALINS, Stanley M., [1976], "An analysis of published financial forecasts," *Atlanta Economic Review,* vol. **26,** pp. 42–46 . . . (*LRF* 454)

BAR-HILLEL, Maya, [1979], "The role of sample size in sample evaluation," *Organizational Behavior and Human Performance,* vol. **24,** pp. 245–257 . . . People's judgments on the accuracy of a statistic depend much more on the ratio of the sample size to the population than on the sample size. That's unfortunate. Keep it in mind when presenting evidence. (*LRF* not cited)

BAR-HILLEL, Maya and FISCHHOFF, Baruch, [1981], "When do base rates affect predictions?" *Journal of Personality and Social Psychology,* vol. **41,** pp. 671–680 . . . A reply to MANIS, et al. [1980]. (*LRF* 625)

BARRETT, Gerald V.; PHILLIPS, James S. and ALEXANDER, Ralph A., [1981], "Concurrent and predictive validity designs: A critical reanalysis," *Journal of Applied Psychology,* vol. **66,** pp. 1–6 . . . This paper argues that for, personnel predictions, the superiority of tests of predictive validity (outside sample time period), has been overestimated relative to concurrent validity. See also GUION and CRANNY [1982]. (*LRF* 342, 613)

BASS, Bernard M., [1977], "Utility of managerial self-planning on a simulated production task with replications in 12 countries," *Journal of Applied Psychology,* vol. **62,** pp. 506–509 . . . This is an important study of planning involving experiments with 1416 managers from 12 countries. Groups that developed their own plans were more effective than those that were presented with plans. As groups gained experience with self-planning, their efficiency improved still more. Modest nationality differences were found, Americans gaining most from self-planning, Germans the least. (*LRF* 36)

BASU, Shankar and SCHROEDER, Roger G., [1977], "Incorporating judgments in sales forecasts: Application of the Delphi method at American Hoist and Derrick," *Interfaces,* vol. **7** [May], pp. 18–27 . . . This study describes how the authors used 23 experts in a three-round Delphi study covering three months. The authors claim that this procedure provided accurate sales forecasts for one and two year horizons. (*LRF* 117)

BECKER, Lawrence J., [1978], "Joint effect of feedback and goal setting on performance: A field study of residential energy conservation," *Journal of Applied Psychology,* vol. **63,** pp. 428–433 . . . Significant gains were achieved when families set high goals for conservation *and* when they also received feedback about their performance in relation to those goals. Those that either did not set high goals or did not receive feedback did not change their use of energy significantly. (*LRF* 37)

BEYTH-MAROM, Ruth, [1982], "How probable is probable? A numerical translation of verbal probability expressions," *Journal of Forecasting,* vol. **1,** pp. 257–269 . . . This experiment took place in a professional forecasting organization accustomed to giving verbal probability assessments ("likely," "probable," etc.). It highlights the communication problems caused by verbal probability expressions. Experts in the organization were first asked to give a numerical translation to 30 different verbal probability expressions, most of which were taken from the organization's own published political forecasts. In a second part of the experiment, the experts were given 15 paragraphs selected from the organization's political publications, each of which contained at least one verbal expression of probability. Subjects were again asked to give a numerical translation to each verbal probability expression. The results indicated that (1) there was a high variability in the interpretation of verbal probability expressions, and (2) the variability is even higher in the problem context. (*LRF* not cited)

BEYTH-MAROM, Ruth and ARKES, Hal R., [1983], "Being accurate but not necessarily Bayesian: Comments on Christensen-Szalanski and Beach," *Organizational Behavior and Human Performance,* vol. **31,** pp. 255–257 . . . See CHRISTENSEN-SZALANSKI and BEACH [1982]. (*LRF* 593)

BINROTH, W.; BURSHSTEIN, I.; HABOUSH, R.K. and HARTZ, J.R., [1979], "A comparison of commodity price forecasting by Box-Jenkins and regression-based techniques," *Technological Forecasting and Social Change,* vol. **14,** pp. 169–180 . . . This paper analyzed three-month-ahead *ex ante* forecasts of rubber commodity prices. It used 72 months of data to develop the models, then forecasted over 26 months. Box-Jenkins was slightly more accurate than the econometric model, but the difference did not appear to be significant. (*LRF* 408)

BOAL, Kimberly B. and WILLIS, Raymond E., [1983], "A note on the Armstrong/Mitroff debate," *Journal of Management,* vol. **9,** pp. 203–216 . . . See ARMSTRONG [1983c]. (*LRF* 583)

BOJE, David M. and MURNIGHAN, J. Keith, [1982], "Group confidence pressures in iterative decisions," *Management Science,* vol.

28, pp. 1187–1196 . . . Individual estimates were compared with ones from group face-to-face interaction and from groups with only written feedback. The experiment involved four estimation problems (two almanac questions and two on heights and weights of people). Participants were 324 undergraduates in group sizes of 3, 7, and 11. The confidence of group members went up over the three rounds in the Delphi-like procedure, which is a typical result. These gains in confidence were unrelated to accuracy, also not surprising. However, no gain was found in the accuracy of the later rounds, which is mildly surprising in light of previous research where small gains were found. Group members preferred the face-to-face interaction and thought it the most effective; however, it was the *least* accurate, a finding that agrees with previous research. I enjoy studies with surprising results. Imagine, then, how pleased I was to find this conclusion in their study . . . "group size had no significant effects on accuracy . . ." This conclusion conflicts with research that dates back to Gordon (1924), and includes Huber and Delbecq (1972), HOGARTH [1978], and LIBBY and BLASHFIELD [1978]. (*LRF* 119, 120, 123)

BOLT, Gordon J., [1982], *Market and Sales Forecasting Manual.* Englewood Cliffs, N.J.: Prentice-Hall . . . This book is aimed at the novice forecaster and is easy to read. It contains step by step descriptions for dealing with some practical issues in forecasting and planning, with emphasis on planning. The author's recommendations are based on face validity. (*LRF* 78)

BOPP, Anthony E. and DURST, Mitchell [1978], "Estimated importance of seasonal adjustment on energy forecasts," *Atlantic Economic Journal,* vol. **6**, pp. 53–59 . . . (*LRF* not cited)

BOPP, Anthony E. and NERI, John A., [1978], "The price of gasoline: Forecasting comparisons," *Quarterly Review of Economics and Business,* vol. **18** [Winter], pp. 23–34 . . . This study makes *ex ante* forecasts for the 18-month period from January 1975 to June 1976 to compare Box-Jenkins, simple econometric, and simultaneous equations models. For one-month ahead, Box-Jenkins tended to be most accurate, but as forecast horizon lengthened, it became least accurate. However, there were too few comparisons to draw statistically significant conclusions. (*LRF* 408)

BORGIDA, Eugene, [1978], "Scientific deduction—evidence is not necessarily informative: A reply to Wells and Harvey," *Journal of Personality and Social Psychology,* vol. **36**, pp. 477–482 . . . This paper extends Nisbett and Borgida [1975]. (*LRF* 557)

BORGIDA, Eugene and NISBETT, Richard E., [1977], "The differential impact of abstract vs. concrete information on decisions,"

Journal of Applied Social Psychology, vol. **7**, pp. 258–271. . . . (*LRF* not cited)

BORMAN, Walter C., [1982], "Validity of behavioral assessment for predicting military recruiter performance," *Journal of Applied Psychology*, vol. **67**, pp. 3–9 . . . Sixteen experienced recruiters assessed 57 soldiers entering the Army's recruiter school. Their assessment ratings were compared with subsequent performance in short training episodes. First impressions, ratings based on a structured interview, and scores on a paper and pencil test of personality and vocational interests, each correlated near zero with the training performance. But an assessment program using role playing, in-basket and the preparation of a short recruiting speech correlated highly with the criteria. Statistical composites of the assessment ratings were less expensive and slightly more valid than clinical judgments based on consensus among the assessors. (*LRF* 123, 126)

BRANDON, Charles; FRITZ, Richard and XANDER, James, [1983]. "Econometric forecasts: Evaluation and revision," *Applied Economics,* vol. **15**, pp. 187–201 . . . (*LRF* 242, 291, 292)

BRANDON, Charles H.; JARRETT, Jeffrey E. and KHUMA-WALA, Saleha, [1983]. "Revising forecasts of accounting earnings: A comparison with the Box-Jenkins method," *Management Science,* vol. **29**, pp. 256–263 . . . (*LRF* 176, 495)

BRANDT, Jon A. and BESSLER, David A., [1983], "Price forecasting and evaluation: An application in agriculture," *Journal of Forecasting*, vol. **2**, pp. 237–248 . . . Seven forecasting methods were used to make one-quarter ahead *ex ante* forecasts of U.S. hog prices for 24 quarters from 1976 to 1981. The errors (MAPES) were: ARIMA (7.96), expert judgment (8.61), econometric (9.98), "no change" (10.07), simple exponential smoothing (10.16), and Holt-Winters (10.28). A combination of ARIMA, econometric and expert judgment was best (7.27). Interestingly, expert forecasts alone did worse than a strategy of never hedging (always selling for cash in the market). The differences in accuracy in this study do *not* appear to be statistically significant. (*LRF* 292, 400, 408)

BRAUN, Michael A. and SRINIVASAN, V., [1975], "Amount of information as a determinant of consumer behavior towards new products," *Proceedings*. Chicago: American Marketing Association, pp. 373–378 . . . Study of intentions to purchase a new product, the Gillette TRAC II twin blade razor. (*LRF* 101)

BROWN, Lawrence D. and ROZEFF, Michael S., [1978], "The superiority of analyst forecasts as measures of expectations: Evidence from earnings," *Journal of Finance*, vol. **33**, pp. 1–16 . . . (*LRF* 176, 494)

BUHMEYER, Kenneth J. and JOHNSON, Alan H., [1978], "Predicting success in a physician-extender training program," *Psychological Reports*, vol. **42**, pp. 507–513 ... I hereby announce this paper as the winner of the 1978 "Tom Swift Award for Data Abuse." It is almost a duplicate of the 1973 award (see Armstrong, 1975a). (*LRF* 56)

BUNN, Derek W., [1979], "The synthesis of predictive models in marketing research," *Journal of Marketing Research*, vol. **16**, pp. 280–28 ... This paper used two small examples to illustrate the value of combining forecasts. (*LRF* 184)

BUNN, Derek W. and SEIGAL, Jeremy P., [1983], "Forecasting the effects of television programming upon electricity loads," *Journal of the Operational Research Society*, vol. **34**, pp. 17–25 ... Small validation sample used to compare econometric and subjective forecasts of peak electricity loads. Mixed results were obtained, so no firm conclusions could be drawn. (*LRF* 397)

BURNS, Michael and PEARL, Judea, [1981], "Causal and diagnostic inferences: A comparison of validity," *Organizational Behavior and Human Performance*, vol. **28**, pp. 379–394 ... The results of this experiment were surprising; better predictions did not result when causal reasoning was used to decompose problems for a group of subjects. Non-causal approaches worked just as well. (*LRF* 59)

BURROWS, Paul, [1971], "Explanatory and forecasting models of inventory investment in Britain," *Applied Economics*, vol. **3**, pp. 275–289 ... Examined forecasts for seven quarters from 1967II to 1968IV. For *ex ante* forecasts, an econometric model did better than an extrapolation model. But for *ex post* forecasts, the extrapolation did better than the econometric model. (*LRF* 408, 409)

CAMERER, Colin, [1981], "General conditions for the success of boot-strapping models," *Organizational Behavior and Human Performance*, vol. **27**, pp. 411–422 ... Camerer examined theoretical arguments and empirical evidence and concluded that bootstrapping models make better predictions than experts in nearly all practical situations in which data on the criteria are missing or vague. (*LRF* 283)

CARBONE, Robert; ANDERSEN, A.; CORRIVEAU, Y. and CORSON, P.P., [1983], "Comparing for different time series methods the value of technical expertise, individualized analysis, and judgmental adjustment," *Management Science*, vol. **29**, pp. 559–566 ... Students with limited training were able to obtain as accurate forecasts when using Box-Jenkins methods as were experts. Subjective adjustments did not improve the accuracy of the extrapolations. (*LRF* 175, 273)

CARBONE, Robert and ARMSTRONG, J. Scott, [1982], "Evaluation of extrapolative forecasting methods: Results of a survey of academicians and practitioners," *Journal of Forecasting*, vol. **1**, pp. 215–217 . . . (*LRF* 359)

CARBONE, Robert and GORR, Wilpen L. [1985], "Accuracy of judgmental forecasting of time series." *Decisions Sciences* (in press) . . . (*LRF* 172)

CAREY, Kenneth J., [1978], "The accuracy of estimates of earnings from naive models," *Journal of Economics and Business*, vol. **30**, No. 3, pp. 182–193 . . . (*LRF* 495)

CATTIN, Philippe, [1980], "Estimation of the predictive power of a regression model," *Journal of Applied Psychology*, vol. **65**, pp. 407–414 . . . Cattin compared standard regression estimates of predictive power with measures obtained from cross-validation. He used theoretical arguments and simulation with two criteria (mean square error and R^2). The formulas, which are less expensive, were often adequate. (*LRF* 342)

CATTIN, Philippe and WITTINK, Dick R., [1982], "Commercial use of conjoint analysis: A survey," *Journal of Marketing*, vol. **46** [Summer], pp. 44–53 . . . This paper reports on a survey of commercial uses of conjoint analysis in determining customer preferences for products. The first commercial application was in 1971. Since then, usage has grown dramatically. The most important application of conjoint analysis is to predict preferences for new products. The authors' survey goes through the various steps in conjoint analysis to determine which techniques are used most often. For example, to develop attributes of a project, some projects used the direct opinions of management while protocols were less popular. To obtain data, the most common approach was to ask customers to choose among products that were described in terms of all key attributes rather than to rely on comparisons of two factors at a time. Most commonly, the question was cast in terms of "intention to buy" rather than preference. The analysis of the data was typically based on some form of regression analysis. Cattin and Wittink encourage research firms to share their experiences with the research community; to date, few published studies have tested the predictive validity of conjoint analysis. (*LRF* 278)

CERF, Christopher and NAVASKY, Victor, [1984], *The Experts Speak*. New York: Pantheon Books . . . A collection of inaccurate statements and forecasts by experts. (*LRF* 87, 91, 103)

CERULLO, Michael J. and AVILA, Alfonso, [1975], "Sales forecasting practices: A survey," *Managerial Planning*, vol. **24** [Sept.-Oct], pp. 33–39 . . . This survey of 110 of the *Fortune* 500 companies yielded replies from 56 companies. Judgmental methods proved to be most popular, as 89% of the companies reported their use. In comparison, 52% said they used extrapolation, 30% econometric, 24% regression, and 20% input-output. The most common approach was to ask each member of the sales force to make a forecast and then to have a group of executives adjust this. The *perceived* accuracy of the forecast was about the same for those who used causal methods as for those who used naive methods. Most firms (77%) said they did not know how much they spend on forecasting. Few firms (4%) used outside consultants. Few firms (9%) forecasted sales beyond one year. (That seems surprising, doesn't it?) About 57% used computers in the forecasting process. Finally, 98% thought that forecasting with causal methods should be taught at business schools. Smile. (*LRF* 73, 426)

CHATFIELD, Christopher, [1978], "The Holt-Winters forecasting procedure," *Applied Statistics*, vol. 27, pp. 264–279 . . . (*LRF* 176, 495)

CHRISTENSEN-SZALANSKI, Jay J.J. and BEACH, Lee Roy, [1982], "Experience and the base-rate fallacy," *Organizational Behavior and Human Performance*, vol. 29, pp. 270–278 *and* **CHRISTENSEN-SZALANSKI, Jay, J.J. and BEACH, Lee Roy, [1983]**, "Believing is not the same as testing," *Organizational Behavior and Human Performance*, vol. 31, pp. 258–261 . . . In the CHRISTENSEN-SZALANSKI and BEACH [1982] experiment, decision makers who *experienced* the relationship between the base rate (i.e., the frequency with which an event occurred in a series of trials) and diagnostic information used this relationship when they made judgments. However, when given the necessary *theoretical* information, they did not use the base rate effectively. (In other words, people may not use Bayes rule; but with experience, they can come close to the Bayesian solution.) BEYTH-MAROM and ARKES [1983] challenge this interpretation. Rather than use Bayes theorem, they suggest that the subjects made direct estimates of the proportions. CHRISTENSEN-SZALANSKI and BEACH [1983], however, say that this is compatible with their interpretation. (*LRF* 98, 588)

CLARKE, Mike; DIX, Martin and GOODWIN, Phil, [1982], "Some; issues of dynamics in forecasting travel behavior: A discussion paper," *Transportation*, vol. 11 [June], pp. 153–172 . . . (*LRF* 261)

CLEARY, James P. and LEVENBACH, Hans, [1982], *The Professional Forecaster: The Forecasting Process Through Data Analysis*. Belmont, Calif.: Lifetime Learning Publications . . . This book was one of a matched set intended for the continuing education market (see LEVENBACH and CLEARY [1981]). It was well received (e.g., see review by Marc S. Meketon in the *Journal of Forecasting*, vol. 2, pp. 319–320).

The matched set was then updated for the college market by a single volume [LEVENBACH and CLEARY, 1984]. (*LRF* 621)

CLIFF, Norman, [1983], "Some cautions concerning the application of causal modeling methods," *Multivariate Behavioral Research*, vol. **18**, pp. 115–126 ... Cautions against expecting too much from sophisticated measurement methods such as LISREL. Sophisticated methods do not change anything fundamental, he says, in the development of causal models. The danger is that people may attribute too much importance to the results and overlook basic principles of scientific inference. (*LRF* 226)

COCOZZA, Joseph J. and STEADMAN, Henry J., [1978], "Prediction in psychiatry: An example of misplaced confidence in experts," *Social Problems*, vol. **25**, pp. 265–276 ... In this study of 256 defendants, psychiatrists were asked to predict which defendants might be violent. The psychiatrists seemed unaware of how they made their ratings. For example, only 11.5% said their rating was related to the violence of the crime of which the defendant was charged. Yet 73% of those charged with a violent crime were rated as dangerous, a much higher figure than for cases where the crime was not violent. A three-year follow-up indicated that there was no difference in violence between those predicted to be dangerous and those predicted not to be dangerous. This agreed with some prior research. Still, courts use psychiatrists, and in 87% of these cases they followed the psychiatrists' recommendations. (*LRF* 96, 278, 649)

COGGIN, T. Daniel and HUNTER, John E., [1982–83], "Analysts' EPS forecasts nearer actual than statistical models," *Journal of Business Forecasting*, vol. **1** [Winter], pp. 20–23 ... This paper reports on a study of one-year-and two-year-ahead forecasts of annual earnings per share for 149 companies in 1978 and 1979. In addition, one-year ahead forcasts were made for another sample of 180 companies for 1979. The accuracy of combined judgmental forecasts by analysts (at least three analysts, but typically about 12 analysts) was compared with the accuracy of three extrapolation models using the mean square percentage error as the criterion (which I converted to root mean square error here to aid in understanding). *Conclusions*: (1) the judgmental forecasts were significantly better than the best of the three extrapolations (RMSE of 33% vs. 37.2% respectively for the one-year-ahead EPS forecasts); (2) even the typical analyst was significantly better than the best of the three extrapolations (33.8% vs. 37.2% respectively); (3) the simpler the extrapolation method, the more acurrate the forecast—especially for the two-year horizon; and (4) the forecast error increased substantially for the two-year-ahead forecast (an increase of

27% for the root mean square percentage error for the best extrapolation method). (*LRF* 495)

COLLINS, Daniel W., [1976], "Predicting earnings with sub-entity data: Some further evidence," *Journal of Accounting Research*, vol. **14**, pp. 163–177 . . . This study examined data on 96 firms for 1968, 1969, and 1970 with two econometric models, five extrapolation models, and two segmented econometric models. The segmented econometric models was more accurate for both sales and profit forecasts. SILHAN [1983] points out that Collins' tests were flawed because different data sets were used for the segmented models as compared to the other models. (*LRF* 287, 644)

COOK, Thomas D. and CAMPBELL, Donald T, [1979], *Quasi-Experimentation*, Boston: Houghton Mifflin. (*LRF* 205)

COOPER, Harris and ROSENTHAL, Robert, [1980], "Statistical versus traditional procedures for summarizing research findings," *Psychological Bulletin*, vol. **87**, pp. 442–449 . . . (*LRF* 445)

COSIER, Richard A., [1978], "The effects of three potential aids for making strategic decisions on prediction accuracy," *Organizational Behavior and Human Performance*, vol. **22**, pp. 295–306 . . . Here is an interesting experiment showing that the Devil's Advocate approach led to better predictions than an approach using an expert who argued in favor of a plan. (*LRF* 143)

COX Eli P., [1980], "The optimal number of response alternatives for a scale: A review," *Journal of Marketing Research*, vol. **17**, pp. 407–422 . . . (*LRF* 106)

CUMMINS, J. David and GRIEPENTROG, Gary L., [1985], "Forecasting automobile insurance paid claim costs using econometric and ARIMA models," *International Journal of Forecasting*, (in press) . . . (*LRF* 409, 412)

CURRIM, Imran S., [1981], "Using segmentation approaches for better prediction and understanding from consumer mode choice models," *Journal of Marketing Research*, vol. **18**, pp. 301–309 . . . The basic proposition of this paper is that segmentation of consumers should allow one to make better predictions because different groups behave differently. That is what we call "common sense" in marketing. Sometimes, of course, our common sense is wrong; hence, the present study seemed like a worthwhile undertaking. The proposition was tested on the prediction of transportation mode choice (e.g., auto or bus) between two geographical points. But it was not the actual choice, merely the mode the consumers *say* they would take if they happened to make that hypothetical trip. The two segmentation schemes, one using 10 "benefit segments" and the other one with nine "situational segments,"

did *not* yield more accurate predictions of overall market shares for
five possible mode choices for a hold-out sample of about 170 subjects.
The average error for the two segmented models was identical to that
of the aggregate model. These results were surprising and disappointing. (*LRF* 250)

CURTIN, Richard T., [1982], "Indicators of consumer behavior: The
University of Michigan surveys of consumers," *Public Opinion Quarterly*, vol. **46**, pp. 340–352 . . . This paper provides a good description
of an important continuing consumer survey. As of 1982, comparable
surveys were being conducted in 11 countries. (*LRF* not cited)

DALRYMPLE, Douglas J., [1975], "Sales forecasting: Methods
and accuracy," *Business Horizons*, vol. **18**, pp. 69–73 . . . This paper
reports on a survey of 500 firms with 175 replies. One finding: Systematic records of forecast accuracy were kept by 61% of the firms that
replied. (*LRF* 454)

DALRYMPLE, Douglas J., [1978], "Using Box-Jenkins in sales
forecasting," *Journal of Business Research*, vol. **6**, pp. 133–145 . . . (*LRF*
176, 494)

DALRYMPLE, Douglas J., [1985], "Sales forecasting practices in
businesses: Results from a 1983 U.S. Survey," Working paper, Graduate School of Business, Indiana University, Bloomington, Indiana
47401 . . . Responses were received from 134 business firms, a 16%
return from a survey of 850 firms in the United States. About 60% of
the respondents were manufacturers, 23% were in distribution, and
14% in retailing. This is the first study I have found that has assessed
the use of *combined forecasts* in business:

20% do it "usually",
19% "frequently",
29% "occasionally", and
32% did not use this strategy.

Also of interest were the results on the use of *upper and lower confidence intervals* when presenting forecasts. They are not widely used:

- not used 48%
- occasional 29%
- frequent 11%
- usual 10%

The survey contains many useful findings on the practice of forecasting.
(*LRF* 73, 288, 426, 427, 429, 454)

DALRYMPLE, Douglas J. and KING, Barry E., [1981], "Selecting parameters for short-term forecasting techniques," *Decision Sciences*, vol. **12**, pp. 661–669 . . . Parameters for extrapolation models are generally selected to reduce the error for a one-period-ahead forecast horizon. Often, however, the forecasts are made for horizons beyond one period. This study asks whether it would be worthwhile to select parameters for the specific forecast horizon. Good question. This is apparently the first study on this issue. The authors examined data for 25 business time series ("mostly monthly" they say). Using cumulative MAPEs for forecast horizons from 1 to 12 periods ahead, their search for optimum parameters led to *no gain* when using either exponential smoothing or trend regression. Dalrymple and King found some benefit for this procedure when using moving averages, but I did not draw the same conclusion from their data. Surprisingly, one-period-ahead searches seem adequate for n-period ahead forecasts. The paper also presents evidence showing an increase in error as the forecast horizon increases. While it did help to use more historical data for the parameter search, their conclusion was unintentionally overstated by a misprint (their p. 668), where they say eight periods of data were optimal for trend regression for a one-period-ahead forecast vs. 27 for a 12-period-ahead forecast. (It should have been 18 periods not eight, for the one-period horizon). (*LRF* 165, 167)

DARLINGTON R.B., [1978], "Reduced variance regression," *Psychological Bulletin*, vol. **85**, pp. 1238–1255 . . . (*LRF* 629).

DANOS, Paul and IMHOFF, Eugene A., [1983], "Factors affecting auditors' evaluations of forecasts," *Journal of Accounting Research*, vol. **21**, pp. 473–494 . . . An experiment consisting of four realistic corporate cases was presented to 81 auditors from the Big Eight accounting firms. The results suggested that auditors tended to have more confidence in forecasting systems that: (1) had centralized financial planning systems; (2) rewarded the managers for accurate forecasts; and, (3) did not make large revisions from the initial to the final forecast. However, the auditors' confidence in the forecasts was significantly increased in cases where the forecasters had a good track record in predicting income statement data. (*LRF* 272)

DAUB, Mervin, [1981], "The accuracy of Canadian short-term economic forecasts revisited," *Canadian Journal of Economics*, vol. **14**, pp. 499–507 . . . Daub compared errors in predicting annual changes in Canadian GNP in the 1970s with those from 1957–69. Forecast errors in the 1970s were *smaller*. (*LRF* see DAUB and PETERSON [1981])

DAUB, Mervin and PETERSON, E., [1981], "The accuracy of a long-term forecast: Canadian energy requirements," *Energy Research*, vol. 5, pp. 141–154 . . . Daub and Peterson analyze the accuracy of a 10-year energy forecast made in Canada in 1966. As we now know, the early 1970s were a period of high turbulence due, first, to environmental concerns, and then to the OPEC petroleum crisis; as a result, it became much more difficult to forecast in general, and especially to forecast energy. According to Daub and Peterson's study, however, the preceeding statement is FALSE! The Canadian National Energy Board's forecasts, based on elaborate data to supplement judgmental procedures, did not deteriorate over time. Surprisingly, the error did not grow over the forecast horizon as one would expect in times of turbulence. This finding corresponds to that reported in forecasts of 1,001 time series in MAKRIDAKIS, et al. [1981] and to DAUB [1981]. It was also interesting that simple extrapolations based on the previous 5 to 10 years did a bit better than forecasts by the five-member Canadian Board. (LRF 4, 397, 597)

DAWES, Robyn M., [1977], "Suppose we measured height with rating scales instead of rulers," Applied Psychological Measurement, vol. 1, pp. 267–273 . . . Average ratings of height by 25 people produced an excellent estimate of true physical height. Of course, it is probably cheaper to use a ruler in such a case. But in many cases it is not possible to measure the concept directly, thus the importance of averaging across many judges. (LRF 135)

DAWES, Robyn M., [1979], "The robust beauty of improper linear models in decision making," American Psychologist, vol. 34, pp. 571–582 . . . This paper is a follow-up on DAWES [1974]. I would like to take credit for my prediction on page 513 of the first edition of LRF when I said that universities would be slow to adopt bootstrapping (or any formal weighting of the variables) for the selection of graduate students. Dawes was aware of only four universities (U. of Illinois, NYU, U. of Oregon, and UC Santa Barbara) that adopted bootstrapping and, even in these places, it was used only for initial screening. However, large state universities with the need to allocate spaces in a politically acceptable manner have been moving in the direction of using linear models. (LRF 282, 530)

DAWES, Robyn M., [1980], "Apologia for using what works," American Psychologist, vol. 35, p. 678 . . . This critiques PRITCHARD [1980].

DENNIS, John D., [1978]. "A performance test of a run-based adaptive exponential forecasting technique," Production and Inventory Management, vol. 19, pp. 43–46 . . . The conclusions of this study were challenged by EKERN [1981]. (LRF 171, 494, 601)

DeSANCTIS, Gerardine, [1984], "Computer graphics as decision aids: directions for research," Decision Sciences, vol. 15, pp. 463–487 . . . (LRF 48).

DICKSON, Gary W.; SENN, James A. and CHERVANY, Norman L., [1977]. "Research in mangement information systems: The Minnesota experiments," *Mangement Science,* vol. **23,** pp. 913–923 . . . Summarizes the Minnesota Experiments on issues such as how computer presentation affects decision making. Some results were surprising. (e.g., decision making seemed to be better among groups given paper output than among those using video screens). (*LRF* 48)

DIELMAN, Terry E., [1985], "Regression forecasts when disturbances are autocorrelated," *International Journal of Forecasting,* (in press) . . . This study uses a Monte Carlo simulation to assess the quality of forecasts obtained from regression models with various degrees of autocorrelation in the error term. Deilman concludes that it is important to correct for autocorrelation, especially for very short-range forecasts. (*LRF* 224)

DILLMAN, Don A., [1978], *Mail and Telephone Surveys.* New York: Wiley . . . A useful set of guidelines for conducting mail and telephone surveys. Reviewed by ARMSTRONG [1981]. (*LRF* 113, 114)

DIPBOYE, Robert L., [1982], "Self-fulfilling prophecies in the selection-recruitment interview," *Academy of Management Review,* vol. **7,** pp. 579–586 . . . This review paper concludes that interviewers are strongly influenced by prior information. (*LRF* not cited)

DORANS, Neil and DRASGOW, Fritz, [1978], "Alternative weighting schemes for linear prediction," *Organizational Behavior and Human Performance,* vol. **21,** pp. 316–345 . . . They examined six approaches to estimating relationships, and tested them on simulated data with three variables. Equal weights performed well across different sample sizes. Regression (OLS) was poorest for small samples in the cross-validation ($n < 30$), but best for large samples. Equal weights are appropriate when (1) sample size is small or moderate; (2) good *a priori* information exists on the direction or the relationship, and (3) positive (not negative) intercorrelations exist among predictors. (*LRF* 231)

DOWNS, Sylvia; FARR, Robert M. and COLBECK, L., [1978], "Self-appraisal: A convergence of selection and guidance," *Journal of Occupational Psychology,* vol. **51,** pp. 271–278 . . . People seem to be able to make good predictions about how successful they will be on a job if they have been given a realistic preview. (*LRF* 155)

DUAN, Naihua; MANNING, W.G.; MORRIS, C.N. and NEWHOUSE, J.P., [1983], "A comparison of alternative models for the demand for medical care," *Journal of Business and Economic Statistics,* vol. **1,** pp. 115–126 . . . Improved forecasts were obtained by segmenting into two or into four subproproblems. The overall problem involved forecasting the effects of different insurance plans. Segmentation seemed especially appropriate because there were such large differences in forecasted behavior for those who had consumed health services and those who had not. The paper is difficult to read as exemplified by this sentence (p. 120): "Moreover, when the normal assumption indeed holds, the nonparametric smearing estimate has high efficiency relative to the parametric normal transformation factor exp ($\alpha/2$) for a wide range of parameter values." (*LRF* 287)

DUDA, Richard O. and SHORTLIFFE, Edward H., [1983], "Expert systems research," *Science*, vol. **220**, pp. 261–268 . . . This paper reviews research on expert systems: (computer systems designed to make diagnoses that rival those of experts). The authors view expert systems as a subset of "knowledge based systems" which, in turn, is a subset of "artificial intelligence." They briefly describe applications of expert systems for medicine, geology, computer design, and chemistry. These programs seemed to perform well in comparison with experts. It appears that the ability of the program to tell the user *why* various questions are being asked is thought to be important for acceptance by the potential user. (*LRF* 277).

EATON, **Warren Q., [1984]**,   "On obtaining data for research integrations," *American Psychologist,* vol. **39**, pp. 1325–1326 . . . (*LRF* 445)

EBERT, Ronald J. and KRUSE, Thomas E., [1978], "Bootstrapping the security analyst," *Journal of Applied Psychology*, vol. **63**, pp. 110–119 . . . (*LRF* 282).

EGGLETON, Ian R.C., [1982], "Intuitive time-series extrapolation," *Journal of Accounting Research*, vol. **20**, pp. 68–102 . . . This paper reports on a laboratory experiment. Subjects were presented with 12 sets of two-digit numbers which were referred to as "monthly production costs." After viewing the series for 15 seconds, each subject forecasted the next observation and provided a confidence interval. Findings: (1) subjects were conservative relative to extrapolation models. That is, they predicted smaller changes than the commonly used extrapolation methods; and (2) the confidence intervals were sensitive to the historical variance. (*LRF* 87, 172)

EHRENBERG, Andrew S.C., [1981],   "The problem of numeracy," *American Statistician*, vol. **35** [May], pp. 67–70 . . . Presents six rules for improving the presentation of data in tables: (1) round to two significant digits, (2) provide row or column averages, (3) arrange the numbers to be compared in a column rather than a row, (4) order the rows and columns by size, (5) use layout to guide the eye and facilitate comparisons, and (6) give verbal summaries about major patterns and exceptions. The first five rules are easy to implement on a personal computer with a spreadsheet program, such as LOTUS. (*LRF* 47)

EINHORN, Hillel J. and HOGARTH, Robin M., [1982], "Prediction diagnosis and causal thinking in forecasting," *Journal of Forecasting*, vol. 1, pp. 23–36 . . . This paper discusses theory and prior research. (*LRF* 75)

EKERN, Steinar, [1981], "Adaptive exponential smoothing revisited," *Journal of the Operational Research Society*, vol. **32**, pp. 775–782 . . . Replicates and challenges the studies by DENNIS [1978] and WHYBARK [1972]. (*LRF* 171, 495, 599, 649)

ELLIOTT, J. Walter and BAIER, Jerome R., [1979], "Econometric models and current interest rates: How well do they predict future rates?" *Journal of Finance*, vol. **34**, pp. 975–986 . . . (*LRF* 339)

ELLIOTT, J.W. and UPHOFF, H.L., [1972], "Predicting the near term profit and loss statement with an econometric model: A feasibility study," *Journal of Accounting Research*, vol. **10**, pp. 259–274 . . . An econometric model provided more accurate *ex post* forecasts of nine variables for one company than did three extrapolation models. However, these were based upon only four monthly forecasts. (*LRF* 409)

ELSTEIN, Arthur S.; SHULMAN, A.S. and SPAFKA, S.A., [1978], *Medical Problem Solving: An Analysis of Clinical Reasoning*. Cambridge, Mass.: Harvard University Press . . . Simple ("low fidelilty") role-playing ("simulations") provided similar results to those from the more realistic ("high fidelity") and more expensive role-playing. (*LRF* 125)

FALCONER, Robert T and SIVESIND, C.M., [1977], "Dealing with conflicting forecasts: The eclectic advantage," *Business Economics*, vol. **12**, No. 4, pp. 5–11 . . . This paper examined combined *ex post* econometric and naive forecasts of U.S. personal income for forecasts up to a six quarter horizon. "Composite" (combined) forecasts, weighted by the relative Root Mean Square Errors, helped in all cases, but especially for the longer forecast horizon. (*LRF* 290)

FEIDLER, Edgar R., [1977], "The three R's of economic forecasting: Irrational, irrelevant and irreverent," *Across the Board*, vol. **14**, No. 6, pp. 62–63 . . . This presents 25 classic quotations poking fun at economic forecasters. Typical selection: "When presenting a forecast, give them a number or give them a date, but never both." Useful material for after-dinner speakers. (*LRF* not cited)

FEILD, Hubert S. and HOLLEY, William H., [1982], "The relationship of performance appraisal system characteristics to verdicts in selected employment discrimination cases," *Academy of Management Journal*, vol. **25**, pp. 392–406 . . . Assume that a worker claims to have received unfair discrimination in termination or promotion, and files suit against your organization. Your organization's action had been based on a performance appraisal. How could you predict your chances of success? This paper reviews relevant research in the field to suggest which factors are important (e.g., an organization that uses specific written instructions will be more successful in defending itself: also, organizations are more successful when they rely on evaluations of *behavior* rather than *personal traits*). The paper also examines 66 new cases in an effort to develop better predictors. Unfortunately, this aspect of the paper did not involve any predictions; it focused on an explanation of historical results. The ability to explain was modest; a linear discriminant function explained only 39% of the variability in the verdicts. Some surprises here: (1) firms that presented evidence on the validity and reliability of their performance appraisal systems received *no* better treatment from the courts, (2) industrial organizations fared *less well* than nonindustrial organizations (such as universities). The study implies that understanding the prejudices of the court will allow one to make better predictions about the outcome. In addition, the results imply actions that organizations can take to reduce the likelihood of losing verdicts. (*LRF* not cited)

FILDES, Robert (with DEWS, D. and HOWELL, S.), [1981], *A Bibliography of Business and Economic Forecasting.* Farnborough, Hants, England: Gower Publishing. (A revised edition was published in 1984 by the Manchester Business School under same title with the subtitle *Part 2, 1979–1981.* Further editions are planned.) My summary draws upon the review by Everette S. Gardner, *Journal of Forecasting*, **1** (1982), (320–321) . . . This is a comprehensive reference source on forecasting methods. Fildes uses a broader definition of forecasting than that used in *LRF*. Many of the studies in Fildes bibliography are only indirectly related to forecasting. More than 4,000 items are indexed in the 1981 edition, mostly articles from 40 journals over the period 1971–1978. Fifteen economics journals were searched. Other areas include: statistics, management science, and marketing—six journals from each field; general business—four; accounting—two; and finance—one. Some articles prior to 1971 were included, along with a selection of books. The bibliography is directed largely toward economic model building. The key words are so extensive that they compose a mini-abstract for most references listed. Here is an illustration under "judgmental forecasting":

YA2657 O'CARROLL, F.M.
"Subjective probabilities and short-term economic forecasts: an empirical investigation," Appl. Stats., vol. 26, 1977, pp. 269–278. APPL-MACRO: INTERNATIONAL FINANCE, EXCHANGE RATES*APPL-MACRO, UK*APPL-SECTOR: FINANCL, STOCK PRICE INDEX*APPL-SECTOR: PRODUCTION, PETROLEUM*PRICE-SECTOR: PRODUCTION*JUDGEMENTAL FORECASTS-SPECIALIST*ERROR DISTRIBUTION-LOGNORMAL*EVALUATION-JUDGEMENTAL FORECASTS*JUDGEMENTAL FORECASTS-UNCERTAINTY

This example shows that macro applications may be located using key words for sector, variable, or country. The key words also indicate that the judgmental forecasts were made by a specialist in the field, using probabilities (key worded as "uncertainty"), and that the article evaluates the effectiveness of the forecasts. A statistical problem related to the lognormal error distribution is also discussed. The key words are based on 14 dimensions or categories of knowledge. These include: (1) applications, (2) variables to forecast, (3) types of models, (4) model interpretation, (5) model estimation, (6) statistical problems, (7) uses and users, (8) forecast effectiveness, (9) forecast monitoring and evaluation, (10) how to develop and select a model, (11) data-related problems, (12) the effects of certain independent variables, (13) the theory underlying a model, and (14) implementation problems. More than 500 examples of applications of forecasting are classified by firm and industry, with subcategories by product. Many of these applications are also cross-referenced to implementation problems and how the forecasts were used. The coverage in inventory control, manpower planning, and portfolio selection is particularly thorough. The listings of comparisons among alternative forecasting methods should be valuable. One can choose any major forecasting method and find references that compare it with other methods. For example, 60 comparisons are listed between ARIMA methods and one or more of the following: autoregressive, causal, decomposition, distributed lag, exponential smoothing, judgmental, and others. Many of these comparisons were not evident from the titles or abstracts of the papers, and this reflects the care that went into this bibliography. Users of this bibliography will be able to spice up their lectures with some of the more exotic references listed. Some classroom examples include papers on forecasting productivity in the Israeli diamond industry (good results), the population of colored foxes in Labrador (also good), and earthquakes (shaky results). Although Fildes does not evaluate the references, some are labeled either basic or advanced, according to mathematical complexity. Basic references can be used by beginners in the field. Articles labeled as advanced have little general value because of their inaccessibility. But many difficult papers on such topics as spectral analysis and statistical testing of simultaneous equations models were not labeled as advanced. The average user will find that papers with advanced labels are incomprehensible. This reference work should help unify the field of forecasting. I found this book to be extremely helpful in updating *LRF*. Because of the extensive literature on forecasting, I believe that it is important to use this book if one expects to do a thorough literature review. The book's problem, however, is similar to that faced by Alice in *Through the Looking Glass*. The White Queen's advice was: "Now, *here*, you see, it takes all the running you can do, to keep in the same place." Its place now is as the leading source book. The 1979–1981 update expanded the coverage from 40 to 70 journals and added 1500 references to the original 4000. (*LRF* 406, 444, 472)

FILDES, Robert, [1982], "Forecasting: The issues," in S. Makridakis and S.C. Wheelwright (Eds.). *The Handbook of Forecasting*. New York: Wiley . . . (*LRF* 7, 366)

FILDES, Robert and FITZGERALD, M. Desmond, [1983], "The use of information in balance of payments forecasting," *Economica*, vol. **50**, pp. 249–258 . . . Fildes and Fitzgerald examined the performance of three economists who each month made one-month-ahead forecasts of the U.K. balance of payments. The period from July 1975 to December 1978 was studied. Some findings were consistent with prior evidence—for example, the combined forecasts of the three economists were better than those by the average forecaster (RMSE of 176 vs. 185). Fildes and Fitzgerald also examined an extrapolation (ARIMA) model and found it equal in accuracy to the average judgmental forecaster (RMSE 184 vs. 185). Then they combined the extrapolation and judgmental forecasts and found little improvement over the combined forecast of three judges (RMSE of 173 vs. 176). Finally, they concluded that bootstrapping models did not improve the forecast accuracy of any of the three judges. But the sample size used (three judges) is too small to allow us to conclude that bootstrapping was less accurate. (*LRF* 283, 290, 292)

FILDES Robert and HOWELL, Syd, [1979], "On selecting a forecasting model," in Spyros Makridakis and Steven C. Wheelwright (Eds.), *Forecasting*. New York: North Holland, pp. 297–312 . . . This literature review, among other things, presents evidence favoring simplicity in econometric models. (*LRF* 231)

FILDES, Robert and LUSK, Edward J., [1984], "The choice of a forecasting model," *Omega*, vol. **12**, pp. 427–435 . . . (*LRF* 176, 441).

FINK, Edward B.; BRADEN, W. and QUALLS, C.B., [1982], "Predicting pharmacotherapy outcome by subjective response," *Journal of Clinical Psychiatry*, vol. **43**, pp. 272–275 . . . How effective will a drug be for a patient? One way to improve this prediction is ask the patient about the benefit of the drug after 24 hours of use. Patients' responses were related to clinical improvement after 8 to 21 days in this experiment. What seems most surprising is that such predictive measures are not used routinely. (*LRF* not cited)

FINKEL, Sidney R. and TUTTLE, Donald L., [1971], "Determinants of the aggregate profits margins," *Journal of Finance*, vol. **26**, pp. 1067–1075 . . . Forecasts (apparently *ex post*) were made for total corporate profits in the U.S. economy. The forecasts were made for the quarters from 1968-I to 1970-II, using a single starting point. An econometric model that had four independent variables was more accurate than a naive model that was based on a weighted moving average. (*LRF* 409)

FISCHER, Gregory W., [1981], "When oracles fail—A comparison of four procedures for aggregating subjective probability forecasts," *Organizational Behavior and Human Performance*, vol. **28**, pp. 96–110 . . . This paper contrasts four methods for obtaining forecasts from a group of experts: (1) statistical average of the individual forecasts, (2) face-to-face discussion to reach consensus, (3) Delphi, and (4) Estimate-Talk-Estimate (E-T-E). Fischer's review of the literature, along with a reanalysis of an important E-T-E study, provided little basis to suggest one method is more accurate than another. Fischer then used the four methods to aggregate opinions on a simple problem, estimating grade point averages of 10 randomly selected students given sex, high school GPA, and SAT scores. The four aggregation methods produced estimates of comparable accuracy. Fischer concluded that in terms of accuracy "it makes little or no difference how one aggregates conflicting opinions of experts." He suggested cost and acceptability are likely to be relevant criteria. These methods differ on cost (#1 being the least expensive) and on acceptability by the group (#2 offering the highest). Fischer omitted mention of Dalkey (1969) who found that method 1 (averaging) was slightly superior to group discussion for simple problems, and of Hall, Mouton, and Blake (1963), who found method 2 (consensus) was superior to unstructured discussion in making predictions in what may have been a more complex case. My conclusion from these studies is that structured group process is superior to unstructured group process, but that a variety of structured approaches yield similar accuracy. (*LRF* 124)

FISCHER, Gregory W., [1982], "Scoring-rule feedback and the overconfidence syndrome in subjective probability forecasting," *Organizational Behavior and Human Performance*, vol. **20**, pp. 352–369 . . . Subjects used information on the sex, SAT scores, and high school grades of 40 college freshmen to predict first-year grades. The feedback on outcome had no effect on overconfidence. Incentives did lead to better scores, but only because subjects were less likely to assign extremely low probabilities, which were heavily penalized. These results must be viewed with caution, because the task proved to be so difficult for the subjects; by assuming an equal probability of being in each of the four categories (a strategy of "pure ignorance"), the subjects would have *improved* their predictions. (*LRF* 380)

FISCHHOFF, Baruch and MacGREGOR, Don, [1982], "Subjective confidence in forecasts," *Journal of Forecasting*, vol. **1**, pp. 155–172 . . . Forecasts have little value to decision makers unless it is known how much confidence to place in them. Those expressions of confidence have, in turn, little value unless forecasters are able to assess the limits of their own knowledge accurately. Previous research has shown patterns in the judgments of individuals who have not received special training in confidence assessment: Knowledge generally increases as confidence increases. However, it increases too swiftly, with a doubling of confidence being associated with perhaps a 50% increase in knowledge. With all but the easiest of tasks, people tend to be overconfident about how much they know. These prior results were derived from studies of judgments of general knowledge. The present study found that they also pertained to confidence in *forecasts*; indeed, the confidence-knowledge curves observed here were strikingly similar to those observed previously. The only deviation was the discovery that a substantial minority of judges never expressed complete confidence in any of their forecasts; these individuals also proved to be better assessors of the extent of their own knowledge. Apparently confidence in forecasts is determined by processes similar to those that determine confidence in general knowledge. Decision makers can use forecasters' assessments in a relative sense, in order to predict when they are more or less likely to be correct. However, they should be hesitant to take confidence assessments literally. Someone is more likely to be right when she is "certain" than when she is "fairly confident," but there is no guarantee that the supposedly certain forecast will come true. The paper includes

a table summarizing 37 studies that have tried to reduce overconfidence. (*LRF* 144, 379)

**FISCHHOFF, Baruch; SLOVIC, Paul and LICHTENSTEIN, Sarah,
[1977],** "Knowing with certainty: The appropriateness of extreme
confidence," *Journal of Experimental Psychology: Human Perception
and Performance*, vol. **3**, pp. 552–564 . . . Overconfidence was found
with a variety of stimulus materials and response modes. Lectures on
how to assess probabilities and how to avoid extreme probability predictions did little to reduce overconfidence. (*LRF* 143)

**FISCHHOFF, Baruch; SLOVIC, Paul and LICHTENSTEIN, Sarah,
[1978],** "Fault trees: Sensitivity of estimated failure probabilities to
problem representation," *Journal of Experimental Psychology: Human
Perception and Performance*, vol. **4**, pp. 330–344 . . . Fault trees involve
the causal decomposition of a complex event as a way to assess its
likelihood. In this paper, the event is "car fails to start." Subjects were
asked to predict the likely causes for failure. When likely causes were
omitted, subjects assigned higher probabilities to the potential causes
remaining, and they made small but insufficient increases in the "other"
category of possible causes. It was just as likely for people with more
expertise to overlook causes that had been omitted. Increasing the
amount of detail about the potential causes had little impact, except
the probabilities for a cause could be increased by presenting it as two
branches rather than one. Fault trees can be used for prediction problems with mechanical systems (e.g., to predict the likelihood of a failure
at a nuclear plant) and for other problems involving multiple causality
(e.g., what is the probability that two people will remain married for
the next 30 years or that a firm will continue for the next 20 years).
(*LRF* 59)

FOSTER, George, [1977], "Quarterly accounting data: Time series
properties and predictive ability results," *Accounting Review*, vol. **52**,
pp. 1–21 . . . This study is based on sales and earnings forecasts for 69
firms. It compares the accuracy of six extrapolation methods. (*LRF* not
cited)

FRALICX, Rodney and RAJU, Namburg S., [1982], "A comparison of five methods for combining multiple criteria into a single composite," *Educational and Psychological Measurement*, vol. **42**, pp. 823–
827 . . . Canonical correlations have been suggested in forecasting problems where a number of criteria are of interest and a number of predictors are available. The canonical weights determine the index that
best predicts a criterion index. Canonical correlation is a method that
is often used when theory is lacking. Theoretically, there is no reason
to expect that a canonical index will be valid. This paper tests the

validity of the canonical index for the formulation of a job performance index. The canonical index was compared with four alternative weighting schemes: managements' subjective weights, equal weights, unit weights, and principal components factor weights. The alternatives yielded *nearly identical weights* for judging the overall performance of 117 bank tellers based on eight performance criteria (e.g., customer relations, attention to detail). In contrast, the canonical weights (which used the eight performance criteria as well as 13 predictor variables such as memory and arithmetic ability) *had almost no correlation to the other methods*. It is distressing that the canonical index bore no relation to methods with high face validity (managements' subjective weights and equal weights). (*LRF* 225)

FRANK, Werner, [1969], "A study of the predictive significance of two income measures," *Journal of Accounting Research*, vol. **7**, pp. 123–136 . . . Exponential smoothing was more accurate than a moving average and also more accurate than a regression against time. (*LRF* 173, 494)

GAETH, Gary J. and SHANTEAU, James, [1984], "Reducing the influence of irrelevant information in experienced decision makers," *Organizational Behavior and Human Performance*, vol. **33**, pp. 263–282 . . . Lectures were not effective in getting judges to ignore irrelevant information in an experiment where 12 judges rated the composition of soil samples. However, experiential learning was effective. Their errors were then noted (negative feedback). The judges were given advice and were then asked to make judgments. Further active training was then provided with an emphasis on positive feedback for good responses. (*LRF* 144, 380)

GARDNER, Everette S., Jr., [1979a], "Box-Jenkins vs. multiple regression: Some adventures in forecasting the demand for blood tests," *Interfaces*, vol. **9** [August], pp. 49–54 . . . On page 54 of Gardner's paper, regression models #23 and #24 should say "*Dependent* variable lagged one period" instead of "*Independent* variable lagged one period." (*LRF* 495)

GARDNER, Everette S., Jr., [1979b], "A note on forecast modification based upon residual analysis," *Decision Sciences*, vol. **10**, pp. 493–494 . . . (*LRF* 623)

GARDNER, Everette S., Jr., [1983a], "Automatic monitoring of forecast errors," *Journal of Forecasting*, vol. **2**, pp. 1–21 . . . This paper evaluates a variety of automatic monitoring schemes to detect biased forecast errors. Backward cumulative sum (CUSUM) tracking signals have been recommended in previous research to monitor exponential smoothing models. This research shows that identical performance can be had with much simpler tracking signals. The smoothed-error signal is recommended for $\alpha = 0.1$, although its performance deteriorates badly as α is increased. For higher α values, the simple CUSUM signal is recommended. Comments by the referees were published along with this paper. See also **GARDNER [1985a]** (*LRF* 187)

GARDNER, Everette S., Jr., [1983b], "Evolutionary operation of the exponential smoothing parameter: Revisited," *Omega*, vol. 11, pp. 621–623 . . . Gardner tried to replicate Chow [1965], but obtained different results. (*LRF* 171, 495, 526)

GARDNER, Everette S., Jr., [1984], "The strange case of the lagging forecasts," *Interfaces*, vol. 14, [May–June], pp. 47–50 . . . Apparently it is difficult to explain exponential smoothing without making some type of error. Gardner found 23 books and articles with errors in model formulations for smoothing a linear trend. (*LRF* 450)

GARDNER, Everette S., Jr., [1985a], "CUSUM vs. Smoothed-error forecast monitoring schemes: Some empirical comparisons," *Journal of the Operational Research Society* , vol. 36, pp. 43–47 . . . (*LRF* 187)

GARDNER, Everette S., Jr., [1985b], "Exponential smoothing: The state of the art," *Journal of Forecasting* (in press) . . . A comprehensive review of the literature. Commentary follows on pages 29–38. (*LRF* 161, 166, 171)

GARDNER, Everette S., Jr. and DANNENBRING, David G., [1980], "Forecasting with exponential smoothing: Some guidelines for model selection," *Decision Sciences*, vol. 11, pp. 370–383 . . . This simulation experiment compared different extrapolation methods (Holt; Gilchrist; Montgomery; Simple Smoothing; Whybark; Trigg and Leach; Roberts and Reed; and Chow) to predict for 9,000 simulated time series (variations in levels, trends and random error). Used a variety of error measures (e.g., MAD, MSE, MAE). Adaptive models generated unstable forecasts, even when average demand was stable. This is an important paper. (*LRF* 171, 495)

GARDNER, Everette S., Jr. and McKENZIE, Ed, [1985], "Forecasting trends in time series," *Management Science* (in press) . . . This paper analyzes data from the M-Competition and demonstrates procedures for automatic dampening of trend factors. (*LRF* 169)

GEURTS, Michael D., [1982], "Forecasting the Hawaiian tourist market," *Journal of Travel Research*, vol. 21 [Summer], pp. 18–21 . . . Replacement of outliers by the estimated values led to dramatic improvements in accuracy in forecasts for the two months following each of four atypical periods occurring over a two year period. (*LRF* 162)

GINZBERG, Michael J., [1979], "A study of the implementation process," in Robert H. Doktor, R.L. Schultz, and D.P. Slevin (Eds.), *The*

Implementation of Management Science. New York: North Holland . . .
This study on the implementation of 29 computer systems showed that
success was higher when the unfreezing, change, and refreezing phases
were each carried out successfully. (*LRF* 32)

GLANTZ, Michael H., [1982], "Consequences and responsibilities
in drought forecasting: The case of Yakima, 1977," *Water Resources
Research*, vol. **18**, pp. 3–13 . . . This paper describes a U.S. Bureau of
Reclamation forecast of a drought. The forecast led to actions to save
crops. As one farmer put it, "Drought is when the government sends
you a report telling you there's no water." However, the forecast was
wrong. (No confidence interval was published, but the actual flow was
much different from the forecast.) It appears, in this case, that the
objective forecasting methods performed well but that subjective adjustments were made. The subjective adjustments led to the prediction
of an extreme event. Attempts are being made to sue the government
for malpractice in forecasting. Some questions: Will such legal actions
lead to a greater reliance on objective methods of forecasting? Should
good practice in forecasting require that confidence limits also be published with the forecast? Should forecasters intentionally bias forecasts
if the loss function seems asymmetric (e.g., the cost of a drought might
be seen as greater than the cost of a flood)? (*LRF* 273)

GLASS, Gene V., [1976], "Primary, secondary and meta-analysis of
research," *Educational Researcher*, vol. **5**, pp. 3–8 . . . (*LRF* 445)

GLASS, Gene V.; McGAW, Barry and SMITH, Mary Lee,
[1981], *Meta-Analysis in Social Research*. Beverly Hills, Calif.:
Sage, . . . (*LRF* 444)

GOMEZ-MEJIA, Luis R.; PAGE, Ronald C. and TORNOW,
Walter W., [1982], "A comparison of the practical utility of traditional, statistical, and hybrid job evaluation approaches," *Academy of
Management Journal*, vol. **25**, pp. 790–809 . . . This paper compares
the predictive accuracy and the acceptability of different methods for
classifying job levels for managers. It first presents an interesting literature review. Three statistical methods were then compared with
three judgmental methods and with a "hybrid" method. The various
methods were calibrated on the same samples and compared on a cross-
validation sample of 150 managers. Some interesting conclusions resulted. *First*, a factor analysis of 235 potential predictor items, followed
by a stepwise regression on the factors, was inferior to a direct stepwise
regression on the variables (cross-validation r^2 of 38% and 58% respectively). *Second*, statistical procedures based on stepwise regression
offered no advantage over traditional methods, such as "assign points
to key factors and calculate a score." *Third*, regression weights on the

variables selected by the experts (their "hybrid model") yielded improvements over the subjective weights (cross-validations of 64% and 55% respectively). And *fourth*, compensation practitioners rated this hybrid model as clearly the most acceptable, the traditional approaches were next most acceptable, and the purely statistical approaches were the least acceptable. My summary: *Use prior theory and judgment to develop a model*, then estimate relationships. (*LRF* 223, 304)

GOULD, John P. and WAUD, R.N., [1973], "The neoclassical model of investment behavior: Another view," *International Economic Review*, vol. **14**, pp. 33–48 . . . The authors examined one-quarter- ahead *ex post* forecasts for eight quarters in 11 industries. No clear-cut winner for accuracy of econometric versus extrapolation forecast accuracy. (*LRF* 408)

GRANGER, C.W.J., [1980], *Forecasting in Business and Economics*. New York: Academic Press . . . This book discusses trend lines, Box-Jenkins, moving averages, regression, econometric analysis, surveys, leading indicators, and the combining of forecasts. It examines population, technology and world models. Designed as a text with "Questions" and "Further Reading" at the end of each chapter, it reads nicely, and has interesting tidbits sprinkled throughout. For example: Q. "Did you know that some people can foretell the future?" A. " I knew you were going to say that." (*LRF* 78)

GRANGER, C.W.J. and NEWBOLD, Paul, [1977], *Forecasting Economic Time Series*. New York: Academic Press . . . This book discusses various techniques for the analysis of time series. It also contains a section on the combining of forecasts. (Granger and Newbold were among the first to do empirical studies on the combination of forecasts.) (*LRF* 224)

GRAY, Clifton W., [1979], "Ingredients of intuitive regression," *Organizational Behavior and Human Performance*, vol. **23**, pp. 30–48 . . . In this experiment, 44 subjects made predictions on a task with a single variable. Their intuitive regressions provided better predictions than did their direct predictions. (*LRF* 278)

GREEN, Paul E. and WIND, Yoram, [1975], "New way to measure consumers' judgments," *Harvard Business Review*, vol. 53 [July-August], pp. 107–117 . . . One of the *Harvard Business Review*'s more popular papers,this provides a short and clear description of conjoint analysis. (*LRF* 278)

GREENLEY, Gordon E., [1983], "Where marketing planning fails," *Long Range Planning*, vol. **16**, pp. 106–115 . . . This paper presents results from personal interviews with high level marketing decision makers in 40 U.K. companies. The companies were selected using a stratified random sample. One question related to the methods the companies used to make forecasts for their marketing plan. This plan typically covered one year, but in about 20% of the cases it extended for two to three years. Their responses were:

Method	Mentioned During Interview	Among Top Three Methods Used by Firm
	(%)	(%)
Judgmental		
Top Management	86	51
Salesforce	89	66
Consumer intentions	57	45
Extrapolation		
Simple projection of trends	83	63
Time series analysis	14	14
Causal methods		
Models	26	20
Correlation	14	11

Simple unaided opinions and crude extrapolations were the most frequently used methods for market forecasting. (*LRF* 426, 427)

GREER, Charles R. and ARMSTRONG, Daniel, [1980], "Human resource forecasting and planning: A state of the art investigation," *Human Resource Planning*, vol. 3, pp. 67–78 . . . Survey of personnel managers at 300 firms drawn randomly from the *1979 College Placement Annual*. Used one follow-up and obtained a 29% response rate. (*LRF* not cited)

GREGORY, W. Larry; CIALDINI, R.B. and CARPENTER, Kathleen M., [1982], "Self-relevant scenarios as mediators of likelihood estimates and compliance: Does imagining make it so?" *Journal of Personality and Social Psychology*, vol. 43, pp. 89–99 . . . (*LRF* 43)

GRIFFITH, John R. and WELLMAN, B.T., [1979], "Forecasting bed needs and recommending facilities plans for community hospitals: A review of past performance," *Medical Care*, vol. 17, pp. 293–303 . . . The authors examined forecasts for six hospitals. The forecasts, prepared by consultants between 1967 and 1971, covered the need for beds in 1975. The clients were often dissatisfied with the consultants' forecasts. They should have used them, however; the formal forecasts were more accurate than the intuitive forecasts used by the decision makers in the hospitals. (*LRF* 40)

GROSS, Charles W. and PETERSON, Robin T., **[1982],** *Business Forecasting*, 2nd Ed. Boston: Houghton-Mifflin . . . A text book aimed at the novice. (*LRF* 78)

GUION, Robert M. and CRANNY, C.J., **[1982],** "A note on concurrent and predictive validity designs: A critical reanalysis," *Journal of Applied Psychology*, vol. **67**, pp. 239–246 . . . A comment on BARRETT, PHILLIPS and ALEXANDER [1981]. (*LRF* 587)

$\mathbf{H}$AGERMAN, Robert L. and RULAND, William, **[1979],** "The accuracy of management forecasts and forecasts of simple alternative models," *Journal of Economics and Business*, vol. **31**, pp. 172–179 . . . Studies 98 one-year earnings forecasts from the *Wall Street Journal*. Compares five extrapolation, one judgment, and one econometric method. (*LRF* 167, 495)

HAMILL, Ruth; WILSON, T.D. and NISBETT, R.E., **[1980],** Insensitivity to sample bias: Generalizing from atypical cases," *Journal of Personality and Social Psychology*, vol. **39**, pp. 578–589 . . . Vivid examples have a strong impact on people's attitudes—much stronger it seems than carefully prepared statistical summaries from large samples. This generalization is drawn from prior research they cite as well as from the two clever experiments reported in this paper. The experiments have implications for the presentation of forecasts, as well as for the use of information to support a forecast. Of particular interest for the *presentation of a forecast* is the use of scenarios. A vivid scenario would be expected to appear to be likely. According to this study, an event described in a scenario will be regarded as more likely even if the scenario was identified as being atypical or unlikely. This might be useful if one is trying to make a case for contingency planning. But scenarios may be dangerous if used to make predictions. Alternatively, vivid scenarios may help to improve estimates in cases where people seriously underestimate the probability. (Perhaps this is the intention of Ground Zero Demonstrations?) In the *presentation of data*, the choice of examples seems to influence people's attitudes more than the statistical information, even when the example is identified as being atypical. To avoid bias in presentation, one should select typical examples. The dangers of atypical examples should be recognized: even more powerful than "lying with statistics" is the opportunity of "lying with examples." (*LRF* 42)

HANKE, John E., [1984], "Forecasting in the business schools," *Journal of Forecasting*, vol. **3**, pp. 229–234 . . . Hanke sent a survey to 620 member institutions of the American Assembly of Collegiate Schools of Business. Responses were received from 52% of the schools. Forecasting courses were offered in 60% of the schools. Regression analysis is the most important technique that is taught in the courses, 83% of the classes use a project, and, surprisingly, judgment methods are hardly ever taught. (*LRF* not cited)

HANKE, John E. and REITSCH, Arthur G., [1981], *Business Forecasting*. Boston: Allyn & Bacon . . . A beginning level textbook with a standard treatment of regression and time series. It contains questions at the end of each chapter, and the answers appear at the end of the book. (*LRF* 78)

HARRIS, R.J., [1973], "Answering questions containing marked and unmarked adjectives and adverbs," *Journal of Experimental Psychology*, vol. **97**, pp. 399–401 . . . (*LRF* 99)

HATJOULLIS, G. and WOOD, D., [1979], "Economic forecasts— An analysis of performance," *Business Economist*, vol. **10** (Spring), pp. 6–21 . . . In general, the econometric models were superior to extrapolation models (either a no-change or an exponential smoothing model). (*LRF* 229, 409)

HERBERT, Theodore T. and YOST, Edward B., [1979], "A comparison of decision quality under nominal interacting consensus group formats: The case of the structured problem," *Decision Sciences*, vol. **10**, pp. 358–370 . . . Provides a good review of the literature on nominal groups (groups that do not actually interact). In an experiment using the NASA moon problem (see *LRF* 462–463), Herbert and Yost found that nominal groups made better decisions than the interacting groups and also made better ones than the best individual. The interacting groups did not have a facilitator nor did they use any formal procedure. (*LRF* 122)

HILL, Gareth and FILDES, Robert, [1984], "The accuracy of extrapolation methods: An automatic Box-Jenkins package (SIFT)," *Journal of Forecasting*, vol. **3**, pp. 319–323 . . . (*LRF* 175)

HINRICHS, John R., [1969], "Comparison of real-life assessments of potential with situational exercises, paper and pencil ability tests, and personality inventories," *Journal of Applied Psychology*, vol. **53**, pp. 425–432 . . . Concludes that an "assessment center" evaluation may be unnecessary if a reliable and relevant employment history is available. However, assessment centers might be useful when no job history exists for an individual. (*LRF* 615)

HINRICHS, John R., [1978], "An eight-year follow-up of a management assessment center," *Journal of Applied Psychology*, vol. **63**, pp. 596–601 . . . Follow-up on HINRICHS [1969]. More evidence that an inexpensive prediction based on a review of personnel files did as well as the assessment center in predicting advancement for a group of sales persons. Not surprising is that those who were promoted in this organization were described as upwardly mobile. (*LRF* 155)

HIRSCH, Albert; GRIMM, B.T. and NARASIMHAM, G.V.L., [1974], "Some multiplier and error characteristics of the BEA Quarterly Model," *International Economic Review*, vol. **15**, pp. 616–631 . . . (*LRF* 237, 241)

HOGARTH, Robin M., [1978], "A note on aggregating opinions," *Organizational Behavior and Human Performance*, vol. **21**, pp. 40–46 . . . How many experts should you use in forecasting a given variable? Hogarth, using theoretical arguments, concludes that one should use at least 6, but no more than 20 experts. You should tend toward the higher side of this range if your experts differ among one another in their forecasts and if they can make good forecasts. A good rule of thumb is to use ten experts. (*LRF* 96, 589)

HOGARTH, Robin M., [1980], *Judgement and Choice: The Psychology of Decision.* New York: Wiley . . . Examples are offered throughout, with attention to personnel decisions, stock purchases, sales strategies and medical prognosis. The literature review is excellent and the writing is clear. Hogarth's Table 9-2 on his pages 166–170 is especially useful. (See Ruth M. Corbin's review in the *Journal of Forecasting*, vol. **1**, (1982), 219–221.) (*LRF* 75, 86, 98)

HOGARTH, Robin M. and MAKRIDAKIS, Spyros, [1981], "Forecasting and planning: An evaluation," *Management Science*, vol. **27**, pp. 115–138 . . . This paper organizes and reviews research on the judgmental aspects of forecasting and planning. It contains 175 references and these were helpful for updating *Long-Range Forecasting*. (*LRF* not cited)

HOLMES, David S., et al., [1980], "Biorhythms: Their utility for predicting post-operative recuperative time, death and athletic performance," *Journal of Applied Psychology*, vol. **65**, pp. 233–236 . . . The marketplace declares biorhythms to be a winner! Unfortunately, research studies do not agree; they find no evidence that biorhythms improve forecast accuracy. Holmes, et al., add three more competent studies. (*LRF* 435)

HOPWOOD, William S.; NEWBOLD, Paul and SILHAN, Peter A., [1982], "The potential for gains in predictive ability through disaggregation: Segmented annual earnings," *Journal of Accounting Research*, vol. **20**, pp. 724–732 . . . This study examined forecasts for fictitious conglomerates (constructed by averaging across two to five actual firms), by extrapolating the composite earnings directly, and comparing the forecasts with those built up from separate extrapolations of each of the components. Minor gains in accuracy were obtained when this was done for the Box-Jenkins and exponential smoothing methods. However, the most accurate forecasts were provided by the no change forecasts (where the issue of segmentation was irrelevant). (*LRF* not cited)

HOWREY, E.P.; KLEIN, L.R. and McCARTHY, M.D., [1974], "Notes on testing the predictive performance of econometric models," *International Economic Review*, vol. **15**, pp. 366–383 . . . A version of the Wharton Econometric Model was found to be more accurate than an autoregressive model in quarterly forecasts of real GNP, 1955–1966. The superiority of the econometric model increased as the forecast horizon was increased. The authors discuss some of the problems in drawing inferences from comparisons of the forecast accuracy of alternative models. (*LRF* 409)

HUNTER, John E.; SCHMIDT, Frank L. and JACKSON, Gregg B., [1982], *Meta-Analysis: Cumulating Research Findings Across Studies.* Beverly Hills, CA: Sage . . . (*LRF* 445)

INCIARDI, James A., [1977], "The parole prediction myth," *International Journal of Criminology and Penology*, vol. **5**, pp. 235–244 . . . (*LRF* 198)

JACKSON, Gregg B., [1980], "Methods for integrative reviews," *Review of Educational Research*, vol. **50**, pp. 438–460 . . . How should you carry out a literature review? The author examined 39 methodology texts and found little guidance. He then examined procedures used in 36 review articles from prestigious social science journals. (*LRF* 445)

JEVONS, William Stanley, [1877], *The Principles of Science: A Treatise on Logic and Scientific Method.* (Reprinted in 1958 by Dover Publications, N.Y.) . . . (*LRF* 52)

JOHNSON, Timothy E. and SCHMITT, Thomas G., [1974], "Effectiveness of earnings per share forecasts," *Financial Management*, vol. **3**, pp. 64–72 . . . Uses data on annual income from 150 industrial companies for 1962–1971 to compare forecast accuracy of no-change, moving average, regression against time, exponential smoothing (with and without trend), adaptive exponential smoothing, and triple smoothing. Basic conclusions: not much difference in accuracy among the various methods, and last year's earnings provided a good forecast of next year's earnings. (*LRF* 495)

JOHNSON, W. Bruce, [1983], "Representativeness in judgmental predictions of corporate bankruptcy," *Accounting Review*, vol. **58**, pp. 78–97 . . . (*LRF* 98)

JONES, Warren H. and RUSSELL, Dan, [1980], "The selective processing of belief disconfirming information," *European Journal of Social Psychology*, vol. **10**, pp. 309–312 . . . Believers and skeptics of ESP (extra sensory perception) were given either confirming or disconfirming evidence in this study that used rigged experiments. Believers were not affected by disconfirming evidence, but the skeptics were. (*LRF* 378, 437)

KAHNEMAN, Daniel; SLOVIC, Paul and TVERSKY, Amos (Eds.), [1982]. *Judgment Under Uncertainty: Heuristics and Biases.* Cambridge, England: Cambridge University Press . . . A useful collection of papers dealing mostly with shortcomings in human judgment. The papers, most of which have been previously published, deal chiefly with the highly influential work by Kahneman and Tversky. Those interested in research on judgmental research should read this book. (For a more detailed review see ARMSTRONG, 1984b.) (*LRF* 86, 516, 569, 583, 646)

KAHNEMAN, Daniel and TVERSKY, Amos, [1979], "Intuitive prediction: Biases and corrective procedures," in Spyros Makridakis and Steven Wheelwright (Eds.), *Forecasting*. Amsterdam: North Holland . . . Provides a good introduction to the work of Kahneman and Tversky and how it relates to forecasting. (*LRF* 43)

KALTON, Graham and SCHUMAN, Howard, [1982], "The effect of the question on survey responses: A review," *Journal of the Royal Statistical Society: Series A,* vol. **145**, Pt 1, pp. 42–73 . . . In addition to providing an overview of recent research on the topic of response error, this paper describes some recent efforts to reduce the errors. These include the use of instructions to the respondent, feedback to the respondent, and the gaining of commitment from the respondent to provide accurate answers. (*LRF* 115)

KALWANI, Manohar and SILK, Alvin J., [1982], "On the reliability and predictive validity of purchase intention measures," *Marketing Science,* vol. **1**, pp. 243–286 . . . In general, intentions understate actual purchase rates. (*LRF* 84)

KEEN, Howard, Jr., [1981], "Who forecasts best? Some evidence from the Livingston survey," *Business Economics*, vol. **16** [September], pp. 24–29 . . . In June and December of each year since 1946, Joseph A. Livingston, a business journalist for the *Philadelphia Inquirer*, has been publishing forecasts of business variables based on a survey of about 50 experts. (Details on the Livingston survey are available from:

Research Department, Federal Reserve Bank of Philadelphia, Philadelphia, Pa. 19105) Keen analyzed forecasts from 1971 to 1978 in an effort to tell which forecasters were best: those from academia, banking, or business? No consistent differences were found in the forecasts of nominal GNP, real GNP, consumer prices, and unemployment when considering size of error and turning points. Another issue Keen examined was whether the Livingston forecasts were better than the no-change model for 6- and 12-month-ahead-forecasts. They were, with the exception of forecasts for the industrial stock price index. This is reassuring and is consistent with findings from previous studies. (See also AHLERS and LAKINISHOK [1983].) (*LRF* 396, 409, 579)

KENNY, Peter B. and DURBIN, James, [1982], "Local trend estimation and seasonal adjustment of economic and social time series" (with discussion), *Journal of the Royal Statistical Society: Series A*, vol. **145**, Pt 1, pp. 1–41. (*LRF* 176, 495)

KEREN, Gideon and NEWMAN, J. Robert, [1978], "Additional considerations with regard to multiple regression and equal weighting," *Organizational Behavior and Human Performance*, vol. **22**, pp. 143–164 . . . Suggests that measurement errors in the criterion (dependent) variable are more damaging to the model than errors in measuring causal variables. Also discusses ridge regression and says that it "shrinks" the estimated relationships towards the origin (or in *LRF* terms, it mitigates the estimate of the forecasted relationship). Finally, this paper presents results of a simulation study with three predictor variables and one criterion. Ridge regression was more accurate than OLS, and OLS was more accurate than unit weights. (*LRF* 222, 231, 239, 327)

KERR, Norbert L.; NERENZ, David R. and HERRICK, David, [1979], "Role playing and the study of jury behavior," *Sociological Methods and Research*, vol. **7**, pp. 337–355 . . . This experiment used 117 mock juries and 108 real juries (at least they *thought* they were real) in a case involving student discipline. Prior to the role playing, 48% of the *individuals* in the mock jury thought the defendant was guilty. For six-person juries, assuming the majority would prevail, this means that 40% of the juries would have been expected to reach a verdict of guilty. But in the real trial, the defendant was never found guilty (0 of 10 juries, though there were 8 hung juries). These results were matched by the mock juries (guilty in 1 of 12 juries with 8 hung juries). (*LRF* 126)

KLEIN, Lawrence R. and YOUNG, Richard M., [1980], *An Introduction to Econometric Forecasting*. Lexington, Mass: D.C. Heath . . . This book describes the Wharton quarterly forecasting model. The authors discuss differences between the time series and econometric model approach to forecasting. They claim that their Wharton model has done well in comparison with other econometric models. (*LRF* not cited)

KORIAT, Asher; LICHTENSTEIN, Sarah and FISCHHOFF, Baruch, [1980], "Reasons for confidence," *Journal of Experimental Psychology: Human Learning and Memory*, vol. **6**, pp. 107–118 . . . People tend to think of the reasons to support a given decision or forecast: this leads to overconfidence. This study traces its roots to an idea of Ben Franklin's: Making an explicit list of the reasons that contradicted their answers in a test of knowledge led subjects to provide more realistic estimates of confidence in their answers. They also found a slight (but not significant) tendency for the resulting answers to be more accurate. This is an important study. (*LRF* 143)

KREILKAMP, Karl, [1971], "*Hindsight* and the real world of science policy," *Science Studies*, vol. **1**, pp. 43–66 . . . (*LRF* 439)

KRUGLANSKI, Arie W., FRIEDLAND, Nehemia and FARKASH, Ettie, [1984], "Lay persons' sensitivity to statistical information: The case of high perceived applicability," *Journal of Personality and Social Psychology*, vol. **46**, pp. 503–518 . . . In these experiments, a number of the judgmental biases were overcome by better wording of the problems. The subjects were able to use statistical information properly if it was clearly shown that the information was relevant. (*LRF* 105)

LARCKER, David F. and LESSIG, V. Parker, [1983], "An examination of the linear and restrospective process tracing approaches to judgment modeling," *Accounting Review*, vol. **58**, pp. 58–77 . . . This study asks people to describe, after the fact, how they made decisions to buy stocks. The authors refer to this as "retrospective process tracing models" an unfortunate term in my opinion. How about calling it a "memory model"? Buy/no-buy decisions were made for 45 stocks by 31 subjects. Each stock was described by six relevant and obvious variables. An indirect bootstrapping, done by discriminant analysis, matched the actual decision in 73% of the cases. The memory model (done immediately after the completion of all stock decisions) was significantly better ($p < .05$), and it matched the actual for 85% of the decisions. The gain came at some cost, as the memory model required ½ hour with each subject. The authors caution that the results may not be applicable to more complex problems or to problems where irrelevant variables are present. They recommend a combined use of discriminant models, memory models, and "concurrent process tracing" (called protocols in *LRF*). It is a thorough study and the literature review brings together a number of relevant findings from accounting, marketing,

and psychology. Although this is a long-winded paper with much jargon, it is important and will be rewarding to those who manage to stay
awake. (*LRF* 276, 278)

LARSON, James R., Jr. and REENAN, A.M., [1979],   "The equiv-
alence interval as a measure of uncertainty," *Organizational Behavior
and Human Performance*, vol. **23**, pp. 49–55 . . . Questions 60 subjects
on number of marbles in cartons and similar tasks. Confidence intervals for a judge became large as the judge's accuracy decreased. Uncertainty intervals (based on the range "outside of which they were
reasonably certain that the correct answer did not lie) contained the
correct answer only about 60% of the time. (*LRF* 140).

LAWRENCE, Michael J., [1983],   "An exploration of some practical
issues in the use of quantitative forecasting models," *Journal of Forecasting*, vol. **2**, pp. 169–179 . . . A small survey of a convenience sample
of firms in Australia indicated that computer-based forecasting systems
are not widely used and, in fact, a number of established systems have
been discarded, due to poor accuracy. Other problem areas mentioned
as contributing to the abandonment of forecasting systems include the
difficulty of manually reviewing the computer forecasts and the effort
required to review carefully the forecast database to adjust for extraor-
dinary events. (*LRF* 172, 426)

**LAWRENCE, Michael J., EDMUNDSON, R.H. and O'CONNOR,
M.J., [1985]**,   "An examination of judgemental extrapolation of time
series," *International Journal of Forecasting* (in press) . . . (*LRF* 48,
172, 175)

LEDOLTER, Johannes and ABRAHAM, Bovas, [1981],
"Parsimony and its importance in time series forecasting," *Techno-
metrics*, vol. **23**, pp. 411–414. (*LRF* 495)

LEE, James A. [1980],   *The Gold and the Garbage in Management
Theories and Prescriptions*. Athens, Ohio: Ohio University Press. An
interesting discussion on the origins of major theories in management
and on the role of evidence in supporting such theories. (*LRF* 4, 28)

**LEIGH, Thomas W.; MacKAY, David B. and SUMMERS, John
O., [1984]**,   "Reliability and validity of conjoint analysis and self-
explicated weights: A comparison," *Journal of Marketing Research*, vol.
21, pp. 456–462 . . . The terms "conjoint analysis" and "self-explicated
weights," used by marketing researchers correspond, respectively, to
the terms "indirect" and "direct" bootstrapping in *LRF*. The technology
for indirect bootstrapping (conjoint analysis) is highly developed by
marketing researchers. Nevertheless, Leigh, et al. were unable to find
a single study that tested the predictive validity of this approach in
comparison to the direct approach. They then made a test by obtaining
data from 122 business students about their preferences for hand held

calculators. Predictions from a variety of indirect approaches were compared with those from a simple and low cost direct approach. The predicted behavior was the choice of a calculator from a list of 10 in a lottery. Few differences were found among the 12 different indirect approaches that were examined, so these were compared, as a group, with the direct approach. The direct approach proved to be slightly more accurate (36.3% correct predictions vs. 34.9%, where chance would be 10%), a result that was statistically significant. The direct approach was also more reliable based on a test-retest with the same subjects. An unfortunate problem with this study is that the direct bootstrapping always followed the indirect bootstrapping for each subject. (*LRF* 278)

LEVENBACH, Hans and CLEARY, James P., [1981], *The Beginning Forecaster: The Forecasting Process Through Data Analysis.* Belmont, Calif: Lifetime Learning . . . Part of the matched set (see CLEARY and LEVENBACH [1982]). An informative (and favorable) review by Don M. Miller appears in the *Journal of Forecasting*, vol. **1**, 1982, pp. 322–324. The matched set has been superceded by LEVENBACH and CLEARY [1984]. (*LRF* 593, 621)

LEVENBACH, Hans and CLEARY, James P., [1984]b, *The Modern Forecaster.* Belmont, Calif. Lifetime Learning . . . Combines and updates LEVENBACH and CLEARY [1981] and CLEARY and LEVENBACH [1982]. It includes problem sets and computer worksheets. (*LRF* 78, 220, 594)

LIBBY, Robert and BLASHFIELD, Roger K., [1978], "Performance of a composite as a function of the number of judges," *Organizational Behavior and Human Performance*, vol. **21**, pp. 121–129 . . . Based on three empirical studies, they show significant gains in accuracy obtained when going from one judge to using an average based on three judges. According to the authors, the optimum number of judges is likely to be between five and nine. (*LRF* 96, 589)

LIBERT, G., [1984], "The M-Competition with a fully automatic Box-Jenkins procedure," *Journal of Forecasting*, vol. **3**, pp. 325–328 . . . (*LRF* 175)

LICHTENSTEIN, Sarah and FISCHHOFF, Baruch, [1980], "Training for calibration," *Organizational Behavior and Human Performance*, vol. **26**, pp. 149–171 . . . Complex paper describing two experiments. Contains a good review of prior literature. (*LRF* not cited)

LINDLEY, D.V., [1982], "The improvement of probability judgments," *Journal of the Royal Statistical Society: Series A*, vol. **145**, pp. 117–126 . . . I was not able to learn much from this study, with the exception of pages 122 and 123 where the responses of a given subject to 500 almanac-type questions are discussed (*LRF* 140)

LONNSTEDT, Lars, [1975], "Factors related to the implementation of operation research solutions," *Interfaces*, vol. **5** (February), pp. 23–30 . . . This study examined the implementation process for 107 operations research projects from 12 companies in Sweden. Lonnstedt conducted personal interviews in 1970 with each head of the operations research department and each project leader, and had telephone interviews with the users. Implementation was more likely to be successful when the users participated in the project. (*LRF* 36)

LORD, Charles G.; ROSS, Lee and LEPPER, Mark R., [1979], "Biased assimilation and attribute polarization: The effects of prior theories on subsequently considered evidence," *Journal of Personality and Social Psychology*, vol. **37**, pp. 2098–2109 . . . Subjects in this study were provided with evidence for and against capital punishment. The methods used in the "study" on capital punishment were rated higher when the results agreed with the subject's prior opinion. (*LRF* 378, 436)

LOUIS, Arthur M., [1978], "Should you buy biorhythms," *Psychology Today*, vol. **11** (April), pp. 93–96 . . . No. Biorhythms did not help in this study for predictions in baseball and boxing. (*LRF* 435)

LUSK, Edward J. and NEVES, Joao S., [1984], "A comparative ARIMA analysis of the 111 series of the Makridakis competition," *Journal of Forecasting*, vol. **3**, pp. 329–332 . . . Of the 111 series fitted, 10 had models that were the same as Andersen's, and 6 of these were simple series. (*LRF* 175)

LYON, Don and SLOVIC, Paul, [1976], "Dominance of accuracy information and neglect of base rates in probability estimation," *Acta Psychologica*, vol. **40**, pp. 287–298 . . . One of the primary tasks of the forecaster is to help the client make better forecasts. As a result of this effort, however, the client may be misled and put too much weight on the conclusions presented by a forecaster. Lyon and Slovic use three problems, including the Blue and Green Cab problem, to show how people can be easily misled; in this case, subjects used new information and ignored prior knowledge of base rates. (*LRF* not cited)

MABERT, Vincent A., [1976], "Statistical versus sales force-executive opinion short range forecasts: A time series case study," *Decision Sciences*, vol. **7**, pp. 310–318 . . . This study compared judgmental forecasts by one company against Winters' exponential smoothing, Brown's harmonic model, and Box-Jenkins on four-week forecasts for five years (1968–1972). Successive updating was used so that 65 monthly (actually four week) forecasts were obtained for each model. The extrapolation methods were cheaper and more accurate than the judgmental forecasts. Few differences were found among the extrapolation methods. (*LRF* 176, 343, 397, 408, 494)

MABERT, Vincent A., [1978], "Forecast modification based upon residual analysis: A case study of check volume estimation," *Decision Sciences*, vol. **9**, pp. 285–296 . . . Looked at daily forecasts of check volume in a commercial bank. Two forecasting procedures were evaluated. First, a dummy variable regression model was used to estimate check volume forecast. A second approach used regression, then used exponential smoothing on the residuals, was used to see if improved results could be obtained. This second approach utilized exponential smoothing in an attempt to adapt to systematic forecast errors that were identified. At best, the latter approach improved the forecasts marginally. For a critique see GARDNER [1979b] followed by Mabert's reply. (*LRF* 171, 495)

MAHONEY, Michael J., [1977], "Publication prejudices: An experimental study of confirmatory bias in the peer review system," *Cognitive Therapy and Research*, vol. **1**, pp. 161–175 . . . (*LRF* 436)

MAHONEY, Michael J. and DeMONBREUN, B.G., [1977], "Psychology of the scientist: An analysis of problem solving bias," *Cognitive Therapy and Research*, vol. **1**, pp. 229–238 . . . Found no difference in the ability of psychologists, physical scientists, and protestant ministers to solve problems involving falsifying experiments. (Used Wason's 2-4-6 study.) (*LRF* 378)

MAHONEY, Michael J. and KIMPER, Terence P., [1976], "From ethics to logic: A survey of scientists," in Michael J. Mahoney (Ed.), *Scientist as Subject*. Cambridge, Mass: Ballinger, pp. 187–193 . . . Physicists, biologists, sociologists and psychologists did not do well in identifying which experiments were logically relevant to an issue. (*LRF* 378)

MAKRIDAKIS, Spyros; ANDERSEN, A.; CARBONE, R.; FILDES, R.; HIBON, M.; LEWANDOWSKI, R.; NEWTON, J.; PARZEN, E. and WINKLER, R., [1982], "The accuracy of extrapolation (time series) methods: Results of a forecasting competition," *Journal of Forecasting*, vol. **1**, pp. 111–153 . . . This study of the comparative accuracy of 21 methods for *ex ante* forecasts of 1001 time series is one of the most important works that has been done on forecasting methods. It is often referred to as the M-Competition. This paper presents the results on the accuracy on each method. MAKRIDAKIS, et al. provide more detail on each of the methods. A discussion by outside commentators, as well as by the original authors can be found in ARMSTRONG and LUSK [1983]. (*LRF* 169, 170, 172, 173, 176, 184, 454, 495, 507, 584, 623)

MAKRIDAKIS, Spyros, et al. [1984], *The Forecasting Accuracy of Major Time Series Methods*. Chichester: Wiley . . . This book provides a detailed report on the M-Competition [MAKRIDAKIS et al., 1984] by having each of the original authors explain each method. (*LRF* 507, 623)

MAKRIDAKIS, Spyros and HIBON, Michele, [1979], "Accuracy of forecasting: An empirical investigation" (with discussion), *Journal of the Royal Statistical Society: Series A*, vol. **142**, pp. 97–145 . . . A study of the comparative accuracy of 111 time series that varied by country, time period, industry, company, and time intervals. A forerunner of MAKRIDAKIS et al. [1983]. Contains numerous interesting conclusions—e.g., adaptive parameters were not useful for exponential smoothing. (*LRF* 176, 495)

MAKRIDAKIS, Spyros and WHEELWRIGHT, Steven C., [1978], *Interactive Forecasting*. San Francisco: Holden-Day . . . Extensive coverage of time series methods. (*LRF* 498)

MAKRIDAKIS, Spyros and WHEELWRIGHT, Steven C. [1979], *Forecasting*. (*TIMS Studies in Management Science*, Volume 12). New York: North Holland . . . Contains 21 papers on a variety of topics in forecasting. The contributions were reviewed by 73 referees. An appendix reviews 40 books on forecasting. (*LRF* not cited)

MAKRIDAKIS, Spyros and WHEELRIGHT, Steven C., [1982], *The Handbook of Forecasting: A Manager's Guide*. New York: Wiley . . . "Handbook" is perhaps not a descriptive title. Instead, this is a collection of papers on a wide variety of subjects in forecasting. Two reviews of this book appeared in the *Journal of Forecasting* (vol. **2**, 1982, pp. 196–202). A revised edition was planned for 1986. (*LRF* 78)

MAKRIDAKIS, Spyros and WHEELWRIGHT, Steven C., [1984], *Forecasting Methods for Management*. 4th Ed. Chichester, England: Wiley . . . Less detailed than MAKRIDAKIS, WHEELWRIGHT and McGEE [1983]. (*LRF* 78)

MAKRIDAKIS, Spyros; WHEELWRIGHT, Steven C. and McGEE, Victor E., [1983], *Forecasting: Methods and Applications*. 2nd Ed. New York: Wiley . . . The first edition quickly became a best selling text. This revised edition is improved in many respects; the book has grown from 713 to 923 pages, the references have been updated, and many changes were made to make the book easier to read. A teacher's manual is available. (*LRF* 78, 175, 220)

MAKRIDAKIS, Spyros and WINKLER, Robert L., [1983], "Averages of forecasts: Some empirical results," *Management Science*, vol. **29**, pp. 987–996 . . . (*LRF* 184, 650)

MANEGOLD, James G., [1981], "Time series properties of earnings: A comparison of extrapolative and component models," *Journal of Accounting Research*, vol. **19** (Autumn), pp. 360–373 . . . Examined one-year-ahead earnings forecasts for 27 firms for 1974 and 1975 and two-year-ahead forecasts for 1975. (*LRF* not cited)

MANIS, Melvin; DOVALINA, Ismael; AVIS, Nancy E. and CAR-DOZE, Steven, [1980], "Base rates can affect individual predictions," *Journal of Personality and Social Psychology*, vol. **38**, pp. 231–248, *and* **MANIS, Melvin; AVIS, Nancy E. and CARDOZE, Steven, [1981],** "Reply to Bar-Hillel and Fischhoff," *Journal of Personality and Social Psychology*, vol. **41**, pp. 681–683 . . . Judgmental forecasters should consider what typically happens in a situation (the "base rate") as well as specific information available about the case in hand. Although the specific information should be considered only if it is valid and reliable, earlier research showed that even irrelevant specific information led people to ignore the base rate. This paper reports on four experiments and reexamines previous studies. From these, the authors defined a set of conditions in which judges showed much sensitivity to base rates. Their study seemed convincing to me until I read the BAR-HILLEL and FISCHHOFF [1981] paper, which reinterpreted MANIS et al. [1980] and concluded that their results were consistent with previous research: Base rates are important when the subject does not receive information on representativeness (evidence that the subject of the prediction fits a stereotype). MANIS et al. [1981] is a well-reasoned reply to Bar-Hillel and Fischhoff. The combination of articles helps to specify the conditions under which forecasters should not trust their intuitions when interpeting base rates plus specific information. An interesting finding in MANIS et al. [1980] was that subjects did not seem to be aware of the occasions on which they used base rates in making their predictions. (*LRF* 587)

MANKTELOW, K.I. and EVANS, J. St. B.T., [1979], "Facilitation of reasoning by realism: Effect or non-effect?" *British Journal of Psychology*, vol. **70**, pp. 477–488 . . . More evidence on the issue of confirming and disconfirming evidence. (*LRF* 378)

MARKS, Robert E., [1980], "The value of 'almost' perfect weather information to the Australian tertiary sector," *Australian Journal of Management*, vol. **5**, pp. 67–85 . . . Marks provides a clear discussion on how to assess the *potential* value of improved forecasts. He then applies this, using a mail survey of 131 corporations in Australia. These "tertiary" (or service) sector corporations consisted mostly of electricity, gas, water, construction, transport, and communications firms. Responses, received from 46% of the firms surveyed, were used to estimate the value of improved forecast accuracy as a percentage of revenues for each type of corporation. These were then compared with estimates from the United States. The paper integrates much previous research, but one relevant omission was SCHNEE [1977]. This would have been interesting because Schnee concluded that the costs of more accurate weather forecasting exceeded its potential benefits, even if the forecasts

were perfect. Marks did not consider the costs of better weather forecasts, only the potential gross benefits. The savings are *potential* because, if people do not act on these forecasts, they are of no value.
Judging from studies, such as BAKER [1979], it appears that weather
forecasts often are not used effectively. (*LRF* 388)

McCLAIN, John O., [1974], "Dynamics of exponential smoothing
with trend and seasonal terms," *Management Science*, vol. **20**, pp.
1300–1304 ... McClain's theoretical analysis leads him to conclude
that Brown's exponential smoothing model responds appropriately to
changes in the data. (*LRF* 168)

McINTYRE, Shelby H., [1981], "An experimental study of the
impact of judgment-based models," *Management Science*, vol. **28**, pp.
17–33. ... Formal processing of information by each of 96 judges did
not lead to better predictions in a management game, although it did
improve their decision making. (*LRF* not cited)

**McINTYRE, Shelby H.; MONTGOMERY, D.B.; SRINIVASAN, V.
and WEITZ, B.A., [1983],** "Evaluating the statistical significance of
models developed by stepwise regression," *Journal of Marketing Research*, vol. **20**, pp. 1–11 ... This paper discusses how to test for statistical significance when stepwise regression is used. Tables are provided for more realistic tests of significance than those typically used.
(*LRF* 205, 330, 351)

**McLEAVEY, Dennis W.; LEE, T.S. and ADAM, E.E., Jr.,
[1981],** "An empirical evaluation of individual item forecasting models,"
Decision Sciences, vol. **12**, pp. 708–714 ... The importance of replication is highlighted by this study. It replicates a study by Adam (1973)
and finds that two of the seven models in the original paper were in
error. However, the general results were similar when seven models
were used to make one-period and 12-period forecasts for five different
simulated demand patterns. It is not easy to make generalizations from
this study, but here are mine: For one-period-ahead forecasts, a two-
period moving average performed well for constant, trend and seasonal
patterns, for a combination of all these patterns, and for a step function.
None of the five exponential models produced significant improvements, and the adaptive smoothing model was less accurate. Double
exponential smoothing performed well for all demand patterns on both
one-period-ahead and twelve-period-ahead forecasts. Which model was
most accurate depended upon the demand pattern and the forecast
horizon, as well as upon the noise level. (*LRF* 171, 174, 495, 516)

**McWHORTER, Archer; NARASIMHAM, G.V.L. and SIMONDS,
R.R., [1977],** "An empirical examination of the predictive performance of an econometric model with random coefficients," *International*

Statistical Review, vol. **45**, pp. 243–255 . . . This study examined *ex post* forecasts using 16 quarters of validation data from 1971.1. The forecasts, made for 1 to 4 quarters in the future, were based on data from 1950.1 to 1970.IV. A variety of extrapolation and econometric models were used. The extrapolation forecasts proved to have much lower errors, about ½ as large as those from the econometric models. (I suspect that this is due to problems in the estimation of the current status.). OLS performed well in comparison with a more complex approach (three-stage least squares). Exponential smoothing with trend did about the same as the more complex ARIMA and better, it appears, than Kalman filter methods, though no significance tests were carried out. (*LRF* 408)

MEADE, Nigel, [1984], "The use of growth curves in forecasting market development—A review and appraisal," *Journal of Forecasting*, vol. **3**, pp. 429–451 . . . (*LRF* 181)

MENTZER, John T. and COX, James E., Jr., [1984], "Familiarity, application, and performance of sales forecasting techniques," *Journal of Forecasting*, vol. **3**, pp. 27–36 . . . Reports on a survey sent to forecasting managers in 500 U.S. companies. Usable replies were received from 32% of the companies. (*LRF* 73, 298, 360, 361, 426, 427, 454, 645)

MILSTEIN, Robert M., et al. [1980], "Prediction of interview ratings in a medical school admission process," *Journal of Medical Education*, vol. **55**, pp. 451–453 and **MILSTEIN, Robert M., et al., [1981],** "Admissions decisions and performance during medical school," *Journal of Medical Education*, vol. **56**, pp. 77–82 . . . Millions of dollars are spent each year on personal interviews for admission to medical school. Milstein's 1980 study found that differences between interviewer and interviewee were of major importance: The greater the difference, the lower the prediction of success. The 1981 study examined 24 applicants who were interviewed and *accepted* at Yale's School of Medicine, but who went elsewhere to medical school (AYEs). They were compared with 27 applicants interviewed and *rejected* by Yale who also went elsewhere to medical school (NAYs). No differences were found between the medical school performance of AYEs and NAYs. That is, for predictive purposes, the interview was worthless. The conclusion is consistent with the research on personnel selection in business. (*LRF* 56)

MITCHELL, Terry W. and KLIMOSKI, Richard J., [1982], "Is it rational to be empirical? A test of methods for scoring biographical data," *Journal of Applied Psychology*, vol. **67**, pp. 411–481 . . . Biographical data on 88 variables (e.g., education, work experience, family background) were used to predict success in obtaining a real estate license for 698 prospective applicants. The researchers compared two methods. The first method, which they call "empirical," used a non-theoretical approach to weighting (the weighted application blank). The weights were obtained from a subsample. The second method, called "rational," used the same subsample, it started with subjective weights for each variable, followed by a factor analysis to yield six factors. The six factors were then entered into a regression model. (I do not agree with the authors who claim this approach to be "rational" and to provide a "better understanding.") The empirical approach provided more accurate forecasts in the cross-validation sample. This result is consistent with the few previously published empirical results: *factor analysis of predictor variables has not been shown to have any demonstrable value in forecasting. (LRF 223)*

MOORE, Geoffrey H., [1983], *Business Cycles, Inflation and Forecasting.* Cambridge, Mass.: Ballanger . . . This book examines the behavior of macroeconomic variables during the course of business cycles in the United States. It also includes an update on leading indicators in the United States, Canada, United Kingdom, West Germany, Italy, France, and Japan. (*LRF* not cited)

MOORE, William L., [1982], "Predictive power of joint space models constructed with composition techniques," *Journal of Business Research,* vol. **10,** pp. 217–236 . . . There has been considerable interest among academics in marketing in the use of composition techniques to build "joint space" models for predicting consumer preferences. In spite of this interest, Moore was unable to locate studies that examined the *predictive ability* of these models; that is, the ability of the models to predict preferences for new brands. However, he did find two studies that compared the *fit* of different composition models. (In both cases, factor analytic models outperformed discriminant analytic models.) Moore obtained data on four product categories and compared the ability of various joint space models to predict performances for brands that were not used to build the spaces. He hypothesized that discriminant models (which build spaces that maximize the among-brand variance in perception and minimize the within brand-variance) should provide better predictions than factor analytic models (that consider only total variance in perception). Although this strikes me as reasonable, it contradicts the assumption behind a number of studies. Moore found that simpler vector representations of preferences gave better predictions than the more complex and theoretically satisfying "ideal point" models. He also found that the models constructed with discriminant analyses were more accurate than the joint space models based on factor analysis. The results held up when considering correlation coefficients, as well as mean absolute deviations. Although the differences were consistent and statistically significant, they were small. (Incidentally, a bit of confusion arose over a typographical error in the second paragraph on his page 229: It should say Table 4 rather than Table 3.) (*LRF* 223)

MORE, Roger A. and LITTLE, Blair, [1980], "The application of discriminant analysis to the prediction of sales forecast uncertainty in new product situations," *Journal of the Operational Research Society*, vol. 31, pp. 71–77 . . . Is it possible to assess the sales forecast uncertainty for a new product introduction? More and Little address this important question, more or less. They present a conceptual model relating the error in the first year's sales forecast to marketing task similarity and marketing task complexity. (Complexity was a function of buyer-risk, distribution difficulty, and competitive advantage.) Data from 185 new product situations were collected by personal interviews and self-administered questionnaires from 152 Canadian firms. The discriminant function did somewhat better than chance in identifying the high risk introductions (over 20% error in unit sales) when tested on a hold-out sample. This test was biased because the respondents knew the outcome. Futher, a more revealing comparison than testing against chance would be to test against the currently used subjective methods. (*LRF* not cited)

MORRIS, John D., [1982], "Ridge regression and some alternative weighting techniques: A comment on Darlington," *Psychological Bulletin*, vol. 91, pp. 203–210 . . . Some researcher have advocated ridge regression as a way to obtain better estimates of parameters and, presumably, better predictions. While advocates have used theoretical arguments, DARLINGTON [1978], in a widely cited paper, provided empirical evidence supporting a ridge regression by showing that it led to more accurate predictions in hold-out samples. ROZEBOOM [1979] challenged the applicability of Darlington's results because they depend on knowing the optimal value of a key constant (k) in the ridge regression, and because Darlington did not consider the effects of such practical considerations as sample sizes. Morris reanalyzed Darlington's results, using Darlington's simulated data, by estimating the constant k from the sample data. He contrasted the predictive validity on hold-out samples with that obtained from four other estimation procedures. Darlington's recommended one-parameter ridge regression technique was found *never* to be superior to the other methods. The best results were nearby always provided by either ordinary least squares or by equal weights. Furthermore, the differences among the predictive

validities of the various methods were small, so one might question
the practical significance of these alternative approaches. (*LRF* 232,
597, 640)

MORRIS, John D., [1981], "Updating the criterion for regression
predictor variable selection," *Educational and Psychological Measurement,* vol. 41, pp. 777–780 . . . Proposals have been made that predictor
variables should be selected on how well they perform on the cross-
validated sample rather than on the calibration sample. (As a propo-
nent of *theory* as the proper way to select predictor variables, I have
not been among those making such suggestions.) This paper reviews
evidence on the use of cross-validated selection procedures. Morris then
describes a computer program which he is willing to provide "for a
nominal cost." (His address is: John D. Morris, Dept. of School Services,
Box 8143, Georgia Southern College, Statesboro, Georgia 30460) The
program can use forward or backward stepwise procedures or it can
examine all possible combinations of variables to obtain the best cross-
validated model. Will such procedures improve our ability to forecast?
That is a good topic for further research. (My guess is "No.") (*LRF* 205)

MORRIS, M.J., [1977], "Forecasting the sunspot cycle," *Journal of
the Royal Statistical Society: Series A,* vol. 140, pp. 437–478 . . . Combinations of two different extrapolation models led to a 50% reduction
in forecast error. However, the weights were selected after the fact.
(*LRF* 184)

**MOSKOWITZ, Herbert; WEISS, Doyle L.; CHENG, K.K. and
REIBSTEIN, David J., [1982],** "Robustness of linear models in dynamic multivariate predictions," *Omega,* vol. 10, pp. 647–661 . . . This
paper shows how, in some cases, unit weights and equal weights are
not identical. (Unit weights differed from equal weights due to the
dynamic nature of their short-range production planning problems.)
They concluded that equal weights were better than human decisions
and almost as good as regression weights. Some interesting ideas sur-
rounded by a complex writing style. For a related paper see REMUS
and JENICKE [1978]. (*LRF* 282, 638)

MOSTELLER, Frederick, [1981], "Innovation and evaluation,"
Science, vol. 211, pp. 881–886 . . . Provides an interesting description
of the prevention of scurvy. (*LRF* 24)

MOSTELLER, Frederick and TUKEY, John W., [1977], *Data
Analysis and Regression.* Reading, Mass.: Addison-Wesley. . . (*LRF* 196,
341)

MOYER, R. Charles, [1977], "Forecasting financial failure: A re-
examination," *Financial Management,* vol. 6 [Spring], pp. 11–17 . . .
This study attempts to predict bankruptcy in a sample of 27 bankrupt

and 27 nonbankrupt firms. Predictive accuracy did not increase when the number of predictor variables was increased from two to five. (*LRF* 198)

MURPHY, Allan H. and BROWN, Barbara G., [1984], "A comparative evaluation of objective and subjective weather forecasts in the United States," *Journal of Forecasting*, vol. **3**, pp. 369–393 . . . Comparisons of objective and subjective forecasts of precipitation occurrence indicate that the latter are more accurate for the short lead-times (12–24 hours), but they are about the same for longer leadtimes (e.g., 36–48 hours). Objective forecasts of cloud cover are more accurate than subjective forecasts for all leadtimes. Forecasts accuracy improved over the period from 1971 to 1982, especially for the objective forecasts. Many weather forecasters make a subjective analysis of the data before examining the objective forecasts not to be unduly influenced by the latter. However, little study has been done on the subjective forecasting process and forecasts that start with the objective forecasts may be just as accurate. This is an excellent review. (*LRF* 272, 424)

MURPHY, Allan H. and DAAN, Harald, [1984], "Impacts of feedback and experience on the quality of subjective probability forecasts: Comparison of results from the first and second years of the Zierikzee experiment," *Monthly Weather Review*, vol. **112**, pp. 413–428 . . . Examines short-range forecasts of wind, fog, and rain that were prepared by four forecasters in 1981 and 1982. (*LRF* 380)

MURPHY, Allan H.; LICHTENSTEIN, S.; FISCHHOFF, B. and WINKLER, R.L., [1980], "Misinterpretations of precipitation probability forecasts," *Bulletin of the American Meterological Society*, vol. **61**, pp. 695–701 . . . Managers often tell me that it introduces too much complexity to use probabilities or distributions when presenting forecasts in their organizations. *Other* managers will be confused, they say. In this survey of 79 residents of Eugene, Oregon, the authors show that the general public has a good understanding of the meaning of precipitation probability forecasts. They even *preferred* probability forecasts. (*LRF* not cited)

MYNATT, Clifford; DOHERTY, M.E. and TWENEY, R.D., [1978], "Consequences of confirmation and disconfirmation in a simulated research environment," *Quarterly Journal of Experimental Psychology*, vol. **30**, pp. 395–406 . . . An interesting experiment where 16 subjects each spent ten hours trying to discover the "laws" governing a complex computer-generated problem. The problem proved so difficult that none of the subjects solved it. Subjects seldom sought disconfirmation of their theories, and they often ignored information that falsified their theories. Commonly, the subjects would record careful mea-

surements with no apparent use of the data they were collecting. Also
they used mathematical approaches with no apparent rationale. Does
this remind you of anything? (*LRF* 378)

NAFTULIN, Donald H.; WARE, J.E., Jr. and DONNELLY, F.A.,
[1973], "The Doctor Fox Lecture: A paradigm of educational seduc-
tion," *Journal of Medical Education*, vol. **48**, pp. 630–635 . . . (*LRF* 46)

NARASIMHAN, Chakravarthi and SEN, Subrata, [1983], "New
product models for test market data," *Journal of Marketing*, vol. **47**,
[Winter], pp. 11–24 . . . Reviews the more widely known models for
predicting the success of new products based on test market data. The
earlier models tend to rely on the extrapolation of trial and repeat
purchase sales. The more recent models also examine the impact of
marketing variables. (*LRF* not cited)

NAYLOR, Thomas H., [1981], "Experience with corporate econometric models: A survey," *Business Economics*, vol. **16** [January], pp.
79–83 . . . Reports on a questionnaire mailed to 1691 corporate members of the National Association of Business Economists on March
1980. The return rate was only 14%! Thus, the findings cannot be called
representative. Some findings: About 2/3 of these respondents used
econometric models, and marketing was the most frequent area for
applications. Ordinary least squares (the standard single equation
regression analysis) was the most commonly used approach to econometric models. Market share was seldom forecast (less than 20% of the
respondents). (*LRF* 200)

NELSON, Charles R., [1984], "A benchmark for the accuracy of
econometric forecasts of GNP," *Business Economics*, vol. **19** [April], pp.
52–58 . . . This paper compares extrapolation and econometric forecasts
of quarterly GNP from 1976–1982 for one-, two-, three-, and four-
quarters-ahead. The econometric forecasts were five of those published
by the Conference Board in its *Statistical Bulletin* (Chase, Conference
Board, DRI, Kent, and Michigan). The econometric forecasts were based
on slightly more recent data than the extrapolations and, as a normal
course, they were subjectively adjusted. So what do you predict as more
accurate for one-quarter forecasts? . . . for four-quarter ahead forecasts?
The answers: The extrapolation method had a higher error for one-
quarter-horizon, but lower errors for the longer horizons, especially
four-quarters-ahead. (No statistical tests were provided.) Nelson also
examined whether a combination of the forecasts would be better than
any single forecast. The answer seems to be "yes." (I say "seems" because the weights were selected in retrospect.) (*LRF* 290, 408)

NESLIN, Scott A., [1981], "Linking product features to perceptions:

Self-stated versus statistically revealed importance weights," *Journal of Marketing Research,* vol. **18**, pp. 80–86 ... The indirect (statistical) bootstrapping was superior to the direct bootstrapping in predicting individual perceptions for an ambulatory health service. This finding emerged from answers given by 112 respondents. The superiority of indirect bootstrapping, shown in a cross-validation test, was statistically significant. (*LRF* 278)

NEVIN, John R., [1974], "Laboratory experiments for estimating consumer demand: A validation study," *Journal of Marketing Research,* vol. **11**, pp. 261–268 ... A lab experiment and a questionnaire each produced good estimates of market share and of market share changes for Coke, Pepsi, and RC, but not such good estimates for brands of coffee. Price elasticity estimates were highest in the questionnaire, followed by simulated shopping and test market methods. (*LRF* 155)

NISBETT, Richard E. and WILSON, T.D., [1977], "Telling more than we can know: Verbal reports on mental processes," *Psychological Review,* vol. **84**, pp. 231–259 ... Contains clever studies suggesting that people are often not aware of how they make decisions or predictions. (*LRF* not cited)

OLNECK, Michael R. and WOLFE, Barbara L., [1980], "Intelligence and family size: Another look," *Review of Economics and Statistics,* vol. **62**, pp. 241–247 ... Good attention given here to multiple hypotheses. (*LRF* 322)

PAGE, Carl V., [1977], "Heuristics for signature table analysis as a pattern recognition technique," *IEEE Transactions on Systems, Man and Cybernetics,* vol. **7**, No. 2 [February], pp. 77–86 ... Cross-classifications were slightly more accurate than regressions in predicting for a cross-validation sample (74% vs. 70% correct predictions). Unfortunately, this paper is filled with jargon. (*LRF* 413)

PALMORE, Erdman, [1979], "Predictors of successful aging," *Gerontologist,* vol. **19**, pp. 427–431 ... Measures of current status (initial health and happiness) were important in predicting health changes over a 9½ year period for older people. (*LRF* 59)

PAN, Judy; NICHOLS, D.R. and JOY, O.M., [1977], "Sales forecasting practices of large U.S. industrial firms," *Financial Management,* vol. **6** [Fall], pp. 72–77 ... The authors conducted a mail survey in 1974 of 251 companies from the *Fortune 500* industrial list and received 139 replies (a 55% response rate). (*LRF* not cited)

PARENTE, Frederick J.; ANDERSON, J.K., MYERS, P. and O'BRIEN, T., [1984], "An examination of factors contributing to Delphi accuracy," *Journal of Forecasting*, vol. 3, pp. 173–182 . . . Draws a distinction between forecasting *if* an event will occur and *when* it will occur. Additional rounds of polling in Delphi did not help to improve "if" predictions, but they did improve predictions for "when." Feedback in Delphi did not improve the accuracy of either *if* or *when* predictions. (*LRF* 119)

PARKER, Barnett R. and SRINIVASAN, V., [1976], "A consumer preference approach to the planning of rural primary health-care facilities," *Operations Research*, vol. 24, pp. 991–1025 . . . Note in particular-pages 1009–1025, which deal with the forecasting issues. They provide tests of face validity, cross-validity, and predictive validity and concluded that differential weights were superior to equal weights in predicting individual patient's choices of health care facilities. (*LRF* 231, 284)

PARSONS, Charles K. and HULIN, Charles L., [1982], "Differentially weighting linear models in organizational research: A cross-validation comparison of four methods," *Organizational Behavior and Human Performance.*, vol. 30, pp. 289–311 . . . Provides a literature review and compares four methods of weighting variables for reenlistment intentions in 51 samples of National Guardsmen. The writing strikes me as obscure and dull. My opinion is that one cannot conclude much from the results. (*LRF* 231)

PEDHAZUR, Elazar J., [1982], *Multiple Regression in Behavioral Research: Explanation and Prediction.* New York: Holt, Rinehart and Winston . . . This is a revision of a book originally published by Fred N. Kerlinger and Pedhazur in 1973. It represents a major revision and the result is impressive. This edition provides descriptions of the latest techniques in measurement (such as LISREL), illustrates step by step usage of three popular computer packages (SPSS, BMDP, and SAS) throughout the book, provides examples, presents the material in a well-written and interesting manner (for a sophisticated text, that is), and addresses practical problems in dealing with data and computer programs. The book provides a philosphical and statistical foundation. It is nice to see that a chapter has been added on prediction. In that chapter, Pedhazur refers to a rule of thumb which calls for the use of 30 observations for each variable in a regression model. However, the excellence of this book creates a problem: Will readers place too much faith in these sophisticated approaches to measurement? (*LRF* 205, 220)

PENCAVEL, John H., [1971], "A note on the predictive performance of wage inflation models of the British economy," *Economic Journal*, vol. 81, pp. 113–119 . . . A "constant change" extrapolation (based on last year's change) was more accurate than five econometric models for 1962–1967. (The econometric forecasts were *ex post.*) The relative accuracy of the five econometric models varied each year. That is, a high rank in one year was not more likely to be followed by a high rank the next year. (*LRF* 228, 408)

PENMAN, Stephen H., [1982], "Insider trader and the dissemination of firms' forecast information," *Journal of Business*, vol. **55**, pp. 479–503 . . . (*LRF* 94)

PERRY, Paul, [1979] "Certain problems in election survey methodology," *Public Opinion Quarterly*, vol. **43**, pp. 312–325 . . . Perry describes various technical advances that have contributed to the improved accuracy of intentions forecasts. (*LRF* 84)

PETERS, Lawrence H.; JACKOFSKY, Ellen F. and SALTER, James R., [1981], "Predicting turnover: A comparison of part-time and full-time employees," *Journal of Occupational Behavior*, vol. **2**, pp. 89–98 . . . This study attempted to predict employee turnover in a telephone sales job over the 12 months following hiring. Separate analytical models were developed for full- and part-time workers. Predictions were based on items from a survey taken two months after the employees started work. Demographic variables were similar for each group with the exception that part-time workers lived closer to their places of employment. Key variables in this study were all derived from previous literature on turnover, and included were job satisfaction, thoughts of quitting, expectation of finding alternative employment, job search behavior, and intention to quit. These five variables all helped to predict turnover for full-timers—but none of them helped to predict turnover among part-timers! As shown in this study, it is frequently useful to segment a problem and then to develop a model for each segment. The segmentation in this study might be thought of in terms of the *importance of the decision*. It is generally easier to predict how people will behave for important decisions. (*LRF* 287)

PFAFF, Philip, [1977], "Evaluation of some money stock forecasting models," *Journal of Finance*, vol. **32**, pp. 1639–1646 . . . Compares four extrapolation models with eight econometric models, all estimated from 1947–1960 quarterly data, in making one- to six-quarter-ahead *ex post* forecasts of the money stock over the 1961 to 1970 period. The extrapolation models were superior to the econometric models, despite the fact that the latter were recognized by academics to be the leading models in the field. The RMSE for the econometric models were cut in half for one-quarter-ahead forecasts by merely adjusting the forecast to compensate for the previous quarter's forecast error. This adjustment was of less value as the forecast horizon increased to six-quarters-ahead where it was of no value. (Instead of this mechanical error adjustment, a lagged dependent variable could be added as a predictor variable.) A decomposed extrapolation, based on extrapolations of its five components, was more accurate than a global extrapolation for the medium-range (six-quarter-ahead) forecasts, but not so for the very short-range (one-quarter-ahead). (*LRF* 237, 408, 409)

PHELPS, Ruth H. and SHANTEAU, James, [1978], "Livestock judges: How much information can an expert use?" *Organizational Behavior and Human Performance*, vol. **21**, pp. 209–219 . . . This study of the judging of female breeding pigs showed that experts were capable of using about ten pieces of information when these variables are not correlated with one another. (*LRF* not cited)

PRISTO, L.J., [1979], "The prediction of graduate school success by the canonical correlation," *Educational and Psychological Measurement*, vol. **39**, pp. 929–933 . . . The correlation between actual and predicted success in the validation sample was *negative*. (*LRF* 225)

PRITCHARD, David A., [1980], "Apologia for clinical/configural decision making," *American Psychologist*, vol. **35** [July], pp. 676–678 . . . See also DAWES [1980] and REMUS [1980] on pages 678–680 of the same issue. (*LRF* 598, 638)

RAO, Vithala and COX, James E., Jr., [1978], *Sales Forecasting Methods: A Survey of Recent Developments*. Cambridge, Mass.: Marketing Science Institute, Report No. 78-119 . . . Contains a listing of 45 books and 147 articles, most of which were published after 1970. Nearly all of these were included in the original edition of *LRF*. However, this gives another viewpoint about which forecasting papers are most relevant for marketing problems. (*LRF* not cited)

RAUSSER, Gordon C. and OLIVEIRA, Ronald A., [1976], "An econometric analysis of wilderness area use," *Journal of the American Statistical Association*, vol. **71**, pp. 276–285 . . . This study examined *ex post* short term forecasts using alternative criteria for accuracy. The econometric model was more accurate than Box-Jenkins, and a combined forecast was even more accurate. (*LRF* 290, 409)

READ, Stephen J., [1983], "Once is enough: Causal reasoning from a single instance," *Journal of Personality and Social Psychology*, vol. **45**, pp. 323–334 . . . A single concrete example had a significant impact on people's predictions in this experiment. The results suggest that predictions by political decision makers may be unduly influenced by single historical events rather than by generalizations from a broad range of situations. The tendency to rely heavily on a single event was higher for more complex situations. (*LRF* 42)

REIBSTEIN, David J. and TRAVER, Phillis A., [1982], "Factors affecting coupon redemption rates," *Journal of Marketing*, vol. **46** [Fall], pp. 102–113 . . . Good illustration of the use of prior research to develop a forecasting model. The Logit model, which transformed the dependent variable from Y to $\ln \frac{Y}{1-Y}$, has often been proposed for situations where Y varies between 0 and 1. Thus, it looked relevant for this study, where the task was to predict the percentage of coupons redeemed. Interestingly, however, the Logit did not provide a better fit than a regression against Y, nor did it do better on the validation sample. (The latter comparison was based on personal communication with Reibstein.) (*LRF* 202)

REID, David J., [1975], "A review of short term projection techniques," in H.A. Gordon (Ed.), *Practical Aspects of Forecasting*. London: Operational Research Society. (*LRF* 176, 494)

REID, Leonard N.; SOLEY, L.C. and WIMMER, R.D., [1981], "Replication in advertising research: 1977, 1978, 1979," *Journal of Advertising Research*, vol. **10**, No. 1, pp. 3–13 . . . (*LRF* 439)

REILLY, Richard R. and CHAO, Georgia T., [1982], "Validity and fairness of some alternative employee selection procedures," *Personnel Psychology*, vol. **35**, pp. 1–62 . . . This systematic and impressive review of the literature includes 41 unpublished papers and 107 published papers. It is well written; but, given the immense material that is covered, be well-rested before you attempt to read it. The authors examined alternatives to standardized tests for predicting which job applicants will be successful. The alternatives were biographical data, peer evaluation, interviews, self-assessments, reference checks, academic achievement, expert judgment, and projective techniques. (Which ones would *you* predict to be most valid?) Of these methods, only the biographical data and peer evaluations had validities comparable to those achieved by using standardized tests; the other methods had little validity—and some involved high costs. However-three new methods appear promising, although the evidence is still limited. One method is the "miniaturized training test," applicable for people without prior experience. The applicant is rated on ability to learn key components of the job in a short training exercise. Second is a structured "situational interview," where job candidates are asked how they would behave in given situations. Third, in "unassembled examinations," job candidates use structured guidelines to assemble a portfolio of verifiable past accomplishments relevant to the job at hand. As implied by the title, Reilly and Chao also examine the extent to which each method avoids prejudice. (*LRF* 155)

REINMUTH, James E. and GEURTS, Michael D., [1979], "Multideterministic approach to forecasting," in S. Makridakis and S.C. Wheelwright (Eds.), *Forecasting*. New York: North Holland ... Large reductions in error were achieved by combining extrapolative forecasts in this *small sample* study involving retail sales in Salt Lake City. (*LRF* 184)

REMUS, William E., [1980], "Measure of fit for unit rules," *American Psychologist*, vol. **35**, pp. 678–680 ... See also PRITCHARD [1980]. In trying to replicate Dawes' (1971) study of graduate admissions, Remus claims different results. He obtained 58% correct predictions for unit rules and 74% for regression (a statistically significant difference). (*LRF* 283)

REMUS, William E. and JENICKE, Lawrence O., [1978], "Unit and random linear models in decision making," *Multivariate Behavioral Research*, vol. **13** [April], 215–221 ... Examined a simulated production scheduling problem and found that "unit rules" and "random" coefficients led to higher costs than these obtained using judgmental decisions. For a related paper, see MOSKOWITZ, et al. [1982]. (*LRF* 630, 636)

RICKETTS, Donald E. and BARRETT, Michael J., [1973], "Corporate operating income forecasting ability," *Financial Management*, vol. **2** [Summer], pp. 53–62 ... Extrapolation of components followed by aggregation was no more accurate than extrapolation of aggregate corporate income. (In fact, it was slightly worse, but the difference was not significant.) (*LRF* 454)

RIGGS, Walter E., [1983] "The Delphi technique: An experimental evaluation," *Technological Forecasting and Social Change*, vol. **23**, pp. 89–94 ... Forecasts for two college football games were obtained from eight traditional groups and eight Delphi groups. Each group had four or five students. The forecasts were made four weeks before the games were played. One game was an intense rivalry well known to the students, while the other was less well known:

	Mean Absolute Error For:	
	Rivalry	Other Game
Delphi (Round 2)	2.2	13.9
Traditional	5.6	17.0

Delphi was significantly more accurate ($p < .05$). (*LRF* 119)

RIMLAND, Bernard and LARSON, Gerald E., [1981], "The manpower quality decline" *Armed Forces and Society*, vol. 8, No. 1, pp. 21–78 . . . (*LRF* 322)

ROBERTSON, Ivan and DOWNS, Sylvia, [1979], "Learning and the prediction of performance: Development of trainability testing in the United Kingdom," *Journal of Applied Psychology*, vol. 64, pp. 42–50 . . . Work sample and trainability tests were found to be superior to written tests for predicting success at semi-skilled manual labor jobs. (*LRF* 335)

ROBERTSON, Ivan T. and KANDOLA, R.S., [1982], "Work sample tests: Validity, adverse impact and applicant reaction," *Journal of Occupational Psychology*, vol. 55, pp. 171–183 . . . This paper examined the validity of psychomotor work samples, job-related information, situational decision making, and group discussion as predictors of job performance, job progress, and training. The conclusions, based on over 60 empirical studies, showed that each of the four methods was of roughly equal validity across all criteria. For the specific criterion of job performance, the psychomotor work samples had the highest predictive validity, followed by group discussion, situational decision making, then job related information tests. When compared with traditional (pencil and paper) psychological tests, work sample tests appeared to have a less adverse impact (i.e., they are not so biased against minorities). Furthermore, work sample tests allow *applicants* to make better predictions of how they would perform a given job. Finally, applicants preferred work samples as a predictive and selection technique. (*LRF* 155)

ROGERS, Everett M., [1983], *Diffusion of Innovations*. New York: Free Press . . . Of particular interest here are the descriptions of the problems involved in implementing what appear to be obvious, effective, important, and low cost solutions. These include the practice of boiling untreated water before drinking, the use of citrus fruits to prevent scurvy, and the Dvorak keyboard for typewriters. These cases are described in his Chapter 1. (*LRF* 24, 154, 425)

ROHRBAUGH, John, [1979], "Improving the quality of group judgment: Social judgment analysis and the Delphi Technique," *Organizational Behavior and Human Performance*," vol. 24, pp. 73–92 . . . This experiment pitted groups that met face-to-face (and discussed the logic of their judgment, as well as the judgment itself) against Delphi groups. Grade point averages of prospective freshmen were predicted by the subjects (172 psychology students). The face-to-face meeting, with some structure, did no better than the Delphi procedure of simply averaging the responses. (*LRF* 123)

ROOSE, Jack E. and DOHERTY, Michael E., [1976], "Judgment theory applied to the selection of life insurance salesmen," *Organizational Behavior and Human Performance*, vol. **16**, pp. 231–249 ... Sixteen agency managers made predictions on the potential success for 200 salespeople who had been hired. A validation sample of another 160 salespeople was used. Conclusions: (1) insight was poor and not related to the managers' experience; (2) commensurate information was weighted too heavily; (3) bootstrapping yielded a small gain for the average judge, but was of little value for the consensus judge; and (4) unit weights did better than bootstrapping. (*LRF* 104, 282, 284)

ROSENBERG, Richard D. and ROSENSTEIN, Eliezer, [1980], "Participation and productivity: An empirical study," *Industrial and Labor Relations Review*, vol. **33**, pp. 355–367 ... An analysis of records from 262 meetings between workers and managers from 1969 to 1975 showed that participation led to increases in productivity. (*LRF* 36)

ROSENBLATT, Aaron, [1968], "The practitioner's use and evaluation of reserarch," *Social Work*, vol. **13**, pp. 53–59 ... Interesting survey of social work practitioners. They ignore many basic concepts of statistics when evaluating research results. (*LRF* 47)

ROZEBOOM, W.W. [1978], "Estimation of cross-validated multiple correlation: A clarification," *Psychological Bulletin*, vol. **85**, pp. 1348–1351 ... (*LRF* 629)

ROTHE, James T., [1978], "Effectiveness of sales forecasting methods," *Industrial Marketing Management*, vol. **7**, pp. 114–118 ... Interviewees from 52 firms were asked about forecasting for production, finance, marketing, purchasing, inventory, and personnel. Opinion techniques were the most popular, as 96% of respondents reported using them. Exponential smoothing was used by 14%, and 6% used regression. About half of the firms kept historical records on accuracy. Only one firm had examined the cost due to inaccurate forecasts. None of the respondents knew how much was being spent on forecasting in their firm. This study addressed many useful questions. Read with care, however, as the conclusions sometimes go beyond the evidence. (*LRF* 73, 426, 427)

RUDELIUS, William; DICKSON, G.W. and HARTLEY, S.W., [1982], "The little model that couldn't: How a decision support system for retail buyers found limbo," *Systems, Objectives, Solutions*, vol. **2**, pp. 115–124 ... Interesting description of a high quality solution that, the authors say, was designed for use by retail buyers without any concern for the implementation *process*. Although it succeeded in meeting the buyers' needs, it was not actually implemented by the firm. Later, the authors talked to newly hired executives in the firm. The authors were asked to design a new model, and the requirements were the same as for the model their colleagues had discarded earlier. The moral, say the authors, is to begin by paying explicit attention to the implementation process. (*LRF* not cited.)

RULAND, William, [1980], "On the choice of simple extrapolative model forecasts of annual earnings," *Financial Management*, vol. **9** [Summer], pp. 30–37 . . . This study compared the forecast accuracy of eight extrapolative models. Simple models were just as accurate. (*LRF* 495)

RUSH, Howard and PAGE, William, [1979], "Long-term metals forecasting: The track record: 1910–1964," *Futures*, vol. **11**, pp. 321–337 . . . The authors examined 372 forecasts and coded them. (Coding was not easy because some original sources did not provide sufficient information.) Judgmental methods were commonly used up to 1939 (about 50% of the published forecasts) and even more so after 1939 (65%). Explicit references to uncertainty were found in 22% of the forecasts published before 1939, but in only 8% afterwards. (*LRF* 372, 426)

Sᴀᴍᴇʟsᴏɴ, **Franz, [1980],** "J.B. Watson's Little Albert, Cyril Burt's twins, and the need for a critical science," *American Psychologist*, vol. **35**, pp. 619–625 . . . (*LRF* 45)

SCHMITT, Neal, [1978], "Comparison of subjective and objective weighting strategies in changing task situations," *Organizational Behavior and Human Performance*, vol. **21**, pp. 171–188 . . . A partial replication of Cook and Stewart (1975). Subjects (112 students) were asked to make predictions of academic success based on three or four variables (contrived data). After practicing on 20 "applicants", subjects made predictions for 30 new "applicants". Interesting results: (1) subjects performed better when they did *not* receive feedback on whether the prediction was right or wrong, (2) three subjective weighting schemes (all direct bootstrapping methods) were tried and found to be of equal accuracy, (3) regression against predicted outcomes (indirect bootstrapping) was more accurate than the direct bootstrapping; and (4) equal weights provided good forecasts. (*LRF* 278, 380, 527)

SCHNAARS, Steven P., [1984], "Situational factors affecting forecast accuracy," *Journal of Marketing Research*, vol. **21**, pp. 290–297 . . . (*LRF* 166, 170, 179, 343, 495)

SCHNAARS, Steven P. and BAVUSO, R. Joseph, [1985], "A comparison of extrapolation models on very short-term forecasts", *Journal of Business Research*, (in press) . . . (*LRF* 170, 495)

SCHNEE, Jerome E., [1977], "Predicting the unpredictable: The impact of meterological satellites on weather forecasting," *Technological Forecasting and Social Change*, vol. **10**, pp. 299–307 . . . (*LRF* 388, 625)

SCHOTT, Kerry, [1978], "The Relations Between Industrial Research and Development and Factor Demands," *Economic Journal*, vol. **88**, pp. 85–106 . . . (*LRF* 241)

SCHREUDER, Hein and KLAASSEN, Jan, [1984], "Confidential revenue and profit forecasts by management and financial analysts: Evidence from the Netherlands," *The Accounting Review*, vol. **59**, pp. 64–77 . . . This study extends the research on the relative accuracy of management and analysts in forecasting next year's annual earnings by examining *confidential* forecasts by a sample of Dutch firms for 1980. Firms were asked to file these confidential forecasts with a notary, with many safeguards provided against misuse. The authors concluded that management was not more accurate. This finding, however, is based on a small sample (38 companies for one year). Furthermore, the *direction* of the results favored management (MAPE of 102.9 vs. 139.4 respectively for management and analysts), a result that seems consistent in relative terms with my meta-analysis of previous studies [ARMSTRONG, 1983b]. Schreuder and Klassen also examined sales forecasts. Again the management errors were a bit smaller than those of analysts (MAPEs of 6.7 vs. 7.7); these results were not significantly different. As might be expected, when the sales forecast was too high (low), the profit forecast tended to be too high (low), but there were many exceptions (38%). Management and analysts estimated 50% and 100% (!) confidence intervals. Consistent with prior research, these confidence intervals were too narrow: 56% of the revenue and 72% of the profit forecasts fell outside the 50% confidence intervals; 35% of the revenue forecasts and 39% of the profit forecasts fell outside the 100% confidence intervals. (*LRF* 143, 454)

SCHULTZ, Randall L., [1984] "The implementation of forecasting models," *Journal of Forecasting*, vol. **3**, pp. 43–55 . . . This paper presents a checklist based on a summary of implementation research drawn from management science literature. (*LRF* 00)

SEWALL, Murphy A., [1981], "Relative information contributions of consumer purchase intentions and management judgment as explanators of sales," *Journal of Marketing Research*, vol. **18**, pp. 249–253 . . . The study is better than the title. It examined U.S. mail order sales from a 1979 catalog for 44 women's blouses priced from $5 to $20. Predictions were made by a buyer for the mail order house, the normal procedure used in deciding on initial orders. Consumer intentions were then obtained from 600 women shoppers in shopping malls.

The intentions were obtained with a 5-point rating scale in response to a set of photographs. Four different methods were considered for summarizing the ratings for each blouse (median, Thurstone, mean, and "fraction in top two categories"). Here are the questions: (1) Which provides the best predictions, the expert (buyer) or the intentions (shoppers) survey? (2) Does it matter how the rating scale is summarized in the intentions survey? The answer to (1) was that each provided useful information for prediction, and the predictive ability of the experts was about equal to that of the intentions survey. Sewall (personal communication) suggests that the combined use of expert and intentions information will improve predictions. He said that it allowed for a 15% reduction in inventory ordering errors in this case. For (2), the method used to summarize the rating scale did not affect the accuracy of the predictions. (*LRF* 85, 136)

SHERMAN, Steven J., [1980], "On the self-erasing nature of errors of prediction," *Journal of Personality and Social Psychology*, vol. **39**, pp. 211–221 . . . This is an interesting and important study relevant to planning, scenarios, and implementation. It is based on the self-fulfilling prophecy. If people are asked how they will respond in a given situation, they tend to cast themselves in a responsible and favorable manner. Then, if presented with that situation or a similar situation, they tend to live up to their predictions. (*LRF* 43)

SHOCKER, Allan and SRINIVASAN, V., [1979], "Multiattribute approaches for product evaluation and generation: A critical review," *Journal of Marketing Research*, vol. **16**, pp. 159–180 . . . Good review of the research on methods to predict preferences for products in the concept phase. See especially their summary Table 1. They cite studies that examined estimation procedures other than ordinary regression analysis. (This paper is reprinted in WIND, MAHAJAN, and CARDOZO [1981].) (*LRF* 202)

SHRADER, Charles B.; TAYLOR, Lew and DALTON, Dan R., [1984], "Strategic Planning and Organizational Performance: A Critical Appraisal," *Journal of Management*, vol. **10**, pp. 147–171 . . . Presents a thorough review of the empirical evidence on the value of formal planning. Includes unpublished as well as published evidence. I used this to update the box score in ARMSTRONG (1982c) to 21 comparisons favoring formal planning, 7 ties, and 2 favoring informal planning. (*LRF* 7)

SILHAN, Peter A., [1983], "The effects of segmenting quarterly sales and margins on extrapolative forecasts of conglomerate earnings: Extension and replication," *Journal of Accounting Research*, vol. **21**, pp. 341–347 . . . This study used quarterly data on income for 60 firms with one-quarter and one-year ahead *ex ante* forecasts for 1976-1978. Supports Kinney (1971) and COLLINS (1976). An excellent study. (*LRF* 287, 595)

SLOVIC, Paul and FISCHHOFF, Baruch, [1977], "On the psychology of experimental surprises," *Journal of Experimental Psychology: Human Perception and Performance*, vol. **3**, pp. 544–551 . . . (*LRF* 39)

SLOVIC, Paul; FISCHHOFF, Baruch and LICHTENSTEIN, Sarah, [1978], "Accident probabilities and seat belt usage: A psychological perspective," *Accident Analysis and Prevention*, vol. **10**, pp. 281–285. . . . The probability of an automobile accident on a single trip is so low that it seems reasonable to many people that they need not wear a seat belt. Only 10% of the people who were given information about the risks for a single trip said that they would increase their use of seat belts. However, when presented with information about the cumulative risks over a lifetime of driving (about 40,000 trips), 39% said such information would increase their seat belt usage. (*LRF* not cited)

SLOVIC, Paul and McPHILLAMY, Douglas J., [1974], "Dimensional commensurability and cue utlization in comparative judgment," *Organizational Behavior and Human Performance*, vol. **11**, pp. 172–194 . . . When asked to make a choice, subjects gave more weight to a dimension that was common to both alternatives and which was precisely measured (e.g., point averages of students in the job application decision). This occurs even when subjects claim they do not want to use this information. (*LRF* 43, 104)

SMITH, David E., [1974], "Adaptive response for exponential smoothing: Comparative system analysis," *Operational Research Quarterly*, vol. **25**, pp. 421–435 . . . (*LRF* 171, 494)

SMITH, Gary and BRAINARD, William, [1976], "The value of *a priori* information in estimating a financial model," *Journal of Finance*, vol. **31**, 1299–1322 . . . Examines *ex post* forecasts over an eight-quarter forecast horizon using RMSE as the criterion for accuracy. Forecasts were made for six variables for banks and four for savings and loan institutions. Extrapolation models were more accurate then econometric models for short-run forecasts, but their performance deteriorated rapidly and seemed worse for the eight-quarter-ahead forecasts. Models based solely on prior information were generally more accurate than those estimated by standard regression analysis. The combination of prior information and data, done in a rigorous manner here, performed well overall. The paper addresses many important issues, but it is difficult to read. (*LRF* 203, 344, 408, 409)

SMITH, M.C., [1976], "A comparison of the value of trainability assessments and other tests for predicting the practical performance of dental students," *International Review of Applied Psychology*, vol. **25**, pp. 125–130 . . . Good description of trainability tests (work sample used to see how long it takes an applicant to learn). The key rules for such a test are that it be (1) based on crucial elements of the job, (2) use skill and knowledge that can be imparted only during a short learning period, and (3) be sufficiently complex to allow for a range of observable errors to be made by the applicants. Presents evidence on validity of this method. (*LRF* 155, 335)

SMYTH, David J., [1983], "Short-run macroeconomic forecasting: The OECD performance," *Journal of Forecasting*, vol. **2**, pp. 37–49 . . . Econometric forecasts for Canada, France, West Germany, Italy, Japan, the United Kingdom, and the United States are published on a regular basis in the OECD's *Economic Outlook*. This paper analyzes the accuracy of the OECD annual forecasts. The forecasts were compared with those generated by a naive model using mean-absolute error, the root-mean-square error, the median-absolute error, and Theil's inequality coefficient. The OECD forecasts of real GNP changes were significantly superior to those generated by a random walk process; however, the OECD price changes and current balance of payments forecasts were not significantly more accurate than those obtained from the naive model. The OECD's forecasting performance has neither improved nor deteriorated over time. (*LRF* 408)

SPARKES, John R. and McHUGH, A.K., [1984], "Awareness and use of forecasting techniques in British industry," *Journal of Forecasting*, vol. **3**, pp. 37–42 . . . Received 76 replies (25%) from a survey mailed to 300 British manufacturing firms. These firms seemed less familiar with objective methods than did the U.S. firms surveyed by MENTZER and COX [1984]. (*LRF* 73, 426, 427)

STAPEL, Jan, [1968], "Predictive attitudes," in Lee Adler and Irving Crespi (Eds.), *Attitude Research on the Rocks*. Chicago: American Marketing Association, pp. 96–115 . . . (*LRF* 81)

STEWART, Thomas R. and GLANTZ, Michael H., [1985], "Expert judgment and climate forecasting: A methodological critique of 'Climate Change to the Year 2000,'" *Climatic Change*, vol. **7**, No. 1, . . . Stewart and Glantz use the existing research on judgmental forecasting to evaluate a widely distributed expert-opinion study by the U.S. National Defense University. This study concluded that climate changes would be small, but, as noted by Stewart and Glantz, the study was not well-designed in light of the research findings on judgmental forecasting. (*LRF* 120)

STUMPF, Stephen A. and ZAND, Dale E., [1981], "Participant estimates of the effectiveness of judgmental decisions," *Journal of Management*, vol. 7, pp. 77–87 . . . Three experiments showed a *negligible* relationship between each participant's ratings of his effectiveness in problem solving and his effectiveness as rated by outside panels. The outside panel members had access to actual results for some problems, and high inter-rater reliability existed among their independent estimates. (*LRF* not cited)

SUDMAN, Seymour and BRADBURN, Norman N., [1983], *Asking Questions*. San Francisco: Jossey-Bass . . . (*LRF* 99)

SULLIVAN, W.G. and CLAYCOMB, W., [1980], *Fundamentals of Forecasting*. Reston, Va.: Reston Publishing. (*LRF* not cited)

TEIGEN, Karl Halvor, [1983], "Studies in subjective probability III: The unimportance of alternatives," *Scandanavian Journal of Psychology*, vol. 24, pp. 97–105 . . . (*LRF* 106)

TIMMERS, Han and WAGENAAR, Willem A., [1977], "Inverse statistics and misperception of exponential growth," *Perception and Psychophysics*, vol. 21, pp. 558–562 . . . Judges tend to greatly underestimate exponential growth. (*LRF* 103)

TRAUGOTT, Michael W. and TUCKER, Clyde, [1984], "Strategies for predicting whether a citizen will vote and estimation of electoral outcomes," *Public Opinion Quarterly*, vol. 48, pp. 330–343 . . . A segmentation approach (eight segments) and a regression (using the logit function) produced almost identical forecasts as to who would vote in the 1980 U.S. presidential election. (*LRF* 413)

TVERSKY, Amos and KAHNEMAN, Daniel, [1981], "The framing of decisions and the psychology of choice," *Science*, vol. 211, pp. 453–458 . . . Seemingly inconsequential changes in the formulation of choice problems can cause major shifts in the preferences of people. (*LRF* 000)

TVERSKY, Amos and KAHNEMAN, Daniel, [1982], "Judgments of and by representativeness," in KAHNEMAN, SLOVIC and TVERSKY [1982] pp. 84–98 . . . Discusses the conjunction effect whereby adding representative descriptors *increases* the perceived probability despite the fact that it violates standard laws of probability. Logically, the added details make the item less general and, thus, less likely. (*A* and *B* is less likely than *A* alone). However, the details seem more representative of what we know and, thus, more likely. (*LRF* 42)

TVERSKY, Amos and KAHNEMAN, Daniel, [1983], "Extensional versus intuitive reasoning: The conjunction fallacy in probability judgment," *Psychological Review*, vol. 90, pp. 293–315 . . . An interesting set of experiments on the conjunction fallacy (*A* and *B* seems more likely than *B* alone, because *A* seems to be a plausible reason). Incidentally, I was a subject in one of these studies and I would not be surprised to find that I was guilty of this fallacy. (*LRF* 43)

TWENEY, Ryan D., et al., [1980], "Strategies of rule discovery in an inference task", *Quarterly Journal of Experimental Psychology,* vol. **32,** pp. 109–123 . . . Subjects were presented with Wason's 2-4-6 problem and were asked to use different strategies. Among these strategies were confirmation, disconfirmation, single hypothesis, and multiple hypotheses. Although a direct application of the multiple hypotheses strategy did not help, a variation of the strategy was useful. In this, subjects were asked to compare two interrelated rules and to examine the evidence favoring each. This strategy avoids the need to label some trials as "wrong"; subjects performed better with these instructions. (*LRF* 437)

TWENEY, Ryan D.; DOHERTY, Michael E. and MYNATT, Clifford R., [1982], "Rationality and disconfirmation: Further evidence," *Social Studies of Science,* vol. **12,** pp. 435–441 . . . This paper reviews the evidence and argues for a mixed strategy of seeking confirming as well as disconfirming evidence. (*LRF* 437)

TWENEY, Ryan D. and YACHANIN, Stephen A., [1985], "Can scientists rationally assess conditional inferences?" *Social Studies of Science* (in press) . . . Scientists performed well, both in absolute terms and relative to nonscientists, in versions of Wason's problem when certain changes were made in the wording of these questions. (*LRF* 378)

WAGENAAR, Willem A., [1978], "Intuitive prediction of growth," in Dietrich F. Burkhardt and William H. Ittelson (Eds.), *Environmental Assessment of Socioeconomic Systems.* New York: Plenum, [1978] . . . This study shows how frequent reference to the latest data led to poorer forecasts in cases of exponential growth. People involved closely with exponential growth would be less likely to be able to predict change. Subjects seem to look at *differences* rather than *ratios* in their subjective forecasts. Mathematical training did not improve accuracy. The following steps were helpful: to (1) observe the process *less* frequently, and (2) use an inverse representation of growth (e.g., instead of people per square mile, try to predict square miles per person). For this inverse representation, the large differences occur early, rather than late, in the sequence. (*LRF* 103)

WAGENAAR, Willem A. and SAGARIA, Sabato D., [1975], "Misperception of exponential growth," *Perception and Psychophysics*, vol. **18**, pp. 416–422 . . . Subjects were presented with exponential growth series and were told that "nothing will stop the growth." Their intuitive predictions were highly conservative. Surprisingly, it did not help when the data were presented to the subjects in graphic form. (*LRF* 102)

WAGENAAR, Willem A.; SCHREUDER, R. and VAN DER HEIJDEN, A.H.C., [1985], "Do TV-pictures help people to remember the weather forecast?" *Ergonomics* (in press) . . . (*LRF* 47)

WAGENAAR, Willem A. and TIMMERS, Han, [1978], "Extrapolation of exponential time series is not enhanced by having more data points," *Perception and Psychophysics*, vol. **24**, pp. 182–184 . . . Subjects were provided with 3, 5 and 7 observations in an exponentially growing series. (All subjects received the same first and last observations.) Those who received more observations made less accurate forecasts. (*LRF* 103)

WAGENAAR, Willem A. and TIMMERS Han, [1979], "The pond-and-duckweed problem: Three experiments in the misperception of exponential growth," *Acta Psychologica*, vol. **43**, pp. 239–251 . . . This study used a computer display screen to display the growth process. (*LRF* 102)

WAGENAAR, Willem A. and VISSER, Jenny G., [1979], "The weather forecast under the weather," *Ergonomics*, vol. **22**, pp. 909–917 . . . Their experiment provided useful guidelines on how to present forecasts effectively: (1) group the forecast information into meaningful blocks, and (2) present current status first (i.e., "what is the weather now?" This was seldom included in the weather reports they analyzed), and (3) shorten the message. (*LRF* 47)

WARSHAW, Paul R., [1980], "Predicting purchase and other behaviors from general and contextually specific intentions," *Journal of Marketing Research*, vol. **17**, pp. 26–33 . . . (*LRF* 61, 140)

WEDLEY, William C. and FERRIE, Adam E.J., [1978], "Perceptual differences and effects of managerial participation on project implementation," *Operational Research Quarterly*, vol. **29**, pp. 199–204 . . . Interestingly, managers and analysts differed substantially on their ratings of whether a given project was a success or a failure. From either perspective, however, higher managerial participation was associated with better project implementation. (*LRF* 35)

WELLS, Gary L. and MURRAY, Donna M., [1984], "Eyewitness Confidence," in Gary L. Wells and E.F. Loftus (Eds.), *Eyewitness Tes-*

timony: Psychological Perspectives. New York: Cambridge University Press . . . (*LRF* 140)

WERNER, Paul D.; ROSE, Terrence L. and YESAVAGE, Jerome A., [1983], "Reliabililty, accuracy, and decision-making strategy in clinical predictions of imminent dangerousness," *Journal of Consulting and Clinical Psychology*, vol. 51, pp. 815–825 . . . The mass media, movies (e.g., *The Parallax View*), and courts assume that is possible to predict who will be violent. But beyond the obvious factor that those who have been violent in the past are more likely to be violent in the future, predictive ability is low, as had been shown previously in CO-COZZA and STEADMAN [1978]. The study by Werner, Rose, and Yesavage adds further evidence. They asked 30 experts (15 psychologists and 15 psychiatrists) to make predictions about physical violence occurring in the first week of hospitalization for 40 newly admitted mental patients. The judges received information on 19 variables about each patient, but they did not meet the patient. The findings: (1) individual judges had modest *reliability* ($r = .42$), and reliability was greatly increased by using a composite of 15 judges ($r = .93$), (2) experience, including experience in a similar situation, *did not* yield better predictions, (3) ratings by individual judges did not have *significant predictive validity* (mean $r = .12$, with only 2 of 30 judges doing better than chance), and (4) the composite of 30 judges tended to be more accurate, but the gain was unexpectedly small ($r = .17$ for composite vs. the mean r of .12). Furthermore, it was not statistically significant (vs. chance). A step-wise regression of the actual violence versus the original variables revealed a different set of factors. Possibly the judges were using the wrong variables? This paper provides an interesting application of the Brunswick Lens Model to the problem. (*LRF* 381)

WHYBARK, D. Clay, [1972], "A comparison of adaptive forecasting techniques," *Logistics and Transportation Review*, vol. 8, No. 3, pp. 13–26 . . . Although the differences were small, adaptive parameters apparently led to improvements. This conclusion was later challenged in a reanalysis of the data by EKERN [1981]. (*LRF* 174, 494, 601)

WILTON, Peter C. and PESSEMIER, Edgar A., [1981], "Forecasting the ultimate acceptance of an innovation: The effects of information," *Journal of Consumer Research*, vol. 8, pp. 162–171 . . . This paper used a mulivariate probit model to predict the *stated choices* for a subcompact electric vehicle for 196 individuals in a hold-out sample. The probit model is an extension to the ordinary regression model that overcomes the problems of heteroscedasticity and negative forecasts when using dummy variables for the dependent variable (such as "1 = Buy" and "0 = Do Not Buy"). The results were not impressive when compared with chance. Actual market behavior was also used as a criterion and here the probit model predictions appeared to be of some value. (*LRF* 202)

WIMSATT, Genevieve B. and WOODWARD, John T., [1970], "Revised estimates of new plant and equipment expenditures in the United States, 1947–1969: Part II," *Survey of Current Business*, vol. **50**, pp. 19–39 . . . For business as a whole, annual expectations correctly predicted the direction of change in investment expenditures in 20 of 21 years (including four years when there was a decline: 1949, 1954, 1958, and 1960). It missed 1950 (big change due to the Korean peace action). The accuracy of forecasts of quarterly changes was also impressive. (*LRF* 83)

WIND, Yoram J., [1982], *Product Policy*. Reading, Mass.: Addison-Wesley . . . (*LRF* 155)

WIND, Yoram; MAHAJAN, Vijay and CARDOZO, Richard N., (Eds.), [1981],*New Product Forecasting*. Lexington, Mass.: Lexington Books. A comprehensive set of readings (12 previously published and 10 prepared for this book) on approaches to new product forecasting. It is an important (and profitable) field and this book presents the state of the art. As pointed out by the editors, validation studies are in dire need in this area. The readings cover forecasting at the various stages of new product development: concept testing, pretest-market, test-market, and early sales. Melvyn Hirst provides an extensive review of this book, along with additional references, in the *Journal of Forecasting*, vol. **2** [1983], 85–87. (*LRF* 643)

WINKLER, Robert L. and MAKRIDAKIS, Spyros, [1983], "The combination of forecasts," *Journal of the Royal Statistical Society: Series A*, vol. **146**, part 2, pp. 150–157 . . . Examines weighting schemes for a large number of time series, many different methods, and several time horizons. See also MAKRIDAKIS and WINKLER [1983]. (*LRF* 184)

WOLIN, Leroy, [1962], "Responsibility for raw data," *American Psychologist*, vol. **17**, pp. 657–658 . . . (*LRF* 439, 445)

WOOD, Gordon, [1978], "The knew-it-all-along effect," *Journal of Experimental Psychology: Human Perception and Performance*, vol. **4**, pp. 345–353 . . . This experiment shows that once the outcome is known, subjects have difficulty remembering their prior beliefs. (*LRF* 39)

WRIGHT, George and WHALLEY, Peter, [1983] "The supra-additivity of subjective probability" in B.P. Stigum and F. Wenstop (Eds.), *Foundations of Utility and Risk Theory with Applications*. London: D.Reidel ... When subjects were asked to estimate the probability of two mutually exclusive and exhaustive events, their probabilities would generally sum to 1. As the number of possibilities were increased, the sum of the probabilities increased:

Possible Outcomes	Total Probabilities
5	1.70
6	1.65
6	1.70
7	2.13
16	3.04

(*LRF* 107)

YETTON, Philip and BOTTGER, Preston, [1983], "The relationships among group size, member ability, social decision schemes, and performance," *Organizational Behavior and Human Performance*, vol. **32**, pp. 145–147 ... This study used the NASA Lost-on-the-Moon exercise. For nominal groups, accuracy improved as group size increased to five people. For interacting groups, accuracy improved up to four people. (*LRF* not cited)

ZAND, Dale E. and SORENSEN, R.E., [1975], "Theory of change and the effective use of management science," *Administrative Science Quarterly*, vol. **20**, pp. 532–545 ... This study used a mail survey to examine change projects in industry. Responses were obtained from 154 management scientists. In the successful projects, the clients were in control during the unfreezing, change, and refreezing phases of change. This seldom occurred for the unsuccessful projects. (*LRF* 32, 36)

ZARNOWITZ, Victor, [1979], "An analysis of annual and multi-period quarterly forecasts of aggregate income, output, and the price level," *Journal of Business*, vol. **52**, pp. 1–33 ... This paper examines errors in forecasting GNP from 1959–1976 (annually) and 1970–1975 (quarterly) using forecast horizons of 1 to 8 quarters. (*LRF* 360)

ZARNOWITZ, Victor, [1984], "The accuracy of individual and group forecasts from business outlook surveys," *Journal of Forecasting*, vol. **3**, pp. 11–26 ... The group mean forecast was more accurate than the typical group member for six economic variables over different forecast horizons. (*LRF* 137)

ZUKIER, Henry, [1982], "The dilution effect: The role of the correlation and the dispersion of predictor variables in the use of diagnostic information," *Journal of Personality and Social Psychology*, vol. **43**, pp. 1163–1174 ... This experiment asks subjects to predict grade point averages of students. When they were given irrelevant information, along with the relevant information, they became more conservative. (*LRF* 104)

PEOPLE INDEX

This index helps you locate your favorite people. It includes authors, well-known personalities (both real and fictional), sources of sayings, and people who helped in the creation of *LRF*. Everyone who is mentioned in *LRF* is listed in this index.

"I couldn't have done it with football players, you know."
> *CASEY STENGEL, after winning the World Series of baseball (New York Times, Nov. 3, 1949, p. 41, col. 2)*

Nor could I have written this book with football players. More than 1500 people are listed here. Without them this book would not exist.

SUBJECT INDEX

This index helps you find specific topics. It includes important technical terms, techniques, organizations, concepts, issues, and forecast areas. For example, if you would like to know about work on the forecasting in the photographic market, you would find about 30 references in this index.

'The time has come,' the Walrus said,
'To talk of many things:
Of shoes   and   ships — and sealing wax —
Of cabbages — and kings —'

LEWIS CARROLL,
Through the Looking Glass

References are provided only to places where the term is *discussed;* that is, the index does not cite every usage of a term in the book. When the term is discussed on a series of pages, the first and last pages are noted with a dash to separate them. Terms that are defined in the glossary are noted with a G, followed by the page number in the glossary.

POSTSCRIPTS

WHY ROME FELL

I n ancient Rome (A.D. 357), the Emperor Constantius made a law forbidding "anyone to consult a soothsayer, a mathematician, or a forecaster ... May curiosity to foretell the future be silenced forever."

Theodosian Code, Book 9, Title 16, Section 4

NEW YORK IS NEXT?

"P ersons pretending to forecast the future" shall be considered disorderly under Subdivision 3, Section 901 of the Criminal Code and liable to a fine of $250 and/or six months in prison.

Section 899, New York State Code of Criminal Procedure (noted in ASCHER & OVERHOLT [1983])